THE BOOK ®

Vauxhall Corsa
Service and Repair Manual

John S. Mead MISTC

Models covered

(3921 - 384)

Corsa models with petrol engines, including special/limited editions
Hatchback, Corsavan & Combo Van

1.0 litre (973cc) 3-cyl petrol
1.2 litre (1196cc & 1199cc), 1.4 litre (1389cc) & 1.6 litre (1598cc) 4-cyl petrol

Does NOT cover diesel engine models
Does NOT cover new Corsa range introduced October 2000

© Haynes Publishing 2002

ABCDE
FGHIJ
K

A book in the **Haynes Service and Repair Manual Series**

ISBN 1 85960 921 X

British Library Cataloguing in Publication Data
A catalogue record for this book is available from the British Library.

Printed in the USA

Haynes Publishing
Sparkford, Yeovil, Somerset BA22 7JJ, England

Haynes North America, Inc
861 Lawrence Drive, Newbury Park, California 91320, USA

Editions Haynes
4, Rue de l'Abreuvoir
92415 COURBEVOIE CEDEX, France

Haynes Publishing Nordiska AB
Box 1504, 751 45 UPPSALA, Sweden

Contents

LIVING WITH YOUR VAUXHALL CORSA

Roadside Repairs

Weekly Checks

MAINTENANCE

Routine maintenance and servicing

Contents

Advanced driving

Many people see the words 'advanced driving' and believe that it won't interest them or that it is a style of driving beyond their own abilities. Nothing could be further from the truth. Advanced driving is straightforward safe, sensible driving - the sort of driving we should all do every time we get behind the wheel.

An average of 10 people are killed every day on UK roads and 870 more are injured, some seriously. Lives are ruined daily, usually because somebody did something stupid. Something like 95% of all accidents are due to human error, mostly driver failure. Sometimes we make genuine mistakes - everyone does. Sometimes we have lapses of concentration. Sometimes we deliberately take risks.

For many people, the process of 'learning to drive' doesn't go much further than learning how to pass the driving test because of a common belief that good drivers are made by 'experience'.

Learning to drive by 'experience' teaches three driving skills:

☐ Quick reactions. (Whoops, that was close!)
☐ Good handling skills. (Horn, swerve, brake, horn).
☐ Reliance on vehicle technology. (Great stuff this ABS, stop in no distance even in the wet...)

Drivers whose skills are 'experience based' generally have a lot of near misses and the odd accident. The results can be seen every day in our courts and our hospital casualty departments.

Advanced drivers have learnt to control the risks by controlling the position and speed of their vehicle. They avoid accidents and near misses, even if the drivers around them make mistakes.

The key skills of advanced driving are **concentration,** effective all-round **observation, anticipation** and **planning.** When **good vehicle handling** is added to

these skills, all driving situations can be approached and negotiated in a safe, methodical way, leaving nothing to chance.

Concentration means applying your mind to safe driving, completely excluding anything that's not relevant. Driving is usually the most dangerous activity that most of us undertake in our daily routines. It deserves our full attention.

Observation means not just looking, but seeing and seeking out the information found in the driving environment.

Anticipation means asking yourself what is happening, what you can reasonably expect to happen and what could happen unexpectedly. (One of the commonest words used in compiling accident reports is 'suddenly'.)

Planning is the link between seeing something and taking the appropriate action. For many drivers, planning is the missing link.

If you want to become a safer and more skilful driver and you want to enjoy your driving more, contact the Institute of Advanced Motorists on 0208 994 4403 or write to IAM House, Chiswick High Road, London W4 4HS for an information pack.

Working on your car can be dangerous. This page shows just some of the potential risks and hazards, with the aim of creating a safety-conscious attitude.

General hazards

Scalding

• Don't remove the radiator or expansion tank cap while the engine is hot.
• Engine oil, automatic transmission fluid or power steering fluid may also be dangerously hot if the engine has recently been running.

Burning

• Beware of burns from the exhaust system and from any part of the engine. Brake discs and drums can also be extremely hot immediately after use.

Crushing

• When working under or near a raised vehicle, always supplement the jack with axle stands, or use drive-on ramps. *Never venture under a car which is only supported by a jack.*
• Take care if loosening or tightening high-torque nuts when the vehicle is on stands. Initial loosening and final tightening should be done with the wheels on the ground.

Fire

• Fuel is highly flammable; fuel vapour is explosive.
• Don't let fuel spill onto a hot engine.
• Do not smoke or allow naked lights (including pilot lights) anywhere near a vehicle being worked on. Also beware of creating sparks (electrically or by use of tools).
• Fuel vapour is heavier than air, so don't work on the fuel system with the vehicle over an inspection pit.
• Another cause of fire is an electrical overload or short-circuit. Take care when repairing or modifying the vehicle wiring.
• Keep a fire extinguisher handy, of a type suitable for use on fuel and electrical fires.

Electric shock

• Ignition HT voltage can be dangerous, especially to people with heart problems or a pacemaker. Don't work on or near the ignition system with the engine running or the ignition switched on.

• Mains voltage is also dangerous. Make sure that any mains-operated equipment is correctly earthed. Mains power points should be protected by a residual current device (RCD) circuit breaker.

Fume or gas intoxication

• Exhaust fumes are poisonous; they often contain carbon monoxide, which is rapidly fatal if inhaled. Never run the engine in a confined space such as a garage with the doors shut.
• Fuel vapour is also poisonous, as are the vapours from some cleaning solvents and paint thinners.

Poisonous or irritant substances

• Avoid skin contact with battery acid and with any fuel, fluid or lubricant, especially antifreeze, brake hydraulic fluid and Diesel fuel. Don't syphon them by mouth. If such a substance is swallowed or gets into the eyes, seek medical advice.
• Prolonged contact with used engine oil can cause skin cancer. Wear gloves or use a barrier cream if necessary. Change out of oil-soaked clothes and do not keep oily rags in your pocket.
• Air conditioning refrigerant forms a poisonous gas if exposed to a naked flame (including a cigarette). It can also cause skin burns on contact.

Asbestos

• Asbestos dust can cause cancer if inhaled or swallowed. Asbestos may be found in gaskets and in brake and clutch linings. When dealing with such components it is safest to assume that they contain asbestos.

Special hazards

Hydrofluoric acid

• This extremely corrosive acid is formed when certain types of synthetic rubber, found in some O-rings, oil seals, fuel hoses etc, are exposed to temperatures above 400°C. The rubber changes into a charred or sticky substance containing the acid. *Once formed, the acid remains dangerous for years. If it gets onto the skin, it may be necessary to amputate the limb concerned.*
• When dealing with a vehicle which has suffered a fire, or with components salvaged from such a vehicle, wear protective gloves and discard them after use.

The battery

• Batteries contain sulphuric acid, which attacks clothing, eyes and skin. Take care when topping-up or carrying the battery.
• The hydrogen gas given off by the battery is highly explosive. Never cause a spark or allow a naked light nearby. Be careful when connecting and disconnecting battery chargers or jump leads.

Air bags

• Air bags can cause injury if they go off accidentally. Take care when removing the steering wheel and/or facia. Special storage instructions may apply.

Diesel injection equipment

• Diesel injection pumps supply fuel at very high pressure. Take care when working on the fuel injectors and fuel pipes.

⚠️ *Warning: Never expose the hands, face or any other part of the body to injector spray; the fuel can penetrate the skin with potentially fatal results.*

Remember...

DO

• Do use eye protection when using power tools, and when working under the vehicle.

• Do wear gloves or use barrier cream to protect your hands when necessary.

• Do get someone to check periodically that all is well when working alone on the vehicle.

• Do keep loose clothing and long hair well out of the way of moving mechanical parts.

• Do remove rings, wristwatch etc, before working on the vehicle – especially the electrical system.

• Do ensure that any lifting or jacking equipment has a safe working load rating adequate for the job.

DON'T

• Don't attempt to lift a heavy component which may be beyond your capability – get assistance.

• Don't rush to finish a job, or take unverified short cuts.

• Don't use ill-fitting tools which may slip and cause injury.

• Don't leave tools or parts lying around where someone can trip over them. Mop up oil and fuel spills at once.

• Don't allow children or pets to play in or near a vehicle being worked on.

Vauxhall Corsavan

Vauxhall Combo Van

The original Corsa models were first introduced to the European market in Spring 1993 and are covered in the companion publication to this manual – SRM 1985. The models covered in this publication are the April 1997 onward models, which were the subject of a model facelift together with extensive mechanical revisions. This manual covers models fitted with petrol engines, but other models in the range are available with diesel engines.

A variety of petrol engines are available in the Corsa range, of 1.0, 1.2, 1.4 and 1.6 litre capacity and with single overhead camshaft (SOHC) or double overhead camshaft (DOHC) configuration. All engines are of the four-cylinder, in-line type, with the exception of the 1.0 litre engine which is a three-cylinder unit. The engines all have fuel injection, and are fitted with a range of emission control systems.

The Corsa is available in 3- and 5-door Hatchback, Corsavan (3-door Van based on Hatchback), and Combo Van body styles, with a wide range of fittings and interior trim depending on the model specification.

Fully-independent front suspension is fitted; the rear suspension is semi-independent, with a torsion beam and trailing arms.

The manual gearbox is of the five-speed all synchromesh type, and a four-speed electronically-controlled transmission is available as an option on certain models.

A wide range of standard and optional equipment is available within the Corsa range to suit most tastes, including central locking, electric windows, electric sunroof, anti-lock braking system, electronic alarm system and supplemental restraint systems.

For the home mechanic, the Corsa is a relatively straightforward vehicle to maintain, and most of the items requiring frequent attention are easily accessible.

Your Vauxhall Corsa Manual

The aim of this manual is to help you get the best value from your vehicle. It can do so in several ways. It can help you decide what work must be done (even should you choose to get it done by a garage), provide information on routine maintenance and servicing, and give a logical course of action and diagnosis when random faults occur. However, it is hoped that you will use the manual by tackling the work yourself. On simpler jobs it may even be quicker than booking the car into a garage and going there twice, to leave and collect it. Perhaps most important, a lot of money can be saved by avoiding the costs a garage must charge to cover its labour and overheads.

The manual has drawings and descriptions to show the function of the various components so that their layout can be understood. Tasks are described and photographed in a clear step-by-step sequence.

Acknowledgements

Certain illustrations are the copyright of Vauxhall Motors Limited, and are used with their permission. Thanks are due to Draper Tools Limited, who provided some of the workshop tools, and to all those people at Sparkford who helped in the production of this Manual.

We take great pride in the accuracy of information given in this manual, but vehicle manufacturers make alterations and design changes during the production run of a particular vehicle of which they do not inform us. No liability can be accepted by the authors or publishers for loss, damage or injury caused by errors in, or omissions from, the information given.

Vauxhall Corsa GLS

Vauxhall Corsa 16V

The following pages are intended to help in dealing with common roadside emergencies and breakdowns. You will find more detailed fault finding information at the back of the manual, and repair information in the main chapters.

If your car won't start and the starter motor doesn't turn

- ☐ If it's a model with automatic transmission, make sure the selector is in the P or N position.
- ☐ Open the bonnet and make sure that the battery terminals are clean and tight.
- ☐ Switch on the headlights and try to start the engine. If the headlights go very dim when you are trying to start, the battery is probably flat. Try 'jump starting' (see next page), using another car.

If your car won't start even though the starter motor turns as normal

- ☐ Is there fuel in the tank?
- ☐ Is there moisture on electrical components under the bonnet? Switch off the ignition, then wipe off any obvious dampness with a dry cloth. Spray a water-repellent aerosol product (WD-40 or equivalent) on ignition and fuel system electrical connectors like those shown in the photos. Pay special attention to the ignition coil, wiring connector and HT leads, as applicable.

A Check that the spark plug HT leads (where applicable) are connected firmly.

B The fuel injection system wiring plug may cause problems if not connected securely.

C Check all multi-plugs and wiring connectors for security, with the ignition switched off.

Check that electrical connections are secure (with the ignition switched off) and spray with water dispersant if you suspect a problem due to damp.

D Check the security and condition of the battery connections.

E Check that the coil's wiring plug is secure and spray with water-dispersant if necessary.

Jump starting

When jump-starting a car using a booster battery, observe the following precautions:

✔ Before connecting the booster battery, make sure that the ignition is switched off.

✔ Ensure that all electrical equipment (lights, heater, wipers, etc) is switched off.

✔ Take note of any special precautions printed on the battery case.

✔ Make sure that the booster battery is the same voltage as the discharged one in the vehicle.

✔ If the battery is being jump-started from the battery in another vehicle, the two vehicles MUST NOT TOUCH each other.

✔ Make sure that the transmission is in neutral (or PARK, in the case of automatic transmission).

 HAYNES HiNT
Jump starting will get you out of trouble, but you must correct whatever made the battery go flat in the first place. There are three possibilities:

1 *The battery has been drained by repeated attempts to start, or by leaving the lights on.*

2 *The charging system is not working properly (alternator drivebelt slack or broken, alternator wiring fault or alternator itself faulty).*

3 *The battery itself is at fault (electrolyte low, or battery worn out).*

1 Connect one end of the red jump lead to the positive (+) terminal of the flat battery

2 Connect the other end of the red lead to the positive (+) terminal of the booster battery.

3 Connect one end of the black jump lead to the negative (-) terminal of the booster battery

4 Connect the other end of the black jump lead to the right-hand engine mounting bracket

5 Make sure that the jump leads will not come into contact with the fan, drive-belts or other moving parts of the engine.

6 Start the engine using the booster battery and run it at idle speed. Switch on the lights, rear window demister and heater blower motor, then disconnect the jump leads in the reverse order of connection. Turn off the lights etc.

Wheel changing

Some of the details shown here will vary according to model.

Warning: Do not change a wheel in a situation where you risk being injured by other traffic. On busy roads, try to stop in a lay-by or gateway. Be wary of passing traffic while changing the wheel. It is easy to become distracted by the job in hand.

Preparation

- ☐ When a puncture occurs, stop when it is safe to do so.
- ☐ Park on firm level ground, if possible, and well out of the way of other traffic.
- ☐ Use hazard warning lights, if necessary.

- ☐ If you have one, use a warning triangle to alert other drivers of your presence.
- ☐ Apply the handbrake and engage first or reverse gear.
- ☐ Chock the wheel diagonally opposite the

one being removed. A couple of large stones will do for this.
- ☐ If the ground is soft, use a flat piece of wood or paving to spread the load under the foot of the jack.

Changing the wheel

1 Remove the tool holder and unscrew the spare wheel clamp.

2 For safety, place the spare wheel under the car near the jacking point.

3 Remove the wheel trim (where fitted) and slacken each wheel bolt by half a turn.

4 Raise the jack whilst locating below the jacking point (ensure that the jack is on firm ground and located on the car correctly).

5 Turn the handle clockwise until the wheel is raised clear of the ground. Remove the bolts and lift the wheel clear.

6 Position the spare wheel and fit the bolts. Hand tighten with the wheel brace and lower the car to the ground. Tighten the wheel bolts in the sequence shown, fit the wheel trim and secure the punctured wheel in the boot.

Finally...

- ☐ Remove the wheel chocks. Stow the jack and tools in the appropriate locations in the car.

- ☐ Check the tyre pressure on the wheel just fitted. If it is low, or if you don't have a pressure gauge with you, drive slowly to the nearest garage and inflate the tyre to the correct pressure.

- ☐ Have the damaged tyre or wheel repaired or replaced, as soon as possible.

Identifying leaks

Puddles on the garage floor or drive, or obvious wetness under the bonnet or underneath the car, suggest a leak that needs investigating. It can sometimes be difficult to decide where the leak is coming from, especially if the engine bay is very dirty already. Leaking oil or fluid can also be blown rearwards by the passage of air under the car, giving a false impression of where the problem lies.

 Warning: Most automotive oils and fluids are poisonous. Wash them off skin, and change out of contaminated clothing, without delay.

 The smell of a fluid leaking from the car may provide a clue to what's leaking. Some fluids are distinctively coloured. It may help to clean the car carefully and to park it over some clean paper overnight as an aid to locating the source of the leak.
Remember that some leaks may only occur while the engine is running.

Sump oil

Engine oil may leak from the drain plug...

Oil from filter

...or from the base of the oil filter.

Gearbox oil

Gearbox oil can leak from the seals at the inboard ends of the driveshafts.

Antifreeze

Leaking antifreeze often leaves a crystalline deposit like this.

Brake fluid

A leak occurring at a wheel is almost certainly brake fluid.

Power steering fluid

Power steering fluid may leak from the pipe connectors on the steering rack.

Towing

When all else fails, you may find yourself having to get a tow home – or of course you may be helping somebody else. Long-distance recovery should only be done by a garage or breakdown service. For shorter distances, DIY towing using another car is easy enough, but observe the following points:
□ Use a proper tow-rope – they are not expensive. The vehicle being towed must display an ON TOW sign in its rear window.
□ Always turn the ignition key to the 'on' position when the vehicle is being towed, so that the steering lock is released, and

that the direction indicator and brake lights work.
□ Only attach the tow-rope to the towing eyes provided.
□ Before being towed, release the handbrake and select neutral on the transmission.
□ Never tow an automatic model backwards. If the automatic transmission appears to be in working order, the vehicle can be towed for a maximum distance of 62 miles (100 km), at no more than 50 mph (80 km/h). The vehicle can be towed greater distances with the front wheels raised.
□ Note that greater-than-usual pedal pressure will be required to operate the brakes, since the vacuum servo unit is only operational with the engine running.

□ On models with power steering, greater-than-usual steering effort will also be required.
□ Make sure that both drivers know the route before setting off.
□ The driver of the car being towed must keep the tow-rope taut at all times to avoid snatching.
□ Only drive at moderate speeds and keep the distance towed to a minimum. Drive smoothly and allow plenty of time for slowing down at junctions.

 Warning: To prevent damage to the catalytic converter, a vehicle must not be push-started, or started by towing, when the engine is at operating temperature; use jump leads (see 'Jump starting').

Introduction

There are some very simple checks that need only take a few minutes to carry out, but that could save you much inconvenience and expense.

These *Weekly checks* require no great skill or special tools and the small amount of time they take to perform could prove to be very well spent, for example.

☐ Keeping an eye on tyre condition and pressures, will not only help to stop them wearing out prematurely but could also save your life.
☐ Many breakdowns are caused by electrical problems. Battery related faults are particularly common and a quick check on a regular basis will often prevent the majority of these.

☐ If your car develops a brake fluid leak, the first time you might know about it is when your brakes don't work properly. Checking the level regularly will give warning of this kind of problem.
☐ If the oil or coolant levels run low, the cost of repairing any engine damage will be far greater than fixing the leak, for example.

Underbonnet check points

SOHC engine

A *Engine oil level dipstick*

B *Engine oil filler cap*

C *Coolant expansion cap*

D *Brake fluid reservoir*

E *Screen washer fluid reservoir*

F *Battery*

Engine oil level

Before you start

✔ Make sure that your car is level ground.
✔ Check the oil level before the car is driven or at least 5 minutes after the engine has been switched off.

The correct oil

Modern engines place great demands on their oil. It is very important that the correct oil for your car is used (See 'Lubricants and Fluids').

Car Care

● If you have to add oil frequently, you should check whether you have any oil leaks. Place some clean paper under the car overnight, and check for stains in the morning. If there are no leaks, the engine may be burning oil.

● Always maintain the level between the upper and lower dipstick marks (see photo 3). If the level is too low severe damage may occur. Oil seal failure may result if the engine is overfilled by adding too much oil.

1 The dipstick is often brightly coloured for easy identification (see *Underbonnet check points* on page 0.11 for exact location). Withdraw the dipstick.

2 Using a clean rag or paper towel remove all oil from the dipstick. Insert the clean dipstick into the tube as far as it will go, then withdraw it again.

3 Note the level on the end of the dipstick, which should be between the upper (MAX) mark (B) and lower (MIN) mark (A).

4 Oil is added through the filler cap. Unscrew the cap and top-up the level. A funnel may help to reduce spillage. Add the oil slowly, checking the level on the dipstick frequently. Avoid overfilling (see *Car Care*).

Coolant level

⚠ **Warning: DO NOT attempt to remove the expansion tank pressure cap when the engine is hot, as there is a very great risk of scalding. Do not leave open containers of coolant about, as it is poisonous.**

Car Care

● Adding coolant should not be necessary on a regular basis. If frequent topping-up is required, it is likely there is a leak. Check the radiator, all hoses and joint faces for signs of staining or wetness and rectify as necessary.

● It is important that antifreeze is used in the cooling system all year round, not just during the winter months. This is due to it's cooling and anti-corrosion properties. Do not top-up with water alone, as the antifreeze will become too diluted.

1 The coolant level varies with the temperature of the engine. When the engine is cold, the coolant level should be near the COLD (or KALT) mark.

2 If topping-up is necessary, **wait until the engine is cold**. Slowly unscrew the cap to release any pressure present in the cooling system and remove it.

3 Add a mixture of water and antifreeze to the expansion tank until the coolant level is up to the COLD/KALT mark.

Brake fluid level

Warning: Brake fluid can harm your eyes and will damage painted surfaces, so use extreme caution when handling and pouring it.

Warning: Do not use fluid that has been standing open for some time, as it absorbs moisture from the air, which can cause a dangerous loss of braking effectiveness.

HAYNES HINT
- **Make sure that your car is on level ground.**
- **The fluid level in the reservoir will drop slightly as the brake pads wear down, but the fluid level must never be allowed to drop below the MIN mark.**

Safety First!

● If the reservoir requires repeated topping-up this indicates a fluid leak somewhere in the system, that should be investigated immediately.

● If a leak is suspected, the car should not be driven until the braking system has been checked. Never take any risks where brakes are concerned.

1 The MIN and MAX marks are indicated on the reservoir. The fluid level must be kept between the marks at all times.

2 If topping-up is necessary, first wipe clean the area around the filler cap to prevent dirt entering the hydraulic system. Unscrew the reservoir cap.

3 Carefully add fluid, taking care not to spill it onto the surrounding components. Use only the specified fluid; mixing different types can cause damage to the system. Then securely refit the cap and wipe off any spilt fluid.

Power steering fluid level

Before you start:

✔ Park the vehicle on level ground.
✔ Set the steering wheel straight-ahead.
✔ The engine should be turned off.

HAYNES HINT *For the check to be accurate, the steering must not be turned once the engine has been stopped.*

Safety First!

● The need for frequent topping-up indicates a leak, which should be investigated immediately.

1 The reservoir is located at the front left-hand side of the engine compartment. The power steering fluid level is checked with a dipstick attached to the reservoir filler cap. Unscrew the filler cap from the top of the reservoir, and wipe all the fluid from the end with a clean rag or paper towel. Refit the reservoir filler cap, then remove it once more. Note the fluid level on the dipstick. When the engine is cold, the fluid level should be up to the lower mark on the dipstick. When the engine is at normal operating temperature, the fluid level should be up to the upper mark on the dipstick.

2 Top-up with the specified type of fluid if necessary and securely refit the reservoir filler cap on completion.

Washer fluid level

Screenwash additives not only keep the windscreen clean during foul weather, they also prevent the washer system freezing in cold weather – which is when you are likely to need it most. Don't top-up using plain water as the screenwash will become too diluted and will freeze during cold weather. **On no account use antifreeze in the washer system as this could discolour or damage the paintwork.**

1 The screenwasher fluid reservoir is located at the rear left-hand corner of the engine compartment.

2 When topping-up the reservoir, a screenwash additive should be added in the quantities recommended on the bottle.

Wiper blades

1 Check the condition of the wiper blades; if they are cracked or show any signs of deterioration, or if the glass swept area is smeared, renew them. Wiper blades should be renewed annually.

2 To remove a windscreen wiper blade, pull the arm fully away from the screen until it locks. Swivel the blade through 90°, press the locking tab with your fingers and slide the blade out of the arm's hooked end.

3 Don't forget to check the tailgate wiper blade as well. To remove the blade, depress the retaining tab and slide the blade out of the hooked end of the arm.

Tyre condition and pressure

It is very important that tyres are in good condition, and at the correct pressure - having a tyre failure at any speed is highly dangerous. Tyre wear is influenced by driving style - harsh braking and acceleration, or fast cornering, will all produce more rapid tyre wear. As a general rule, the front tyres wear out faster than the rears. Interchanging the tyres from front to rear ("rotating" the tyres) may result in more even wear. However, if this is completely effective, you may have the expense of replacing all four tyres at once! Remove any nails or stones embedded in the tread before they penetrate the tyre to cause deflation. If removal of a nail does reveal that the tyre has been punctured, refit the nail so that its point of penetration is marked. Then immediately change the wheel, and have the tyre repaired by a tyre dealer.

Regularly check the tyres for damage in the form of cuts or bulges, especially in the sidewalls. Periodically remove the wheels, and clean any dirt or mud from the inside and outside surfaces. Examine the wheel rims for signs of rusting, corrosion or other damage. Light alloy wheels are easily damaged by "kerbing" whilst parking; steel wheels may also become dented or buckled. A new wheel is very often the only way to overcome severe damage.

New tyres should be balanced when they are fitted, but it may become necessary to re-balance them as they wear, or if the balance weights fitted to the wheel rim should fall off. Unbalanced tyres will wear more quickly, as will the steering and suspension components. Wheel imbalance is normally signified by vibration, particularly at a certain speed (typically around 50 mph). If this vibration is felt only through the steering, then it is likely that just the front wheels need balancing. If, however, the vibration is felt through the whole car, the rear wheels could be out of balance. Wheel balancing should be carried out by a tyre dealer or garage.

1 Tread Depth - visual check
The original tyres have tread wear safety bands (B), which will appear when the tread depth reaches approximately 1.6 mm. The band positions are indicated by a triangular mark on the tyre sidewall (A).

2 Tread Depth - manual check
Alternatively, tread wear can be monitored with a simple, inexpensive device known as a tread depth indicator gauge.

3 Tyre Pressure Check
Check the tyre pressures regularly with the tyres cold. Do not adjust the tyre pressures immediately after the vehicle has been used, or an inaccurate setting will result. Tyre pressures are shown on page 0•18.

Tyre tread wear patterns

Shoulder Wear

Underinflation (wear on both sides)
Under-inflation will cause overheating of the tyre, because the tyre will flex too much, and the tread will not sit correctly on the road surface. This will cause a loss of grip and excessive wear, not to mention the danger of sudden tyre failure due to heat build-up.
Check and adjust pressures
Incorrect wheel camber (wear on one side)
Repair or renew suspension parts
Hard cornering
Reduce speed!

Centre Wear

Overinflation
Over-inflation will cause rapid wear of the centre part of the tyre tread, coupled with reduced grip, harsher ride, and the danger of shock damage occurring in the tyre casing.
Check and adjust pressures

If you sometimes have to inflate your car's tyres to the higher pressures specified for maximum load or sustained high speed, don't forget to reduce the pressures to normal afterwards.

Uneven Wear

Front tyres may wear unevenly as a result of wheel misalignment. Most tyre dealers and garages can check and adjust the wheel alignment (or "tracking") for a modest charge.
Incorrect camber or castor
Repair or renew suspension parts
Malfunctioning suspension
Repair or renew suspension parts
Unbalanced wheel
Balance tyres
Incorrect toe setting
Adjust front wheel alignment
Note: *The feathered edge of the tread which typifies toe wear is best checked by feel.*

Battery

Warning: Before carrying out any work on the vehicle battery, read the precautions given in the 'Safety First' at the beginning of this manual.

✔ Make sure that the battery tray is in good condition and that the clamp is tight. Corrosion on the tray, retaining clamp and the battery itself can be removed with a solution of water and baking soda. Thoroughly rinse all cleaned areas with water. Any metal parts damaged by corrosion should be coated with a zinc based primer, then painted.

✔ Periodically (approximately every three months), check the charge condition of the battery, as described in Chapter 5A.

✔ If the battery is flat and you need to jump start your vehicle, see *Roadside Repairs*.

Battery corrosion can be kept to a minimum by applying a layer of petroleum jelly to the clamps and terminals after they are reconnected.

1 The battery is located at the rear left-hand side of the engine compartment. The exterior of the battery should be inspected periodically for damage such as a cracked case or cover.

2 Check the tightness of the battery cable clamps to ensure good electrical connections. You should not be able to move them. Also check each cable for cracks and frayed conductors.

Electrical systems

✔ Check all external lights and the horn. Refer to the appropriate Sections of Chapter 12 for details if any of the circuits are found to be inoperative.

✔ Visually check all accessible wiring connectors, harnesses and retaining clips for security and for signs of chafing or damage.

If you need to check your brake lights and indicators unaided, back up to a wall or garage door and operate the lights. The reflected light should show if they are working properly.

1 If a single indicator light, brake stop-light or headlight has failed, it is likely that a bulb has blown and will need to be replaced. Refer to Chapter 12 for details. If both brake lights have failed, it is possible that the stop-light switch operated by the brake pedal has failed. Refer to Chapter 9 for details.

2 If more than one indicator light or tail light has failed it is likely that either a fuse has blown or that there is a fault in the circuit (see Chapter 12). The main fuses are located in the fusebox situated behind the cover in the facia on the driver's side.

3 To replace a blown fuse, remove it, where applicable, using the plastic tool provided. Fit a new fuse of the same rating, available from car accessory shops. It is important that you find the reason that the fuse blew (see *Electrical fault finding* in Chapter 12).

Lubricants and fluids

Engine . . . . Multigrade engine oil, viscosity SAE 5W/40 or 10W/40,
to API SH and ACEA-A3.96
(Duckhams QXR Premium Petrol Engine Oil)

Manual gearbox . . . . Vauxhall/Opel gear oil No 90 540 998

Automatic transmission . . . . Dexron type II automatic transmission fluid
(Duckhams ATF Autotrans III)

Power steering fluid reservoir . . . . Dexron type II automatic transmission fluid
(Duckhams ATF Autotrans III)

Cooling system . . . . Clean water and antifreeze to Vauxhall/Opel specification
GME L 1301
(Duckhams Antifreeze and Summer Coolant)

Brake fluid reservoir . . . . Hydraulic fluid to DOT 4
(Duckhams Universal Brake and Clutch Fluid)

Choosing your engine oil

Engines need oil, not only to lubricate moving parts and minimise wear, but also to maximise power output and to improve fuel economy. By introducing a simplified and improved range of engine oils, Duckhams has taken away the confusion and made it easier for you to choose the right oil for your engine.

HOW ENGINE OIL WORKS

• *Beating friction*

Without oil, the moving surfaces inside your engine will rub together, heat up and melt, quickly causing the engine to seize. Engine oil creates a film which separates these moving parts, preventing wear and heat build-up.

• *Cooling hot-spots*

Temperatures inside the engine can exceed 1000° C. The engine oil circulates and acts as a coolant, transferring heat from the hot-spots to the sump.

• *Cleaning the engine internally*

Good quality engine oils clean the inside of your engine, collecting and dispersing combustion deposits and controlling them until they are trapped by the oil filter or flushed out at oil change.

OIL CARE - FOLLOW THE CODE

To handle and dispose of used engine oil safely, always:

OIL CARE
FOLLOW THE CODE
OIL BANK LINE
0800 66 33 66
www.oilbankline.org.uk

• *Avoid skin contact with used engine oil. Repeated or prolonged contact can be harmful.*
• *Dispose of used oil and empty packs in a responsible manner in an authorised disposal site. Call 0800 663366 to find the one nearest to you. Never tip oil down drains or onto the ground.*

Note: *Pressures are quoted for standard tyre fitments (see Chapter 10); consult a dealer or tyre specialist for alternative or revised recommendations.*

	Front	Rear
Corsa and Corsavan		
Normal load (up to 3 passengers):		
1.0 litre models:		
145/80 R 13-75 T tyres	2.2 bars (32 psi)	1.8 bars (26 psi)
All other tyres	2.0 bars (29 psi)	1.6 bars (23 psi)
1.2 litre SOHC models:		
145/80 R 13-75 T tyres	2.1 bars (30 psi)	1.9 bars (28 psi)
All other tyres	1.9 bars (28 psi)	1.7 bars (24 psi)
1.2 litre DOHC models	2.2 bars (32 psi)	2.0 bars (29 psi)
1.4 litre SOHC models with single-point fuel injection (X 14 SZ):		
145/80 R 13-75 T tyres	2.4 bars (35 psi)	2.2 bars (32 psi)
All other tyres	2.1 bars (30 psi)	1.9 bars (28 psi)
1.4 litre SOHC models with multi-point fuel injection (C 14 SE):		
All tyres sizes	2.3 bars (33 psi)	2.1 bars (30 psi)
1.4 litre DOHC model	2.4 bars (35 psi)	2.2 bars (32 psi)
1.6 litre models	2.2 bars (32 psi)	2.0 bars (29 psi)
Fully laden:		
1.0 litre models	2.3 bars (33 psi)	2.7 bars (39 psi)
1.2 litre SOHC models:		
145/80 R 13-75 T tyres	2.1 bars (30 psi)	2.4 bars (35 psi)
All other tyres	1.9 bars (28 psi)	2.2 bars (32 psi)
1.2 litre DOHC models	2.3 bars (33 psi)	2.9 bars (42 psi)
1.4 litre SOHC models with single-point fuel injection (X 14 SZ):		
145/80 R 13-75 T tyres	2.4 bars (35 psi)	2.8 bars (41 psi)
All other tyres	2.1 bars (30 psi)	2.5 bars (36 psi)
1.4 litre SOHC models with multi-point fuel injection (C 14 SE):		
All tyres sizes	2.3 bars (33 psi)	2.1 bars (30 psi)
1.4 litre DOHC models	2.4 bars (35 psi)	2.2 bars (32 psi)
1.6 litre models	2.2 bars (32 psi)	2.0 bars (29 psi)
Combo Van		
Normal load (up to 3 passengers)	2.1 bars (30 psi)	2.1 bars (30 psi)
Fully laden	2.1 bars (30 psi)	3.5 bars (51 psi)

Chapter 1
Routine maintenance and servicing

Contents

Degrees of difficulty

Easy, suitable for novice with little experience		Fairly easy, suitable for beginner with some experience		Fairly difficult, suitable for competent DIY mechanic		Difficult, suitable for experienced DIY mechanic		Very difficult, suitable for expert DIY or professional	

Lubricants and fluids

Refer to end of *Weekly checks*

Capacities

Engine oil

Oil change, including filter:

1.0 litre DOHC engines	3.0 litres
1.2 litre DOHC engines	3.5 litres
1.2 and 1.4 litre SOHC engines:	
Without air conditioning	3.5 litres
With air conditioning	3.25 litres
1.4 and 1.6 litre DOHC engines	3.25 litres
Difference between MAX and MIN dipstick marks	1.0 litre

Cooling system

1.0 and 1.2 litre DOHC engines	4.3 litres
1.2 and 1.4 litre SOHC engines:	
Without air conditioning	5.8 litres
With air conditioning	6.1 litres
1.4 and 1.6 litre DOHC engines:	
Without air conditioning	5.6 litres
With air conditioning	5.8 litres

Fuel tank

All models except Combo Van	46.0 litres
Combo Van models	50.0 litres

Manual gearbox .... 1.6 litres

Automatic transmission

Drain and refill .... 3.0 to 3.5 litres

Power steering fluid reservoir .... 1.0 litre

Cooling system

Antifreeze mixtures (Vauxhall/Opel specification antifreeze):	Antifreeze	Water
Protection to –10°C	20%	80%
Protection to –20°C	34%	66%
Protection to –30°C	44%	56%
Protection to –40°C	52%	48%

Fuel grade

Note: *95 RON (Premium) unleaded fuel is the fuel recommended by the manufacturers. 98 RON (Super) unleaded may also be used but there will be no performance gain, or economy savings, by doing so.*

Fuel octane requirement:

1.0 litre engine[1]	95 RON (Premium) or 98 RON (Super) unleaded
1.2 litre DOHC engine[1]	95 RON (Premium) or 98 RON (Super) unleaded
1.2 litre SOHC engine[2]	95 RON (Premium) or 98 RON (Super) unleaded
1.4 litre SOHC engine with multi-point fuel injection (C 14 SE)[3]	95 RON (Premium) or 98 RON (Super) unleaded
1.4 litre SOHC engine with single-point fuel injection (X 14 SZ)[2]	95 RON (Premium) or 98 RON (Super) unleaded
1.4 litre DOHC engine[1]	95 RON (Premium) or 98 RON (Super) unleaded
1.6 litre engine[1]	95 RON (Premium) or 98 RON (Super) unleaded

1 If no higher-octane unleaded fuel is available, 91 RON (Regular) unleaded fuel can be used, but there will be a reduction in engine power and torque.

2 If no higher-octane unleaded fuel is available, 91 RON (Regular) unleaded fuel can be used, provided severe engine loads (including towing and heavy payloads) and full-throttle operation are avoided, but there will be a reduction in engine power and torque.

3 The octane coding plug must be positioned correctly in accordance with the octane rating of the fuel being used – refer to Chapter 4B, Section 1, for details. If no higher-octane unleaded fuel is available, 91 RON (Regular) unleaded fuel can be used, provided a special octane plug (available from a Vauxhall/Opel dealer) is used, but there will be a reduction in engine power and torque.

Ignition system

Spark plugs:	Type	Electrode gap
1.0 litre DOHC engines	Bosch FR8LDC	1.0 mm
1.2 litre DOHC engines	Bosch FR8LDC	1.0 mm
1.2 litre DOHC engines	Bosch WR8DC	0.7 mm
1.4 litre SOHC engines with multi-point fuel injection (C 14 SE)	Bosch WR7DC	0.7 mm
1.4 litre SOHC engines with single-point fuel injection (X 14 SZ)	Bosch FR8LDC4	0.8 mm
1.4 litre DOHC engines	Bosch FR8LDC	0.7 mm
1.6 litre DOHC engines	Bosch FLR8LDC	0.7 mm

Clutch

Clutch pedal travel . . . . 126.0 to 132.0 mm

Braking system

Minimum front brake pad lining thickness (including backing plate) . . . 7.0 mm
Minimum rear brake shoe lining thickness . . . . 2.5 mm

Suspension and steering

Tyre pressures . . . . Refer to end of *Weekly checks*

Torque wrench settings

	Nm	lbf ft
Cooling system bleed screw	15	11
Crankshaft pulley-to-sprocket bolts:		
1.0 and 1.2 litre DOHC engines	8	6
Oil filter housing cap to filter housing:		
1.0 and 1.2 litre DOHC engines	15	11
Right-hand engine mounting block-to-engine bracket bolt/nut	60	44
Right-hand engine mounting bracket-to-engine bolts:		
SOHC engines without power steering	65	48
SOHC engines with power steering	60	44
DOHC engines	60	44
Roadwheel bolts	110	81
Spark plugs	25	18
Sump drain plug:		
1.0 and 1.2 litre DOHC engines	10	7
All other engines:		
Engines with steel sump	55	41
Engines with aluminium sump	45	33

Underbonnet view of a Vauxhall Corsa 1.0 litre DOHC engine

1 Air cleaner assembly
2 Front suspension strut top mounting
3 Brake fluid reservoir
4 Air box
5 Coolant expansion tank
6 Washer fluid reservoir
7 Battery negative (earth) terminal
8 Battery condition indicator
9 Distributorless ignition system DIS module
10 Clutch cable adjuster
11 Oil filter housing
12 Oil filler cap
13 Oil level dipstick
14 Thermostat housing
15 Air intake trunking
16 Resonator
17 Air mass meter

Underbonnet view of a Vauxhall Corsa 1.2 litre DOHC engine

1 Air cleaner assembly
2 Front suspension strut top mounting
3 Brake fluid reservoir
4 Air box
5 Coolant expansion tank
6 Washer fluid reservoir
7 Battery negative (earth) terminal
8 Battery condition indicator
9 Distributorless ignition system DIS module
10 Clutch cable adjuster
11 Oil filter housing
12 Oil filler cap
13 Oil level dipstick
14 Thermostat housing
15 Air intake trunking
16 Air mass meter

Underbonnet view of a Vauxhall Corsa 1.2 litre SOHC engine

1 Air cleaner assembly
2 Timing belt covers
3 Front suspension strut top mounting
4 Brake fluid reservoir
5 Air box
6 Exhaust gas recirculation (EGR) valve
7 Manifold absolute pressure (MAP) sensor
8 Coolant expansion tank
9 Washer fluid reservoir
10 Battery negative (earth) terminal
11 Battery condition indicator
12 Electronic modules
13 Coolant hose
14 Radiator
15 Cooling fan
16 Oil level dipstick
17 Oxygen sensor
18 Hot air tube
19 Camshaft cover breather hose
20 Alternator
21 Camshaft cover
22 Oil filler cap
23 Distributorless ignition system (DIS) module

Underbonnet view of a Vauxhall Corsa 1.6 litre DOHC engine

1 Air cleaner assembly
2 Front suspension strut top mounting
3 Brake fluid reservoir
4 Intake air temperature sensor
5 Inlet manifold upper section
6 Manifold absolute pressure (MAP) sensor
7 Coolant expansion tank
8 Washer fluid reservoir
9 Battery negative (earth) terminal
10 Battery condition indicator
11 Bonnet anti-theft alarm switch
12 Secondary air injection switchover valve
13 Secondary air injection pump
14 Power steering fluid reservoir
15 Secondary air injection air duct
16 Distributorless ignition system (DIS)
   module
17 Oil level dipstick
18 Secondary air injection combination valve
19 Oil filler cap
20 Thermostat housing
21 Air intake trunking
22 Timing belt covers

Front underbody view of a Vauxhall Corsa 1.2 litre DOHC engine

1 Petrol pipes
2 Front suspension lower arm
3 Front brake caliper
4 Front suspension tie-bar front mounting
5 Radiator hose
6 Anti-roll bar
7 Catalytic converter
8 Radiator electric cooling fan
9 Left-hand engine mounting
10 Left-hand driveshaft
11 Brake fluid pipes
12 Driveshaft gaiter
13 Differential cover plate
14 Rear engine/gearbox mounting
15 Engine oil drain plug
16 Steering rack
17 Alternator
18 Right-hand driveshaft

Front underbody view of a Vauxhall Corsa 1.6 litre DOHC engine

1 Petrol pipes
2 Front suspension lower arm
3 Front brake caliper
4 Charcoal canister
5 Front suspension tie-bar front mounting
6 Radiator hose
7 Anti-roll bar
8 Oil filter
9 Left-hand engine mounting
10 Left-hand driveshaft
11 Brake fluid pipes
12 Driveshaft gaiter
13 Differential cover plate
14 Rear engine/gearbox mounting
15 Exhaust front pipe connection
16 Engine oil drain plug
17 Steering rack
18 Right-hand driveshaft
19 Exhaust front pipe

Rear underbody view of a Vauxhall Corsa Hatchback model

1 Brake fluid pipe
2 Rear suspension trailing arm
3 Rear brake backplate
4 Coil spring
5 Rear exhaust silencer
6 Exhaust heat shield
7 Rear axle
8 Fuel filler and vent pipes
9 Fuel pipe
10 Fuel filter
11 Fuel tank
12 Fuel tank securing strap
13 Exhaust rear section
14 Handbrake cable

The maintenance intervals in this manual are provided with the assumption that you, not the dealer, will be carrying out the work. These are the minimum maintenance intervals based on the schedule recommended by the manufacturer for vehicles driven daily. If you wish to keep your vehicle in peak condition at all times, you may wish to perform some of these procedures more often. We encourage frequent maintenance, because it enhances the efficiency, performance and resale value of your vehicle.

If the vehicle is driven in dusty areas, used to tow a trailer, or driven frequently at slow speeds (idling in traffic) or on short journeys, more frequent maintenance intervals are recommended.

When the vehicle is new, it should be serviced by a factory-authorised dealer service department, in order to preserve the factory warranty.

Every 250 miles (400 km) or weekly

☐ Refer to *Weekly checks*

Every 5000 miles (7500 km) or 6 months – whichever comes first

☐ Renew the engine oil and filter (Section 3)

Note: *Frequent oil and filter changes are good for the engine. We recommend changing the oil at the mileage specified here, or at least twice a year if the mileage covered is a less.*

Every 10 000 miles (15 000 km) or 12 months – whichever comes first

☐ Check all underbonnet and underbody components, pipes and hoses for leaks (Section 4)
☐ Check the condition of the auxiliary drivebelt, and renew if necessary (Sections 5 and 6)
☐ Check the condition and security of the ignition HT system components (Section 7)
☐ Check the operation of the engine management system (Section 8)
☐ Check the operation and condition of the emission control system components (Section 9)
☐ Renew the pollen filter (Section 10)
☐ Check the operation of the horn, all lights, and the wipers and washers (Section 11)
☐ Check the headlight beam alignment (Section 12)
☐ Check the tightness of the roadwheel bolts (Section 13)
☐ Check the condition of the front brake pads (renew if necessary), the calipers and discs (Section 14)
☐ Check the rear brake pressure-regulating valve adjustment – 1.4 and 1.6 litre engine models (Section 15)
☐ Check the condition of all brake fluid pipes and hoses (Section 16)
☐ Check the bodywork and underbody for damage and corrosion, and check the condition of the underbody corrosion protection (Section 17)
☐ Check the condition of the exhaust system components (Section 18)
☐ Carry out a road test (Section 19)

Every 20 000 miles (30 000 km) or 2 years – whichever comes first

☐ Renew the air cleaner filter element (Section 20)
☐ Renew the fuel filter (Section 21)
☐ Check the manual gearbox oil level – where applicable (Section 22)
☐ Check the automatic transmission fluid level – where applicable (Section 23)
☐ Check the operation of the automatic transmission – where applicable (Section 24)
☐ Renew the coolant (Section 25)
☐ Check the clutch cable adjustment – where applicable (Section 26)
☐ Lubricate all door, bonnet and tailgate hinges and locks (Section 27)
☐ Check the condition of the rear brake shoes (renew if necessary), the drums and wheel cylinders (Section 28)
☐ Renew the brake fluid (Section 29)
☐ Check the condition of the front suspension and steering components, particularly the rubber gaiters and seals (Section 30)
☐ Check the condition of the rear suspension components (Section 31)
☐ Check the condition of the driveshaft joint gaiters, and the driveshaft joints (Section 32)

Every 30 000 miles (45 000 km) or 3 years – whichever comes first

☐ Renew the automatic transmission fluid – where applicable (Section 33)

Every 40 000 miles (60 000 km) or 4 years – whichever comes first

☐ Renew the spark plugs (Section 34)
☐ Renew the timing belt – 1.4 and 1.6 litre DOHC engines (Section 35)

Note: *Although the normal interval for timing belt renewal on these engines is 60 000 miles (90 000 km), it is strongly recommended that the interval is reduced to 40 000 miles (60 000 km) on vehicles which are subjected to intensive use, ie, mainly short journeys or a lot of stop-start driving. The actual belt renewal interval is therefore very much up to the individual owner, but bear in mind that severe engine damage will result if the belt breaks.*

☐ Renew the timing belt – 1.2 and 1.4 litre SOHC engines (Section 36)

Note: *Although the normal interval for timing belt renewal on these engines is 80 000 miles (120 000 km), it is strongly recommended that the interval is reduced to 40 000 miles (60 000 km) on vehicles which are subjected to intensive use, ie, mainly short journeys or a lot of stop-start driving. The actual belt renewal interval is therefore very much up to the individual owner, but bear in mind that severe engine damage will result if the belt breaks.*

1 General information

This Chapter is designed to help the home mechanic maintain his/her vehicle for safety, economy, long life and peak performance.

The Chapter contains a master maintenance schedule, followed by sections dealing specifically with each task on the schedule. Visual checks, adjustments, component renewal and other helpful items are included. Refer to the accompanying Illustrations of the engine compartment and the underside of the vehicle for the locations of the various components.

Servicing of your vehicle in accordance with the mileage/time maintenance schedule and the following sections will provide a planned maintenance programme, which should result in a long and reliable service life. This is a comprehensive plan, so maintaining some items but not others at the specified service intervals, will not produce the same results.

As you service your vehicle, you will discover that many of the procedures can – and should – be grouped together, because of the particular procedure being performed, or because of the close proximity of two otherwise-unrelated components to one another. For example, if the vehicle is raised for any reason, the exhaust can be inspected at the same time as the suspension and steering components.

The first step in this maintenance programme is to prepare yourself before the actual work begins. Read through all the sections relevant to the work to be carried out, then make a list and gather together all the parts and tools required. If a problem is encountered, seek advice from a parts specialist, or a dealer service department.

2 Regular maintenance

1 If, from the time the vehicle is new, the routine maintenance schedule is followed closely, and frequent checks are made of fluid levels and high-wear items, as suggested throughout this manual, the engine will be kept in relatively good running condition, and the need for additional work will be minimised.
2 It is possible that there will be times when the engine is running poorly due to the lack of regular maintenance. This is even more likely if a used vehicle, which has not received regular and frequent maintenance checks, is purchased. In such cases, additional work may need to be carried out, outside of the regular maintenance intervals.
3 If engine wear is suspected, a compression test (Chapter 2A, 2B or 2C) will provide valuable information regarding the overall performance of the main internal components. Such a test can be used as a basis to decide on the extent of the work to be carried out. If for example a compression test indicates serious internal engine wear, conventional maintenance as described in this Chapter will not greatly improve the performance of the engine, and may prove a waste of time and money, unless extensive overhaul work (Chapter 2D or 2E) is carried out first.
4 The following series of operations are those most often required to improve the performance of a generally poor-running engine:

Primary operations

a) Clean, inspect and test the battery ('Weekly checks').
b) Check all the engine-related fluids ('Weekly checks').
c) Check the condition and tension of the auxiliary drivebelt (Sections 5 or 6).
d) Renew the spark plugs (Section 34).
e) Inspect the ignition HT leads – where applicable (Section 7).
f) Check the condition of the air cleaner filter element, and renew if necessary (Section 20).
g) Check the condition of all hoses, and check for fluid leaks (Section 4).

5 If the above operations do not prove fully effective, carry out the following secondary operations:

Secondary operations

All items listed under *Primary operations*, plus the following:
a) Check the ignition system (Chapter 5B).
b) Check the charging system (Chapter 5A).
c) Check the fuel system (Chapter 4A or 4B).
d) Renew the ignition HT leads – where applicable (Section 7).

Every 5000 miles (7500 km) or 6 months – whichever comes first

3 Engine oil and filter renewal

 Frequent oil and filter changes are the most important preventative maintenance procedures which can be undertaken by the DIY owner. As engine oil ages, it becomes diluted and contaminated, which leads to premature engine wear.

1 Before starting this procedure, gather together all the necessary tools and materials. Also make sure that you have plenty of clean rags and newspapers handy, to mop up any spills. Ideally, the engine oil should be warm, as it will drain more easily, and more built-up sludge will be removed with it. Take care not to touch the exhaust or any other hot parts of the engine when working under the vehicle. To avoid any possibility of scalding, and to protect yourself from possible skin irritants and other harmful contaminants in used engine oils, it is advisable to wear gloves when carrying out this work.
2 Access to the underside of the vehicle will be greatly improved if it can be raised on a lift, driven onto ramps, or jacked up and supported on axle stands (see *Jacking and vehicle support*). Whichever method is chosen, make sure that the vehicle remains level, or if it is at an angle, that the drain plug is at the lowest point. The drain plug is located at the rear of the sump.
3 Remove the oil filler cap from the camshaft cover (twist it through a quarter-turn anti-clockwise and withdraw it).
4 Using a spanner, or preferably a suitable socket and bar, slacken the drain plug about half a turn **(see illustration)**. Position the draining container under the drain plug, then remove the plug completely. If possible, try to keep the plug pressed into the sump while unscrewing it by hand the last couple of turns.

3.4 Engine oil drain plug (arrowed) – SOHC engine with steel sump

3.14a Fit a new sealing O-ring to the oil filter housing cap . . .

 As the plug releases from the threads, move it away sharply, so that the stream of oil from the sump runs into the container, not up your sleeve.

5 Allow some time for the oil to drain, noting that it may be necessary to reposition the container as the oil flow slows to a trickle.

6 After all the oil has drained, wipe the drain plug and the sealing washer with a clean rag. Examine the condition of the sealing washer, and renew it if it shows signs of scoring or other damage which may prevent an oil-tight seal. Clean the area around the drain plug opening, and refit the plug complete with the washer. Tighten the plug securely, preferably to the specified torque, using a torque wrench.

7 Two different types of oil filter will be encountered on engines covered by this manual. On 1.0 and 1.2 litre DOHC engines, the oil filter is of the element type, which is removed from the oil filter housing and then a new element is fitted to the housing. On all other engines, the filter is of the metal container type, which is unscrewed and removed as a unit from the engine, and then a new container is screwed into position. Proceed as described under the following sub-Sections, according to engine type.

3.14b . . . then clip the new oil filter element to the cap – 1.0 and 1.2 litre DOHC engines

1.0 & 1.2 litre DOHC engines

8 The oil filter housing is located at the front left-hand side of the engine.

9 Move the container into position under the oil filter housing.

10 Unscrew the oil filter housing cap and withdraw the cap together with the filter from the oil filter housing.

11 Withdraw the filter from the oil filter housing cap.

12 Use clean rags to remove all remaining oil, dirt and sludge from the oil filter housing.

13 Remove the sealing O-ring from the oil filter housing cap.

14 Fit a new sealing O-ring to the oil filter housing cap then clip the new oil filter element to the cap **(see illustrations)**.

15 Fit the cap and filter element assembly to the oil filter housing and screw the cap into position. Finally, tighten the cap to the specified torque **(see illustrations)**.

1.2 SOHC, 1.4 & 1.6 litre engines

16 The oil filter is located at the front left-hand side of the engine. Note that on 1.4 and 1.6 litre DOHC engine models, access is most easily obtained from underneath the front of the vehicle.

17 Move the container into position under the oil filter.

18 Using an oil filter removal tool if necessary, slacken the filter initially, then unscrew it by hand the rest of the way **(see**

illustration). Empty the oil in the old filter into the container. To ensure that the old filter is completely empty before disposal, puncture the filter dome in at least two places and allow any remaining oil to drain through the punctures and into the container.

19 Use a clean rag to remove all oil, dirt and sludge from the filter sealing area on the engine. Check the old filter to make sure that the rubber sealing ring has not stuck to the engine. If it has, carefully remove it.

20 Apply a light coating of clean engine oil to the sealing ring on the new filter, then screw the filter into position on the engine. Tighten the filter firmly by hand only – **do not** use any tools.

21 Remove the old oil and all tools from under the vehicle then, if applicable, lower the vehicle to the ground.

All engines

22 Fill the engine through the filler hole in the camshaft cover, using the correct grade and type of oil (refer to *Weekly checks* for details of topping-up). Pour in half the specified quantity of oil first, then wait a few minutes for the oil to drain into the sump. Continue to add oil, a small quantity at a time, until the level is up to the lower mark on the dipstick. Adding a further 1.0 litre will bring the level up to the upper mark on the dipstick.

23 Start the engine and run it for a few minutes, while checking for leaks around the oil filter and the sump drain plug. Note that there may be a delay of a few seconds before the oil pressure warning light goes out when the engine is first started, as the oil circulates through the new oil filter and the engine oil galleries before the pressure builds up.

24 Stop the engine, and wait a few minutes for the oil to settle in the sump once more. With the new oil circulated and the filter now completely full, recheck the level on the dipstick, and add more oil as necessary.

25 Dispose of the used engine oil and filter safely, with reference to *General repair procedures* in the Reference Chapter of this manual. Do not discard the old filter with domestic household waste. The facility for waste oil disposal provided by many local council refuse tips generally has a filter receptacle alongside.

3.15a Fit the cap and filter element assembly to the oil filter housing . . .

3.15b . . . screw the assembly into place and tighten the cap to the specified torque – 1.0 and 1.2 litre DOHC engines

3.18 Using an oil filter removal tool to slacken the filter – 1.2 SOHC, 1.4 and 1.6 litre engines

Every 10 000 miles (15 000 km) or 12 months – whichever comes first

4 Hose and fluid leak check

1 Visually inspect the engine joint faces, gaskets and seals for any signs of water or oil leaks. Pay particular attention to the areas around the camshaft cover, cylinder head, oil filter and sump joint faces. Bear in mind that, over a period of time, some very slight seepage from these areas is to be expected; what you are really looking for is any indication of a serious leak. Should a leak be found, renew the offending gasket or oil seal by referring to the appropriate Chapters in this manual.

2 Also check the security and condition of all the engine-related pipes and hoses. Ensure that all cable ties or securing clips are in place, and in good condition. Clips which are broken or missing can lead to chafing of the hoses pipes or wiring, which could cause more serious problems in the future.

3 Carefully check the radiator hoses and heater hoses along their entire length. Renew any hose which is cracked, swollen or deteriorated. Cracks will show up better if the hose is squeezed. Pay close attention to the hose clips that secure the hoses to the cooling system components. Hose clips can pinch and puncture hoses, resulting in cooling system leaks. If wire-type hose clips are used, it may be a good idea to replace them with screw-type clips.

4 Inspect all the cooling system components (hoses, joint faces, etc) for leaks. Where any problems of this nature are found on system components, renew the component or gasket with reference to Chapter 3.

HAYNES HiNT
A leak in the cooling system will usually show up as white- or rust-coloured deposits on the area adjoining the leak.

5 Where applicable, inspect the automatic transmission fluid cooler hoses for leaks or deterioration.

6 With the vehicle raised, inspect the petrol tank and filler neck for punctures, cracks and other damage. The connection between the filler neck and tank is especially critical. Sometimes, a rubber filler neck or connecting hose will leak due to loose retaining clamps or deteriorated rubber.

7 Carefully check all rubber hoses and metal fuel lines leading away from the petrol tank. Check for loose connections, deteriorated hoses, crimped lines and other damage. Pay particular attention to the vent pipes and hoses, which often loop up around the filler neck and can become blocked or crimped. Follow the lines to the front of the vehicle, carefully inspecting them all the way. Renew damaged sections as necessary.

8 From within the engine compartment, check the security of all fuel hose attachments and pipe unions, and inspect the fuel hoses and vacuum hoses for kinks, chafing and deterioration.

9 Where applicable, check the condition of the power steering fluid hoses and pipes.

5 Auxiliary drivebelt check and renewal – 1.0 and 1.2 litre DOHC engines

Checking

1 The ribbed type auxiliary drivebelt drives the alternator, coolant pump and the power steering pump and/or air conditioning compressor where applicable. An automatic drivebelt tensioner is fitted, and there is no requirement to check the drivebelt tension.

2 For improved access, remove the air cleaner assembly as described in Chapter 4A.

3 The belt should be inspected along its entire length, and if it is found to be worn, frayed or cracked, it should be renewed as a precaution against breakage in service.

Removal, renewal and refitting

4 To remove the drivebelt, remove the air cleaner assembly (if not already done) for improved access, as described in Chapter 4A.

5 Mark the running direction of the belt if it is to be refitted.

6 On models without air conditioning, obtain a wire rod, or roll pin, of approximately 4 mm diameter which can be used to lock the tensioner in the released position. Using a suitable spanner or socket and wrench engaged with the tensioner roller bolt, lever the tensioner roller clockwise against the spring pressure, until the hole in the tensioner roller arm is aligned with the corresponding hole in the tensioner body (it may be necessary to use a mirror to accurately observe the position of the hole). The roller can then be locked in position by inserting the rod or roll pin through the two holes (see illustrations).

7 On models with air conditioning, using a suitable spanner or socket and wrench engaged with the tensioner roller bolt, lever the tensioner roller clockwise against the spring pressure, until the tensioner can be heard to audibly lock in its end position.

1.0 litre engine

8 Attach a suitable hoist and lifting tackle to the engine lifting brackets on the cylinder head, and support the weight of the engine.

9 Undo the three bolts securing the right-hand engine mounting bracket to the timing cover.

10 Working under the vehicle, remove the nut and bolt securing the right-hand engine mounting bracket to the mounting block on the body and withdraw the mounting bracket.

11 Withdraw the auxiliary drivebelt from the pulleys.

12 Refit the drivebelt by slipping the belt over the pulleys. If the original belt is being refitted, ensure that the running direction marks made

5.6a Lever the drivebelt tensioner roller clockwise, until the hole in the tensioner arm (arrowed) is aligned with the corresponding hole in the tensioner body – 1.2 litre DOHC engine

5.6b Insert the 4 mm rod or drill bit through the two holes . . .

5.6c . . . to lock the tensioner in the released position – 1.2 litre DOHC engine

on the belt are positioned as noted before removal.

13 Using the method described previously, lever the tensioner roller until the locking tool (where used) can be removed from the backplate. Use the spanner or wrench to gradually release the tensioner in order to tension the belt. **Do not** allow the tensioner to spring back unrestrained.

14 Check that the belt is correctly located on all the pulleys.

15 Refit the engine mounting bracket, and tighten the three securing bolts to the specified torque.

16 Refit the nut and bolt securing the right-hand engine mounting bracket to the mounting block on the body, and tighten the nut and bolt to the specified torque.

17 Disconnect the hoist and lifting tackle.

18 Refit the air cleaner assembly as described in Chapter 4A.

1.2 litre engine

19 Firmly apply the handbrake, then jack up the front of the car and support it securely on axle stands (see *Jacking and vehicle support*). Remove the right-hand roadwheel and the wheelarch liner for access to the crankshaft pulley.

20 Prevent the crankshaft from turning using a spanner or socket on the crankshaft sprocket bolt, then undo the six bolts securing the crankshaft pulley to the pulley hub. Slip the auxiliary drivebelt off the pulley and remove the pulley from the hub.

21 Attach a suitable hoist and lifting tackle to the engine lifting brackets on the cylinder head, and support the weight of the engine.

22 Undo the three bolts securing the right-hand engine mounting bracket to the timing cover.

23 Working under the vehicle, remove the nut and bolt securing the right-hand engine mounting bracket to the mounting block on the body.

24 Twist the mounting bracket downwards, approximately 90°, then twist it to the left, towards the bulkhead, approximately 90°. Lower the bracket and manipulate it out from under the car.

25 Withdraw the auxiliary drivebelt from the remaining pulleys.

26 Refit the drivebelt by laying it in place over the pulleys. If the original belt is being refitted, ensure that the running direction marks made on the belt are positioned as noted before removal.

27 Insert the retaining bolts into the engine mounting bracket and manipulate the bracket back into position using the reverse of the removal sequence.

28 Screw in the three mounting bolts and tighten them to the specified torque.

29 Refit the nut and bolt securing the right-hand engine mounting bracket to the mounting block on the body, and tighten the nut and bolt to the specified torque.

30 Refit the crankshaft pulley to the pulley

hub and tighten the six bolts to the specified torque.

31 Engage the auxiliary drivebelt with the crankshaft pulley and check that the belt is correctly located on all the other pulleys.

32 Using the method described previously, lever the tensioner roller until the locking tool (where used) can be removed from the backplate. Use the spanner or wrench to gradually release the tensioner in order to tension the belt. **Do not** allow the tensioner to spring back unrestrained.

33 Refit the wheelarch liner and the roadwheel, tightening the roadwheel bolts to the specified torque.

34 Disconnect the hoist and lifting tackle, then lower the car to the ground.

35 Refit the air cleaner assembly as described in Chapter 4A.

---

6 Auxiliary drivebelt check and renewal – 1.2 SOHC, 1.4 and 1.6 litre engines

V-belt models

Checking and adjustment

1 Correct tensioning of the auxiliary drivebelt will ensure that it has a long life. Beware, however, of overtightening, as this can cause excessive wear in the alternator.

2 The auxiliary drivebelt drives the alternator, and the power steering pump and/or air conditioning compressor where applicable.

3 For improved access, remove the air cleaner assembly as described in Chapter 4B.

4 The belt should be inspected along its entire length, and if it is found to be worn, frayed or cracked, it should be renewed as a precaution against breakage in service. It is advisable to carry a spare drivebelt of the correct type in the vehicle at all times.

5 Although special tools are available for measuring the belt tension, a good approximation can be achieved if the belt is tensioned so that there is approximately 13.0 mm of total free movement under firm thumb and finger pressure at the mid-point of the longest run between pulleys.

6 If adjustment is required, slacken the alternator mounting bolt nut(s) and the bolt securing the adjuster strut to the top of the

alternator. Turn the adjuster bolt as necessary to apply tension to the belt, until the correct tension is achieved. Tighten the adjuster strut and alternator mountings on completion.

Removal, renewal and refitting

7 To remove the belt, simply loosen the mounting bolt nut(s), and fully slacken the adjuster bolt, as described previously, then slip the belt from the pulleys.

8 Refit the belt, and tension it as described previously.

Ribbed belt models without power steering or air conditioning

Checking and adjustment

9 Proceed as described in paragraphs 1 to 4.

10 An automatic drivebelt tensioner is fitted, and there is no requirement to check the drivebelt tension.

Removal, renewal and refitting

11 To remove the drivebelt, remove the air cleaner assembly (if not already done) for improved access, as described in Chapter 4B.

12 Mark the running direction of the belt if it is to be refitted.

13 Using a suitable spanner or socket and wrench engaged with the tensioner roller bolt, lever the tensioner roller against the spring pressure. The roller can then be locked in position, using a suitable pin punch or similar tool inserted through the lug on the roller assembly, to engage with the corresponding hole in the tensioner backplate **(see illustrations)**.

14 With the tensioner locked in position, slip the drivebelt from the pulleys.

15 Refit the drivebelt by slipping the belt over the pulleys. If the original belt is being refitted, ensure that the running direction marks made on the belt are positioned as noted before removal.

16 Using the method described previously, lever the tensioner roller until the locking tool can be removed from the backplate. Use the spanner or wrench to gradually release the tensioner in order to tension the belt. **Do not**

6.13a Lever the tensioner roller against the spring pressure . . .

6.13b . . . until the roller can be locked in position using a suitable tool (arrowed)

6.22 Tools used to lock tensioner in position – models with power steering and air conditioning

A Lever the tensioner against the spring pressure
B Dimensions of locking tool
C Locking tool (arrowed) in position
1 30.0 mm
2 Radius 30.0 mm
3 Radius 35.0 mm
4 150.0 mm

allow the tensioner to spring back unrestrained.

17 Check that the belt is correctly located on all the pulleys.

18 Refit the air cleaner assembly.

6.25 Remove the nut and bolt (arrowed) securing the right-hand engine mounting bracket to the mounting block

Ribbed belt models with power steering and air conditioning

Checking and adjustment

19 Proceed as described in paragraphs 1 to 4.

20 An automatic drivebelt tensioner is fitted, and there is no requirement to check the drivebelt tension.

Removal, renewal and refitting

21 Proceed as described in paragraphs 11 and 12.

22 Obtain a wire rod of approximately 4 mm (0.16 in) diameter x 280 mm (11 in). Make up a suitable tool to lock the tensioner in position as the belt is removed **(see illustration)**.

23 Using a suitable spanner or socket and wrench engaged with the tensioner roller bolt, lever the tensioner roller against the spring pressure. The roller can then be locked in position, using the tool inserted through the lug on the roller assembly, to engage with the corresponding hole in the tensioner backplate.

24 Attach a suitable hoist and lifting tackle to the engine lifting brackets on the cylinder head, and support the weight of the engine.

25 Working under the vehicle, remove the nut and bolt securing the right-hand engine mounting bracket to the mounting block on the body **(see illustration)**.

26 Remove the right-hand front suspension tie-bar as described in Chapter 10.

27 Using the lifting tackle, lower the engine approximately 50.0 mm.

28 Unbolt the engine bracket from the power steering pump bracket **(see illustration)**, and withdraw it downwards from the engine compartment.

29 Withdraw the auxiliary drivebelt from the pulleys.

30 Proceed as described in paragraphs 15 to 17 inclusive.

31 Refit the engine bracket, and tighten the securing bolts.

32 Raise the engine, using the lifting tackle, and refit the right-hand front suspension tie-bar with reference to Chapter 10.

33 Refit the nut and bolt securing the right-hand engine mounting to the mounting block on the body, and tighten the nut and bolt to the specified torque.

6.28 Unbolt the engine bracket (bolts arrowed) and withdraw it downwards

34 Disconnect the hoist and lifting tackle.

35 Refit the air cleaner assembly.

7 Ignition HT system check

1 To check the HT leads, proceed as follows, noting that there are no HT leads on 1.0 and 1.2 litre DOHC engines.

2 On 1.4 and 1.6 litre DOHC engines, unscrew the two securing screws, and lift off the plastic shield which fits over the camshaft cover.

 HAYNES HiNT *Ensure that the leads are numbered before removing them, to avoid confusion when refitting (No 1 is at the timing belt end of the engine).*

3 Working on each HT lead in turn, pull the end of the lead from the spark plug by gripping the end connector, not the lead, otherwise the lead connection may be fractured. Note that on DOHC engines a plastic tool is provided (attached to one of the HT leads) to pull the leads from the spark plugs.

4 Check inside the connector for signs of corrosion, which will look like a white crusty powder. Push the connector back onto the spark plug, ensuring that it is a tight fit on the plug. If it is not, remove the lead again, and use pliers to carefully crimp the metal terminal inside the connector until it fits securely on the end of the spark plug.

5 Using a clean rag, wipe the entire length of the lead to remove any built-up dirt and grease. Once the lead is clean, check for burns, cracks and other damage. Do not bend the lead excessively, or pull the lead lengthwise – the conductor inside might break.

6 Disconnect the other end of the lead from the DIS module. Again, pull only on the connector. Check for corrosion and a tight fit, as described previously for the spark plug end of the lead. Refit the lead securely on completion.

7 Check the remaining HT leads one at a time, in the same way.

8 If new HT leads are required, purchase a set for your specific vehicle and engine type.

9 Even with the ignition system in first-class condition, some engines may still occasionally experience poor starting, attributable to damp ignition components.

8 Engine management system check

1 This check is part of the manufacturer's maintenance schedule, and involves testing the engine management system using special dedicated test equipment. Such testing will allow the test equipment to read any fault codes stored in the electronic control unit memory.

2 Unless a fault is suspected, this test is not essential, although it should be noted that it is recommended by the manufacturers.

3 If access to suitable test equipment is not possible, make a thorough check of all ignition, fuel and emission control system components, hoses, and wiring, for security and obvious signs of damage. Further details of the fuel system, emission control system and ignition system can be found in the relevant Parts of Chapters 4 and 5.

9 Emission control system check

1 Check all emission control system components for condition and security, with reference to Chapter 4C. Pay particular attention to all wiring and hoses.

10 Pollen filter renewal

1 Peel the bonnet seal off the engine compartment bulkhead, and remove it from the vehicle.

2 Undo the retaining screws from the windscreen cowl panels, and remove the left-hand panel from the vehicle.

3 Lift the right-hand cowl panel, and prise out the two plugs from the centre of the water deflector shield.

4 Lift the water deflector shield, then release the two retaining clips and lift the pollen filter out from its housing, noting which way round it is fitted **(see illustration)**.

5 Wipe clean the filter housing and install the new filter, making sure it is the correct way up. Ensure that the filter is correctly seated, and secure it in position with the retaining clips.

6 Refitting is the reverse of the removal procedure.

10.4 Withdrawing the pollen filter

11 Electrical system check

1 Check the operation of all the electrical equipment, ie, lights, direction indicators, horn, etc. Refer to the appropriate sections of Chapter 12 for details if any of the circuits are found to be inoperative.

2 Note that stop-light switch adjustment is described in Chapter 9.

3 Check all accessible wiring connectors, harnesses and retaining clips for security, and for signs of chafing or damage. Rectify any faults found.

12 Headlight beam alignment check

1 Accurate adjustment of the headlight beam is only possible using optical beam-setting equipment, and this work should therefore be carried out by a Vauxhall/Opel dealer or service station with the necessary facilities.

2 Basic adjustments can be carried out in an emergency, and further details are given in Chapter 12.

13 Roadwheel bolt tightness check

1 Using a torque wrench on each wheel bolt in turn, ensure that the bolts are tightened to the specified torque.

14 Front brake pad, caliper and disc check

1 Apply the handbrake, then jack up the front of the vehicle and support securely on axle stands; remove the roadwheels (see *Jacking and vehicle support*).

2 For a quick check, the thickness of friction material remaining on each pad can be measured through the slot in the front of the caliper body. If any pad is worn to the specified minimum thickness or less, all four pads must be renewed (see Chapter 9).

3 For a comprehensive check, the brake pads should be removed and cleaned. This will allow the operation of the caliper to be checked, and the condition of the brake disc itself to be fully examined on both sides (see Chapter 9).

15 Rear brake pressure-regulating valve adjustment check – 1.4 and 1.6 litre engines

Check the operation of the valve and adjust it as described in Chapter 9.

16 Brake fluid pipe and hose check

1 The brake hydraulic system includes a number of metal pipes, which run from the master cylinder to the front and rear brake assemblies, and the hydraulic modulator on models with an anti-lock braking system (ABS). Flexible hoses are fitted between the pipes and the front and rear brake assemblies, to allow for steering and suspension movement.

2 When checking the system, first look for signs of leakage at the pipe or hose unions, then examine the flexible hoses for signs of cracking, chafing or deterioration of the rubber. Bend the hoses sharply between the fingers (but do not actually bend them double, or the casing may be damaged) and check that this does not reveal previously-hidden cracks, cuts or splits. Check that the pipes and hoses are securely fastened in their clips.

3 Carefully working along the length of the metal pipes, look for dents, kinks, damage of any sort, or corrosion. Light corrosion can be polished off, but if the depth of pitting is significant, the pipe must be renewed.

17 Bodywork and underbody condition check

Bodywork damage/corrosion check

1 Once the car has been washed, and all tar spots and other surface blemishes have been cleaned off, carefully check all paintwork, looking closely for chips or scratches. Pay particular attention to vulnerable areas such as the front panels (bonnet and spoiler), and around the wheelarches. Any damage to the paintwork must be rectified as soon as possible, to comply with the terms of the manufacturer's anti-corrosion warranties; check with a Vauxhall/Opel dealer for details.

2 If a chip or light scratch is found which is recent and still free from rust, it can be touched-up using the appropriate touch-up stick which can be obtained from Vauxhall/Opel dealers. Any more serious damage, or rusted stone chips, can be repaired as described in Chapter 11, but if damage or corrosion is so severe that a panel must be renewed, seek professional advice as soon as possible.

3 Always check that the door and ventilation opening drain holes and pipes are completely clear, so that water can drain out.

Underbody corrosion protection check

4 The wax-based underbody protective coating should be inspected annually, preferably just prior to Winter, when the

18.3 Check the condition of the exhaust system mountings (typical example arrowed)

underbody should be washed down as thoroughly as possible without disturbing the protective coating. Any damage to the coating should be repaired using a suitable wax-based sealer. If any of the body panels are disturbed for repair or renewal, do not forget to re-apply the coating. Wax should be injected into door cavities, sills and box sections, to maintain the level of protection provided by the vehicle manufacturer – seek the advice of a Vauxhall/Opel dealer.

18 Exhaust system check

1 With the engine cold (at least an hour after the vehicle has been driven), check the complete exhaust system from the engine to the end of the tailpipe. The exhaust system is most easily checked with the vehicle raised on a hoist, or suitably supported on axle stands, so that the exhaust components are readily visible and accessible (see *Jacking and vehicle support*).

2 Check the exhaust pipes and connections for evidence of leaks, severe corrosion and damage. Make sure that all brackets and mountings are in good condition, and that all relevant nuts and bolts are tight. Leakage at any of the joints or in other parts of the system

will usually show up as a black sooty stain in the vicinity of the leak.

3 Rattles and other noises can often be traced to the exhaust system, especially the brackets and mountings (see illustration). Try to move the pipes and silencers. If the components are able to come into contact with the body or suspension parts, secure the system with new mountings. Otherwise separate the joints (if possible) and twist the pipes as necessary to provide additional clearance.

19 Road test

Instruments and electrical equipment

1 Check the operation of all instruments and electrical equipment.

2 Make sure that all instruments read correctly, and switch on all electrical equipment in turn, to check that it functions properly.

Steering and suspension

3 Check for any abnormalities in the steering, suspension, handling or road 'feel'.

4 Drive the vehicle, and check that there are no unusual vibrations or noises.

5 Check that the steering feels positive, with no excessive 'sloppiness', or roughness, and check for any suspension noises when cornering and driving over bumps.

Drivetrain

6 Check the performance of the engine, clutch (where applicable), gearbox/transmission and driveshafts.

7 Listen for any unusual noises from the engine, clutch and gearbox/transmission.

8 Make sure that the engine runs smoothly when idling, and that there is no hesitation when accelerating.

9 Check that, where applicable, the clutch action is smooth and progressive, that the

drive is taken up smoothly, and that the pedal travel is not excessive. Also listen for any noises when the clutch pedal is depressed.

10 On manual gearbox models, check that all gears can be engaged smoothly without noise, and that the gear lever action is smooth and not abnormally vague or 'notchy'.

11 On automatic transmission models, make sure that all gearchanges occur smoothly, without snatching, and without an increase in engine speed between changes. Check that all the gear positions can be selected with the vehicle at rest. If any problems are found, they should be referred to a Vauxhall/Opel dealer.

12 Listen for a metallic clicking sound from the front of the vehicle, as the vehicle is driven slowly in a circle with the steering on full-lock. Carry out this check in both directions. If a clicking noise is heard, this indicates wear in a driveshaft joint, in which case renew the joint if necessary.

Check the operation and performance of the braking system

13 Make sure that the vehicle does not pull to one side when braking, and that the wheels do not lock prematurely when braking hard.

14 Check that there is no vibration through the steering when braking.

15 Check that the handbrake operates correctly without excessive movement of the lever, and that it holds the vehicle stationary on a slope.

16 Test the operation of the brake servo unit as follows. With the engine off, depress the footbrake four or five times to exhaust the vacuum. Hold the brake pedal depressed, then start the engine. As the engine starts, there should be a noticeable 'give' in the brake pedal as vacuum builds up. Allow the engine to run for at least two minutes, and then switch it off. If the brake pedal is depressed now, it should be possible to detect a hiss from the servo as the pedal is depressed. After about four or five applications, no further hissing should be heard, and the pedal should feel considerably harder.

Every 20 000 miles (30 000 km) or 2 years – whichever comes first

20 Air cleaner filter element renewal

1 The air cleaner assembly is located at the front right-hand corner of the engine compartment.

2 Release the securing clips, and lift the air

cleaner cover sufficiently to enable removal of the filter element. Where applicable, take care not to strain the wiring for the air mass meter, or the intake air temperature sensor, as applicable.

3 Lift out the filter element (see illustration).

4 Wipe out the casing and the cover. Fit the new filter, noting that the rubber locating flange should be uppermost, and secure the cover with the clips.

20.3 Removing the air cleaner filter element

21.1 Fuel filter – Combo Van model

21.5 Loosening the fuel filter clamp bolt – Hatchback model

21.7a Release the connectors . . .

21 Fuel filter renewal

1 The fuel filter is located under the rear of the vehicle **(see illustration)**.
2 Disconnect the battery negative terminal (refer to *Disconnecting the battery* in the Reference Chapter).
3 Depressurise the fuel system as described in Chapter 4A or 4B.
4 Chock the front wheels, then jack up the rear of the vehicle, and support securely on axle stands (see *Jacking and vehicle support*).
5 Loosen the clamp nut and bolt, and withdraw the filter from its clamp **(see illustration)**. Note the orientation of the fuel flow direction arrow.
6 Position a suitable container below the fuel filter, to catch spilt fuel.
7 Release the connectors and disconnect the fuel hoses from the fuel filter, noting their locations to ensure correct refitting **(see illustrations)**. A Vauxhall/Opel special tool is available to disconnect the hose connectors, but provided care is taken, the connections can be released using a pair of pliers. Be prepared for fuel spillage, and take adequate precautions.
8 Recover the mounting rubber from the old filter, and transfer it to the new filter.
9 Fitting the new filter is a reversal of removal, bearing in mind the following points.

  a) *Ensure that the filter is fitted with the flow direction arrow on the filter body pointing in the direction of fuel flow (see illustration).*
  b) *Ensure that the hoses are reconnected to their correct locations, as noted before removal.*
  c) *On completion, run the engine and check for leaks. If leakage is evident, stop the engine immediately and rectify the problem without delay.*

22 Manual gearbox oil level check

1 Ensure that the vehicle is standing on level ground and the handbrake applied.
2 Working underneath the vehicle, unscrew the gearbox oil level plug, which is located in the rear left of the differential housing **(see illustration)**.
3 The oil level should be up to the lower edge of the level plug hole.
4 If necessary, top-up with oil through the breather/filler orifice in the gear selector cover. Unscrew the breather/filler plug, and top-up with the specified grade of oil, until oil just begins to run from the level plug hole. A funnel may be helpful, to avoid spillage **(see illustrations)**. Do not overfill – if too much oil is added, wait until the excess has run out of the level plug hole. Refit the level plug and the breather/filler plug on completion.

21.7b . . . and disconnect the fuel hoses from the filter. Depress the catches (1) to release the locking tags (2) from the locating holes (3)

21.9 Ensure that the flow direction arrow points in the direction of fuel flow

22.2 Manual gearbox oil level plug (arrowed)

22.4a Unscrew the breather/filler plug . . .

22.4b . . . and top-up with the specified grade of oil

23 Automatic transmission fluid level check

1 To check the fluid level, the vehicle must be parked on level ground. Apply the handbrake.
2 If the transmission fluid is cold (ie, if the engine is cold), the level check must be completed with the engine idling, within one minute of the engine being started.
3 With the engine idling, fully depress the brake pedal, and move the gear selector lever smoothly through all positions, finishing in position P.
4 With the engine still idling, withdraw the transmission fluid level dipstick (located at the left-hand side of the engine compartment, next to the engine oil level dipstick). Pull up the lever on the top of the dipstick to release it from the tube. Wipe the dipstick clean with a lint-free rag, re-insert it and withdraw it again.
5 If the transmission fluid was cold at the beginning of the procedure, the fluid level should be on the MAX mark on the side of the dipstick marked +20°C. Note that 0.4 litres of fluid is required to raise the level from the MIN to the MAX mark **(see illustration)**.
6 If the transmission fluid was at operating temperature at the beginning of the procedure (ie, if the vehicle had been driven for at least 12 miles/20 km), the fluid level should be between the MIN and MAX marks on the side of the dipstick marked +80°C. Note that 0.2 litres of fluid is required to raise the level from the MIN to the MAX mark.
7 If topping-up is necessary, stop the engine, and top-up with the specified type of fluid through the transmission dipstick tube.
8 Recheck the level, and refit the dipstick on completion.

24 Automatic transmission system check

1 This check is part of the manufacturer's maintenance schedule, and involves testing the automatic transmission control system

23.5 Automatic transmission fluid level dipstick markings

A Markings for fluid at operating temperature
B Markings for cold fluid

using special dedicated test equipment. Such testing will allow the test equipment to read any fault codes stored in the electronic control unit memory.
2 Unless a fault is suspected, this test is not essential, although it should be noted that it is recommended by the manufacturers.
3 If access to suitable test equipment is not possible, make a thorough check of all control system components and wiring for security and obvious signs of damage. Further details of the control system can be found in Chapter 7B.

25 Coolant renewal

Note: *Vauxhall/Opel do not specify renewal intervals for the antifreeze mixture, as the mixture used to fill the system when the vehicle is new is designed to last the lifetime of the vehicle. However, it is strongly recommended that the coolant is renewed at the intervals specified in the 'Maintenance schedule', as a precaution against possible engine corrosion problems. This is particularly advisable if the coolant has been renewed, using an antifreeze other than that specified by Vauxhall/Opel. With many antifreeze types, the corrosion inhibitors become progressively less effective with age. It is up to the individual owner whether or not to follow this advice.*

Cooling system draining

 Warning: Wait until the engine is cold before starting this procedure. Do not allow antifreeze to come in contact with your skin, or with the painted surfaces of the vehicle. Rinse off spills immediately with plenty of water. Never leave antifreeze lying around in an open container, or in a puddle on the driveway or garage floor. Children and pets are attracted by its sweet smell, but antifreeze is fatal if ingested.
1 To drain the cooling system, first cover the expansion tank cap with a wad of rag, and slowly turn the cap anti-clockwise to relieve the pressure in the cooling system (a hissing sound will normally be heard). Wait until any pressure remaining in the system is released, then continue to turn the cap until it can be removed.
2 Position a suitable container beneath the radiator bottom hose connection, then slacken the hose clip and ease the hose from the radiator stub. If the hose joint has not been disturbed for some time, it will be necessary to gently manipulate the hose to break the joint. Do not use excessive force, or the radiator stub could be damaged. Allow the coolant to drain into the container.
3 As no cylinder block drain plug is fitted, and the radiator bottom hose may be situated above the bottom of the radiator, the system

cannot be drained completely. Care should therefore be taken when refilling the system, to maintain antifreeze strength. If the system is being drained for coolant renewal, it is recommended that the cooling fan switch is unscrewed from the radiator (see Chapter 3) in order to allow the maximum possible quantity of coolant to be drained.
4 If the coolant has been drained for a reason other than renewal, then provided it is clean and less than two years old, it can be re-used.

Cooling system flushing

5 If coolant renewal has been neglected, or if the antifreeze mixture has become diluted, then in time, the cooling system may gradually lose efficiency, as the coolant passages become restricted due to rust, scale deposits, and other sediment. The cooling system efficiency can be restored by flushing the system clean.
6 The radiator should be flushed independently of the engine, to avoid unnecessary contamination.
7 To flush the radiator, disconnect the top hose at the radiator, then insert a garden hose into the radiator top inlet. Direct a flow of clean water through the radiator, and continue flushing until clean water emerges from the radiator bottom outlet (the bottom radiator hose should have been disconnected to drain the system). If after a reasonable period, the water still does not run clear, the radiator can be flushed with a good proprietary cleaning agent. It is important that the cleaning agent manufacturer's instructions are followed carefully. If the contamination is particularly bad, insert the hose in the radiator bottom outlet, and flush the radiator in the reverse direction ('reverse-flushing').
8 To flush the engine block, the thermostat must be removed, because it will be shut, and would otherwise prevent the flow of water around the engine. On SOHC engines, remove the thermostat as described in Chapter 3, then temporarily refit the thermostat cover. On DOHC engines, the thermostat cannot be removed from the cover. In order to flush the block, the thermostat cover must be removed as described in Chapter 3, and the aperture temporarily covered over. Take care not to introduce dirt or debris into the system if this approach is used.
9 With the radiator top and bottom hoses disconnected from the radiator, insert a hose into the radiator bottom hose. Direct a clean flow of water through the engine, and continue flushing until clean water emerges from the radiator top hose.
10 On completion of flushing, refit the thermostat and/or cover with reference to Chapter 3, and reconnect the hoses.

Cooling system filling

11 Before attempting to fill the cooling system, make sure that all hoses and clips are in good condition, and that the clips are tight. Note that an antifreeze mixture must be used all year round, to prevent corrosion of the

alloy engine components. Where applicable, also ensure that the cooling fan switch has been refitted to the radiator.

12 On SOHC engines, disconnect the wire and unscrew the coolant temperature sender from the inlet manifold **(see illustration)**. On 1.4 and 1.6 litre DOHC engines, unscrew the bleed screw which is situated in the thermostat housing cover.

13 Remove the expansion tank cap, and fill the system by slowly pouring the coolant into the expansion tank to prevent airlocks from forming.

14 If the coolant is being renewed, begin by pouring in a couple of litres of water, followed by the correct quantity of antifreeze, then top-up with more water.

15 When coolant free of air bubbles emerges from the orifice, refit the coolant temperature sender and tighten it securely (SOHC engines), or refit the bleed screw and tighten it to the specified torque setting (1.4 and 1.6 litre DOHC engines) **(see illustration)**.

16 Top-up the coolant level to the KALT (or COLD) mark on the expansion tank, then refit the expansion tank cap.

17 Start the engine and run it until it reaches normal operating temperature, then stop the engine and allow it to cool.

18 Check for leaks, particularly around disturbed components. Check the coolant level in the expansion tank, and top-up if necessary. Note that the system must be cold before an accurate level is indicated in the expansion tank. If the expansion tank cap is removed while the engine is still warm, cover the cap with a thick cloth, and unscrew the cap slowly to gradually relieve the system pressure (a hissing sound will normally be heard). Wait until any pressure remaining in the system is released, then continue to turn the cap until it can be removed.

Antifreeze mixture

19 Always use an ethylene-glycol based antifreeze which is suitable for use in mixed-metal cooling systems. The quantity of antifreeze and levels of protection are indicated in the Specifications.

20 Before adding antifreeze, the cooling system should be completely drained,

25.12 On SOHC engines, remove the coolant temperature sender (arrowed) before filling the cooling system

preferably flushed, and all hoses and clips checked for condition and security.

21 After filling with antifreeze, a label should be attached to the radiator or expansion tank, stating the type and concentration of antifreeze used, and the date installed. Any subsequent topping-up should be made with the same type and concentration of antifreeze.

22 Do not use engine antifreeze in the windscreen/tailgate washer system, as it will cause damage to the vehicle paintwork. A screenwash should be added to the washer system in the quantities recommended on the bottle.

26 Clutch cable adjustment check

1 Working inside the vehicle, ensure that the clutch pedal is in its normal rest position, then measure the distance from the centre of the top edge of the pedal to the lowest point of the steering wheel. Fully depress the pedal, and repeat the measurement **(see illustrations)**. The measurements can be taken using a suitable strip of wood or metal, as the important figure is the *difference* between the two measurements, ie the movement (stroke) of the pedal.

2 The difference between the two measurements must be as given in the Specifications – if not, adjust the clutch cable as follows to achieve the specified pedal movement.

25.15 Refitting the thermostat housing bleed screw – 1.6 litre DOHC engine

3 Working in the engine compartment, remove the clip from the threaded rod at the clutch release arm on the gearbox, then turn the threaded rod end fitting as required, using a spanner on the flats provided to hold the threaded rod as the end fitting is turned **(see illustration)**. Turn the end fitting clockwise to decrease pedal movement, or anti-clockwise to increase pedal movement. Recheck the pedal movement, and then refit the clip to the threaded rod on completion.

4 On a vehicle in which the clutch has covered a high mileage, it may no longer be possible to adjust the cable to achieve the specified pedal movement, and this indicates that the clutch friction disc requires renewal. Note that when correctly adjusted, the clutch pedal will rest slightly higher than the brake pedal – it is incorrect for the two pedals to be in alignment. If the pedals are aligned, the clutch cable requires adjustment.

27 Hinge and lock lubrication

1 Lubricate the hinges of the bonnet, doors and tailgate with a light general-purpose oil. Similarly, lubricate all latches, locks and lock strikers. At the same time, check the security and operation of all the locks, adjusting them if necessary (see Chapter 11).

2 Lightly lubricate the bonnet release mechanism and cable with a suitable grease.

26.1a Measure the dimension (A) from the top edge of the pedal to the lowest point of the steering wheel . . .

26.1b . . . then fully depress the pedal and repeat the measurement (B)

26.3 Removing the clip from the clutch pedal threaded rod. Threaded rod adjuster flats arrowed

28 Rear brake shoe, drum and wheel cylinder check

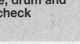

1 Chock the front wheels, then jack up the rear of the vehicle, and support it securely on axle stands (see *Jacking and vehicle support*).
2 For a quick check, the thickness of friction material remaining on one of the brake shoes can be observed through the hole in the brake backplate which is exposed by prising out the sealing grommet **(see illustration)**. If a rod of the same diameter as the specified minimum friction material thickness is placed against the shoe friction material, the amount of wear can be assessed. An electric torch or inspection light will probably be required. If the friction material on any shoe is worn down to the specified minimum thickness or less, all four shoes must be renewed as a set.
3 For a comprehensive check, the brake drum should be removed and cleaned. This will allow the wheel cylinders to be checked, and the condition of the brake drum itself to be fully examined (see Chapter 9).

29 Brake fluid renewal

1 The procedure is similar to that for the bleeding of the hydraulic system as described in Chapter 9, except that the brake fluid reservoir should be emptied by syphoning, using a (clean) old battery hydrometer or similar before starting, and allowance should be made for the old fluid to be expelled from the circuit when bleeding each section of the circuit.

30 Front suspension and steering check

1 Apply the handbrake, then raise the front of the vehicle and securely support it on axle stands (see *Jacking and vehicle support*).
2 Inspect the balljoint dust covers and the steering gear gaiters for splits, chafing or deterioration. Any wear of these components will cause loss of lubricant, and may allow water to enter the components, resulting in rapid deterioration of the balljoints or steering gear.
3 On vehicles with power steering, check the fluid hoses for chafing or deterioration, and the pipe and hose unions for fluid leaks. Also check for signs of fluid leakage under pressure from the steering gear rubber gaiters, which would indicate failed fluid seals within the steering gear.
4 Grasp each roadwheel at the 12 o'clock and 6 o'clock positions, and try to rock it **(see illustration)**. Very slight free play may be felt, but if the movement is appreciable, further investigation is necessary to determine the

28.2 Removing the sealing grommet from a brake backplate

source. Continue rocking the wheel while an assistant depresses the footbrake. If the movement is now eliminated or significantly reduced, it is likely that the hub bearings are at fault. If the free play is still evident with the footbrake depressed, then there is wear in the suspension joints or mountings.
5 Now grasp each wheel at the 9 o'clock and 3 o'clock positions, and try to rock it as before. Any movement felt now may again be caused by wear in the hub bearings or the steering track-rod end balljoints. If the track-rod end balljoint is worn, the visual movement will be obvious.
6 Using a large screwdriver or flat bar, check for wear in the suspension mounting bushes by levering between the relevant suspension component and its attachment point. Some movement is to be expected, as the mountings are made of rubber, but excessive wear should be obvious. Also check the condition of any visible rubber bushes, looking for splits, cracks or contamination of the rubber.
7 Check for any signs of fluid leakage around the suspension strut/shock absorber bodies, or from the rubber gaiters around the piston rods. Should any fluid be noticed, the suspension strut/shock absorber is defective internally, and should be renewed. **Note:** *Suspension struts/shock absorbers should always be renewed in pairs on the same axle.*
8 With the vehicle standing on its wheels, have an assistant turn the steering wheel back-and-forth about an eighth of a turn each way. There should be very little, if any, lost movement between the steering wheel and roadwheels. If this is not the case, closely observe the joints and mountings previously described, but in addition check the steering column rubber coupling for wear, and also check the steering gear itself.
9 The efficiency of each suspension strut/shock absorber may be checked by bouncing the vehicle at each corner. Generally speaking, the body will return to its normal position and stop after being depressed. If it rises and returns on a rebound, the suspension strut/shock absorber is probably suspect. Also examine the suspension strut/shock absorber upper and lower mountings for any signs of wear.

30.4 Rocking a roadwheel to check steering/suspension component wear

31 Rear suspension check

1 Chock the front wheels, then jack up the rear of the vehicle and support securely on axle stands (see *Jacking and vehicle support*).
2 Inspect the rear suspension components for any signs of obvious wear or damage. Pay particular attention to the rubber mounting bushes, and renew if necessary (see Chapter 10).
3 Grasp each roadwheel at the 12 o'clock and 6 o'clock positions, and try to rock it. Any excess movement indicates incorrect adjustment or wear in the wheel bearings. Wear may also be accompanied by a rumbling sound when the wheel is spun, or a noticeable roughness if the wheel is turned slowly. The wheel bearing can be renewed as described in Chapter 10, Section 10.
4 Check the rear shock absorbers in a similar manner to that described previously for the front shock absorbers.

32 Driveshaft check

1 With the vehicle raised and securely supported on stands, turn the steering onto full-lock, then slowly rotate each front roadwheel. Inspect the condition of the outer constant velocity (CV) joint rubber gaiters, while squeezing the gaiters to open out the folds. Check for signs of cracking, splits or deterioration of the rubber, which may allow the grease to escape and lead to water and grit entering the joint. Also check the security and condition of the retaining clips. Repeat these checks on the inner CV joints. If any damage or deterioration is found, the gaiters should be renewed as described in Chapter 8.
2 At the same time, check the general condition of the CV joints themselves by first holding the driveshaft and attempting to rotate the wheel. Repeat this check by holding the inner joint and attempting to rotate the driveshaft. Any appreciable movement indicates wear in the joints, wear in the driveshaft splines, or a loose front hub nut.

Every 30 000 miles (45 000 km) or 3 years – whichever comes first

33 Automatic transmission fluid renewal

1 Firmly apply the handbrake, then jack up the front of the car and support it securely on axle stands (see *Jacking and vehicle support*).
2 Place a suitable container under the drain plug located at the lower right-hand side of the transmission housing.
3 Wipe clean the area around the drain plug, then unscrew the plug and allow the fluid to drain into the container.
4 After all the fluid has drained, wipe the drain plug and the sealing washer with a clean rag. Examine the condition of the sealing washer, and renew it if it shows signs of scoring or other damage which may prevent a perfect seal. Clean the area around the drain plug opening, and refit the plug complete with the washer. Tighten the plug securely and lower the car to the ground.
5 Refill the transmission through the dipstick tube with the correct quantity and type of fluid, using the procedures described in Section 23.

Every 40 000 miles (60 000 km) or 4 years – whichever comes first

34 Spark plug check and renewal

General

1 The correct functioning of the spark plugs is vital for the correct running and efficiency of the engine. It is essential that the plugs fitted are appropriate for the engine, the suitable type being specified at the beginning of this Chapter. If the correct type of plug is used and the engine is in good condition, the spark plugs should not need attention between scheduled renewal intervals, except for adjustment of their gaps. Spark plug cleaning is rarely necessary, and should not be attempted unless specialised equipment is available, as damage can easily be caused to the firing ends.
2 To check and renew the spark plugs, proceed as described under the following sub-headings.

1.0 and 1.2 litre DOHC engines

3 To gain access to the spark plugs, remove the DIS module as described in Chapter 5B.
4 Unscrew the plugs using a spark plug spanner, a suitable box spanner, or a deep socket and extension bar. Keep the socket in alignment with the spark plugs, otherwise if it is forcibly moved to either side, the porcelain top of the spark plug may be broken off. As each plug is removed, examine it as follows.
5 Examination of the spark plugs will give a good indication of the condition of the engine. If the insulator nose of the spark plug is clean and white, with no deposits, this is indicative of a weak mixture or too hot a plug (a hot plug transfers heat away from the electrode slowly, while a cold plug transfers heat away quickly).
6 If the tip and insulator nose are covered with hard black-looking deposits, then this is indicative that the idle mixture is too rich. Should the plug be black and oily, then it is likely that the engine is fairly worn, as well as the mixture being too rich.
7 If the insulator nose is covered with light-tan to greyish-brown deposits, then the mixture is correct and it is likely that the engine is in good condition.
8 The spark plug gap is of considerable importance as, if it is too large or too small, the size of the spark and its efficiency will be seriously impaired. For the best results, the spark plug gap should be set in accordance with the Specifications at the beginning of this Chapter.
9 To set the spark plug gap, measure the gap between the electrodes with a feeler blade, and then bend open, or close, the outer plug electrode until the correct gap is achieved **(see illustrations)**. The centre electrode should never be bent, as this may crack the insulation and cause plug failure, if nothing worse.
10 Special spark plug electrode gap adjusting tools are available from most motor accessory shops **(see illustration)**.
11 Before fitting the new spark plugs, check that the threaded connector sleeves on the top of the plug are tight, and that the plug exterior surfaces and threads are clean.

34.9a Measuring a spark plug electrode gap using a feeler blade

34.9b Measuring a spark plug electrode gap using a wire gauge

34.10 Adjusting a spark plug electrode gap using a special tool

34.18a Removing the plastic cover from the camshaft cover – 1.4 and 1.6 litre DOHC engines

34.18b Using the plastic tool to pull an HT lead from a spark plug – 1.4 and 1.6 litre DOHC engines

It's often difficult to insert spark plugs into their holes without cross-threading them. To avoid this possibility, fit a short piece of rubber hose over the end of the spark plug. The flexible hose acts as a universal joint, to help align the plug with the plug hole. Should the plug begin to crossthread, the hose will slip on the spark plug, preventing thread damage.

12 Screw in the spark plugs by hand where possible, then tighten them to the specified torque. Take extra care to enter the plug threads correctly, as the cylinder head is of light alloy construction **(see Haynes Hint)**.

13 Refit the DIS module as described in Chapter 5B.

1.2 and 1.4 litre SOHC engines

14 If necessary, mark the HT leads 1 to 4, to correspond to the cylinder the lead serves (No 1 cylinder is nearest the timing belt end of the engine).

Caution: Pull the HT leads from the plugs by gripping the end connectors, not the leads, otherwise the lead connections may be fractured.

15 It is advisable to remove any dirt from the spark plug recesses using a clean brush, vacuum cleaner or compressed air, before

removing the plugs, to prevent the dirt dropping into the cylinders.

16 Proceed as described in paragraphs 3 to 12.

17 Reconnect the HT leads in their correct order.

1.4 and 1.6 litre DOHC engines

18 Proceed as described in paragraphs 3 to 12, noting the following points **(see illustrations)**.

a) *For access to the spark plugs, the oil filler cap and the plastic cover must be removed from the top of the camshaft cover. The plastic cover is secured by two screws.*

b) *A plastic tool is provided (attached to one of the spark plug leads) to pull the HT leads from the spark plugs.*

c) *Take great care, when removing and refitting the spark plugs, to use a suitable long-reach socket, which locates in the spark plug hole (the manufacturers recommend the use of Vauxhall/Opel special tool KM-194-B). If a standard spark plug removal socket is used, which does not provide adequate guidance in*

the spark plug's hole, it is possible for the socket to touch the ceramic body of the spark plug, causing hairline cracks – this may cause intermittent misfiring and possible damage to the catalytic converter.

d) *Tighten the spark plugs to the specified torque.*

e) *Reconnect the HT leads in their correct order.*

f) *When refitting the plastic cover, ensure that the lugs on the plastic cover engage with the rubbers on the camshaft cover.*

35 Timing belt renewal –
1.4 and 1.6 litre DOHC engines

Refer to Chapter 2C.

36 Timing belt renewal –
1.2 and 1.4 litre SOHC engines

Refer to Chapter 2B.

34.18c Use a suitable long-reach socket to remove the spark plugs – 1.4 and 1.6 litre DOHC engines

34.18d Tighten the spark plugs to the specified torque – 1.4 and 1.6 litre DOHC engines

34.18e Ensure that the plastic cover lugs (1) engage with the camshaft cover rubbers (2) – 1.4 and 1.6 litre DOHC engines

Chapter 2 Part A: 1.0 & 1.2 litre DOHC engine in-car repair procedures

Contents

Degrees of difficulty

Easy, suitable for novice with little experience	**Fairly easy,** suitable for beginner with some experience	**Fairly difficult,** suitable for competent DIY mechanic	**Difficult,** suitable for experienced DIY mechanic	**Very difficult,** suitable for expert DIY or professional

Specifications

General

Engine type:

1.0 litre engine .... Three-cylinder, in-line, water-cooled. Double overhead camshafts, chain-driven, acting on rocker arms and hydraulic valve lifters

1.2 litre engine .... Four-cylinder, in-line, water-cooled. Double overhead camshafts, chain-driven, acting on rocker arms and hydraulic valve lifters

Manufacturer's engine codes:*

1.0 litre engine .... X 10 XE

1.2 litre engine .... X 12 XE

Bore .... 72.50 mm

Stroke:

1.0 litre engine .... 78.60 mm

1.2 litre engine .... 72.60 mm

Capacity:

1.0 litre engine .... 973 cc

1.2 litre engine .... 1199 cc

Firing order:

1.0 litre engine .... 1-2-3 (No 1 cylinder at timing chain end of engine)

1.2 litre engine .... 1-3-4-2 (No 1 cylinder at timing chain end of engine)

Direction of crankshaft rotation .... Clockwise (viewed from timing chain end of engine)

Compression ratio 10.0:1

For details of engine code location, see 'Vehicle identification' in the Reference Chapter.

Lubrication system

Minimum oil pressure at 80°C .... 1.5 bars at idle speed

Oil pump type .... Gear-type, driven directly from crankshaft

Gear-to-housing clearance (endfloat) : .... 0.035 to 0.070 mm

Flywheel

Maximum permissible lateral run-out of starter ring gear . . . . 0.500 mm
Refinishing limit – maximum depth of material which may be
  removed from clutch friction surface . . . . 0.300 mm

Torque wrench settings

	Nm	lbf ft
Air conditioning compressor to cylinder block	20	15
Auxiliary drivebelt tensioner to cylinder block:		
M8 bolt	20	15
M10 bolt	55	41
Big-end bearing cap bolts:*		
Stage 1	10	7
Stage 2	Angle-tighten a further 60°	
Camshaft bearing cap bolts	8	6
Camshaft cover bolts	8	6
Camshaft position sensor to timing cover	6	4
Camshaft sprocket bolt:*		
Stage 1	50	37
Stage 2	Angle-tighten a further 60°	
Catalytic converter support bracket bolts	20	15
Catalytic converter-to-exhaust manifold nuts	35	26
Coolant pump bolts	8	6
Coolant pump pulley bolts	20	15
Crankshaft pulley hub-to-crankshaft bolt:*		
Stage 1	150	111
Stage 2	Angle-tighten a further 45°	
Crankshaft pulley-to-pulley hub bolts	8	6
Cylinder block baseplate to cylinder block:*		
M6 bolts:		
Stage 1	10	7
Stage 2	Angle-tighten a further 60°	
M8 bolts:		
Stage 1	25	18
Stage 2	Angle-tighten a further 60°	
Cylinder block closure bolt (for TDC setting tool)	60	44
Cylinder head bolts:*		
Stage 1	25	18
Stage 2	Angle-tighten a further 60°	
Stage 3	Angle-tighten a further 60°	
Stage 4	Angle-tighten a further 60°	
Cylinder head cover bolts	8	6
Engine mountings:		
Left-hand:		
Gearbox/transmission bracket-to-gearbox/transmission bolts . . .	60	44
Gearbox/transmission bracket-to-mounting block bolts	60	44
Mounting block-to-body bolts**	65	48
Rear:		
Gearbox/transmission bracket-to-gearbox/transmission bolts . . .	70	52
Gearbox/transmission bracket-to-mounting block bolts	65	48
Mounting block-to-body bolts	65	48
Right-hand:		
Engine bracket-to-engine bolts:		
Models without power steering	65	48
Models with power steering	60	44
Engine bracket-to-mounting block bolt/nut	60	44
Mounting block-to-body bolts:		
Models without power steering	65	48
Models with power steering	20	15
Engine-to-automatic transmission bolts	60	44
Engine-to-manual gearbox bolts	45	33
Flywheel/driveplate bolts:*		
Stage 1	35	26
Stage 2	Angle-tighten a further 30°	
Fuel feed and return hose unions	15	11
Fuel injector wiring trough to inlet manifold	8	6
Heat shield to exhaust manifold	8	6
Inlet manifold support bracket to cylinder block	20	15

Torque wrench settings (continued)

	Nm	lbf ft
Inlet manifold support bracket to manifold:		
1.0 litre engines	10	7
1.2 litre engines	6	4
Oil baffle plate bolts	8	6
Oil dipstick guide tube to exhaust manifold	8	6
Oil filter housing to cylinder block	20	15
Oil filter housing cap to filter housing	15	11
Oil pump cover to timing cover	8	6
Oil pick-up pipe-to-sump bolts	14	10
Sump to cylinder block baseplate and timing cover	10	7
Sump to gearbox/transmission:		
M10 bolts	40	30
M8 bolts	20	15
Thermostat housing cover bolts	8	6
Timing chain guide rail to cylinder block	8	6
Timing chain sliding rail to cylinder head	8	6
Timing chain tension rail pivot bolt	20	15
Timing chain tensioner closure bolt (for locking pin access)	50	37
Timing chain tensioner to cylinder head	8	6
Timing cover bolts:		
M10	35	26
M6	8	6
Timing cover oil fill channel closure plug	50	37
Torque converter to driveplate*	50	37

*Use new bolts.
**Use thread-locking compound.

1 General information

How to use this Chapter

This Part of Chapter 2 describes the repair procedures which can reasonably be carried out on the engine while it remains in the vehicle. If the engine has been removed from the vehicle and is being dismantled as described in Chapter 2D, any preliminary dismantling procedures can be ignored.

Note that, while it may be *possible* physically to overhaul items such as the piston/connecting rod assemblies while the engine is in the vehicle, such tasks are not usually carried out as separate operations, and usually require the execution of several additional procedures (not to mention the cleaning of components and of oilways); for this reason, all such tasks are classed as major overhaul procedures, and are described in Chapter 2D.

Chapter 2D describes the removal of the engine/transmission unit from the vehicle, and the full overhaul procedures which can then be carried out.

Engine description

The engine is of three-cylinder (1.0 litre) or four-cylinder (1.2 litre) in-line type, with double overhead camshafts (DOHC). The engine is mounted transversely at the front of the vehicle. Apart from the obvious difference in the number of cylinders, the two engines are virtually identical in all other respects.

The crankshaft runs in five shell-type main bearings with crankshaft endfloat being controlled by thrustwashers which are an integral part of No 3 main bearing shells (1.0 litre engines), or No 4 main bearing shells (1.2 litre engines).

The connecting rods are attached to the crankshaft by horizontally-split shell-type big-end bearings. The pistons are attached to the connecting rods by gudgeon pins, which are an interference fit in the connecting rod small-end bores. The aluminium-alloy pistons are fitted with three piston rings – two compression rings and an oil control ring.

The camshafts are driven from the crankshaft by a hydraulically tensioned timing chain. Each cylinder has four valves (two inlet and two exhaust), operated via rocker arms which are supported at their pivot ends by hydraulic self-adjusting valve lifters (tappets). One camshaft operates the inlet valves, and the other operates the exhaust valves.

The inlet and exhaust valves are each closed by a single valve spring, and operate in guides pressed into the cylinder head.

A rotor-type oil pump is located in the timing cover attached to the cylinder block, and is driven directly from the crankshaft.

The coolant pump is located externally on the timing cover, and is driven by the auxiliary drivebelt.

Repair operations possible with the engine in the vehicle

The following operations can be carried out without having to remove the engine from the vehicle.

a) Removal and refitting of the cylinder head.
b) Removal and refitting of the timing cover.
c) Removal and refitting of the timing chain, tensioner and sprockets.
d) Removal and refitting of the camshafts.
e) Removal and refitting of the sump.
f) Removal and refitting of the big-end bearings, connecting rods, and pistons*.
g) Removal and refitting of the oil pump.
h) Renewal of the crankshaft oil seals.
i) Renewal of the engine mountings.
j) Removal and refitting of the flywheel/driveplate.

*Although the operation marked with an asterisk can be carried out with the engine in the vehicle (after removal of the sump), it is preferable for the engine to be removed, in the interests of cleanliness and improved access. For this reason, the procedure is described in Chapter 2D.

2 Compression test – description and interpretation

Note: *A suitable compression gauge will be required to carry out this test.*

1 When engine performance is down, or if misfiring occurs which cannot be attributed to the ignition or fuel systems, a compression test can provide diagnostic clues as to the engine's condition. If the test is performed regularly, it can give warning of trouble before any other symptoms become apparent

2 The engine must be fully warmed-up to normal operating temperature, and the battery must be fully charged. The aid of an assistant will also be required.

3 Remove the DIS module from the top of the camshaft cover as described in Chapter 5B. Ensure that the ignition is switched off then disconnect the two wiring plugs from the engine management electronic control unit

3.2a Disconnect the wiring connectors at the air mass meter (arrowed) . . .

3.2b . . . coolant temperature sensor (A) and camshaft position sensor (B) . . .

3.2c . . . and at the oil pressure switch (arrowed)

located on the left-hand side of the inlet manifold.

4 Remove all of the spark plugs from the engine (see Chapter 1).

5 Fit a compression tester to the No 1 spark plug hole (No 1 cylinder is nearest the timing chain end of the engine) – the type of tester which screws into the plug thread is to be preferred.

6 Have an assistant hold the accelerator pedal fully depressed, at the same time cranking the engine over for approximately four seconds on the starter motor. After one or two revolutions, the compression pressure reading on the gauge should build up to a maximum figure and then stabilise. Record the highest reading obtained.

7 Repeat the test on the remaining cylinders, recording the pressure in each.

8 All cylinders should produce very similar pressures; any difference greater than that specified indicates the existence of a fault. Note that the compression should build-up quickly in a healthy engine; low compression on the first stroke, followed by gradually-increasing pressure on successive strokes, indicates worn piston rings. A low compression reading on the first stroke, which does not build-up during successive strokes, indicates leaking valves or a blown head gasket (a cracked head could also be the cause). Deposits on the undersides of the valve heads can also cause low compression.

9 If the pressure in any cylinder is significantly lower than that in the remaining cylinders, carry out the following test to isolate the cause. Introduce a teaspoonful of clean engine oil into the relevant cylinder through its spark plug hole, and repeat the test.

10 If the addition of oil temporarily improves the compression pressure, this indicates that bore or piston wear is responsible for the pressure loss. No improvement suggests that leaking or burnt valves, or a blown head gasket may be to blame.

11 A low reading from two adjacent cylinders is almost certainly due to the head gasket having blown between them; the presence of coolant in the engine oil will confirm this.

12 If one cylinder is about 20 percent lower than the others, and the engine has a slightly rough idle, a worn camshaft lobe could be the cause.

13 If the compression reading is unusually high, the combustion chambers are probably coated with carbon deposits. If this is the case, the cylinder head should be removed and decarbonised (see Chapter 2D).

14 On completion of the test, refit the spark plugs, reconnect the electronic control unit wiring plugs (ensure that the ignition is switched off), and refit the DIS module.

3 Camshaft cover –
removal and refitting

Note: *A new camshaft cover rubber seal will be required for refitting, and a suitable silicone sealant (Vauxhall/Opel No 90 543 772, or equivalent) will be required to seal the timing cover-to-cylinder head upper joint.*

Removal

1 Disconnect the battery negative terminal (refer to *Disconnecting the battery* in the Reference Chapter).

2 Disconnect the wiring connectors at the air mass meter, coolant temperature sensor, camshaft position sensor and oil pressure switch **(see illustrations)**.

3 Lift the wiring harness trough from the camshaft cover and move it to one side **(see illustration)**.

4 Disconnect the two breather hoses at the right-hand rear of the camshaft cover.

5 Remove the DIS module from the centre of the camshaft cover as described in Chapter 5B.

6 Progressively slacken the camshaft cover retaining bolts until they are all fully unscrewed. Note that the bolts are captive and will remain in place in the cover as it is removed.

7 Lift the camshaft cover up and off the cylinder head **(see illustration)**.

Refitting

8 Remove the old seal from the camshaft cover, then examine the inside of the cover for a build-up of oil sludge or any other contamination, and if necessary clean the cover with paraffin, or a water-soluble solvent. Dry the cover thoroughly before refitting.

9 Check the condition of the rubber seals on the camshaft cover retaining bolts. If the seals are in any way damaged or deformed, carefully tap the bolts out of the camshaft cover using a soft-faced mallet and fit new seals to the bolts **(see illustrations)**.

3.3 Lift the wiring harness trough from the camshaft cover and move it to one side

3.7 Lift the camshaft cover up and off the cylinder head

3.9a If necessary, tap the bolts out of the camshaft cover . . .

10 Fit a new rubber seal to the cover ensuring that it is correctly located in the camshaft cover groove **(see illustration)**.

11 Inspect the joint between the timing cover and cylinder head, and cut off any projecting timing cover gasket using a sharp knife **(see illustration)**.

12 Thoroughly clean the mating faces of the camshaft cover and cylinder head.

13 Apply a 2 mm diameter bead of silicone sealant (Vauxhall/Opel No 90 543 772, or equivalent) to the joint between the timing cover and cylinder head on each side **(see illustration)**.

14 Locate the camshaft cover on the cylinder head and screw in the retaining bolts. Progressively and evenly tighten the retaining bolts to the specified torque.

15 Refit the DIS module from the centre of the camshaft cover as described in Chapter 5B.

16 Reconnect the two breather hoses to the right-hand rear of the camshaft cover.

17 Locate the wiring harness trough in the camshaft cover slots then reconnect the air mass meter, coolant temperature sensor, camshaft position sensor and oil pressure switch wiring connectors.

18 Reconnect the battery negative terminal on completion.

3.9b . . . and fit new seals to the bolts

3.10 Fit a new rubber seal to the camshaft cover ensuring that it is correctly located in the cover groove

3.11 Cut off any projecting timing cover gasket using a sharp knife

3.13 Apply a bead of silicone sealant to the joint between the timing cover and cylinder head on each side

4 Valve timing – checking and adjustment

Note: *Certain special tools will be required for this operation. Read through the entire procedure to familiarise yourself with the work involved, then either obtain the manufacturer's special tools, or use the alternatives described. New gaskets and sealing rings will also be required for all disturbed components.*

Checking

1 Disconnect the battery negative terminal (refer to *Disconnecting the battery* in the Reference Chapter).

2 Remove the air cleaner assembly as described in Chapter 4A.

4.6 Turn the crankshaft until the TDC notch (A) on the crankshaft pulley is located just before the cast lug (B) on the timing cover

3 Remove the camshaft cover as described in Section 3.

4 Firmly apply the handbrake, then jack up the front of the car and support it securely on axle stands (see *Jacking and vehicle support*). Remove the right-hand front roadwheel and the wheelarch liner for access to the crankshaft pulley.

5 On models with air conditioning, release the tension on the auxiliary drivebelt and lock the tensioner in the released position as described in the auxiliary drivebelt renewal procedure in Chapter 1. Note that it is not necessary to completely remove the drivebelt, as this would entail removal of the right-hand engine mounting bracket. With the drivebelt tension released, slip the belt off the

4.7 With No 1 piston on the compression stroke, the camshaft lobes for No 1 cylinder should be pointing outwards

compressor pulley. Unbolt the compressor from the cylinder block, release the refrigerant lines from their brackets and support the compressor clear of the engine. **Do not** disconnect the refrigerant lines from the compressor.

6 Using a socket or spanner on the crankshaft pulley hub bolt, turn the crankshaft in the normal direction of rotation (clockwise as viewed from the right-hand side of the car) until the TDC notch on the crankshaft pulley is located just before the cast lug on the timing cover **(see illustration)**.

7 Check that No 1 piston is on the compression stroke by observing No 1 cylinder camshaft lobes. All four lobes should be pointing outwards (away from the engine) **(see illustration)**. If they are not, No 1 piston is on the exhaust stroke and the crankshaft should be turned through a further full turn, stopping once again just before the TDC notch aligns with the lug on the timing cover.

8 Undo the closure bolt from the crankshaft TDC position setting hole. The plug is located on the front facing side of the cylinder block baseplate, adjacent to the timing cover joint. Note that a new closure bolt sealing ring will be required for refitting.

9 If the Vauxhall/Opel TDC positioning pin KM-952 is available, insert the tool into the TDC position setting hole. Slowly turn the crankshaft in the normal direction of rotation until the tool engages with the TDC slot in the crankshaft, and moves fully in, up to its stop.

10 In the absence of the Vauxhall/Opel tool, a

TOOL TiP 1

A commercially available clutch aligning tool can be used as a TDC positioning tool

4.10a The end of the tool must engage with the slot in the crankshaft web (arrowed) – shown with engine partially dismantled

4.10b Clutch aligning tool in position in the TDC setting hole

4.12 Camshaft setting tool (arrowed) made from steel strip and inserted into the camshaft slots

typical commercially available clutch aligning tool of the type having interchangeable cones and collars of various diameters can be used as an alternative (see Tool Tip 1). Assemble the tool so that the end collar (the part that normally engages with the crankshaft spigot bearing) is of 12 mm diameter, and the sliding cone (the part that normally engages with the clutch disc hub) is of 17.5 mm diameter. Insert the tool into the TDC position setting hole, and slowly turn the crankshaft in the normal direction of rotation until the end collar engages with the TDC slot in the crankshaft web. Push the cone fully into the

setting hole as far as it will go, and the crankshaft should now be locked in the TDC position (see illustrations).

11 If the Vauxhall/Opel camshaft setting tool KM-953 is available, insert the tool into the slots in the left-hand end of the camshafts. Ensure that the tool is inserted fully, up to its stop, to lock both camshafts.

12 In the absence of the Vauxhall/Opel tool, a camshaft setting tool can be made out of 5 mm thick flat steel strip, approximately 20 mm wide and long enough to engage both camshaft slots. Insert the setting tool into the camshaft slots to lock the camshafts in the TDC position (see illustration). Note that a ready-made equivalent is available from tool stockists.

13 If it is not possible to insert the camshaft setting tool, then the valve timing must be adjusted as described in paragraphs 17 to 35 below.

14 If all is satisfactory so far, the position of the camshaft position sensor phase disc on the inlet camshaft should be checked as follows. This check entails the use of Vauxhall/Opel camshaft sensor phase disc positioning tool KM-954. If this tool is not available, an alternative can be fabricated as follows.

15 The Vauxhall/Opel positioning tool (KM-954) is a relatively substantial die-casting, the purpose of which is to check the position of the phase disc, and also to hold the phase disc in the correct position on the camshaft sprocket if adjustment is required. During the workshop procedures undertaken for the preparation of this manual, we discovered that a tool made from stiff cardboard (such that used for the cover of a Haynes manual) worked just as well as the factory tool (see illustrations and Tool Tip 2).

16 Using the Vauxhall/Opel positioning tool, or the home-made alternative, check to see if the tool will engage with the phase disc on the camshaft, and also seat squarely on the timing cover surface. If it does, proceed to paragraph 31. If adjustment is required, proceed as follows.

Adjustment

Note: New camshaft sprocket retaining bolts will be required for this operation.

17 Remove the camshaft sensor phase disc positioning tool, and the tool used to lock the camshafts in position.

18 Unscrew the timing chain tensioner closure plug from the timing cover, located just below the heater hose union on the

4.15a Vauxhall/Opel camshaft sensor phase disc positioning tool (KM-954)

4.15b Home-made cardboard alternative camshaft sensor phase disc positioning tool in place

TOOL TIP 2

ALL DIMENSIONS IN MM

60° 84° R=35 8 2 63 127

H32566

A home-made camshaft sensor phase disc positioning tool can be fabricated using the dimensions shown

coolant pump. Note that a new closure bolt sealing ring will be required for refitting **(see illustration)**.

19 Using a suitable spanner engaged with the flats provided on the inlet camshaft, apply tension in a clockwise direction (as viewed from the right-hand side of the car) to the camshaft, to take up any slack in the timing chain **(see illustration)**. This will push the timing chain tensioner plunger fully into its bore.

20 Hold the camshaft in this position and retain the tensioner plunger in the released position by inserting a 2 mm diameter roll pin, approximately 30 mm long, through the closure plug aperture and into the hole on the tensioner body **(see illustrations)**.

21 Slacken and remove the sprocket retaining bolts for both camshafts, using a spanner to counterhold each camshaft as the bolts are slackened.

22 Fit the new bolts to both camshaft sprockets and tighten them finger tight only at this stage. Check that the phase disc on the inlet camshaft can still be turned.

23 Again, using the spanner on the camshaft flats, turn the camshafts slightly, as necessary, until the camshaft setting tool can be reinserted into the slots in the ends of the camshafts.

24 Remove the roll pin used to hold the timing chain tensioner plunger in the retracted position.

25 Turn the camshaft sensor phase disc slightly, as necessary, and locate the Vauxhall/Opel positioning tool (KM-954), or the home-made alternative over the disc and in contact with the timing cover. If the

Vauxhall/Opel tool is being used, bolt it into position on the timing cover.

26 Tighten the camshaft sprocket retaining bolts to 10 Nm/7 lbf ft. Note that this is just an

initial torque loading to hold the sprockets and the phase disc in position when the setting tools are removed.

27 Remove the crankshaft, camshaft and

4.18 Unscrew the timing chain tensioner closure plug from the timing cover

4.19 Using a spanner on the flats of the inlet camshaft, apply tension in a clockwise direction, to take up any slack in the timing chain

4.20a Insert a 2 mm diameter roll pin, approximately 30 mm long, through the closure plug aperture . . .

4.20b . . . and into the hole on the tensioner body (arrowed)

5.5 Undo the six bolts and remove the crankshaft pulley from the pulley hub

phase disc setting tools, then tighten the camshaft sprocket retaining bolts to the specified torque in the stages given in the Specifications. Counterhold the camshafts using the spanner on the camshaft flats as the sprocket bolts are tightened.

28 Turn the crankshaft through two complete revolutions, stopping just before the TDC notch on the crankshaft pulley aligns with the cast lug on the timing cover **(see illustration 4.6)**. Check that all four lobes for No 1 cylinder are pointing outwards (away from the engine).

29 Slowly turn the crankshaft further until the TDC position setting tool can once again be inserted to lock the crankshaft.

30 It should now be possible to re-insert the camshaft setting tool into the slots in the camshafts, and to fit the camshaft sensor phase disc setting tool over the disc. If this is not possible repeat the entire adjustment procedure.

31 If all is satisfactory, remove all the setting/aligning tools and refit the timing chain tensioner and cylinder block closure bolts using new sealing rings. Tighten both closure bolts to the specified torque.

32 On models with air conditioning, refit the compressor to the cylinder block and tighten the mounting bolts to the specified torque. Refit the refrigerant lines to their relevant clips or brackets, then refit the auxiliary drivebelt as described in Chapter 1.

33 Refit the wheelarch liner and the roadwheel. Tighten the roadwheel bolts to the specified torque, then lower the vehicle to the ground.

34 Refit the camshaft cover as described in Section 3.

35 Refit the air cleaner assembly as described in Chapter 4A, then reconnect the battery negative terminal.

5 Crankshaft pulley – removal and refitting

Removal

1 Firmly apply the handbrake, then jack up the front of the car and support it securely on axle stands (see *Jacking and vehicle support*).

Remove the right-hand roadwheel and the wheelarch liner.

2 Release the tension on the auxiliary drivebelt and lock the tensioner in the released position as described in the auxiliary drivebelt renewal procedure in Chapter 1. Note that it is not necessary to completely remove the drivebelt, as this would entail removal of the right-hand engine mounting bracket.

3 With the drivebelt tension released, slip the belt off the crankshaft pulley.

4 Using quick-drying paint, or similar, make an alignment mark between the crankshaft pulley and the pulley hub. It should only be possible to refit the pulley in one position, but it is advisable to make an alignment mark anyway.

5 Unscrew the six crankshaft pulley retaining bolts and remove the pulley from the hub **(see illustration)**. If necessary, prevent the crankshaft from turning as the pulley bolts are slackened using a spanner or socket on the pulley hub bolt.

Refitting

6 Align the marks made on removal and locate the pulley on the hub.

7 Refit the six retaining bolts and progressively tighten them to the specified torque.

8 Refit the auxiliary drivebelt over the crankshaft pulley and ensure that it is correctly seated in the other pulleys.

9 Unlock the auxiliary drivebelt tensioner as described in Chapter 1 to retension the drivebelt.

10 Refit the wheelarch liner and the roadwheel and tighten the wheel bolts to the specified torque.

11 Lower the car to the ground.

6 Timing cover – removal and refitting

Note: *The special tools described in Section 4 will also be required for this operation. Read through the entire procedure and also the procedures contained in Section 4 to familiarise yourself with the work involved, then either obtain the manufacturer's special tools, or use the alternatives described. New gaskets and sealing rings will also be required for all disturbed components, together with new camshaft sprocket retaining bolts. A tube of silicone sealant (Vauxhall/Opel No 90 543 772, or equivalent) will also be needed to seal the joint between the cylinder block and cylinder head.*

Removal

1 Disconnect the battery negative terminal (refer to *Disconnecting the battery* in the Reference Chapter).

2 Remove the air cleaner assembly as described in Chapter 4A.

3 Remove the camshaft cover as described in Section 3.

4 Slacken, but do not remove, the three coolant pump pulley retaining bolts.

5 Remove the auxiliary drivebelt, together with the right-hand engine mounting bracket, as described in Chapter 1.

6 On models without air conditioning, undo the auxiliary drivebelt tensioner lower mounting bolt and the tensioner roller arm upper pivot bolt. Remove the tensioner from the timing cover.

7 On models with air conditioning, using a suitable spanner or socket and wrench engaged with the tensioner roller bolt, gradually release the tensioner by levering the tensioner roller anti-clockwise. Undo the tensioner lower mounting bolt and upper pivot bolt, then remove the tensioner from the timing cover. Store the tensioner upright in its normally fitted position after removal.

8 Remove the alternator as described in Chapter 5A.

9 Drain the cooling system as described in Chapter 1.

10 Undo the three bolts securing the thermostat housing cover to the coolant pump. Release the clip securing the top hose to the radiator and remove the top hose and thermostat housing cover together. Remove the sealing ring from the housing cover noting that a new one will be required for refitting.

11 Release the clips and disconnect the bottom hose from the radiator, expansion tank and coolant pump.

12 Release the clips and disconnect the heater and expansion tank hoses from the coolant pump.

13 Remove the previously slackened coolant pump pulley bolts and remove the pulley from the pump.

14 Using a socket or spanner on the crankshaft pulley hub bolt, turn the crankshaft in the normal direction of rotation (clockwise as viewed from the right-hand side of the car) until the TDC notch on the crankshaft pulley is located just before the cast lug on the timing cover **(see illustration 4.6)**.

15 Check that No 1 piston is on the compression stroke by observing No 1 cylinder camshaft lobes. All four lobes should be pointing outwards (away from the engine). If they are not, No 1 piston is on the exhaust stroke and the crankshaft should be turned through a further full turn, stopping once again just before the TDC notch aligns with the lug on the timing cover.

16 On models with air conditioning, unbolt the compressor from the cylinder block, release the refrigerant lines from their brackets and support the compressor clear of the engine. **Do not** disconnect the refrigerant lines from the compressor.

17 Using quick-drying paint, or similar, make an alignment mark between the crankshaft pulley and the pulley hub. It should only be possible to refit the pulley in one position, but

6.19 Slacken the crankshaft pulley hub retaining bolt (arrowed)

6.31 Push back the timing chain tensioner plunger and secure it in the released position with a 2 mm diameter roll pin

6.32 Undo the two bolts (arrowed) and remove the timing chain sliding rail from the cylinder head

it is advisable to make an alignment mark anyway.

18 Unscrew the six crankshaft pulley retaining bolts and remove the pulley from the hub. If necessary, prevent the crankshaft from turning as the pulley bolts are slackened, using a spanner or socket on the pulley hub bolt.

19 Using a suitable socket, initially slacken (but do not remove) the crankshaft pulley hub retaining bolt **(see illustration)**. The crankshaft can be prevented from turning as the bolt is slackened, using Vauxhall/Opel special tool KM-956 or a similar tool which will engage with the flats on each side of the pulley hub. Alternatively, remove the starter motor, and lock the flywheel ring gear teeth using a suitable hooked tool bolted to the bellhousing.

20 Undo the closure bolt from the crankshaft TDC position setting hole. The plug is located on the front facing side of the cylinder block baseplate, adjacent to the timing cover joint. Note that a new closure bolt sealing ring will be required for refitting.

21 Temporarily place the crankshaft pulley back on the hub and check that the TDC notch is still positioned just before the lug on the timing cover.

22 Slowly turn the crankshaft in the normal direction of rotation until the TDC positioning pin (or suitable alternative) described in paragraphs 9 and 10 of Section 4, engages with the TDC slot in the crankshaft.

23 Remove the crankshaft pulley, if still in place, and check that the punch mark on the pulley hub is in the 11 o-clock position.

24 Insert the camshaft setting tool described in paragraphs 11 and 12 of Section 4 into the slots in the ends of the camshafts.

25 Unscrew the coolant pump retaining bolts, noting the locations of the three short bolts. The short bolts secure the pump to the timing cover, and the long bolts secure the pump and the timing cover to the cylinder block and cylinder head.

26 Withdraw the coolant pump from the timing cover, noting that it may be necessary to tap the pump lightly with a soft-faced mallet to free it from the locating dowels.

27 Recover the pump sealing ring noting that a new one must be used for refitting.

28 Unscrew the previously slackened crankshaft pulley hub retaining bolt and remove the hub from the crankshaft. Note that a new bolt will be required for refitting.

29 Remove the sump as described in Section 11.

30 Undo the timing cover retaining bolts and remove the timing cover from the engine. The cover will be initially tight as it is located on dowels and secured by sealant. If necessary, gently tap it off using a soft-faced mallet.

31 Fully push back the timing chain tensioner plunger and secure it in the released position by inserting a 2 mm diameter roll pin, approximately 30 mm long, in the hole on the

tensioner body **(see illustration)**.

32 Undo the two bolts and remove the timing chain sliding rail from the top of the cylinder head **(see illustration)**.

33 Undo the two bolts and remove the timing chain (front) guide rail from the cylinder block **(see illustration)**.

34 Undo the lower pivot bolt and remove the timing chain (rear) tension rail from the cylinder block **(see illustration)**.

35 Lift the timing chain off the sprockets and remove the chain, then remove the drive sprocket from the crankshaft **(see illustrations)**.

36 Remove the composite gasket from the cylinder block baseplate, cylinder block, and cylinder head, using a plastic spatula if

6.33 Undo the two bolts (arrowed) and remove the timing chain guide rail from the cylinder block

6.34 Undo the lower pivot bolt and remove the timing chain tension rail from the cylinder block

6.35a Lift the timing chain off the sprockets and remove the chain . . .

6.35b . . . then remove the drive sprocket from the crankshaft

6.36 Remove the timing cover composite gasket from the cylinder block baseplate, cylinder block, and cylinder head

6.44 Apply a 2 mm diameter bead of silicone sealant to the joint between the cylinder block and cylinder head on each side

6.46 Slide the timing chain drive sprocket onto the crankshaft with the markings facing outwards

necessary to release the sealant **(see illustration)**. Note that if the cylinder head has ever been previously removed, the gasket will be a two-piece type, with a split at the cylinder head-to cylinder block joint. A new gasket will be required for refitting.

37 Thoroughly clean the timing cover and remove all traces of gasket and sealant from all the mating surfaces. Similarly clean the cylinder block baseplate, cylinder block and cylinder head mating surfaces. Ensure that all traces of old sealant are removed, particularly from the area of the cylinder head-to-cylinder block joint.

38 Inspect the timing chain, sprockets, sliding rail, guide rail and tension rail for any sign of wear or deformation, and renew any suspect components as necessary. Renew the crankshaft timing chain end oil seal in the timing cover as a matter of course using the procedures described in Section 13.

39 It is advisable also, to check the condition of the timing chain tensioner at this stage, as described in Section 7.

40 Obtain all new gaskets and components as necessary ready for refitting.

Refitting

41 Commence refitting by inserting a new

coolant pump seal into the groove in the timing cover.

42 Check that the locating dowels are in place, and that the mating surfaces are clean and dry, then locate the pump in position on the timing cover.

43 Refit the three coolant pump short retaining bolts, ensuring that the bolts are fitted to their correct locations (refer to Chapter 3 if necessary). Tighten the bolts to the specified torque.

44 Apply a 2 mm diameter bead of silicone sealant (Vauxhall/Opel No 90 543 772, or equivalent) to the joint between the cylinder block and cylinder head on each side **(see illustration)**. The bead should be long enough to fill the joint in the area covered by the timing cover gasket.

45 Ensure that the locating dowels are in position, then locate the new timing cover gasket in place on the cylinder head, cylinder block and baseplate.

46 Slide the timing chain drive sprocket onto the crankshaft with the markings facing outwards **(see illustration)**.

47 Engage the timing chain with the drive sprocket then, keeping it tight on the exhaust camshaft side, feed the chain up and over the camshaft sprockets **(see illustration)**.

48 Place the timing chain tension rail in position, refit the lower pivot bolt and tighten the bolt to the specified torque.

49 Attach the timing chain guide rail to the cylinder block and secure with the two bolts tightened to the specified torque.

50 Refit the timing chain sliding rail to the cylinder head and secure with the two bolts tightened to the specified torque.

51 Remove the roll pin used to secure the timing chain tensioner plunger in the released position.

52 Locate the timing cover in position and refit all the retaining bolts, finger tight only at this stage. Now tighten all the bolts to the specified torque, starting with the bolts around the coolant pump first, followed by the bolts around the periphery of the cover.

53 Refit the sump as described in Section 11.

54 Remove the position setting tools used to lock the crankshaft and camshafts in the TDC position.

55 Lubricate the crankshaft pulley hub with engine oil, then refit the hub to the crankshaft, ensuring that the punch mark on the hub is in the 11 o-clock position **(see illustration)**.

56 Screw in the new pulley hub retaining bolt and tighten it to the specified torque, in the stages given in the Specifications **(see**

6.47 Keeping the timing chain tight on the exhaust camshaft side, locate the chain over the sprockets

6.55 Lubricate the crankshaft pulley hub, then refit the hub to the crankshaft

6.56a Screw in the new pulley hub retaining bolt . . .

6.56b . . . tighten it to the specified torque . . .

6.56c . . . then through the specified angle in the stages given in the Specifications

illustrations). Prevent crankshaft rotation as the bolt is tightened, using the method employed for removal.

57 Refit the crankshaft pulley to the pulley hub, with the marks made on removal aligned, and tighten the six bolts to the specified torque.

58 Turn the crankshaft through two complete revolutions, stopping just before the TDC notch on the crankshaft pulley aligns with the cast lug on the timing cover. Check that all four lobes for No 1 cylinder are pointing outwards (away from the engine).

59 Slowly turn the crankshaft further until the TDC position setting tool can once again be inserted to lock the crankshaft.

60 It should now be possible to re-insert the camshaft setting tool into the slots in the camshafts. If the setting tool cannot be inserted, carry out the valve timing adjustment procedures contained in Section 4.

61 If all is satisfactory, remove all the setting/aligning tools and refit the closure bolt to the cylinder block using a new sealing ring. Tighten the closure bolt to the specified torque.

62 Refit the coolant pump pulley and tighten the three bolts to the specified torque. To prevent the pulley turning as the bolts are tightened, hold the pulley using a screwdriver engaged with one of the bolts and the pump centre spindle. Alternatively, wait until the auxiliary drivebelt has been refitted and tighten the bolts then.

63 On models with air conditioning, refit the compressor to the cylinder block and tighten the mounting bolts to the specified torque. Refit the refrigerant lines to their relevant clips or brackets.

64 Refit the alternator as described in Chapter 5A.

65 Refit the auxiliary drivebelt tensioner and

tighten the mounting bolts to the specified torque. On models with air conditioning, using a suitable spanner or socket and wrench engaged with the tensioner roller bolt, lever the tensioner roller clockwise against the spring pressure, until the tensioner can be heard to audibly lock in its end position.

66 Refit the auxiliary drivebelt (together with the right-hand engine mounting bracket) as described in Chapter 1.

67 Refit the camshaft cover as described in Section 3.

68 Ensure that the mating surfaces are clean, then fit a new sealing ring to the thermostat housing cover. Refit the cover to the coolant pump and tighten the bolts to the specified torque.

69 Reconnect the radiator top and bottom hoses, expansion tank hoses and heater hose to their respective connections.

70 Refit the air cleaner assembly as described in Chapter 4A.

71 Refill the cooling system as described in Chapter 1, then reconnect the battery negative terminal.

---

7 Timing chain tensioner –
removal, inspection and
refitting

Removal

1 Remove the timing cover as described in Section 6.

2 Undo the two tensioner retaining bolts and remove the tensioner from the cylinder head (see illustration).

3 Extract the roll pin used to retain the tensioner plunger in the retracted position and withdraw the tensioner plunger and spring (see illustrations).

Inspection

4 Examine the components for any sign of wear, deformation or damage and, if evident, renew the complete tensioner assembly.

Refitting

5 Lubricate the tensioner spring and plunger, then insert the spring, followed by the plunger into the tensioner body.

6 Fully compress the tensioner plunger and reinsert the retaining roll pin (see illustration).

7.2 Undo the two retaining bolts and remove the timing chain tensioner from the cylinder head

7.3a Extract the roll pin used to retain the tensioner plunger in the retracted position . . .

7.3b . . . and withdraw the tensioner plunger and spring

7.6 Timing chain tensioner plunger fully retracted and locked with the roll pin

7 Refit the tensioner assembly to the cylinder head and tighten the retaining bolts to the specified torque.

8 Camshaft sprockets – removal and refitting

Note: *The special tools described in Section 4 will also be required for this operation. Read through the entire procedure and also the procedures contained in Section 4 to familiarise yourself with the work involved, then either obtain the manufacturer's special tools, or use the alternatives described. New gaskets and sealing rings will also be required for all disturbed components, together with new camshaft sprocket retaining bolts.*

Removal

1 Disconnect the battery negative terminal (refer to *Disconnecting the battery* in the Reference Chapter).

2 Remove the air cleaner assembly as described in Chapter 4A.

3 Remove the camshaft cover as described in Section 3.

4 Firmly apply the handbrake, then jack up the front of the car and support it securely on axle stands (see *Jacking and vehicle support*). Remove the right-hand front roadwheel and the wheelarch liner for access to the crankshaft pulley.

5 On models with air conditioning, release the tension on the auxiliary drivebelt and lock the tensioner in the released position as described in the auxiliary drivebelt renewal procedure in Chapter 1. Note that it is not necessary to completely remove the drivebelt, as this entails removal of the right-hand engine mounting bracket. With the drivebelt tension released, slip the belt off the compressor pulley. Unbolt the compressor from the cylinder block, release the refrigerant lines from their brackets and support the compressor clear of the engine. **Do not disconnect the refrigerant lines from the compressor.**

6 Using a socket or spanner on the crankshaft pulley hub bolt, turn the crankshaft

8.13 Slacken the camshaft sprocket retaining bolts using a spanner to counterhold each camshaft as the bolts are slackened

in the normal direction of rotation (clockwise as viewed from the right-hand side of the car) until the TDC notch on the crankshaft pulley is located just before the cast lug on the timing cover **(see illustration 4.6)**.

7 Check that No 1 piston is on the compression stroke by observing No 1 cylinder camshaft lobes. All four lobes should be pointing outwards (away from the engine). If they are not, No 1 piston is on the exhaust stroke and the crankshaft should be turned through a further full turn, stopping once again just before the TDC notch aligns with the lug on the timing cover.

8 Unscrew the timing chain tensioner closure bolt from the front of the timing cover, below the heater hose union on the coolant pump. Note that a new closure bolt sealing ring will be required for refitting.

9 Obtain a suitable roll pin or similar of 2 mm diameter and approximately 30 mm long to use as a timing chain tensioner locking tool.

10 Using a suitable spanner engaged with the flats provided on the inlet camshaft, apply tension in a clockwise direction (as viewed from the right-hand side of the car) to the camshaft, to take up any slack in the timing chain. This will push the timing chain tensioner plunger fully into its bore.

11 Hold the camshaft in this position and retain the tensioner plunger in the released position by inserting the roll pin through the closure plug aperture and into the hole on the tensioner body.

12 Undo the two bolts and remove the timing chain sliding rail from the top of the cylinder head.

13 Slacken the sprocket retaining bolts for both camshafts, using the spanner to counterhold each camshaft as the bolts are slackened **(see illustration)**. Remove the bolt for the sprocket(s) being removed together with the camshaft position sensor phase disc, if removing the inlet camshaft. Withdraw the relevant sprocket(s) from the camshaft(s), disengage the timing chain and remove the sprocket(s) from the engine.

Refitting

14 Engage the sprocket(s) with the timing chain and locate the sprocket(s) on the camshaft(s). Fit the new retaining bolt(s) together with the phase disc, if working on the inlet camshaft. Note that new retaining bolts must be fitted to both sprockets, even if only one sprocket was removed. Tighten the bolts finger tight only at this stage and check that the phase disc on the inlet camshaft can still be turned.

15 Refit the timing chain sliding rail to the top of the cylinder head and secure with the two bolts tightened to the specified torque.

16 Using the spanner on the camshaft flats, turn the camshafts slightly, as necessary, until the camshaft setting tool described in paragraphs 11 and 12 of Section 4 can be inserted into the slots in the ends of the camshafts.

17 Turn the camshaft sensor phase disc as necessary until the phase disc positioning tool

(or suitable alternative) described in paragraphs 14 and 15 of Section 4 can be located over the phase disc. If the Vauxhall/Opel tool is being used, bolt it to the top of the timing cover. If the alternative tool described is being used, ensure that its base is in contact with the timing cover.

18 Remove the roll pin used to hold the timing chain tensioner plunger in the retracted position.

19 Undo the closure bolt from the crankshaft TDC position setting hole. The plug is located on the front facing side of the cylinder block baseplate, adjacent to the timing cover joint. Note that a new closure bolt sealing ring will be required for refitting.

20 Slowly turn the crankshaft in the normal direction of rotation until the TDC positioning pin (or suitable alternative), described in paragraphs 9 and 10 of Section 4, engages with the TDC slot in the crankshaft.

21 Tighten the camshaft sprocket retaining bolts to 10 Nm/7 lbf ft. Note that this is just an initial torque loading to hold the sprockets and the phase disc in position when the setting tools are removed.

22 Remove the crankshaft, camshaft and phase disc setting tools, then tighten the camshaft sprocket retaining bolts to the specified torque in the stages given in the Specifications. Counterhold the camshafts using the spanner on the camshaft flats as the sprocket bolts are tightened.

23 Turn the crankshaft through two complete revolutions, stopping just before the TDC notch on the crankshaft pulley aligns with the cast lug on the timing cover. Check that all four lobes for No 1 cylinder are pointing outwards (away from the engine).

24 Slowly turn the crankshaft further until the TDC position setting tool can once again be inserted to lock the crankshaft.

25 It should now be possible to re-insert the camshaft setting tool into the slots in the camshafts, and to fit the camshaft sensor phase disc setting tool over the disc. If this is not possible carry out the valve timing adjustment procedure contained in Section 4.

26 If all is satisfactory, remove all the setting/aligning tools and refit the timing chain tensioner and cylinder block closure bolts using new sealing rings. Tighten both closure bolts to the specified torque.

27 On models with air conditioning, refit the compressor to the cylinder block and tighten the mounting bolts to the specified torque. Refit the refrigerant lines to their relevant clips or brackets, then refit the auxiliary drivebelt as described in Chapter 1.

28 Refit the wheelarch liner and the roadwheel. Tighten the roadwheel bolts to the specified torque, then lower the vehicle to the ground.

29 Refit the camshaft cover as described in Section 3.

30 Refit the air cleaner assembly as described in Chapter 4A, then reconnect the battery negative terminal.

9.2 Camshaft bearing cap identification numbers (arrowed)

9.4 Lift off the camshaft bearing caps, keeping them in order – shown with cylinder head removed

9.5 Lift the camshaft(s) from their locations in the cylinder head. If both camshafts are removed, identify them as exhaust and inlet – shown with cylinder head removed

9 Camshafts, tappets and rocker arms – removal and refitting

Removal

1 Remove the camshaft sprocket(s) as described in Section 8.

2 Observe the identification numbers and markings on the camshaft bearing caps **(see illustration)**. On the project car used during the compilation of this manual, the bearing caps with odd numbers were fitted to the exhaust camshaft, and the caps with the even numbers were fitted to the inlet camshaft. However, this may not be the case on other engines. Also, as it is possible to fit the caps either way round, it will be necessary to mark the caps with quick-drying paint, or identify them in some way, so that they can be refitted in exactly the same position. On the project car, all the numbers could be read the correct way up, when viewed from the exhaust camshaft side of the engine. Again, this may not always be the case.

3 With the bearing caps correctly identified, and working in a spiral pattern from the outside to the inside, initially slacken the bearing cap bolts, one at a time, by half a turn. When all the bolts have been initially slackened, repeat the procedure, slackening the bolts by a further half a turn. Continue until all the bolts have been fully slackened. The camshaft will rise up under the action of the valve springs as the bolts are slackened. Ensure that the camshaft rises uniformly and does not jam in its bearings.

4 When all the bolts have been slackened, remove the bolts and lift off the bearing caps, keeping them in order according to the identification method decided on **(see illustration)**.

5 Note the installed position of the camshaft(s) before removal – the cam lobes for No 1 cylinder should be pointing outwards (ie, away from the centre). Carefully lift the camshaft(s) from their locations in the cylinder head. If both camshafts are removed, identify them as exhaust and inlet **(see illustration)**.

6 Obtain eight (or sixteen) small, clean plastic containers, and number them inlet 1 to 8 and exhaust 1 to 8; alternatively, divide a larger container into sixteen compartments and number each compartment accordingly. Withdraw each rocker arm and hydraulic tappet in turn, and place them in their respective container **(see illustrations)**. Do not interchange the rocker arms and tappets, or the rate of wear will be much increased.

Inspection

7 Examine the camshaft bearing surfaces and cam lobes for signs of wear ridges and scoring. Renew the camshaft if any of these conditions are apparent. Examine the condition of the bearing surfaces, both on the camshaft journals and in the cylinder head/bearing caps. If the head bearing surfaces are worn excessively, the cylinder head will need to be renewed.

8 Examine the rocker arm and hydraulic tappet bearing surfaces for wear ridges and

scoring. Renew any rocker arm or tappet on which these conditions are apparent.

9 If either camshaft is being renewed, it will be necessary to renew all the rocker arms and tappets for that particular camshaft also.

Refitting

10 Before refitting, thoroughly clean all the components and the cylinder head and bearing cap journals.

11 Liberally oil the cylinder head hydraulic tappet bores and the tappets. Carefully refit the tappets to the cylinder head, ensuring that each tappet is refitted to its original bore.

12 Lay each rocker arm in position over its respective tappet.

13 Liberally oil the camshaft bearings in the cylinder head and the camshaft lobes, then place the camshafts in the cylinder head. Turn the camshafts so that the cam lobes for No 1 cylinder are pointing outwards as noted during removal.

14 Refit all the bearing caps to their respective locations ensuring they are fitted the correct way round as noted during removal.

15 Working in a spiral pattern from the inside to the outside, initially tighten the bearing cap bolts, one at a time, by half a turn. When all the bolts have been initially tightened, repeat the procedure, tightening the bolts by a further half a turn. Continue until all the bearing caps are in contact with the cylinder head and the bolts are lightly tightened.

16 Again, working in a spiral pattern from inside to outside, tighten all the bolts to the specified torque.

17 Refit the camshaft sprockets as described in Section 8.

10 Cylinder head – removal and refitting

Note 1: *The engine must be cold when removing the cylinder head. A new cylinder head gasket, timing cover gasket, cylinder head bolts, camshaft sprocket bolts and*

9.6a Withdraw each rocker arm . . .

9.6b . . . and hydraulic tappet in turn, and place them in their respective containers – shown with cylinder head removed

10.27 Undo the bolt (arrowed) securing the support bracket to the base of the inlet manifold. Slacken the bolt securing the bracket to the block and twist the bracket to one side – shown with engine removed

10.31 Undo the two bolts (arrowed) and remove the exhaust manifold heat shield

10.33 Undo the three bolts and remove the oil filter housing from the cylinder block

numerous seals and sealing rings will be required for refitting. A suitable sealant (Vauxhall/Opel No 90 543 772, or equivalent) will also be needed to seal the timing cover-to-cylinder block joint.

Note 2: The special tools described in Section 4 will also be required for this operation. Read through the entire procedure and also the procedures contained in Section 4 to familiarise yourself with the work involved, then either obtain the manufacturer's special tools, or use the alternatives described.

Note 3: The following procedure describes removal and refitting of the cylinder head with the manifolds attached. If required, the manifolds may be removed first, as described in Chapter 4A.

Removal

1 Disconnect the battery negative terminal (refer to Disconnecting the battery in the Reference Chapter).

2 On right-hand drive models, remove the battery and battery tray as described in Chapter 5A.

3 Remove the air cleaner assembly as described in Chapter 4A.

4 Drain the cooling system as described in Chapter 1.

5 Undo the three bolts securing the thermostat housing cover to the coolant pump.

6 Release the clip securing the top hose to the radiator and remove the top hose and thermostat housing cover together. Remove the sealing ring from the housing cover noting that a new one will be required for refitting.

7 Release the clips and disconnect the bottom hose from the radiator, expansion tank and coolant pump.

8 Release the clips and disconnect the heater and expansion tank hoses from the coolant pump.

9 Remove the throttle body as described in Chapter 4A, Section 11.

10 Undo the two bolts, one at each end, securing the plastic fuel injector wiring trough to the top of the fuel rail. Note that these bolts also secure the fuel rail to the inlet manifold.

11 Release the retaining clips at each

injector, then lift the wiring trough up and off the injectors. Place the trough to one side.

12 Depressurise the fuel system as described in Chapter 4A, then disconnect the fuel feed and return hoses from the fuel rail, noting their locations to aid refitting. Be prepared for fuel spillage, and take adequate precautions. Clamp or plug the open ends of the hoses, to minimise further fuel loss.

13 Disconnect the coolant hoses from the coolant expansion tank, then undo the retaining bolts and remove the expansion tank.

14 Disconnect the wiring plug from the top of the EGR valve, and the wiring connector from the adjacent temperature gauge sender.

15 Disconnect the coolant hose from the side of the EGR valve.

16 Release the DIS ignition module cover from the centre of the camshaft cover and remove it toward the transmission end of the engine.

17 Disconnect the wiring plug from the left-hand end of the DIS module.

18 Disconnect the fuel injector wiring trough wiring connector.

19 Undo the retaining bolt and release the left-hand engine lifting bracket from the cylinder head, complete with attached wiring harness.

20 Release the wiring harness from its locating clips to gain access to the electronic control unit wiring connectors.

21 Lift up the locking levers and disconnect the engine management and main body wiring harness connectors from the electronic control unit.

22 Undo the retaining screw and release the earth cable from the electronic control unit bracket.

23 Detach the fuel tank vent valve from its mounting bracket and move the valve to one side.

24 Disconnect the brake servo vacuum hose connection at the inlet manifold. On 1.0 litre engines the connection is by a conventional union nut. On 1.2 litre engines a quick-release fitting is used. Depress the two tags on the side of the fitting and withdraw the fitting from the manifold pipe stub.

25 Undo the two bolts and release the wiring harness support bracket from the rear of the inlet manifold.

26 If not already done, firmly apply the handbrake, then jack up the front of the car and support it securely on axle stands (see Jacking and vehicle support).

27 From under the car, undo the bolt securing the support bracket to the base of the inlet manifold. Slacken the bolt securing the bracket to the cylinder block and twist the bracket to one side **(see illustration)**.

28 On 1.0 litre engines, detach the additional lower wiring harness bracket from the inlet manifold.

29 Undo the bolts and remove the remaining engine lifting brackets from the cylinder head.

30 Undo the bolt securing the oil dipstick guide tube to the exhaust manifold and withdraw the dipstick and guide tube from the cylinder block baseplate. Suitably cover or plug the guide tube aperture in the cylinder block baseplate to prevent dirt ingress.

31 Undo the two bolts and remove the exhaust manifold heat shield **(see illustration)**.

32 Remove the oil filter from the filter housing as described in Chapter 1. Remove as much of the oil remaining in the filter housing as possible using clean rags.

33 Undo the three bolts and remove the oil filter housing from the cylinder block **(see illustration)**. Place absorbent rags below the housing as it is removed to catch any remaining oil. Recover the filter housing seal noting that a new seal will be required for refitting.

34 Remove the camshaft cover as described in Section 3.

35 Undo the three nuts securing the catalytic converter flange to the exhaust manifold. Undo the two bolts securing the converter support bracket to the cylinder block baseplate and separate the converter from the manifold. Lower the exhaust system clear of the manifold and support it in this position. Recover the flange gasket.

36 Using a socket or spanner on the crankshaft pulley hub bolt, turn the crankshaft in the normal direction of rotation (clockwise as viewed from the right-hand side of the car) until the TDC notch on the crankshaft pulley is located just before the cast lug on the timing cover **(see illustration 4.6)**.

37 Check that No 1 piston is on the

compression stroke by observing No 1 cylinder camshaft lobes. All four lobes should be pointing outwards (away from the engine). If they are not, No 1 piston is on the exhaust stroke and the crankshaft should be turned through a further full turn, stopping once again just before the TDC notch aligns with the lug on the timing cover.

38 Slacken, but do not remove, the three coolant pump pulley retaining bolts. Release the tension on the auxiliary drivebelt and lock the tensioner in the released position as described in the auxiliary drivebelt renewal procedure in Chapter 1. Note that it is not necessary to completely remove the drivebelt, as this would entail removal of the right-hand engine mounting bracket. With the drivebelt tension released, slip the belt off the pulleys.

39 On models with air conditioning, unbolt the compressor from the cylinder block, release the refrigerant lines from their brackets and support the compressor clear of the engine. **Do not** disconnect the refrigerant lines from the compressor.

40 Remove the previously slackened coolant pump pulley bolts and remove the pulley from the pump.

41 Undo the closure bolt from the crankshaft TDC position setting hole. The plug is located on the front facing side of the cylinder block baseplate, adjacent to the timing cover joint. Note that a new closure bolt sealing ring will be required for refitting.

42 Slowly turn the crankshaft in the normal direction of rotation until the TDC positioning pin (or suitable alternative), described in paragraphs 9 and 10 of Section 4, engages with the TDC slot in the crankshaft.

43 Obtain a suitable roll pin, or similar, of 2 mm diameter and approximately 30 mm long, to use as a timing chain tensioner locking tool.

44 Using a suitable spanner engaged with the flats provided on the inlet camshaft, apply tension in a clockwise direction (as viewed from the right-hand side of the car) to the camshaft, to take up any slack in the timing chain. This will push the timing chain tensioner plunger fully into its bore.

45 Hold the camshaft in this position and retain the tensioner plunger in the released position by inserting the roll pin through the closure plug aperture and into the hole on the tensioner body.

46 Undo the two bolts and remove the timing chain sliding rail from the top of the cylinder head.

47 Slacken the sprocket retaining bolts for both camshafts, using the spanner to counterhold each camshaft as the bolts are slackened. Remove both sprocket bolts together with the camshaft position sensor phase disc from the inlet camshaft. Ease the sprockets and chain off the camshafts and rest the sprockets on the top of the timing cover.

48 Undo the retaining bolt and remove the camshaft position sensor from the front of the timing cover.

10.49 Undo the bolts (1) securing the coolant pump, and the bolts (arrowed) securing timing cover to the cylinder head

49 Undo the bolts securing the coolant pump and timing cover to the cylinder head **(see illustration)**. Note that it is not necessary to remove all the coolant pump bolts as three are shorter than the rest, and only secure the pump to the timing cover.

50 Working in the sequence shown, progressively slacken the cylinder head retaining bolts half a turn at a time until all the bolts are loose **(see illustration)**. Remove the

bolts from their locations noting that new bolts will be required for refitting.

51 Slightly raise the cylinder head so it just clears the cylinder block face and move the head toward the transmission end of the engine. The head will be initially tight due to the sealant on the timing cover gasket and head gasket. Note that the locating dowel holes on the cylinder head are elongated to allow the head to move sideways slightly.

10.50 Cylinder head bolt slackening sequence

10.57 Before refitting the cylinder head, insert the camshaft setting tool (arrowed) into the slots in the ends of the camshafts

10.60 Position the cylinder head gasket on the block with the words OBEN/TOP uppermost

52 As soon as sufficient clearance exists, lift the cylinder head up and off the cylinder block. At the same time, release the timing chain guide rail from the peg on the cylinder head, and guide the chain tensioner clear of the tensioning rail. Check that the tensioner locking pin is not dislodged as the cylinder head is lifted up. Place the cylinder head on wooden blocks after removal to avoid damage to the valves. Recover the cylinder head gasket.

Preparation for refitting

53 The mating faces of the cylinder head and cylinder block must be perfectly clean before refitting the head. Scouring agents are available for this purpose, but acceptable results can be achieved by using a hard plastic or wood scraper to remove all traces of gasket and carbon. The same method can be used to clean the piston crowns. Take particular care to avoid scoring or gouging the cylinder head mating surfaces during the cleaning operations, as aluminium alloy is easily damaged. Make sure that the carbon is not allowed to enter the oil and water passages – this is particularly important for the lubrication system, as carbon could block the oil supply to the engine's components. Using adhesive tape and paper, seal the water, oil and bolt holes in the cylinder block. To prevent carbon entering the gap between the pistons and bores, smear a little grease in the gap. After cleaning each piston, use a small brush to remove all traces of grease and carbon from the gap, then wipe away the remainder with a clean rag.

54 Check the mating surfaces of the cylinder block and the cylinder head for nicks, deep scratches and other damage. If slight, they may be removed carefully with a file, but if excessive, machining may be the only alternative to renewal. If warpage of the cylinder head gasket surface is suspected, use a straight-edge to check it for distortion. Refer to Part D of this Chapter if necessary.

55 Thoroughly clean the threads of the cylinder head bolt holes in the cylinder block. Ensure that the bolts run freely in their threads, and that all traces of oil and water are removed from each bolt hole.

56 Using a sharp knife, partially cut through the timing cover gasket flush with the top of the cylinder block. Release the gasket from the timing cover and bend it in half to break it off at the cut line. Remove the upper part of the gasket, and thoroughly clean the mating surface, paying particular attention to the cylinder block edge where it contacts the timing cover.

57 Before refitting the cylinder head, using the spanner on the camshaft flats, turn the camshafts slightly, as necessary, until the camshaft setting tool described in paragraphs 11 and 12 of Section 4 can be inserted into the slots in the ends of the camshafts **(see illustration)**. With the tool in position, the camshaft lobes for No 1 cylinder should be pointing outward.

Refitting

58 Prior to locating the cylinder head gasket on the cylinder block, cut off the two protruding tabs at the timing cover end of the gasket, flush with the gasket edge.

59 Apply a 2 mm diameter bead of silicone sealant (Vauxhall/Opel No 90 543 772, or equivalent) to the joint between the cylinder block and the timing cover on each side.

60 Check that the locating dowels are in position in the cylinder block, then lay the new gasket on the block face, with the words OBEN/TOP uppermost **(see illustration)**. Push the gasket hard up against the timing cover so that is engages with the sealant.

61 Position the new timing cover gasket upper part on the timing cover, so that its lower ends engage with the sealant. Temporarily insert the left- and right-hand upper timing cover mounting bolts to locate the gasket in the correct position.

62 Apply a further 2 mm diameter bead of silicone sealant (Vauxhall/Opel

No 90 543 772, or equivalent) to the joint between the cylinder block and the timing cover on each side.

63 Carefully lower the cylinder head into position on the gasket, guiding the chain tensioner past the tensioning rail and guiding the tensioner locking pin into the timing cover access hole. Check also that the timing chain guide rail engages with cylinder head peg.

64 Once the head is seated on its dowels, tap it towards the timing cover with a rubber mallet.

65 Refit the three lower timing cover retaining bolts (one at each side, and one below the coolant pump). Tighten the three bolts to the specified torque.

66 Remove the camshaft setting tool from the camshaft slots.

67 Fit the new cylinder head retaining bolts and screw in the bolts until they contact the cylinder head. Working in the reverse order to that shown in illustration 10.50, tighten the cylinder head bolts to the Stage one torque setting given in the Specifications, using a torque wrench. Again working in the correct order, tighten all the bolts through the Stage two angle using angle measuring gauge **(see illustrations)**. Repeat for Stage three and Stage four.

68 Slacken the three previously fitted bolts

10.67a Tighten the cylinder head bolts to the Stage 1 torque setting using a torque wrench

10.67b Tighten the cylinder head bolts through the Stage two, three and four angles using an angle tightening gauge

securing the timing cover to the cylinder head.

69 Refit the bolts around the coolant pump and tighten them to the specified torque.

70 Refit the remaining timing cover retaining bolts and tighten them to the specified torque.

71 Using the spanner on the camshaft flats, turn the camshafts slightly, as necessary, until the camshaft setting tool can once again be inserted into the camshaft slots.

72 Engage the camshaft sprockets with their respective camshafts, and fit the new retaining bolts together with the phase disc on the inlet camshaft. Tighten the bolts finger tight only at this stage and check that the phase disc on the inlet camshaft can still be turned.

73 Refit the timing chain sliding rail to the top of the cylinder head and secure with the two bolts tightened to the specified torque.

74 Remove the roll pin used to hold the timing chain tensioner plunger in the retracted position.

75 Turn the camshaft sensor phase disc as necessary until the phase disc positioning tool (or suitable alternative), described in paragraphs 14 and 15 of Section 4, can be located over the phase disc. If the Vauxhall/Opel tool is being used, bolt it to the top of the timing cover. If the alternative tool described is being used, ensure that its base is in contact with the timing cover.

76 Tighten the camshaft sprocket retaining bolts to 10 Nm/7 lbf ft. Note that this is just an initial torque loading to hold the sprockets and the phase disc in position when the setting tools are removed. Tighten the inlet camshaft sprocket bolt first, followed by the exhaust camshaft sprocket bolt.

77 Remove the crankshaft, camshaft and phase disc setting tools, then tighten the camshaft sprocket retaining bolts to the specified torque in the stages given in the Specifications. Counterhold the camshafts using the spanner on the camshaft flats as the sprocket bolts are tightened.

78 Turn the crankshaft through two complete revolutions, stopping just before the TDC notch on the crankshaft pulley aligns with the cast lug on the timing cover. Check that all four lobes for No 1 cylinder are pointing outwards (away from the engine).

79 Slowly turn the crankshaft further until the TDC position setting tool can once again be inserted to lock the crankshaft.

80 It should now be possible to re-insert the camshaft setting tool into the slots in the camshafts, and to fit the camshaft sensor phase disc setting tool over the disc. If this is not possible carry out the valve timing adjustment procedure contained in Section 4.

81 If all is satisfactory, remove all the setting/aligning tools and refit the timing chain tensioner and cylinder block closure bolts using new sealing rings. Tighten both closure bolts to the specified torque.

82 Refit the camshaft position sensor using a new sealing ring and tighten the retaining bolt to the specified torque.

83 Thoroughly clean the mating surfaces of the oil pump housing and cylinder block, and refit the housing using a new seal. Refit and tighten the retaining bolts to the specified torque.

84 Fit a new sealing O-ring to the oil filter housing cap, then clip the new oil filter element to the cap.

85 Fit the cap and filter element assembly to the oil filter housing and screw the cap into position. Finally, tighten the cap to the specified torque.

86 Refit the coolant pump pulley and tighten the three bolts to the specified torque. To prevent the pulley turning as the bolts are tightened, hold the pulley using a screwdriver engaged with one of the bolts and the pump centre spindle. Alternatively, wait until the auxiliary drivebelt has been refitted and tighten the bolts then.

87 On models with air conditioning, refit the compressor to the cylinder block and tighten the mounting bolts to the specified torque. Refit the refrigerant lines to their relevant clips or brackets.

88 Refit the auxiliary drivebelt as described in Chapter 1.

89 Reconnect the catalytic converter to the exhaust manifold using a new flange gasket. Tighten the converter-to-manifold nuts to the specified torque first, followed by the support bracket bolts.

90 From under the car, reposition the inlet manifold support bracket and refit the bolt securing the bracket to the manifold. Tighten this bolt, and the bolt securing the bracket to the cylinder block, to the specified torque.

91 Refit the wiring harness support bracket(s) to the inlet manifold.

92 Reconnect the brake servo vacuum hose to the inlet manifold.

93 Refit the exhaust manifold heat shield and secure with the two bolts.

94 Renew the oil dipstick guide tube O-rings and lubricate the O-rings with petroleum jelly. Insert the guide tube into the cylinder block baseplate then secure the tube to the exhaust manifold with the retaining bolt.

95 Refit the engine lifting brackets to the cylinder head.

96 Reconnect the coolant hose to the side of the EGR valve.

97 Refit the fuel tank vent valve to its mounting bracket.

98 Reconnect the two wiring connectors to the electronic control unit and secure the earth lead to the control unit bracket with the retaining screw. Reposition the wiring harness moved clear for access.

99 Reconnect the wiring plug to the top of the EGR valve and the wiring connector to the adjacent temperature gauge sender.

100 Reconnect the wiring plugs at the oil pressure switch, coolant temperature sensor and camshaft position sensor.

101 Refit the throttle body as described in Chapter 4A, Section 11.

102 Reconnect the wiring plug to the left-hand end of the DIS module, then refit the module cover.

103 Refit the coolant expansion tank and reconnect the coolant hoses.

104 Reconnect the fuel feed and return hoses to the fuel rail.

105 Locate the plastic fuel injector wiring trough over the injectors ensuring that the wiring connectors correctly engage. Secure the trough with the two retaining bolts, then reconnect the wiring connector.

106 Ensure that the mating surfaces are clean, then fit a new sealing ring to the thermostat housing cover. Refit the cover to the coolant pump and tighten the bolts to the specified torque.

107 Reconnect the radiator top and bottom hoses, expansion tank hoses and heater hose to their respective connections.

108 Refit the camshaft cover as described in Section 3.

109 Refit the air cleaner assembly as described in Chapter 4A.

110 On right-hand drive models, refit the battery and battery tray as described in Chapter 5A.

111 Refill the cooling system as described in Chapter 1, then reconnect the battery.

11 Sump and oil pick-up pipe – removal and refitting

Note: *A new sump gasket must be used on refitting. If the oil pick-up pipe is removed, a new O-ring should be used on refitting.*

Removal

1 Drain the engine oil, with reference to Chapter 1 if necessary, then refit and tighten the sump drain plug.

2 Firmly apply the handbrake, then jack up the front of the car and support it securely on axle stands (see *Jacking and vehicle support*).

3 Disconnect the exhaust system catalytic converter from the manifold, and disconnect the system from the forward rubber mountings (Chapter 4A). Lower the system sufficiently to enable removal of the sump (support the exhaust using wire or string).

4 Undo the bolts securing the sump to the

11.7a Undo the bolts (arrowed) . . .

11.7b . . . remove the oil pick-up pipe . . .

11.7c . . . and recover the O-ring from the flange

11.11a Apply a 2 mm diameter bead of silicone sealant to the joint between the timing cover and cylinder block on each side . . .

11.11b . . . then place a new gasket on the sump and locate the sump on the cylinder block base plate – shown with engine removed

11.12 If the engine has been separated from the transmission, use a straight-edge to check the gearbox/transmission mating face alignment when refitting the sump

cylinder block baseplate, timing cover and gearbox/transmission bellhousing, then withdraw the sump. If necessary, tap the sump with a soft-faced mallet to free it from its location – **do not** lever between the sump and cylinder block baseplate mating faces.

5 Recover the gasket.

6 To remove the oil baffle plate, undo the retaining bolts and remove the baffle plate from the cylinder block baseplate.

7 If desired, the oil pick-up pipe can be removed from the sump by unscrewing the two support bracket retaining bolts and the two bolts securing the flange to the end face of the sump. Lift out the pick-up pipe and recover the O-ring from the flange **(see illustrations)**. Note that a new O-ring will be required for refitting.

Refitting

8 Thoroughly clean the inside and outside of the sump ensuring that all traces of old gasket are removed from the mating face. Also clean the cylinder block baseplate mating face to remove all traces of old gasket.

9 If the oil pick-up pipe has been removed, fit a new O-ring to the flange, then refit the pipe to the sump. Refit the flange bolts and support bracket bolts, then tighten the flange bolts to the specified torque. Tighten the support bracket bolts securely.

10 If removed, refit the oil baffle plate and

secure with the retaining bolts tightened to the specified torque.

11 Apply a 2 mm diameter bead of silicone sealant (Vauxhall/Opel No 90 543 772, or equivalent) to the joint between the timing cover and cylinder block, on each side. Place a new gasket on the sump, then locate the sump on the cylinder block baseplate **(see illustrations)**. Refit the securing bolts and tighten them finger tight at this stage.

12 If the engine has been removed from the car and separated from the transmission, use a straight-edge to check that the gearbox/transmission mating face is aligned with the cylinder block baseplate mating face **(see illustration)**.

12.2 Remove the securing screws and withdraw the oil pump cover from the rear of the timing cover

13 Tighten the bolts securing the sump to the cylinder block baseplate and timing cover, progressively to the specified torque. Now tighten the bolts securing the sump to the gearbox/transmission bellhousing to the specified torque.

14 Reconnect the exhaust system catalytic converter to the manifold as described in Chapter 4A.

15 Lower the car to the ground and refill the engine with oil as described in Chapter 1.

12 Oil pump – removal, inspection and refitting

Note: *A new pressure relief valve cap sealing ring and new oil fill channel closure plug sealing ring will be required for refitting.*

Removal

1 Remove the timing cover as described in Section 6.

2 Remove the securing screws and withdraw the oil pump cover from the rear of the timing cover **(see illustration)**.

3 Remove the inner and outer rotor from the timing cover and wipe them clean. Also clean the rotor location in the timing cover.

4 The oil pressure relief valve components can also be removed from the timing cover by unscrewing the cap. Withdraw the cap and

12.4a Unscrew the oil pressure relief valve cap and sealing ring . . .

12.4b . . . then withdraw the spring and plastic pin . . .

12.4c . . . and the plunger

sealing ring, the spring and plastic pin, and the plunger **(see illustrations)**.

Inspection

5 Locate the inner and outer rotor back in the timing cover, noting that the chamfer on the outer rotor outside diameter must face the timing cover.

6 Check the clearance between the end faces of the gears and the housing (endfloat) using a straight-edge and a feeler gauge **(see illustration)**.

7 If the clearance is outside the specified limits, renew the components as necessary.

8 Examine the pressure relief valve spring and plunger, and renew if any sign of damage or wear is evident.

9 Ensure that the rotor location in the interior of the timing cover is scrupulously clean before commencing reassembly.

Refitting

10 Thoroughly clean the pressure relief valve components, and lubricate them with clean engine oil before refitting. Insert the plunger, the spring and plastic pin, then refit the cap using a new sealing ring. Tighten the cap securely.

11 Ensure that the gears are clean, then lubricate them with clean engine oil, and refit them to the pump body. Ensure that the chamfer on the outer rotor outside diameter faces the timing cover.

12 Ensure that the mating faces of the rear cover and the pump housing are clean, then refit the rear cover. Refit and tighten the securing screws to the specified torque.

12.6 Check the oil pump gear endfloat using a straight-edge and feeler gauge

13 Fit a new crankshaft oil seal to the timing cover as described in Section 13.

14 Refit the timing cover to the engine as described in Section 6.

15 After refitting the timing cover, unscrew the oil fill channel closure bolt from the lower front facing side of the timing cover. Using a pump type oil can filled with clean engine oil, insert the oil can spout into the oil channel, so that the spout pushes back the internal ball valve. Prime the pump by filling it with oil until the oil runs out of the fill channel. Refit the closure plug using a new sealing ring and tighten it to the specified torque.

13 Crankshaft oil seals – renewal

Timing chain end oil seal

Note: *A new crankshaft pulley hub retaining bolt will be required for refitting.*

1 Disconnect the battery negative terminal (refer to *Disconnecting the battery* in the Reference Chapter).

2 Remove the air cleaner assembly as described in Chapter 4A.

3 Firmly apply the handbrake, then jack up the front of the car and support it securely on axle stands (see *Jacking and vehicle support*). Remove the right-hand front roadwheel and

13.10 Carefully prise out the crankshaft oil seal from the timing cover using a screwdriver or similar tool – shown with timing cover removed

the wheelarch liner for access to the crankshaft pulley.

4 Release the tension on the auxiliary drivebelt and lock the tensioner in the released position as described in the auxiliary drivebelt renewal procedure in Chapter 1. Note that it is not necessary to completely remove the drivebelt, as this would entail removal of the right-hand engine mounting bracket. With the drivebelt tension released, slip the belt off the crankshaft pulley.

5 Using a socket or spanner on the crankshaft pulley hub bolt, turn the crankshaft in the normal direction of rotation (clockwise as viewed from the right-hand side of the car) until the TDC notch on the crankshaft pulley is located just before the cast lug on the timing cover **(see illustration 4.6)**.

6 Using quick-drying paint, or similar, make an alignment mark between the crankshaft pulley and the pulley hub. It should only be possible to refit the pulley in one position, but it is advisable to make an alignment mark anyway.

7 Unscrew the six crankshaft pulley retaining bolts and remove the pulley from the hub. If necessary, prevent the crankshaft from turning as the pulley bolts are slackened, using a spanner or socket on the pulley hub bolt.

8 Using a suitable socket, slacken the crankshaft pulley hub retaining bolt. The crankshaft can be prevented from turning as the bolt is slackened, using Vauxhall/Opel special tool KM-956 or a similar tool which will engage with the flats on each side of the pulley hub. Alternatively, remove the starter motor, and lock the flywheel ring gear teeth using a suitable hooked tool bolted to the bellhousing.

9 Unscrew the slackened crankshaft pulley hub retaining bolt and remove the hub from the crankshaft. Note that a new bolt will be required for refitting.

10 The seal can now be carefully prised out with a screwdriver or similar hooked tool **(see illustration)**.

11 Clean the oil seal seat with a wooden or plastic scraper.

12 Grease the lips of the new seal, and tap it into position until it is flush with the outer face

13.12 Tap the new seal into position until it is flush with the outer face of the timing cover – shown with timing cover removed

13.23 Locate the crankshaft seal over the crankshaft and into the recess in the cylinder block and baseplate – shown with engine removed

13.24 Tap the seal into position until it is flush with the outer faces of the cylinder block and baseplate – shown with engine removed

of the timing cover, using a suitable socket or tube, or a wooden block **(see illustration)**.

13 Refit the crankshaft pulley hub to the crankshaft, ensuring that the punch mark on the pulley hub is in the 11 o-clock position.

14 Screw in the new pulley hub retaining bolt and tighten it to the specified torque, in the stages given in the Specifications. Prevent crankshaft rotation as the bolt is tightened, using the method employed for removal.

15 Refit the crankshaft pulley to the pulley hub, with the marks made on removal aligned, and tighten the six bolts to the specified torque.

16 Refit the auxiliary drivebelt as described in Chapter 1.

17 Refit the air cleaner assembly as described in Chapter 4A.

18 Refit the wheelarch liner and roadwheel tightening the wheel bolts to the specified torque.

19 Lower the car to the ground, then reconnect the battery negative terminal.

Flywheel end oil seal

20 Remove the flywheel/driveplate as described in Section 14.

21 Carefully prise out the old seal from its location using a screwdriver or similar hooked tool.

22 Proceed as described in paragraphs 2 to 4 inclusive of this Section.

23 Grease the lips of the new seal, then carefully locate the seal over the crankshaft and into the recess in the cylinder block and baseplate **(see illustration)**.

24 Tap the seal into position using a suitable socket or tube, or a wooden block, until it is flush with the outer faces of the cylinder block and baseplate **(see illustration)**.

25 Refit the flywheel/driveplate as described in Section 14.

14 Flywheel/driveplate – removal, inspection and refitting

Note: New flywheel/driveplate securing bolts must be used on refitting.

Removal

1 Remove the manual gearbox or automatic transmission as described in Chapter 7A or 7B, as applicable.

2 On manual gearbox models, remove the clutch assembly as described in Chapter 6.

3 Although the flywheel/driveplate bolt holes are offset so that the flywheel/driveplate can only be fitted in one position, it will make

refitting easier if alignment marks are made between the flywheel/driveplate and the end of the crankshaft.

4 Prevent the flywheel/driveplate from turning by jamming the ring gear teeth using a suitable tool **(see illustration)**.

5 Unscrew the securing bolts, and remove the flywheel/driveplate **(see illustration)**. *Take care, as the flywheel is heavy.*

Inspection

6 If the teeth on the flywheel starter ring are badly worn, or if some are missing, then it will be necessary to remove the ring and fit a new one.

7 The old ring can be split with a cold chisel, after making a cut with a hacksaw blade between two gear teeth. Take great care not to damage the flywheel during this operation, and wear eye protection at all times. Once the ring has been split, it will spread apart, and can be lifted from the flywheel.

8 The new ring gear must be heated evenly to between 180 and 230ºC. Unless facilities for heating by oven or flame are available, leave the fitting to a Vauxhall/Opel dealer or engineering works. The new ring gear must not be overheated during this work, or the temper of the metal will be affected.

9 The ring should be tapped gently down

14.4 If the engine is removed, lock the flywheel with a suitable tool

14.5 Unscrew the securing bolts, and remove the flywheel/driveplate – shown with engine removed

14.12a Tighten the flywheel bolts to the specified torque using a torque wrench . . .

14.12b . . . then through the specified angle using an angle tightening gauge

onto its register, and left to cool naturally – the contraction of the metal on cooling will ensure that it is a secure and permanent fit.

10 If the clutch friction disc contact surface of the flywheel is scored, or on close inspection shows signs of small hair cracks (caused by overheating), it may be possible to have the flywheel surface-ground, provided the overall thickness of the flywheel is not reduced too much. Consult a Vauxhall/Opel dealer or a specialist engine repairer and, if grinding is not possible, renew the flywheel complete.

Refitting

11 Offer the flywheel/driveplate to the end of the crankshaft, and align the previously-made marks on the flywheel and crankshaft.

12 Coat the threads of the new flywheel bolts with thread-locking compound (note that new bolts may be supplied ready-coated), then fit the bolts and tighten them to the specified torque, whilst preventing the flywheel from turning as during removal **(see illustrations)**.

13 Where applicable refit the clutch as described in Chapter 6, then refit the manual gearbox or automatic transmission as described in Chapter 7A or 7B, as applicable.

15 Engine/gearbox mountings – inspection and renewal

Note: *References to 'engine/gearbox' in this Section may be taken to be equally applicable for vehicles with automatic transmission.*

Inspection

1 To improve access, firmly apply the handbrake, then jack up the front of the car and support it securely on axle stands (see *Jacking and vehicle support*).

2 Check the mounting blocks (rubbers) to see if they are cracked, hardened or separated from the metal at any point. Renew the mounting block if any such damage or deterioration is evident.

3 Check that all the mounting securing nuts and bolts are securely tightened, using a torque wrench to check if possible.

4 Using a large screwdriver, or a similar tool, check for wear in the mounting blocks by

carefully levering against them to check for free play. Where this is not possible, enlist the aid of an assistant to move the engine/gearbox unit back-and-forth, and from side-to-side, while you observe the mountings. While some free play is to be expected, even from new components, excessive wear should be obvious. If excessive free play is found, check first to see that the securing nuts and bolts are correctly tightened, then renew any worn components as described in the following paragraphs.

Renewal

Right-hand mounting – 1.0 litre engines

5 Remove the air cleaner as described in Chapter 4A.

6 Attach a suitable hoist and lifting tackle to the engine lifting brackets on the cylinder head, and support the weight of the engine.

7 Undo the three bolts securing the right-hand engine mounting bracket to the timing cover.

8 Working under the vehicle, remove the nut and bolt securing the right-hand engine mounting bracket to the mounting block on the body, then remove the mounting bracket.

9 Undo the four bolts and remove the mounting block from the body.

10 Locate the new mounting block on the body and tighten the bolts to the specified torque.

11 Refit the right-hand engine mounting bracket then screw in the three mounting bolts and tighten them to the specified torque.

15.20 Remove the nut and bolt securing the right-hand engine mounting bracket to the mounting block on the body

12 Refit the nut and bolt securing the engine mounting bracket to the mounting block on the body, and tighten the nut and bolt to the specified torque.

13 Disconnect the hoist and lifting tackle, then refit the air cleaner assembly as described in Chapter 4A.

Right-hand mounting – 1.2 litre engines

14 Firmly apply the handbrake, then jack up the front of the car and support it securely on axle stands (see *Jacking and vehicle support*). Remove the right-hand roadwheel and the wheelarch liner for access to the crankshaft pulley.

15 Remove the air cleaner as described in Chapter 4A.

16 Release the tension on the auxiliary drivebelt and lock the tensioner in the released position as described in the auxiliary drivebelt renewal procedure in Chapter 1.

17 Prevent the crankshaft from turning using a spanner or socket on the crankshaft sprocket bolt, then undo the six bolts securing the crankshaft pulley to the pulley hub. Slip the auxiliary drivebelt off the pulley and remove the pulley from the hub.

18 Attach a suitable hoist and lifting tackle to the engine lifting brackets on the cylinder head, and support the weight of the engine.

19 Undo the three bolts securing the right-hand engine mounting bracket to the timing cover.

20 Working under the vehicle, remove the nut and bolt securing the right-hand engine mounting bracket to the mounting block on the body **(see illustration)**.

21 Twist the mounting bracket downwards, approximately 90°, then twist it to the left, towards the bulkhead, approximately 90°. Lower the bracket and manipulate it out from under the car.

22 Undo the four bolts and remove the mounting block from the body.

23 Locate the new mounting block on the body and tighten the bolts to the specified torque.

24 Insert the retaining bolts into the engine mounting bracket and manipulate the bracket back into position using the reverse of the removal sequence.

25 Screw in the three mounting bolts and tighten them to the specified torque.

26 Refit the nut and bolt securing the right-hand engine mounting bracket to the mounting block on the body, and tighten the nut and bolt to the specified torque.

27 Refit the crankshaft pulley to the pulley hub and tighten the six bolts to the specified torque.

28 Engage the auxiliary drivebelt with the crankshaft pulley and check that the belt is correctly located on all the other pulleys.

29 Using the method used during removal, lever the drivebelt tensioner roller until the locking tool (where used) can be removed from the backplate. Use the spanner or

15.34 Left-hand gearbox mounting bracket-to-mounting block retaining bolts – manual gearbox models

15.45 Remove the nut and bolt securing the rear engine mounting block to the gearbox/transmission bracket

wrench to gradually release the tensioner in order to tension the belt. **Do not** allow the tensioner to spring back unrestrained.

30 Refit the wheelarch liner and the roadwheel, tightening the roadwheel bolts to the specified torque.

31 Disconnect the hoist and lifting tackle, then lower the car to the ground.

32 Refit the air cleaner assembly as described in Chapter 4A.

Left-hand mounting – manual gearbox models

33 Attach a suitable hoist and lifting tackle to the engine lifting brackets on the cylinder head, and support the weight of the engine.

34 Working under the vehicle, unbolt the mounting bracket from the gearbox, and from the mounting block, and withdraw the bracket **(see illustration)**.

35 Unbolt the mounting block from the body.

36 Refit the mounting block to the body, and tighten the bolts to the specified torque.

37 Refit the mounting bracket, and tighten the securing bolts to the specified torque.

38 Disconnect the hoist and lifting tackle.

Left-hand mounting – automatic transmission models

39 Attach a suitable hoist and lifting tackle to the engine lifting brackets on the cylinder head, and support the weight of the engine.

40 Working under the vehicle, unbolt the mounting block from the body and unbolt the mounting bracket from the transmission. Withdraw the bracket and mounting block from under the vehicle.

41 Undo the two bolts and separate the mounting block from the bracket.

42 Refitting is a reversal of removal, ensuring that all mounting bolts are tightened to the specified torque.

Rear mounting

43 Firmly apply the handbrake, then jack up the front of the car and support it securely on axle stands (see *Jacking and vehicle support*). Remove the right-hand roadwheel and the wheelarch liner for access to the crankshaft pulley.

44 Attach a suitable hoist and lifting tackle to the engine lifting brackets on the cylinder head, and support the weight of the engine.

45 Working under the vehicle, remove the nut and bolt securing the mounting block to the gearbox/transmission bracket **(see illustration)**.

46 Remove the bolts securing the mounting block to the body, and withdraw the mounting block.

47 Refitting is a reversal of removal, but ensure that the arrow on the mounting block points towards the front of the vehicle.

Chapter 2 Part B: 1.2 & 1.4 litre
SOHC engine in-car repair procedures

Contents

Degrees of difficulty

Easy, suitable for novice with little experience	**Fairly easy,** suitable for beginner with some experience	**Fairly difficult,** suitable for competent DIY mechanic	**Difficult,** suitable for experienced DIY mechanic	**Very difficult,** suitable for expert DIY or professional

Specifications

General

Engine type . . . . Four-cylinder, in-line, water-cooled. Single overhead camshaft, belt-driven, acting on hydraulic valve lifters

Manufacturer's engine codes:*
  1.2 litre engine . . . . X 12 SZ
  1.4 litre multi-point fuel injection engine . . . . C 14 SE
  1.4 litre single-point fuel injection engine . . . . X 14 SZ
Bore:
  1.2 litre engines . . . . 72.00 mm
  1.4 litre engines . . . . 77.60 mm
Stroke . . . . 73.40 mm
Capacity:
  1.2 litre engines . . . . 1196 cc
  1.4 litre engines . . . . 1389 cc
Firing order . . . . 1-3-4-2 (No 1 cylinder at timing belt end)
Direction of crankshaft rotation . . . . Clockwise (viewed from timing belt end of engine)
Compression ratio:
  1.2 litre engine 10.0:1
  1.4 litre multi-point fuel injection engine 10.0:1
  1.4 litre single-point fuel injection engine 9.6:1

For details of engine code location, see 'Vehicle identification' in the Reference Chapter.

Camshaft

Endfloat	0.090 to 0.210 mm
Camshaft bearing journal diameter:	
No 1	39.435 to 39.455 mm
No 2	39.685 to 39.705 mm
No 3	39.935 to 39.955 mm
No 4	40.185 to 40.205 mm
No 5	40.435 to 40.455 mm
Camshaft housing bearing journal diameter:	
No 1	39.500 to 39.525 mm
No 2	39.750 to 39.775 mm
No 3	40.000 to 40.025 mm
No 4	40.250 to 40.275 mm
No 5	40.500 to 40.525 mm
Maximum permissible radial run-out	0.040 mm

Lubrication system

Minimum oil pressure at 80°C	1.5 bars at idle speed
Oil pump type	Gear-type, driven directly from crankshaft
Oil pump clearances:	
Inner-to-outer gear teeth clearance (backlash)	0.100 to 0.200 mm
Gear-to-housing clearance (endfloat)	0.080 to 0.150 mm

Flywheel

Maximum permissible lateral run-out of starter ring gear	0.500 mm
Refinishing limit – maximum depth of material which may be removed from clutch friction surface	0.300 mm

Torque wrench settings

	Nm	lbf ft
Big-end bearing cap bolts:		
Bolts with 15.0 mm thread length	25	18
Bolts with 40.0 mm thread length:*		
Stage 1	25	18
Stage 2	Angle-tighten a further 30°	
Camshaft cover bolts	8	6
Camshaft sprocket bolt	45	33
Camshaft thrust plate bolts	8	6
Clutch bellhousing cover plate	7	5
Coolant pump bolts	8	6
Crankshaft pulley bolt:*		
Stage 1	95	70
Stage 2	Angle-tighten a further 30°	
Stage 3	Angle-tighten a further 15°	
Cylinder head bolts:*		
Stage 1	25	18
Stage 2	Angle-tighten a further 60°	
Stage 3	Angle-tighten a further 60°	
Stage 4	Angle-tighten a further 60°	
Engine mountings:		
Left-hand:		
Gearbox/transmission bracket-to-gearbox/transmission bolts	60	44
Gearbox/transmission bracket-to-mounting block bolts	60	44
Mounting block-to-body bolts**	65	48
Rear:		
Gearbox/transmission bracket-to-gearbox/transmission bolts	70	52
Gearbox/transmission bracket-to-mounting block bolts	65	48
Mounting block-to-body bolts	65	48
Right-hand:		
Engine bracket-to-engine bolts:		
Models without power steering	65	48
Models with power steering	60	44
Engine bracket-to-mounting block bolt/nut	60	44
Mounting block-to-body bolts:		
Models without power steering	65	48
Models with power steering	20	15

Torque wrench settings (continued)

	Nm	lbf ft
Engine-to-gearbox/transmission bolts	60	44
Flywheel/driveplate bolts:*		
Stage 1	35	26
Stage 2	Angle-tighten a further 30°	
Stage 3	Angle-tighten a further 15°	
Main bearing cap bolts:*		
Stage 1	50	37
Stage 2	Angle-tighten a further 45°	
Stage 3	Angle-tighten a further 15°	
Oil pick-up pipe bracket-to-cylinder block bolt	8	6
Oil pick-up pipe-to-oil pump bolts**	8	6
Oil pressure relief valve plug to oil pump	30	22
Oil pump cover screws	6	4
Oil pump-to-cylinder block bolts	10	7
Sump-to-cylinder block bolts:**		
Steel sump	8	6
Aluminium sump	10	7
Sump to gearbox/transmission (aluminium sump):		
M8 bolts	20	15
M10 bolts	40	30
Timing belt cover bolts:		
Outer cover	4	3
Rear cover	6	4
Timing belt tension indicator bolt	20	15
Torque converter to driveplate*	50	37

*Use new bolts.
**Use thread-locking compound.

1 General information

How to use this Chapter

This Part of Chapter 2 describes the repair procedures which can reasonably be carried out on the engine while it remains in the vehicle. If the engine has been removed from the vehicle and is being dismantled as described in Chapter 2E, any preliminary dismantling procedures can be ignored.

Note that, while it may be *possible* physically to overhaul items such as the piston/connecting rod assemblies while the engine is in the vehicle, such tasks are not generally carried out as separate operations, and usually require the execution of several additional procedures (not to mention the cleaning of components and of oilways); for this reason, all such tasks are classed as major overhaul procedures, and are described in Chapter 2E.

Chapter 2E describes the removal of the engine/transmission unit from the vehicle, and the full overhaul procedures which can then be carried out.

Engine description

The engine is of the in-line four-cylinder, single overhead camshaft (SOHC) type, mounted transversely at the front of the car, with the transmission attached to its left-hand end **(see illustrations)**.

The crankshaft runs in five shell-type bearings, and the centre bearing incorporates

H.22822

1.4a Front sectional view of the engine

1.4b Side sectional view of the engine

2.4 Compression tester fitted to No 1 spark plug hole

thrust bearing shells to control crankshaft endfloat.

The connecting rods are attached to the crankshaft by horizontally-split shell-type big-end bearings. The pistons are attached to the connecting rods by gudgeon pins, which are an interference fit in the connecting rod small-end bores. The aluminium-alloy pistons are fitted with three piston rings – two compression rings and an oil control ring.

The camshaft rotates in a housing attached to the top of the cylinder head, and is driven from the crankshaft by a toothed composite-rubber timing belt.

Each cylinder has two valves (one inlet and one exhaust), operated via rocker arms which are supported at their pivot ends by hydraulic self-adjusting valve lifters (tappets). The inlet and exhaust valves are each closed by a single valve spring, and operate in guides pressed into the cylinder head.

A gear-type oil pump is located in a housing attached to the front of the cylinder block, and is driven directly from the crankshaft.

The coolant pump is located at the front of the cylinder block, and is driven by the timing belt.

Repair operations possible with the engine in the vehicle

The following operations can be carried out without having to remove the engine from the vehicle.

a) *Removal and refitting of the cylinder head.*
b) *Removal and refitting of the timing belt and sprockets.*
c) *Removal and refitting of the camshaft.*
d) *Removal and refitting of the sump.*
e) *Removal and refitting of the big-end bearings, connecting rods, and pistons.**
f) *Removal and refitting of the oil pump.*
g) *Renewal of the engine mountings.*
h) *Removal and refitting of the flywheel/driveplate.*

*Although the operation marked with an asterisk can be carried out with the engine in the vehicle (after removal of the sump), it is preferable for the engine to be removed, in the interests of cleanliness and improved access. For this reason, the procedure is described in Chapter 2E.

2 Compression test – description and interpretation

Note: *A suitable compression gauge will be required to carry out this test.*

1 When engine performance is down, or if misfiring occurs which cannot be attributed to the ignition or fuel systems, a compression test can provide diagnostic clues as to the engine's condition. If the test is performed regularly, it can give warning of trouble before any other symptoms become apparent.

2 The engine must be fully warmed-up to normal operating temperature, the battery must be fully charged, and all the spark plugs must be removed (see Chapter 1). The aid of an assistant will also be required.

3 Disconnect the wiring plug from the DIS module, and remove the fuel pump relay (see Chapter 12 for details of relay locations).

4 Fit a compression tester to the No 1 spark plug hole (No 1 cylinder is nearest the timing belt end of the engine) – the type of tester which screws into the plug thread is to be preferred **(see illustration)**.

5 Have an assistant hold the accelerator pedal fully depressed, at the same time cranking the engine over for approximately four seconds on the starter motor. After one or two revolutions, the compression pressure reading on the gauge should build-up to a maximum figure and then stabilise. Record the highest reading obtained.

6 Repeat the test on the remaining cylinders, recording the pressure in each.

7 All cylinders should produce very similar pressures; a difference of more than 1 bar between any two cylinders indicates a fault. Note that the compression should build-up quickly in a healthy engine; low compression on the first stroke, followed by gradually-increasing pressure on successive strokes, indicates worn piston rings. A low compression reading on the first stroke, which does not build-up during successive strokes, indicates leaking valves or a blown head gasket (a cracked head could also be the cause). Deposits on the undersides of the valve heads can also cause low compression.

8 If the pressure in any cylinder is significantly lower than that in the remaining cylinders, carry out the following test to isolate the cause. Introduce a teaspoonful of clean engine oil into the relevant cylinder through its spark plug hole, and repeat the test.

9 If the addition of oil temporarily improves the compression pressure, this indicates that bore or piston wear is responsible for the pressure loss. No improvement suggests that leaking or burnt valves, or a blown head gasket may be to blame.

10 A low reading from two adjacent cylinders

3.6a Camshaft sprocket timing mark aligned with notch in rear timing belt cover (No 1 piston at TDC)

3.6b Notch in crankshaft pulley (A) aligned with timing pointer (B) on timing belt cover (No 1 piston at TDC)

3.6c Crankshaft sprocket timing mark aligned with mark on rear timing belt cover and oil pump lower flange (No 1 piston at TDC)

is almost certainly due to the head gasket having blown between them; the presence of coolant in the engine oil will confirm this.

11 If one cylinder is about 20 percent lower than the others, and the engine has a slightly rough idle, a worn camshaft lobe could be the cause.

12 If the compression reading is unusually high, the combustion chambers are probably coated with carbon deposits. If this is the case, the cylinder head should be removed and decarbonised (see Chapter 2E).

13 On completion of the test, refit the spark plugs, reconnect the DIS module wiring plug, and refit the fuel pump relay.

3 Top dead centre (TDC) for No 1 piston – locating

1 Top dead centre (TDC) is the highest point in the cylinder that a piston reaches as the crankshaft turns. Each piston reaches TDC at the end of the compression stroke, and again at the end of the exhaust stroke. For the purpose of timing the engine, TDC refers to the position of No 1 piston at the end of its compression stroke. On all engines in this Chapter, No 1 piston and cylinder are at the timing belt end of the engine.

2 All engine overhaul procedures use the factory timing marks, which vary according to engine type.

3 Disconnect the battery negative terminal (refer to *Disconnecting the battery* in the Reference Chapter).

4 Remove the upper outer timing belt cover as described in Section 6.

5 Using a suitable spanner or socket on the crankshaft pulley bolt, rotate the crankshaft to bring No 1 piston to TDC as follows, according to engine type. Note that turning the engine will be made much easier if the spark plugs are removed first (see Chapter 1).

6 The timing marks must be aligned as follows:

a) The timing mark on the camshaft sprocket must be aligned with the notch in the rear timing belt cover **(see illustration)**.

b) The notch in the crankshaft pulley, or the timing mark on the crankshaft speed/position sensor wheel (as applicable) must be aligned with the pointer (raised line) on the timing belt cover **(see illustration)**. Note that if the crankshaft pulley and lower outer timing belt cover have been removed, the timing mark on the crankshaft sprocket can be used instead of the mark on the pulley. The mark on the crankshaft sprocket must align with the corresponding mark on the rear timing belt cover, and the oil pump lower flange **(see illustration)**.

4 Camshaft cover – removal and refitting

Removal

1 Disconnect the breather hose(s) from the stub(s) on the camshaft cover **(see illustrations)**.

2 Take note of the positions of any brackets and/or clips secured by the camshaft cover bolts, then unscrew and remove the bolts, along with the clips and/or brackets, as applicable.

3 Lift the camshaft cover from the camshaft housing **(see illustration)**. If the cover is stuck, do not lever between the cover and camshaft housing mating surfaces – if necessary, gently tap the cover sideways to

free it. Recover the cork gasket or rubber seal, as applicable.

Refitting

4 Before refitting, examine the inside of the cover for a build-up of oil sludge or any other contamination, and if necessary clean the cover with paraffin, or a water-soluble solvent. Where applicable, examine the condition of the crankcase ventilation filter inside the camshaft cover, and clean as described for the inside of the cover if clogging is evident (if desired, the filter can be removed from the cover, after removing the securing bolts). Dry the cover thoroughly before refitting.

5 Where applicable, examine the condition of the rubber seal, and if necessary renew it. Note that on certain models, the seal rests in a groove in the cover, and a tag on the seal engages with the notch in the cover when the

4.1a Disconnect the breather hoses . . .

4.1b . . . from the camshaft cover

4.3 Lifting the camshaft cover from the camshaft housing

4.5 Tag on seal (arrowed) engages with notch in camshaft cover

4.8 Ensure that the brackets (arrowed) are in place on the camshaft cover bolts

5.4 Removing the crankshaft pulley – note notch in pulley and locating lug on sprocket (arrowed)

seal is correctly positioned (see illustration). If a cork gasket was fitted, it should always be renewed on refitting.

6 Thoroughly clean the mating faces of the camshaft housing and the cover.

7 Position the cover on the camshaft housing, noting that the breather pipe stub(s) should be nearest the timing belt end of the engine.

8 Refit the securing bolts, ensuring that any clips and/or brackets are in place under their heads as noted before removal, and tighten the bolts to the specified torque in a diagonal sequence (see illustration).

9 Reconnect the breather hose(s) to the stub(s) on the cover.

5 Crankshaft pulley – removal and refitting

Note: A new crankshaft pulley bolt will be required for refitting.

Removal

1 Access is most easily obtained from under the wheelarch, after jacking up the vehicle and removing the right-hand front wheel (see Jacking and vehicle support). If necessary for subsequent operations, rotate the crankshaft to position No 1 piston to TDC as described in Section 3.

2 Remove the auxiliary drivebelt as described in Chapter 1.

3 To prevent the crankshaft from turning as the pulley bolt is unscrewed, select top gear

and have an assistant apply the brakes hard (manual gearbox models only). Alternatively, remove the starter motor, and lock the flywheel ring gear teeth using a suitable tool.

4 Unscrew the pulley bolt and recover the washer fitted behind it, then remove the pulley (see illustration).

Refitting

5 On refitting, ensure that the notch in the pulley fits over the locating lug on the crankshaft sprocket.

6 Prevent the crankshaft from turning as during removal, then fit the new pulley securing bolt, ensuring that the washer is in place under the bolt head.

7 Tighten the bolt to the specified torque, in the stages given in the Specifications.

8 Refit and tension the auxiliary drivebelt, as described in Chapter 1.

6 Timing belt covers – removal and refitting

Upper outer cover

Removal

1 For improved access, remove the air cleaner assembly, and the air inlet trunking, as described in Chapter 4B.

2 Remove the auxiliary drivebelt, as described in Chapter 1.

3 Unscrew the three securing bolts, and unclip the lower edge of the upper cover from

the lower cover. Withdraw the upper cover (see illustration).

Refitting

4 Refitting is a reversal of removal, but refit and tension the auxiliary drivebelt as described in Chapter 1.

Lower outer cover

Removal

5 For improved access, firmly apply the handbrake, then jack up the front right-hand side of the car and support it securely on axle stands (see Jacking and vehicle support). Remove the roadwheel.

6 If desired, to further improve access, remove the wheelarch liner (see Chapter 11, Section 22).

7 Remove the crankshaft pulley as described in Section 5.

8 Where applicable, unclip the crankshaft speed/position sensor wiring from the lower timing belt cover.

9 Unscrew the three securing bolts, and remove the lower timing belt cover (see illustrations).

Refitting

10 Refitting is a reversal of removal. Refit the crankshaft pulley as described in Section 5.

Rear cover

Removal

11 Remove the outer covers as described previously in this Section.

6.3 Upper timing belt cover securing bolts (arrowed)

6.9a Unscrew the three securing bolts (arrowed) . . .

6.9b . . . and remove the lower timing belt cover

6.14 Unscrewing a rear timing belt cover upper securing screw

6.15 Crankshaft speed/position sensor wiring clipped to rear timing belt cover

7.4a Insert a tool into the hole (arrowed) in the tension indicator arm . . .

7.4b . . . then lever the arm clockwise and lock in position

12 Remove the timing belt and sprockets as described in Sections 7 and 8.

13 Unscrew the securing bolt, and remove the timing belt tension indicator assembly from the cylinder block.

14 Unscrew the two upper and two lower screws securing the rear timing belt cover **(see illustration)**.

15 Withdraw the rear cover, and where applicable, unclip the crankshaft speed/position sensor wiring from the rear of the cover **(see illustration)**.

Refitting

16 Refitting is a reversal of removal, bearing in mind the following points.

a) *Refit the timing belt sprockets as described in Section 8.*

b) *Refit and tension the timing belt as described in Section 7.*

c) *Refit the outer timing belt covers as described previously in this Section.*

7 Timing belt – removal, refitting and adjustment

Removal

1 Disconnect the battery negative terminal (refer to *Disconnecting the battery* in the Reference Chapter).

2 Remove the outer timing belt covers as described in Section 6. To enable the crankshaft to be turned, temporarily refit the crankshaft pulley retaining bolt.

3 If not already done, turn the crankshaft to bring No 1 piston to top dead centre, as described in Section 3.

4 Insert a suitable tool (such as a pin punch) into the hole in the timing belt tension indicator arm, then lever the arm clockwise to its stop, and lock in position by inserting the tool into the corresponding hole in the tension indicator backplate **(see illustrations)**. Leave the tool in position to lock the tension indicator until the belt is refitted.

5 Loosen the three coolant pump securing bolts, using a suitable Allen key or hexagon bit, then turn the pump to relieve any remaining tension in the timing belt **(see illustration)**.

6 Slide the timing belt from the sprockets, and withdraw it from the engine **(see illustration)**. Take note of any arrows marked on the belt to indicate the direction of rotation (if necessary, mark the belt to aid correct refitting).

Refitting

7 Ensure that No 1 piston is still positioned at top dead centre, as described in Section 3.

8 Refit the timing belt around the sprockets, starting at the crankshaft sprocket.

9 Adjust the timing belt tension, as described in paragraphs 11 to 20 inclusive.

10 On completion, reconnect the battery negative terminal.

Adjustment

Note: *The engine must be cold when checking and adjusting the timing belt tension.*

11 With the outer timing belt covers removed as described in Section 6, proceed as follows.

12 To enable the crankshaft to be turned, temporarily refit the crankshaft pulley retaining bolt.

13 If not already done, turn the crankshaft to bring No 1 piston to top dead centre, as described in Section 3.

14 Loosen the three coolant pump securing bolts, using a suitable Allen key or hexagon bit, but do not remove them.

15 Turn the coolant pump clockwise to increase the belt tension until the tensioner indicator arm moves fully clockwise to its stop (ie, the holes in the indicator arm and the tensioner backplate are aligned). Note that a special tool is available to turn the coolant pump (Vauxhall/Opel tool KM-421-A or equivalent) **(see illustration)**.

16 Tighten the coolant pump securing bolts

7.5 Loosening a coolant pump securing bolt

7.6 Sliding the timing belt from the camshaft sprocket

7.15 Using special tool KM-421-A to turn the coolant pump

7.18 Turn the coolant pump (special tool shown) anti-clockwise until the tension indicator pointer (1) is positioned in the centre of the V (2)

sufficiently to prevent the pump from moving during the following operation.

17 Turn the crankshaft clockwise through two complete revolutions, until No 1 piston is again positioned at top dead centre. Turn the crankshaft smoothly without jerking, to avoid the belt jumping on the sprockets. Check that the timing marks are correctly aligned as described in Section 3.

18 Carefully turn the coolant pump anti-clockwise to slacken the belt, until the tension indicator pointer is positioned in the centre of the V on the tensioner backplate (see illustration), then tighten the coolant pump securing bolts to the specified torque.

19 Turn the crankshaft clockwise through two

8.11 Refit the crankshaft sprocket with the locating flange and locating lug for pulley outermost

8.14 Withdrawing the timing belt tension indicator

8.2 Improvised tool being used to hold the camshaft sprocket stationary

complete revolutions, as described previously, and check that the tension indicator pointer is still positioned as described in paragraph 18 – if not, the procedure described in paragraphs 14 to 18 inclusive must be repeated until the pointer aligns correctly.

20 On completion, refit the spark plugs (where applicable), and refit the outer timing belt covers as described in Section 6.

8 Timing belt sprockets and tension indicator – removal and refitting

Camshaft sprocket

Removal

1 Remove the timing belt as described in Section 7. Note that if only the camshaft sprocket is to be removed, the timing belt can be left engaged with the remaining sprockets, and slipped from the camshaft sprocket once the tension has been relieved.

2 The camshaft must be prevented from turning as the sprocket bolt is unscrewed, and this can be achieved in one of two ways as follows.

a) Make up a tool similar to that shown (see illustration), and use it to hold the sprocket stationary by means of the holes in the sprocket face.

b) With the camshaft cover removed as described in Section 4, prevent the camshaft from turning by holding it with a suitable spanner on the flats provided between Nos 3 and 4 camshaft lobes.

8.15 Lug (1) on tension indicator backplate must engage with hole (2) in oil pump

8.5 Lug (1) on camshaft engages with hole (2) in sprocket

3 Unscrew the camshaft sprocket bolt and withdraw it, noting the washer under the bolt head.

4 Withdraw the sprocket from the end of the camshaft, where applicable manipulating the timing belt from the sprocket as it is withdrawn.

Refitting

5 Commence refitting by offering the camshaft sprocket to the camshaft, making sure that the lug on the end of the camshaft engages with the corresponding hole in the camshaft sprocket (see illustration).

6 Refit the sprocket securing bolt, ensuring that the washer is in place, and tighten the bolt to the specified torque, preventing the camshaft from turning as during removal (see illustration).

7 Where applicable, refit the camshaft cover as described in Section 4.

8 Refit and tension the timing belt as described in Section 7.

Crankshaft sprocket

Note: A new crankshaft pulley retaining bolt will be required for refitting – see Section 5.

Removal

9 Remove the timing belt as described in Section 7.

10 Remove the sprocket from the end of the crankshaft.

Refitting

11 Refit the crankshaft sprocket with the locating flange and locating lug for the crankshaft pulley outermost (see illustration).

12 Refit and tension the timing belt as described in Section 7.

Tension indicator

Removal

13 Remove the timing belt as described in Section 7.

14 Unscrew the central securing bolt, and withdraw the tension indicator (see illustration).

Refitting

15 Refit the tension indicator, ensuring that the lug on the indicator backplate engages with the corresponding hole in the oil pump (see illustration).

9.3 Extracting the camshaft oil seal using a self-tapping screw

9.6 Fitting a new camshaft oil seal using a large socket

9.10 DIS module mounting plate removed for access to O-ring/camshaft oil seal (arrowed)

16 Refit the tension indicator securing bolt and tighten it to the specified torque.

17 Refit and tension the timing belt, as described in Section 7.

9 Camshaft oil seals – renewal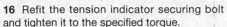

Timing belt end oil seal

1 Remove the camshaft sprocket as described in Section 8.

2 Punch or drill a small hole in the centre of the now-exposed oil seal.

3 Screw in a self-tapping screw, and pull on the screw with pliers to extract the seal **(see illustration)**.

4 Clean the oil seal seat with a wooden or plastic scraper.

5 Wind a thin band of tape around the end of the camshaft, to protect the lips of the new oil seal as it is fitted.

6 Grease the lips of the new seal, then fit it to the housing. Ideally, the seal should be drawn into position using a suitable socket or tube and washer, and a suitable bolt. Alternatively, the seal can be tapped into position **(see illustration)**. The seal should be fitted with its outer face flush with the housing. Take care not to damage the seal lips during fitting.

7 Carefully remove the tape from the end of the camshaft.

8 Refit the camshaft sprocket as described in Section 8.

Flywheel end oil seal

9 Remove the DIS module from the end of the camshaft housing, as described in Chapter 5B.

10 The camshaft flywheel end oil seal takes the form of an O-ring on the rear of the DIS module mounting plate. Unscrew the three module mounting plate securing bolts, and withdraw the plate from the end of the camshaft housing **(see illustration)**. Prise off the old O-ring

using a screwdriver, then fit the new O-ring, and refit the module mounting plate. Refit the DIS module to the mounting plate, with reference to Chapter 5B if necessary.

10 Camshaft – removal, inspection and refitting

Note: *The camshaft timing belt end oil seal should be renewed on refitting.*

Removal

1 The camshaft can only be removed without disturbing the housing if a special tool (Vauxhall/Opel No 603 850, or equivalent) is available to depress the rocker arms whilst the camshaft is withdrawn.

2 Assuming that such a tool is not available, the camshaft housing must be removed. Since the cylinder head bolts must be removed, it is strongly recommended that a new cylinder head gasket is fitted. If the gasket is not renewed, and it 'blows' on reassembly, the cylinder head will have to be removed in order to renew the gasket, and another set of new bolts will have to be obtained for refitting.

3 Removal and refitting of the camshaft housing is described in Section 11 along with cylinder head removal and refitting. If it is decided not to disturb the cylinder head, the

relevant paragraphs referring specifically to cylinder head removal and refitting can be ignored; it is strongly recommended that the cylinder head is clamped to the cylinder block using four head bolts and some spacers, to reduce the possibility of the seal between the head and the block being broken.

4 With the camshaft housing removed, proceed as follows.

5 Remove the DIS module from the end of the camshaft housing, with reference to Chapter 5B if necessary.

6 Unscrew the three securing bolts, and remove the DIS module mounting plate from the end of the camshaft housing.

7 Working at the DIS module end of the camshaft, unscrew the two camshaft thrustplate securing bolts, using a suitable Allen key or hexagon bit **(see illustration)**.

8 Withdraw the thrustplate, noting which way round it is fitted.

9 Carefully withdraw the camshaft from the DIS module end of the housing, taking care not to damage the bearing journals **(see illustration)**.

Inspection

10 With the camshaft removed, examine the bearings in the camshaft housing for signs of obvious wear or pitting. If evident, a new camshaft housing will probably be required. Also check that the oil supply holes in the

10.7 Camshaft thrustplate and securing bolts

10.9 Withdrawing the camshaft from the housing

10.10 Oil supply hole (arrowed) in camshaft housing

10.16 Checking the camshaft endfloat using a feeler gauge

11 Cylinder head – removal and refitting

Note: *The engine must be cold when removing the cylinder head. A new cylinder head gasket and new cylinder head bolts must be used on refitting, and a suitable sealant (Vauxhall/Opel No 90 542 114, or equivalent) will be required to coat the camshaft housing-to-cylinder head mating faces.*

Removal

1 Depressurise the fuel system as described in Chapter 4B.
2 Disconnect the battery negative terminal (refer to *Disconnecting the battery* in the Reference Chapter).
3 Drain the cooling system as described in Chapter 1.
4 Remove the camshaft sprocket as described in Section 8.
5 Disconnect the exhaust front section from the manifold, with reference to Chapter 4B.
6 Where applicable, unbolt the wiring harness earth lead(s) from the camshaft housing **(see illustration)**.
7 Loosen the alternator mountings, then unbolt the upper alternator mounting bracket(s) from the inlet manifold and camshaft housing, as applicable **(see illustration)**. Note that on certain models it will be necessary to remove the upper alternator mounting nut and bolt, and pivot the alternator away from the upper mounting bracket, leaving the bracket attached to the inlet manifold (the bracket securing bolt cannot be reached with the manifold fitted to the cylinder head).
8 Disconnect the crankcase breather hose from the stub at the rear of the camshaft housing **(see illustration)**.
9 Where applicable, unclip the wiring harness from the brackets on the camshaft cover, and move the harness to one side **(see illustration)**.
10 Where applicable, separate the two halves of the wiring harness connector, and release the connector from the clip on the camshaft cover **(see illustration)**.
11 On single-point fuel injection engines,

camshaft housing are free from obstructions **(see illustration)**.
11 The camshaft itself should show no marks or scoring on the journal or cam lobe surfaces. If evident, renew the camshaft. Note that if the camshaft is renewed, all the rocker arms should also be renewed.
12 Check the camshaft thrustplate for signs of wear or grooves, and renew if evident.

Refitting

13 It is advisable to renew the camshaft timing belt end oil seal as a matter of course if the camshaft has been removed. Prise out the old seal using a screwdriver, and tap in the new seal until it is flush with the housing, using a suitable socket or tube.
14 Commence refitting by lubricating the bearings in the housing, and also the oil seal lip.

15 Carefully insert the camshaft into the housing from the DIS module end, taking care to avoid damage to the bearings.
16 Refit the thrustplate, and tighten the securing bolts. Check the camshaft endfloat by inserting a feeler gauge between the thrustplate and the camshaft end flange. If the endfloat exceeds that specified, renew the thrustplate **(see illustration)**.
17 Examine the condition of the O-ring on the rear of the DIS module mounting plate, and renew it if necessary. Refit the mounting plate.
18 Refit the DIS module as described in Chapter 5B.
19 Where applicable, remove the bolts and spacers clamping the cylinder head to the block.
20 Refit the camshaft housing, as described in Section 11.

11.6 Unbolting a wiring harness earth lead from the camshaft housing

11.7 Unbolt the upper alternator mounting bracket bolt (arrowed) from the inlet manifold

11.8 Loosening the crankcase breather hose clamp from the camshaft housing stub

11.9 Unclip the fuel injector wiring harness from the brackets on the camshaft cover

11.10 Separate the two halves of the wiring connector

11.21 Disconnecting the coolant hose from the thermostat housing

11.22 Disconnecting the wiring plug from the coolant temperature sensor – engines with multi-point fuel injection

disconnect the hot-air hose from the shroud on the exhaust manifold.

12 The cylinder head can be removed complete with the manifolds, or the manifolds can be detached from the cylinder head prior to removal, with reference to Chapter 4B. If no work is to be carried out on the inlet manifold, it can be unbolted from the cylinder head and supported to one side out of the way, thus avoiding the need to disconnect the relevant hoses, pipes and wiring.

13 If the cylinder head is to be removed complete with the manifolds, disconnect all relevant hoses, pipes and wiring from the inlet manifold and associated components, with reference to Chapter 4B.

14 If the inlet manifold is to be left in the engine compartment, proceed as follows – otherwise proceed to paragraph 18.

15 Disconnect the breather hose(s) from the camshaft cover.

16 Make a final check to ensure that all necessary hoses, pipes and wires have been disconnected. Unscrew the inlet manifold securing nuts, noting the location of any brackets (eg, engine lifting bracket) attached to the studs in the cylinder head, and lift the inlet manifold from the cylinder head. Ensure that the manifold is properly supported, taking care not to strain any of the hoses, pipes and wires, etc, which are still connected.

17 Recover the manifold gasket from the cylinder head.

18 If desired, remove the exhaust manifold with reference to Chapter 4B.

19 Unscrew the two upper rear timing belt cover securing bolts from the camshaft housing.

20 Disconnect the HT leads from the spark plugs and the DIS module, and remove the leads, labelling them if necessary to aid refitting. Disconnect the DIS module wiring plug.

21 Disconnect the coolant hose from the thermostat housing **(see illustration)**.

22 On multi-point fuel injection models, disconnect the wiring plug from the coolant

temperature sensor located in the end of the cylinder head **(see illustration)**.

23 Where applicable, unscrew the nuts securing the fuel tank vent valve mounting bracket and the earth wiring to the left-hand end of the camshaft housing. Move the valve assembly and the wiring to one side, clear of the working area.

24 Make a final check to ensure that all relevant hoses, pipes and wires, etc, have been disconnected.

25 Working from the outside inwards in a

11.25 Cylinder head bolt loosening sequence

spiral pattern as shown, loosen all the cylinder head bolts by a quarter of a turn, then loosen all the bolts by half a turn, and finally loosen and remove the bolts **(see illustration)**. Recover the washers.

26 Lift the camshaft housing from the cylinder head **(see illustration)**. If necessary, tap the housing gently with a soft-faced mallet to free it from the cylinder head, but **do not** lever at the mating faces. Note that the camshaft housing is located on dowels.

27 Lift the rocker arms and their thrust pads from the cylinder head, keeping them in order so that they can be refitted in their original positions **(see illustrations)**.

11.26 Lifting the camshaft housing from the cylinder head

11.27a Lift the rocker arms . . .

11.27b . . . and their thrust pads from the cylinder head

11.28 Lift the hydraulic valve lifters from the cylinder head

11.29 Lifting the cylinder head from the cylinder block

11.32a Cylinder head gasket OBEN/TOP markings

11.32b Cylinder head gasket correctly located over dowels (arrowed) in cylinder block

11.35 Lubricate the valve lifter contact faces

28 Lift the hydraulic valve lifters from the cylinder head, and keep the lifters in order, so that they can be refitted in their original positions **(see illustration)**.

29 Lift the cylinder head from the cylinder block **(see illustration)**. If necessary, tap the cylinder head gently with a soft-faced mallet to free it from the block, but **do not** lever at the mating faces. Note that the cylinder head is located on dowels.

30 Recover the cylinder head gasket, and discard it.

Refitting

31 Clean the cylinder head and block mating

faces, and the camshaft housing and cylinder head mating faces, by careful scraping. Take care not to damage the cylinder head and camshaft housing, which are made of light alloy, and are easily scored. Cover the coolant passages and other openings with masking tape or rag, to prevent dirt and carbon falling in. Mop out all the oil from the bolt holes; if oil is left in the holes, hydraulic pressure could crack the block when the bolts are refitted.

32 Commence refitting by locating a new cylinder head gasket on the block so that the word OBEN or TOP can be read from above **(see illustrations)**.

33 With the mating faces scrupulously clean,

locate the cylinder head on the block so that the positioning dowels engage in their holes.

34 Before refitting the hydraulic valve lifters, it is advisable to dismantle and clean them as described in Chapter 2E, Section 8.

35 Refit the hydraulic valve lifters, thrust pads and rocker arms to the cylinder head in their original positions. Liberally oil the valve lifter bores. Lubricate the contact faces of the valve lifters, thrust pads and rocker arms with a little molybdenum disulphide grease **(see illustration)**.

36 Temporarily refit the camshaft sprocket, and ensure that the timing marks are still positioned with No 1 piston at top dead centre (the mark on the sprocket should be uppermost – see Section 3).

37 Apply sealing compound (Vauxhall/Opel No 90 542 114, or equivalent) to the cylinder head top mating face, then refit the camshaft housing to the cylinder head **(see illustration)**.

38 Fit the **new** cylinder head bolts, ensuring that the washers are in place under their heads, and screw the bolts in by hand as far as possible **(see illustration)**.

39 Tighten the cylinder head bolts, working from the inside outwards in a spiral pattern. Tighten the bolts in the four stages given in the Specifications – ie, tighten all bolts to the

11.37 Apply sealing compound to the cylinder head top mating face

11.38 Fit new cylinder head bolts, ensuring that the washers are in place

11.39a Cylinder head bolt tightening sequence

11.39b Tighten the cylinder head bolts to the specified torque . . .

11.39c . . . then through the specified angles

Stage 1 torque, then tighten all bolts to Stage 2, and so on **(see illustrations)**.

40 Further refitting is a reversal of the removal procedure, bearing in mind the following points.

41 Ensure that the ignition HT leads are reconnected to their correct cylinders.

42 Where applicable, refit the manifolds to the cylinder head with reference to Chapter 4B, using new gaskets.

43 Reconnect the exhaust front section to the manifold, using a new gasket, with reference to Chapter 4B.

44 Refit the camshaft sprocket as described in Section 8.

45 Refill the cooling system as described in Chapter 1.

46 On completion, check that all relevant hoses, pipes and wires, etc, have been reconnected.

12.6 Removing the engine-to-gearbox/transmission blanking plate

12.7 Withdrawing the sump

47 When the engine is started, check for signs of leaks.

12 Sump and oil pick-up pipe – removal and refitting

Note: *A new sump gasket must be used on refitting. Suitable sealant (Vauxhall/Opel No 90 485 251, or equivalent) will be required to coat the cylinder block face (see text), and suitable thread-locking compound will be required to coat the sump securing bolt threads (and the oil pick-up pipe bolt threads, where applicable). If the oil pick-up pipe is removed, a new O-ring should be used on refitting.*

Engines with steel sump

Removal

1 Disconnect the battery negative terminal (refer to *Disconnecting the battery* in the Reference Chapter).

2 Drain the engine oil, with reference to Chapter 1 if necessary, then refit and tighten the sump drain plug.

3 Firmly apply the handbrake, then jack up the front of the car and support it securely on axle stands (see *Jacking and vehicle support*).

4 Disconnect the exhaust system from the manifold, and disconnect the system from the

12.11 Apply sealing compound to oil pump and flywheel end main bearing cap joints before refitting sump

forward rubber mountings (Chapter 4B). Lower the system sufficiently to enable removal of the sump.

5 Where applicable, disconnect the wiring from the oil level sensor mounted in the sump.

6 Unscrew the securing bolts, and remove the engine-to-gearbox/transmission blanking plate from the bellhousing **(see illustration)**.

7 Unscrew the securing bolts, and withdraw the sump **(see illustration)**. If necessary, tap the sump with a soft-faced mallet to free it from the cylinder block – **do not** lever between the sump and cylinder block mating faces.

8 Recover the gasket.

9 If desired, the oil pick-up pipe can be removed by unscrewing the single bolt securing the support bracket to the cylinder block, and the two bolts securing the end of the pipe to the oil pump. Recover the O-ring.

Refitting

10 Clean all traces of old gasket from the mating faces of the cylinder block and sump.

11 Commence refitting by applying sealing compound (Vauxhall/Opel No 90 485 251, or equivalent) to the joints between the oil pump and cylinder block, and the flywheel end main bearing cap and cylinder block **(see illustration)**.

12 If the oil pick-up pipe has been removed, clean the threads of the securing bolts (including the bracket securing bolt), and coat them with thread-locking compound before refitting. Refit the pick-up pipe to the oil pump using a new O-ring, then refit the bracket securing the pipe to the cylinder block **(see illustration)**.

12.12 Fit a new O-ring to the oil pick-up pipe

12.20 Aluminium sump-to-gearbox securing bolts (arrowed)

12.21 Prising a plug from the cylinder block for access to a sump end securing bolt – aluminium sump

13 Clean the threads of the sump securing bolts and coat them with thread-locking compound. Refit the sump using a new gasket, and tighten the securing bolts progressively to the specified torque.

14 Further refitting is a reversal of removal, but refit the front section of the exhaust system with reference to Chapter 4B, and on completion, refill the engine with oil as described in Chapter 1.

Engines with aluminium sump

Removal

15 Disconnect the battery negative terminal (refer to *Disconnecting the battery* in the Reference Chapter).

16 Drain the engine oil, with reference to Chapter 1 if necessary, then refit and tighten the sump drain plug.

17 Firmly apply the handbrake, then jack up the front of the car and support it securely on axle stands (see *Jacking and vehicle support*).

18 Remove the exhaust system front section as described in Chapter 4B.

19 Where applicable, disconnect the wiring from the oil level sensor mounted in the sump.

20 Unscrew the three bolts securing the sump to the gearbox/transmission bell-housing **(see illustration)**.

21 Using a screwdriver or similar tool, prise out the two plastic blanking plugs from the cylinder block for access to the two end sump securing bolts **(see illustration)**.

22 Unscrew the securing bolts, and withdraw the sump. If necessary, tap the sump with a soft-faced mallet to free it from the cylinder block – **do not** lever between the sump and cylinder block mating faces.

23 Recover the gasket.

24 If desired, the oil pick-up pipe can be removed by unscrewing the single bolt securing the support bracket to the cylinder block, and the two bolts securing the end of the pipe to the oil pump. Recover the O-ring.

Refitting

25 Clean all traces of old gasket from the mating faces of the cylinder block and sump.

26 Commence refitting by applying sealing compound (Vauxhall/Opel No 90 485 251, or equivalent) to the joints between the oil pump and cylinder block, and the flywheel end main bearing cap and cylinder block **(see illustration 12.11)**.

27 If the oil pick-up pipe has been removed, clean the threads of the securing bolts (including the bracket securing bolt), and coat them with thread-locking compound before refitting. Refit the pick-up pipe to the oil pump using a new O-ring, then refit the bracket securing the pipe to the cylinder block **(see illustration 12.12)**.

28 Clean the threads of the sump securing bolts and coat them with thread-locking compound. Place the sump in position and refit all the securing bolts finger tight only at this stage.

29 To ensure a good seal between the sump and the gearbox/transmission, tighten the sump-to-gearbox/transmission bolts to the specified torque first, then tighten the sump-to-cylinder block bolts to the specified torque.

30 Further refitting is a reversal of removal, but refit the front section of the exhaust system with reference to Chapter 4B, and on completion, refill the engine with oil as described in Chapter 1.

13 Oil pump – removal, inspection and refitting

Note: *A new oil pump gasket and a new timing belt end crankshaft oil seal must be used on refitting.*

Removal

1 Remove the rear timing belt cover as described in Section 6.

2 Remove the sump and oil pick-up pipe as described in Section 12.

3 Disconnect the wiring from the oil pressure switch mounted in the oil pump.

4 Unbolt the crankshaft speed/position sensor bracket from the oil pump. Move the sensor/bracket assembly to one side, taking care not to damage the sensor.

5 Remove the securing bolts, and withdraw the oil pump from the cylinder block **(see illustration)**. Recover the gasket.

13.5 Oil pump securing bolts (arrowed)

13.7 Removing an oil pump rear cover securing screw

13.8 Oil pressure relief valve components

1 Plunger   3 Sealing ring
2 Spring   4 Plug

13.10 Check the clearance between the inner and outer gear teeth . . .

Inspection

Note: *A new pressure relief valve sealing ring should be used on reassembly, and sealing compound (Vauxhall/Opel No 90 485 251, or equivalent) will be required to coat the pump housing mating face.*

6 With the oil pump removed, proceed as follows.

7 Remove the securing screws and withdraw the rear cover **(see illustration)**. The screws may be very tight, in which case it may be necessary to use an impact driver to remove them.

8 The oil pressure relief valve components can be removed from the pump by unscrewing the cap. Withdraw the cap, sealing ring, spring and plunger **(see illustration)**.

9 Prise the crankshaft timing belt end oil seal from the pump using a screwdriver.

13.11 . . . and between the end faces of the gears and the housing

10 Check the clearance between the inner and outer gear teeth (backlash) using a feeler gauge **(see illustration)**.

11 Check the clearance between the end faces of the gears and the housing (endfloat) using a straight-edge and a feeler gauge **(see illustration)**.

12 If any of the clearances are outside the specified limits, renew the components as necessary.

13 Examine the pressure relief valve spring and plunger, and renew if any sign of damage or wear is evident.

14 Ensure that the interior of the pump body is scrupulously clean before commencing reassembly.

15 Discard the old pressure relief valve sealing ring, then thoroughly clean the pressure relief valve components, and lubricate them with clean engine oil before refitting. Use a new sealing ring.

16 Ensure that the gears are clean, then lubricate them with clean engine oil, and refit them to the pump body, noting that the outer gear is marked with a punch dot to indicate its outer face (ie, the face nearest the pump cover) **(see illustration)**.

17 Ensure that the mating faces of the rear cover and the pump housing are clean, then coat the pump housing mating face with suitable sealing compound (Vauxhall/Opel No 90 485 251, or equivalent), and refit the

rear cover. Refit and tighten the securing screws.

18 Fit a new crankshaft timing belt end oil seal to the recess in the pump body, using a suitable socket or tube, so that the seal is flush with the outer face of the housing **(see illustration)**.

Refitting

19 Thoroughly clean the mating faces of the oil pump and cylinder block, then locate a new gasket on the block.

20 Wind a thin layer of tape around the end of the crankshaft, to prevent damage to the oil seal lips as the pump is refitted.

21 With a new oil seal fitted to the pump, as described previously in this Section, grease the oil seal lips, then refit the pump, ensuring that the inner gear engages with the flats on the crankshaft **(see illustration)**.

22 Tighten the securing bolts to the specified torque, then carefully remove the tape from the crankshaft.

23 Refit the crankshaft speed/position sensor and its securing bracket, and tighten the securing bolt.

24 Reconnect the wiring to the oil pressure switch.

25 Refit the oil pick-up pipe and sump, as described in Section 12.

26 Refit the rear timing belt cover as described in Section 6.

13.21 Refitting the oil pump (shown with engine removed from vehicle and inverted)

1 Tape wound around crankshaft
2 Flats on crankshaft engage with inner oil pump gear

13.16 Gear outer face identification mark (arrowed)

13.18 Fitting a new crankshaft oil seal to the oil pump

14.3 Using a self-tapping screw and a pair of pliers to extract the crankshaft oil seal

14 Crankshaft oil seals – renewal

Timing belt end oil seal

1 Remove the crankshaft sprocket as described in Section 8.
2 Punch or drill a small hole in the centre of the now-exposed oil seal.
3 Screw in a self-tapping screw, and pull on the screw with pliers to extract the seal **(see illustration)**. Several attempts may be necessary. Be careful not to damage the sealing face of the crankshaft.
4 Clean the oil seal seat with a wooden or plastic scraper.
5 Wind a thin band of tape around the end of the crankshaft, to protect the lips of the new oil seal as it is fitted.
6 Grease the lips of the new seal, and tap it into position until it is flush with the outer face of the oil pump body, using a suitable socket or tube **(see illustration)**. Take care not to damage the seal lips during fitting.
7 Carefully remove the tape from the end of the crankshaft.
8 Refit the crankshaft sprocket, as described in Section 8.

Flywheel end oil seal

9 Remove the flywheel/driveplate as described in Section 15.
10 Proceed as described in paragraphs 2 to 4 inclusive of this Section.

15.5 Removing the flywheel

14.6 Tapping a new crankshaft oil seal into position

11 Grease the lips of the new seal, then tap the seal into position using a suitable tube, until flush with the outer faces of the cylinder block and main bearing cap.

 HAYNES HINT *Wind a length of tape around the end of the crankshaft to reduce the possibility of damage to the lips of the oil seal as the seal is fitted.*

12 Refit the flywheel/driveplate as described in Section 15.

15 Flywheel/driveplate – removal, inspection and refitting

Note: *New flywheel/driveplate securing bolts must be used on refitting.*

Removal

1 Remove the manual gearbox as described in Chapter 7A, or the automatic transmission as described in Chapter 7B, as applicable.
2 On manual gearbox models, remove the clutch as described in Chapter 6.
3 Although the flywheel/driveplate bolt holes are offset so that the flywheel/driveplate can only be fitted in one position, it will make refitting easier if alignment marks are made between the flywheel/driveplate and the end of the crankshaft.

15.12a Tool for preventing the flywheel from turning, secured using an engine-to-gearbox bolt

4 Prevent the flywheel/driveplate from turning by locking the ring gear teeth using a suitable tool.
5 Unscrew the securing bolts, and remove the flywheel/driveplate **(see illustration)**. *Take care, as the flywheel is heavy.*

Inspection

6 If the teeth on the flywheel starter ring are badly worn, or if some are missing, then it will be necessary to remove the ring and fit a new one.
7 The old ring can be split with a cold chisel, after making a cut with a hacksaw blade between two gear teeth. Take great care not to damage the flywheel during this operation, and wear eye protection at all times. Once the ring has been split, it will spread apart, and can be lifted from the flywheel.
8 The new ring gear must be heated evenly to between 180 and 230°C. Unless facilities for heating by oven or flame are available, leave the fitting to a Vauxhall/Opel dealer or engineering works. The new ring gear must not be overheated during this work, or the temper of the metal will be affected.
9 The ring should be tapped gently down onto its register, and left to cool naturally – the contraction of the metal on cooling will ensure that it is a secure and permanent fit.
10 If the clutch friction disc contact surface of the flywheel is scored, or on close inspection, shows signs of small hair cracks (caused by overheating), it may be possible to have the flywheel surface-ground, provided the overall thickness of the flywheel is not reduced too much. Consult a Vauxhall/Opel dealer or a specialist engine repairer, and if grinding is not possible, renew the flywheel complete.

Refitting

11 Offer the flywheel to the end of the crankshaft, and align the previously-made marks on the flywheel and crankshaft.
12 Coat the threads of the new flywheel bolts with thread-locking compound (note that new bolts may be supplied ready-coated), then fit the bolts and tighten them to the three stages given in the Specifications, whilst preventing the flywheel from turning as during removal **(see illustrations)**.

15.12b Tighten the flywheel securing bolts to the specified torque . . .

15.12c . . . and then through the specified angle

13 Where applicable, refit the clutch as described in Chapter 6.

14 Refit the manual gearbox, or automatic transmission as described in Chapter 7A or 7B, as applicable.

16 Engine/gearbox mountings – inspection and renewal

Note: *References to 'engine/gearbox' in this Section may be taken to be equally applicable for vehicles with automatic transmission.*

Inspection

1 To improve access, firmly apply the handbrake, then jack up the front of the car and support it securely on axle stands (see *Jacking and vehicle support*).

2 Check the mounting blocks (rubbers) to see if they are cracked, hardened or separated from the metal at any point **(see illustrations)**. Renew the mounting block if any such damage or deterioration is evident.

3 Check that all the mounting securing nuts and bolts are securely tightened, using a torque wrench to check if possible.

4 Using a large screwdriver, or a similar tool, check for wear in the mounting blocks by carefully levering against them to check for free play. Where this is not possible, enlist the aid of an assistant to move the engine/gearbox unit back-and-forth, and from side-to-side, while you observe the mountings. While some free play is to be expected, even from new components, excessive wear should be obvious. If excessive free play is found, check first to see that the securing nuts and bolts are correctly tightened, then renew any worn components as described in the following paragraphs.

Renewal

Right-hand mounting – models without power steering

Note: *Suitable thread-locking compound will be required to coat the threads of the mounting block-to-body bolts on refitting.*

5 If not already done, firmly apply the handbrake, then jack up the front of the car

16.2a Engine/gearbox mountings – models without power steering
1 Right-hand mounting   2 Rear mounting   3 Left-hand mounting

16.2b Engine/gearbox mountings – models with power steering
1 Right-hand mounting   2 Rear mounting   3 Left-hand mounting

16.7 Right-hand engine/gearbox mounting-to-body bolts (arrowed) – models without power steering

16.18 Lower the engine until the mounting bracket is clear of the stud

and support it securely on axle stands (see *Jacking and vehicle support*).

6 Attach suitable lifting tackle to the engine lifting brackets on the cylinder head, and support the weight of the engine.

7 Working under the vehicle, unbolt the engine mounting bracket from the cylinder block. Now unbolt the mounting block from the body, then withdraw the bracket/mounting block assembly **(see illustration)**.

8 Unbolt the mounting block from the bracket.

9 Fit the new mounting block to the bracket, and tighten the securing bolts to the specified torque.

10 Before refitting the bracket/mounting block assembly, clean the threads of the mounting block-to-body bolts, then check that the bolts rotate freely in their threaded holes in the body. If necessary, re-cut the threaded holes in the body using a suitable-size tap.

11 Refit the mounting bracket to the cylinder block, and tighten the securing bolts to the specified torque.

12 Coat the threads of the mounting block-to-body bolts with suitable thread-locking compound, then refit them and tighten to the specified torque.

13 Disconnect the lifting tackle and hoist from the engine.

14 Lower the vehicle to the ground.

Right-hand mounting – models with power steering

Note: *Suitable thread-locking compound will be required to coat the threads of the mounting block-to-body bolts on refitting.*

15 Proceed as described in paragraphs 5 and 6.

16 On models with air conditioning, remove the air cleaner assembly (Chapter 4B) and the auxiliary drivebelt (Chapter 1). Unbolt the power steering pump and support it clear of the engine, taking care not to strain the fluid lines.

17 Working under the vehicle, remove the nut and bolt securing the engine mounting bracket to the mounting block.

18 Using the lifting tackle, carefully lower the right-hand side of the engine, until the engine mounting bracket is clear of the mounting block stud **(see illustration)**.

19 Unbolt the mounting block from the body.

20 Before refitting the mounting block, clean the threads of the mounting block-to-body bolts, then check that the bolts rotate freely in their threaded holes in the body. If necessary,

re-cut the threaded holes in the body using a suitable tap.

21 Coat the threads of the mounting block-to-body bolts with suitable thread-locking compound, then refit the mounting block to the body, and tighten the bolts to the specified torque.

22 Carefully raise the right-hand side of the engine until the mounting block stud protrudes through the bracket sufficiently to refit the nut.

23 Refit the nut and bolt securing the engine mounting bracket to the mounting block, and tighten them to the specified torque.

24 On models with air conditioning, refit the power steering pump, tightening the mounting bolts to the specified torque (Chapter 10). Refit the air cleaner assembly (Chapter 4B) and the auxiliary drivebelt (Chapter 1).

25 Proceed as described in paragraphs 13 and 14.

Left-hand mounting

Note: *Suitable thread-locking compound will be required to coat the threads of the mounting block-to-body bolts on refitting.*

26 Proceed as described in paragraphs 5 and 6.

27 Working under the vehicle, unbolt the mounting bracket from the gearbox, and from the mounting block, and withdraw the bracket **(see illustration)**.

28 Unbolt the mounting block from the body.

29 Before refitting the mounting block, clean the threads of the mounting block-to-body bolts, then check that the bolts rotate freely in their threaded holes in the body. If necessary, re-cut the threaded holes in the body using a suitable tap.

30 Coat the threads of the mounting block-to-body bolts with suitable thread-locking compound, then refit the mounting block to the body, and tighten the bolts to the specified torque.

31 Refit the mounting bracket, and tighten the securing bolts to the specified torque.

32 Proceed as described in paragraphs 13 and 14.

Rear mounting

33 Proceed as described in paragraphs 5 and 6.

34 Working under the vehicle, remove the nut and bolt securing the mounting block to the gearbox/transmission bracket.

35 Remove the bolts securing the mounting block to the body, and withdraw the mounting block.

36 Refitting is a reversal of removal, but ensure that the arrow on the mounting block points towards the front of the vehicle **(see illustration)**.

16.26 Unbolting the left-hand engine/gearbox mounting bracket from the gearbox

16.36 The arrow on the rear engine/gearbox mounting block must point towards the front of the vehicle

Chapter 2 Part C: 1.4 & 1.6 litre
DOHC engine in-car repair procedures

Contents

Degrees of difficulty

Easy, suitable for novice with little experience	**Fairly easy,** suitable for beginner with some experience	**Fairly difficult,** suitable for competent DIY mechanic 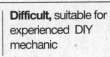	**Difficult,** suitable for experienced DIY mechanic	**Very difficult,** suitable for expert DIY or professional

Specifications

General

Engine type	Four-cylinder, in-line, water-cooled. Double overhead camshafts, belt-driven, acting on hydraulic valve lifters
Manufacturer's engine codes*:	
1.4 litre engine	X 14 XE
1.6 litre engine	X 16 XE
Bore:	
1.4 litre engine	77.60 mm
1.6 litre engine	79.00 mm
Stroke:	
1.4 litre engine	73.40 mm
1.6 litre engine	81.50 mm
Capacity:	
1.4 litre engine	1389 cc
1.6 litre engine	1598 cc
Firing order	1-3-4-2 (No 1 cylinder at timing belt end)
Direction of crankshaft rotation	Clockwise (viewed from timing belt end of engine)
Compression ratio	10.5:1

*For details of engine code location, see 'Vehicle identification' in the Reference Chapter.

Camshaft

Endfloat	0.040 to 0.144 mm
Camshaft bearing journal diameter	27.939 to 27.960 mm
Maximum permissible radial run-out	0.040 mm

Lubrication system

Minimum oil pressure at 80°C	1.5 bars at idle speed
Oil pump type	Gear-type, driven directly from crankshaft
Oil pump clearances:	
Inner-to-outer gear teeth clearance (backlash)	0.100 to 0.200 mm
Gear-to-housing clearance (endfloat)	0.080 to 0.150 mm

Flywheel

Maximum permissible lateral run-out of starter ring gear . . . . 0.500 mm
Refinishing limit – maximum depth of material which may be
  removed from clutch friction surface . . . . 0.300 mm

Torque wrench settings

	Nm	lbf ft
Big-end bearing cap bolts:*		
Stage 1	25	18
Stage 2	Angle-tighten a further 30°	
Camshaft bearing cap bolts	8	6
Camshaft cover bolts	8	6
Camshaft sprocket bolt:*		
Stage 1	50	37
Stage 2	Angle-tighten a further 60°	
Stage 3	Angle-tighten a further 15°	
Clutch bellhousing cover plate	7	5
Coolant pump bolts	8	6
Crankshaft pulley bolt:*		
Stage 1	95	70
Stage 2	Angle-tighten a further 30°	
Stage 3	Angle-tighten a further 15°	
Cylinder head bolts:*		
Stage 1	25	18
Stage 2	Angle-tighten a further 90°	
Stage 3	Angle-tighten a further 90°	
Stage 4	Angle-tighten a further 90°	
Stage 5	Angle-tighten a further 45°	
Engine mountings:		
Left-hand:		
Gearbox/transmission bracket-to-gearbox/transmission bolts	60	44
Gearbox/transmission bracket-to-mounting block bolts	60	44
Mounting block-to-body bolts**	65	48
Rear:		
Gearbox/transmission bracket-to-gearbox/transmission bolts . . .	70	52
Gearbox/transmission bracket-to-mounting block bolts	65	48
Mounting block-to-body bolts	65	48
Right-hand:		
Engine bracket-to-engine bolts	60	44
Engine bracket-to-mounting block bolt/nut	60	44
Mounting block-to-body bolts	20	15
Engine-to-gearbox/transmission bolts	60	44
Flywheel/driveplate bolts:*		
Stage 1	35	26
Stage 2	Angle-tighten a further 30°	
Stage 3	Angle-tighten a further 15°	
Main bearing cap bolts:*		
Stage 1	50	37
Stage 2	Angle-tighten a further 45°	
Stage 3	Angle-tighten a further 15°	
Oil pick-up pipe bracket-to-cylinder block bolt	8	6
Oil pick-up pipe-to-oil pump bolts**	8	6
Oil pressure relief valve plug to oil pump	30	22
Oil pump cover screws	6	4
Oil pump-to-cylinder block bolts	10	7
Plastic shield-to-camshaft cover screws	4	3
Sump-to-cylinder block bolts:**		
Aluminium sump	10	7
Steel sump	8	6
Sump-to-gearbox/transmission (aluminium sump):		
M8 bolts	20	15
M10 bolts	40	30
Timing belt cover bolts:		
Outer cover	4	3
Rear cover	6	4
Timing belt idler roller bolts	25	18
Timing belt tensioner bolt	20	15
Torque converter to driveplate*	50	37

*Use new bolts.
**Use thread-locking compound.

1 General information

How to use this Chapter

This Part of Chapter 2 describes the repair procedures which can reasonably be carried out on the engine while it remains in the vehicle. If the engine has been removed from the vehicle and is being dismantled as described in Chapter 2E, any preliminary dismantling procedures can be ignored.

Note that, while it may be *possible* physically to overhaul items such as the piston/connecting rod assemblies while the engine is in the vehicle, such tasks are not generally carried out as separate operations, and usually require the execution of several additional procedures (not to mention the cleaning of components and of oilways); for this reason, all such tasks are classed as major overhaul procedures, and are described in Chapter 2E.

Chapter 2E describes the removal of the engine/transmission unit from the vehicle, and the full overhaul procedures which can then be carried out.

Engine description

The engine is of the in-line four-cylinder, double overhead camshaft (DOHC) type, mounted transversely at the front of the car, with the transmission attached to its left-hand end **(see illustrations)**.

The crankshaft runs in five shell-type bearings, and the centre bearing incorporates thrust bearing shells to control crankshaft endfloat.

The connecting rods are attached to the crankshaft by horizontally-split shell-type big-end bearings. The pistons are attached to the connecting rods by gudgeon pins, which are an interference fit in the connecting rod small-end bores. The aluminium-alloy pistons are fitted with three piston rings – two compression rings and an oil control ring.

Both camshafts are driven from the crankshaft by a toothed composite-rubber belt. Each cylinder has four valves (two inlet and two exhaust), operated directly from the camshafts via hydraulic self-adjusting valve lifters (tappets). One camshaft operates the inlet valves, and the other operates the exhaust valves. The inlet and exhaust valves are each closed by a single valve spring, and operate in guides pressed into the cylinder head.

A gear-type oil pump is located in a housing attached to the front of the cylinder block, and is driven directly from the crankshaft.

The coolant pump is located at the front of the cylinder block, and is driven by the timing belt.

1.4a Front sectional view of engine

1.4b Side sectional view of engine

Repair operations possible with the engine in the vehicle

The following operations can be carried out without having to remove the engine from the vehicle.

a) *Removal and refitting of the cylinder head.*
b) *Removal and refitting of the timing belt and sprockets.*
c) *Removal and refitting of the camshaft.*
d) *Removal and refitting of the sump.*
e) *Removal and refitting of the big-end bearings, connecting rods, and pistons*.*
f) *Removal and refitting of the oil pump.*
g) *Renewal of the engine mountings.*
h) *Removal and refitting of the flywheel/driveplate.*

Although the operation marked with an asterisk can be carried out with the engine in the vehicle (after removal of the sump), it is preferable for the engine to be removed, in the interests of cleanliness and improved access. For this reason, the procedure is described in Chapter 2E.

2 Compression test – description and interpretation

Note: *A suitable compression gauge will be required to carry out this test.*

1 When engine performance is down, or if misfiring occurs which cannot be attributed to the ignition or fuel systems, a compression test can provide diagnostic clues as to the engine's condition. If the test is performed regularly, it can give warning of trouble before any other symptoms become apparent.

2 The engine must be fully warmed-up to normal operating temperature, the battery must be fully charged, and all the spark plugs must be removed (see Chapter 1). The aid of an assistant will also be required.

3 Disconnect the wiring plug from the DIS module, and remove the fuel pump relay (see Chapter 12 for details of relay locations).

4 Fit a compression tester to the No 1 spark plug hole (No 1 cylinder is nearest the timing belt end of the engine) – the type of tester which screws into the plug thread is to be preferred.

5 Have an assistant hold the accelerator pedal fully depressed, at the same time cranking the engine over for approximately four seconds on the starter motor. After one or two revolutions, the compression pressure reading on the gauge should build-up to a maximum figure and then stabilise. Record the highest reading obtained.

6 Repeat the test on the remaining cylinders, recording the pressure in each.

7 All cylinders should produce very similar pressures; a difference of more than 1 bar between any two cylinders indicates a fault. Note that the compression should build-up quickly in a healthy engine; low compression on the first stroke, followed by gradually-increasing pressure on successive strokes,

indicates worn piston rings. A low compression reading on the first stroke, which does not build-up during successive strokes, indicates leaking valves or a blown head gasket (a cracked head could also be the cause). Deposits on the undersides of the valve heads can also cause low compression.

8 If the pressure in any cylinder is significantly lower than that in the remaining cylinders, carry out the following test to isolate the cause. Introduce a teaspoonful of clean engine oil into the relevant cylinder through its spark plug hole, and repeat the test.

9 If the addition of oil temporarily improves the compression pressure, this indicates that bore or piston wear is responsible for the pressure loss. No improvement suggests that leaking or burnt valves, or a blown head gasket may be to blame.

10 A low reading from two adjacent cylinders is almost certainly due to the head gasket having blown between them; the presence of coolant in the engine oil will confirm this.

11 If one cylinder is about 20 percent lower than the others, and the engine has a slightly rough idle, a worn camshaft lobe could be the cause.

12 If the compression reading is unusually high, the combustion chambers are probably coated with carbon deposits. If this is the case, the cylinder head should be removed and decarbonised (see Chapter 2E).

13 On completion of the test, refit the spark plugs, reconnect the DIS module wiring plug, and refit the fuel pump relay.

3 Top dead centre (TDC) for No 1 piston – locating

1 Top dead centre (TDC) is the highest point in the cylinder that a piston reaches as the crankshaft turns. Each piston reaches TDC at the end of the compression stroke, and again at the end of the exhaust stroke. For the purpose of timing the engine, TDC refers to the position of No 1 piston at the end of its compression stroke. On all engines in this Chapter, No 1 piston and cylinder are at the timing belt end of the engine.

2 All engine overhaul procedures use the factory timing marks, which vary according to engine type.

3 Disconnect the battery negative terminal (refer to *Disconnecting the battery* in the Reference Chapter).

4 Remove the upper outer timing belt cover as described in Section 6.

5 Using a suitable spanner or socket on the crankshaft pulley bolt, rotate the crankshaft to bring No 1 piston to TDC as follows, according to engine type. Note that turning the engine will be made much easier if the spark plugs are removed first (see Chapter 1).

6 The timing marks must be aligned as follows **(see illustrations)**.

a) *The timing marks on the camshaft sprockets must be directly opposite each*

1 *Camshaft sprocket timing marks aligned with top edge of cylinder head*
2 *TDC sensor wheel timing mark aligned with mark on timing belt cover*
3 *Crankshaft sprocket timing mark aligned with mark on timing belt cover*
4 *Timing belt tensioner bolt*
5 *Coolant pump mark aligned with mark on cylinder block (see Chapter 3)*

3.6a Timing mark positions with No 1 piston at TDC

3.6b Camshaft sprocket timing marks (A) aligned with top edge of cylinder head (B)

3.6c Crankshaft sprocket timing mark (A) aligned with mark (B) on timing belt cover

other, and aligned with the top edge of the cylinder head.

b) The timing mark on the crankshaft speed/position sensor wheel must be aligned with the pointer (raised line) on the timing belt cover. Note that if the crankshaft pulley and lower outer timing belt cover have been removed, the timing mark on the crankshaft sprocket can be used instead of the mark on the pulley. The mark on the crankshaft sprocket must align with the corresponding mark on the rear timing belt cover (there may be two marks on the sprocket, in which case ignore the mark with a cross stamped across it).

4 Camshaft cover – removal and refitting

Removal

1 Remove the upper section of the inlet manifold as described in Chapter 4B.
2 Disconnect the breather hoses from the camshaft cover (see illustration).
3 Using the tool provided (attached to one of the spark plug HT lead connectors), pull the HT leads from the spark plugs, and lay them to one side, clear of the camshaft cover.

4 Progressively loosen the camshaft cover securing bolts (preferably working from the ends of the cover towards the centre, in a spiral pattern), then withdraw the bolts (see illustration).
5 Lift the camshaft cover from the cylinder head (see illustration), and recover the rubber gaskets and O-rings.

Refitting

6 Commence refitting by examining the condition of the rubber gaskets and O-rings. If necessary, renew the gaskets and O-rings.
7 Ensure that the gaskets and O-rings are correctly located on the camshaft cover (see illustrations).

HAYNES HiNT *Smear the O-rings with a little light grease to hold them in position as the cover is refitted.*

8 Fit the cover to the cylinder head, then refit the securing bolts. Tighten the bolts to the specified torque, working from the centre to the ends of the cover, in a spiral pattern.
9 Reconnect the HT leads to the spark plugs.
10 Reconnect the breather hose to the camshaft cover.
11 Refit the upper section of the inlet manifold as described in Chapter 4B.

4.2 Disconnect the breather hoses (arrowed) from the camshaft cover

4.4 Unscrew the bolts . . .

4.5 . . . and lift the camshaft cover from the cylinder head

4.7a Ensure that the gaskets are correctly located

4.7b Hold the O-rings in position using a little grease

6.3 Removing the upper outer timing belt cover

6.9a Lower outer timing belt cover upper securing bolt (arrowed) . . .

6.9b . . . and lower (arrowed) securing bolt

5 Crankshaft pulley – removal and refitting

Note: *A new crankshaft pulley bolt will be required for refitting.*

Removal

1 Access is most easily obtained from under the wheelarch, after jacking up the vehicle and removing the right-hand front wheel (see *Jacking and vehicle support*). If necessary for subsequent operations, rotate the crankshaft to position No 1 piston to TDC as described in Section 3.
2 Remove the auxiliary drivebelt as described in Chapter 1.
3 To prevent the crankshaft from turning as the pulley bolt is unscrewed, select top gear and have an assistant apply the brakes hard (manual gearbox models only). Alternatively, remove the starter motor, and lock the flywheel ring gear teeth using a suitable tool.
4 Unscrew the pulley bolt and recover the washer fitted behind it, then remove the pulley.

Refitting

5 On refitting, ensure that the notch in the pulley fits over the locating lug on the crankshaft sprocket.
6 Prevent the crankshaft from turning as during removal, then fit the new pulley securing bolt, ensuring that the washer is in place under the bolt head.
7 Tighten the bolt to the specified torque, in the stages given in the Specifications.

8 Refit and tension the auxiliary drivebelt, as described in Chapter 1.

6 Timing belt covers – removal and refitting

Upper outer cover
Removal

1 For improved access, remove the air cleaner assembly, as described in Chapter 4B.
2 Where applicable, unclip the wiring harness from the timing belt cover, noting its routing.
3 Unscrew the three securing bolts, and remove the cover (see illustration).

Refitting

4 Refitting is a reversal of removal, ensuring that the wiring harness is routed as noted before removal.

Lower outer cover
Removal

5 For improved access, firmly apply the handbrake, then jack up the front right-hand side of the car and support it securely on axle stands (see *Jacking and vehicle support*). Remove the roadwheel.
6 If desired, to further improve access, remove the wheelarch liner (see Chapter 11, Section 22).
7 Remove the upper outer timing belt cover, as described previously in this Section.
8 Remove the crankshaft pulley, as described in Section 5.

9 Remove the two securing bolts, then release the four clips, and withdraw the lower outer cover (see illustrations).

Refitting

10 Refitting is a reversal of removal, but fit the crankshaft pulley with reference to Section 5.

Rear cover
Removal

11 Remove the upper and lower outer covers as described previously in this Section.
12 Remove the timing belt, sprockets and inlet-side idler roller, as described in Sections 7 and 8.
13 Unscrew the securing bolt and remove the timing belt tensioner.
14 Unscrew the two upper and two lower securing screws, and withdraw the rear cover from the engine (see illustration).

Refitting

15 Refitting is a reversal of removal, bearing in mind the following points:
a) *Refit the timing belt sprockets as described in Section 8.*
b) *Refit and tension the timing belt as described in Section 7.*
c) *Refit the outer timing belt covers as described previously in this Section.*

7 Timing belt – removal, refitting and adjustment

Removal

1 Disconnect the battery negative terminal (refer to *Disconnecting the battery* in the Reference Chapter).
2 Remove the upper and lower outer timing belt covers as described in Section 6. To enable the crankshaft to be turned, temporarily refit the crankshaft pulley retaining bolt.
3 If not already done, turn the crankshaft to bring No 1 piston to top dead centre, as described in Section 3.
4 Unscrew the two bolts securing the camshaft position sensor mounting bracket to the cylinder head, and move the sensor/bracket assembly to one side (see illustration).

6.14 Rear timing belt cover securing bolts – arrowed (seen with timing belt and sprockets still fitted)

7.4 Withdraw the camshaft position sensor

5 Loosen the belt tensioner securing bolt sufficiently to completely relieve the tension in the belt. If necessary, turn the tensioner clockwise to relieve the tension, using a suitable hexagon bit or Allen key engaged with the hole provided in the tensioner front plate **(see illustration)**.

6 Slide the timing belt from the sprockets, and withdraw it from the engine **(see illustration)**. Take note of any arrows marked on the belt to indicate the direction of rotation (if necessary, mark the belt to aid correct refitting).

Refitting

7 Ensure that No 1 piston is still positioned at top dead centre, as described in Section 3.

8 If the coolant pump has been disturbed, check the position of the pump. The mark on the edge of the pump must be aligned with the corresponding mark on the cylinder block (see Chapter 3). If necessary, loosen the securing bolts, and turn the pump as required to align the marks, then tighten the bolts to the specified torque.

9 Refit the timing belt around the sprockets, starting at the crankshaft sprocket, and

7.5 Timing belt tensioner securing bolt (1) and hexagon hole (2) in front plate

7.6 Sliding the timing belt from the sprockets

working in the order shown **(see illustration)**.
Note: *When fitting the belt over the inlet camshaft sprocket, ensure that the belt does not jump a tooth on the sprocket, and make sure that the timing marks on both camshaft sprockets stay positioned directly opposite each other, and aligned with the top edge of the cylinder head.*

10 Adjust the timing belt tension, as described in paragraphs 12 to 20 inclusive.

11 On completion, reconnect the battery negative terminal.

Adjustment

Note: *The engine must be cold when checking and adjusting the timing belt tension.*

12 With the outer timing belt covers removed as described in Section 6, proceed as follows.

13 To enable the crankshaft to be turned, temporarily refit the crankshaft pulley retaining bolt.

14 If not already done, turn the crankshaft to bring No 1 piston to top dead centre, as described in Section 3.

15 With the tensioner securing bolt loosened, engage a suitable hexagon bit or Allen key with the hole provided in the tensioner front plate, and turn the tensioner anti-clockwise until maximum tension is attained. On early type tensioners, the tension indicator pointer should be positioned to the right of the V on the tensioner backplate **(see illustration)**. On later type tensioners, the tension indicator pointer should be positioned to the right of the notch marked NEW on the tensioner backplate. Note that there is no stop on the tensioner front plate, so it is possible to turn the plate beyond the maximum tension position.

16 Tighten the tensioner securing bolt in this position.

17 Using a suitable socket or spanner on the crankshaft pulley bolt, turn the crankshaft

7.9 Fit the timing belt around the sprockets in the order shown

1 Crankshaft sprocket	4 Exhaust-side idler roller	6 Inlet camshaft sprocket
2 Timing belt tensioner	5 Exhaust camshaft	7 Inlet-side idler roller
3 Coolant pump sprocket	sprocket	

7.15 Turn the tensioner anti-clockwise until maximum tension is attained, with the pointer positioned to the right of the V (inset) – early type tensioner shown

7.18 To set the belt tension on a new belt, turn the tensioner clockwise until the pointer is positioned in the centre of the V – early type tensioner shown

8.2a Using a Torx bit engaged with the rear timing belt cover bolt hole to counterhold the inlet camshaft sprocket

8.2b Counterholding the inlet camshaft using a spanner on the flats in front of No 1 cam lobe

clockwise through two complete revolutions, until No 1 piston is again positioned at top dead centre. Turn the crankshaft smoothly without jerking, to avoid the belt jumping on the sprockets. Check that the timing marks are correctly aligned as described in Section 3.

18 Engage the hexagon bit or Allen key with the hole in the tensioner front plate, then slacken the tensioner securing bolt, and carefully turn the front plate clockwise to slacken the belt. If a new timing belt has been fitted, the tension indicator pointer should be positioned in the centre of the V, or aligned with the notch marked NEW, on the tensioner backplate **(see illustration)**. If a 'run-in' belt has been fitted (one that has been used for more than a few hours), the tension indicator pointer should be positioned approximately 4 mm to the left of the centre of the V, or aligned with the notch marked USED. Tighten the tensioner securing bolt to the specified torque.

19 Turn the crankshaft clockwise through two complete revolutions, as described previously, and check that the tension indicator pointer is still positioned as described in paragraph 18 – if not, the procedure described in paragraphs 15 to 19 inclusive must be repeated until the pointer aligns correctly.

20 On completion, refit the spark plugs (where applicable), and refit the outer timing belt covers as described in Section 6.

8 Timing belt sprockets, tensioner and idler rollers – removal and refitting

Camshaft sprockets
Removal

1 Remove the timing belt as described in Section 7.

2 The camshaft sprocket bolt must be prevented from turning as the sprocket bolt is unscrewed, and this can be achieved in one of three ways as follows **(see illustrations)**.
a) Pass a suitable Torx bit and extension bar through one of the holes in the camshaft

sprocket, to engage with the rear timing belt cover bolt. Use the Torx bit and extension bar to counterhold the sprocket as the bolt is loosened.
b) With the camshaft cover removed as described in Section 4, prevent the camshaft from turning by holding it with a suitable spanner on the flats provided in front of No 1 cam lobe.
c) Make up a forked tool and use it to hold the sprocket stationary by means of the holes in the sprocket face (see Section 8 in Part B of this Chapter).

3 Unscrew the camshaft sprocket bolt and withdraw it, noting the washer under the bolt head **(see illustration)**.

4 Withdraw the sprocket from the end of the camshaft.

Refitting

5 Commence refitting by offering the camshaft sprocket(s) to the camshaft(s), noting the following points:
a) Ensure that each sprocket is fitted so that the timing mark is visible on the outer face.
b) If both camshaft sprockets have been removed, ensure that they are refitted to their correct camshafts – the exhaust camshaft sprocket is fitted with lugs which activate the camshaft position sensor.

6 Refit the sprocket securing bolt, ensuring that the washer is in place, and tighten the bolt to the specified torque, preventing the camshaft from turning as during removal.

8.3 Removing the inlet camshaft sprocket

7 Where applicable, refit the camshaft cover as described in Section 4.

8 Refit and tension the timing belt as described in Section 7.

Crankshaft sprocket

Note: *A new crankshaft pulley retaining bolt will be required for refitting – see Section 5.*

Removal

9 Remove the timing belt as described in Section 7.

10 Remove the sprocket from the end of the crankshaft.

Refitting

11 Refit the crankshaft sprocket with the locating flange and locating lug for the crankshaft pulley outermost **(see illustration)**.

12 Refit and tension the timing belt as described in Section 7.

Tensioner

Removal

13 Remove the timing belt as described in Section 7.

14 Unscrew the central securing bolt, and withdraw the tensioner.

Refitting

15 Refit the tensioner, ensuring that the lug on the tensioner backplate engages with the corresponding hole in the oil pump.

16 Refit the tensioner securing bolt, but do not tighten the bolt fully until the timing belt has been tensioned.

8.11 Refit the crankshaft sprocket with the locating flange and pulley locating lug outermost

8.20 Timing belt idler rollers (arrowed)

9.6 Fitting a new camshaft oil seal using a socket and bolt

10.3a Camshaft bearing cap numbering sequence (No 1 at timing belt end)

17 Refit and tension the timing belt, as described in Section 7.

Idler rollers

Removal

18 Remove the timing belt as described in Section 7.
19 Unscrew the securing bolt, and remove the relevant idler roller.

Refitting

20 If both idler rollers have been removed, note that the larger-diameter roller fits on the inlet side of the engine (see illustration).
21 Refit the relevant idler roller, and tighten the securing bolt to the specified torque.
22 Refit the timing belt as described in Section 7.

9 Camshaft oil seals – renewal

1 Remove the relevant camshaft sprocket as described in Section 8.
2 Punch or drill a small hole in the centre of the now-exposed oil seal.
3 Screw in a self-tapping screw, and pull on the screw with pliers to extract the seal.
4 Clean the oil seal seat with a wooden or plastic scraper.
5 Wind a thin band of tape around the end of the camshaft, to protect the lips of the new oil seal as it is fitted.
6 Grease the lips of the new seal, then fit it to the housing. Ideally, the seal should be drawn

into position using a suitable socket or tube and a washer, and a suitable bolt (see illustration). Alternatively, the seal can be tapped into position. The seal should fitted with its outer face flush with the housing. Take care not to damage the seal lips during fitting.
7 Carefully remove the tape from the end of the camshaft.
8 Refit the camshaft sprocket as described in Section 8.

10 Camshafts – removal, inspection and refitting

Removal

Note: *A new timing belt end oil seal, and a tube of suitable sealant (Vauxhall/Opel No 90 542 114, or equivalent) will be required when refitting.*
1 Remove the camshaft cover as described in Section 4.
2 Remove the relevant camshaft sprocket as described in Section 8.
3 Check the camshaft bearing caps for identification marks, and if none are present, make corresponding marks on the bearing caps and the top surface of the cylinder head using a centre-punch (take care not to damage the cylinder head or bearing caps). Note the orientation of the bearing caps before removal, as they must be refitted in exactly the same positions from which they are removed. The inlet camshaft caps are usually numbered 1 to 5, and the exhaust

camshaft caps 6 to 10, with corresponding numbers cast into the cylinder head (see illustrations).
4 Before removing the camshaft, check the endfloat using a dial gauge or a feeler gauge. If the endfloat is outside the specified limits, the camshaft must be renewed.
5 If removing the inlet camshaft, loosen Nos 1, 3 and 5 bearing cap bolts progressively by half a turn, then by a full turn, then remove the bolts. Similarly, if removing the exhaust camshaft, loosen and then remove Nos 6, 8 and 10 bearing cap bolts. Lift the relevant bearing caps from the cylinder head (see illustration).
6 Progressively loosen the remaining bearing cap bolts (bearing caps 2 and 4, or 7 and 9, as applicable) in half-turn stages, working in a crosswise pattern (this is necessary to progressively relieve the tension in the valve springs), then remove the bolts.
7 Lift the remaining bearing caps from the cylinder head, then lift out the camshaft, complete with the oil seal (see illustration). If both camshafts are removed, identify them as exhaust and inlet.

Inspection

8 With the camshaft removed, examine the bearing surfaces in the cylinder head for signs of obvious wear or pitting. If evident, the cylinder head and all the bearing caps must be renewed as a matched set, as it is not possible to renew the bearings individually.

10.3b Camshaft bearing cap numbers (exhaust camshaft shown)

10.5 Removing a camshaft bearing cap

10.7 Lifting the exhaust camshaft from the cylinder head

10.11 Lubricate the contact faces of the valve lifters, camshaft lobes and bearings with molybdenum disulphide paste

10.12 Coat the timing belt end bearing cap mating faces of the cylinder head (arrowed) with sealing compound

10.17 Camshaft bearing cap bolt tightening sequence (exhaust camshaft shown)

9 The camshaft should show no marks or scoring on the journal or cam lobe surfaces. If evident, renew the camshaft.

10 It is advisable to renew the oil seal as a matter of course. Prise the old seal from the camshaft and discard it.

Refitting

11 Commence refitting by liberally coating the contact faces of the hydraulic valve lifters, the camshaft lobes, and the bearing surfaces with molybdenum disulphide paste **(see illustration)**.

12 Coat the timing belt end bearing cap mating faces of the cylinder head (No 1 and/or 6, depending on the camshaft(s) removed) with sealing compound (Vauxhall/Opel No 90 542 114, or equivalent) **(see illustration)**.

13 Place the camshaft in position on the cylinder head, temporarily refit the camshaft sprocket, and check that the timing marks are still aligned with No 1 piston at TDC, as described in Section 3.

14 Loosely refit the bearing caps in their original positions as noted during removal.

15 If refitting the inlet camshaft, refit Nos 2 and 4 bearing cap bolts, and progressively tighten them in half-turn stages, working in a crosswise pattern. Tighten the bolts until the bearing caps just contact the mating faces of the cylinder head – **do not** fully tighten the bolts at this stage. Similarly, if refitting the exhaust camshaft, refit and tighten Nos 7 and 9 bearing cap bolts.

16 Refit the remaining bearing cap bolts, and tighten them progressively until the bearing caps just contact the mating faces of the cylinder head – **do not** fully tighten the bolts at this stage.

17 Working from the centre outwards in a spiral pattern, tighten the bearing cap bolts to the specified torque **(see illustration)**.

18 Lubricate the lips of a new camshaft oil seal with a little grease, and fit the oil seal as described in Section 9.

19 Refit the relevant camshaft sprocket as described in Section 8.

20 Refit the camshaft cover as described in Section 4.

11 Cylinder head –
removal and refitting

Removal

Note: *The engine must be cold when removing the cylinder head. A new cylinder head gasket and new cylinder head bolts must be used on refitting.*

1 Depressurise the fuel system as described in Chapter 4B.

2 Disconnect the battery negative terminal (refer to *Disconnecting the battery* in the Reference Chapter).

3 Drain the cooling system as described in Chapter 1, then remove the coolant expansion tank from its location on the bulkhead.

4 Remove the camshaft cover as described in Section 4.

5 Remove the camshaft sprockets, timing belt tensioner, and the timing belt idler rollers, as described in Section 8.

6 Remove the rear timing belt cover with reference to Section 6.

7 Unscrew the union nut, and disconnect the return hose from the fuel pressure regulator **(see illustration)**. Be prepared for fuel spillage, and clamp or plug the hose to reduce fuel loss and to prevent dirt ingress.

8 Similarly, disconnect the fuel supply hose from the fuel rail.

9 Refer to Chapter 4B, Section 14, and remove the throttle body and the manifold absolute pressure sensor.

10 Refer to Chapter 4C, and remove the secondary air injection pump assembly.

11 Disconnect the wiring plug and the spark plug HT leads from the DIS module.

12 Disconnect the wiring from the coolant temperature sensor and the temperature gauge sender, located in the thermostat housing **(see illustration)**.

13 Disconnect the coolant hose from the thermostat housing **(see illustration)**.

14 Remove the front section of the exhaust system as described in Chapter 4B.

15 Unclip the following wiring connectors from their brackets, and separate the two

11.7 Disconnecting the fuel return hose from the fuel pressure regulator

11.12 Disconnect the wiring from the coolant temperature sensor (1) and the temperature gauge sender (2)

11.13 Disconnect the coolant hose from the thermostat housing

11.15a Disconnect the wiring connectors for the fuel injector . . .

11.15b . . . camshaft position sensor . . .

11.15c . . . and crankshaft speed/position sensor

11.17a Disconnect the earth wiring from the stud on the alternator upper mounting bracket . . .

11.17b . . . and the inlet manifold

11.18 Disconnect the coolant hose (arrowed) from the timing belt end of the manifold

halves of the connector in each case **(see illustrations)**:

  a) *Fuel injector wiring connector.*
  b) *Camshaft position sensor wiring connector.*
  c) *Crankshaft speed/position sensor wiring connector.*
  d) *Knock sensor wiring connector.*
  e) *Oxygen sensor wiring connector (from its bracket on the gearbox).*

16 Unclip the crankshaft speed/position sensor wiring from the lower section of the inlet manifold, and feed the wiring down through the clips on the manifold, so that the wiring can be left in the engine compartment. Note the routing of the wiring.

11.19a Note the location of the stud for the earth wiring . . .

11.19b . . . and remove the upper alternator mounting bracket

17 Disconnect the earth wiring from the studs on the alternator upper mounting bracket, and the gearbox end of the inlet manifold **(see illustrations)**.

11.22b Remove the cylinder head bolts and washers

18 Disconnect the coolant hose from the timing belt end of the lower section of the inlet manifold **(see illustration)**.

19 Unscrew the three securing bolts, and remove the upper alternator mounting bracket (note that one of the bolts doubles as a stud for the earth wiring) **(see illustrations)**.

20 Pivot the alternator away from the manifold as far as it will go.

21 Make a final check to ensure that all relevant hoses, pipes and wires have been disconnected.

22 Working in a spiral pattern from the outside inwards, progressively loosen the cylinder head bolts. First loosen all the bolts by quarter of a turn, then loosen all the bolts by half a turn, then finally slacken all the bolts fully and withdraw them from the cylinder head. Recover the washers **(see illustrations)**.

11.22a Cylinder head bolt loosening sequence

11.23 Lifting the cylinder head from the cylinder block

23 Lift the cylinder head from the cylinder block **(see illustration)**. If necessary, tap the cylinder head gently with a soft-faced mallet to free it from the block, but **do not** lever at the mating faces. Note that the cylinder head is located on dowels.

24 Recover the cylinder head gasket, and discard it.

Refitting

25 Clean the cylinder head and block mating faces by careful scraping. Take care not to damage the cylinder head, which is made of light alloy, and is easily scored. Cover the coolant passages and other openings with masking tape or rag, to prevent dirt and

11.30a Cylinder head bolt tightening sequence

11.30b Tightening a cylinder head bolt using an angle gauge

11.27 Cylinder head gasket OBEN/TOP marking should be at timing belt end of engine

carbon falling in. Mop out all the oil from the bolt holes; if oil is left in the holes, hydraulic pressure could crack the block when the bolts are refitted.

26 Temporarily refit the crankshaft pulley retaining bolt and turn the crankshaft so that all the pistons are positioned approximately half way down their bores. This will prevent the possibility of the valves contacting the pistons as the cylinder head is refitted.

27 Commence refitting by locating a new cylinder head gasket on the block, so that the word OBEN or TOP is uppermost at the timing belt end of the engine **(see illustration)**.

28 With the mating faces scrupulously clean, locate the cylinder head on the block so that the positioning dowels engage in their holes.

29 Fit the **new** cylinder head bolts, ensuring that the washers are in place under their heads, and screw in the bolts *by hand* as far as possible.

30 Tighten the bolts in the order shown. Tighten the bolts in the five stages given in the Specifications – ie, tighten all bolts to the Stage 1 torque using a torque wrench, then tighten all bolts to Stage 2, and so on using an angle tightening gauge **(see illustrations)**.

31 Temporarily refit the camshaft sprockets, and reposition the camshafts, then the crankshaft to the No 1 piston at top dead centre position (see Section 3).

32 Further refitting is a reversal of removal, bearing in mind the following points.

33 Ensure that all hoses, wires and cables are routed as noted during removal.

34 Refit the front section of the exhaust system as described in Chapter 4B.

35 Refit the throttle body as described in Chapter 4B.

36 Refit the camshaft sprockets and the timing belt idler rollers, as described in Section 8.

37 Refit the camshaft cover as described in Section 4.

38 Refill and bleed the cooling system as described in Chapter 1.

39 On completion, check that all relevant hoses, pipes and wires, etc, have been reconnected (check the security of the fuel hose connections)

40 When the engine is started, check for signs of leaks.

12 Sump and oil pick-up pipe – removal and refitting

Refer to Chapter 2B, Section 12.

13 Oil pump – removal, inspection and refitting

Note: *A new oil pump gasket and a new crankshaft oil seal must be used on refitting.*

Removal

1 Remove the rear timing belt cover as described in Section 6.

2 Remove the sump and oil pick-up pipe as described in Section 12.

3 Disconnect the wiring from the oil pressure switch mounted in the oil pump.

4 Unbolt the crankshaft speed/position sensor bracket from the oil pump. Move the sensor/bracket assembly to one side, taking care not to damage the sensor.

5 Remove the securing bolts, and withdraw the oil pump from the cylinder block **(see illustration)**. Recover the gasket.

13.5 Oil pump securing bolts (arrowed)

13.7 Removing an oil pump rear cover securing screw

13.8 Oil pressure relief valve components

1 Plunger   3 Sealing ring
2 Spring   4 Plug

13.10 Check the clearance between the inner and outer gear teeth . . .

Inspection

Note: *A new pressure relief valve sealing ring should be used on reassembly, and sealing compound (Vauxhall/Opel No 90 485 251, or equivalent) will be required to coat the pump housing mating face.*

6 With the oil pump removed, proceed as follows.

7 Remove the securing screws and withdraw the rear cover **(see illustration)**. The screws may be very tight, in which case it may be necessary to use an impact driver to remove them.

8 The oil pressure relief valve components can be removed from the pump by unscrewing the cap. Withdraw the cap, sealing ring, spring and plunger **(see illustration)**.

9 Prise the oil seal from the pump using a screwdriver.

10 Check the clearance between the inner and outer gear teeth (backlash) using a feeler gauge **(see illustration)**.

11 Check the clearance between the end faces of the gears and the housing (endfloat) using a straight-edge and a feeler gauge **(see illustration)**.

12 If any of the clearances are outside the specified limits, renew the components as necessary.

13 Examine the pressure relief valve spring and plunger, and renew if any sign of damage or wear is evident.

14 Ensure that the interior of the pump body

is scrupulously clean before commencing reassembly.

15 Discard the old pressure relief valve sealing ring, then thoroughly clean the pressure relief valve components, and lubricate them with clean engine oil before refitting. Use a new sealing ring.

16 Ensure that the gears are clean, then lubricate them with clean engine oil, and refit them to the pump body, noting that the outer gear is marked with a punch dot to indicate its outer face (ie, the face nearest the pump cover) **(see illustration)**.

17 Ensure that the mating faces of the rear cover and the pump housing are clean, then coat the pump housing mating face with suitable sealing compound (Vauxhall/Opel No 90 485 251, or equivalent), and refit the rear cover. Refit and tighten the securing screws.

18 Fit a new crankshaft oil seal to the recess in the pump body, using a suitable socket or tube, so that the seal is flush with the outer face of the housing **(see illustration)**.

Refitting

19 Thoroughly clean the mating faces of the oil pump and cylinder block, then locate a new gasket on the block.

20 Wind a thin layer of tape around the end of the crankshaft, to prevent damage to the oil seal lips as the pump is refitted.

21 With a new oil seal fitted to the pump, as described previously in this Section, grease the oil seal lips, then refit the pump, ensuring

13.11 . . . and between the end faces of the gears and the housing

that the inner gear engages with the flats on the crankshaft **(see illustration)**.

22 Tighten the securing bolts to the specified torque, then carefully remove the tape from the crankshaft.

23 Refit the crankshaft speed/position sensor and its securing bracket, and tighten the securing bolt.

24 Reconnect the wiring to the oil pressure switch.

25 Refit the oil pick-up pipe and sump, as described in Section 12.

26 Refit the rear timing belt cover as described in Section 6.

13.16 Gear outer face identification mark (arrowed)

13.18 Fitting a new crankshaft oil seal to the oil pump

13.21 Refitting the oil pump (shown with engine removed from vehicle and inverted)

1 Tape wound around crankshaft
2 Flats on crankshaft engage with inner oil pump gear

11 Grease the lips of the new seal, then tap the seal into position using a suitable tube, until flush with the outer faces of the cylinder block and main bearing cap.

> **HAYNES HiNT**
> *Wind a length of tape around the end of the crankshaft to reduce the possibility of damage to the lips of the oil seal as the seal is fitted.*

12 Refit the flywheel/driveplate as described in Section 15.

14.3 Using a self-tapping screw and a pair of pliers to extract the crankshaft oil seal

14.6 Tapping a new crankshaft oil seal into position

14 Crankshaft oil seals – renewal

Timing belt end oil seal

1 Remove the crankshaft sprocket as described in Section 8.
2 Punch or drill a small hole in the centre of the now-exposed oil seal.
3 Screw in a self-tapping screw, and pull on the screw with pliers to extract the seal **(see illustration)**. Several attempts may be necessary. Be careful not to damage the sealing face of the crankshaft.
4 Clean the oil seal seat with a wooden or plastic scraper.

5 Wind a thin band of tape around the end of the crankshaft, to protect the lips of the new oil seal as it is fitted.
6 Grease the lips of the new seal, and tap it into position until it is flush with the outer face of the oil pump body, using a suitable socket or tube **(see illustration)**. Take care not to damage the seal lips during fitting.
7 Carefully remove the tape from the end of the crankshaft.
8 Refit the crankshaft sprocket, as described in Section 8.

Flywheel end oil seal

9 Remove the flywheel/driveplate as described in Section 15.
10 Proceed as described in paragraphs 2 to 4 inclusive of this Section.

15 Flywheel/driveplate – removal, inspection and refitting

Refer to Chapter 2B, Section 15.

16 Engine/gearbox mountings – inspection and renewal

Note: *References to 'engine/gearbox' in this Section may be taken to be equally applicable for vehicles with automatic transmission.*

Inspection

1 To improve access, firmly apply the handbrake, then jack up the front of the car and support it securely on axle stands (see *Jacking and vehicle support*).
2 Check the mounting blocks (rubbers) to see if they are cracked, hardened or separated from the metal at any point **(see illustration)**. Renew the mounting block if any such damage or deterioration is evident.
3 Check that all the mounting securing nuts and bolts are securely tightened, using a torque wrench to check if possible.
4 Using a large screwdriver, or a similar tool, check for wear in the mounting blocks by carefully levering against them to check for free play. Where this is not possible, enlist the aid of an assistant to move the engine/gearbox unit back-and-forth, and from side-to-side, while you observe the mountings. While some free play is to be expected, even from new components, excessive wear should be obvious. If excessive free play is found, check first to see that the securing nuts and bolts are correctly tightened, then renew any worn components as described in the following paragraphs.

Renewal

Right-hand mounting – models without air conditioning

5 Remove the air cleaner and the air inlet trunking, as described in Chapter 4B.
6 Remove the two securing screws, and lift off the plastic shield with fits over the top of the camshaft cover.

16.2 Engine/gearbox mountings

1 Right-hand mounting   *2 Rear mounting*   *3 Left-hand mounting*

7 If not already done, firmly apply the handbrake, then jack up the front of the car and support it securely on axle stands (see *Jacking and vehicle support*).
8 Attach suitable lifting tackle to the engine lifting brackets on the cylinder head, and support the weight of the engine.
9 Depressurise the cooling system by removing the expansion tank cap.

Warning: Do not attempt to remove the expansion tank filler cap while the engine is hot, as there is a high risk of scalding. If the expansion tank filler cap must be removed before the engine and radiator have fully cooled (even thought this is NOT recommended) the pressure in the cooling system must be relieved as follows. Cover the cap with a thick layer of cloth, to avoid scalding, and slowly unscrew the filler cap until a hissing sound can be heard. When the hissing has stopped, indicating that the pressure has reduced, slowly unscrew the filler cap until it can be removed; if more hissing sounds are heard, wait until they have stopped before unscrewing the cap completely. At all times, keep well away from the filler cap opening.

10 Have a container ready to collect escaping coolant, then disconnect the radiator top hose from the thermostat housing. If desired, the cooling system can be partially drained as described in Chapter 1 before disconnecting the hose.
11 Disconnect the exhaust front section from the manifold as described in Chapter 4B, and support the exhaust system using wire or string.
12 Working under the vehicle, remove the nut and bolt securing the engine mounting bracket to the mounting block.
13 Using the lifting tackle, carefully lower the right-hand side of the engine, until the engine mounting bracket is clear of the mounting block stud **(see illustration)**. On models fitted with power steering, take care not to strain the power steering pump fluid hoses when lowering the engine.
14 Unbolt the mounting block from the body.
15 Before refitting the mounting block, clean the threads of the mounting block-to-body bolts, then check that the bolts rotate freely in their threaded holes in the body. If necessary, re-cut the threaded holed in the body using a suitable tap.
16 Coat the threads of the mounting block-to-body bolts with suitable thread-locking compound, then refit the mounting block to the body, and tighten the bolts to the specified torque.
17 Carefully raise the right-hand side of the engine until the mounting block stud protrudes through the bracket sufficiently to refit the nut.
18 Refit the nut and bolt securing the engine mounting bracket to the mounting block, and tighten them to the specified torque.
19 Reconnect the front section of the exhaust system to the manifold, using a new gasket, with reference to Chapter 4B if necessary.
20 Reconnect the radiator top hose to the thermostat housing.
21 Disconnect the lifting tackle and hoist from the engine.
22 Lower the vehicle to the ground.
23 Refit the plastic shield to the camshaft cover.
24 Refit the air cleaner and the air inlet trunking.
25 Reconnect the battery negative terminal.
26 Top-up and bleed the cooling system as described in Chapter 1.

Right-hand mounting – models with air conditioning

27 Proceed as described in paragraphs 1 to 7 inclusive, but completely remove the radiator top hose.

16.13 Lower the engine until the mounting bracket is clear of the stud

28 Remove the auxiliary drivebelt as described in Chapter 1.
29 Unbolt the power steering pump from its mounting bracket, as described in Chapter 10, and move the pump to one side, leaving the fluid lines connected. Support the pump (using wire or string if necessary) to avoid straining the fluid lines.
30 Remove the right-hand front suspension tie-bar as described in Chapter 10.
31 Proceed as described in paragraphs 8 to 14 inclusive.
32 Refit the front suspension tie-bar as described in Chapter 10.
33 Refit the power steering pump to its bracket as described in Chapter 10.
34 Refit the auxiliary drivebelt as described in Chapter 1.
35 Proceed as described in paragraphs 15 to 22 inclusive, but reconnect the radiator top hose to the thermostat housing and to the radiator.

Left-hand mounting

36 Refer to Chapter 2B, Section 16.

Rear mounting

37 Refer to Chapter 2B, Section 16.

Notes

Chapter 2 Part D: 1.0 & 1.2 litre
DOHC engine removal and overhaul procedures

Contents

Degrees of difficulty

Easy, suitable for novice with little experience	**Fairly easy,** suitable for beginner with some experience	**Fairly difficult,** suitable for competent DIY mechanic	**Difficult,** suitable for experienced DIY mechanic	**Very difficult,** suitable for expert DIY or professional

Specifications

Cylinder block
Material	Cast iron
Maximum cylinder bore ovality	0.013 mm
Maximum cylinder bore taper	0.013 mm
Maximum permissible rebore oversize	0.500 mm

Cylinder bore diameters:
Standard size:
Identification mark 99	72.485 to 72.495 mm
Identification mark 00	72.495 to 72.505 mm
Identification mark 01	72.505 to 72.515 mm

0.500 mm oversize:
Identification mark 9 + 0.5	72.965 to 72.975 mm

Pistons
Piston-to-bore clearance:
New	0.020 to 0.030 mm
After rebore (oversize)	0.010 to 0.030 mm

Note: *Piston diameters – pistons carry identification marks corresponding to those listed previously for cylinder bore diameters. The appropriate piston diameter is 0.020 mm less than the corresponding bore diameter.*

Piston rings
Number of rings (per piston)	2 compression, 1 oil control

Ring end gap:
Compression	0.200 to 0.400 mm
Oil control (top and bottom sections)	0.400 to 1.400 mm
Ring gap offset (to gap of adjacent ring)*	180°

For oil control ring sections, see text (Section 17).

Cylinder head
Material	Light alloy
Maximum permissible distortion of sealing face	0.025 mm
Overall height of cylinder head (sealing surface-to-sealing surface) . . .	126.000 mm

Valve seat width:
Inlet	1.000 to 1.400 mm
Exhaust	1.400 to 1.800 mm
Valve seat angle	45°

Crankshaft and bearings

Number of main bearings:	
1.0 litre engines	5
1.2 litre engines	4
Main bearing journal diameter:	
Standard size – 1 (green)	50.004 to 50.010 mm
Standard size – 2 (brown)	50.010 to 50.017 mm
0.250 mm undersize – 1 (brown/blue)	49.754 to 49.760 mm
0.250 mm undersize – 2 (green/blue)	49.760 to 49.767 mm
0.500 mm undersize – 1 (green/white)	49.504 to 49.510 mm
0.500 mm undersize – 2 (brown/white)	49.510 to 49.517 mm
Main bearing shell colour codes (upper and lower):	
Standard – 1	Green
Standard – 2	Brown
0.250 mm undersize – 1	Brown/blue
0.250 mm undersize – 2	Green/blue
0.500 mm undersize – 1	Green/white
0.500 mm undersize – 2	Brown/white
Main bearing thrust journal width:	
Standard	23.000 to 23.252 mm
0.200 mm undersize	23.200 to 23.252 mm
0.400 mm undersize	23.400 to 23.452 mm
Big-end bearing journal diameter:	
Standard	42.971 to 42.987 mm
0.250 mm undersize (blue)	42.721 to 42.737 mm
0.500 mm undersize (white)	42.471 to 42.487 mm
Big-end bearing shell colour codes:	
Standard	None
0.250 mm undersize	Blue
0.500 mm undersize	White
Maximum main and big-end bearing journal out-of-round	0.040 mm
Main and big-end bearing running clearance	0.007 to 0.036 mm
Crankshaft endfloat	0.100 to 0.200 mm
Connecting rod endfloat	0.013 to 0.049 mm

Valves and guides

Stem diameter:	
Inlet valve:	
Standard	4.955 to 4.970 mm
0.075 mm oversize	5.030 to 5.045 mm
0.150 mm oversize	5.105 to 5.120 mm
Exhaust valve:	
Standard – 1	4.930 to 4.945 mm
Standard – 2	4.945 to 4.960 mm
0.075 mm oversize – 1	5.005 to 5.020 mm
0.075 mm oversize – 2	5.020 to 5.035 mm
0.150 mm oversize – 1	5.080 to 5.095 mm
0.150 mm oversize – 2	5.095 to 5.110 mm
Valve head diameter:	
Inlet valve	27.900 to 28.100 mm
Exhaust valve	24.900 to 25.100 mm
Maximum permissible valve stem play in guide:	
Inlet	0.018 to 0.052 mm
Exhaust	0.028 to 0.062 mm
Valve seat angle (included)	90°40'
Valve clearances	Automatic adjustment by hydraulic valve lifters
Valve guide bore:	
Standard	4.988 to 5.007 mm
0.075 mm oversize	5.063 to 5.082 mm
0.150 mm oversize	5.138 to 5.157 mm
Valve guide length	38.750 to 39.250 mm
Valve guide fitted height (above cylinder head)	11.700 to 12.000 mm

Torque wrench settings

Refer to Specifications for Chapter 2A.

1 General information

This Part of Chapter 2 includes details of engine removal and refitting, and general overhaul procedures for the cylinder head, cylinder block/crankcase, and internal engine components.

The information ranges from advice concerning preparation for an overhaul and the purchase of replacement parts, to detailed step-by-step procedures covering removal, inspection, renovation and refitting of internal engine components.

The following Sections have been compiled based on the assumption that the engine has been removed from the vehicle. For information concerning in-vehicle engine repair, as well as information on the removal and refitting of the external components necessary to facilitate overhaul, refer to Chapter 2A, and to Section 6 of this Part.

2 Engine overhaul – general information

It is not always easy to determine when, or if, an engine should be completely overhauled, as a number of factors must be considered.

High mileage is not necessarily an indication that an overhaul is needed, while low mileage does not preclude the need for an overhaul. Frequency of servicing is probably the most important consideration. An engine which has had regular and frequent oil and filter changes, as well as other required maintenance, will most likely give many thousands of miles of reliable service. Conversely, a neglected engine may require an overhaul very early in its life.

Excessive oil consumption is an indication that piston rings, valve seals and/or valve guides are in need of attention. Make sure that oil leaks are not responsible before deciding that the rings and/or guides are bad. Perform a cylinder compression check to determine the extent of the work required.

Check the oil pressure with a gauge fitted in place of the oil pressure sender, and compare it with the Specifications (Chapter 2A). If it is extremely low, the main and big-end bearings and/or the oil pump are probably worn out.

Loss of power, rough running, knocking or metallic engine noises, excessive valve gear noise and high fuel consumption may also point to the need for an overhaul, especially if they are all present at the same time. If a complete tune-up does not remedy the situation, major mechanical work is the only solution.

An engine overhaul involves restoring the internal parts to the specifications of a new engine. During an overhaul, new pistons and/or rings are fitted, and the cylinder bores are reconditioned. New main bearings and connecting rod big-end bearings are generally fitted, and if necessary, the crankshaft may be reground to restore the journals. The valves are also serviced as well, since they are usually in less-than-perfect condition at this point. While the engine is being overhauled, other components, such as the starter and alternator, can be overhauled too. The end result should be a like-new engine that will give many trouble-free miles. **Note:** *Critical cooling system components such as the hoses, drivebelts, thermostat and coolant pump MUST be renewed when an engine is overhauled. The radiator should be checked carefully to ensure that it is not clogged or leaking. Also it is a good idea to renew the oil pump whenever the engine is overhauled.*

Before beginning the engine overhaul, read through the entire procedure to familiarise yourself with the scope and requirements of the job. Overhauling an engine is not difficult if you follow all of the instructions carefully, have the necessary tools and equipment, and pay close attention to all specifications; however, it can be time-consuming. Plan on the vehicle being tied up for a minimum of two weeks, especially if parts must be taken to an engineering works for repair or reconditioning. Check on the availability of parts, and make sure that any necessary special tools and equipment are obtained in advance. Most work can be done with typical hand tools, although a number of precision measuring tools are required for inspecting parts to determine if they must be renewed. Often the engineering works will handle the inspection of parts, and offer advice concerning reconditioning and renewal. **Note:** *Always wait until the engine has been completely dismantled and all components, especially the cylinder block, have been inspected before deciding what service and repair operations must be performed by an engineering works. Since the condition of the block will be the major factor to consider when determining whether to overhaul the original engine or buy a reconditioned unit, do not purchase parts or have overhaul work done on other components until the block has been thoroughly inspected. As a general rule, time is the primary cost of an overhaul, so it does not pay to fit worn or sub-standard parts.*

As a final note, to ensure maximum life and minimum trouble from a reconditioned engine, everything must be assembled with care in a spotlessly-clean environment.

3 Engine removal – methods and precautions

If you have decided that an engine must be removed for overhaul or major repair work, several preliminary steps should be taken.

Locating a suitable place to work is extremely important. Adequate work space, along with storage space for the vehicle, will be needed. If a garage is not available, at the very least a flat, level, clean work surface is required.

Cleaning the engine compartment and engine before beginning the removal procedure will help keep tools clean and organised.

An engine hoist or A-frame will also be necessary. Make sure the equipment is rated in excess of the combined weight of the engine and transmission. Safety is of primary importance, considering the potential hazards involved in lifting the engine out of the vehicle.

If this is the first time you have removed an engine, an assistant should be available. Advice and aid from someone more experienced would also be helpful. There are many instances when one person cannot simultaneously perform all of the operations required when lifting the engine out of the vehicle.

Plan the operation ahead of time. Arrange for, or obtain, all of the tools and equipment you will need, prior to beginning the job. Some of the equipment necessary to perform engine removal and installation safely and with relative ease are (in addition to an engine hoist) a heavy-duty trolley jack, complete sets of spanners and sockets as described at the end of this manual, wooden blocks, and plenty of rags and cleaning solvent for mopping-up spilled oil, coolant and fuel. If the hoist must be hired, make sure that you arrange for it in advance, and perform all of the operations possible without it beforehand. This will save you money and time.

Plan for the vehicle to be out of use for quite a while. An engineering works will be required to perform some of the work which the do-it-yourselfer cannot accomplish without special equipment. These places often have a busy schedule, so it would be a good idea to consult them before removing the engine, in order to accurately estimate the amount of time required to rebuild or repair components that may need work.

Always be extremely careful when removing and refitting the engine. Serious injury can result from careless actions. Plan ahead, take your time, and you will find that a job of this nature, although major, can be accomplished successfully.

On all Corsa models, the engine must be removed complete with the gearbox/transmission as an assembly. There is insufficient clearance in the engine compartment to remove the engine leaving the gearbox/transmission in the vehicle. The assembly is removed by raising the front of the vehicle, and lowering the assembly from the engine compartment.

4 Engine/manual gearbox assembly – removal and refitting

Note: *Suitable equipment will be required to support the engine and gearbox during this procedure – see text.*

Removal

1 Disconnect the battery negative terminal (refer to *Disconnecting the battery* in the Reference Chapter).
2 To improve access, remove the bonnet as described in Chapter 11.
3 On right-hand drive models, remove the battery and battery tray as described in Chapter 5A.
4 Remove the air cleaner assembly as described in Chapter 4A.
5 Drain the cooling system as described in Chapter 1.
6 Drain the engine oil as described in Chapter 1.
7 Release the clips and disconnect the top hose from the radiator and thermostat housing.

HAYNES HINT *If the engine is to be removed for some time, making sketches or taking a few photographs of wire and hose runs and connections before disconnection will prove helpful when refitting.*

8 Release the clips and disconnect the bottom hose from the radiator, expansion tank and coolant pump.
9 Release the clips and disconnect the heater and expansion tank hoses from the coolant pump.
10 Release the retaining clips and disconnect the two coolant hoses from the rear of the throttle body.
11 Turn the throttle disc and disconnect the throttle cable end fitting from the disc. Release the cable grommet from its bracket on the inlet manifold.
12 Disconnect the wiring plugs at the idle speed control motor and throttle position sensor located on the throttle body.
13 Disconnect the wiring connectors at the coolant temperature sensor, camshaft position sensor and oil pressure switch. Lift the wiring harness trough from the camshaft cover and move it to one side.
14 Depressurise the fuel system as described in Chapter 4A, then disconnect the fuel feed and return hoses from the fuel rail, noting their locations to aid refitting. Be prepared for fuel spillage, and take adequate precautions. Clamp or plug the open ends of the hoses, to minimise further fuel loss.
15 Disconnect the coolant hoses from the coolant expansion tank, then undo the retaining bolts and remove the expansion tank (see illustration).

4.15 Disconnect the expansion tank coolant hoses then undo the bolts and remove the expansion tank

16 Disconnect the wiring plug from the top of the EGR valve, and the wiring connector from the adjacent temperature gauge sender.
17 Disconnect the coolant hose from the side of the EGR valve.
18 Release the DIS ignition module cover from the centre of the camshaft cover and remove it toward the transmission end of the engine.
19 Disconnect the wiring plug from the left-hand end of the DIS module.
20 Disconnect the fuel injector wiring trough wiring connector.
21 Release the wiring harness from its locating clips to gain access to the electronic control unit wiring connectors.
22 Lift up the locking levers and disconnect the engine management and main body wiring harness connectors from the electronic control unit.
23 Undo the retaining screw and release the earth cable from the electronic control unit bracket.
24 Disconnect the oxygen sensor wiring connector from the top of the transmission, and release the adjacent grey wiring connector from its support bracket (see illustration).
25 Disconnect the wiring from the reversing light switch, located at the front of the gearbox, above the mounting bracket.
26 Disconnect the hoses and wiring plug from the fuel tank vent valve.
27 Disconnect the brake servo vacuum hose connection at the inlet manifold. On 1.0 litre engines the connection is by a conventional

4.32a Disconnect the wiring from the alternator . . .

4.24 Disconnect the oxygen sensor wiring connector and release the adjacent wiring connector from its support bracket

union nut. On 1.2 litre engines a quick-release fitting is used. Depress the two tags on the side of the fitting and withdraw the fitting from the manifold pipe stub.
28 Undo the two bolts and release the wiring harness support bracket from the rear of the inlet manifold.
29 If not already done, apply the handbrake, then jack up the front of the vehicle and support securely on axle stands (see *Jacking and vehicle support*). Note that the vehicle must be raised sufficiently high (approximately 650 mm) to enable the engine/gearbox assembly to be withdrawn from under the front of the vehicle. Remove the roadwheels.
30 On 1.0 litre engines, detach the additional lower wiring harness bracket from the inlet manifold.
31 At the rear of the engine, disconnect the wiring plugs for the crankshaft speed/position sensor and knock sensor.
32 Disconnect the wiring from the alternator and the starter motor, and unbolt the earth lead from the starter motor upper mounting (see illustrations).
33 Where applicable, unscrew the securing sleeve and disconnect the speedometer cable from the top of the gearbox. Note that on certain models, the cable is in two sections, joined by a connector near the engine compartment bulkhead – in this case, it may be easier to separate the two cable sections at the connector, rather than to disconnect the cable from the gearbox.
34 On later models, disconnect the wiring

4.32b . . . and from the starter motor solenoid (arrowed)

4.40 Remove the front suspension lower arms, tie-bars and anti-roll bar as an assembly

4.60 Raise the engine/gearbox assembly into the engine compartment and reconnect the mountings

connector from the electronic speedometer sensor.

35 Undo the three nuts securing the catalytic converter flange to the exhaust manifold. Undo the two bolts securing the converter support bracket to the cylinder block baseplate and separate the converter from the manifold. Lower the exhaust system clear of the manifold and support it in this position. Recover the flange gasket.

36 On models with air conditioning, release the tension on the auxiliary drivebelt and lock the tensioner in the released position as described in the auxiliary drivebelt renewal procedures in Chapter 1. Slip the drivebelt off the pulleys.

37 On models with air conditioning, unbolt the compressor from the cylinder block, release the refrigerant lines from their brackets and support the compressor clear of the engine. **Do not** disconnect the refrigerant lines from the compressor.

38 Remove the retaining clip (where applicable), then slide the clutch cable from the release lever, pushing the release lever back towards the bulkhead if necessary, to allow the cable to be disconnected. Pull the cable support from the bracket on the gearbox casing, then move the cable to one side out of the way, taking note of its routing.

Measure the length of the threaded rod protruding through the plastic block at the release arm end of the cable. This will enable approximate pre-setting of the cable when refitting.

39 Working under the front of the vehicle, loosen the clamp nut and bolt securing the gear selector rod to the linkage, then pull the selector tube towards the engine compartment bulkhead to separate it from the linkage.

40 Remove the front suspension lower arms,

tie-bars, and anti-roll bar, as described in Chapter 10 **(see illustration)**.

41 Disconnect the inner ends of the driveshafts from the gearbox, as described in Chapter 8. There is no need to disconnect the driveshafts from the swivel hubs. Be prepared for oil spillage, and plug the openings in the gearbox to prevent dirt ingress and further oil loss. Do not allow the driveshafts to hang down under their own weight, or the joints may be damaged; support the driveshafts with wire or string.

42 Attach a suitable hoist and lifting tackle to the engine lifting brackets on the cylinder head, and support the weight of the engine.

43 Make a final check to ensure that all relevant pipes, hoses, wires, etc, have been disconnected, and that they are positioned clear of the engine and gearbox.

44 To stabilise the engine/gearbox assembly as it is removed, it is advisable to support the assembly from underneath using a jack and interposed block of wood, in addition to the engine hoist and lifting tackle.

45 Ensure that the engine/gearbox assembly is adequately supported, then proceed as follows.

46 Unscrew the through-bolt and nut securing the rear engine/gearbox mounting bracket to the mounting on the body.

47 Unscrew the nut and bolt securing the right-hand engine mounting bracket to the mounting block on the body.

48 Unbolt the left-hand engine/transmission mounting block from the body.

49 Carefully lower the engine/gearbox assembly from the engine compartment.

50 Ensure that the assembly is adequately supported using jacks, or a suitable trolley, then disconnect the engine hoist and lifting tackle, and withdraw the engine/gearbox assembly from under the front of the vehicle.

51 With the engine/gearbox assembly removed, support the assembly on suitable blocks of wood positioned on a workbench, or failing that, on a clean area of the workshop floor.

52 Clean away any external dirt using paraffin or a water-soluble solvent and a stiff brush.

53 Where applicable, unscrew the securing bolts, and remove the engine-to-gearbox blanking plate from the bellhousing.

54 Ensure that both engine and gearbox are adequately supported, then unscrew and remove the engine-to-gearbox bolts, noting the locations of the brackets which are be secured by the bolts.

55 Carefully withdraw the gearbox from the engine, ensuring that the weight of the gearbox is not allowed to hang on the input shaft while it is engaged with the clutch friction disc. Note that the gearbox locates on dowels positioned in the cylinder block.

Refitting

56 Carefully offer the gearbox to the engine until the bellhousing is located on the dowels in the cylinder block, then refit the engine-to-gearbox bolts, and tighten them to the specified torque. Make sure that the brackets secured by the bolts are correctly positioned, as noted before removal. Ensure that the weight of the gearbox is not allowed to hang on the input shaft as it is engaged with the clutch friction disc.

57 Where applicable, refit the engine-to-gearbox blanking plate to the bellhousing.

58 With the front of the vehicle raised and supported on axle stands, move the engine/gearbox assembly under the vehicle, ensuring that the assembly is adequately supported.

59 Reconnect the hoist and lifting tackle to the engine lifting brackets.

60 Raise the engine/gearbox assembly, and reconnect the left-hand engine/transmission mounting block to the body **(see illustration)**. Reconnect the right-hand engine mounting bracket to the mounting block, then refit the rear engine/gearbox mounting bracket through-bolt and nut. Tighten all mounting nuts and bolts to the specified torque.

61 Disconnect the hoist and lifting tackle from the engine lifting brackets.
62 Reconnect the inner ends of the driveshafts to the gearbox as described in Chapter 8.
63 Refit the front suspension anti-roll bar, tie-bars and lower arms, as described in Chapter 10.
64 Reconnect the exhaust front section to the manifold as described in Chapter 4A.
65 Reconnect the wiring to the alternator and the starter motor, and reconnect the earth strap to the starter motor upper mounting.
66 Reconnect the gear selector rod to the gear linkage, and adjust the linkage as described in Chapter 7A.
67 Reconnect and if necessary adjust the clutch cable, as described in Chapter 6.
68 On models with air conditioning, refit the compressor to the cylinder block and tighten the mounting bolts to the specified torque. Refit the refrigerant lines to their relevant clips or brackets.
69 Refit the auxiliary drivebelt as described in Chapter 1.
70 Reconnect the speedometer cable to the gearbox, or reconnect the speedometer cable connector (as applicable). On later models, reconnect the wiring connector to the electronic speedometer sensor.
71 Reconnect the wiring plugs for the crankshaft speed/position sensor and knock sensor.
72 Refit the wiring harness support brackets to the rear of the inlet manifold.
73 Refit the roadwheels, and lower the vehicle to the ground.
74 Reconnect all relevant wiring to the engine and associated components using a reverse of the removal sequence, ensuring that the wiring is routed and secured as noted before removal.
75 Reconnect the fuel lines, ensuring that they are connected to their correct locations, and securely tighten the unions.
76 Reconnect the coolant hoses to the coolant pump, thermostat, EGR valve, throttle body and radiator.
77 Reconnect the coolant hoses to the expansion tank, and refit the expansion tank to the bulkhead.
78 Reconnect the hoses and the wiring plug to the fuel tank vent valve.
79 Reconnect the brake servo vacuum hose to the inlet manifold.
80 Reconnect the throttle cable to the throttle linkage, and if necessary adjust the cable, as described in Chapter 4A.
81 Refit the radiator cooling fan and shroud assembly as described in Chapter 3.
82 On right-hand drive models, refit the battery tray and battery.
83 Refit the air cleaner assembly as described in Chapter 4A.
84 Refill the engine with oil, as described in Chapter 1.
85 Refill and bleed the cooling system as described in Chapter 1.

86 Check and if necessary top-up the gearbox oil level as described in Chapter 1.
87 Make a final check to ensure that all relevant hoses, pipes and wires have been correctly reconnected.
88 Refit the bonnet as described in Chapter 11.
89 Reconnect the battery positive lead, followed by the negative lead.

5 Engine/automatic transmission assembly – removal and refitting

Note: *Suitable equipment will be required to support the engine and transmission during this procedure – see text. New torque converter-to-driveplate bolts must be used on refitting.*

Removal

1 Disconnect the battery negative terminal (refer to *Disconnecting the battery* in the Reference Chapter).
2 To improve access, remove the bonnet as described in Chapter 11.
3 On right-hand drive models, remove the battery and battery tray as described in Chapter 5A.
4 Remove the air cleaner assembly as described in Chapter 4A.
5 Drain the cooling system as described in Chapter 1.
6 Drain the engine oil as described in Chapter 1.
7 Release the clips and disconnect the top hose from the radiator and thermostat housing.

 HAYNES HiNT *If the engine is to be removed for some time, making sketches or taking a few photographs of wire and hose runs and connections before disconnection will prove helpful when refitting.*

8 Release the clips and disconnect the bottom hose from the radiator, expansion tank and coolant pump.
9 Release the clips and disconnect the heater and expansion tank hoses from the coolant pump.
10 Release the retaining clips and disconnect the two coolant hoses from the rear of the throttle body.
11 Turn the throttle disc and disconnect the throttle cable end fitting from the disc. Release the cable grommet from its bracket on the inlet manifold.
12 Disconnect the wiring plugs at the idle speed control motor and throttle position sensor located on the throttle body.
13 Disconnect the wiring connectors at the coolant temperature sensor, camshaft position sensor and oil pressure switch. Lift

the wiring harness trough from the camshaft cover and move it to one side.
14 Depressurise the fuel system as described in Chapter 4A, then disconnect the fuel feed and return hoses from the fuel rail, noting their locations to aid refitting. Be prepared for fuel spillage, and take adequate precautions. Clamp or plug the open ends of the hoses, to minimise further fuel loss.
15 Disconnect the coolant hoses from the coolant expansion tank, then undo the retaining bolts and remove the expansion tank.
16 Disconnect the wiring plug from the top of the EGR valve, and the wiring connector from the adjacent temperature gauge sender.
17 Disconnect the coolant hose from the side of the EGR valve.
18 Release the DIS ignition module cover from the centre of the camshaft cover and remove it toward the transmission end of the engine.
19 Disconnect the wiring plug from the left-hand end of the DIS module.
20 Disconnect the fuel injector wiring trough wiring connector.
21 Release the wiring harness from its locating clips to gain access to the electronic control unit wiring connectors.
22 Lift up the locking levers and disconnect the engine management and main body wiring harness connectors from the electronic control unit.
23 Undo the retaining screw and release the earth cable from the electronic control unit bracket.
24 Disconnect the oxygen sensor wiring connector from the top of the transmission, and release the adjacent grey wiring connector from its support bracket.
25 Carefully prise the selector cable end fitting from the ball stud on the selector lever position switch actuating lever.
26 Using a screwdriver, extract the retaining clip securing the selector cable trunion to the bracket on the transmission. Depress the two locking tags on the side of the trunion and release the cable from the bracket.
27 Disconnect the vent hose from the front of the transmission.
28 Disconnect the transmission wiring harness plugs, and unbolt the wiring harness brackets from the transmission.
29 Disconnect the hoses and wiring plug from the fuel tank vent valve.
30 Disconnect the brake servo vacuum hose quick-release fitting by depressing the two tags and withdrawing the fitting from the manifold pipe stub.
31 Undo the two bolts and release the wiring harness support bracket from the rear of the inlet manifold.
32 If not already done, apply the handbrake, then jack up the front of the vehicle and support securely on axle stands (see *Jacking and vehicle support*). Note that the vehicle must be raised sufficiently high (approximately 650 mm) to enable the

engine/transmission assembly to be withdrawn from under the front of the vehicle. Remove the roadwheels.

33 At the rear of the engine, disconnect the wiring plugs for the crankshaft speed/position sensor and knock sensor.

34 Disconnect the wiring from the alternator and the starter motor, and unbolt the earth lead from the starter motor upper mounting.

35 Disconnect the wiring connector from the electronic speedometer vehicle speed sensor.

36 Undo the three nuts securing the catalytic converter flange to the exhaust manifold. Undo the two bolts securing the converter support bracket to the cylinder block baseplate and separate the converter from the manifold. Lower the exhaust system clear of the manifold and support it in this position. Recover the flange gasket.

37 On models with air conditioning, release the tension on the auxiliary drivebelt and lock the tensioner in the released position as described in the auxiliary drivebelt renewal procedures in Chapter 1. Slip the drivebelt off the pulleys.

38 On models with air conditioning, unbolt the compressor from the cylinder block, release the refrigerant lines from their brackets and support the compressor clear of the engine. **Do not** disconnect the refrigerant lines from the compressor.

39 Remove the front suspension lower arms, tie-bars, and anti-roll bar, as described in Chapter 10.

40 Disconnect the inner ends of the driveshafts from the transmission, as described in Chapter 8. There is no need to disconnect the driveshafts from the swivel hubs. Be prepared for oil spillage, and plug the openings in the transmission to prevent dirt ingress and further oil loss. Do not allow the driveshafts to hang down under their own weight, or the joints may be damaged; support the driveshafts with wire or string.

41 Place a suitable container beneath the transmission fluid cooler hose connections at the transmission. Clamp the transmission fluid cooler hoses, then disconnect them from the transmission, noting their locations. Be prepared for fluid spillage, and plug the open ends of the hoses and transmission to minimise fluid loss and prevent dirt ingress.

42 Attach a suitable hoist and lifting tackle to the engine lifting brackets on the cylinder head, and support the weight of the engine.

43 Make a final check to ensure that all relevant pipes, hoses, wires, etc, have been disconnected, and that they are positioned clear of the engine and transmission.

44 To stabilise the engine/transmission assembly as it is removed, it is advisable to support the assembly from underneath using a jack and interposed block of wood, in addition to the engine hoist and lifting tackle.

45 Ensure that the engine/transmission assembly is adequately supported, then proceed as follows.

46 Unscrew the through-bolt and nut securing the rear engine/transmission mounting bracket to the mounting on the body.

47 Unscrew the nut and bolt securing the right-hand engine mounting bracket to the mounting block on the body.

48 Unbolt the left-hand engine/transmission mounting block from the body.

49 Carefully lower the engine/transmission assembly from the engine compartment.

50 Ensure that the assembly is adequately supported using jacks, or a suitable trolley, then disconnect the engine hoist and lifting tackle, and withdraw the engine/transmission assembly from under the front of the vehicle.

51 With the engine/transmission assembly removed, support the assembly on suitable blocks of wood positioned on a workbench, or failing that, on a clean area of the workshop floor.

52 Clean away any external dirt using paraffin or a water-soluble solvent and a stiff brush.

53 Pull out the rubber access plug from the bellhousing.

54 If the original torque converter and driveplate are to be refitted, make alignment marks between the torque converter and the driveplate, to ensure that the components are reassembled in their original positions.

55 Working through the bottom of the bellhousing, unscrew the three torque converter-to-driveplate bolts. It will be necessary to turn the engine, using a suitable spanner or socket on the crankshaft pulley bolt, to gain access to each bolt in turn through the aperture. Turning the engine will be much easier if the spark plugs are removed first (see Chapter 1). Use a screwdriver or a similar tool to jam the driveplate ring gear, preventing the driveplate from rotating as the bolts are loosened. Discard the bolts.

56 Ensure that the engine and transmission are adequately supported, then unscrew and remove the engine-to-transmission bolts (note the locations of the brackets secured by the bolts). Carefully pull the engine and transmission apart, ensuring that the torque converter is held firmly in place in the transmission casing as the engine and transmission are separated, otherwise it could fall out, resulting in fluid spillage and possible damage. Retain the torque converter while the transmission is removed by bolting a strip of metal across the transmission bellhousing end face.

Refitting

57 If the original torque converter is being refitted, commence refitting by re-cutting the torque converter-to-driveplate bolt threads in the torque converter, using an M10 x 1.25 mm tap.

58 If a new transmission is being fitted, the manufacturers recommend that the radiator fluid cooler passages are flushed clean before the new transmission is installed. Ideally, compressed air should be used (in which case, ensure that adequate safety precautions are taken). Alternatively, the cooler can be flushed with clean automatic transmission fluid, until all the old fluid has been expelled, and fresh fluid runs clear from the cooler outlet.

59 Carefully offer the transmission to the engine until the bellhousing is located on the dowels in the cylinder block (ensure that the torque converter is held firmly in place in the transmission casing as the engine and transmission are connected), then refit the engine-to-transmission bolts, and tighten them to the specified torque. Make sure that any brackets secured by the bolts are correctly positioned, as noted before removal.

60 If the original torque converter and driveplate are being refitted, carefully turn the crankshaft to align the marks made before removal, before refitting the torque converter-to-driveplate bolts.

61 Fit **new** torque converter-to-driveplate bolts, and tighten them to the specified torque. Turn the crankshaft for access to each bolt in turn, and prevent the driveplate from turning as during removal.

62 Refit the rubber access plug from the bellhousing.

63 With the front of the vehicle raised and supported on axle stands, move the engine/transmission assembly under the vehicle, ensuring that the assembly is adequately supported.

64 Reconnect the hoist and lifting tackle to the engine lifting brackets.

65 Raise the engine/transmission assembly, and reconnect the left-hand engine/transmission mounting block to the body. Reconnect the right-hand engine mounting bracket to the mounting block, then refit the rear engine/transmission mounting bracket through-bolt and nut. Tighten all mounting nuts and bolts to the specified torque.

66 Disconnect the hoist and lifting tackle from the engine lifting brackets.

67 Reconnect the fluid cooler hoses to the transmission. Ensure that the hoses are reconnected to their correct locations, as noted before removal.

68 Reconnect the inner ends of the driveshafts to the transmission as described in Chapter 8.

69 Refit the front suspension anti-roll bar, tie-bars and lower arms, as described in Chapter 10.

70 Reconnect the exhaust front section to the manifold as described in Chapter 4A.

71 Reconnect the wiring to the alternator and the starter motor, and reconnect the earth strap to the starter motor upper mounting.

72 On models with air conditioning, refit the compressor to the cylinder block and tighten the mounting bolts to the specified torque. Refit the refrigerant lines to their relevant clips or brackets.

73 Refit the auxiliary drivebelt as described in Chapter 1.

74 Reconnect the wiring connector to the electronic speedometer vehicle speed sensor.

75 Reconnect the wiring plugs for the crankshaft speed/position sensor and knock sensor.

76 Refit the wiring harness support brackets to the rear of the inlet manifold.

77 Refit the roadwheels, and lower the vehicle to the ground.

78 Reconnect all relevant wiring to the engine and associated components using a reverse of the removal sequence, ensuring that the wiring is routed and secured as noted before removal.

79 Reconnect the transmission wiring harness plugs, and secure the wiring harness brackets to the transmission.

80 Reconnect the transmission vent hose.

81 Refit the selector cable trunion and refit the retaining clip securing the trunion to the bracket on the transmission. Refit the selector cable end fitting to the ball stud on the selector lever position switch actuating lever

82 Reconnect the fuel lines, ensuring that they are connected to their correct locations, and securely tighten the unions.

83 Reconnect the coolant hoses to the coolant pump, thermostat, EGR valve, throttle body and radiator.

84 Reconnect the coolant hoses to the expansion tank, and refit the expansion tank to the bulkhead.

85 Reconnect the hoses and the wiring plug to the fuel tank vent valve.

86 Reconnect the brake servo vacuum hose to the inlet manifold.

87 Reconnect the throttle cable to the throttle linkage, and if necessary adjust the cable, as described in Chapter 4A.

88 On right-hand drive models, refit the battery tray and battery.

89 Refit the air cleaner assembly as described in Chapter 4A.

90 Refill the engine with oil, as described in Chapter 1.

91 Refill and bleed the cooling system as described in Chapter 1.

92 Check and if necessary top-up the transmission oil level as described in Chapter 1.

93 Make a final check to ensure that all relevant hoses, pipes and wires have been correctly reconnected.

94 Refit the bonnet as described in Chapter 11.

95 Reconnect the battery positive lead, followed by the negative lead.

6 Engine overhaul – dismantling sequence

1 It is far easier to dismantle and work on the engine if it is mounted on a portable engine stand. These stands can often be hired from a tool hire shop. Depending on the type of stand used, the flywheel/driveplate may have

to be removed from the engine to allow the engine stand bolts to be tightened into the end of the cylinder block.

2 If a stand is not available, it is possible to dismantle the engine while supported on blocks on a sturdy workbench or on the floor. Be extra-careful not to tip or drop the engine when working without a stand.

3 Before starting the overhaul procedure, the external ancillary components must be removed (this is the case even if a reconditioned engine is to be fitted, in which case, the components from the old engine must be transferred to the reconditioned unit). These components include the following:

a) *Alternator and mounting bracket (see Chapter 5A).*
b) *Auxiliary drivebelt tensioner (see Chapter 1)*
c) *Starter motor (see Chapter 5A).*
d) *Coolant hoses.*
e) *Inlet and exhaust manifolds (see Chapter 4A).*
f) *Oil filter housing (see Chapter 2A).*
g) *DIS module and spark plugs (see Chapters 1 and 5B).*
h) *Engine mounting brackets (where applicable) (see Chapter 2A).*
i) *Oil pressure switch (see Chapter 5A).*
j) *Engine lifting brackets.*
k) *Crankshaft speed/position sensor (see Chapter 4A).*
l) *Camshaft position sensor (see Chapter 4A).*
m) *Coolant temperature sensor (see Chapter 4A).*
n) *Knock sensor (see Chapter 5B).*
o) *Coolant temperature gauge sender (see Chapter 3).*
p) *EGR valve housing (see Chapter 4C).*
q) *Wiring harnesses.*
r) *Dipstick.*
s) *Coolant pump and thermostat (see Chapter 3).*

Note: *When removing the ancillary components from the engine, pay close attention to details which may be helpful or important during refitting. Note the fitted position of gaskets, seals, spacers, washers, bolts, brackets and other relevant items.*

4 If a 'short' engine is being obtained (which consists of the cylinder block, crankshaft, pistons and connecting rods all assembled as a unit), then the cylinder head, sump, timing chain, timing cover, and possibly other components will have to be removed from the old unit and fitted to the new unit.

5 If a complete overhaul is being planned, the engine can be dismantled using the following sequence.

a) *Inlet and exhaust manifolds (see Chapter 4A).*
b) *Timing cover, timing chain, sprockets and tensioner (see Chapter 2A).*
c) *Cylinder head, camshafts, rocker arms and tappets (see Chapter 2A).*
d) *Flywheel/driveplate (see Chapter 2A).*
e) *Sump (see Chapter 2A).*

f) *Piston/connecting rod assemblies (see Section 10).*
g) *Crankshaft (see Section 11).*

6 Before beginning the dismantling and overhaul procedures, make sure that all the correct tools have been obtained. Refer to the preliminary Sections of this manual for further information.

7 Cylinder head – dismantling

Note: *New and reconditioned cylinder heads are available from the manufacturers, and from engine overhaul specialists. Due to the fact that some specialist tools are required for the dismantling and inspection procedures, and new components may not be readily available, it may be more practical and economical for the home mechanic to purchase a reconditioned head rather than to dismantle, inspect and recondition the original head. A valve spring compressor tool will be required for this operation.*

1 With the cylinder head removed as described in Chapter 2A, clean away all external dirt, and remove the following components, if not already done:

a) *Manifolds (see Chapter 4A).*
b) *Spark plugs (see Chapter 1).*
c) *Timing chain tensioner (see Chapter 2A).*
d) *Camshafts, rocker arms and tappets (see Chapter 2A).*
e) *EGR valve housing (see Chapter 4C).*
f) *Oil pressure switch (see Chapter 5A).*
g) *Engine lifting brackets.*

2 To remove a valve, fit a valve spring compressor tool. Ensure that the arms of the compressor tool are securely positioned on the head of the valve and the spring cap **(see illustration)**. The valves deeply-recessed, and a suitable extension piece may be required for the spring compressor.

3 Compress the valve spring to relieve the pressure of the spring cap acting on the collets.

7.2 Fit a valve spring compressor tool, ensuring that the arms of the compressor are securely positioned on the valve head and spring cap

HAYNES HiNT *If the spring cap sticks to the valve stem, support the compressor tool, and give the end a light tap with a soft-faced mallet to help free the spring cap.*

4 Extract the two split collets by hooking them out using a small screwdriver, then slowly release the compressor tool **(see illustration)**.

5 Remove the valve spring cap and the spring, then withdraw the valve through the combustion chamber. Remove the valve stem oil seal (using long-nosed pliers if necessary), and the spring seat **(see illustrations)**.

6 Repeat the procedure for the remaining valves, keeping all components in strict order so that they can be refitted in their original positions, unless all the components are to be renewed. If the components are to be kept and used again, place each valve assembly in a labelled polythene bag or a similar small container **(see illustration)**. Note that as with cylinder numbering, the valves are normally numbered from the timing chain end of the engine. Make sure that the valve components are identified as inlet and exhaust, as well as numbered.

8 Cylinder head and valve components – cleaning and inspection

1 Thorough cleaning of the cylinder head and valve components, followed by a detailed inspection, will enable a decision to be made on whether further work is necessary before reassembling the components.

Cleaning

2 Scrape away all traces of old gasket material and sealing compound from the cylinder head surfaces. Take care not to damage the cylinder head surfaces, as the head is made of light alloy.

3 Scrape away the carbon from the combustion chambers and ports, then wash the cylinder head thoroughly with paraffin or a suitable solvent.

4 Scrape off any heavy carbon deposits that may have formed on the valves, then use a power-operated wire brush to remove deposits from the valve heads and stems.

Inspection

Note: *Be sure to perform all the following inspection procedures before concluding that the services of a machine shop or engine overhaul specialist are required. Make a list of all items that require attention.*

Cylinder head

5 Inspect the head very carefully for cracks, evidence of coolant leakage, and other

7.4 Compress the valve spring and hook out the split collets using a small screwdriver

7.5a Remove the valve spring cap . . .

7.5b . . . spring and valve . . .

7.5c . . . then remove the valve stem oil seal . . .

7.5d . . . and spring seat

7.6 Place each valve assembly in a labelled polythene bag or similar container

damage. If cracks are found, a new cylinder head should be obtained.

6 Use a straight-edge and feeler blade to check that the cylinder head surface is not distorted. If the specified distortion limit is exceeded, the cylinder head must be renewed, as machining is not possible.

7 Examine the valve seats in each of the combustion chambers. If the seats are severely pitted, cracked or burned, then they will need to be re-cut by an engine overhaul specialist. If only slight pitting is evident, this can be removed by grinding the valve heads and seats together with coarse, then fine, grinding paste, as described later in this Section.

8 If the valve guides are worn, indicated by a side-to-side motion of the valve, oversize valve guides are available, and valves with

oversize stems can be fitted. This work is best carried out by an engine overhaul specialist. A dial gauge may be used to determine whether the amount of side play of a valve exceeds the specified maximum.

9 Check the hydraulic tappet bores in the cylinder head for wear. If excessive wear is evident, the cylinder head must be renewed. Also check the tappet oil holes in the cylinder head for obstructions.

Valves

10 Examine the head of each valve for pitting, burning, cracks and general wear, and check the valve stem for scoring and wear ridges. Rotate the valve, and check for any obvious indication that it is bent. Look for pitting and excessive wear on the end of each valve stem. If the valve appears satisfactory at

8.10 Measuring a valve stem diameter

this stage, measure the valve stem diameter at several points using a micrometer **(see illustration)**. Any significant difference in the readings obtained indicates wear of the valve stem. Should any of these conditions be apparent, the valve(s) must be renewed. If the valves are in satisfactory condition, they should be ground (lapped) onto their respective seats to ensure a smooth gas-tight seal.

11 Valve grinding is carried out as follows. Place the cylinder head upside-down on a bench, with a block of wood at each end to give clearance for the valve stems.

 HAYNES HINT *A light spring placed under the valve head will greatly ease the grinding operation.*

12 Smear a trace of coarse carborundum paste on the seat face in the cylinder head, and press a suction grinding tool onto the relevant valve head. With a semi-rotary action, grind the valve head to its seat, lifting the valve occasionally to redistribute the grinding paste. When a dull, matt, even surface is produced on the faces of both the valve seat and the valve, wipe off the paste and repeat the process with fine carborundum paste. When a smooth unbroken ring of light grey matt finish is produced on both the valve and seat faces, the grinding operation is complete. Carefully clean away every trace of grinding paste, taking great care to leave none in the ports or in the valve guides. Clean the valves

and valve seats with a paraffin-soaked rag, then with a clean rag, and finally, if an air line is available, blow the valves, valve guides and cylinder head ports clean.

Valve springs

13 Check that all the valve springs are intact. If any one is broken, all should be renewed.

14 If possible, check the free height of the springs against new ones, then stand each spring on a flat surface and check it for squareness. If a spring is found to be too short, or damaged in any way, renew all the springs as a set. Springs suffer from fatigue, and it is a good idea to renew them even if they look serviceable.

Rocker arm components

15 Check the rocker arm thrust faces (the areas that contact the tappets and valve stems) for pits, wear, score-marks or any indication that the surface-hardening has worn through. Check the rocker arm camshaft roller in the same manner. Renew any rocker arms which appear suspect.

Hydraulic tappets

16 Proceed as described in paragraph 9.

17 Inspect the tappets for obvious signs of wear on the contact faces, and check the oil holes for obstructions, particularly for oil sludge. If excessive wear is evident, or if any tappet has been noisy in operation, all the tappets must be renewed as a set.

9 Cylinder head – reassembly

Note: New valve stem oil seals should be used on reassembly. A valve spring compressor tool will be required for this operation.

1 With all the components cleaned, starting at one end of the cylinder head, fit the valve components as follows.

2 Insert the appropriate valve into its guide (if new valves are being fitted, insert each valve into the location to which it has been ground), ensuring that the valve stem is well-lubricated with clean engine oil **(see illustration)**. If the original components are being refitted, all

components must be refitted in their original positions.

3 Fit the spring seat.

4 New valve stem oil seals may be supplied with a fitting sleeve, which fits over the collet groove in the valve stem, to prevent damage to the oil seal as it is slid down the valve stem. If no sleeve is supplied, wind a short length of tape round the top of the valve stem to cover the collet groove.

5 Lubricate the valve stem oil seal with clean engine oil, then push the oil seal down the valve stem using a suitable tube or socket, until the seal is fully engaged with the spring seat **(see illustration)**. Remove the fitting sleeve or the tape, as applicable, from the valve stem.

6 Fit the valve spring and the spring cap.

7 Fit the spring compressor tool, and compress the valve spring until the spring cap passes beyond the collet groove in the valve stem **(see illustration)**.

8 Refit the split collets to the groove in the valve stem, with the narrow ends nearest the spring.

 HAYNES HINT *Apply a little grease to the split collets, then fit the split collets into the groove. The grease should hold the collets in the groove.*

9 Slowly release the compressor tool, ensuring that the collets are not dislodged from the groove. When the compressor is fully released, give the top of the valve assembly a tap with a soft-faced mallet to settle the components.

10 Repeat the procedure for the remaining valves, ensuring that if the original components are being used, they are all refitted in their original positions.

11 Refit the following components as applicable (if desired, these components can be refitted after refitting the cylinder head).

a) *Engine lifting brackets.*
b) *Oil pressure switch (see Chapter 5A).*
c) *EGR valve housing (see Chapter 4C).*
d) *Camshafts, rocker arms and tappets (see Chapter 2A).*
e) *Timing chain tensioner (see Chapter 2A).*
f) *Spark plugs (see Chapter 1).*
g) *Manifolds (see Chapter 4A).*

9.2 Insert the appropriate valve into its guide ensuring that the valve stem is well-lubricated

9.5 Push the oil seal into position using a suitable tube or socket

9.7 Compress the valve spring until the spring cap passes beyond the collet groove in the valve stem then refit the collets

10.3 Undo the bolts and remove the oil baffle plate from the cylinder block baseplate

10.5 Unscrew the big-end cap bolts from the first connecting rod, and remove the cap

10.7 Push the piston/rod assembly up and out of the top of the cylinder bore

10 Piston/connecting rod assemblies – removal

Note: *The mating faces of the connecting rods and the big-end bearing caps are 'rough' (not machined), which ensures perfect mating of each individual rod and bearing cap. When the components have been removed from the engine, extreme care should be taken not to damage the mating surfaces – eg, do not rest the bearing caps on the mating faces. Ensure that each bearing cap is kept together with its respective rod, to prevent any possibility of the components being refitted incorrectly. Note that new big-end cap retaining bolts will be required for reassembly.*

1 Remove the cylinder head as described in Chapter 2A.
2 Remove the sump and oil pick-up pipe, as described in Chapter 2A.
3 Undo the retaining bolts and remove the oil baffle plate from the cylinder block baseplate **(see illustration)**.
4 If the connecting rods and big-end caps are not marked to indicate their positions in the cylinder block (ie, marked with cylinder numbers), suitably mark both the rod and cap with quick-drying paint or similar. Note to which side of the engine the marks face and accurately record this also. There may not be any other way of identifying which way round the cap fits on the rod, when refitting.
5 Unscrew the big-end cap bolts from the

first connecting rod, and remove the cap **(see illustration)**. If the bearing shells are to be re-used, tape the cap and the shell together.
6 Check the top of the cylinder bore for a wear ridge. If evident, carefully scrape it away with a ridge reamer tool, otherwise the piston rings may jam against the ridge as the piston is pushed out of the block.
7 Place the wooden handle of a hammer against the bottom of the connecting rod, and push the piston/rod assembly up and out of the cylinder bore **(see illustration)**. Recover the bearing shell, and tape it to the connecting rod if it is to be re-used.
8 Remove the remaining three assemblies in a similar way. Rotate the crankshaft as necessary to bring the big-end bolts to the most accessible position.

11 Crankshaft – removal

Note: *New cylinder block baseplate retaining bolts will be required for refitting.*

1 Remove the flywheel/driveplate as described in Chapter 2A.
2 Remove the pistons and connecting rods, as described in Section 10.
3 Invert the engine so that the crankshaft is uppermost.
4 Before removing the crankshaft, check the endfloat using a dial gauge in contact with the end of the crankshaft. Push the crankshaft fully one way, and then zero the gauge. Push

the crankshaft fully the other way, and check the endfloat **(see illustration)**. The result should be compared with the specified limit, and will give an indication as to the size of the main bearing shell thrust journal width which will be required for reassembly.
5 Working in a diagonal sequence, progressively slacken the outer (M6) bolts securing the cylinder block baseplate to the cylinder block.
6 When all the outer bolts have been slackened, repeat the procedure on the inner (M8) retaining bolts.
7 Remove all the bolts and lift the cylinder block baseplate off the cylinder block **(see illustration)**. If the baseplate is initially tight to remove, carefully tap it free using a soft-faced mallet.
8 As the baseplate is withdrawn check that the lower main bearing shells come away with the baseplate. If they remain on the crankshaft journals, lift them off and refit them to their respective locations in the baseplate.
9 Lift the crankshaft from the cylinder block and remove the crankshaft oil seal.
10 Extract the upper bearing shells, and identify them for position if they are to be re-used.

12 Cylinder block and baseplate – cleaning and inspection

Cleaning

1 For complete cleaning, remove all external components (senders, sensors, brackets, etc) from the cylinder block.
2 Scrape all traces of gasket and/or sealant from the cylinder block and cylinder block baseplate, taking particular care not to damage the cylinder head and sump mating faces.
3 Remove all oil gallery plugs, where fitted. The plugs are usually very tight – they may have to be drilled out and the holes re-tapped. Use new plugs when the engine is reassembled.
4 If the block and baseplate are extremely dirty, they should both be steam-cleaned.

11.4 Using a dial gauge to check the crankshaft endfloat

11.7 Lift the cylinder block baseplate off the cylinder block

5 If the components have been steam-cleaned, clean all oil holes and oil galleries one more time on completion. Flush all internal passages with warm water until the water runs clear. Dry the block and baseplate thoroughly, and wipe all machined surfaces with a light oil. If you have access to compressed air, use it to speed the drying process, and to blow out all the oil holes and galleries.

 Warning: Wear eye protection when using compressed air.

6 If the block and baseplate are relatively clean, an adequate cleaning job can be achieved with hot soapy water and a stiff brush. Take plenty of time, and do a thorough job. Regardless of the cleaning method used, be sure to clean all oil holes and galleries very thoroughly, dry everything completely, and coat all cast-iron machined surfaces with light oil.

7 The threaded holes in the cylinder block and baseplate must be clean, to ensure accurate torque readings when tightening fixings during reassembly. Run the correct-size tap (which can be determined from the size of the relevant bolt) into each of the holes to remove rust, corrosion, thread sealant or other contamination, and to restore damaged threads. If possible, use compressed air to clear the holes of debris produced by this operation. Do not forget to clean the threads of all bolts and nuts which are to be re-used, as well.

8 Where applicable, apply suitable sealant to the new oil gallery plugs, and insert them into the relevant holes in the cylinder block. Tighten the plugs securely.

9 If the engine is to be left dismantled for some time, refit the baseplate, tighten the bolts finger-tight, and cover the cylinder block with a large plastic bag to keep it clean and prevent corrosion.

Inspection

10 Visually check the block for cracks, rust and corrosion. Look for stripped threads in the threaded holes (it may be possible to re-cut stripped threads using a suitable tap). If there has been any history of internal coolant leakage, it may be worthwhile asking an engine overhaul specialist to check the block using special equipment. If defects are found, have the block repaired if possible, otherwise a new block may be the only option.

11 Examine the cylinder bores for taper, ovality, scoring and scratches. Start by carefully examining the top of the cylinder bores. If they are at all worn, a very slight ridge will be found on the thrust side. This marks the top of the piston ring travel.

12 Measure the bore diameter of each cylinder at the top (just under the wear ridge), centre and bottom of the cylinder bore, parallel to the crankshaft axis.

13 Next, measure the bore diameter at the same three locations, at right-angles to the crankshaft axis. Compare the results with the figures given in the Specifications.

14 Repeat the procedure for the remaining cylinders.

15 If the cylinder wear exceeds the permitted tolerances, or if the cylinder walls are badly scored or scuffed, then the cylinders will have to be rebored by a suitably-qualified specialist, and new oversize pistons will have to be fitted. In this case, note the following points:

a) *Pistons and cylinder bores are closely matched in production. The actual diameter of the piston is indicated by numbers on its crown; the same numbers on the crankcase indicate the cylinder bore diameter.*

b) *After reboring has taken place, the cylinder bores should be measured accurately, and oversize pistons selected from the grades available to give the specified piston-to-bore clearance.*

c) *For grading purposes, the piston diameter is measured across the bottom of the skirt.*

16 If the bore wear is marginal, and within the specified tolerances, new special piston rings can be fitted to offset the wear.

17 If this is the case, the bores should be honed in order to allow the new rings to bed in correctly and provide the best possible seal. An engine overhaul specialist will be able to carry out this work at moderate cost, if required.

13 Piston/connecting rod assemblies – inspection

1 Before the inspection process can begin, the piston/connecting rod assemblies must be cleaned, and the original piston rings removed from the pistons.

2 Carefully expand the old rings over the top of the pistons. The use of two or three old feeler gauges will be helpful in preventing the rings dropping into empty grooves **(see illustration)**. Take care, however, as piston rings are sharp.

3 Scrape away all traces of carbon from the top of the piston. A hand-held wire brush, or a piece of fine emery cloth, can be used once

13.2 Using a feeler gauge to aid removal of a piston ring

the majority of the deposits have been scraped away.

4 Remove the carbon from the ring grooves in the piston, using an old ring. Break the ring in half to do this (be careful not to cut your fingers – piston rings are sharp). Be very careful to remove only the carbon deposits – do not remove any metal, and do not nick or scratch the sides of the ring grooves.

5 Once the deposits have been removed, clean the piston/connecting rod assembly with paraffin or a suitable solvent, and dry thoroughly. Make sure that the oil return holes in the ring grooves are clear.

6 If the pistons and cylinder bores are not damaged or worn excessively, and if the cylinder block does not need to be rebored, the original pistons can be refitted. Normal piston wear shows up as even vertical wear on the piston thrust surfaces, and slight looseness of the top ring in its groove. New piston rings should always be used when the engine is reassembled.

7 Carefully inspect each piston for cracks around the skirt, at the gudgeon pin bosses, and at the piston ring lands (between the ring grooves).

8 Look for scoring and scuffing on the thrust faces of the piston skirt, holes in the piston crown, and burned areas at the edge of the crown. If the skirt is scored or scuffed, the engine may have been suffering from overheating, and/or abnormal combustion ('pinking') which caused excessively-high operating temperatures. The cooling and lubrication systems should be checked thoroughly. A hole in the piston crown, or burned areas at the edge of the piston crown indicates that abnormal combustion (pre-ignition, 'pinking', knocking or detonation) has been occurring. If any of the above problems exist, the causes must be investigated and corrected, or the damage will occur again. The causes may include leaks in the intake air tracts, incorrect fuel/air mixture, or an incorrect grade of spark plug.

9 Corrosion of the piston, in the form of pitting, indicates that coolant has been leaking into the combustion chamber and/or the crankcase. Again, the cause must be corrected, or the problem may persist in the rebuilt engine.

10 Check the piston-to-bore clearance by measuring the cylinder bore (see Section 12) and the piston diameter. Measure the piston across the bottom of the skirt, at a 90° angle to the gudgeon pin. Subtract the piston diameter from the bore diameter to obtain the clearance. If this is greater than the figures given in the Specifications, the block will have to be rebored, and new oversize pistons and rings, together with new gudgeon pins and connecting rods will have to be fitted (see paragraph 12).

11 Check the fit of the gudgeon pin by twisting the piston and connecting rod in opposite directions. Any noticeable play indicates excessive wear, which must be corrected. If the pistons or connecting rods are to be renewed, it is necessary to have this work carried out by a Vauxhall/Opel dealer or a suitable engine overhaul specialist, who will have the necessary tooling to remove the gudgeon pins.

12 It should be noted that if any of the components of a piston, gudgeon pin and connecting rod assembly are to be renewed, the manufacturers state that all the components of that assembly must be renewed as well (ie, if a new piston is required, a new gudgeon pin and connecting rod will be required also). A new piston must not be fitted to an old connecting rod and *vice versa*.

13 Check the alignment of the connecting rods visually, and if the rods are not straight, take them to an engine overhaul specialist for a more detailed check.

14 Crankshaft – inspection

1 Clean the crankshaft using paraffin or a suitable solvent, and dry it, preferably with compressed air if available. Be sure to clean the oil holes with a pipe cleaner or similar probe, to ensure that they are not obstructed.

 Warning: Wear eye protection when using compressed air.

2 Check the main and big-end bearing journals for uneven wear, scoring, pitting and cracking.

3 Big-end bearing wear is accompanied by distinct metallic knocking when the engine is running (particularly noticeable when the engine is pulling from low revs), and some loss of oil pressure.

4 Main bearing wear is accompanied by severe engine vibration and rumble – getting progressively worse as engine revs increase – and again by loss of oil pressure.

5 Check the bearing journal for roughness by running a finger lightly over the bearing surface. Any roughness (which will be accompanied by obvious bearing wear) indicates that the crankshaft requires regrinding.

6 If the crankshaft has been reground, check for burrs around the crankshaft oil holes (the holes are usually chamfered, so burrs should not be a problem unless regrinding has been carried out carelessly). Remove any burrs with a fine file or scraper, and thoroughly clean the oil holes as described previously.

7 Using a micrometer, measure the diameter of the main and big-end bearing journals, and compare the results with the Specifications at the beginning of this Chapter **(see illustration)**. By measuring the diameter at a number of points around each journal's circumference, you will be able to determine whether or not the journal is out-of-round. Take the measurement at each end of the journal, near the webs, to determine if the

14.7 Measuring the diameter of a crankshaft journal

journal is tapered. If the crankshaft journals are damaged, tapered, out-of-round or excessively-worn, the crankshaft will have to be reground and undersize bearings fitted.

8 Check the oil seal contact surfaces at each end of the crankshaft for wear and damage. If the seal has worn an excessive groove in the surface of the crankshaft, consult an engine overhaul specialist, who will be able to advise whether a repair is possible, or whether a new crankshaft is necessary.

9 If a new crankshaft is to be fitted, undo the screws securing the crankshaft speed/ position sensor pulse pick-up ring to the crankshaft, and transfer the ring to the new crankshaft **(see illustration)**.

15 Main and big-end bearings – inspection

1 Even though the main and big-end bearing shells should be renewed during engine overhaul, the old bearing shells should be retained for close examination, as they may reveal valuable information about the condition of the engine. The bearing shells carry identification marks to denote their size in the form of a colour code, and/or a letter/number code marked on the back of the shell **(see illustrations)**. If the shells are to be renewed, without carrying out any crankshaft regrinding, the old shells should be taken along when obtaining new shells, to ensure that the correct shells are obtained.

2 Bearing failure occurs because of lack of

14.9 If a new crankshaft is to be fitted, transfer the crankshaft speed/position sensor pulse pick-up ring to the new crankshaft

lubrication, the presence of dirt or other foreign particles, overloading the engine, or corrosion. If a bearing fails, the cause must be found and eliminated before the engine is reassembled, to prevent the failure from happening again.

3 To examine the bearing shells, remove them from the cylinder block, the cylinder block baseplate, the connecting rods and the big-end bearing caps, and lay them out on a clean surface in the same order as they were fitted to the engine. This will enable any bearing problems to be matched with the corresponding crankshaft journal.

4 Dirt and other foreign particles can enter the engine in a variety of ways. Contamination may be left in the engine during assembly, or it may pass through filters or the crankcase ventilation system. Normal engine wear produces small particles of metal, which can eventually cause problems. If particles find their way into the lubrication system, it is likely that they will eventually be carried to the bearings. Whatever the source, these foreign particles often end up embedded in the soft bearing material, and are easily recognised. Large particles will not embed in the bearing, and will score or gouge the bearing and journal. To prevent possible contamination, clean all parts thoroughly, and keep everything spotlessly-clean during engine assembly. Once the engine has been installed in the vehicle, ensure that engine oil and filter changes are carried out at the recommended intervals.

5 Lack of lubrication (or lubrication breakdown) has a number of interrelated causes. Excessive

15.1a Typical main bearing shell . . .

15.1b . . . and main thrust bearing shell identification marks

heat (which thins the oil), overloading (which squeezes the oil from the bearing face), and oil leakage (from excessive bearing clearances, worn oil pump or high engine speeds) all contribute to lubrication breakdown. Blocked oil passages, which may be the result of misaligned oil holes in a bearing shell, will also starve a bearing of oil and destroy it. When lack of lubrication is the cause of bearing failure, the bearing material is wiped or extruded from the steel backing of the bearing. Temperatures may increase to the point where the steel backing turns blue from overheating.

6 Driving habits can have a definite effect on bearing life. Full-throttle, low-speed operation (labouring the engine) puts very high loads on bearings, which tends to squeeze out the oil film. These loads cause the bearings to flex, which produces fine cracks in the bearing face (fatigue failure). Eventually the bearing material will loosen in places, and tear away from the steel backing. Regular short journeys can lead to corrosion of bearings, because insufficient engine heat is produced to drive off the condensed water and corrosive gases which form inside the engine. These products collect in the engine oil, forming acid and sludge. As the oil is carried to the bearings, the acid attacks and corrodes the bearing material.

7 Incorrect bearing installation during engine assembly will also lead to bearing failure. Tight-fitting bearings leave insufficient bearing lubrication clearance, and will result in oil starvation. Dirt or foreign particles trapped behind a bearing shell results in high spots on the bearing which can lead to failure.

8 If new bearings are to be fitted, the bearing running clearances should be measured before the engine is finally reassembled, to ensure that the correct bearing shells have been obtained (see Sections 18 and 19). If the crankshaft has been reground, the engineering works should be able to advise on the correct-size bearing shells to suit the work carried out. If there is any doubt as to which bearing shells should be used, seek advice from a Vauxhall/Opel dealer.

16 Engine overhaul –
reassembly sequence

1 Before reassembly begins, ensure that all necessary new parts have been obtained (particularly gaskets, and various bolts which must be renewed), and that all the tools required are available. Read through the entire procedure to familiarise yourself with the work involved, and to ensure that all items necessary for reassembly of the engine are to hand. In addition to all normal tools and materials, a thread-locking compound will be required. A tube of silicone sealant (Vauxhall/Opel No 90 543 772, or equivalent) will be required to seal certain joint faces which are not fitted with gaskets.

2 In order to save time and avoid problems,

17.5 Measuring a piston ring end gap using a feeler gauge

engine reassembly can be carried out in the following order:
   a) *Piston rings (see Section 17).*
   b) *Crankshaft and main bearings (see Section 18).*
   c) *Piston/connecting rod assemblies (see Section 19).*
   d) *Sump (see Chapter 2A).*
   e) *Flywheel/driveplate (see Chapter 2A).*
   f) *Cylinder head, camshafts, rocker arms and tappets (see Chapter 2A).*
   g) *Timing chain, sprockets, tensioner and cover (see Chapter 2A).*
   h) *Engine external components.*

17 Piston rings – refitting

1 Before refitting the new piston rings, the ring end gaps must be checked as follows.

2 Lay out the piston/connecting rod assemblies and the new piston ring sets, so that the ring sets will be matched with the same piston and cylinder during the end gap measurement and subsequent engine reassembly.

3 Insert the top ring into the first cylinder, and push it down the bore using the top of the piston. This will ensure that the ring remains square with the cylinder walls. Position the ring near the bottom of the cylinder bore, at the lower limit of ring travel.

4 Measure the end gap using feeler gauges.

5 Repeat the procedure with the ring at the top of the cylinder bore, at the upper limit of its travel, and compare the measurements with the figures given in the Specifications **(see illustration)**.

6 If the gap is too small (unlikely if genuine Vauxhall/Opel parts are used), it must be enlarged or the ring ends may contact each other during engine operation, causing serious damage. Ideally, new piston rings providing the correct end gap should be fitted, but as a last resort, the end gap can be increased by filing the ring ends very carefully with a fine file. Mount the file in a vice equipped with soft jaws, slip the ring over the file with the ends contacting the file face, and slowly move the ring to remove material from

17.10 Fitting an oil control spreader ring

the ends – take care, as piston rings are sharp, and are easily broken.

7 With new piston rings, it is unlikely that the end gap will be too large. If they are too large, check that you have the correct rings for your engine and for the particular cylinder bore size.

8 Repeat the checking procedure for each ring in the first cylinder, and then for the rings in the remaining cylinders. Remember to keep rings, pistons and cylinders matched up.

9 Once the ring end gaps have been checked and if necessary corrected, the rings can be fitted to the pistons.

10 The oil control ring (lowest one on the piston) is composed of three sections, and should be installed first. Fit the lower steel ring, then the spreader ring, followed by the upper steel ring **(see illustration)**.

11 With the oil control ring components installed, the second (middle) ring can be fitted. It is usually stamped with a mark (TOP) which must face up, towards the top of the piston. **Note:** *Always follow the instructions supplied with the new piston ring sets – different manufacturers may specify different procedures. Do not mix up the top and middle rings, as they have different cross-sections.* Using two or three old feeler blades, as for removal of the old rings, carefully slip the ring into place in the middle groove.

12 Fit the top ring in the same manner, ensuring that, where applicable, the mark on the ring is facing up. If a stepped ring is being fitted, fit the ring with the smaller diameter of the step uppermost **(see illustration)**.

13 Repeat the procedure for the remaining pistons and rings.

17.12 Sectional view showing correct orientation of piston rings

18.4a Fit the plain main bearing shells . . .

18.4b . . . and the shells with thrust flanges to their correct locations in the cylinder block

18.4c Similarly, fit the bearing shells to the cylinder block baseplate

18 Crankshaft – refitting and main bearing running clearance check

1 Refitting the crankshaft is the first step in the engine reassembly procedure. It is assumed at this point that the cylinder block, baseplate and crankshaft have been cleaned, inspected and repaired or reconditioned as necessary.
2 Position the cylinder block with the baseplate mating face uppermost.

Main bearing running clearance check

Note: *When finally refitting the crankshaft, new cylinder block baseplate bolts must be used. However, when checking the bearing running clearance, the original bolts may be used, and then discarded. A vernier dial indicator, an internal micrometer, or Plastigauge will be required for this check – see text.*

3 Clean the bearing shells and the bearing recesses in both the cylinder block and the baseplate. If new shells are being fitted, ensure that all traces of the protective grease are cleaned off using paraffin. Wipe the shells dry with a clean lint-free cloth.
4 Note that No 4 (1.2 litre engines) or No 3 (1.0 litre engines) bearing shells have thrust flanges which control crankshaft endfloat. If the original bearing shells are being re-used,

they must be refitted to their original locations in the block and baseplate **(see illustrations)**.
5 Before the crankshaft can be permanently installed, the main bearing running clearance should be checked, and this can be done in either of two ways. One method is to fit the baseplate to the cylinder block, with bearing shells in place. With the original baseplate retaining bolts tightened to the specified torque, measure the internal diameter of each assembled pair of bearing shells using a vernier dial indicator or an internal micrometer. If the diameter of each corresponding crankshaft journal is measured and then subtracted from the bearing internal diameter, the result will give the main bearing running clearance. The second (and more accurate) method is to use a product known as Plastigauge. This consists of a fine thread of perfectly-round plastic, which is compressed between the baseplate shell and the crankshaft journal. When the baseplate is removed, the deformed plastic can be measured with a special card gauge supplied with the Plastigauge kit. The running clearance is determined from this gauge. Plastigauge is sometimes difficult to obtain in this country, but enquiries at one of the larger specialist chains of quality motor factors should produce the name of a stockist in your area. The procedure for using Plastigauge is as follows.
6 With the upper main bearing shells in place in the cylinder block, carefully lay the

crankshaft in position **(see illustration)**. Do not use any lubricant; the crankshaft journals and bearing shells must be perfectly clean and dry.
7 Cut several pieces of the appropriate-size Plastigauge (they should be slightly shorter than the width of the main bearings) and place one piece on each crankshaft journal axis **(see illustration)**.
8 With the bearing shells in position in the cylinder block baseplate, fit the baseplate to the cylinder block. Take care not to disturb the Plastigauge.
9 Using the original bolts, and working progressively and in a diagonal sequence, tighten the inner (M8) baseplate retaining bolts to the specified torque, then through the specified angle, in the two stages given in the Specifications (see Chapter 2A). Now similarly tighten the outer (M6) retaining bolts. Do not rotate the crankshaft at any time during this operation.
10 Remove the baseplate bolts (outer bolts first, then the inner bolts) and carefully lift off the baseplate. Do not disturb the Plastigauge or rotate the crankshaft.
11 Compare the width of the deformed Plastigauge on each journal with the scale printed on the card gauge to obtain the main bearing running clearance **(see illustration)**.
12 If the clearance is not as specified, the bearing shells may be the wrong size (or excessively-worn if the original shells are being re-used). Before deciding that different

18.6 With the upper main bearing shells in place in the cylinder block, carefully lay the crankshaft in position

18.7 Lay the length of Plastigauge on the journal to be measured, parallel to the crankshaft centre-line

18.11 Using the scale on the envelope provided to check the width of the crushed Plastigauge (at its widest point)

18.15 Liberally lubricate each bearing shell in the cylinder block then lower the crankshaft into position

18.17 Lubricate the bearing shells in the baseplate

18.18 Apply a 2 mm diameter bead of silicone sealant to the outside of the groove (not in the groove itself), in the baseplate

shells are required, make sure that no dirt or oil was trapped between the bearing shells and the baseplate or block when the clearance was measured. If the Plastigauge was wider at one end than at the other, the crankshaft journal may be tapered.

13 Carefully remove all traces of the Plastigauge material from the crankshaft and bearing shells, using a fingernail or other improvised tool which is unlikely to score the shells.

Final crankshaft refitting

Note: *New cylinder block baseplate bolts must be used when refitting the crankshaft. A tube of silicone sealant (Vauxhall/Opel*

No 90 543 772, or equivalent) will be required when fitting the baseplate to the cylinder block.
14 Carefully lift the crankshaft out of the cylinder block once more.
15 Liberally lubricate each bearing shell in the cylinder block, and lower the crankshaft into position **(see illustration).**
16 If necessary, seat the crankshaft using light taps from a soft-faced mallet on the crankshaft balance webs.
17 Lubricate the crankshaft journals, and the bearing shells in the baseplate **(see illustration).**
18 Ensure that the cylinder block and baseplate mating surfaces are clean and dry, then apply a 2 mm diameter bead of silicone

sealant (Vauxhall/Opel No 90 543 772, or equivalent) to the outside of the groove (not in the groove itself), in the baseplate **(see illustration).**
19 Locate the baseplate over the crankshaft and onto the cylinder block.
20 Fit the new baseplate retaining bolts, then working progressively and in a diagonal sequence, tighten the inner (M8) bolts to the specified torque, then through the specified angle, in the two stages given in the Specifications. Now similarly tighten the outer (M6) retaining bolts **(see illustrations).**
21 Now rotate the crankshaft, and check that it turns freely, with no signs of binding or tight spots.

18.20a Fit the new baseplate inner bolts . . .

18.20b . . . and outer bolts

18.20c Tighten the inner bolts to the specified Stage 1 torque setting using a torque wrench . . .

18.20d . . . then through the specified Stage 2 angle using an angle tightening gauge

18.20e Similarly tighten the outer bolts to the specified torque . . .

18.20f . . . and through the specified angle

19.2 Press the bearing shells into the connecting rods and caps in their correct positions

22 Check the crankshaft endfloat with reference to Section 11.
23 Fit a new crankshaft flywheel end oil seal as described in Chapter 2A.
24 Refit the pistons and connecting rods as described in Section 19.

19 Piston/connecting rod assemblies – refitting and big-end bearing clearance check

1 Clean the backs of the big-end bearing shells and the recesses in the connecting rods and big-end caps. If new shells are being fitted, ensure that all traces of the protective grease are cleaned off using paraffin. Wipe the shells, caps and connecting rods dry with a lint-free cloth.
2 Press the bearing shells into the connecting rods and caps in their correct positions **(see illustration)**.

Big-end bearing running clearance check

Note: *When finally refitting the piston/connecting rod assemblies, new big-end bearing cap bolts must be used. However, when checking the bearing running clearance, the original bolts may be used, and then discarded. A piston ring compressor tool will be required for this operation.*

3 Lubricate No 1 piston and piston rings, and check that the ring gaps are correctly positioned **(see illustration)**.
4 Liberally lubricate the cylinder bore with clean engine oil.
5 Fit a ring compressor to No 1 piston, then insert the piston and connecting rod into the cylinder bore so that the base of the compressor stands on the block. With the crankshaft big-end bearing journal positioned at its lowest point, tap the piston carefully into the cylinder bore with the wooden handle of a hammer, and at the same time guide the connecting rod onto the bearing journal **(see illustration)**. Note that the arrow on the piston crown should point towards the timing chain end of the engine, and the lugs on the connecting rod should point towards the flywheel end of the engine **(see illustrations)**.

19.3 Piston ring end gap positions

1 *Top compression ring end gap*
2 *Oil control ring lower steel ring end gap*
3 *Oil control ring upper steel ring end gap*
4 *Second compression ring end gap*
5 *Oil control ring spreader ring end gap*

6 To measure the big-end bearing running clearance, refer to the information contained in Section 18, as the same general procedures apply. If the Plastigauge method is being used, ensure that the big-end bearing journal and the bearing shells are clean and dry, then engage the connecting rod with the bearing journal. Lay the Plastigauge strip on the bearing journal, fit the bearing cap in its original location (as marked on removal), then tighten the original bearing cap bolts to the specified torque and angle, in the two stages given in the Specifications (see Chapter 2A). Do not rotate the crankshaft during this operation. Remove the bearing cap, and check the running clearance by measuring the Plastigauge as previously described.
7 Repeat the checking procedures on the remaining piston/connecting rod assemblies.

Final piston/connecting rod assembly refitting

Note: *New big-end bearing cap bolts must be used when refitting the piston/connecting rod assemblies.*

19.9a Tighten the big-end bearing cap bolts to the specified torque . . .

19.5a Tap the piston carefully into the cylinder bore with the wooden handle of a hammer . . .

19.5b . . . ensuring that the arrow on the piston (1) points toward the timing chain and the lug (2) on the connecting rod is toward the flywheel

8 After checking the running clearance of all the big-end bearings and taking any corrective action necessary, clean off all traces of Plastigauge from the bearing shells and journals.
9 Liberally lubricate the bearing journals and bearing shells, and refit the bearing caps once more, ensuring correct positioning as previously described. Tighten the new bearing cap bolts to the Stage 1 torque setting, then tighten all bolts through the specified Stage 2 angle **(see illustrations)**.

19.9b . . . then through the specified angle

10 After refitting each piston/connecting rod assembly, rotate the crankshaft, and check that it turns freely, with no signs of binding or tight spots.

11 Refit the oil baffle plate and tighten the retaining bolts to the specified torque.

12 Refit the sump and oil pick-up pipe as described in Chapter 2A.

13 Refit the flywheel/driveplate as described in Chapter 2A.

14 Refit the cylinder head as described in Chapter 2A.

15 Refit the timing chain, sprockets, tensioner and cover as described in Chapter 2A.

16 Refit the engine external components.

20 Engine – initial start-up after overhaul

1 With the engine refitted to the vehicle, check the engine oil and coolant levels.

2 With the spark plugs removed, disable the fuel and ignition system by disconnecting the two wiring plugs from the engine management electronic control unit located on the left-hand side of the inlet manifold.

3 Crank the engine over on the starter until the oil pressure light goes out, noting that this may take a few seconds as the new oil filter fills with oil.

4 Refit the spark plugs, and with the ignition switched off, reconnect all the wiring connectors.

5 Start the engine, and allow it to idle. It may be initially noisy at the top-end as the hydraulic tappets fill with oil, and this may take some time.

6 While the engine is idling, check for fuel, coolant and oil leaks. Where applicable, check the automatic transmission fluid pipe/hose unions for leakage. Do not be alarmed if there are some odd smells and smoke from parts getting hot and burning off oil deposits.

7 Keep the engine idling until hot coolant is felt circulating through the radiator top hose, indicating that the engine is at normal operating temperature, then check as far as possible that the engine is running smoothly. Ideally, the engine management system should be checked using suitable diagnostic equipment with reference to Chapter 4A.

8 Stop the engine.

9 Allow the engine to cool, then recheck the oil and coolant levels, and top-up as necessary.

10 If new pistons, rings or bearings have been fitted, the engine must be run-in at reduced speeds and loads for the first 500 miles (800 km). Do not operate the engine at full-throttle, or allow it to labour in any gear during this period. It is beneficial to change the engine oil and filter at the end of this period.

Chapter 2 Part E: 1.2 SOHC, 1.4 & 1.6 litre engine removal and overhaul procedures

Contents

Degrees of difficulty

Easy, suitable for novice with little experience	**Fairly easy,** suitable for beginner with some experience	**Fairly difficult,** suitable for competent DIY mechanic	**Difficult,** suitable for experienced DIY mechanic	**Very difficult,** suitable for expert DIY or professional 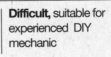

Specifications

Cylinder block

Material	Cast iron
Maximum cylinder bore ovality	0.013 mm
Maximum cylinder bore taper	0.013 mm
Maximum permissible rebore oversize	0.500 mm

Cylinder bore diameters:
  1.2 litre engines:
    Standard size:

Identification mark 8	71.975 to 71.985 mm
Identification mark 99	71.985 to 71.995 mm
Identification mark 00	71.995 to 72.005 mm
Identification mark 01	72.005 to 72.015 mm
Identification mark 02	72.015 to 72.025 mm

    0.500 mm oversize:

Identification mark 7 + 0.5	72.465 to 72.475 mm

  1.4 litre engines:
    Standard size:

Identification mark 8	77.575 to 77.585 mm
Identification mark 99	77.585 to 77.595 mm
Identification mark 00	77.595 to 77.605 mm
Identification mark 01	77.605 to 77.615 mm
Identification mark 02	77.615 to 77.625 mm

    0.500 mm oversize:

Identification mark 7 + 05	78.065 to 78.075 mm

  1.6 litre engines:
    Standard size:

Identification mark 8	78.975 to 78.985 mm
Identification mark 99	78.985 to 78.995 mm
Identification mark 00	78.995 to 79.005 mm
Identification mark 01	79.005 to 79.015 mm
Identification mark 02	79.015 to 79.025 mm

    0.500 mm oversize:

Identification mark 7 + 0.5	79.465 to 79.475 mm

Crankshaft and bearings

Number of main bearings 5

Main bearing journal diameter:
  Standard (all engines) .... 54.980 to 54.997 mm
  0.250 mm undersize (all engines) .... 54.730 to 54.747 mm
  0.500 mm undersize (all engines) .... 54.482 to 54.495 mm

Main bearing shell colour codes:

	Cylinder block	Bearing cap
Standard	Brown	Green
0.250 mm undersize	Brown/blue	Green/blue
0.500 mm undersize	Brown/white	Green/white

Centre (thrust) main bearing journal width:
  Standard .... 26.000 to 26.052 mm
  0.250 mm undersize .... 26.200 to 26.252 mm
  0.500 mm undersize .... 26.400 to 26.452 mm

Big-end bearing journal diameter:
  Standard .... 42.971 to 42.987 mm
  0.250 mm undersize .... 42.721 to 42.737 mm
  0.500 mm undersize .... 42.471 to 42.487 mm

Big-end bearing shell colour codes:
  Standard .... None
  0.250 mm undersize .... Blue
  0.500 mm undersize .... White

Maximum main and big-end bearing journal out-of-round .... 0.040 mm
Main bearing running clearance .... 0.013 to 0.043 mm
Big-end bearing running clearance .... 0.019 to 0.071 mm
Crankshaft endfloat .... 0.100 to 0.200 mm
Connecting rod endfloat .... 0.070 to 0.142 mm

Valves and guides – SOHC engines

Stem diameter:

	Inlet	Exhaust
Standard	6.998 to 7.012 mm	6.978 to 6.992 mm
0.075 mm oversize	7.073 to 7.087 mm	7.053 to 7.067 mm
0.150 mm oversize	7.148 to 7.162 mm	7.128 to 7.142 mm
0.250 mm oversize	7.248 to 7.262 mm	7.228 to 7.242 mm

Valve guide bore:
  Standard .... 7.030 to 7.050 mm
  0.075 mm oversize .... 7.105 to 7.125 mm
  0.150 mm oversize .... 7.180 to 7.200 mm
  0.250 mm oversize .... 7.280 to 7.300 mm

Maximum permissible valve stem play in guide:
  Inlet .... 0.018 to 0.052 mm
  Exhaust .... 0.038 to 0.072 mm
Valve seat angle .... 46°
Valve clearances .... Automatic adjustment by hydraulic valve lifters

Valves and guides – DOHC engine

Stem diameter:

	Inlet	Exhaust
Standard	5.955 to 5.970 mm	5.935 to 5.950 mm
0.075 mm oversize	6.030 to 6.045 mm	6.010 to 6.025 mm
0.150 mm oversize	6.105 to 6.120 mm	6.085 to 6.100 mm

Valve guide bore:
  Standard .... 6.000 to 6.012 mm
  0.075 mm oversize .... 6.075 to 6.090 mm
  0.150 mm oversize .... 6.150 to 6.165 mm

Maximum permissible valve stem play in guide:
  Inlet .... 0.030 to 0.060 mm
  Exhaust .... 0.040 to 0.070 mm
Valve seat angle .... 45°
Valve clearances .... Automatic adjustment by hydraulic valve lifters

Pistons

Piston-to-bore clearance:
  New .... 0.020 mm
  After rebore (oversize) .... 0.010 to 0.030 mm

Note: *Piston diameters – pistons carry identification marks corresponding to those listed previously for cylinder bore diameters. The appropriate piston diameter is 0.020 mm less than the corresponding bore diameter.*

Piston rings

Number of rings (per piston)	2 compression, 1 oil control
Ring end gap:	
Compression	0.300 to 0.500 mm
Oil control (top and bottom sections)	0.400 to 1.400 mm
Ring gap offset (to gap of adjacent ring)*	180°

*For oil control ring sections, see text (Section 19).

Cylinder head

Material	Light alloy
Maximum permissible distortion of sealing face	0.025 mm
Overall height of cylinder head (sealing surface-to-sealing surface):	
SOHC engines	95.250 ± 0.450 mm
DOHC engine	134.900 to 135.100 mm
Valve seat width:	
SOHC engines:	
Inlet	1.300 to 1.500 mm
Exhaust	1.600 to 1.800 mm
DOHC engine:	
Inlet	1.000 to 1.400 mm
Exhaust	1.400 to 1.800 mm

Torque wrench settings

Refer to Specifications for Chapter 2B (SOHC engines) or 2C (DOHC engines).

1 General information

This Part of Chapter 2 includes details of engine removal and refitting, and general overhaul procedures for the cylinder head, cylinder block/crankcase, and internal engine components.

The information ranges from advice concerning preparation for an overhaul and the purchase of replacement parts, to detailed step-by-step procedures covering removal, inspection, renovation and refitting of internal engine components.

The following Sections have been compiled based on the assumption that the engine has been removed from the vehicle. For information concerning in-vehicle engine repair, as well as information on the removal and refitting of the external components necessary to facilitate overhaul, refer to Chapter 2B or 2C, and to Section 8 of this Part.

2 Engine overhaul – general information

It is not always easy to determine when, or if, an engine should be completely overhauled, as a number of factors must be considered.

High mileage is not necessarily an indication that an overhaul is needed, while low mileage does not preclude the need for an overhaul. Frequency of servicing is probably the most important consideration. An engine which has had regular and frequent oil and filter changes, as well as other required

maintenance, will most likely give many thousands of miles of reliable service. Conversely, a neglected engine may require an overhaul very early in its life.

Excessive oil consumption is an indication that piston rings, valve seals and/or valve guides are in need of attention. Make sure that oil leaks are not responsible before deciding that the rings and/or guides are bad. Perform a cylinder compression check to determine the extent of the work required.

Check the oil pressure with a gauge fitted in place of the oil pressure sender, and compare it with the Specifications. If it is extremely low, the main and big-end bearings and/or the oil pump are probably worn out.

Loss of power, rough running, knocking or metallic engine noises, excessive valve gear noise and high fuel consumption may also point to the need for an overhaul, especially if they are all present at the same time. If a complete tune-up does not remedy the situation, major mechanical work is the only solution.

An engine overhaul involves restoring the internal parts to the specifications of a new engine. During an overhaul, new pistons and/or rings are fitted, and the cylinder bores are reconditioned. New main bearings, connecting rod bearings and camshaft bearings are generally fitted, and if necessary, the crankshaft may be reground to restore the journals. The valves are also serviced as well, since they are usually in less-than-perfect condition at this point. While the engine is being overhauled, other components, such as the distributor, starter and alternator, can be overhauled too. The end result should be a like-new engine that will give many trouble-free miles. **Note:** *Critical cooling system components such as the hoses, drivebelts, thermostat and water pump MUST be renewed when an engine is overhauled.*

The radiator should be checked carefully to ensure that it is not clogged or leaking. Also it is a good idea to renew the oil pump whenever the engine is overhauled.

Before beginning the engine overhaul, read through the entire procedure to familiarise yourself with the scope and requirements of the job. Overhauling an engine is not difficult if you follow all of the instructions carefully, have the necessary tools and equipment, and pay close attention to all specifications; however, it can be time-consuming. Plan on the vehicle being tied up for a minimum of two weeks, especially if parts must be taken to an engineering works for repair or reconditioning. Check on the availability of parts, and make sure that any necessary special tools and equipment are obtained in advance. Most work can be done with typical hand tools, although a number of precision measuring tools are required for inspecting parts to determine if they must be renewed. Often the engineering works will handle the inspection of parts, and offer advice concerning reconditioning and renewal. **Note:** *Always wait until the engine has been completely dismantled and all components, especially the engine block, have been inspected before deciding what service and repair operations must be performed by an engineering works. Since the condition of the block will be the major factor to consider when determining whether to overhaul the original engine or buy a reconditioned unit, do not purchase parts or have overhaul work done on other components until the block has been thoroughly inspected. As a general rule, time is the primary cost of an overhaul, so it does not pay to fit worn or sub-standard parts.*

As a final note, to ensure maximum life and minimum trouble from a reconditioned engine, everything must be assembled with care in a spotlessly-clean environment.

3 Engine removal –
methods and precautions

If you have decided that an engine must be removed for overhaul or major repair work, several preliminary steps should be taken.

Locating a suitable place to work is extremely important. Adequate work space, along with storage space for the vehicle, will be needed. If a garage is not available, at the very least a flat, level, clean work surface is required.

Cleaning the engine compartment and engine before beginning the removal procedure will help keep tools clean and organised.

An engine hoist or A-frame will also be necessary. Make sure the equipment is rated in excess of the combined weight of the engine and transmission. Safety is of primary importance, considering the potential hazards involved in lifting the engine out of the vehicle.

If this is the first time you have removed an engine, an assistant should be available. Advice and aid from someone more experienced would also be helpful. There are many instances when one person cannot simultaneously perform all of the operations required when lifting the engine out of the vehicle.

Plan the operation ahead of time. Arrange for, or obtain, all of the tools and equipment you will need, prior to beginning the job. Some of the equipment necessary to perform engine removal and installation safely and with relative ease are (in addition to an engine hoist) a heavy-duty trolley jack, complete sets of spanners and sockets as described at the back of this manual, wooden blocks, and plenty of rags and cleaning solvent for mopping-up spilled oil, coolant and fuel. If the hoist must be hired, make sure that you arrange for it in advance, and perform all of the operations possible without it beforehand. This will save you money and time.

Plan for the vehicle to be out of use for quite a while. An engineering works will be required to perform some of the work which the do-it-yourselfer cannot accomplish without special equipment. These places often have a busy schedule, so it would be a good idea to consult them before removing the engine, in order to accurately estimate the amount of time required to rebuild or repair components that may need work.

Always be extremely careful when removing and refitting the engine. Serious injury can result from careless actions. Plan ahead, take your time, and you will find that a job of this nature, although major, can be accomplished successfully.

On all Corsa models, the engine must be removed complete with the gearbox/transmission as an assembly. There is insufficient clearance in the engine compartment to remove the engine leaving the gearbox/transmission in the vehicle. The assembly is removed by raising the front of the vehicle, and lowering the assembly from the engine compartment.

4.14 Removing the expansion tank – DOHC engine

4 Engine/manual gearbox assembly –
removal and refitting

Note: *Suitable equipment will be required to support the engine and gearbox during this procedure – see text.*

Removal

1 Depressurise the fuel system as described in Chapter 4B.
2 Disconnect the battery negative terminal, followed by the positive terminal (refer to *Disconnecting the battery* in the Reference Chapter).
3 To improve access, remove the bonnet as described in Chapter 11.
4 Drain the cooling system as described in Chapter 1.
5 Drain the engine oil as described in Chapter 1.
6 Remove the air cleaner assembly, as described in Chapter 4B.
7 On right-hand-drive models, remove the battery, as described in Chapter 5A.
8 Disconnect the coolant hoses connecting the radiator to the thermostat housing, coolant gallery (at the gearbox end of the engine), and expansion tank.
9 Remove the radiator cooling fan and shroud assembly as described in Chapter 3.
10 Disconnect the throttle cable from the throttle linkage, as described in Chapter 4B, and move the cable clear of the engine, noting its routing.
11 Disconnect the vacuum pipe(s) from the

4.16 Disconnect the clutch cable from the release lever

4.15 Disconnect the heater coolant hoses (arrowed) at the bulkhead

fuel injection unit or the throttle body (as applicable), noting their locations.
12 Disconnect the brake servo vacuum hose from the inlet manifold.
13 Where applicable, disconnect the hoses and the wiring plug from the fuel tank vent valve (see Chapter 4C, Section 4).
14 Unscrew the securing nuts, then remove the coolant expansion tank from the engine compartment bulkhead, disconnect the coolant hoses, and withdraw the expansion tank **(see illustration)**.
15 Disconnect the heater coolant hoses from the heater matrix pipes at the engine compartment bulkhead **(see illustration)**. Be prepared for coolant spillage.
16 Remove the retaining clip (where applicable), then slide the clutch cable from the release lever, pushing the release lever back towards the bulkhead if necessary to allow the cable to be disconnected **(see illustration)**. Pull the cable support from the bracket on the gearbox casing, then move the cable to one side out of the way, taking note of its routing.

> **HAYNES HINT** *Measure the length of the threaded rod protruding through the plastic block at the release arm end of the cable. This will enable approximate pre-setting of the cable when refitting.*

17 Disconnect the wiring from the reversing light switch, located at the front of the gearbox, above the mounting bracket **(see illustration)**.

4.17 Disconnect the wiring from the reversing light switch (arrowed)

4.19 Disconnect the fuel lines (arrowed) – DOHC engine

4.20 Fuel line bracket securing bolt location (arrowed) – SOHC engine with multi-point fuel injection

4.21a Disconnecting the wiring from the oil pressure warning light switch (viewed from underneath vehicle)

18 Where applicable, unscrew the securing sleeve and disconnect the speedometer cable from the top of the gearbox, as described in Chapter 12. Note that on certain models, the cable is in two sections, joined by a connector near the engine compartment bulkhead – in this case, it may be easier to separate the two cable sections at the connector, rather than to disconnect the cable from the gearbox. On later models, disconnect the wiring connector from the electronic speedometer sensor.

19 Identify the fuel supply and return lines, then unscrew the unions, or loosen the clamps, as applicable, and disconnect the fuel lines from the fuel injection unit (single-point fuel injection models) or the fuel rail/fuel

pressure regulator (multi-point fuel injection models), as applicable (see illustration). Be prepared for fuel spillage, and take adequate fire precautions. Plug or clamp the open ends of the pipes and hoses, to prevent dirt ingress and further fuel leakage.

20 On SOHC engine models with multi-point fuel injection, unbolt the fuel line bracket from the lower rear of the inlet manifold (see illustration).

21 Identify and disconnect all relevant wiring from the engine and associated components, using the following list as a guide (see illustrations). Make careful notes of the routing of the wiring, and the positions of any brackets or cable-ties. In some cases, it may be necessary to

separate wiring harness connectors, in which case identify the connectors.

a) Oil pressure warning light switch (see Chapter 5A).
b) Temperature gauge sender (see Chapter 3, Section 6).
c) DIS module (see Chapter 5B).
d) Engine earth wiring (bolted to inlet manifold and/or cylinder head).
e) Disconnect the auxiliary battery leads from the main battery leads (secured by nuts).
f) Fuel injectors (see Chapter 4B).
g) Throttle position sensor (see Chapter 4B, Section 12, 13 or 14).
h) Idle speed control motor (see Chapter 4B, Section 12, 13 or 14).

4.21b Disconnecting the wiring from the temperature gauge sender (arrowed) – DOHC engine

4.21c Disconnect the auxiliary leads from the battery positive . . .

4.21d . . . and negative leads – DOHC engine

4.21e Disconnecting the fuel injector wiring harness connector – DOHC engine

4.21f Disconnect the crankshaft speed/position sensor (1) and camshaft position sensor (2) wiring connectors – DOHC engine

4.21g Oxygen sensor wiring connector location (arrowed) on engine-to-gearbox bolt bracket

i) Coolant temperature sensor (see Chapter 4B, Section 12, 13 or 14).

j) Crankshaft speed/position sensor (see Chapter 4B, Section 13 or 14).

k) Camshaft position sensor (see Chapter 4B, Section 14).

l) Oxygen sensor (see Chapter 4B, Section 12, 13 or 14).

m) Knock sensor (see Chapter 5B, Section 5).

 HAYNES HINT *If the engine is to be removed for some time, making sketches or taking a few photographs of wire and hose runs and connections before disconnection will prove helpful when refitting.*

22 On models with power steering, remove the auxiliary drivebelt as described in Chapter 1.

23 On models with power steering (but not power steering *and* air conditioning), unbolt the power steering pump from the bracket on the engine as described in Chapter 10. The pump can be moved to one side and left in the engine compartment, avoiding the need to disconnect the fluid hoses, but note the routing of the hoses to aid refitting.

24 Apply the handbrake, then jack up the front of the vehicle and support securely on axle stands (see *Jacking and vehicle support*). Note that the vehicle must be raised sufficiently high (approximately 650 mm) to enable the engine/gearbox assembly to be withdrawn from under the front of the vehicle **(see illustration)**. Remove the roadwheels.

25 Attach a suitable hoist and lifting tackle to the engine lifting brackets on the cylinder head, and support the weight of the engine.

26 Working under the front of the vehicle, loosen the clamp nut and bolt securing the gear selector rod to the linkage, then pull the selector tube towards the engine compartment bulkhead to separate it from the linkage.

27 Where applicable, unscrew the retaining nut, and disconnect the earth strap from the gearbox endplate.

28 Disconnect the wiring from the alternator and the starter motor.

29 Disconnect the exhaust front section from the manifold, with reference to Chapter 4B. Release the exhaust system from its forward rubber mountings, and move the system to one side, clear of the engine and gearbox. On DOHC engine models, remove the exhaust front section.

30 Remove the front suspension lower arms, tie-bars and anti-roll bar, as described in Chapter 10.

31 Disconnect the inner ends of the driveshafts from the gearbox, as described in Chapter 8. There is no need to disconnect the driveshafts from the swivel hubs. Be prepared for oil spillage, and plug the openings in the gearbox to prevent dirt ingress and further oil loss. Do not allow the driveshafts to hang down under their own weight, or the joints may be damaged; support the driveshafts with wire or string.

32 Make a final check to ensure that all relevant pipes, hoses, wires, etc, have been disconnected, and that they are positioned clear of the engine and gearbox.

33 To stabilise the engine/gearbox assembly as it is removed, it is advisable to support the assembly from underneath using a jack and interposed block of wood, in addition to the engine hoist and lifting tackle.

34 Ensure that the engine/gearbox assembly is adequately supported, then proceed as follows:

35 Unscrew the through-bolt and nut securing the rear engine/gearbox mounting bracket to the mounting on the body.

36 Release the spring clip, then pull the gear linkage pivot pin from the bracket on the rear engine/gearbox mounting **(see illustration)**.

37 Remove the two bolts securing the rear engine/gearbox mounting bracket to the gearbox, and withdraw the mounting bracket.

38 Unbolt the left-hand and right-hand engine/gearbox mountings from the body, with reference to Chapter 2B if necessary.

39 On models with air conditioning and power steering, proceed as follows:

a) Carefully lower the engine/gearbox assembly by approximately 100 mm.

b) Unbolt the compressor from the bracket on the engine (see Chapter 3), and move the compressor to one side, leaving the refrigerant lines connected. Suspend the compressor from the front body crossmember using wire or string.

c) Similarly, unbolt the power steering pump from the bracket (see Chapter 10), and suspend the pump in the engine compartment, leaving the fluid lines connected.

 Warning: Do not under any circumstances attempt to disconnect the refrigerant lines.

40 Carefully lower the engine/gearbox assembly from the engine compartment.

41 Ensure that the assembly is adequately supported using jacks, or a suitable trolley, then disconnect the engine hoist and lifting tackle, and withdraw the engine/gearbox assembly from under the front of the vehicle.

42 With the engine/gearbox assembly removed, support the assembly on suitable blocks of wood positioned on a workbench, or failing that, on a clean area of the workshop floor.

43 Clean away any external dirt using paraffin or a water-soluble solvent and a stiff brush.

44 Where applicable, unscrew the securing bolts, and remove the engine-to-gearbox blanking plate from the bellhousing.

45 Ensure that both engine and gearbox are adequately supported, then unscrew and remove the engine-to-gearbox bolts, noting the locations of any brackets which may be secured by the bolts.

46 Carefully withdraw the gearbox from the engine, ensuring that the weight of the gearbox is not allowed to hang on the input shaft while it is engaged with the clutch friction disc. Note that the gearbox locates on dowels positioned in the cylinder block.

Refitting

47 Carefully offer the gearbox to the engine until the bellhousing is located on the dowels in the cylinder block, then refit the engine-to-gearbox bolts, and tighten them to the specified torque. Make sure that any brackets secured by the bolts are correctly positioned, as noted before removal. If the clutch is still bolted to the flywheel, ensure that the weight of the gearbox is not allowed to hang on the input shaft as it is engaged with the clutch friction disc.

48 Where applicable, refit the engine-to-gearbox blanking plate to the bellhousing.

49 With the front of the vehicle raised and supported on axle stands, move the engine/gearbox assembly under the vehicle, ensuring that the assembly is adequately supported.

50 Reconnect the hoist and lifting tackle to the engine lifting brackets.

51 On models with air conditioning, proceed as follows:

a) Raise the engine/gearbox assembly sufficiently to enable the power steering

4.24 The front of the vehicle must be raised approximately 650 mm to enable engine/gearbox removal

4.36 Pull the gear linkage pivot pin (arrowed) from the rear engine/gearbox mounting

pump and air conditioning compressor to be refitted.

b) *Refit the power steering pump, with reference to Chapter 10 if necessary.*

c) *Refit the air conditioning compressor, with reference to Chapter 3 if necessary.*

52 Raise the engine/gearbox assembly, and reconnect the left-hand and right-hand engine/gearbox mountings to the body, with reference to Chapter 2B or 2C, if necessary.

53 Refit the rear engine/gearbox mounting bracket to the gearbox, and tighten the bolts to the specified torque.

54 Refit the through-bolt and nut securing the rear engine/gearbox mounting to the mounting on the body.

55 Refit the gear linkage to the bracket on the rear engine/gearbox mounting, and secure with the pivot pin.

56 Reconnect the inner ends of the driveshafts to the gearbox as described in Chapter 8.

57 Refit the front suspension anti-roll bar, tie-bars and lower arms, as described in Chapter 10.

58 Reconnect the exhaust front section to the manifold, or refit the exhaust front section, as applicable, as described in Chapter 4B. Where applicable, reconnect the exhaust system to the forward rubber mountings.

59 Reconnect the wiring to the alternator and the starter motor.

60 Where applicable, reconnect the gearbox earth strap.

61 Reconnect the gear selector rod to the gear linkage, and adjust the linkage as described in Chapter 7A.

62 Disconnect the hoist and lifting tackle from the engine lifting brackets.

63 Refit the roadwheels, and lower the vehicle to the ground.

64 On models with power steering, refit the power steering pump to the bracket on the engine, routing the fluid hoses as noted before removal.

65 Where applicable, refit and tension the auxiliary drivebelt as described in Chapter 1.

66 Reconnect all relevant wiring to the engine and associated components, ensuring that the wiring is routed and secured as noted before removal.

67 On SOHC engine models with multi-point fuel injection, refit the fuel line bracket to the inlet manifold.

68 Reconnect the fuel lines, ensuring that they are connected to their correct locations, and tighten the unions or hose clamps, as applicable.

69 Reconnect the speedometer cable to the gearbox, or reconnect the speedometer cable connector (as applicable), with reference to Chapter 12 if necessary. On later models, reconnect the wiring connector to the electronic speedometer sensor.

70 Reconnect the reversing light switch wiring.

71 Reconnect and if necessary adjust the clutch cable, as described in Chapter 6.

72 Reconnect the heater coolant hoses to the pipes at the engine compartment bulkhead.

73 Reconnect the coolant hoses to the expansion tank, and refit the expansion tank to the bulkhead.

74 Where applicable, reconnect the hoses and the wiring plug to the fuel tank vent valve.

75 Reconnect the brake servo vacuum hose to the inlet manifold.

76 Reconnect the vacuum pipe(s) to the fuel injection unit or the throttle body, as applicable.

77 Reconnect the throttle cable to the throttle linkage, and if necessary adjust the cable, as described in Chapter 4B.

78 Refit the radiator cooling fan and shroud assembly as described in Chapter 3.

79 Reconnect the coolant hoses to the radiator, thermostat housing, coolant gallery, and expansion tank.

80 On right-hand drive models, refit the battery.

81 Refit the air cleaner assembly.

82 Refill the engine with oil, as described in Chapter 1.

83 Refill and bleed the cooling system as described in Chapter 1.

84 Check and if necessary top-up the gearbox oil level as described in Chapter 1.

85 Make a final check to ensure that all relevant hoses, pipes and wires have been correctly reconnected.

86 Refit the bonnet as described in Chapter 11.

87 Reconnect the battery leads.

5 Engine/automatic transmission assembly – removal and refitting

Note: *Suitable equipment will be required to support the engine and transmission during this procedure – see text. New torque converter-to-driveplate bolts must be used on refitting.*

Removal

1 Proceed as described in Section 4, paragraphs 1 to 23 inclusive, ignoring paragraphs 16 and 17.

2 Working in the engine compartment, remove the retaining clip, and disconnect the selector cable from the actuating lever on the transmission **(see illustration)**. Unclip the cable sheath from the bracket on the transmission, then move the cable to one side, clear of the transmission.

3 Disconnect the vent hose from the front of the transmission.

4 Disconnect the transmission wiring harness plugs, and unbolt the wiring harness brackets from the transmission.

5 Apply the handbrake, then jack up the front of the vehicle and support securely on axle stands (see *Jacking and vehicle support*). Note that the vehicle must be raised

sufficiently high (approximately 650 mm) to enable the engine/transmission assembly to be withdrawn from under the front of the vehicle. Remove the roadwheels.

6 Attach a suitable hoist and lifting tackle to the engine lifting brackets on the cylinder head, and support the weight of the engine.

7 Place a suitable container beneath the transmission fluid cooler hose connections at the transmission. Clamp the transmission fluid cooler hoses, then disconnect them from the transmission, noting their locations. Be prepared for fluid spillage, and plug the open ends of the hoses and transmission connections, to minimise fluid loss and prevent dirt ingress.

8 Proceed as described in Section 4, paragraphs 28 to 43 inclusive, ignoring paragraph 36, and substituting 'transmission' for 'gearbox'.

9 Unscrew the securing bolts, and remove the transmission bellhousing cover plate.

10 If the original torque converter and driveplate are to be refitted, make alignment marks between the torque converter and the driveplate, to ensure that the components are reassembled in their original positions.

11 Working through the bottom of the bellhousing, unscrew the three torque converter-to-driveplate bolts. It will be necessary to turn the crankshaft using a suitable spanner or socket on the crankshaft pulley or sprocket bolt (as applicable), to gain access to each bolt in turn through the aperture. Use a screwdriver or a similar tool to jam the driveplate ring gear, preventing the driveplate from rotating as the bolts are loosened. Discard the bolts.

12 Ensure that the engine and transmission are adequately supported, then unscrew and remove the engine-to-transmission bolts (note the location of any brackets secured by the bolts). Carefully pull the engine and transmission apart, ensuring that the torque converter is held firmly in place in the transmission casing as the engine and transmission are separated, otherwise it could fall out, resulting in fluid spillage and possible damage. Retain the torque converter while the transmission is removed by bolting a strip of metal across the transmission bellhousing end face.

5.2 Remove the retaining clip (arrowed) and disconnect the selector cable

Refitting

13 Before refitting begins, check that the left-hand engine/transmission mounting-to-body bolts rotate freely in their threaded holes in the body. If necessary, re-cut the threaded holes in the body, using a suitable tap.

14 If the original torque converter is being refitted, commence refitting by re-cutting the torque converter-to-driveplate bolt threads in the torque converter, using an M10 x 1.25 mm tap.

15 If a new transmission is being fitted, the manufacturers recommend that the radiator fluid cooler passages are flushed clean before the new transmission is installed. Ideally, compressed air should be used (in which case, ensure that adequate safety precautions are taken). Alternatively, the cooler can be flushed with clean automatic transmission fluid, until all the old fluid has been expelled, and fresh fluid runs clear from the cooler outlet.

16 Carefully offer the transmission to the engine until the bellhousing is located on the dowels in the cylinder block (ensure that the torque converter is held firmly in place in the transmission casing as the engine and transmission are connected), then refit the engine-to-transmission bolts, and tighten them to the specified torque. Make sure that any brackets secured by the bolts are correctly positioned, as noted before removal.

17 If the original torque converter and driveplate are being refitted, carefully turn the crankshaft to align the marks made before removal, before refitting the torque converter-to-driveplate bolts.

18 Fit **new** torque converter-to-driveplate bolts, and tighten them to the specified torque (see Chapter 7B). Turn the crankshaft for access to each bolt in turn, and prevent the driveplate from turning as during removal.

19 Refit the transmission bellhousing cover plate.

20 Proceed as described in Section 4, paragraphs 49 to 59 inclusive, substituting 'transmission' for 'gearbox', and ignoring paragraph 55.

21 Reconnect the transmission fluid cooler hoses to the transmission, ensuring that they are correctly reconnected, as noted before removal.

22 Disconnect the hoist and lifting tackle from the engine lifting brackets.

23 Refit the roadwheels, and lower the vehicle to the ground.

24 Reconnect the transmission wiring harness plugs, and secure the wiring harness brackets to the transmission.

25 Reconnect the vent hose to the transmission.

26 Reconnect the selector cable to the actuating lever on the transmission, and refit the cable sheath to the transmission bracket.

27 On models with power steering, refit the power steering pump to the bracket on the engine, routing the fluid hoses as noted before removal.

28 Where applicable, refit and tension the auxiliary drivebelt as described in Chapter 1.

29 Reconnect all relevant wiring to the engine and associated components, ensuring that the wiring is routed and secured as noted before removal.

30 On SOHC engine models with multi-point fuel injection, refit the fuel line bracket to the inlet manifold.

31 Reconnect the fuel lines, ensuring that they are connected to their correct locations, and tighten the unions or hose clamps, as applicable.

32 Reconnect the speedometer cable to the transmission, or reconnect the speedometer cable connector (as applicable), with reference to Chapter 12 if necessary. On later models, reconnect the wiring connector to the electronic speedometer sensor.

33 Proceed as described in Section 4, paragraphs 70 to 80 inclusive.

34 Check and if necessary top-up the transmission fluid level as described in Chapter 1.

35 Check the adjustment of the selector cable as described in Chapter 7B.

36 Make a final check to ensure that all relevant hoses, pipes and wires have been correctly reconnected.

37 Refit the bonnet as described in Chapter 11.

38 Reconnect the battery leads.

6 Engine overhaul – dismantling sequence

1 It is far easier to dismantle and work on the engine if it is mounted on a portable engine stand. These stands can often be hired from a tool hire shop. Depending on the type of stand used, the flywheel/driveplate may have to be removed from the engine to allow the engine stand bolts to be tightened into the end of the cylinder block.

2 If a stand is not available, it is possible to dismantle the engine while supported on blocks on a sturdy workbench or on the floor. Be extra-careful not to tip or drop the engine when working without a stand.

3 Before starting the overhaul procedure, the external ancillary components must be removed (this is the case even if a reconditioned engine is to be fitted, in which case, the components from the old engine must be transferred to the reconditioned unit). These components include the following:

a) *Alternator and mounting bracket (see Chapter 5A).*
b) *Starter motor (see Chapter 5A).*
c) *Rear coolant gallery and hoses.*
d) *Inlet and exhaust manifolds (see Chapter 4B).*
e) *Oil filter (see Chapter 1).*
f) *DIS module components, HT leads and spark plugs (see Chapters 1 and 5B).*

g) *Engine mountings (where applicable) (see Chapter 2B or 2C).*
h) *Oil pressure switch (see Chapter 5A).*
i) *Crankcase breather tube.*
j) *Engine lifting brackets.*
k) *Crankshaft speed/position sensor and bracket (where applicable) (see Chapter 4B, Section 13 or 14).*
l) *Coolant temperature sensor (see Chapter 4B, Section 12, 13 or 14).*
m) *Knock sensor (where applicable) (see Chapter 5B, Section 5).*
n) *Power steering pump and mounting bracket (where applicable) (see Chapter 10).*
o) *Wiring harnesses.*
p) *Dipstick.*
q) *Coolant pump and thermostat (the timing belt and rear timing belt cover must be removed for access to these components) (see Chapter 3).*

Note: *When removing the ancillary components from the engine, pay close attention to details which may be helpful or important during refitting. Note the fitted position of gaskets, seals, spacers, washers, bolts and other small items.*

4 If a 'short' engine is being obtained (which consists of the cylinder block, crankshaft, pistons and connecting rods all assembled as a unit), then the cylinder head, sump, timing belt, and possibly other components (such as the oil pump) will have to be removed from the old unit and fitted to the new one.

5 If a complete overhaul is being planned, the engine can be dismantled using the following sequence.

a) *Inlet and exhaust manifolds (see Chapter 4B).*
b) *Timing belt and sprockets (see Chapter 2B or 2C).*
c) *Cylinder head, valve lifters, camshaft(s) and rocker components (as applicable) (see Chapter 2B or 2C).*
d) *Flywheel/driveplate (see Chapter 2B or 2C).*
e) *Sump (see Chapter 2B or 2C).*
f) *Oil pump (see Chapter 2B or 2C).*
g) *Piston/connecting rod assemblies (see Section 10).*
h) *Crankshaft (see Section 11).*

6 Before beginning the dismantling and overhaul procedures, make sure that all the correct tools have been obtained. Refer to the preliminary Sections of this manual for further information.

7 Cylinder head – dismantling

Note: *New and reconditioned cylinder heads are available from the manufacturers, and from engine overhaul specialists. Due to the fact that some specialist tools are required for the dismantling and inspection procedures, and new components may not be readily*

7.2 Remove the valve lifters from the cylinder head, and store with the oil groove (arrowed) at the bottom – DOHC engine

7.3 Valve spring compressor fitted to No 1 exhaust valve – SOHC engine

7.5 Extracting a split collet – SOHC engine

available, it may be more practical and economical for the home mechanic to purchase a reconditioned head rather than to dismantle, inspect and recondition the original head. A valve spring compressor tool will be required for this operation.

1 With the cylinder head removed as described in Chapter 2B or 2C, clean away all external dirt, and remove the following components, if not already done:

a) Manifolds (see Chapter 4B).
b) Spark plugs (see Chapter 1).
c) Thermostat housing, and the thermostat (see Chapter 3).
d) On DOHC engines, remove the camshafts (see Chapter 2C), the DIS module and its bracket (see Chapter 5B), and the coolant housing (mounted on the inlet manifold side of the cylinder head).

2 On DOHC engines, remove the hydraulic valve lifters from their bores, using a rubber suction plunger tool – do not invert the cylinder head in order to remove the valve lifters. Keep the valve lifters upright at all times, with the oil groove at the bottom **(see illustration)**. Immerse them, in order of removal, in a container of clean engine oil until they are to be refitted.

3 To remove a valve, fit a valve spring compressor tool. Ensure that the arms of the compressor tool are securely positioned on the head of the valve and the spring cap **(see illustration)**. The valves on the DOHC engine are deeply-recessed, and a suitable extension piece may be required for the spring compressor.

4 Compress the valve spring to relieve the pressure of the spring cap acting on the collets.

> **HAYNES HiNT** *If the spring cap sticks to the valve stem, support the compressor tool, and give the end a light tap with a soft-faced mallet to help free the spring cap.*

5 Extract the two split collets, then slowly release the compressor tool **(see illustration)**.
6 Remove the spring cap, spring, valve stem oil seal (using long-nosed pliers if necessary), and the spring seat, then withdraw the valve through the combustion chamber **(see illustrations)**.
7 Repeat the procedure for the remaining valves, keeping all components in strict order so that they can be refitted in their original positions, unless all the components are to be renewed. If the components are to be kept

and used again, place each valve assembly in a labelled polythene bag or a similar small container **(see illustration)**. Note that as with cylinder numbering, the valves are normally numbered from the timing belt end of the engine. Make sure that on DOHC engines, the valve components are identified as inlet and exhaust, as well as numbered.

8 Cylinder head and valve components – cleaning and inspection

1 Thorough cleaning of the cylinder head and valve components, followed by a detailed inspection, will enable a decision to be made on whether further work is necessary before reassembling the components.

7.6a Remove the spring cap . . .

7.6b . . . spring . . .

7.6c . . . valve stem oil seal . . .

7.6d . . . and the spring seat – DOHC engine

7.7 Place each valve assembly in a labelled polythene bag

8.6 Checking the cylinder head surface for distortion

8.9a Valve lifter oil holes (arrowed) in cylinder head – DOHC engine

8.9b Check the oil holes (arrowed) in the oil jets for obstructions – DOHC engine

Cleaning

2 Scrape away all traces of old gasket material and sealing compound from the cylinder head surfaces. Take care not to damage the cylinder head surfaces, as the head is made of light alloy.

3 Scrape away the carbon from the combustion chambers and ports, then wash the cylinder head thoroughly with paraffin or a suitable solvent.

4 Scrape off any heavy carbon deposits that may have formed on the valves, then use a power-operated wire brush to remove deposits from the valve heads and stems.

Inspection

Note: *Be sure to perform all the following inspection procedures before concluding that the services of a machine shop or engine overhaul specialist are required. Make a list of all items that require attention.*

Cylinder head

5 Inspect the head very carefully for cracks, evidence of coolant leakage, and other damage. If cracks are found, a new cylinder head should be obtained.

6 Use a straight-edge and feeler blade to check that the cylinder head surface is not distorted **(see illustration)**. If the specified distortion limit is exceeded, it may be possible to have the cylinder head resurfaced, provided that the overall height of the head is not reduced to less than the specified minimum.

7 Examine the valve seats in each of the combustion chambers. If the seats are severely pitted, cracked or burned, then they will need

to be re-cut by an engine overhaul specialist. If only slight pitting is evident, this can be removed by grinding the valve heads and seats together with coarse, then fine, grinding paste, as described later in this Section.

8 If the valve guides are worn, indicated by a side-to-side motion of the valve, the guides can be reamed, and valves with oversize stems can be fitted. This work is best carried out by an engine overhaul specialist. A dial gauge may be used to determine whether the amount of side play of a valve exceeds the specified maximum.

9 Check the valve lifter bores in the cylinder head for wear. If excessive wear is evident, the cylinder head must be renewed. Also check the valve lifter oil holes in the cylinder head for obstructions. On DOHC engines, unscrew the oil jets from the cylinder head, and check the oil holes for obstruction. Clean the jets if necessary, then refit and tighten them. If desired, the oil gallery plugs (where applicable) can be removed, and the oil galleries can be cleaned by blowing through with compressed air **(see illustrations)**.

⚠ *Warning: Wear eye protection when using compressed air.*

Valves

10 Examine the head of each valve for pitting, burning, cracks and general wear, and check the valve stem for scoring and wear ridges. Rotate the valve, and check for any obvious indication that it is bent. Look for pitting and excessive wear on the end of each valve stem. If the valve appears satisfactory at this stage,

measure the valve stem diameter at several points using a micrometer **(see illustration)**. Any significant difference in the readings obtained indicates wear of the valve stem. Should any of these conditions be apparent, the valve(s) must be renewed. If the valves are in satisfactory condition, they should be ground (lapped) onto their respective seats to ensure a smooth gas-tight seal.

⚠ *Warning: The exhaust valves fitted to DOHC engines are filled with sodium, to improve heat transfer. Sodium is a highly-reactive metal, which will ignite or explode spontaneously on contact with water (including water vapour in the air). Valves containing sodium must NOT be disposed of with ordinary scrap – seek advice from a Vauxhall/Opel dealer if the valves are to be disposed of.*

11 Valve grinding is carried out as follows. Place the cylinder head upside-down on a bench, with a block of wood at each end to give clearance for the valve stems.

> **HAYNES HINT** *A light spring placed under the valve head will greatly ease the grinding operation.*

12 Smear a trace of coarse carborundum paste on the seat face in the cylinder head, and press a suction grinding tool onto the relevant valve head. With a semi-rotary action, grind the valve head to its seat, lifting the valve occasionally to redistribute the grinding paste **(see illustration)**. When a dull, matt,

8.9c Cylinder head oil gallery plugs (arrowed) – DOHC engine

8.10 Measuring a valve stem diameter

8.12 Grinding-in a valve seat

8.17 Hydraulic valve lifter components – SOHC engine

1 Collar   5 Plunger cap
2 Plunger   6 Large spring
3 Ball   7 Cylinder
4 Small spring

8.23 Locate the ball (1) on its seat (2) in the base of the plunger

8.24a Spring (1) located in plunger cap, and ball (2) located on seat in plunger

even surface is produced on the faces of both the valve seat and the valve, wipe off the paste and repeat the process with fine carborundum paste. When a smooth unbroken ring of light grey matt finish is produced on both the valve and seat faces, the grinding operation is complete. Carefully clean away every trace of grinding paste, taking great care to leave none in the ports or in the valve guides. Clean the valves and valve seats with a paraffin-soaked rag, then with a clean rag, and finally, if an air line is available, blow the valves, valve guides and cylinder head ports clean.

Valve springs

13 Check that all the valve springs are intact. If any one is broken, all should be renewed.
14 If possible, check the free height of the springs against new ones, then stand each spring on a flat surface and check it for squareness. If a spring is found to be too short, or damaged in any way, renew all the springs as a set. Springs suffer from fatigue, and it is a good idea to renew them even if they look serviceable.

Rocker arm components – SOHC engines

15 Check the rocker arm and thrust pad

faces (the areas that contact the valve lifters and valve stems) for pits, wear, score-marks or any indication that the surface-hardening has worn through. Check the rocker arm camshaft contact faces in the same manner. Clean the oil hole in the top of each rocker arm using a length of wire. Renew any rocker arms or thrust pads which appear suspect.

Valve lifters – SOHC engines

16 Proceed as described in paragraph 9.
17 On engines which have covered a high mileage, or for which the service history (particularly oil changes) is suspect, it is possible for the valve lifters to suffer internal contamination, which in extreme cases may result in increased engine top-end noise and wear. To minimise the possibility of problems occurring later in the life of the engine, it is advisable to dismantle and clean the hydraulic valve lifters as follows whenever the cylinder head is overhauled. Note that this procedure is not recommended by the manufacturers, and no spare parts are available for the valve lifters – if any of the components are unserviceable, the complete assembly must be renewed (see illustration).
18 Carefully pull the collar from the top of the valve lifter cylinder. It should be possible to remove the collar by hand – if a tool is used, take care not to distort the collar.
19 Withdraw the plunger from the cylinder, and recover the spring.
20 Using a small screwdriver, carefully prise

the cap from the base of the plunger. Recover the spring and ball from under the cap, taking care not to lose them as the cap is removed.
21 Carefully clean all the components using paraffin or a suitable solvent, paying particular attention to the machined surfaces of the cylinder (internal surfaces), and piston (external surfaces). Thoroughly dry all the components using a lint-free cloth. Carefully examine the springs for damage or distortion – the complete valve lifter must be renewed if the springs are not in perfect condition.
22 Lubricate the components sparingly with clean engine oil of the correct grade (see Weekly checks), then reassemble as follows.
23 Invert the plunger, and locate the ball on its seat in the base of the plunger (see illustration).
24 Locate the smaller spring on its seat in the plunger cap, then carefully refit the cap and spring, ensuring that the spring locates on the ball. Carefully press around the flange of the cap, using a small screwdriver if necessary, until the flange is securely located in the groove in the base of the plunger (see illustrations).
25 Locate the larger spring over the plunger cap, ensuring that the spring is correctly seated, and slide the plunger and spring assembly into the cylinder (see illustrations).
26 Slide the collar over the top of the plunger, and carefully compress the plunger by hand, until the collar can be pushed down

8.24b Locate the cap flange in the plunger groove

8.25a Locate the spring over the plunger cap . . .

8.25b . . . then slide the plunger and spring assembly into the cylinder

8.26 Slide the collar (1) over the top of the plunger and engage with the groove (2) in the cylinder

9.1 Inlet (1) and exhaust (2) valve components – SOHC engine

9.2 Inserting an exhaust valve into its guide – SOHC engine

9.3 Fitting a spring seat (exhaust valve) – SOHC engine

9.4 Slide the oil seal fitting sleeve down the valve stem . . .

9.5a . . . then fit the valve stem oil seal . . .

9.5b . . . and push onto the spring seat using a suitable socket – SOHC engine

9.6a Fit the valve spring . . .

9.6b . . . and spring cap – SOHC engine

to engage securely with the groove in the cylinder (**see illustration**).

Valve lifters – DOHC engines

Note: *The valve lifters should always be stored upright in a container of clean engine oil while removed from the cylinder head.*

27 Inspect the valve lifters for obvious signs of wear on the contact faces, and check the valve lifter oil holes for obstructions, particularly for oil sludge. If excessive wear is evident (this is unlikely), all the valve lifters must be renewed as a set.

9 Cylinder head – reassembly

Note: *New valve stem oil seals should be used on reassembly. A valve spring compressor tool will be required for this operation.*

1 With all the components cleaned, starting at one end of the cylinder head, fit the valve components as follows (**see illustration**).

2 Insert the appropriate valve into its guide (if new valves are being fitted, insert each valve into the location to which it has been ground), ensuring that the valve stem is well-lubricated with clean engine oil (**see illustration**). If the original components are being refitted, all components must be refitted in their original positions.

3 Fit the spring seat (**see illustration**).

4 New valve stem oil seals should be supplied with a fitting sleeve, which fits over the collet groove in the valve stem, to prevent damage to the oil seal as it is slid down the valve stem (**see illustration**). If no sleeve is supplied, wind a short length of tape round the top of the valve stem to cover the collet groove.

5 Lubricate the valve stem oil seal with clean engine oil, then push the oil seal down the valve stem using a suitable tube or socket, until the seal is fully engaged with the spring seat (**see illustrations**). Remove the fitting sleeve or the tape, as applicable, from the valve stem.

6 Fit the valve spring and the spring cap (**see illustrations**).

9.8 Refit the split collets – DOHC engine

9.11 Oil the valve lifters before refitting – DOHC engine

10.3 Big-end cap centre-punched identification marks. Note that lug on bearing cap faces flywheel end of engine

7 Fit the spring compressor tool, and compress the valve spring until the spring cap passes beyond the collet groove in the valve stem.

8 Refit the split collets to the groove in the valve stem, with the narrow ends nearest the spring **(see illustration)**.

 HAYNES HiNT *Apply a little grease to the split collets, then fit the split collets into the groove. The grease should hold the collets in the groove.*

9 Slowly release the compressor tool, ensuring that the collets are not dislodged from the groove. When the compressor is fully released, give the top of the valve assembly a tap with a soft-faced mallet to settle the components.

10 Repeat the procedure for the remaining valves, ensuring that if the original components are being used, they are all refitted in their original positions.

11 On DOHC engines, refit the hydraulic valve lifters to the cylinder head in their original positions. Liberally oil the valve lifters and their bores **(see illustration)**. If new valve lifters are being fitted, initially immerse each one in a container of clean engine oil, and compress it (by hand) several times to charge it.

12 Refit the following components as applicable (if desired, these components can be refitted after refitting the cylinder head).

a) On DOHC engines, refit the camshafts

(see Chapter 2C), the DIS module and its mounting bracket (see Chapter 5B), and the coolant housing.

b) Refit the thermostat housing and thermostat, using a new sealing ring, where applicable – see Chapter 3.

c) Refit the spark plugs (see Chapter 1).

d) Refit the manifolds (see Chapter 4B).

10 Piston/connecting rod assemblies – removal

Note: *On DOHC engines, the mating faces of the connecting rods and the big-end bearing caps are 'rough' (not machined), which ensures perfect mating of each individual rod and bearing cap. When the components have been removed from the engine, extreme care should be taken not to damage the mating surfaces – eg, do not rest the bearing caps on the mating faces. Ensure that each bearing cap is kept together with its respective rod, to prevent any possibility of the components being refitted incorrectly.*

1 Remove the cylinder head as described in Chapter 2B or 2C.

2 Remove the sump and oil pick-up pipe, as described in Chapter 2B or 2C.

3 If the connecting rods and big-end caps are not marked to indicate their positions in the cylinder block (ie, marked with cylinder numbers), centre-punch them at adjacent points either side of the cap/rod joint. Note to

which side of the engine the marks face **(see illustration)**.

4 Unscrew the big-end cap bolts from the first connecting rod, and remove the cap. If the bearing shells are to be re-used, tape the cap and the shell together.

5 Check the top of the cylinder bore for a wear ridge. If evident, carefully scrape it away with a ridge reamer tool, otherwise the piston rings may jam against the ridge as the piston is pushed out of the block.

6 Place the wooden handle of a hammer against the bottom of the connecting rod, and push the piston/rod assembly up and out of the cylinder bore. Recover the bearing shell, and tape it to the connecting rod if it is to be re-used.

7 Remove the remaining three assemblies in a similar way. Rotate the crankshaft as necessary to bring the big-end bolts to the most accessible position.

11 Crankshaft – removal

1 Remove the flywheel/driveplate as described in Chapter 2B or 2C.

2 Remove the pistons and connecting rods, as described in Section 10.

3 Remove the oil pump as described in Chapter 2B or 2C.

4 Invert the engine so that the crankshaft is uppermost.

5 Before removing the crankshaft, check the endfloat using a dial gauge in contact with the end of the crankshaft. Push the crankshaft fully one way, and then zero the gauge. Push the crankshaft fully the other way, and check the endfloat **(see illustration)**. The result should be compared with the specified limit, and will give an indication as to whether new thrust bearing shells are required.

6 If a dial gauge is not available, a feeler gauge can be used to measure crankshaft endfloat. Push the crankshaft fully towards one end of the crankcase, and insert a feeler gauge between the thrust flange of the centre main bearing shell and the machined surface of the crankshaft web **(see illustration)**.

11.5 Check the crankshaft endfloat using a dial gauge . . .

11.6 . . . or a feeler gauge

11.7 Main bearing cap identification marks (arrowed)

11.9 Lifting the crankshaft from the crankcase

12.17 Piston diameter marking (arrowed) on piston crown

Before measuring, ensure that the crankshaft is fully forced towards one end of the crankcase, to give the widest possible gap at the measuring location.

7 The main bearing caps are normally numbered 1 to 4 from the timing belt end of the engine. The flywheel end cap is not marked. The numbers are read from the coolant pump side of the engine **(see illustration)**. If the bearing caps are not marked, centre-punch them to indicate their locations, and note to which side of the engine the marks face.

8 Unscrew and remove the main bearing cap bolts, and withdraw the bearing caps. If the bearing caps are stuck, tap them gently with a soft-faced mallet to free them. If the bearing shells are to be re-used, tape them to their respective caps.

9 Lift the crankshaft from the crankcase **(see illustration)**.

10 Extract the upper bearing shells, and identify them for position if they are to be re-used.

---

12 Cylinder block/crankcase – cleaning and inspection

Cleaning

1 For complete cleaning, ideally the core plugs should be removed, where fitted. Drill a small hole in the plugs, then insert a self-tapping screw, and pull out the plugs using a pair of grips or a slide hammer. Also remove all external components (senders, sensors, brackets, etc).

2 Note that, where applicable, the rubber plug located next to the bellhousing flange on the cylinder block covers the aperture for the installation of a diagnostic TDC sensor (used by Vauxhall/Opel dealers). The sensor, when connected to a suitable monitoring unit, indicates TDC from the position of the pins set into the crankshaft balance weight.

3 Scrape all traces of gasket from the cylinder block, taking particular care not to damage the cylinder head and sump mating faces.

4 Remove all oil gallery plugs, where fitted.

The plugs are usually very tight – they may have to be drilled out and the holes re-tapped. Use new plugs when the engine is reassembled.

5 If the block is extremely dirty, it should be steam-cleaned.

6 If the block has been steam-cleaned, clean all oil holes and oil galleries one more time on completion. Flush all internal passages with warm water until the water runs clear. Dry the block thoroughly, and wipe all machined surfaces with a light oil. If you have access to compressed air, use it to speed the drying process, and to blow out all the oil holes and galleries.

 Warning: Wear eye protection when using compressed air.

7 If the block is relatively clean, an adequate cleaning job can be achieved with hot soapy water and a stiff brush. Take plenty of time, and do a thorough job. Regardless of the cleaning method used, be sure to clean all oil holes and galleries very thoroughly, dry the block completely, and coat all machined surfaces with light oil.

8 The threaded holes in the cylinder block must be clean, to ensure accurate torque readings when tightening fixings during reassembly. Run the correct-size tap (which can be determined from the size of the relevant bolt) into each of the holes to remove rust, corrosion, thread sealant or other contamination, and to restore damaged threads. If possible, use compressed air to clear the holes of debris produced by this operation. Do not forget to clean the threads of all bolts and nuts as well.

9 After coating the mating surfaces of the new core plugs with suitable sealant, fit them to the cylinder block. Make sure that they are driven in straight and seated correctly, or leakage could result.

> **HAYNES HiNT** *Special tools are available to fit the core plugs, but a large socket, with an outside diameter which will just fit into the core plug, will work just as well.*

10 Where applicable, apply suitable sealant to the new oil gallery plugs, and insert them into the relevant holes in the cylinder block. Tighten the plugs securely.

11 If the engine is to be left dismantled for some time, refit the main bearing caps, tighten the bolts finger-tight, and cover the cylinder block with a large plastic bag to keep it clean and prevent corrosion.

Inspection

12 Visually check the block for cracks, rust and corrosion. Look for stripped threads in the threaded holes (it may be possible to re-cut stripped threads using a suitable tap). If there has been any history of internal coolant leakage, it may be worthwhile asking an engine overhaul specialist to check the block using special equipment. If defects are found, have the block repaired if possible, otherwise a new block may be the only option.

13 Examine the cylinder bores for taper, ovality, scoring and scratches. Start by carefully examining the top of the cylinder bores. If they are at all worn, a very slight ridge will be found on the thrust side. This marks the top of the piston ring travel.

14 Measure the bore diameter of each cylinder at the top (just under the wear ridge), centre and bottom of the cylinder bore, parallel to the crankshaft axis.

15 Next, measure the bore diameter at the same three locations, at right-angles to the crankshaft axis. Compare the results with the figures given in the Specifications.

16 Repeat the procedure for the remaining cylinders.

17 If the cylinder wear exceeds the permitted tolerances, or if the cylinder walls are badly scored or scuffed, then the cylinders will have to be rebored by a suitably-qualified specialist, and new oversize pistons will have to be fitted. In this case, note the following points:

a) *Pistons and cylinder bores are closely matched in production. The actual diameter of the piston is indicated by numbers on its crown* **(see illustration)**; *the same numbers on the crankcase indicate the cylinder bore diameter.*

b) *After reboring has taken place, the*

cylinder bores should be measured accurately, and oversize pistons selected from the grades available to give the specified piston-to-bore clearance.

c) *For grading purposes, the piston diameter is measured across the bottom of the skirt.*

18 If the bore wear is marginal, and within the specified tolerances, new special piston rings can be fitted to offset the wear.

19 If this is the case, the bores should be honed in order to allow the new rings to bed in correctly and provide the best possible seal. The conventional type of hone has spring-loaded stones, and is used with a power drill. You will also need some paraffin or honing oil, and rags. The hone should be moved up and down the cylinder bore to produce a crosshatch pattern, and plenty of honing oil should be used. Ideally, the cross-hatch lines should intersect at approximately a 60° angle. Do not remove more material than is necessary to produce the required finish. If new pistons are being fitted, the piston manufacturers may specify a finish with a different angle, so their instructions should be followed. Do not withdraw the hone from the cylinder while it is still being turned – stop it first. After honing a cylinder, wipe out all traces of the honing oil. An engine overhaul specialist will be able to carry out this work at moderate cost, if required.

13 Piston/connecting rod assemblies – inspection

1 Before the inspection process can begin, the piston/connecting rod assemblies must be cleaned, and the original piston rings removed from the pistons.

2 Carefully expand the old rings over the top of the pistons. The use of two or three old feeler gauges will be helpful in preventing the rings dropping into empty grooves **(see illustration)**. Take care, however, as piston rings are sharp.

3 Scrape away all traces of carbon from the top of the piston. A hand-held wire brush, or a piece of fine emery cloth, can be used once the majority of the deposits have been scraped away.

4 Remove the carbon from the ring grooves in the piston, using an old ring. Break the ring in half to do this (be careful not to cut your fingers – piston rings are sharp). Be very careful to remove only the carbon deposits – do not remove any metal, and do not nick or scratch the sides of the ring grooves.

5 Once the deposits have been removed, clean the piston/connecting rod assembly with paraffin or a suitable solvent, and dry thoroughly. Make sure that the oil return holes in the ring grooves are clear.

6 If the pistons and cylinder bores are not damaged or worn excessively, and if the cylinder block does not need to be rebored, the original pistons can be refitted. Normal piston wear shows up as even vertical wear on the piston thrust surfaces, and slight looseness of the top ring in its groove. New piston rings should always be used when the engine is reassembled.

7 Carefully inspect each piston for cracks around the skirt, at the gudgeon pin bosses, and at the piston ring lands (between the ring grooves).

8 Look for scoring and scuffing on the thrust faces of the piston skirt, holes in the piston crown, and burned areas at the edge of the crown. If the skirt is scored or scuffed, the engine may have been suffering from overheating, and/or abnormal combustion ('pinking') which caused excessively-high operating temperatures. The cooling and lubrication systems should be checked thoroughly. A hole in the piston crown, or burned areas at the edge of the piston crown indicates that abnormal combustion (pre-ignition, 'pinking', knocking or detonation) has been occurring. If any of the above problems exist, the causes must be investigated and corrected, or the damage will occur again. The causes may include leaks in the intake air tracts, incorrect fuel/air mixture, incorrect grade of spark plug, or incorrect ignition timing.

9 Corrosion of the piston, in the form of pitting, indicates that coolant has been leaking into the combustion chamber and/or the crankcase. Again, the cause must be corrected, or the problem may persist in the rebuilt engine.

10 Check the piston-to-bore clearance by measuring the cylinder bore (see Section 12)

and the piston diameter. Measure the piston across the bottom of the skirt, at a 90° angle to the gudgeon pin. Subtract the piston diameter from the bore diameter to obtain the clearance. If this is greater than the figures given in the Specifications, the block will have to be rebored, and new pistons and rings fitted.

11 Check the fit of the gudgeon pin by twisting the piston and connecting rod in opposite directions. Any noticeable play indicates excessive wear, which must be corrected. If the pistons or connecting rods are to be renewed, it is necessary to have this work carried out by a Vauxhall/Opel dealer or a suitable engine overhaul specialist, who will have the necessary tooling to remove the gudgeon pins.

12 Check the alignment of the connecting rods visually, and if the rods are not straight, take them to an engine overhaul specialist for a more detailed check.

14 Crankshaft – inspection

1 Clean the crankshaft using paraffin or a suitable solvent, and dry it, preferably with compressed air if available. Be sure to clean the oil holes with a pipe cleaner or similar probe, to ensure that they are not obstructed.

⚠ **Warning: Wear eye protection when using compressed air.**

2 Check the main and big-end bearing journals for uneven wear, scoring, pitting and cracking.

3 Big-end bearing wear is accompanied by distinct metallic knocking when the engine is running (particularly noticeable when the engine is pulling from low revs), and some loss of oil pressure.

4 Main bearing wear is accompanied by severe engine vibration and rumble – getting progressively worse as engine revs increase – and again by loss of oil pressure.

5 Check the bearing journal for roughness by running a finger lightly over the bearing surface. Any roughness (which will be accompanied by obvious bearing wear) indicates the that the crankshaft requires regrinding.

6 If the crankshaft has been reground, check for burrs around the crankshaft oil holes (the holes are usually chamfered, so burrs should not be a problem unless regrinding has been carried out carelessly). Remove any burrs with a fine file or scraper, and thoroughly clean the oil holes as described previously.

7 Using a micrometer, measure the diameter of the main and big-end bearing journals, and compare the results with the Specifications at the beginning of this Chapter **(see illustration)**. By measuring the diameter at a number of points around each journal's

13.2 Using a feeler gauge to aid removal of a piston ring

14.7 Measuring the diameter of a crankshaft journal

circumference, you will be able to determine whether or not the journal is out-of-round. Take the measurement at each end of the journal, near the webs, to determine if the journal is tapered. If the crankshaft journals are damaged, tapered, out-of-round or excessively-worn, the crankshaft will have to be reground and undersize bearings fitted.

8 Check the oil seal contact surfaces at each end of the crankshaft for wear and damage. If the seal has worn an excessive groove in the surface of the crankshaft, consult an engine overhaul specialist, who will be able to advise whether a repair is possible, or whether a new crankshaft is necessary.

9 Where applicable, check the condition of the pins in the front crankshaft balance weight, which serve as detent points for the plug-in diagnostic sensor used by Vauxhall/Opel dealers.

15 Main and big-end bearings – inspection

1 Even though the main and big-end bearing shells should be renewed during engine overhaul, the old bearing shells should be retained for close examination, as they may reveal valuable information about the condition of the engine. The bearing shells carry identification marks to denote their size in the form of a colour code, or a letter/number code marked on the back of the shell **(see illustrations)**. If the shells are to be renewed, without carrying out any crankshaft regrinding, the old shells should be taken along when obtaining new shells, to ensure that the correct shells are obtained.

2 Bearing failure occurs because of lack of lubrication, the presence of dirt or other foreign particles, overloading the engine, or corrosion. If a bearing fails, the cause must be found and eliminated before the engine is reassembled, to prevent the failure from happening again.

3 To examine the bearing shells, remove them from the cylinder block, the main bearing caps, the connecting rods and the big-end bearing caps, and lay them out on a clean surface in the same order as they were

fitted to the engine. This will enable any bearing problems to be matched with the corresponding crankshaft journal.

4 Dirt and other foreign particles can enter the engine in a variety of ways. Contamination may be left in the engine during assembly, or it may pass through filters or the crankcase ventilation system. Normal engine wear produces small particles of metal, which can eventually cause problems. If particles find their way into the lubrication system, it is likely that they will eventually be carried to the bearings. Whatever the source, these foreign particles often end up embedded in the soft bearing material, and are easily recognised. Large particles will not embed in the bearing, and will score or gouge the bearing and journal. To prevent possible contamination, clean all parts thoroughly, and keep everything spotlessly-clean during engine assembly. Once the engine has been installed in the vehicle, ensure that engine oil and filter changes are carried out at the recommended intervals.

5 Lack of lubrication (or lubrication breakdown) has a number of interrelated causes. Excessive heat (which thins the oil), overloading (which squeezes the oil from the bearing face), and oil leakage (from excessive bearing clearances, worn oil pump or high engine speeds) all contribute to lubrication breakdown. Blocked oil passages, which may be the result of misaligned oil holes in a bearing shell, will also starve a bearing of oil and destroy it. When lack of lubrication is the cause of bearing failure, the bearing material is wiped or extruded from the steel backing of the bearing. Temperatures may increase to the point where the steel backing turns blue from overheating.

6 Driving habits can have a definite effect on bearing life. Full-throttle, low-speed operation (labouring the engine) puts very high loads on bearings, which tends to squeeze out the oil film. These loads cause the bearings to flex, which produces fine cracks in the bearing face (fatigue failure). Eventually the bearing material will loosen in places, and tear away from the steel backing. Regular short journeys can lead to corrosion of bearings, because insufficient engine heat is produced to drive off the condensed water and corrosive gases

which form inside the engine. These products collect in the engine oil, forming acid and sludge. As the oil is carried to the bearings, the acid attacks and corrodes the bearing material.

7 Incorrect bearing installation during engine assembly will also lead to bearing failure. Tight-fitting bearings leave insufficient bearing lubrication clearance, and will result in oil starvation. Dirt or foreign particles trapped behind a bearing shell results in high spots on the bearing which can lead to failure.

8 If new bearings are to be fitted, the bearing running clearances should be measured before the engine is finally reassembled, to ensure that the correct bearing shells have been obtained (see Sections 18 and 19). If the crankshaft has been reground, the engineering works should be able to advise on the correct-size bearing shells to suit the work carried out. If there is any doubt as to which bearing shells should be used, seek advice from a Vauxhall/Opel dealer.

16 Engine overhaul – reassembly sequence

1 Before reassembly begins, ensure that all necessary new parts have been obtained (particularly gaskets, and various bolts which must be renewed), and that all the tools required are available. Read through the entire procedure to familiarise yourself with the work involved, and to ensure that all items necessary for reassembly of the engine are to hand. In addition to all normal tools and materials, a thread-locking compound will be required. A tube of RTV sealing compound will also be required, to seal certain joint faces which are not fitted with gaskets.

2 In order to save time and avoid problems, engine reassembly can be carried out in the following order:

a) *Piston rings (see Section 17).*
b) *Crankshaft and main bearings (see Section 18).*
c) *Piston/connecting rod assemblies (see Section 19).*
d) *Oil pump (see Chapter 2B or 2C).*
e) *Sump (see Chapter 2B or 2C).*
f) *Flywheel/driveplate (see Chapter 2B or 2C).*
g) *Cylinder head, valve lifters, camshaft(s) and rocker components (as applicable) (see Chapter 2B or 2C).*
h) *Timing belt and sprockets (see Chapter 2B or 2C).*
i) *Engine external components.*

17 Piston rings – refitting

1 Before refitting the new piston rings, the ring end gaps must be checked as follows.

15.1a Typical main bearing shell . . .

15.1b . . . and main thrust bearing shell identification marks

17.5 Measuring a piston ring end gap using a feeler gauge

17.10 Fitting an oil control spreader ring

17.12 Sectional view showing correct orientation of piston rings

2 Lay out the piston/ connecting rod assemblies and the new piston ring sets, so that the ring sets will be matched with the same piston and cylinder during the end gap measurement and subsequent engine reassembly.

3 Insert the top ring into the first cylinder, and push it down the bore using the top of the piston. This will ensure that the ring remains square with the cylinder walls. Position the ring near the bottom of the cylinder bore, at the lower limit of ring travel.

4 Measure the end gap using feeler gauges.

5 Repeat the procedure with the ring at the top of the cylinder bore, at the upper limit of its travel, and compare the measurements with the figures given in the Specifications (see illustration).

6 If the gap is too small (unlikely if genuine Vauxhall/Opel parts are used), it must be enlarged or the ring ends may contact each other during engine operation, causing serious damage. Ideally, new piston rings providing the correct end gap should be fitted, but as a last resort, the end gap can be increased by filing the ring ends very carefully with a fine file. Mount the file in a vice equipped with soft jaws, slip the ring over the file with the ends contacting the file face, and slowly move the ring to remove material from the ends – take care, as piston rings are sharp, and are easily broken.

7 With new piston rings, it is unlikely that the end gap will be too large. If they are too large, check that you have the correct rings for your engine and for the particular cylinder bore size.

8 Repeat the checking procedure for each ring in the first cylinder, and then for the rings in the remaining cylinders. Remember to keep rings, pistons and cylinders matched up.

9 Once the ring end gaps have been checked and if necessary corrected, the rings can be fitted to the pistons.

10 The oil control ring (lowest one on the piston) is composed of three sections, and should be installed first. Fit the lower steel ring, then the spreader ring, followed by the upper steel ring (see illustration).

11 With the oil control ring components installed, the second (middle) ring can be fitted. It is usually stamped with a mark (TOP)

which must face up, towards the top of the piston. **Note:** *Always follow the instructions supplied with the new piston ring sets – different manufacturers may specify different procedures. Do not mix up the top and middle rings, as they have different cross-sections.* Using two or three old feeler blades, as for removal of the old rings, carefully slip the ring into place in the middle groove.

12 Fit the top ring in the same manner, ensuring that, where applicable, the mark on the ring is facing up. If a stepped ring is being fitted, fit the ring with the smaller diameter of the step uppermost (see illustration).

13 Repeat the procedure for the remaining pistons and rings.

18 Crankshaft – refitting and main bearing running clearance check

1 Refitting the crankshaft is the first step in the engine reassembly procedure. It is assumed at this point that the cylinder block and crankshaft have been cleaned, inspected and repaired or reconditioned as necessary.

2 Position the cylinder block with the sump mating face uppermost.

Main bearing running clearance check

Note: *When finally refitting the crankshaft, new main bearing cap bolts must be used. However, when checking the bearing running clearance, the original bolts may be used, and*

then discarded. A vernier dial indicator, an internal micrometer, or Plastigauge will be required for this check – see text.

3 Clean the bearing shells and the bearing recesses in both the cylinder block and main bearing caps. If new shells are being fitted, ensure that all traces of the protective grease are cleaned off using paraffin. Wipe the shells dry with a clean lint-free cloth.

4 Note that the central bearing shells have thrust flanges which control crankshaft endfloat. If the original bearing shells are being re-used, they must be refitted to their original locations in the block and caps (see illustrations).

5 Before the crankshaft can be permanently installed, the main bearing running clearance should be checked, and this can be done in either of two ways. One method is to fit the main bearing caps to the cylinder block, with bearing shells in place. With the original cap retaining bolts tightened to the specified torque, measure the internal diameter of each assembled pair of bearing shells using a vernier dial indicator or an internal micrometer. If the diameter of each corresponding crankshaft journal is measured and then subtracted from the bearing internal diameter, the result will give the main bearing running clearance. The second (and more accurate) method is to use a product known as Plastigauge. This consists of a fine thread of perfectly-round plastic, which is compressed between the bearing cap shell and the crankshaft journal. When the bearing cap is removed, the deformed plastic can be

18.4a Main bearing shell (A) and central main bearing shell (B) with thrust flange

18.4b Fitting a main bearing shell to the cylinder block

18.7 Lay the length of Plastigauge on the journal to be measured, parallel to the crankshaft centre-line

18.11 Using the scale on the envelope provided to check the width of the crushed Plastigauge (at its widest point)

18.16 Lubricate the main bearing shells before fitting the crankshaft

measured with a special card gauge supplied with the Plastigauge kit. The running clearance is determined from this gauge. Plastigauge is sometimes difficult to obtain in this country, but enquiries at one of the larger specialist chains of quality motor factors should produce the name of a stockist in your area. The procedure for using Plastigauge is as follows.

6 With the upper main bearing shells in place in the cylinder block, carefully lay the crankshaft in position. Do not use any lubricant; the crankshaft journals and bearing shells must be perfectly clean and dry.

7 Cut several pieces of the appropriate-size Plastigauge (they should be slightly shorter than the width of the main bearings) and place one piece on each crankshaft journal axis **(see illustration)**.

8 With the bearing shells in position in the caps, fit the caps to their original locations. Take care not to disturb the Plastigauge.

9 Starting with the centre main bearing and working outwards, tighten the main bearing cap bolts (use the original bolts) progressively to their specified torque. Do not rotate the crankshaft at any time during this operation.

10 Remove the bearing cap bolts and carefully lift off the caps, keeping them in order. Do not disturb the Plastigauge or rotate the crankshaft. If any of the bearing caps are difficult to remove, free them by carefully tapping with a soft-faced mallet.

11 Compare the width of the deformed Plastigauge on each journal with the scale printed on the card gauge to obtain the main bearing running clearance **(see illustration)**.

12 If the clearance is not as specified, the bearing shells may be the wrong size (or excessively-worn if the original shells are being re-used). Before deciding that different shells are required, make sure that no dirt or oil was trapped between the bearing shells and the caps or block when the clearance was measured. If the Plastigauge was wider at one end than at the other, the crankshaft journal may be tapered.

13 Carefully remove all traces of the Plastigauge material from the crankshaft and bearing shells, using a fingernail or other improvised tool which is unlikely to score the shells.

Final crankshaft refitting

Note: *New main bearing cap bolts must be used when refitting the crankshaft. Suitable sealants (Vauxhall/Opel Nos 15 03 295 and 15 03 170, or equivalents) will be required to coat the end main bearing caps.*

14 Carefully lift the crankshaft out of the cylinder block once more.

15 Lubricate the lips of a new crankshaft flywheel end oil seal, and carefully slip it over the end of the crankshaft. Do this carefully, as

the seal lips are very delicate. Ensure that the open side of the seal faces the inside of the engine.

16 Liberally lubricate each bearing shell in the cylinder block **(see illustration)**, and lower the crankshaft into position. Check that the oil seal is positioned correctly.

17 If necessary, seat the crankshaft using light taps from a soft-faced mallet on the crankshaft balance webs.

18 Lubricate the bearing shells in the bearing caps, and the crankshaft journals, then fit Nos 2, 3 and 4 bearing caps, and tighten the new bolts as far as possible by hand **(see illustration)**.

19 Fill the side grooves of the timing belt end (where applicable – not all engines have grooves in the timing belt end main bearing cap) and flywheel end main bearing caps with RTV jointing compound (Vauxhall/Opel part No 15 03 295, or equivalent). Coat the lower surfaces of the bearing caps with sealing compound (Vauxhall/Opel part No 15 03 170, or equivalent). Fit the bearing caps, and tighten the new bolts as far as possible by hand **(see illustrations)**. Ensure that the timing belt end main bearing cap is exactly flush with the end face of the cylinder block.

20 Working from the centre main bearing cap outwards, tighten the bearing cap bolts to the specified torque in the three stages given in the Specifications; ie, tighten all bolts to

18.18 Fitting the centre main bearing cap

18.19a Fill the side grooves of the flywheel end main bearing cap with RTV jointing compound . . .

18.19b . . . and coat the lower surfaces with sealing compound

18.20a Tighten the main bearing cap bolts to the specified torque . . .

18.20b . . . then through the specified angle

19.5a Piston crown arrow must point towards timing belt end of engine – SOHC engine

Stage 1, then tighten all bolts to Stage 2, and so on **(see illustrations)**.

21 When all bolts have been fully tightened, inject further RTV jointing compound into the side grooves of the timing belt end (where applicable) and flywheel end main bearing caps until it is certain that they are full.

22 Now rotate the crankshaft, and check that it turns freely, with no signs of binding or tight spots.

23 Check the crankshaft endfloat with reference to Section 11.

24 Refit the pistons and connecting rods as described in Section 19.

25 Refit the oil pump as described in Chapter 2B or 2C.

26 Refit the sump and oil pick-up pipe as described in Chapter 2B or 2C.

27 Refit the flywheel/driveplate as described in Chapter 2B or 2C.

28 Refit the cylinder head as described in Chapter 2B or 2C.

19 Piston/connecting rod assemblies – refitting and big-end bearing clearance check

1 Clean the backs of the big-end bearing shells and the recesses in the connecting rods and big-end caps. If new shells are being fitted, ensure that all traces of the protective grease are cleaned off using paraffin. Wipe the shells, caps and connecting rods dry with a lint-free cloth.

2 Press the bearing shells into the connecting rods and caps in their correct positions.

Big-end bearing running clearance check

Note: *When finally refitting the piston/connecting rod assemblies, new big-end bearing cap bolts must be used. However, when checking the bearing running clearance, the original bolts may be used, and then discarded. A piston ring compressor tool will be required for this operation. On DOHC engines, ensure that the mating faces of the connecting rods and big-end bearing caps are clean before refitting (refer to the note at the beginning of Section 10.*

3 Lubricate No 1 piston and piston rings, and check that the ring gaps are correctly positioned. The gap in the lower steel ring of the oil control ring should be offset 25.0 to 50.0 mm to the right of the spreader ring gap, and the upper steel ring gap should be offset by the same distance to the left of the spreader ring gap. The upper compression ring should be positioned with the ring gap offset by 180° to the lower compression ring gap.

4 Liberally lubricate the cylinder bore with clean engine oil.

5 Fit a ring compressor to No 1 piston, then insert the piston and connecting rod into the cylinder bore so that the base of the compressor stands on the block. With the crankshaft big-end bearing journal positioned at its lowest point, tap the piston carefully into the cylinder bore with the wooden handle of a

hammer, and at the same time guide the connecting rod onto the bearing journal. Note that the arrow or notch, as applicable, on the piston crown should point towards the timing belt end of the engine, and the lugs on the connecting rod and big-end bearing cap should point towards the flywheel end of the engine **(see illustrations)**. The oil spray hole in the connecting rod should be on the coolant pump side of the engine.

6 To measure the big-end bearing running clearance, refer to the information contained in Section 18, as the same general procedures apply. If the Plastigauge method is being used, ensure that the big-end bearing journal and the bearing shells are clean and dry, then engage the connecting rod with the bearing journal. Lay the Plastigauge strip on the bearing journal, fit the bearing cap in its original location (noting that the lug on the bearing cap should point towards the flywheel end of the engine), then tighten the original bearing cap bolts to the specified torque. Do not rotate the crankshaft during this operation. Remove the bearing cap, and check the running clearance by measuring the Plastigauge as previously described.

7 Repeat the checking procedures on the remaining piston/connecting rod assemblies.

Final piston/connecting rod assembly refitting

Note: *New big-end bearing cap bolts must be used when refitting the piston/connecting rod assemblies.*

19.5b Piston crown arrow and piston identification markings – DOHC engine

19.5c Lugs (arrowed) on connecting rod and big-end cap must point towards flywheel end of engine

19.5d Tapping a piston into its bore

19.9a Tighten the big-end bearing cap bolts to the specified torque . . .

19.9b . . . then through the specified angle

8 After checking the running clearance of all the big-end bearings and taking any corrective action necessary, clean off all traces of Plastigauge from the bearing shells and journals.

9 Liberally lubricate the bearing journals and bearing shells, and refit the bearing caps once more, ensuring correct positioning as previously described. Tighten the new bearing cap bolts to the specified torque (where two stages are specified, tighten all bolts to Stage 1, then tighten all bolts to Stage 2) **(see illustrations)**.

10 After refitting each piston/connecting rod assembly, rotate the crankshaft, and check that it turns freely, with no signs of binding or tight spots.

11 Refit the oil pick-up pipe and sump, as described in Chapter 2B or 2C.

12 Refit the cylinder head as described in Chapter 2B or 2C.

20 Engine – initial start-up after overhaul

1 With the engine refitted to the vehicle, check the engine oil and coolant levels.

2 With the spark plugs removed and the ignition system disabled by disconnecting the DIS module wiring plug, crank the engine over on the starter until the oil pressure light goes out. This may take a few seconds as the new oil filter fills with oil.

3 Refit the spark plugs, and reconnect all ignition wiring.

4 Start the engine, noting that this may take a little longer than usual as fuel is pumped to the engine.

5 While the engine is idling, check for fuel, coolant and oil leaks. Where applicable, check the power steering and/or automatic transmission fluid pipe/hose unions for leakage. Do not be alarmed if there are some odd smells and smoke from parts getting hot and burning off oil deposits.

6 Keep the engine idling until hot coolant is felt circulating through the radiator top hose, indicating that the engine is at normal operating temperature, then check as far as possible that the engine is running smoothly. Ideally, the engine management system should be checked using suitable diagnostic equipment with reference to Chapter 4B.

7 Stop the engine.

8 Allow the engine to cool, then recheck the oil and coolant levels, and top-up as necessary.

9 If new pistons, rings or bearings have been fitted, the engine must be run-in at reduced speeds and loads for the first 500 miles (800 km). Do not operate the engine at full-throttle, or allow it to labour in any gear during this period. It is beneficial to change the engine oil and filter at the end of this period.

Chapter 3
Cooling, heating and ventilation systems

Contents

Degrees of difficulty

Easy, suitable for novice with little experience	Fairly easy, suitable for beginner with some experience	Fairly difficult, suitable for competent DIY mechanic	Difficult, suitable for experienced DIY mechanic	Very difficult, suitable for expert DIY or professional

Specifications

General
Expansion tank cap opening pressure . . . . 1.20 to 1.35 bars

Thermostat
Opening temperatures:
SOHC engines:
  Starts to open . . . . 88°C
  Fully-open . . . . 106°C
DOHC engines:
  Starts to open . . . . 92°C
  Fully-open . . . . 107°C

Electric cooling fan(s) operating temperatures
Cooling fan(s) on:
  Models without air conditioning . . . . 100°C
  Models with air conditioning:
    Slow speed . . . . 100°C
    Fast speed . . . . 105°C
Cooling fan(s) off:
  Models without air conditioning . . . . 95°C
  Models with air conditioning:
    Slow speed . . . . 95°C
    Fast speed . . . . 100°C

Torque wrench settings

	Nm	lbf ft
Automatic transmission fluid cooler pipe unions to radiator	25	18
Coolant pump bolts	8	6
Coolant pump cover bolts:		
1.0 and 1.2 litre DOHC engines	8	6
Coolant pump pulley bolts:		
1.0 and 1.2 litre DOHC engines	20	15
Radiator upper mounting brackets to crossmember	6	4
Thermostat housing bolts:		
1.2 and 1.4 litre SOHC engines	10	7
1.4 and 1.6 litre DOHC engines	20	15
Thermostat housing cover bolts (DOHC engines)	8	6

1 General information and precautions

General information

The cooling system is of pressurised type, comprising a pump driven by the timing belt (on all except 1.0 and 1.2 litre DOHC engines) or by the auxiliary drivebelt (on 1.0 and 1.2 litre DOHC engines), an aluminium crossflow radiator, electric cooling fan, and a thermostat. The system functions as follows. Cold coolant from the radiator passes through the hose to the coolant pump, where it is pumped around the cylinder block and head passages. After cooling the cylinder bores, combustion surfaces and valve seats, the coolant reaches the underside of the thermostat, which is initially closed. The coolant passes through the heater, and is returned via the cylinder block to the coolant pump.

When the engine is cold, the coolant circulates only through the cylinder block, cylinder head, expansion tank and heater. When the coolant reaches a predetermined temperature, the thermostat opens and the coolant passes through to the radiator. As the coolant circulates through the radiator, it is cooled by the inrush of air when the car is in forward motion. Airflow is supplemented by the action of the electric cooling fan when necessary. Once the coolant has passed through the radiator, and has cooled, the cycle is repeated.

The electric cooling fan, mounted on the rear of the radiator, is controlled by a thermostatic switch. At a predetermined coolant temperature, the switch actuates the fan.

Refer to Section 11 for information on the air conditioning system.

Precautions

 Warning: Do not attempt to remove the expansion tank filler cap, or disturb any part of the cooling system, while the engine is hot; there is a high risk of scalding. If the expansion tank filler cap must be removed before the engine and radiator have fully cooled (even though this is not recommended) the pressure in the cooling system must first be relieved. Cover the cap with a thick layer of cloth, to avoid scalding, and slowly unscrew the filler cap until a hissing sound can be heard. When the hissing has stopped, indicating that the pressure has reduced, slowly unscrew the filler cap until it can be removed; if more hissing sounds are heard, wait until they have stopped before unscrewing the cap completely. At all times, keep well away from the filler cap opening.

 Warning: Do not allow antifreeze to come into contact with skin, or with the painted surfaces of the vehicle. Rinse off spills immediately, with plenty of water. Never leave antifreeze lying around in an open container, or in a puddle on the driveway or garage floor. Children and pets are attracted by its sweet smell, but antifreeze can be fatal if ingested.

 Warning: If the engine is hot, the electric cooling fan may start rotating even if the engine is not running; be careful to keep hands, hair and loose clothing well clear when working in the engine compartment.

Warning: Refer to Section 11 for precautions to be observed when working on models equipped with air conditioning.

2 Cooling system hoses – disconnection and renewal

Note: *Refer to the warnings given in Section 1 of this Chapter before proceeding. Do not attempt to disconnect any hose while the system is still hot.*

1 If the checks described in Chapter 1 reveal a faulty hose, it must be renewed as follows.
2 First drain the cooling system (see Chapter 1). If the coolant is not due for renewal, it may be re-used if it is collected in a clean container.
3 Before disconnecting a hose, first note its routing in the engine compartment, and whether it is secured by any additional retaining clips or cable ties. Use a pair of pliers to release the clamp-type clips, or a screwdriver to slacken the screw-type clips, then move the clips along the hose, clear of the relevant inlet/outlet union. Carefully work the hose free.
4 Note that the radiator inlet and outlet unions are fragile; do not use excessive force when attempting to remove the hoses. If a hose proves to be difficult to remove, try to release it by rotating the hose ends before attempting to free it.

 If all else fails, cut the coolant hose with a sharp knife, then slit it so that it can be peeled off in two pieces. Although this may prove expensive if the hose is otherwise undamaged, it is preferable to buying a new radiator.

5 When fitting a hose, first slide the clips onto the hose, then work the hose into position. If clamp-type clips were originally fitted, it is a good idea to replace them with screw-type clips when refitting the hose. If the hose is stiff, use a little soapy water (washing-up liquid is ideal) as a lubricant, or soften the hose by soaking it in hot water.
6 Work the hose into position, checking that it is correctly routed and secured. Slide each clip along the hose until it passes over the flared end of the relevant inlet/outlet union, before tightening the clips securely.
7 Refill the cooling system with reference to Chapter 1.
8 Check thoroughly for leaks as soon as possible after disturbing any part of the cooling system.

3 Radiator – removal, inspection and refitting

 If leakage is the reason for wanting to remove the radiator, bear in mind that minor leaks can often be cured using a radiator sealant without removing the radiator.

Removal

Note: *On models with automatic transmission fluid cooler unions attached to the radiator, new copper washers will be required for refitting.*

1 Disconnect the battery negative terminal (refer to *Disconnecting the battery* in the Reference Chapter).
2 Drain the cooling system as described in Chapter 1.
3 Undo the plastic stud securing the air cleaner air intake trunking to the engine compartment front crossmember.
4 Disconnect the wiring connector(s) from the cooling fan switch(es) on the right-hand end of the radiator (see illustration).
5 Remove the engine oil dipstick and, where applicable, the automatic transmission fluid dipstick.
6 On 1.4 and 1.6 litre DOHC engines, remove the secondary air injection air pipe and combination valve as described in Chapter 4C.
7 On engines with air conditioning, free the refrigerant pipe from the support bracket, then unbolt the support bracket from the exhaust manifold or cylinder head, as applicable.

3.4 Cooling fan switch screwed into the right-hand end of the radiator

3.11a Slacken the retaining clips, and disconnect the coolant hose (A) and expansion tank hose (B) from the left-hand end of the radiator . . .

3.11b . . . and the coolant hose from the right-hand end of the radiator

3.12a Unscrew the retaining bolt . . .

8 On all except 1.0 and 1.2 litre DOHC engines with air conditioning, remove the cooling fan assembly as described in Section 5. On 1.0 and 1.2 litre DOHC engines with air conditioning, unbolt the fan shroud from the radiator.

9 On 1.2 litre DOHC engines, where applicable, unbolt the automatic transmission fluid cooler banjo unions from the radiator. Recover the copper washers, noting that new washers will be required for refitting. On all other models with automatic transmission, disconnect the fluid cooler hoses at the quick-release fittings on the transmission.

10 To improve clearance on models with power steering, unbolt the power steering fluid reservoir, and place it clear of the radiator.

11 Slacken the retaining clips, and disconnect the coolant and expansion tank hoses from the left-hand end of the radiator. Also disconnect the coolant hose from the radiator right-hand end **(see illustrations)**.

12 Undo the retaining bolts, and remove the left- and right-hand mounting brackets from the top of the radiator **(see illustrations)**.

13 Free the radiator from its lower mounting rubbers, and lift it out of the engine compartment **(see illustration)**. On 1.0 and 1.2 litre DOHC engines with air conditioning, the fan motor and shroud can now be withdrawn.

Inspection

14 If the radiator has been removed due to suspected blockage, reverse-flush it as described in Chapter 1, Section 25. Clean dirt and debris from the radiator fins, using an air line (in which case, wear eye protection) or a soft brush. Be careful, as the fins are easily damaged, and are sharp.

15 If necessary, a radiator specialist can perform a 'flow test' on the radiator, to establish whether an internal blockage exists.

16 A leaking radiator must be referred to a specialist for permanent repair. Do not attempt DIY repairs to a leaking radiator, as damage may result.

17 In an emergency, minor leaks from the radiator can be cured by using a suitable radiator sealant (in accordance with its manufacturer's instructions) with the radiator in situ.

18 If the radiator is to be sent for repair, or is to be renewed, remove the cooling fan switch(es).

19 Inspect the radiator mounting rubbers, and renew them if necessary **(see illustration)**.

Refitting

20 Refitting is a reversal of removal, bearing in mind the following points:

a) Ensure that the lower lugs on the radiator

3.12b . . . and remove each radiator upper mounting bracket and rubber

are correctly engaged with the mounting rubbers in the body panel **(see illustration)**.

b) Ensure that all hoses are correctly reconnected, and their retaining clips securely tightened.

c) Where applicable, reconnect the automatic transmission fluid cooler banjo unions using new copper washers.

d) On completion, refill the cooling system as described in Chapter 1.

e) On models with automatic transmission, check and, if necessary, top-up the automatic transmission fluid as described in Chapter 1.

3.13 Free the radiator from its lower mounting rubbers, and lift it out of the engine compartment

3.19 Inspect the mounting rubbers for signs of damage, and renew if necessary

3.20 On refitting, ensure that the radiator pegs engage with lower mounting rubbers (arrowed)

4.5 Remove the thermostat housing cover from the coolant pump – 1.0 and 1.2 litre DOHC engines

4.17 Slacken the retaining clip and disconnect the coolant hose from the thermostat housing cover . . .

4.18 . . . then undo the three bolts and remove the thermostat housing cover from the engine. The thermostat is integral with the cover – 1.4 and 1.6 litre DOHC engines

4 Thermostat – removal, testing and refitting

Removal

1.0 and 1.2 litre DOHC engines

1 Disconnect the battery negative terminal (refer to *Disconnecting the battery* in the Reference Chapter).
2 Drain the cooling system as described in Chapter 1.
3 Undo the plastic stud securing the air cleaner air intake trunking to the engine compartment front crossmember and move the trunking clear of the thermostat housing.
4 Slacken the retaining clip, and disconnect the coolant hose from the thermostat housing cover.
5 Slacken and remove the three retaining bolts, and remove the thermostat housing cover from the coolant pump **(see illustration)**.
6 The thermostat is an integral part of the housing cover, and cannot be removed.

If a thermometer is available, the precise opening temperature of the thermostat may be determined, and compared with the figures given in the Specifications.

7 Remove the sealing ring from the housing cover and discard it; a new one should be used on refitting.

1.2 and 1.4 litre SOHC engines

8 Disconnect the battery negative terminal (refer to *Disconnecting the battery* in the Reference Chapter).
9 Drain the cooling system as described in Chapter 1.
10 Remove the rear timing belt cover as described in Chapter 2B.
11 Slacken the retaining clip, and disconnect the coolant hose from the thermostat housing.
12 Slacken and remove the two retaining bolts, and remove the thermostat housing from the engine.
13 Withdraw the thermostat from the cylinder head.
14 Remove the sealing ring from the edge of the thermostat and discard it; a new one should be used on refitting.

1.4 and 1.6 litre DOHC engines

15 Disconnect the battery negative terminal (refer to *Disconnecting the battery* in the Reference Chapter).
16 Drain the cooling system as described in Chapter 1.
17 Slacken the retaining clip, and disconnect the coolant hose from the thermostat housing cover **(see illustration)**.
18 Slacken and remove the three retaining

4.23 Fitting a new sealing ring to the thermostat cover groove – 1.0 and 1.2 litre DOHC engines

bolts, and remove the thermostat housing cover from the housing on the front of the cylinder head **(see illustration)**. The thermostat is an integral part of the housing cover, and cannot be removed.
19 Remove the housing cover sealing ring, and discard it; a new one should be used on refitting.

Testing

20 A rough test of the thermostat's operation may be made by suspending it with a piece of string in a container full of water. Heat the water to bring it to the boil – the thermostat must open by the time the water boils. If not, renew it.
21 The opening temperature is marked on the thermostat.
22 A thermostat which fails to close as the water cools must also be renewed.

Refitting

1.0 and 1.2 litre DOHC engines

23 Refitting is a reversal of removal, bearing in mind the following points:
a) Fit the new sealing ring to the thermostat housing cover, and fit the cover to the coolant pump **(see illustration)**.
b) Tighten the thermostat housing cover bolts to the specified torque setting.
c) On completion, refill the cooling system as described in Chapter 1.

1.2 and 1.4 litre SOHC engines

24 Refitting is a reversal of removal, bearing in mind the following points:
a) Fit the new sealing ring to the thermostat, and fit the thermostat to the cylinder head. Ensure that the thermostat is fitted the correct way round, and that its lugs are correctly engaged with the slots in the cylinder head.
b) Tighten the thermostat housing bolts to the specified torque setting.
c) Refit the rear timing belt cover as described in Chapter 2B.
d) On completion, refill the cooling system as described in Chapter 1.

4.25 Fitting a new sealing ring to the thermostat cover groove – 1.4 and 1.6 litre DOHC engines

5.7 Disconnecting the wiring connector from the cooling fan motor (viewed from underneath)

5.9 Undo the retaining bolts, and lift the cooling fan assembly out from the engine compartment

1.4 and 1.6 litre DOHC engine

25 Refitting is the reverse of the removal sequence, noting the following points:
a) *Fit a new sealing ring to the thermostat housing cover* **(see illustration)**.
b) *Tighten the thermostat housing cover bolts to the specified torque setting.*
c) *On completion, refill the cooling system as described in Chapter 1.*

5 Electric cooling fan – testing, removal and refitting

Testing

1 The cooling fan is supplied with current via the ignition switch, relay(s) and a fuse (see Chapter 12). The circuit is completed by the cooling fan thermostatic switch, which is mounted in the right-hand end of the radiator. **Note:** *On models with air conditioning, there are two switches fitted to the radiator; both switches operate the cooling fan and the air conditioning auxiliary cooling fan simultaneously. The lower switch operates at 100°C, switching the fans on at a slow speed. If the coolant temperature reaches 105°C, the upper switch operates both fans at full speed.*

2 If a fan does not appear to work, run the engine until normal operating temperature is reached, then allow it to idle. If the fan does not cut in within a few minutes (or before the temperature gauge indicates overheating), switch off the ignition and disconnect the wiring plug from the cooling fan switch. Bridge the two contacts in the wiring plug using a length of spare wire, and switch on the ignition. If the fan now operates, the switch is probably faulty, and should be renewed.

3 If the fan still fails to operate, check that full battery voltage is available at the feed wire to the switch; if not, then there is a fault in the feed wire (possibly due to a fault in the fan motor, or a blown fuse). If there is no problem with the feed, check that there is continuity between the switch earth terminal and a good earth point on the body. If not, then the earth connection is faulty, and must be re-made.

4 If the switch and the wiring are in good condition, the fault must lie in the motor itself. The motor can be checked by disconnecting the motor wiring connector and connecting a 12 volt supply directly to the motor terminals. If the motor fails this test, it is proved faulty, and must be renewed complete.

Removal

Models without air conditioning

5 Disconnect the battery negative terminal (refer to *Disconnecting the battery* in the Reference Chapter).
6 Undo the plastic stud securing the air cleaner air intake trunking to the engine compartment front crossmember.
7 Disconnect the wiring connector from the cooling fan **(see illustration)**.
8 On 1.2 litre DOHC engines, where applicable, unbolt the automatic transmission fluid cooler upper banjo union from the radiator. Recover the copper washers, noting that new washers will be required for refitting.
9 Unscrew the fan shroud retaining bolts, then tilt the assembly back slightly towards the engine, and withdraw it upwards away from the radiator **(see illustration)**. Where necessary, push the coolant hoses aside to provide sufficient clearance for removal.
10 To separate the fan motor from the shroud, unscrew the three retaining nuts, and remove the fan motor from the shroud.
11 No spare parts are available for the motor, and if the unit is faulty, it must be renewed complete.

Models with air conditioning

12 Disconnect the battery negative terminal (refer to *Disconnecting the battery* in the Reference Chapter).
13 On 1.0 and 1.2 litre DOHC engines, remove the radiator as described in Section 3, then proceed to paragraph 20. On all other models, proceed as follows.
14 Undo the plastic stud securing the air cleaner air intake trunking to the engine compartment front crossmember.
15 Undo the retaining bolts, and remove the left- and right-hand mounting brackets from the top of the radiator.
16 Unbolt the refrigerant pipe support

bracket from the engine lifting bracket, then remove the engine lifting bracket from the cylinder head.
17 Remove the engine oil dipstick and, where applicable, the automatic transmission fluid dipstick.
18 On 1.4 and 1.6 litre DOHC engines, unbolt the condenser left-hand mounting bracket from the front crossmember.
19 Unscrew the fan shroud retaining bolts, carefully push the top of the radiator towards the front of the car and withdraw the fan and shroud upwards from the radiator.
20 To separate the fan motor from the shroud, unscrew the three retaining nuts, and remove the fan motor from the shroud.
21 No spare parts are available for the motor, and if the unit is faulty, it must be renewed complete.

Refitting

22 Refitting is a reversal of removal, ensuring that the shroud is correctly located in the radiator clips.
23 On completion, start the engine and run it until it reaches normal operating temperature; continue to run the engine, and check that the cooling fan cuts in and functions correctly.

6 Cooling system electrical switches – testing, removal and refitting

Electric cooling fan thermostatic switch(es)

Testing

1 Testing of the switch(es) is described in Section 5, as part of the electric cooling fan test procedure.

Removal

2 The switch(es) is/are located in the right-hand side of the radiator **(see illustration 3.4)**. The engine and radiator should be cold before removing the switch.
3 Disconnect the battery negative terminal (refer to *Disconnecting the battery* in the Reference Chapter). Firmly apply the handbrake, then jack up the front of the car

6.6 Unscrew the cooling fan switch from the radiator, and recover the sealing washer (arrowed)

6.10 Coolant temperature gauge sender (arrowed) – 1.0 and 1.2 litre DOHC engines

and support it securely on axle stands (see *Jacking and vehicle support*). Access to the switch can then be gained from underneath the vehicle.

4 Either drain the cooling system to below the level of the switch (as described in Chapter 1), or have a suitable plug ready which can be used to block the switch aperture in the radiator whilst the switch is removed. If a plug is used, take great care not to damage the radiator, and do not use anything which will allow foreign matter to enter the radiator.

5 Disconnect the wiring plug from the switch.

6 Carefully unscrew the switch from the radiator, and recover the sealing ring/washer (see illustration).

Refitting

7 Refitting is a reversal of removal, using a new sealing ring/washer. Securely tighten the switch, and top-up/refill the cooling system as described in Chapter 1.

8 On completion, start the engine and run it until it reaches normal operating temperature; continue to run the engine, and check that the cooling fan cuts in and functions correctly.

Coolant temperature gauge sender

Testing

9 The coolant temperature gauge is fed with a stabilised voltage supply from the instrument panel feed (via the ignition switch and a fuse), and its earth is controlled by the sender.

10 The sender is screwed into the exhaust gas

recirculation valve housing on 1.0 and 1.2 litre DOHC engines, into the inlet manifold on 1.2 and 1.4 litre SOHC engines, or into the thermostat housing on 1.4 and 1.6 litre DOHC engines (see illustration). The sender contains a thermistor (thermal resistor), an electronic component whose electrical resistance decreases at a predetermined rate as its temperature rises. When the coolant is cold, the sender resistance is high, current flow through the gauge is reduced, and the gauge needle points towards the 'cold' end of the scale. If the sender is faulty, it must be renewed.

11 If the gauge develops a fault, first check the other instruments; if they do not work at all, check the instrument panel electrical feed. If the readings are erratic, there may be a fault in the voltage stabiliser, which will necessitate renewal of the stabiliser (see Chapter 12, Section 10). If the fault lies in the temperature gauge alone, check it as follows.

12 If the gauge needle remains at the 'cold' end of the scale, disconnect the sender wire, and earth it to the cylinder head. If the needle then deflects when the ignition is switched on, the sender unit is proved faulty, and should be renewed. If the needle still does not move, remove the instrument panel (Chapter 12) and check the continuity of the wiring between the sender unit and the gauge, and the feed to the gauge unit. If continuity is shown, and the fault still exists, then the gauge is faulty, and the gauge unit should be renewed.

13 If the gauge needle remains at the 'hot' end of the scale, disconnect the sender wire. If the

needle then returns to the 'cold' end of the scale when the ignition is switched on, the sender unit is proved faulty, and should be renewed. If the needle still does not move, check the remainder of the circuit as described previously.

Removal

14 Either partially drain the cooling system to just below the level of the sender (as described in Chapter 1), or have a suitable plug ready which can be used to block the sender aperture whilst it is removed. If a plug is used, take great care not to damage the internal threads, and do not use anything which will allow foreign matter to enter the cooling system.

15 Disconnect the battery negative terminal (refer to *Disconnecting the battery* in the Reference Chapter).

16 Disconnect the wiring from the sender, then unscrew the unit from its location.

Refitting

17 Ensure the sender threads are clean, and apply a smear of suitable sealant to them.

18 Refit the sender, tightening it securely, and reconnect the wiring.

19 Top-up/refill the cooling system as described in Chapter 1.

20 On completion, start the engine and check the operation of the temperature gauge. Also check for coolant leaks.

Fuel injection system coolant temperature sensor

21 Refer to the relevant Part of Chapter 4.

7 Coolant pump – removal and refitting

Removal

1.0 and 1.2 litre DOHC engines

1 Drain the cooling system as described in Chapter 1.

2 Slacken the three coolant pump pulley retaining bolts.

3 Remove the auxiliary drivebelt as described in Chapter 1.

4 Release the retaining clips and disconnect the radiator top and bottom hoses, heater hose and expansion tank hose from the coolant pump and thermostat housing.

5 Disconnect the coolant temperature sensor wiring plug.

6 Unscrew the previously slackened coolant pump pulley bolts and withdraw the pulley from the pump.

7 Unscrew the coolant pump retaining bolts, noting the locations of the three short bolts (see illustration). The short bolts secure the pump to the timing cover, and the long bolts secure the pump and the timing cover to the cylinder block and cylinder head.

8 Withdraw the coolant pump from the timing cover, noting that it may be necessary to tap the pump lightly with a soft-faced hammer to free it from the locating dowels (see illustration).

7.7 Coolant pump short retaining bolt locations (arrowed) – 1.0 and 1.2 litre DOHC engines (shown with timing cover removed)

7.8 Withdraw the coolant pump from the timing cover – 1.0 and 1.2 litre DOHC engines (shown with timing cover removed)

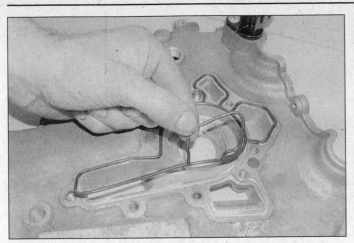

7.20 Locate a new coolant pump rubber seal in the timing cover groove – 1.0 and 1.2 litre DOHC engines (shown with timing cover removed)

7.30 Align the flange edge with the mark on the cylinder block (arrowed) when refitting the coolant pump – 1.4 and 1.6 litre DOHC engines

9 Recover the pump sealing ring, and discard it; a new one must be used on refitting.

10 Note that it is not possible to overhaul the pump. If it is faulty, the unit must be renewed complete.

11 If the pump is being renewed, remove the thermostat housing and transfer it to the new pump, referring to the procedures in Section 4.

12 Similarly, unscrew the two bolts and withdraw the coolant pump cover from the old pump and fit the cover to the new pump using a new seal. Tighten the cover bolts to the specified torque.

1.2 SOHC, 1.4 & 1.6 litre engines

13 Drain the cooling system with reference to Chapter 1.

14 On 1.2 and 1.4 litre SOHC engines, remove the timing belt and rear timing belt cover as described in Chapter 2B.

15 On 1.4 and 1.6 litre DOHC engines, remove the timing belt as described in Chapter 2C.

16 Unscrew and remove the three coolant pump securing bolts.

17 Withdraw the coolant pump from the cylinder block, noting that it may be necessary to tap the pump lightly with a soft-faced hammer to free it from the cylinder block.

18 Recover the pump sealing ring, and discard it; a new one must be used on refitting.

19 Note that it is not possible to overhaul the pump. If it is faulty, the unit must be renewed complete.

Refitting

1.0 and 1.2 litre DOHC engines

20 Ensure that the pump and timing cover mating faces are clean and dry and locate a new seal in the timing cover groove **(see illustration)**.

21 Check that the locating dowels are in

place and locate the pump in position on the timing cover.

22 Refit the pump retaining bolts, ensuring that the short bolts are fitted to their correct locations. Tighten the bolts to the specified torque.

23 Refit the coolant pump pulley and tighten the three bolts to the specified torque. To prevent the pulley turning as the bolts are tightened, hold the pulley using a screwdriver engaged with one of the bolts and the pump centre spindle. Alternatively, wait until the auxiliary drivebelt has been refitted and tighten the bolts then.

24 Reconnect the coolant hoses and the coolant temperature sensor wiring plug.

25 Refit the auxiliary drivebelt and refill the cooling system as described in Chapter 1.

26 If not already done, tighten the coolant pump pulley bolts to the specified torque.

1.2 SOHC, 1.4 & 1.6 litre engines

27 Ensure that the pump and cylinder block mating surfaces are clean and dry, and apply a smear of silicone grease to the pump mating surface in the cylinder block. Vauxhall/Opel recommend the use of their grease (Part No 90 167 353); in the absence of this, ensure a good-quality equivalent is used.

28 Fit a new sealing ring to the pump, and install the pump in the cylinder block.

29 On 1.2 and 1.4 litre SOHC engines, refit the pump retaining bolts, tightening them by hand only at this stage. Refit the rear timing belt cover and install the timing belt as described in Chapter 2B.

30 On 1.4 and 1.6 litre DOHC engines, align the edge of the coolant pump flange with the mark on the cylinder block, then tighten the coolant pump bolts to the specified torque setting **(see illustration)**. Refit the timing belt as described in Chapter 2C.

31 On all models, refill the cooling system as described in Chapter 1.

8 Heater/ventilation system – general information

The heater/ventilation system consists of a four-speed blower motor (housed in the engine compartment), face-level vents in the centre and at each end of the fascia, and air ducts to the front footwells.

The control unit is located in the fascia, and the controls operate flap valves to deflect and mix the air flowing through the various parts of the heater/ventilation system. The flap valves are contained in the air distribution housing, which acts as a central distribution unit, passing air to the various ducts and vents.

Cold air enters the system through the grille at the rear of the engine compartment. On most models (depending on specification) a pollen filter is fitted to the ventilation intake, to filter out dust, soot, pollen and spores from the air entering the vehicle.

The air (boosted by the blower fan if required) then flows through the various ducts, according to the settings of the controls. Stale air is expelled through ducts behind the doors. If warm air is required, the cold air is passed through the heater matrix, which is heated by the engine coolant.

A recirculation lever enables the outside air supply to be closed off, while the air inside the vehicle is recirculated. This can be useful to prevent unpleasant odours entering from outside the vehicle, but should only be used briefly, as the recirculated air inside the vehicle will soon deteriorate.

Certain models may be fitted with heated front seats. The heat is produced by electrically-heated mats in the seat and backrest cushions (see Chapter 12). The temperature is regulated automatically by a thermostat, and cannot be adjusted.

9.4a Lever off the knob from the air recirculation lever . . .

9.4b . . . then carefully prise out the lever surround. Note the use of a piece of card to avoid marking the facia panel

9.5a Undo the four retaining screws (arrowed) . . .

9 Heater/ventilation system components – removal and refitting

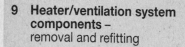

Control unit

Removal

1 Disconnect the battery negative terminal (refer to *Disconnecting the battery* in the Reference Chapter).

2 Remove the two centre vents from the facia panel as described in Section 10.

3 Remove the hazard warning light and heated rear window switches as described in Chapter 12. On models with heated front seats, also remove the seat heating switches.

4 Carefully lever the knob off the air recirculation lever, then prise the lever surround out of the centre facia panel, taking great care not to mark the panel **(see illustrations)**.

5 Undo the four retaining centre facia panel retaining screws, then withdraw the panel from the facia until access can be gained to the rear of the control panel **(see illustrations)**.

6 Unclip the four control cables, and release each cable from the control unit, noting each cable's correct fitted location and routing. **Note:** *The control cable end fittings are colour-coded for identification purposes.* The outer cables are released by simply lifting the retaining clips.

7 Disconnect the wiring connectors from the

control panel, and unclip the switch wiring connectors from the rear of the centre facia panel **(see illustration)**. Remove the centre facia panel from the vehicle.

8 If necessary, carefully prise off the remaining control knobs, then undo the two retaining screws, and unclip the heater control unit and vent from the centre facia panel **(see illustrations)**.

Refitting

9 Refitting is reversal of removal. Ensure that the control cables are correctly routed and reconnected to the control panel, as noted before removal. Clip the outer cables in position, and check the operation of each knob/lever before refitting the centre facia panel.

Control cables renewal

Lower air distribution control

10 Remove the heater/ventilation control unit from the facia, as described above in paragraphs 1 to 5.

11 Unclip the lower air distribution cable (with the grey end fitting) and free the cable from the right-hand side of the control unit. The outer cable is released by simply lifting the retaining clip **(see illustration)**.

12 Follow the run of the cable behind the facia, taking note of its routing, and disconnect the cable from the lever on the air distribution housing. Note that the method of fastening is the same as that used at the control unit. On right-hand drive models, if

9.5b . . . then withdraw the centre facia panel from the facia

9.7 Free the wiring connectors from the rear of the centre facia panel and control unit, and remove the assembly from the facia

9.8a Unclip the remaining control knobs . . .

9.8b . . . then undo the two retaining screws (arrowed) . . .

9.8c . . . and separate the vent and control unit from the facia panel

9.11 Unclipping the lower air distribution cable from the heater control unit. The rear cable (arrowed) is the upper air distribution cable

9.30 Disconnecting the air recirculation cable from the rear of the control unit

necessary, undo the two screws and remove the trim panel from the right-hand side of the facia centre panel to improve access to the cable.

13 Fit the new cable, ensuring that it is correctly routed, and free from kinks and obstructions.

14 Connect the cable to the control unit and air distribution housing, making sure the outer cable is clipped securely in position.

15 Check the operation of the control knob, then refit the control unit as described previously in this Section.

Upper air distribution control

16 Remove the heater/ventilation control unit from the facia, as described above in paragraphs 1 to 5.

17 Unclip the upper air distribution cable (with the brown end fitting) and free the cable from the right-hand side of the control unit **(see illustration 9.11)**. The outer cable is released by simply lifting the retaining clip.

18 On left-hand drive models, remove the storage compartment (where fitted) from underneath the passenger side of the facia. The compartment is secured in position by a retaining screw and clip.

19 On all models, follow the run of the cable behind the facia, taking note of its routing, and disconnect the cable from the lever on the air distribution housing. Note that the method of fastening is the same as that used at the control unit. Release the cable from its retaining clip on the air distribution housing, and remove it from behind the facia.

20 Fit the new cable as described in paragraphs 13 to 15.

Air temperature control

21 Remove the heater/ventilation control unit from the facia, as described above in paragraphs 1 to 5.

22 Unclip and detach the upper and lower air distribution cables from the control unit (see paragraphs 11 and 17), noting the correct fitted location of each cable. Swing the

control panel away from the facia, and disconnect the air temperature cable (with the black end fitting) from the left-hand side of the control unit.

23 On right-hand drive models, remove the storage compartment (where fitted) from underneath the passenger side of the facia. The compartment is secured in position by a retaining screw and clip.

24 On all models, follow the run of the cable behind the facia, taking note of its routing, and disconnect the cable from the lever on the air distribution housing. Note that the method of fastening is the same as that used at the control unit. Release the cable from its retaining clip on the air distribution housing, and remove it from behind the facia.

25 Fit the new cable, ensuring that it is correctly routed, and free from kinks and obstructions.

26 Connect the cable to the control unit and air distribution housing, making sure the outer cable is clipped securely in position. Also clip the air distribution cables into their correct positions.

27 Check the operation of the control knobs, then refit the control unit as described previously in this Section.

Air recirculation control

28 Remove the heater/ventilation control unit from the facia, as described above in paragraphs 1 to 5.

29 Unclip and detach the upper and lower air distribution cables from the control unit (see paragraphs 11 and 17), noting the correct fitted location of each cable.

30 Swing the control panel away from the facia, and disconnect the air recirculation cable (with the blue or yellow end fitting) from the rear of the control unit **(see illustration)**.

31 On left-hand drive models, remove the storage compartment (where fitted) from underneath the passenger side of the facia. The compartment is secured in position by a retaining screw and clip.

32 On all models, remove the cable and install the new one as described in paragraphs 24 to 27. Note that, on models with air conditioning, it will also be necessary to remove the glovebox (see Chapter 11, Section 26) and detach the cable from the evaporator housing.

Heater matrix

Removal

33 With the engine cold, unscrew the expansion tank cap (referring to the warning note in Section 1) to release any pressure present in the cooling system, then securely refit the cap.

34 On right-hand drive vehicles, remove the battery as described in Chapter 5A.

35 Undo the expansion tank retaining nuts, and free the tank from the engine compartment bulkhead. Place the tank clear of the bulkhead to gain access to the heater matrix hose unions.

36 Clamp both heater hoses as close to the bulkhead as possible, to minimise coolant loss. Alternatively, drain the cooling system as described in Chapter 1.

37 Slacken the retaining clips, and disconnect both hoses from the heater matrix unions. Unscrew the retaining screw which is situated between the unions.

38 Working inside the vehicle, remove the storage compartment (where fitted) from underneath the passenger side of the facia. The compartment is secured in position by a retaining screw and clip.

39 On left-hand drive models, undo the two screws and remove the trim panel from the centre of the facia, on the driver's side. Unbolt the support strut (where fitted, this is situated on the driver's side of the air distribution housing) from the floor, and swing the strut away from the housing.

40 Undo the five retaining screws (two on the left-hand side, and three on the right-hand side), securing the lower cover to the base of

9.40a Undo the two left-hand retaining screws (arrowed) . . .

9.40b . . . and the three right-hand screws (arrowed) . . .

9.40c . . . then detach the air distribution housing base and remove it from the left-hand side

the air distribution housing. Unclip the cover and remove it from the vehicle **(see illustrations)**.

41 Detach the intermediate housing from bottom of the distribution housing, and remove it towards the left-hand side of the vehicle **(see illustration)**. On left-hand drive models, it may be necessary to depress the brake and clutch pedals to allow the housing to be removed.

42 Cover the carpet directly underneath the air distribution housing, to catch any coolant which may be spilt from the matrix as it is removed. Alternatively, release the carpet fasteners, and fold the carpet back from the bulkhead so that any spilt coolant will go behind the carpet.

43 Lower the heater matrix out from the air distribution housing, swing it to the left, then

disengage the matrix unions from the bulkhead and remove the matrix from the vehicle **(see illustration)**. Note: *Keep the matrix unions uppermost as the matrix is removed, to prevent coolant spillage. Mop up any spilt coolant immediately, and wipe the affected area with a damp cloth to prevent staining.*

44 Where necessary, recover the sealing grommets from the matrix unions, and refit them to the bulkhead.

Refitting

45 Refitting is a reversal of the removal procedure, bearing in mind the following points:

a) *Apply a smear of oil to the matrix sealing grommets, to ease installation.*

b) *Ensure that the heater hose retaining clips are securely tightened.*

c) *On completion, top-up/refill the cooling system as described in Chapter 1.*

Heater blower motor renewal

Models without air conditioning

46 Disconnect the battery negative terminal (refer to *Disconnecting the battery* in the Reference Chapter).

47 Remove both windscreen wiper arms as described in Chapter 12.

48 Carefully prise out the wiper spindle sealing grommets from the windscreen cowl panel.

49 Undo the retaining screws, and remove both halves of the windscreen cowl panel from the vehicle.

50 Peel the bonnet seal off the engine compartment bulkhead, and remove it from the vehicle.

51 Unscrew the large plastic nut from each wiper spindle.

52 Prise out the two clips from the centre of the water deflector shield. Release the deflector from the engine compartment bulkhead and wiper spindles, and remove it from the vehicle.

53 Where necessary, release the retaining clips and lift out the pollen filter **(see illustration)**.

54 Undo the screws, and remove the frame from the top of the heater/ventilation intake duct **(see illustrations)**.

55 Set the air recirculation control to the 'fresh air' position.

56 Release the retaining clips, and remove

9.41 Unclip the air distribution intermediate housing, and remove it from the left-hand side

9.43 Lower the heater matrix out of position, and swing it to the left to disengage its unions from the bulkhead

9.53 Where necessary, remove the pollen filter from the heater/ventilation intake

9.54a Undo the four retaining screws (arrowed) . . .

9.54b . . . and lift out the frame

9.56a Release the retaining clips . . .

9.56b . . . and remove the right-hand . . .

9.56c . . . and left-hand covers from the blower motor

the blower motor right-hand, then left-hand covers from inside the intake duct **(see illustrations)**.

57 Unhook the blower motor retaining clip, noting how the wiring is routed through the clip **(see illustration)**.

58 Disconnect the motor wiring connectors from the resistor, noting the correct routing of the wiring, and manoeuvre the blower motor out from its housing **(see illustration)**.

59 Refitting is a reversal of the removal procedure, noting the following points:

a) *Make sure that the motor wiring is correctly routed underneath the blower motor retaining clip (see illustration) so that there is no danger of the wiring contacting the fan blades.*

b) *Make sure that the blower motor covers are correctly engaged with each other, and clipped securely in position.*

Models with air conditioning

60 Remove the windscreen wiper motor as described in Chapter 12.

61 Where necessary, release the retaining clips and remove the pollen filter.

62 Undo the screws, and remove the frame from the top of the heating/ventilation intake duct. Where necessary, also cut the intake mesh to allow access to the motor assembly.

63 Set the air recirculation control to the 'fresh air' position.

9.57 Unhook the retaining clip (arrowed) . . .

64 Undo the retaining screws, and remove both halves of the blower motor cover.

65 Disconnect the wiring connectors from the resistor, then undo the two screws and remove the blower motor retaining clamp.

66 Lift the blower motor assembly out of position.

67 Refitting is a reverse of the removal procedure, noting the following points:

a) *Make sure that the motor wiring is correctly routed underneath the blower motor retaining clamp, so that there is no danger of the wiring contacting the fan blades.*

b) *Make sure that the blower motor covers are correctly engaged with each other, and clipped securely in position.*

9.58 . . . and lift the blower motor out from its housing

Heater blower motor resistor

Removal

68 On models without air conditioning, carry out the operations described above in paragraphs 46 to 56. On models with air conditioning, carry out the operations described in paragraphs 60 to 64.

69 From inside the vehicle, reach up behind the facia, and disconnect the wiring connector from the underside of the blower motor resistor, which is on the left-hand side of the air distribution housing **(see illustration)**.

70 Return to the engine compartment, then undo the retaining screw and disconnect the blower motor wiring connectors from the

9.59 Secure the blower motor in position with the retaining clip, making sure its wiring is correctly routed through the clip (arrowed)

9.69 Disconnecting the wiring connector from the blower motor resistor (viewed through glovebox aperture)

9.70a Disconnect the wiring connectors . . .

9.70b . . . then undo the retaining screw (arrowed) . . .

9.70c . . . and lift the blower motor resistor out of position

9.78 Removing the air distribution housing

resistor. Remove the resistor from the vehicle **(see illustrations)**.

Refitting

71 Refitting is the reverse of removal.

Air distribution housing renewal

Models without air conditioning

72 Remove the facia assembly as described in Chapter 11.

73 Carry out the operations described in paragraphs 33 to 37.

74 Where necessary, release the retaining clips and remove the pollen filter.

75 Undo the screws, and remove the frame from the top of the heating/ventilation intake duct.

76 Cover the carpet directly underneath the air distribution housing, to catch any coolant which may be spilt from the matrix as the housing assembly is removed.

77 Disconnect the wiring connector from the blower motor resistor on the left-hand side of the housing.

78 Disconnect the duct from the driver's side of the housing, and remove the housing from the vehicle **(see illustration)**. Note: *Keep the matrix unions uppermost as the housing is removed, to prevent coolant spillage. Mop up any spilt coolant immediately, and wipe the affected area with a damp cloth to prevent staining. Recover the foam spacers from behind the housing.*

79 Refitting is the reverse of removal. On completion, top-up the cooling system as described in Chapter 1.

Models with air conditioning

80 On models with air conditioning, it is not possible to remove the air distribution housing without opening the refrigerant circuit (see Section 11). Therefore, this task must be entrusted to a Vauxhall/Opel dealer.

10 Heater/ventilation vents and ducts – removal and refitting

Vents

1 Point the vent fully downwards then, using a suitable screwdriver, carefully lever between the top of the vent and the vent housing until a gap of approximately 2 mm appears. Position a piece of card behind screwdriver blade, to avoid damaging the housing.

2 Insert a small, flat-bladed screwdriver in through the gap, and carefully lever between the sides of the vent and the housing to release the vent from its locating pegs **(see illustration)**.

3 Once the vent is free from both its locating pegs, it can be withdrawn from the facia **(see illustration)**.

4 On refitting, carefully manoeuvre the vent back into the facia, ensuring it is correctly engaged with the locating pegs.

Driver's side heater/ventilation housing

5 Disconnect the battery negative terminal (refer to *Disconnecting the battery* in the Reference Chapter).

10.2 Remove the heater/ventilation ducts as described in text . . .

10.3 . . . to release them from their locating pegs (arrowed)

10.9a Undo the four retaining screws (arrowed) . . .

10.9b . . . then withdraw the vent housing/switch assembly from the facia . . .

6 Remove the cover from the fusebox.

7 Remove the driver's side vent as described in paragraphs 1 to 3.

8 Remove the lighting switch as described in Chapter 12.

9 Undo the four retaining screws, and withdraw the vent housing/switch assembly from the facia, disconnecting its wiring connectors as they become accessible (see illustrations).

10 Refitting is a reversal of the removal procedure, ensuring that the housing is correctly located with the duct.

Passenger side duct

11 Remove the glovebox as described in Chapter 11, Section 26.

12 Undo the three retaining screws, and remove the vent housing from the facia (see illustrations).

10.9c . . . and free the wiring connectors from the rear of the housing

13 Disconnect the duct from the air distribution housing, and manoeuvre the duct out through the glovebox aperture, or from underneath the facia (see illustration).

10.12a Undo the three retaining screws (arrowed) . . .

14 Refitting is a reversal of the removal procedure, ensuring that the duct is securely reconnected to the air distribution housing.

10.12b . . . and remove the vent housing from the facia

10.13 Disconnect the duct from the air distribution housing, and remove it from underneath the facia

11.1 Air conditioning system components

1 High-pressure refrigerant pipe
2 Low-pressure refrigerant hose
3 Thermostatically-controlled expansion valve
4 Evaporator
5 Recirculation air duct
6 Blower motor
7 Heater matrix unions
8 Low-pressure refrigerant hose
9 High pressure refrigerant hose
10 Cooling fan
11 Idle-up switch
12 Auxiliary cooling fan switch
13 Radiator
14 High-pressure refrigerant hose
15 Condenser
16 Accumulator
17 Auxiliary cooling fan
18 Coolant temperature switch
19 Coolant temperature switch
20 Compressor drive pulley with integral clutch
21 Compressor
22 Low-pressure service connection
23 High-pressure service connection

11 Air conditioning system – general information and precautions

General information

1 Air conditioning is available on certain models (see illustration). It enables the temperature of incoming air to be lowered, and also dehumidifies the air, which makes for rapid demisting and increased comfort.

2 The cooling side of the system works in the same way as a domestic refrigerator. Refrigerant gas is drawn into a belt-driven compressor, and passes into a condenser mounted in front of the radiator, where it loses heat and becomes liquid. The liquid passes through an expansion valve to an evaporator, where it changes from liquid under high pressure to gas under low pressure. This change is accompanied by a drop in temperature, which cools the evaporator. The refrigerant returns to the compressor, and the cycle begins again.

3 Air blown through the evaporator passes to the air distribution unit, where it is mixed with hot air blown through the heater matrix, to achieve the desired temperature in the passenger compartment.

4 The heating side of the system works in the same way as on models without air conditioning (see Section 8).

5 The operation of the system is controlled electronically by the coolant temperature switches (see Section 5), which are screwed into the right-hand end of the radiator, and pressure switches which are screwed into the compressor high-pressure line. Any problems with the system should be referred to a Vauxhall/Opel dealer.

Precautions

6 It is necessary to observe special precautions whenever dealing with any part of the system, its associated components, and any items which necessitate disconnection of the system.

 Warning: The refrigeration circuit contains a liquid refrigerant. This refrigerant is potentially dangerous, and should only be handled by qualified persons. If it is splashed onto the skin, it can cause frostbite. It is not itself poisonous, but in the presence of a naked flame it forms a poisonous gas; inhalation of the vapour through a lighted cigarette could prove fatal. Uncontrolled discharging of the refrigerant is dangerous, and potentially damaging to the environment. It is therefore dangerous to disconnect any part of the system without specialised knowledge and equipment. If for any reason the system must be disconnected, entrust this task to your Vauxhall/Opel dealer or a refrigeration engineer.

7 Do not operate the air conditioning system if it is known to be short of refrigerant, as this may damage the compressor.

12 Air conditioning system components – removal and refitting

 Warning: Do not attempt to open the refrigerant circuit. Refer to the precautions given in Section 11.

1 The only operation which can be carried out easily, without discharging the refrigerant, is renewal of the compressor drivebelt, which is covered in Chapter 1. All other operations must be referred to a Vauxhall/Opel dealer or an air conditioning specialist.

2 Where required for improved access, the compressor can be unbolted and moved aside, **without disconnecting its flexible hoses,** after removing the drivebelt.

Chapter 4 Part A: Fuel and exhaust systems – 1.0 & 1.2 litre DOHC engines

Contents

Degrees of difficulty

Easy, suitable for novice with little experience

Fairly easy, suitable for beginner with some experience

Fairly difficult, suitable for competent DIY mechanic

Difficult, suitable for experienced DIY mechanic

Very difficult, suitable for expert DIY or professional

Specifications

General
System type . . . . Bosch Motronic M 1.5.5 sequential multi-point fuel injection

Fuel pump
Type . . . . Electric, mounted in fuel tank

Fuel injection system data
Idle speed (not adjustable – for reference only):
   1.0 litre engines . . . . 800 to 1100 rpm
   1.2 litre engines . . . . 730 to 890 rpm
Idle mixture CO content (not adjustable – for reference only) . . . . 0.4% maximum

Torque wrench settings

	Nm	lbf ft
Air conditioning compressor mounting bolts	20	15
Brake servo vacuum hose to inlet manifold (1.0 litre engines)	18	13
Catalytic converter-to-exhaust manifold nuts	35	26
Catalytic converter support bracket bolts	20	15
Camshaft position sensor to timing cover	6	4
Coolant temperature sensor	18	13
Crankshaft speed/position sensor to cylinder block baseplate	8	6
EGR pipe to EGR valve housing	8	6
Exhaust manifold securing nuts*	22	16
Fuel feed and return hose unions	15	11
Fuel injector wiring trough to inlet manifold	8	6
Heat shield to exhaust manifold	8	6
Inlet manifold to cylinder head:		
1.0 litre engines	22	16
1.2 litre engines	8	6
Inlet manifold support bracket to cylinder block	20	15
Inlet manifold support bracket to manifold:		
1.0 litre engines	10	7
1.2 litre engines	6	4
Oil dipstick guide tube to exhaust manifold	8	6
Oxygen sensor	30	22
Throttle body to inlet manifold	8	6

*Use new nuts

1 General information and precautions

General information

1 The fuel supply system consists of a fuel tank (which is mounted under the rear of the car, with an electric fuel pump immersed in it), a fuel filter, fuel feed and return lines. The fuel pump supplies fuel to the fuel rail, which acts as a reservoir for the fuel injectors which inject fuel into the inlet tracts. The fuel filter incorporated in the feed line from the pump to the fuel rail ensures that the fuel supplied to the injectors is clean.

2 The electronic control unit controls both the fuel injection system and the ignition system, integrating the two into a complete engine management system. Refer to Section 9 for further information on the operation of the fuel system and to Chapter 5B for details of the ignition side of the system.

3 The exhaust system incorporates a catalytic converter to reduce exhaust gas emissions. Further details can be found in Chapter 4C, along with details of the other emission control systems and components.

Precautions

Note: *Refer to Part C of this Chapter for general information and precautions relating to the catalytic converter.*

4 Before disconnecting any fuel lines, or working on any part of the fuel system, the system must be depressurised as described in Section 5.

5 Care must be taken when disconnecting the fuel lines. When disconnecting a fuel union or hose, loosen the union or clamp screw slowly, to avoid sudden uncontrolled fuel spillage. Take adequate fire precautions.

6 When working on fuel system components, scrupulous cleanliness must be observed, and care must be taken not to introduce any foreign matter into fuel lines or components.

7 After carrying out any work involving disconnection of fuel lines, it is advisable to check the connections for leaks; pressurise the system by switching the ignition on and off several times.

8 Electronic control units are very sensitive components, and certain precautions must be taken to avoid damage to these units as follows.

a) *When carrying out welding operations on the vehicle using electric welding equipment, the battery and alternator should be disconnected.*

b) *Although the underbonnet-mounted control units will tolerate normal underbonnet conditions, they can be adversely affected by excess heat or moisture. If welding equipment or pressure-washing equipment in the vicinity of an electronic control unit, take care not to direct heat, or jets of water or steam, at the unit. If this cannot be avoided, remove the control unit from the vehicle, and protect its wiring plug with a plastic bag.*

c) *Before disconnecting any wiring, or removing components, always ensure that the ignition is switched off.*

d) *Do not attempt to improvise fault diagnosis procedures using a test light or multi-meter, as irreparable damage could be caused to the control unit.*

e) *After working on fuel injection/engine management system components, ensure that all wiring is correctly reconnected before reconnecting the battery or switching on the ignition.*

⚠ **Warning: Many of the procedures in this Chapter require the disconnection of fuel line connections, and the removal of components, which may result in some fuel spillage. Before carrying out any operation on the fuel system, refer to the precautions given in 'Safety first!' at the beginning of this manual, and follow them implicitly. Petrol is a highly-dangerous and volatile liquid, and the precautions necessary when handling it cannot be overstressed.**

2 Air cleaner assembly – removal and refitting

Removal

1 Disconnect the battery negative terminal (refer to *Disconnecting the battery* in the Reference Chapter).

2 Disconnect the wiring plug from the air mass meter, located in the air inlet trunking **(see illustration)**.

3 Release the hose clamp and disconnect the breather hose from the side of the airbox **(see illustration)**.

4 Undo the three bolts and lift off the airbox and inlet trunking from the throttle body **(see illustration)**.

5 Release the securing clips, lift off the air cleaner cover, and remove the cover, inlet trunking and airbox from the vehicle **(see illustration)**.

6 Lift out the air cleaner element.

7 Undo the plastic stud securing the air intake trunking to the engine compartment front crossmember. Detach the trunking from

2.2 Disconnect the wiring plug from the air mass meter

2.3 Disconnect the breather hose from the side of the airbox

2.4 Undo the bolts and lift the airbox and inlet trunking off the throttle body

2.5 Release the clips and lift off the air cleaner cover

2.7a Undo the plastic stud securing the air intake trunking to the front crossmember

2.7b Detach the trunking from the air cleaner casing and withdraw the trunking

2.8 Pull the air cleaner front locating grommet (arrowed) to release it from the hole in the air cleaner casing

2.9 Release the air cleaner casing rear locating rubbers, and withdraw the assembly from the engine compartment

the front of the air cleaner casing (and from the resonator on 1.0 litre engines), and withdraw the trunking **(see illustrations)**.

8 Pull the air cleaner front locating grommet to release it from the hole in the air cleaner casing, then pull the casing upwards over the grommet **(see illustration)**.

9 Pull the assembly forwards to release the rear locating rubbers, and withdraw the assembly from the engine compartment **(see illustration)**.

Refitting

10 Refitting is a reversal of removal.

3 Throttle cable – removal, refitting and adjustment

Removal

1 Disconnect the battery negative terminal (refer to *Disconnecting the battery* in the Reference Chapter).

2 Remove the airbox from the top of the throttle body, with reference to Section 2 if necessary.

3 Turn the throttle disc and disconnect the throttle cable end fitting from the disc. Release the cable grommet from its bracket on the inlet manifold.

4 On automatic transmission models, disconnect the kickdown switch wiring connector and release the kickdown switch from the bulkhead.

5 Working inside the driver's footwell, pull the cable end from the top of the throttle pedal.

6 Where applicable, remove the circlip securing the cable grommet at the bulkhead in the footwell.

7 Make a careful note of the cable routing, then pull the cable through the bulkhead into the engine compartment.

Refitting

8 Refitting is a reversal of removal, bearing in mind the following points:

a) Ensure that the cable is correctly routed, as noted during removal.

b) Ensure that the bulkhead grommet is

correctly seated in its aperture, and that, where applicable, the circlip is engaged with the grommet.

c) Check the throttle mechanism for satisfactory operation, and if necessary adjust the cable as described in the following paragraphs.

Adjustment

9 The cable adjustment is controlled by the position of the metal clip on the cable sheath at the bracket on the inlet manifold **(see illustration)**.

10 The cable should be adjusted so that when the throttle pedal is released, there is very slight free play in the cable at the fuel injection unit/throttle body end.

11 Check that when the throttle pedal is fully depressed, the throttle valve is fully open.

12 Adjust the position of the clip on the cable sheath to achieve the desired results.

4 Throttle pedal – removal and refitting

Removal

1 Unclip the throttle cable end from the top of the pedal.

2 Remove the spring clip from the end of the throttle pedal pivot shaft.

3 Unhook the return spring from the pedal, and slide the pedal from the end of the pivot shaft.

3.9 Throttle cable adjustment clip (arrowed)

Refitting

4 Refitting is a reversal of removal, but on completion, check and if necessary adjust the throttle cable free play as described in Section 3.

5 Fuel system – depressurising

> ⚠ **Warning: The fuel system is pressurised all the time the ignition is switched on, and will remain so for a considerable time after switching off. It is therefore essential to depressurise the system before disconnecting fuel lines, or carrying out any work on the fuel system components. Failure to do this before carrying out work may result in a sudden release of pressure which may cause fuel spray – this constitutes a serious fire hazard, and a health risk. Note that, even when the system has been depressurised, fuel will still be present in the system fuel lines and components, and adequate precautions should still be taken when carrying out work.**

1 The fuel system referred to in this Section is defined as the tank-mounted fuel pump, the fuel filter, the fuel injectors, the fuel rail and the pressure regulator, and the metal pipes and flexible hoses of the fuel lines between these components. All these contain fuel which will be under pressure while the engine is running, and/or while the ignition is switched on. The pressure will remain for some time after the ignition has been switched off, and must be relieved in a controlled fashion when any of these components are disturbed for servicing work.

2 Disconnect the battery negative terminal (refer to *Disconnecting the battery* in the Reference Section of this manual).

3 Place a container beneath the connection/union to be disconnected, and have a large rag ready to soak up any escaping fuel not being caught by the container.

6.8 Disconnect the fuel hoses (arrowed) from the rear of the tank

6.10 Fuel filter-to-fuel tank securing bolt (arrowed)

6.17 Fuel tank strap securing nut (1) and handbrake cable bracket (2)

4 Slowly loosen the connection or union nut to avoid a sudden release of pressure, and position the rag around the connection, to catch any fuel spray which may be expelled. Once the pressure is released, disconnect the fuel line. Plug the pipe ends, to minimise fuel loss and prevent the entry of dirt into the fuel system.

6 Fuel tank – removal and refitting

Note: *Refer to the precautions given in Section 1 before proceeding.*

Removal

Note: *During this procedure, the rear of the vehicle must be raised sufficiently to enable the fuel tank securing straps to be lowered far enough to allow the fuel tank to pass below the rear axle – the front ends of the tank securing straps are mounted on hinge pins on the vehicle underside, and cannot be removed.*

1 Depressurise the fuel system as described in Section 5.
2 Disconnect the battery negative terminal if not already done (refer to *Disconnecting the battery* in the Reference Chapter).
3 Syphon out any remaining fuel in the tank through the filler pipe into a clean metal container which can be sealed.
4 Chock the front wheels, then jack up the rear of the vehicle and support securely on axle stands (see *Jacking and vehicle support*).
5 Disconnect the rear of the exhaust system from its rubber mountings, and lower the system, or move it to one side sufficiently to enable removal of the fuel tank. Alternatively, remove the exhaust system completely to provide greater clearance – refer to Section 14 for details on removing the exhaust mountings and components.
6 Where applicable, remove the handbrake cable heat shield.
7 Slacken the handbrake cable adjuster with reference to Chapter 9, then pull the rubber grommet from the connecting link under the

vehicle floor, and disconnect the rear section of the handbrake cable from the connecting link. Release the cable from the brackets on the underbody and fuel tank, as applicable, and move the cable clear of the working area.
8 Working under the vehicle, release the hose clamps, and disconnect the fuel hoses from the rear of the fuel tank **(see illustration)**.
9 Release the connectors and disconnect the fuel hoses from the fuel filter, noting their locations to ensure correct refitting. A Vauxhall/Opel special tool is available to release the fuel line connectors, but provided care is taken, the connectors can be released using a pair of long-nosed pliers, or similar tool, to depress the retaining tangs. Refer to *Fuel filter renewal* in Chapter 1 for further details.
10 Unscrew the securing bolt and remove the fuel filter, complete with its clamp, from the fuel tank **(see illustration)**.
11 Fold the rear seat cushions forwards.
12 Lift the carpet panel on the right-hand side of the floor to expose the plastic fuel pump cover.
13 Carefully prise the plastic cover from the floor to expose the fuel pump.
14 Disconnect the pump wiring plug.
15 Clamp the fuel feed and return hoses to prevent fuel spillage, then release the hose clips, and carefully disconnect the fuel hoses from the top of the pump. Be prepared for fuel spillage, and take adequate precautions.
16 Support the weight of the fuel tank on a jack with interposed block of wood.
17 Remove the two nuts from the securing straps at the rear of the fuel tank **(see illustration)**. Lower the straps clear of the rear axle to allow sufficient clearance to withdraw the fuel tank.
18 Lower the tank sufficiently to enable access to the fuel hoses clipped to the tank. Unclip the relevant hoses from the tank, noting their locations to ensure correct refitting.
19 Continue to lower the tank until it can be removed from under the vehicle.

Refitting

20 If the tank contains sediment or water, it

may cleaned out with two or three rinses of clean fuel. Remove the fuel filter, fuel gauge sender unit and fuel pump as described in Sections 7 and 8 respectively. Shake the tank vigorously, and change the fuel as often as is necessary to remove all contamination from the tank. *This procedure should be carried out in a well-ventilated area, and it is vital to take adequate fire precautions.*
21 Any repairs to the fuel tank should be carried out by a professional. Do not under any circumstances attempt any form of DIY repair to a fuel tank.
22 Refitting is a reversal of removal, bearing in mind the following points:
a) *Ensure that all hoses are securely reconnected to their correct locations, as noted before removal.*
b) *Check the handbrake cable adjustment, as described in Chapter 9.*
c) *On completion, fill the fuel tank, then run the engine and check for leaks. If leakage is evident, stop the engine immediately and rectify the problem without delay.*

7 Fuel gauge sender unit – removal and refitting

Note: *Refer to the precautions given in Section 1 before proceeding.*

Removal

Note: *The fuel tank should be as empty as possible when carrying out this procedure. If the fuel level in the tank is high, fuel should be syphoned out through the filler pipe to avoid any possibility of spillage – syphon the fuel into a clean metal container which can be sealed.*

1 Disconnect the battery negative terminal (refer to *Disconnecting the battery* in the Reference Chapter).
2 Working inside the vehicle, fold the rear seat cushion forwards, and where applicable lift the carpet panel to expose the plastic fuel pump cover.
3 Carefully prise the plastic cover from the

7.3a Prise the plastic cover from the floor . . .

7.3b . . . to expose the fuel pump cover. Locking ring arrowed

7.5 Disconnect the fuel gauge sender wiring plug

floor to expose the fuel pump cover (see illustrations).

4 Release the fuel pump cover locking ring. A special tool (Vauxhall/Opel tool No KM-797) is available for this, but the ring can be removed by tapping anti-clockwise until the locking clips release.

 Warning: To prevent the possibility of any sparks which could ignite fuel vapour, use a plastic, wooden or brass tool to release the locking ring.

5 Withdraw the cover locking ring, then lift the pump cover from the top of the pump, and disconnect the fuel gauge sender unit wiring plug from the underside of the pump cover (see illustration).

6 Using the hook provided, pull the sender unit from the clips on the side of the fuel pump housing (see illustrations).

Refitting

7 Refitting is a reversal of removal, bearing in mind the following points:

 a) Ensure that the sender unit engages correctly with the clips on the fuel pump housing.

 b) Check the condition of the sealing ring on the underside of the fuel pump cover, and renew if necessary.

 c) Refit the fuel pump cover locking ring by tapping it anti-clockwise until the locking clips 'click' into position.

---

8 Fuel pump – testing, removal and refitting

Testing

1 If the pump is functioning, it should be possible to hear it 'buzzing' by listening under the rear of the vehicle when the ignition is switched on. Unless the engine is started, the fuel pump should switch off after approximately two seconds. If the noise produced is excessive, this may indicate a faulty pump.

2 If the pump appears to have failed completely, check the wiring to the pump, and check the appropriate fuse and relay.

3 To test the performance of the pump, special equipment is required, and it is

7.6a Using the hook . . .

recommended that any suspected faults are referred to a Vauxhall/Opel dealer.

Removal

Note: *Refer to the precautions given in Section 1 before proceeding. The fuel tank should be as empty as possible when carrying out this procedure. If the fuel level in the tank is high, fuel should be syphoned out through the filler pipe to avoid any possibility of spillage – syphon the fuel into a clean metal container which can be sealed.*

4 Depressurise the fuel system as described in Section 5.

5 Disconnect the battery negative terminal (refer to *Disconnecting the battery* in the Reference Chapter).

6 Working inside the vehicle, fold the rear seat cushion forwards, and where applicable, lift the carpet panel to expose the plastic fuel pump cover.

8.9 Disconnect the fuel pump wiring plug

7.6b . . . pull the sender unit from the fuel pump housing

7 Carefully prise the plastic cover from the floor to expose the fuel pump cover.

8 Release the hose clips, and carefully disconnect the fuel hoses from the top of the pump cover. Be prepared for fuel spillage, and take adequate precautions. Clamp or plug the open ends of the hoses, to prevent dirt ingress and further fuel spillage.

9 Disconnect the pump wiring plug (see illustration).

10 Release the fuel pump locking ring. A special tool (Vauxhall/Opel tool No KM-797) is available for this, but the ring can be removed by tapping anti-clockwise until the locking clips release (see illustration).

 Warning: To prevent the possibility of any sparks which could ignite fuel vapour, use a plastic, wooden or brass tool to release the locking ring.

8.10 Releasing the fuel pump locking ring using a brass drift

8.11 Disconnect the wiring plugs from the underside of the cover

8.13a Press the three pump housing retaining lugs (1 – one shown), and pull the housing from the tank using a hook engaged with the eyelet (2)

8.13b Withdrawing the fuel pump housing from the fuel tank

11 Lift the pump cover from the housing, then disconnect the two wiring plugs from the underside of the cover (see illustration).

12 Loosen the hose clip, and disconnect the fuel hose from the top of the fuel pump.

13 Press the three pump housing retaining lugs to release them, and simultaneously pull the pump housing from the tank using a wire hook engaged with the eyelet provided (see illustrations).

14 To remove the pump from the housing, first pull the filter from the base of the pump (see illustration), and disconnect the wires from the pump. Note the wire locations to ensure correct refitting.

15 Compress the three locking tabs, and pull the pump mounting plate and the pump from the housing (see illustrations).

Refitting

16 Refitting is a reversal of removal, bearing in mind the following points:

a) Before refitting the filter to the bottom of the pump, inspect the filter for contamination or blockage, and renew if necessary.

b) Ensure that the pump mounting plate engages correctly with the retaining clips on the housing.

c) Check the condition of the sealing ring on the underside of the fuel pump cover, and renew if necessary.

d) Refit the fuel pump cover locking ring by tapping it anti-clockwise until the locking clips 'click' into position.

9 Fuel injection system – general information

1 The system is under the overall control of the Motronic M 1.5.5 engine management system, which also controls the ignition system (see Chapter 5B).

2 Fuel is supplied from the rear-mounted tank, via a fuel filter and a pressure regulator, to the fuel rail. Excess fuel is returned from the regulator to the tank. The fuel rail acts as a reservoir for the fuel injectors, which inject fuel into the cylinder inlet tracts, upstream of the inlet valves. The Motronic M 1.5.5 system is a 'sequential' fuel injection system. This means that each of the three (1.0 litre engines), or four (1.2 litre engines) fuel injectors is triggered individually, just before the inlet valve on the relevant cylinder opens.

3 The duration of the electrical pulses to the fuel injectors determines the quantity of fuel injected. The pulse duration is computed by the Motronic electronic control unit (ECU) on the basis of information received from the following sensors:

a) Throttle position sensor – informs the ECU of throttle position, and the rate of throttle opening/closing.

b) Air mass meter – informs the ECU of the load on the engine (expressed in terms of the mass of air passing from the air cleaner to the throttle body).

c) Crankshaft speed/position sensor – informs the ECU of the crankshaft speed and position.

d) Camshaft position sensor – informs the ECU when No 1 cylinder is at top dead centre (TDC) on the firing stroke (expressed in terms of the position of the inlet camshaft).

e) Coolant temperature sensor – informs the ECU of engine temperature.

f) Exhaust gas oxygen sensor – informs the ECU of the oxygen content of the exhaust gases (explained in greater detail in Chapter 4C).

g) Vehicle speed sensor – informs the ECU of the vehicle speed.

h) Knock sensor – informs the ECU when engine 'knock' (pre-ignition) occurs (explained in greater detail in Chapter 5B).

4 The signals from the various sensors are processed by the ECU, and the optimum fuelling and ignition settings are selected for the prevailing engine operating conditions.

5 Idle speed is controlled by the idle speed control motor, which directly regulates the position of the throttle valve. The motor is controlled by the electronic control unit; there is no provision for direct adjustment of the idle speed.

6 Similarly, the fuel/air mixture is controlled within fine limits by the electronic control unit, via the fuel injectors. No manual adjustment of fuel/air mixture is possible.

7 A catalytic converter is fitted, to reduce harmful exhaust gas emissions. Details of this

8.14 Removing the fuel filter from the base of the fuel pump

8.15a Compress the three locking tabs (arrowed) . . .

8.15b . . . and withdraw the pump from the housing

and other emissions control system equipment are given in Chapter 4C.

8 If certain sensors fail, and send abnormal signals to the ECU, the ECU has a back-up programme. In this event, the abnormal signals are ignored, and a pre-programmed value is substituted for the sensor signal, allowing the engine to continue running, albeit at reduced efficiency. If the ECU enters its back-up mode, a warning light on the instrument panel will illuminate, and a fault code will be stored in the ECU memory. This fault code can be read using suitable specialist test equipment.

10 Fuel injection system components – testing

In order to safely test the fuel injection system components without the risk of damage to the components or electronic control unit, specialist test equipment is required.

The systems have a self-diagnosis function, and any faults are stored as codes in the electronic control unit memory. These fault codes can be read using suitable test equipment such as a fault code reader. If a fault code reader is available, it should be connected and operated according to the instructions supplied with the reader.

System sensors and actuators can be tested for continuity and resistance using a suitable multi-meter, but always ensure that the ignition is switched off, and that the relevant sensor or actuator is disconnected from the engine management system. Refer to the precautions given in Section 1 before attempting to carry out any fault diagnosis.

In the event of a suspected fault, and suitable test and diagnostic equipment is not available, the best course of action is to seek advice from a Vauxhall/Opel dealer, who will have access to the necessary equipment.

11 Fuel injection system components – removal and refitting

Throttle body

Removal

1 Disconnect the battery negative terminal (refer to *Disconnecting the battery* in the Reference Chapter).

2 Remove the air cleaner cover, inlet trunking and airbox as described in Section 2.

3 Partially drain the cooling system as described in Chapter 1 (drain sufficient coolant to empty the coolant expansion tank).

4 Release the retaining clips and disconnect the two coolant hoses from the rear of the throttle body.

Engine management system fault codes

Code	Cause of fault
P0100	Air mass meter (voltage high/low)
P0110	Intake air temperature (voltage high/low)
P0115	Coolant temperature sensor (voltage high/low)
P0120	Throttle position sensor (voltage high/low)
P0130	Oxygen sensor (voltage high/low or open-circuit)
P0170	Oxygen sensor (exhaust gases rich/lean)
P0201	Fuel injector 1 (voltage high/low or open circuit)
P0202	Fuel injector 2 (voltage high/low or open circuit)
P0203	Fuel injector 3 (voltage high/low or open circuit)
P0204	Fuel injector 4 (voltage high/low or open circuit)
P0230	Fuel pump relay (voltage high/low or open circuit)
P0325	Knock sensor (incorrect signal)
P0335	Incorrect engine speed (rpm) signal
P0340	Camshaft position sensor (voltage high/low)
P0403	EGR valve (voltage high/low or open-circuit)
P0443	Fuel tank vent valve (voltage high/low or open-circuit)
P0505	Idle speed control motor (voltage high/low)
P0550	Electronic power steering (voltage high/low)
P0560	Battery (voltage high/low
P0602	Electronic control unit (program error)
P1230	Relay circuit
P1405	EGR valve (actual value voltage high/low or open-circuit)
P1501	Electronic immobiliser (incorrectly coded)
P1502	Electronic immobiliser (no signal)
P1503	Electronic immobiliser (incorrect signal)
P1530	Air conditioning relay (voltage high/low)
P1600	Electronic control unit (defective)
P1602	Electronic control unit (knock control circuit fault)
P1640	Electronic control unit (unidentifiable fault)
P1690	Warning light (voltage high/low or open-circuit)

5 Turn the throttle disc and disconnect the throttle cable end fitting from the disc. Release the cable grommet from its bracket on the inlet manifold.

6 Release the retaining clips and disconnect the crankcase breather hose and the fuel tank vent valve vacuum hose from the throttle body.

7 Disconnect the wiring plugs at the idle speed control motor and throttle position sensor.

8 Undo the four bolts and lift the throttle body off the inlet manifold **(see illustration)**. Recover the gasket.

Refitting

9 Refitting is a reversal of removal, bearing in mind the following points:
 a) Thoroughly clean the mating faces and use a new throttle body gasket.
 b) On completion, check and if necessary

adjust the throttle cable free play as described in Section 3, and top-up the coolant level as described in 'Weekly checks'.

11.8 Throttle body retaining bolts (arrowed)

11.17a Disconnect the wiring plugs at the coolant temperature sensor (A), and camshaft position sensor (B) . . .

11.17b . . . and at the oil pressure switch (arrowed)

11.11 Air mass meter inlet trunking retaining clips (1) and direction of fitting arrow (2). Arrow must point toward the throttle body

Air mass meter

Removal

10 Remove the air cleaner cover, inlet trunking and airbox as described in Section 2.
11 Release the retaining clips securing the inlet trunking to the air mass meter and withdraw the meter (see illustration).

Refitting

12 Refitting is a reversal of removal, but ensure that the arrow on the air mass meter body points toward the throttle body when fitted.

Fuel injectors

Note: *Refer to the precautions given in Section 1 before proceeding. The seals at both ends of the fuel injectors must be renewed on refitting.*

Removal

13 Depressurise the fuel system as described in Section 5.
14 Remove the throttle body as described previously in this Section.
15 Detach the fuel tank vent valve from its mounting bracket and move the valve to one side.
16 Disconnect the two engine breather hoses from the left-hand end of the camshaft cover.
17 Disconnect the wiring plugs at the coolant temperature sensor, camshaft position sensor and oil pressure switch (see illustrations).

18 Undo the two bolts, one at each end, securing the plastic fuel injector wiring trough to the top of the fuel rail (see illustration). Note that these bolts also secure the fuel rail to the inlet manifold.
19 Release the retaining clips at each injector, then lift the wiring trough up and off the injectors. Place the trough to one side.
20 Disconnect the fuel feed and return hoses from the fuel rail, noting their locations to aid refitting (see illustration). Be prepared for fuel spillage, and take adequate precautions. Clamp or plug the open ends of the hoses, to minimise further fuel loss.
21 Disconnect the vacuum hose from the fuel pressure regulator (see illustration).
22 Undo the bolt securing the fuel rail hose union plate to the inlet manifold, then lift the fuel rail complete with the injectors off the manifold (see illustration).
23 To remove an injector from the fuel rail, prise out the metal securing clip using a screwdriver or a pair of pliers, and pull the injector from the fuel rail.
24 Overhaul of the fuel injectors is not possible, as no spares are available. If faulty, an injector must be renewed.

Refitting

25 Commence refitting by fitting new O-ring seals to both ends of the fuel injectors (see illustration). Coat the seals with a thin layer of petroleum jelly before fitting.
26 Refitting is a reversal of removal, bearing in mind the following points:

11.18 Fuel injector wiring trough right-hand securing bolt (arrowed)

11.20 Fuel feed and return hose connections at the fuel rail

11.21 Disconnect the vacuum hose from the fuel pressure regulator

11.22 Undo the bolt securing the fuel rail hose union plate to the manifold

11.25 Fit new O-rings (arrowed) to the fuel injectors before refitting

11.36 Idle speed control motor retaining bolts (arrowed)

11.41 Throttle position sensor retaining screws (arrowed)

11.43 Crankshaft speed/position sensor location

a) When refitting the injectors to the fuel rail, note that the groove in the metal securing clip must engage with the lug on the injector body.

b) Refit the throttle body as described previously in this Section.

c) Ensure that all wiring connectors are securely reconnected, and that the wiring is secured in the relevant clips and brackets.

Fuel pressure regulator

Note: *Refer to the precautions given in Section 1 before proceeding. New regulator O-ring seals must be used on refitting.*

Removal

27 Depressurise the fuel system as described in Section 5.

28 Disconnect the battery negative terminal if not already done (refer to *Disconnecting the battery* in the Reference Chapter).

29 Disconnect the two engine breather hoses from the left-hand end of the camshaft cover.

30 Disconnect the vacuum hose from the fuel pressure regulator.

31 Place some rags under the regulator, to catch any spilt fuel. Extract the retaining clip and ease the regulator out from the fuel rail.

Refitting

32 Refitting is a reversal of removal, but fit new O-ring seals to the regulator and coat the seals with a thin layer of petroleum jelly before fitting.

Idle speed control motor

Note: *If a new idle speed control motor is to be fitted, it will be necessary to erase the adaptive value settings for the old motor, stored in the engine management ECU memory. This can only be done using Vauxhall/Opel diagnostic test equipment.*

Removal

33 Disconnect the battery negative terminal (refer to *Disconnecting the battery* in the Reference Chapter).

34 Remove the air cleaner cover, inlet trunking and airbox as described in Section 2.

35 Disconnect the wiring plug from the idle speed control motor.

36 Undo the two retaining bolts and withdraw the motor from the throttle body **(see illustration)**.

Refitting

37 Refitting is a reversal of removal. On completion, it will be necessary to take the car to a Vauxhall/Opel dealer to enable the ECU memory to be cleared (see the note at the start of this sub-Section).

Throttle position sensor

Note: *If a new throttle position sensor is to be fitted, it will be necessary to erase the adaptive value settings for the old sensor stored in the engine management ECU memory. This can only be done using Vauxhall/Opel diagnostic test equipment.*

Removal

38 Disconnect the battery negative terminal (refer to *Disconnecting the battery* in the Reference Chapter).

39 Remove the air cleaner cover, inlet trunking and airbox as described in Section 2.

40 Disconnect the wiring plug from the throttle position sensor, located at the rear of the throttle body.

41 Undo the two retaining screws and withdraw the sensor from the throttle body **(see illustration)**.

Refitting

42 Refitting is a reversal of removal. On completion, it will be necessary to take the car to a Vauxhall/Opel dealer to enable the ECU memory to be cleared (see the note at the start of this sub-Section).

Crankshaft speed/position sensor

Note: *A new O-ring seal must be used on refitting.*

43 The crankshaft speed/position sensor is located at the rear right-hand end of the cylinder block baseplate, below the starter motor **(see illustration)**.

44 Disconnect the battery negative terminal (refer to *Disconnecting the battery* in the Reference Chapter).

45 Firmly apply the handbrake, then jack up the front of the car and support it securely on axle stands (see *Jacking and vehicle support*).

46 Disconnect the sensor wiring connector, then undo the retaining bolt and withdraw the sensor from the cylinder block baseplate.

Refitting

47 Refitting is a reversal of removal, but ensure that the mating surfaces of the sensor and baseplate are clean and fit a new O-ring seal to the sensor before refitting.

Camshaft position sensor

Removal

48 The camshaft position sensor is located on the timing cover, on the inlet camshaft side.

49 Disconnect the battery negative terminal (refer to *Disconnecting the battery* in the Reference Chapter).

50 Disconnect the sensor wiring connector.

51 Undo the retaining bolt and withdraw the sensor from the timing cover.

Refitting

52 Refitting is a reversal of removal, but ensure that the mating surfaces of the sensor and timing cover are clean before fitting.

Coolant temperature sensor

53 The coolant temperature sensor is located in the top of the coolant pump housing.

54 Disconnect the battery negative terminal (refer to *Disconnecting the battery* in the Reference Chapter).

55 Partially drain the cooling system as described in Chapter 1.

56 Disconnect the sensor wiring plug.

57 Unscrew the sensor, and withdraw it from the coolant pump. Recover the sealing ring.

Refitting

58 Refitting is a reversal of removal, but use a new sealing ring, and on completion, top-up the cooling system as described in *Weekly checks*.

Exhaust gas oxygen sensor

Note: *The sensor must be removed and refitted with the exhaust system at normal operating temperature; take great care to avoid burns, and damage to tools or surrounding components during the procedure – the exhaust system and sensor will be very hot. If the original sensor is to be re-used, the threads must be lubricated with special grease on refitting – see text.*

Removal

59 If the engine is cold, start the engine, and run it until it reaches normal operating temperature. Stop the engine.

60 Disconnect the battery negative terminal (refer to *Disconnecting the battery* in the Reference Chapter).

61 Unclip the sensor wiring connector from the bracket adjacent to the oil filter housing, then separate the two halves of the connector.

62 Using a suitable spanner, unscrew the sensor from the catalytic converter. It is advisable to wear suitable gloves, as the exhaust system will be extremely hot.

63 Withdraw the sensor and its wiring, taking care not to burn the wiring on the exhaust system.

Refitting

64 The sensor must be refitted with the engine and exhaust system still at normal operating temperature.

65 If a new sensor is being fitted, it will be supplied with the threads coated in a special grease to prevent the sensor seizing in the exhaust manifold.

66 If the original sensor is being refitted, clean the threads carefully. The threads must be coated with Vauxhall/Opel special grease (No 19 48 602). Use only the specified grease, which consists of liquid graphite and glass beads. As the exhaust system heats up, the graphite will burn off, leaving the glass beads between the threads to prevent the sensor from seizing.

67 Refitting is a reversal of removal, ensuring that the sensor is tightened to the specified torque.

Vehicle speed sensor

68 The vehicle speed sensor is located in the transmission casing and removal and refitting details are given in Chapter 7A, Section 5.

Knock sensor

69 The sensor is part of the knock control system, details of which are given in Chapter 5B.

Electronic control unit

Removal

70 The electronic control unit is attached to the inlet manifold on the left-hand side.

71 Disconnect the battery negative terminal (refer to *Disconnecting the battery* in the Reference Chapter).

72 Release the adjacent wiring harness from its locating clips to gain access to the control unit wiring connectors.

73 Lift up the locking levers and disconnect the engine management and body harness wiring connectors from the control unit **(see illustration)**.

74 Undo the retaining screw and release the earth cable from the control unit bracket.

75 Undo the two remaining screws and remove the control unit from the inlet manifold.

Refitting

76 Refitting is a reversal of removal. Ensure that the earth lead is securely connected and the wiring harness is correctly routed and retained by the relevant clips.

Emission control system components

77 Details are given in Chapter 4C. Removal and refitting details for the oxygen sensor are given earlier in this Section.

12 Inlet manifold – removal and refitting

Removal

Note: *A new manifold gasket(s) and, on 1.2 litre engines, a new EGR pipe gasket must be used on refitting.*

1 Depressurise the fuel system as described in Section 5.

2 Disconnect the battery negative terminal (refer to *Disconnecting the battery* in the Reference Chapter).

3 Remove the throttle body as described in Section 11.

4 Disconnect the wiring plugs at the oil pressure switch, coolant temperature sensor and camshaft position sensor.

5 Release the wiring harness from its locating clips to gain access to the electronic control unit wiring connectors.

6 Lift up the locking levers and disconnect the engine management and main body wiring harness connectors from the electronic control unit.

7 Undo the retaining screw and release the earth cable from the electronic control unit bracket.

8 Detach the fuel tank vent valve from its mounting bracket and move the valve to one side.

9 Disconnect the brake servo vacuum hose connection at the inlet manifold. On 1.0 litre engines the connection is by a conventional union nut. On 1.2 litre engines a quick-release fitting is used. Depress the two tags on the

side of the fitting and withdraw the fitting from the manifold pipe stub.

10 Undo the two bolts and release the wiring harness support bracket from the rear of the inlet manifold.

11 Firmly apply the handbrake, then jack up the front of the car and support it securely on axle stands (see *Jacking and vehicle support*).

12 From under the car, undo the bolt securing the support bracket to the base of the inlet manifold. Slacken the bolt securing the bracket to the cylinder block and twist the bracket to one side.

13 On 1.0 litre engines, detach the additional lower wiring harness bracket from the inlet manifold.

14 Undo the two bolts, one at each end, securing the plastic fuel injector wiring trough to the top of the fuel rail. Note that these bolts also secure the fuel rail to the inlet manifold.

15 Release the retaining clips at each injector, then lift the wiring trough up and off the injectors. Place the trough to one side.

16 Disconnect the fuel feed and return hoses from the fuel rail, noting their locations to aid refitting. Be prepared for fuel spillage, and take adequate precautions. Clamp or plug the open ends of the hoses, to minimise further fuel loss.

17 Disconnect the wiring plug from the top of the EGR valve and the wiring connector from the adjacent temperature gauge sender.

18 Release the DIS ignition module cover from the centre of the camshaft cover and remove it toward the transmission end of the engine.

19 Disconnect the wiring plug from the left-hand end of the DIS module.

20 Disconnect the fuel injector wiring trough wiring connector.

21 Undo the retaining bolt and release the left-hand engine lifting bracket from the cylinder head, complete with attached wiring harness.

22 On 1.2 litre engines, undo the two bolts securing the EGR pipe to the side of the EGR valve housing at the left-hand end of the cylinder head. When the inlet manifold has been removed, recover the gasket between the pipe flange and valve housing.

23 Undo the six nuts (1.0 litre engines) or six

11.73 Disconnect the wiring connectors from the electronic control unit. Note the location of the earth lead (arrowed)

12.26 Fit new individual rubber seals to the grooves in the inlet manifold on 1.2 litre engines

tubular bolts (1.2 litre engines) securing the manifold to the cylinder head. Note that on 1.2 litre engines, the tubular bolts are internally retained and cannot be removed completely from the manifold.

24 Withdraw the inlet manifold from the cylinder head studs, and recover the one-piece gasket or the four individual rubber seals, as applicable.

Refitting

25 Thoroughly clean the mating face of the inlet manifold and cylinder head, ensuring that all traces of old gasket are removed (where applicable).

26 Locate a new one-piece gasket over the manifold studs, or fit the individual rubber seals to the grooves in the manifold mating face **(see illustration)**.

27 Locate the manifold over the cylinder head studs and secure with the nuts or tubular bolts tightened progressively to the specified torque.

28 On 1.2 litre engines, refit the EGR pipe to the EGR housing using a new gasket. Secure the pipe with the two bolts tightened to the specified torque.

29 Refit the left-hand engine lifting bracket and wiring harness.

30 Reconnect the wiring plug to the DIS module and refit the module cover.

31 Reconnect the EGR valve wiring plug and the temperature gauge sender wiring connector.

32 Reconnect the fuel feed and return hoses to the fuel rail.

33 Locate the plastic fuel injector wiring trough over the injectors ensuring that the wiring connectors correctly engage. Secure the trough with the two retaining bolts, then reconnect the wiring connector.

34 From under the car, reposition the inlet manifold support bracket and refit the bolt securing the bracket to the manifold. Tighten this bolt, and the bolt securing the bracket to the cylinder block, to the specified torque.

35 Refit the wiring harness support bracket(s) to the inlet manifold.

36 Reconnect the brake servo vacuum hose to the inlet manifold.

37 Refit the fuel tank vent valve to its mounting bracket.

13.5 Remove the engine lifting brackets from the front of the cylinder head

38 Reconnect the two wiring connectors to the electronic control unit and secure the earth lead to the control unit bracket with the retaining screw. Reposition the wiring harness moved clear for access.

39 Reconnect the wiring plugs at the oil pressure switch, coolant temperature sensor and camshaft position sensor.

40 Refit the throttle body as described in Section 11.

13 Exhaust manifold – removal and refitting

Removal

Note: *New manifold retaining nuts, a new manifold gasket, catalytic converter flange gasket and oil dipstick guide tube O-rings must be used on refitting.*

1 Disconnect the battery negative terminal (refer to *Disconnecting the battery* in the Reference Chapter).

2 On models equipped with air conditioning, carry out the following:

a) *Remove the auxiliary drivebelt from the air conditioning compressor pulley as described in Chapter 1. Note that it is not necessary to remove the belt completely, as long as it is free of the pulley.*

b) *Undo the bolt securing the refrigerant pipe/hose bracket to the front of the cylinder head.*

c) *Undo the bolts securing the air conditioning compressor to the timing*

13.6 Undo the bolt (arrowed) and remove the oil dipstick guide tube

cover and cylinder block. Release the refrigerant hoses and pipes from the retaining clips as necessary and move the compressor to one side, clear of the manifold. Tie or support the compressor in this position. **Do not** *disconnect the refrigerant pipes/hoses from the compressor.*

3 Unclip the oxygen sensor wiring connector from the bracket adjacent to the oil filter housing, then separate the two halves of the connector.

4 Undo the three nuts securing the catalytic converter flange to the exhaust manifold. Undo the two bolts securing the converter support bracket to the cylinder block baseplate and separate the converter from the manifold. Lower the exhaust system clear of the manifold and support it in this position. Recover the flange gasket.

5 Undo the two bolts and remove the engine lifting brackets from the front of the cylinder head **(see illustration)**.

6 Undo the bolt securing the oil dipstick guide tube to the exhaust manifold and withdraw the dipstick and guide tube from the cylinder block baseplate **(see illustration)**. Suitably cover or plug the guide tube aperture in the cylinder block baseplate to prevent dirt ingress.

7 Undo the two bolts and remove the exhaust manifold heat shield **(see illustration)**.

8 Undo the retaining nuts and withdraw the exhaust manifold from the cylinder head studs **(see illustrations)**. Recover the manifold gasket.

13.7 Remove the exhaust manifold heat shield

13.8a Undo the exhaust manifold retaining nuts . . .

13.8b . . . and withdraw the manifold from the cylinder head studs

14.7 Exhaust system cutting point

1 Exhaust front section
2 Intermediate silencer
3 Cutting point – 254 to 256 mm from intermediate silencer

Refitting

9 Refitting is a reversal of removal, bearing in mind the following points:
a) Clean the gasket faces of the manifold and the cylinder head.
b) Refit the manifold using a new gasket and new retaining nuts.
c) Renew the oil dipstick guide tube O-rings and lubricate the O-rings with petroleum jelly before refitting.
d) Reconnect the catalytic converter to the manifold using a new flange gasket. Tighten the converter-to-manifold nuts to the specified torque first, followed by the support bracket bolts.
e) On engines with air conditioning, refit the auxiliary drivebelt as described in Chapter 1.

14 Exhaust system – general information and component renewal

General information

1 With the exception of the rear silencer box, the exhaust system originally fitted to the vehicle at the factory is a single-section welded unit, which includes the integral catalytic converter.
2 Periodically, the exhaust system should be checked for signs of leaks or damage. Also inspect the system rubber mountings, and renew if necessary.
3 Small holes or cracks can be repaired using proprietary exhaust repair products.
4 Before renewing an individual section of the exhaust system, it is wise to inspect the remaining sections. If corrosion or damage is evident on more than one section of the system, it may prove more economical to renew the entire system.

Component renewal

5 With the exception of the rear silencer box, individual sections of the system can only be removed by cutting the system, and using suitable clamps and sleeves to join the new section to the remainder of the system. Individual front, intermediate and rear sections of the exhaust system are available from Vauxhall/Opel dealers.
6 If any part of the system is to be renewed, it is important to ensure that the correct replacement components are obtained for the particular model concerned.

7 If it proves necessary to cut the system in order to renew particular components, the cutting point is 254 to 256 mm in front of the intermediate silencer **(see illustration)**. It is strongly recommended that any such work is entrusted to a Vauxhall/Opel dealer, or exhaust specialist.
8 If work is to be carried out on the exhaust system, first jack up the vehicle and support securely on axle stands (see *Jacking and vehicle support*).
9 The exhaust front section (catalytic converter) can be disconnected from the manifold after removing the three securing nuts and two support bracket bolts. Recover the gasket after separating the flange joint and renew the gasket on refitting.
10 To remove the entire exhaust system, disconnect the joints, or cut the system as necessary (with regard to the spare sections available), then unhook the rubber mountings, and withdraw the relevant section of the system.
11 When refitting the catalytic converter to the manifold, refit and loosely tighten the three flange nuts and the two support bracket bolts. The three flange nuts should then be tightened to the specified torque first, followed by the support bracket bolts.

Chapter 4 Part B: Fuel and exhaust systems – 1.2 SOHC, 1.4 & 1.6 litre engines

Contents

Degrees of difficulty

| Easy, suitable for novice with little experience | Fairly easy, suitable for beginner with some experience | Fairly difficult, suitable for competent DIY mechanic | Difficult, suitable for experienced DIY mechanic | Very difficult, suitable for expert DIY or professional |

Specifications

General

System type:*
  1.2 litre SOHC (X 12 SZ) engines . . . . Multec single-point fuel injection
  1.4 litre SOHC engines:
    X 14 SZ engines . . . . Multec single-point fuel injection
    C 14 SE engine . . . . Multec M multi-point fuel injection
  1.4 and 1.6 litre DOHC (X 14 XE and X 16 XE) engines . . . . Multec S sequential multi-point fuel injection
*For details of engine code location, see 'Vehicle identification' in the Reference Chapter.

Fuel pump

Type .... Electric, mounted in fuel tank

Fuel grade

Note: *95 RON (Premium) unleaded fuel is the fuel recommended by the manufacturers. 98 RON (Super) unleaded may also be used but there will be no performance gain, or economy savings, by doing so.*

Fuel octane requirement:

1.2 litre SOHC engine[2]	95 RON (Premium) or 98 RON (Super) unleaded
1.4 litre SOHC engine with multi-point fuel injection (C 14 SE)[3]	95 RON (Premium) or 98 RON (Super) unleaded
1.4 litre SOHC engine with single-point fuel injection (X 14 SZ)[2]	95 RON (Premium) or 98 RON (Super) unleaded
1.4 litre DOHC engine[1]	95 RON (Premium) or 98 RON (Super) unleaded
1.6 litre engine[1]	95 RON (Premium) or 98 RON (Super) unleaded

1 If no higher-octane unleaded fuel is available, 91 RON (Regular) unleaded fuel can be used, but there will be a reduction in engine power and torque.

2 If no higher-octane unleaded fuel is available, 91 RON (Regular) unleaded fuel can be used, provided severe engine loads (including towing and heavy payloads) and full-throttle operation are avoided, but there will be a reduction in engine power and torque.

3 The octane coding plug must be positioned correctly in accordance with the octane rating of the fuel being used – refer to Section 1, for details. If no higher-octane unleaded fuel is available, 91 RON (Regular) unleaded fuel can be used, provided a special octane plug (available from a Vauxhall/Opel dealer) is used, but there will be a reduction in engine power and torque.

Multec single-point fuel injection system data

Idle speed (not adjustable – for reference only)	820 to 980 rpm
Idle mixture CO content (not adjustable – for reference only)	0.4% maximum
Crankshaft speed/position sensor-to-sensor wheel air gap	1.0 ± 0.7 mm

Multec M multi-point fuel injection system data

Idle speed (not adjustable – for reference only)	850 to 1010 rpm
Idle mixture CO content (not adjustable – for reference only)	0.4% maximum
Crankshaft speed/position sensor-to-sensor wheel air gap	1.0 ± 0.7 mm

Multec S sequential multi-point fuel injection system data

Idle speed (not adjustable – for reference only)	820 to 980 rpm
Idle mixture CO content (not adjustable – for reference only)	0.3 % maximum
Crankshaft speed/position sensor-to-sensor wheel air gap	1.0 ± 0.7 mm

Torque wrench settings

	Nm	lbf ft
Single-point fuel injection system		
Coolant temperature sensor	20	15
Exhaust front section-to-manifold nuts	25	18
Exhaust manifold securing nuts	22	16
Fuel line-to-fuel injection unit union nuts	30	22
Fuel injection unit-to-inlet manifold nuts	22	16
Inlet manifold nuts/bolts	22	16
Oxygen sensor	30	22
Multec M multi-point fuel injection system		
Coolant temperature sensor	20	15
Exhaust front section-to-manifold nuts	25	18
Exhaust manifold securing nuts	22	16
Inlet manifold nuts/bolts	22	16
Oxygen sensor	30	22
Multec S sequential multi-point fuel injection system		
Coolant temperature sensor	14	10
Exhaust front section-to-manifold nuts	25	18
Exhaust manifold securing nuts	22	16
Heat shield to exhaust manifold	8	6
Lower section of inlet manifold-to-cylinder head nuts	20	15
Oxygen sensor	30	22

1 General information and precautions

General information

1 Three different basic types of fuel injection system are used on the engines covered in this Part of Chapter 4, these being Multec single-point fuel injection, Multec M multi-point fuel injection, and Multec S sequential multi-point fuel injection. The systems are described in more detail in Section 10.

2 Fuel is supplied from a tank, mounted under the rear of the vehicle, by an electric fuel pump mounted in the tank. The fuel passes through a filter to the fuel injection system, which incorporates various sensors, actuators, and an electronic control unit.

3 The inducted air passes through an air cleaner, which incorporates a paper filter element to filter out potentially-harmful particles (serious internal engine damage can be caused if foreign particles enter through the air intake system). On single-point fuel injection engines, the air cleaner has a vacuum-controlled air intake, supplying a blend of hot and cold air to suit the prevailing engine operating conditions.

4 The electronic control unit controls both the fuel injection system and the ignition system, integrating the two into a complete engine management system. Refer to Chapter 5B for details of the ignition side of the system.

5 The exhaust system on all models incorporates a catalytic converter to reduce exhaust gas emissions. Further details can be found in Chapter 4C, along with details of the other emission control systems and components.

Octane plug adjustment

6 The fuel octane recommendations for each engine are given in Chapter 1 Specifications.

7 On the C 14 SE engine, an octane coding plug is provided. The plug is located in the engine compartment, in a bracket attached to the right-hand suspension strut top mounting **(see illustration)**. The coding plug allows the engine management system to optimise the ignition timing for the type of fuel in use.

1.7 Octane coding plug location (arrowed) in engine compartment – C 14 SE engine

8 By reversing the position of the octane coding plug in its connector, it is possible to choose between two octane ratings. The number visible on the plug should correspond to the octane rating of the fuel in use.

9 It is also possible to select a third octane rating by using a special coding plug, available from a Vauxhall/Opel dealer.

10 If the octane rating of the fuel being used is to be changed, allow the fuel tank to become practically empty, then fill the tank with the new type of fuel. Ensure that the ignition is switched off, then release the octane coding plug from its bracket and reverse the position of the plug in its connector to correspond with the octane rating of the new type of fuel.

11 On all other engines, the engine management system automatically adjusts the ignition timing for the type of fuel in use, via the knock control system (see Chapter 5B).

Precautions

Note: *Refer to Part C of this Chapter for general information and precautions relating to the catalytic converter.*

12 Before disconnecting any fuel lines, or working on any part of the fuel system, the system must be depressurised as described in Section 6.

13 Care must be taken when disconnecting the fuel lines. When disconnecting a fuel union or hose, loosen the union or clamp screw slowly, to avoid sudden uncontrolled fuel spillage. Take adequate fire precautions.

14 When working on fuel system components, scrupulous cleanliness must be observed, and care must be taken not to introduce any foreign matter into fuel lines or components.

15 After carrying out any work involving disconnection of fuel lines, it is advisable to check the connections for leaks; pressurise the system by switching the ignition on and off several times.

16 Electronic control units are very sensitive components, and certain precautions must be taken to avoid damage to these units as follows.

a) *When carrying out welding operations on the vehicle using electric welding equipment, the battery and alternator should be disconnected.*

b) *Although the underbonnet-mounted control units will tolerate normal underbonnet conditions, they can be adversely affected by excess heat or moisture. If using welding equipment or pressure-washing equipment in the vicinity of an electronic control unit, take care not to direct heat, or jets of water or steam, at the unit. If this cannot be avoided, remove the control unit from the vehicle, and protect its wiring plug with a plastic bag.*

c) *Before disconnecting any wiring, or removing components, always ensure that the ignition is switched off.*

d) *Do not attempt to improvise fault diagnosis procedures using a test light or multi-meter, as irreparable damage could be caused to the control unit.*

e) *After working on fuel injection/engine management system components, ensure that all wiring is correctly reconnected before reconnecting the battery or switching on the ignition.*

 Warning: Many of the procedures in this Chapter require the disconnection of fuel line connections, and the removal of components, which may result in some fuel spillage. Before carrying out any operation on the fuel system, refer to the precautions given in 'Safety first!' at the beginning of this manual, and follow them implicitly. Petrol is a highly-dangerous and volatile liquid, and the precautions necessary when handling it cannot be overstressed.

2 Air cleaner intake air temperature control (single-point fuel injection) – testing

1 The air cleaner is thermostatically-controlled, to provide air at the most suitable temperature for combustion with minimum exhaust emission levels.

2 The optimum air temperature is achieved by drawing in cold air from an air intake at the front of the vehicle, and blending it with hot air from a shroud on the exhaust manifold. The proportion of hot air and cold air is varied by the position of a flap valve in the air cleaner intake spout, which is controlled by a vacuum diaphragm unit. The vacuum applied to the diaphragm is regulated by a heat sensor located within the air cleaner body.

3 To check the operation of the air temperature control, the engine must be cold. First check the position of the flap valve. The air cleaner cover and the air filter element must be removed in order to view the flap valve **(see illustration)**. Check that the flap is initially closed, to admit only cold air from outside the vehicle. Start the engine, and check that the flap now opens to admit only hot air from the exhaust manifold.

2.3 Intake air temperature control flap valve (arrowed) in air cleaner casing

3.6 Disconnecting the intake air temperature control vacuum pipe from the air cleaner

3.7 Disconnecting the hot-air trunking from the exhaust manifold hot-air shroud

3.8a Undo the air intake trunking plastic stud from the crossmember . . .

3.8b . . . and disconnect the trunking from the air cleaner casing

3.9 Pull the front locating grommet (arrowed) upwards . . .

4 Temporarily refit the filter element and the air cleaner cover.
5 Run the engine until it reaches normal operating temperature.
6 Remove the cover and the filter element once more, and check that the flap is now closed, to admit only cold air from outside the vehicle, or in cold weather, a mixture of hot and cold air. Refit the filter element and the cover after making the check.
7 If the flap does not function correctly, the air cleaner must be renewed, as parts are not available individually.

3 Air cleaner assembly – removal and refitting

Removal

1 Disconnect the battery negative terminal (refer to *Disconnecting the battery* in the Reference Chapter).
2 Where applicable, disconnect the wiring plug from the intake air temperature sensor, located in the air inlet trunking.
3 Disconnect the air inlet trunking from the

airbox on the fuel injection unit (single-point fuel injection models), or the throttle body (multi-point fuel injection models), as applicable.
4 Release the securing clips, then lift off the air cleaner cover, and remove it from the vehicle.
5 Lift out the air cleaner element.
6 Where applicable, disconnect the intake air temperature control vacuum pipe from the air cleaner casing **(see illustration)**.
7 Where applicable, disconnect the hot-air trunking from the exhaust manifold hot-air shroud **(see illustration)**.
8 Undo the plastic stud securing the air intake trunking to the engine compartment front crossmember, then disconnect the trunking from the front of the air cleaner casing, and withdraw the trunking **(see illustrations)**.
9 Pull the air cleaner front locating grommet to release it from the hole in the air cleaner casing, then pull the casing upwards over the grommet **(see illustration)**.
10 Pull the assembly forwards to release the rear locating rubbers, and withdraw the assembly from the engine compartment **(see illustrations)**.

Refitting

11 Refitting is a reversal of removal.

3.10a . . . then pull the air cleaner assembly forwards to release the rear locating rubbers (arrowed) . . .

3.10b . . . and withdraw the assembly

4 Throttle cable – removal, refitting and adjustment

SOHC engine models

Removal

1 On models with single-point fuel injection, remove the airbox from the top of the fuel injection unit, with reference to Section 12 if necessary.

2 Release the securing clip, and disconnect the cable end balljoint from the throttle linkage **(see illustration)**.

3 Release the cable grommet from its bracket on the inlet manifold **(see illustration)**. On automatic transmission models, disconnect the kickdown switch wiring connector and release the kickdown switch from the bulkhead.

4 Working inside the driver's footwell, pull the cable end from the top of the throttle pedal **(see illustration)**.

5 Where applicable, remove the circlip securing the cable grommet at the bulkhead in the footwell.

6 Make a careful note of the cable routing, then pull the cable through the bulkhead into the engine compartment.

Refitting

7 Refitting is a reversal of removal, bearing in mind the following points:

a) Ensure that the cable is correctly routed, as noted during removal.

b) Ensure that the bulkhead grommet is correctly seated in its aperture, and that, where applicable, the circlip is engaged with the grommet.

c) Check the throttle mechanism for satisfactory operation, and if necessary adjust the cable as described in the following paragraphs.

Adjustment

8 The cable adjustment is controlled by the position of the metal clip on the cable sheath at the bracket on the inlet manifold.

9 The cable should be adjusted so that when the throttle pedal is released, there is very slight free play in the cable at the fuel injection unit/throttle body end.

10 Check that when the throttle pedal is fully depressed, the throttle valve is fully open.

11 Adjust the position of the clip on the cable sheath to achieve the desired results.

DOHC engine models

Removal

12 Disconnect the battery negative terminal (refer to *Disconnecting the battery* in the Reference Chapter). If desired, for improved access, remove the battery completely as described in Chapter 5A.

13 Partially drain the cooling system as described in Chapter 1 (drain sufficient coolant to empty the coolant expansion tank).

4.2 Releasing the throttle cable end balljoint clip (arrowed)

4.3 Releasing the throttle cable grommet from the bracket. Note clip (arrowed) provided for cable adjustment

4.4 Pull the end of the throttle cable from the pedal – note cable grommet securing circlip (arrowed) at bulkhead

4.14 Release the throttle cable grommet from the throttle body bracket

14 Disconnect the hoses from the coolant expansion tank, then unscrew the securing nuts, and withdraw the expansion tank. Note that the lower hose is more easily disconnected once the tank has been removed.

15 Disconnect the cable end from the throttle linkage.

16 Release the cable grommet from the throttle body bracket **(see illustration)**.

17 On automatic transmission models, disconnect the kickdown switch wiring connector and release the kickdown switch from the bulkhead.

18 Release the cable from the clips in the engine compartment. Note that the cable is routed around the front of the engine compartment, above the radiator.

19 Proceed as described in paragraphs 4 to 6 inclusive.

Refitting

20 Refitting is a reversal of removal, bearing in mind the following points:

a) Ensure that the cable is correctly routed, as noted during removal.

b) Ensure that the bulkhead grommet is correctly seated in its aperture, and that, where applicable, the circlip is engaged with the grommet.

c) Check the throttle mechanism for satisfactory operation, and if necessary adjust the cable with reference to paragraph 21.

d) Refit the battery, if removed, and/or reconnect the battery lead(s).

e) Refit the coolant expansion tank then top-up the cooling system with reference to 'Weekly checks'.

Adjustment

21 Proceed as described in paragraphs 8 to 11 inclusive, noting that the adjustment is controlled by the position of the metal clip on the cable sheath at the throttle body bracket.

5 Throttle pedal – removal and refitting

Removal

1 Unclip the throttle cable end from the top of the pedal.

2 Remove the spring clip from the end of the throttle pedal pivot shaft.

3 Unhook the return spring from the pedal, and slide the pedal from the end of the pivot shaft.

Refitting

4 Refitting is a reversal of removal, but on completion, check and if necessary adjust the throttle cable free play as described in Section 4.

6 Fuel system – depressurising

⚠ Warning: The fuel system is pressurised all the time the ignition is switched on, and will remain so for a considerable time after switching off. It is therefore essential to depressurise the system before disconnecting fuel lines, or carrying out any work on the fuel system components. Failure to do this before carrying out work may result in a sudden release of pressure which may cause fuel spray – this constitutes a serious fire hazard, and a health risk. Note that, even when the system has been depressurised, fuel will still be present in the system fuel lines and components, and adequate precautions should still be taken when carrying out work.

1 The fuel system referred to in this Section is defined as the tank-mounted fuel pump, the fuel filter, the fuel injectors, the fuel rail and the pressure regulator, and the metal pipes and flexible hoses of the fuel lines between these components. All these contain fuel which will be under pressure while the engine is running, and/or while the ignition is switched on. The pressure will remain for some time after the ignition has been switched off, and must be relieved in a controlled fashion when any of these components are disturbed for servicing work.

2 Disconnect the battery negative terminal (refer to *Disconnecting the battery* in the Reference Section of this manual).

3 Place a container beneath the connection/union to be disconnected, and have a large rag ready to soak up any escaping fuel not being caught by the container.

4 Slowly loosen the connection or union nut to avoid a sudden release of pressure, and position the rag around the connection, to catch any fuel spray which may be expelled. Once the pressure is released, disconnect the fuel line. Plug the pipe ends, to minimise fuel loss and prevent the entry of dirt into the fuel system.

7 Fuel tank – removal and refitting

Corsa models

Note: *During this procedure, the rear of the vehicle must be raised sufficiently to enable the fuel tank securing straps to be lowered far enough to allow the fuel tank to pass below the rear axle – the front ends of the tank securing straps are mounted on hinge pins on the vehicle underside, and cannot be removed.*

Removal

1 Depressurise the fuel system as described in Section 6.

2 Disconnect the battery negative terminal if not already done (refer to *Disconnecting the battery* in the Reference Chapter).

3 Syphon out any remaining fuel in the tank through the filler pipe into a clean metal container which can be sealed.

4 Chock the front wheels, then jack up the rear of the vehicle and support securely on axle stands (see *Jacking and vehicle support*).

5 Disconnect the rear of the exhaust system from its rubber mountings, and lower the system, or move it to one side sufficiently to enable removal of the fuel tank. On certain models, it may be necessary to remove the exhaust system completely to allow sufficient clearance – refer to Section 17 for details on removing the exhaust mountings and components.

6 Where applicable, remove the handbrake cable heat shield.

7 Slacken the handbrake cable adjuster with reference to Chapter 9, then pull the rubber grommet from the connecting link under the vehicle floor, and disconnect the rear section of the handbrake cable from the connecting link. Release the cable from the brackets on the underbody and fuel tank, as applicable, and move the cable clear of the working area.

8 Working under the vehicle, release the hose clamps, and disconnect the fuel hoses from the rear of the fuel tank **(see illustration)**.

9 Release the connectors and disconnect the fuel hoses from the fuel filter, noting their locations to ensure correct refitting. A Vauxhall/Opel special tool is available to release the fuel line connectors, but provided care is taken, the connectors can be released using a pair of long-nosed pliers, or similar tool, to depress the retaining tangs. Refer to *Fuel filter renewal* in Chapter 1 for further details.

10 Unscrew the securing bolt and remove the fuel filter, complete with its clamp, from the fuel tank **(see illustration)**.

11 Fold the rear seat cushions forwards.

12 Lift the carpet panel on the right-hand side of the floor to expose the plastic fuel pump cover.

13 Carefully prise the plastic cover from the floor to expose the fuel pump.

14 Disconnect the pump wiring plug.

15 Clamp the fuel feed and return hoses to prevent fuel spillage, then release the hose clips, and carefully disconnect the fuel hoses from the top of the pump. Be prepared for fuel spillage, and take adequate fire precautions.

16 Support the weight of the fuel tank on a jack with interposed block of wood.

17 Remove the two nuts from the securing straps at the rear of the fuel tank **(see illustration)**. Lower the straps clear of the rear axle to allow sufficient clearance to withdraw the fuel tank.

18 Lower the tank sufficiently to enable access to the fuel hoses clipped to the tank. Unclip the relevant hoses from the tank, noting their locations to ensure correct refitting.

19 Continue to lower the tank until it can be removed from under the vehicle.

Refitting

20 If the tank contains sediment or water, it may cleaned out with two or three rinses of clean fuel. Remove the fuel filter, fuel gauge sender unit and fuel pump as described in Sections 8 and 9 respectively. Shake the tank vigorously, and change the fuel as often as is necessary to remove all contamination from the tank. *This procedure should be carried out in a well-ventilated area, and it is vital to take adequate fire precautions.*

21 Any repairs to the fuel tank should be carried out by a professional. Do not under

7.8 Disconnect the fuel hoses (arrowed) from the rear of the tank – Hatchback models

7.10 Fuel filter-to-fuel tank securing bolt (arrowed) – Hatchback models

7.17 Fuel tank strap securing nut (1) and handbrake cable bracket (2) – Hatchback models

7.24 Disconnect the fuel hoses (arrowed) from the rear of the tank – Combo Van models

7.25 Disconnect the fuel line connectors (arrowed) – Combo Van models

30 Continue to lower the tank until it can be removed from under the vehicle.

Refitting

31 Refer to paragraphs 20 and 21.
32 Refitting is a reversal of removal, bearing in mind the following points:
  a) *Ensure that all hoses are securely reconnected to their correct locations, as noted before removal.*
  b) *On completion, fill the fuel tank, then run the engine and check for leaks. If leakage is evident, stop the engine immediately and rectify the problem without delay.*

---

any circumstances attempt any form of DIY repair to a fuel tank.
22 Refitting is a reversal of removal, bearing in mind the following points:
  a) *Ensure that all hoses are securely reconnected to their correct locations, as noted before removal.*
  b) *Check the handbrake cable adjustment, as described in Chapter 9.*
  c) *On completion, fill the fuel tank, then run the engine and check for leaks. If leakage is evident, stop the engine immediately and rectify the problem without delay.*

Combo Van models

Note: *During this procedure, the rear of the vehicle must be raised sufficiently to enable the fuel tank securing straps to be lowered far enough to allow the fuel tank to pass below the rear axle – the front ends of the tank securing straps are mounted on hinge pins on the vehicle underside, and cannot be removed.*

Removal

23 Proceed as described in paragraphs 1 to 4 inclusive.
24 Working under the vehicle, release the hose clamps, and disconnect the fuel hoses

from the rear of the fuel tank **(see illustration)**.
25 Working at the front right-hand corner of the fuel tank, release the connectors, and disconnect the fuel lines which run around the side of the tank, noting their locations to ensure correct refitting **(see illustration)**. Be prepared for fuel spillage, and take adequate fire precautions. A Vauxhall/Opel special tool is available to release the fuel line connectors, but provided care is taken, the connectors can be released using a pair of long-nosed pliers, or similar tool, to depress the retaining tangs. Refer to *Fuel filter renewal* in Chapter 1 for further details.
26 Unscrew the securing nut and withdraw the fuel filter, complete with its bracket, from the fuel tank securing strap stud at the rear of the fuel tank. Support the filter to one side, clear of the working area.
27 Support the weight of the fuel tank on a jack with interposed block of wood.
28 Remove the two nuts from the securing straps at the rear of the fuel tank. Lower the straps clear of the rear axle to allow sufficient clearance to withdraw the fuel tank.
29 Lower the tank sufficiently to enable access to the fuel pump wiring plug, and disconnect the plug.

---

8 Fuel gauge sender unit – removal and refitting

Corsa models

Removal

Note: *The fuel tank should be as empty as possible when carrying out this procedure. If the fuel level in the tank is high, fuel should be syphoned out through the filler pipe to avoid any possibility of spillage – syphon the fuel into a clean metal container which can be sealed.*

1 Disconnect the battery negative terminal (refer to *Disconnecting the battery* in the Reference Chapter).
2 Working inside the vehicle, fold the rear seat cushion forwards, and where applicable lift the carpet panel to expose the plastic fuel pump cover.
3 Carefully prise the plastic cover from the floor to expose the fuel pump cover **(see illustrations)**.
4 Release the fuel pump cover locking ring. A special tool (Vauxhall/Opel tool No KM-797) is available for this, but the ring can be removed by tapping anti-clockwise until the locking clips release.

8.3a Prise the plastic cover from the floor . . .

8.3b . . . to expose the fuel pump cover. Locking ring arrowed – Hatchback models

8.5 Disconnect the fuel gauge sender wiring plug – Hatchback models

8.6a Using the hook . . .

8.6b . . . pull the sender unit from the fuel pump housing – Hatchback models

 Warning: To prevent the possibility of any sparks which could ignite fuel vapour, use a plastic, wooden or brass tool to release the locking ring.

5 Withdraw the cover locking ring, then lift the pump cover from the top of the pump, and disconnect the fuel gauge sender unit wiring plug from the underside of the pump cover **(see illustration)**.

6 Using the hook provided, pull the sender unit from the clips on the side of the fuel pump housing **(see illustrations)**.

Refitting

7 Refitting is a reversal of removal, bearing in mind the following points:
  a) *Ensure that the sender unit engages correctly with the clips on the fuel pump housing.*
  b) *Check the condition of the sealing ring on the underside of the fuel pump cover, and renew if necessary.*
  c) *Refit the fuel pump cover locking ring by tapping it anti-clockwise until the locking clips 'click' into position.*

Combo Van models

Removal

8 Remove the fuel tank as described in Section 7.

9 Release the connectors, and disconnect the fuel lines from the fuel pump cover, noting their locations to ensure correct refitting. Be prepared for fuel spillage, and take adequate fire precautions. A Vauxhall/Opel special tool is available to release the fuel line connectors, but

in the absence of this tool, the connectors can be released using a pair of long-nosed pliers, or similar tool, to depress the retaining tangs.

10 Proceed as described in paragraphs 4 to 6 inclusive.

Refitting

11 Proceed as described in paragraph 7.

12 On completion, refit the fuel tank as described in Section 7.

---

9 Fuel pump –
testing, removal and refitting

Corsa models

Testing

1 If the pump is functioning, it should be possible to hear it 'buzzing' by listening under the rear of the vehicle when the ignition is switched on. Unless the engine is started, the fuel pump should switch off after approximately two seconds. If the noise produced is excessive, this may indicate a faulty pump.

2 If the pump appears to have failed completely, check the wiring to the pump, and check the appropriate fuse and relay.

3 To test the performance of the pump, special equipment is required, and it is recommended that any suspected faults are referred to a Vauxhall/Opel dealer.

Removal

Note: *The fuel tank should be as empty as possible when carrying out this procedure. If the fuel level in the tank is high, fuel should be*

syphoned out through the filler pipe to avoid any possibility of spillage – syphon the fuel into a clean metal container which can be sealed.

4 Depressurise the fuel system as described in Section 6.

5 Disconnect the battery negative terminal (refer to *Disconnecting the battery* in the Reference Chapter).

6 Working inside the vehicle, fold the rear seat cushion forwards, and where applicable, lift the carpet panel to expose the plastic fuel pump cover.

7 Carefully prise the plastic cover from the floor to expose the fuel pump cover.

8 Release the hose clips, and carefully disconnect the fuel hoses from the top of the pump cover. Be prepared for fuel spillage, and take adequate fire precautions. Clamp or plug the open ends of the hoses, to prevent dirt ingress and further fuel spillage.

9 Disconnect the pump wiring plug **(see illustration)**.

10 Release the fuel pump locking ring. A special tool (Vauxhall/Opel tool No KM-797) is available for this, but the ring can be removed by tapping anti-clockwise until the locking clips release **(see illustration)**.

 Warning: To prevent the possibility of any sparks which could ignite fuel vapour, use a plastic, wooden or brass tool to release the locking ring.

11 Lift the pump cover from the housing, then disconnect the two wiring plugs from the underside of the cover **(see illustration)**.

12 Loosen the hose clip, and disconnect the fuel hose from the top of the fuel pump.

9.9 Disconnect the fuel pump wiring plug – Hatchback models

9.10 Releasing the fuel pump locking ring using a brass drift – Hatchback models

9.11 Disconnect the wiring plugs from the underside of the cover – Hatchback models

9.13a Press the three pump housing retaining lugs (1 – one shown), and pull the housing from the tank using a hook engaged with the eyelet (2) – Hatchback models

9.13b Withdrawing the fuel pump housing from the fuel tank – Hatchback models

9.14 Removing the fuel filter from the base of the fuel pump – Hatchback models

13 Press the three pump housing retaining lugs to release them, and simultaneously pull the pump housing from the tank using a wire hook engaged with the eyelet provided (see illustrations).

14 To remove the pump from the housing, first pull the filter from the base of the pump (see illustration), and disconnect the wires from the pump. Note the wire locations to ensure correct refitting.

15 Compress the three locking tabs, and pull the pump mounting plate and the pump from the housing (see illustrations).

Refitting

16 Refitting is a reversal of removal, bearing in mind the following points:

a) Before refitting the filter to the bottom of the pump, inspect the filter for contamination or blockage, and renew if necessary.

b) Ensure that the pump mounting plate engages correctly with the retaining clips on the housing.

c) Check the condition of the sealing ring on

9.15a Compress the three locking tabs (arrowed) . . .

the underside of the fuel pump cover, and renew if necessary.

d) Refit the fuel pump cover locking ring by tapping it anti-clockwise until the locking clips 'click' into position.

Combo Van models

Testing

17 Proceed as described in paragraphs 1 to 3 inclusive.

9.15b . . . and withdraw the pump from the housing – Hatchback models

Removal

18 Remove the fuel tank as described in Section 7.

19 Release the connectors, and disconnect the fuel lines from the top of the fuel pump cover, noting their locations to ensure correct refitting. Be prepared for fuel spillage, and take adequate fire precautions. A Vauxhall/Opel special tool is available to release the fuel line connectors, but in the absence of this tool, the connectors can be released using a pair of long-nosed pliers, or similar tool, to depress the retaining tangs. Be prepared for fuel spillage, and take adequate fire precautions.

20 Proceed as described in paragraphs 10 to 15 inclusive.

Refitting

21 Proceed as described in paragraph 16.

22 On completion, refit the fuel tank as described in Section 7.

10.1 Layout of Multec single-point fuel injection system/engine management system components

1 Fuel tank vent valve (see Chapter 4C)	3 Exhaust gas recirculation (EGR) valve (see Chapter 4C)	5 Distributorless ignition system (DIS) module (see Chapter 5B)
2 Fuel injection unit	4 Manifold absolute pressure (MAP) sensor	6 Exhaust gas oxygen sensor

10 Fuel injection systems – general information

Single-point fuel injection

1 The system is under the overall control of the Multec engine management system, which also controls the ignition system (see Chapter 5B) (see illustration).

2 Fuel is supplied from the rear-mounted fuel tank by an electric pump mounted in the tank, via a fuel filter, to the Multec injection unit. A fuel pressure regulator mounted on the injection unit maintains a constant fuel pressure to the fuel injector. Excess fuel is returned from the regulator to the tank.

3 The fuel injection unit (resembling a carburettor) houses the throttle valve, idle speed control motor, throttle position sensor, fuel injector, and pressure regulator.

4 The duration of the electrical pulse supplied to the fuel injector determines the time for which the injector is open, and hence the quantity of fuel injected. Pulse duration is computed by the Multec electronic control unit (ECU) on the basis of information received from the following sensors:

a) *Throttle position sensor – informs the ECU of throttle position, and the rate of throttle opening/closing.*

b) *Manifold absolute pressure (MAP) sensor – informs the ECU of the load on the engine (expressed in terms of inlet manifold vacuum).*

c) *Crankshaft speed/position sensor – informs the ECU of the crankshaft speed and position.*

d) *Coolant temperature sensor – informs the ECU of engine temperature.*

e) *Exhaust gas oxygen sensor – informs the ECU of the oxygen content of the exhaust gases (explained in greater detail in Chapter 4C).*

f) *Vehicle speed sensor – informs the ECU of the vehicle speed.*

g) *Knock sensor – informs the ECU when engine 'knock' (pre-ignition) occurs (explained in greater detail in Chapter 5B).*

5 The signals from the various sensors are processed by the ECU, and the optimum fuelling and ignition settings are selected for the prevailing engine operating conditions.

6 Idle speed is controlled by the idle speed control motor, which regulates the quantity of air bypassing the throttle valve. The motor is controlled by the electronic control unit; there is no provision for direct adjustment of idle speed.

7 Similarly, the fuel/air mixture is controlled within fine limits by the electronic control unit, via the fuel injector. No manual adjustment of fuel/air mixture is possible.

8 A catalytic converter is fitted, to reduce harmful exhaust gas emissions. Details of this and other emissions control system equipment are given in Chapter 4C.

9 If certain sensors fail, and send abnormal signals to the ECU, the ECU has a back-up programme. In this event, the abnormal signals are ignored, and a pre-programmed value is substituted for the sensor signal, allowing the engine to continue running, albeit at reduced efficiency. If the ECU enters its back-up mode, a warning light on the instrument panel will illuminate, and a fault code will be stored in the ECU memory. This fault code can be read using suitable specialist test equipment.

Multi-point fuel injection – SOHC engines

10 The system is under the overall control of the Multec M engine management system, which also controls the ignition system (see Chapter 5B) **(see illustration)**.

11 Fuel is supplied from the rear-mounted fuel tank, via a fuel filter and a pressure regulator, to the fuel rail. Excess fuel is returned from the regulator to the tank. The fuel rail acts as a reservoir for the four fuel injectors, which inject fuel into the cylinder inlet tracts, upstream of the inlet valves. The fuel injectors operate in pairs. The injectors for cylinder Nos 1 and 2 operate simultaneously, as do the injectors for cylinder Nos 3 and 4.

12 The duration of the electrical pulses to the fuel injectors determines the quantity of fuel injected. The pulse duration is computed by the Multec M electronic control unit (ECU) on the basis of information received from the following sensors:

a) *Throttle position sensor – informs the ECU of throttle position, and the rate of throttle opening/closing.*

b) *Manifold absolute pressure (MAP) sensor – informs the ECU of the load on the engine (expressed in terms of inlet manifold vacuum).*

c) *Crankshaft speed/position sensor – informs the ECU of the crankshaft speed and position.*

d) *Intake air temperature sensor – informs the ECU of the temperature of the air passing through the air intake ducting.*

e) *Coolant temperature sensor – informs the ECU of engine temperature.*

f) *Exhaust gas oxygen sensor – informs the ECU of the oxygen content of the exhaust gases (explained in greater detail in Chapter 4C).*

g) *Vehicle speed sensor – informs the ECU of the vehicle speed.*

13 The signals from the various sensors are processed by the ECU, and the optimum fuelling and ignition settings are selected for the prevailing engine operating conditions.

14 Idle speed is controlled by the idle speed control motor, which regulates the quantity of air bypassing the throttle valve. The motor is controlled by the electronic control unit; there is no provision for direct adjustment of the idle speed.

15 Similarly, the fuel/air mixture is controlled within fine limits by the electronic control unit, via the fuel injector. No manual adjustment of fuel mixture is possible.

16 A catalytic converter is fitted to reduce harmful exhaust gas emissions. Details of this and other emissions control system equipment are given in Chapter 4C.

17 If certain sensors fail, and send abnormal signals to the ECU, the ECU has a back-up programme. In this event, the abnormal signals are ignored, and a pre-programmed value is substituted for the sensor signal, allowing the engine to continue running, albeit at reduced efficiency. If the ECU enters its back-up mode, a warning light on the instrument panel will illuminate, and a fault code will be stored in the ECU memory. This fault code can be read using suitable specialist test equipment.

Multi-point fuel injection – DOHC engines

18 The system is under the overall control of the Multec S engine management system,

10.10 Layout of Multec M multi-point fuel injection system/engine management system components

1 *Idle speed control motor*   3 *Fuel pressure regulator*   4 *Distributorless ignition*
2 *Throttle body*   *system (DIS) module*

which also controls the ignition system (see Chapter 5B).

19 Fuel is supplied from the rear-mounted tank, via a fuel filter and a pressure regulator, to the fuel rail. Excess fuel is returned from the regulator to the tank. The fuel rail acts as a reservoir for the four fuel injectors, which inject fuel into the cylinder inlet tracts, upstream of the inlet valves. The Multec S system is a 'sequential' fuel injection system. This means that each of the four fuel injectors is triggered individually, just before the inlet valve on the relevant cylinder opens.

20 The duration of the electrical pulses to the fuel injectors determines the quantity of fuel injected. The pulse duration is computed by the Multec S electronic control unit (ECU) on the basis of information received from the following sensors:

a) *Throttle position sensor – informs the ECU of throttle position, and the rate of throttle opening/closing.*

b) *Manifold absolute pressure (MAP) sensor – informs the ECU of the load on the engine (expressed in terms of inlet manifold vacuum).*

c) *Crankshaft speed/position sensor – informs the ECU of the crankshaft speed and position.*

d) *Intake air temperature sensor – informs the ECU of the temperature of the air passing through the air intake ducting.*

e) *Camshaft position sensor – informs the ECU when No 1 cylinder is at top dead centre (TDC) on the firing stroke (expressed in terms of the position of the exhaust camshaft).*

f) *Coolant temperature sensor – informs the ECU of engine temperature.*

g) *Exhaust gas oxygen sensor – informs the ECU of the oxygen content of the exhaust gases (explained in greater detail in Chapter 4C).*

h) *Vehicle speed sensor – informs the ECU of the vehicle speed.*

i) *Knock sensor – informs the ECU when engine 'knock' (pre-ignition) occurs (explained in greater detail in Chapter 5B).*

21 The signals from the various sensors are processed by the ECU, and the optimum fuelling and ignition settings are selected for the prevailing engine operating conditions.

22 Idle speed is controlled by the idle speed control motor, which regulates the quantity of air bypassing the throttle valve. The motor is controlled by the electronic control unit; there is no provision for direct adjustment of the idle speed.

23 Similarly, the fuel/air mixture is controlled within fine limits by the electronic control unit, via the fuel injectors. No manual adjustment of fuel/air mixture is possible.

24 A catalytic converter is fitted to reduce harmful exhaust gas emissions. Details of this and other emissions control system equipment are given in Chapter 4C.

25 If certain sensors fail, and send abnormal signals to the ECU, the ECU has a back-up programme. In this event, the abnormal signals are ignored, and a pre-programmed value is substituted for the sensor signal, allowing the engine to continue running, albeit at reduced efficiency. If the ECU enters its back-up mode, a warning light on the instrument panel will illuminate, and a fault code will be stored in the ECU memory. This fault code can be read using suitable specialist test equipment.

11 Fuel injection system components – testing

General

In order to safely test the fuel injection system components without the risk of damage to the components or electronic control unit, specialist test equipment is required.

The systems have a self-diagnosis function, and any faults are stored as codes in the electronic control unit memory. These fault codes can be read using suitable test equipment such as a fault code reader. If a fault code reader is available, it should be connected and operated according to the instructions supplied with the reader. The applicable fault codes and causes are given below.

System sensors and actuators can be tested for continuity and resistance using a suitable multi-meter, but always ensure that the ignition is switched off, and that the relevant sensor or actuator is disconnected from the engine management system. Refer to the precautions given in Section 1 before attempting to carry out any fault diagnosis.

In the event of a suspected fault, and suitable test and diagnostic equipment is not available, the best course of action is to seek advice from a Vauxhall/Opel dealer, who will have access to the necessary equipment.

Engine management system fault codes

Code	Cause of fault
12	Start of diagnosis
13	Oxygen sensor (open-circuit)
14	Coolant temperature sensor (voltage low)
15	Coolant temperature sensor (voltage high)
16	Knock sensor
18	Knock control system module
19	Incorrect engine speed (rpm) signal
21	Throttle position sensor (voltage high)
22	Throttle position sensor (voltage low)
24	No vehicle speed signal
25	Fuel injector (voltage low)
28	Fuel pump relay (faulty contact)
29	Fuel pump relay (voltage low)
32	Fuel pump relay (voltage high)
33	MAP sensor (voltage high)
34	MAP sensor (voltage low)
35	Idle speed control
41	DIS ignition signal – cylinders 2 and 3 (voltage high)
42	DIS ignition signal – cylinders 1 and 4 (voltage high)
44	Exhaust gases lean
45	Exhaust gases rich
46	DIS ignition control signal (voltage high)
49	Battery (voltage high)
51	Electronic control unit
55	Electronic control unit
63	DIS ignition signal – cylinders 2 and 3 (voltage low)
64	DIS ignition signal – cylinders 1 and 4 (voltage low)
69	Intake air temperature sensor (voltage low)
71	Intake air temperature (voltage high)
72	DIS ignition control signal (open-circuit)
75	Automatic transmission torque control (voltage low)
76	Automatic transmission continuous torque control
81	Fuel injector (voltage high)
93	Electronic control unit

12.1 Disconnecting the breather hose from the camshaft cover

12.3a Remove the securing screws . . .

12.3b . . . and lift off the airbox and sealing ring

12 Single-point fuel injection system components – removal and refitting

Airbox

Removal

1 Disconnect the breather hose from the airbox or the camshaft cover, as desired (**see illustration**).

2 Loosen the clamp screw, and disconnect the air trunking from the end of the airbox, or from the air cleaner casing, as desired.

3 Remove the two securing screws, and lift the airbox from the fuel injection unit. Recover the sealing ring (**see illustrations**).

4 Disconnect the two vacuum pipes from the rear of the airbox, or from the fuel injection unit and the air cleaner casing, as desired,

noting their locations, then withdraw the airbox (**see illustration**).

Refitting

5 Refitting is a reversal of removal, bearing in mind the following points:

a) *Inspect the sealing ring for damage or deterioration, and renew if necessary. Ensure that the sealing ring locates correctly in the grooves in the base of the airbox.*

b) *Ensure that the vacuum pipes are correctly reconnected, as noted before removal.*

Fuel injection unit

Note: *Refer to the precautions given in Section 1 before proceeding. All gaskets and seals must be renewed on refitting, and suitable thread-locking compound will be*

required to coat the fuel injection unit securing nut threads.

Removal

6 Depressurise the fuel system as described in Section 6.

7 Disconnect the battery negative terminal if not already done (refer to *Disconnecting the battery* in the Reference Chapter).

8 Remove the airbox from the top of the fuel injection unit, as described earlier in this Section.

9 Release the securing lugs, and disconnect the wiring plug from the fuel injector (**see illustration**).

10 Remove the rubber seal from the top of the fuel injection unit (if not already done), then slide the fuel injector wiring rubber grommet from the slot in the side of the fuel injection unit (**see illustration**). Move the wiring to one side.

11 Disconnect the wiring plugs from the idle speed control motor and the throttle position sensor.

12 Disconnect the fuel feed and return hoses from the fuel injection unit, noting their locations to aid refitting. Be prepared for fuel spillage, and take adequate fire precautions. Clamp or plug the open ends of the hoses, to minimise further fuel loss.

13 Disconnect the vacuum hoses from the fuel injection unit, noting their locations and routing to ensure correct refitting.

14 Disconnect the MAP sensor hose from the rear of the fuel injection unit (**see illustration**).

15 Disconnect the operating rod from the throttle valve lever (**see illustration**).

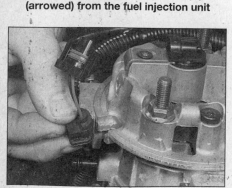

12.4 Disconnecting the vacuum pipe (arrowed) from the fuel injection unit

12.9 Releasing the fuel injector wiring plug retaining lugs

12.10 Sliding the fuel injector wiring rubber grommet from the fuel injection unit

12.14 Disconnecting the MAP sensor hose from the fuel injection unit

12.15 Disconnect the operating rod (arrowed) from the throttle valve lever

12.17a Recover the sleeves which fit over the manifold studs

12.17b Lifting the fuel injection unit from the inlet manifold

12.18 Removing a fuel injection unit upper-to-lower section securing screw

16 Make a final check to ensure that all relevant hoses and wires have been disconnected to facilitate removal of the fuel injection unit.

17 Unscrew the two securing nuts, recovering the washers and the sleeves which fit over the manifold studs, then carefully lift the fuel injection unit from the inlet manifold **(see illustrations)**. Recover the gasket.

18 If desired, the fuel injection unit may now be split into its upper and lower sections by removing the two securing screws **(see illustration)**. The vacuum hose flange and the fuel hose unions can also be removed if desired.

Refitting

19 Refitting is a reversal of removal, bearing in mind the following points.

20 Where applicable, when reassembling the two sections of the fuel injection unit, use a new gasket. Similarly, where applicable, use a new gasket when refitting the vacuum hose flange. If the fuel hose unions have been removed, make sure that the washers are in place when refitting.

21 Refit the fuel injection unit to the manifold using a new gasket, ensuring that the sleeves are in place over the manifold studs. Coat the threads of the securing nuts with a suitable thread-locking compound before fitting. Ensure that the washers are in place under the nuts.

22 Ensure that all hoses are reconnected and routed correctly, as noted before removal.

23 On completion, check and if necessary adjust the throttle cable free play as described in Section 4.

Fuel injector

Note: *Refer to the precautions given in Section 1 before proceeding. If the original injector is being refitted, new O-rings must be used. Suitable thread-locking compound will be required to coat the clamp bracket screw threads.*

Removal

24 Depressurise the fuel system as described in Section 6.

25 Disconnect the battery negative terminal if not already done (refer to *Disconnecting the battery* in the Reference Chapter).

26 Remove the airbox from the top of the fuel injection unit, as described earlier in this Section.

27 Squeeze the securing lugs, and disconnect the wiring plug from the fuel injector **(see illustration)**.

12.27 Disconnecting the wiring plug from the fuel injector

28 Remove the Torx type securing screw, and withdraw the injector clamp bracket **(see illustrations)**.

29 Carefully withdraw the injector from the fuel injection unit **(see illustration)**.

Refitting

30 If the original injector is to be refitted, renew the two O-rings at the base of the injector.

31 Carefully install the injector in the fuel injection unit, with the wiring socket pointing towards the clamp bracket screw hole.

32 Refit the injector clamp bracket, ensuring that it engages correctly with the injector (the bracket should engage with the slot below the wiring socket in the injector).

33 Coat the threads of the clamp bracket screw with a suitable thread-locking compound, then refit and tighten the screw **(see illustration)**.

12.28a Remove the securing screw . . .

12.28b . . . and withdraw the injector clamp bracket

12.29 Removing the fuel injector. Note the O-rings (arrowed)

12.33 Coat the fuel injector clamp bracket screw with thread-locking compound

12.39a Unscrew the fuel pressure regulator securing screws (arrowed) . . .

12.39b . . . and remove the cover

12.40 Fuel pressure regulator components

1 Diaphragm   *3 Spring seat*
2 Spring   *4 Cover*

34 Reconnect the injector wiring plug.
35 Refit the airbox to the fuel injection unit.
36 Reconnect the battery negative terminal.

Fuel pressure regulator

Note: *Refer to the precautions given in Section 1 before proceeding. The pressure regulator diaphragm must be renewed whenever the regulator cover is removed. Suitable thread-locking compound will be required to coat the regulator cover securing bolts.*

Removal

37 Depressurise the fuel system as described in Section 6.
38 Remove the airbox from the top of the fuel injection unit, as described earlier in this Section.
39 Unscrew the four Torx-type pressure regulator cover securing screws, and carefully withdraw the cover **(see illustrations)**.
40 Recover the spring seat and spring assembly, and lift out the diaphragm **(see illustration)**.

Refitting

41 Refitting is a reversal of removal, but ensure that the diaphragm is correctly located in the groove in the fuel injection unit, and coat the threads of the cover securing screws with a suitable thread-locking compound before fitting.

Idle speed control motor

Note: *A new O-ring must be used on refitting, and suitable thread-locking compound will be required to coat the motor securing bolt threads.*

Removal

42 Disconnect the battery negative terminal (refer to *Disconnecting the battery* in the Reference Chapter).
43 Remove the airbox from the top of the fuel injection unit, as described earlier in this Section.
44 Release the securing lugs, and disconnect the wiring plug from the idle speed control motor **(see illustration)**.

45 Remove the two securing screws, and withdraw the motor from the side of the fuel injection unit. Where applicable, recover the O-ring seal **(see illustrations)**.

Refitting

46 Refitting is a reversal of removal, bearing in mind the following points:
a) *To avoid damaging the housing or the motor during refitting, the distance between the end of the motor piston and the end face of the motor body flange should not be greater than 28.0 mm. Measure the distance shown, and if greater than 28.0 mm, carefully push the piston into the motor body as far as its stop* **(see illustration)**.
b) *Refit the motor using a new O-ring seal, with the wiring socket facing downwards.*
c) *Coat the threads of the motor securing bolts with a suitable thread-locking compound before fitting.*

Throttle position sensor

Note: *Suitable thread-locking compound will be required to coat the sensor securing bolt threads on refitting.*

Removal

47 Disconnect the battery negative terminal (refer to *Disconnecting the battery* in the Reference Chapter).
48 Remove the airbox from the top of the fuel injection unit, as described earlier in this Section.

12.44 Disconnecting the wiring plug from the idle speed control motor

12.45a Remove the securing screws . . .

12.45b . . . and withdraw the idle speed control motor. Note O-ring (arrowed)

12.46 Measure the distance (A) between the end of the idle speed control motor piston and the end face of the motor body flange

12.49 Disconnecting the wiring plug from the throttle position sensor

12.50 Removing the throttle position sensor

12.56 Disconnecting the vacuum pipe from the MAP sensor

49 Disconnect the wiring plug from the throttle position sensor **(see illustration)**.
50 Remove the two securing screws, and withdraw the sensor from its housing in the fuel injection unit **(see illustration)**.

Refitting

51 Ensure that the throttle valve is closed, then refit the sensor to the housing, making sure that the sensor arm is correctly engaged with the throttle valve shaft.
52 Coat the sensor securing bolts with suitable thread-locking compound, then insert and tighten them.
53 Further refitting is a reversal of removal.

Manifold absolute pressure (MAP) sensor

Removal

54 The sensor is located on the engine compartment bulkhead, under the scuttle flange.
55 Disconnect the battery negative terminal (refer to *Disconnecting the battery* in the Reference Chapter).
56 Disconnect the sensor wiring plug and the vacuum pipe **(see illustration)**. Note the routing of the vacuum pipe.
57 Unscrew the two securing nuts, and withdraw the sensor from the bulkhead **(see illustrations)**.

Refitting

58 Refitting is a reversal of removal. It is important to ensure that when reconnecting

the vacuum pipe, the pipe is routed with a downward slope from the sensor to the fuel injection housing. This is to prevent the possibility of the pipe becoming blocked from condensation freezing in the pipe during cold weather.

Crankshaft speed/position sensor

Removal

59 The sensor is located in a bracket attached to the oil pump at the lower timing belt end of the engine.
60 Access is most easily obtained from underneath the vehicle.
61 Disconnect the battery negative terminal (refer to *Disconnecting the battery* in the Reference Chapter).
62 Firmly apply the handbrake, then jack up the front of the car and support it securely on axle stands (see *Jacking and vehicle support*).
63 Separate the two halves of the sensor wiring connector, located in the bracket attached to the camshaft cover **(see illustration)**.
64 Feed the wiring down behind the rear timing belt cover, and unclip the wiring from the lugs on the cover.
65 Remove the securing bolt, and withdraw the sensor from the bracket on the oil pump **(see illustration)**.

Refitting

66 Refitting is a reversal of removal, but ensure that the sensor and bracket are scrupulously clean before refitting, as any

contamination may affect the air gap between the sensor and the toothed sensor wheel.
67 On completion, check the air gap between the end face of the sensor and the toothed sensor wheel, using a suitable feeler gauge. If the air gap is outside the specified limits (see Specifications), the sensor bracket must be renewed.

Coolant temperature sensor

Note: *A new sealing ring must be used on refitting.*

Removal

68 The sensor is located in the rear right-hand side of the inlet manifold.
69 Disconnect the battery negative terminal (refer to *Disconnecting the battery* in the Reference Chapter).
70 Partially drain the cooling system, as described in Chapter 1.

12.57a Unscrew the securing nuts . . .

12.57b . . . and withdraw the MAP sensor

12.63 Separating the two halves of the crankshaft speed/position sensor wiring connector

12.65 Crankshaft speed/position sensor securing bolt (arrowed) – viewed from underneath vehicle

12.71 Disconnecting the wiring plug from the coolant temperature sensor (arrowed)

12.76 Disconnecting the oxygen sensor wiring connector

12.77 Oxygen sensor location (arrowed) in exhaust manifold

71 Disconnect the sensor wiring plug (see illustration).

72 Unscrew the sensor, and withdraw it from the inlet manifold. Recover the sealing ring.

Refitting

73 Refitting is a reversal of removal, but use a new sealing ring, and on completion, top-up the cooling system as described in *Weekly checks*.

Exhaust gas oxygen sensor

Note: *The sensor must be removed and refitted with the exhaust system at normal operating temperature; take great care to avoid burns, and damage to tools or surrounding components during the procedure – the exhaust system and sensor will be very hot. If the original sensor is to be re-used, the threads must be lubricated with special grease on refitting – see text.*

Removal

74 If the engine is cold, start the engine, and run it until it reaches normal operating temperature. Stop the engine.

75 Disconnect the battery negative terminal (refer to *Disconnecting the battery* in the Reference Chapter).

76 Unclip the sensor wiring connector from the bracket on the gearbox/transmission, then separate the two halves of the connector (see illustration).

77 Using a suitable spanner, unscrew the sensor from the exhaust manifold. It is advisable to wear suitable gloves, as the exhaust system will be extremely hot (see illustration).

78 Withdraw the sensor and its wiring, taking care not to burn the wiring on the exhaust system.

Refitting

79 The sensor must be refitted with the engine and exhaust system still at normal operating temperature.

80 If a new sensor is being fitted, it will be supplied with the threads coated in a special grease to prevent the sensor seizing in the exhaust manifold.

81 If the original sensor is being refitted, clean the threads carefully. The threads must be coated with Vauxhall/Opel special grease (No 19 48 602). Use only the specified grease, which consists of liquid graphite and glass beads. As the exhaust system heats up, the graphite will burn off, leaving the glass beads between the threads to prevent the sensor from seizing.

82 Refitting is a reversal of removal.

Vehicle speed sensor

83 On early models, the sensor is an integral part of the speedometer assembly, and no individual spare parts are available. If the sensor is faulty, the complete speedometer assembly must be renewed. Removal and refitting details for the speedometer are given in Chapter 12. On later models, the sensor is located in the transmission casing and removal and refitting details are given in Chapter 7A, Section 5.

Knock sensor

84 The sensor is part of the knock control system, details of which are given in Chapter 5B.

Electronic control unit (ECU)

Note: *The control unit consists of two components – the basic control unit, and the programme memory, which clips into a circuit board in the control unit. The two components can be renewed independently, if a fault is suspected, but the source of the fault can only be established using specialist test equipment available to a Vauxhall/Opel dealer.*

Removal

85 The control unit is located behind the right-hand footwell trim panel.

86 Disconnect the battery negative terminal (refer to *Disconnecting the battery* in the Reference Chapter).

87 Open the right-hand front door.

88 Where applicable, remove the storage tray from under the facia.

89 Remove the screw securing the front of the sill trim panel, and lift up the front edge of the sill trim panel.

90 Remove the screw and the plastic clip securing the footwell trim panel.

91 Carefully pull back the weatherstrip from the front edge of the door aperture to expose the edge of the footwell trim panel, then withdraw the trim panel from the footwell.

92 Remove the two securing nuts, and move the wiring connector/relay bracket assembly to one side, clear of the control unit. It may be necessary to pull back the edge of the footwell rubber for access to the rear nut (see illustrations).

93 Release the clip at the front of the control unit bracket, then pull the control unit forwards from the bracket (see illustration).

12.92a Remove the side . . .

12.92b . . . and rear nuts securing the wiring connector/relay bracket assembly

12.93 Releasing the electronic control unit securing clip

12.94 Disconnecting an electronic control unit wiring connector

12.95a Remove the control unit rear cover . . .

12.95b . . . for access to the program memory

94 Disconnect the wiring connectors, and withdraw the unit from the footwell **(see illustration)**.
95 The programme memory can be unclipped from its circuit board in the control unit, after removing the cover from the rear of the control unit. The cover is secured by two screws **(see illustrations)**. Do not touch the memory plug contacts.

Refitting

96 Refitting is a reversal of removal.

Emission control system components

97 Details are given in Chapter 4C. Removal and refitting details for the oxygen sensor are given earlier in this Section.

13 Multi-point fuel injection system components (SOHC engines) – removal and refitting

Throttle body

Note: A new gasket must be used on refitting.

Removal

1 Disconnect the battery negative terminal (refer to Disconnecting the battery in the Reference Chapter).
2 Disconnect the wiring plug from the intake air temperature sensor located in the inlet air trunking.
3 Loosen the clamp screw securing the air

trunking to the throttle body, then release the air cleaner cover securing clips, and withdraw the air cleaner cover complete with the air trunking. If desired, to improve access, the complete air cleaner assembly can be removed, as described in Section 3.
4 Disconnect the camshaft cover breather hoses from the throttle body **(see illustration)**.
5 Disconnect the fuel tank vent valve vacuum hose from the throttle body **(see illustration)**.
6 Disconnect the manifold absolute pressure (MAP) sensor vacuum hose from the throttle body.
7 Disconnect the coolant hoses from the throttle body. Be prepared for coolant spillage, and clamp or plug the open ends of the hoses, to prevent further coolant loss.
8 Disconnect the wiring plugs from the throttle position sensor and the idle speed control motor.
9 Release the securing clip, then disconnect the throttle cable end balljoint from the throttle valve lever.
10 Slide the throttle cable grommet from the bracket on the inlet manifold, then unhook the throttle return spring from the bracket. If desired, unhook the spring from the grommet in the throttle valve linkage, and lay the spring to one side out of the way (in this case, note the orientation of the spring to enable correct refitting) **(see illustration)**.
11 Make a final check to ensure that all relevant hoses and wires have been disconnected to facilitate removal of the throttle body.

12 Unscrew the four securing nuts, and withdraw the throttle body from the inlet manifold.
13 Recover the gasket.
14 If desired, the throttle position sensor and the idle speed control motor can be removed from the throttle body, as described later in this Section.

Refitting

15 Refitting is a reversal of removal, bearing in mind the following points:
 a) Where applicable, refit the throttle position sensor and/or the idle speed control motor, as described later in this Section.
 b) Thoroughly clean the mating faces of the throttle body and inlet manifold, and refit the throttle body using a new gasket.
 c) Ensure that all wires and hoses are correctly reconnected and routed.
 d) Check and if necessary top-up the coolant level, as described in 'Weekly checks'.
 e) On completion, check and if necessary adjust the throttle cable free play as described in Section 4.

Fuel injectors

Note: Refer to the precautions given in Section 1 before proceeding. The seals at both ends of the fuel injectors must be renewed on refitting.

13.4 Disconnecting a camshaft cover breather hose from the throttle body

13.5 Disconnecting the fuel tank vent valve vacuum hose from the throttle body

13.10 Throttle linkage – Multec M multi-point fuel injection system

1 Cable end balljoint
2 Cable grommet
3 Throttle return spring (note orientation)

13.18 Disconnecting a fuel injector wiring plug

13.20 Disconnect the fuel feed (1) and fuel return (2) lines from the end of the fuel rail

13.21 Fuel rail securing bolts (arrowed)

Removal

16 Depressurise the fuel system as described in Section 6.

17 Disconnect the battery negative terminal if not already done (refer to *Disconnecting the battery* in the Reference Chapter).

18 Disconnect the wiring plugs from the fuel injectors, then move the wiring clear of the fuel rail **(see illustration)**.

19 Disconnect the vacuum pipe from the end of the fuel pressure regulator.

20 Unscrew the union nuts, and disconnect the fuel supply and return lines from the unions at the end of the fuel rail **(see illustration)**. Be prepared for fuel spillage, and take adequate fire precautions. Plug the open ends of the fuel lines, to prevent dirt ingress and further fuel spillage.

21 Remove the two fuel rail securing bolts,

13.22 Removing a fuel injector securing clip (arrowed)

then lift the fuel rail, complete with fuel injectors, from the inlet manifold **(see illustration)**.

22 To remove an injector from the fuel rail, prise out the metal securing clip using a screwdriver or pair of pliers, then pull the injector from the fuel rail **(see illustration)**.

23 Overhaul of the fuel injectors is not possible, as no spares are available. If faulty, an injector must be renewed.

Refitting

24 Commence refitting by fitting new seals to both ends of the fuel injectors. Coat the seals with a thin layer of petroleum jelly before fitting **(see illustration)**.

25 Refitting is a reversal of removal.

Fuel pressure regulator

Removal

Note: *Refer to the precautions given in Section 1 before proceeding. New fuel injector sealing rings, and a new pressure regulator sealing ring, must be used on refitting.*

26 Proceed as described in paragraphs 16 to 21 inclusive.

27 Unscrew the three securing bolts, and withdraw the fuel pressure regulator from the fuel rail **(see illustration)**. Recover the sealing ring.

Refitting

28 Refitting is a reversal of removal, bearing in mind the following points:

a) Use a new sealing ring when refitting the pressure regulator, and coat the sealing ring with a thin layer of petroleum jelly before fitting.

b) Ensure that all pipes and wires are correctly reconnected.

Idle speed control motor

Note: *A new sealing ring may be required on refitting.*

Removal

29 Disconnect the battery negative terminal (refer to *Disconnecting the battery* in the Reference Chapter).

30 Release the securing clip, and disconnect the wiring plug from the idle speed control motor **(see illustration)**.

31 Remove the two securing screws, and withdraw the motor from the throttle body. Recover the O-ring seal.

Refitting

32 Before refitting the motor, examine the condition of the sealing ring, and renew if necessary.

33 Refitting is a reversal of removal, ensuring that the sealing ring is correctly located, and that the motor wiring socket faces downwards.

Throttle position sensor

Removal

34 Disconnect the battery negative terminal (refer to *Disconnecting the battery* in the Reference Chapter).

13.27 Fuel pressure regulator securing bolts (arrowed)

13.30 Disconnecting the wiring plug from the idle speed control motor

13.24 Fitting a new seal to a fuel injector

13.36 Throttle position sensor securing screws (arrowed)

13.40 Intake air temperature sensor location (arrowed)

13.45 Coolant temperature sensor location (arrowed) in end of cylinder head

35 Release the securing clips, and disconnect the wiring plug from the throttle position sensor.

36 Remove the securing screws, and withdraw the sensor from the throttle body **(see illustration)**.

Refitting

37 Refitting is a reversal of removal. Ensure that the sensor wiper engages correctly with the throttle valve shaft, and that the sensor is correctly seated in its location on the throttle body.

Manifold absolute pressure (MAP) sensor

38 Proceed as described in Section 12 for models with single-point fuel injection.

Crankshaft speed/position sensor

39 Proceed as described in Section 12 for models with single-point fuel injection.

Intake air temperature sensor

Removal

40 The sensor is located in the air inlet trunking, upstream of the throttle body **(see illustration)**.

41 Disconnect the battery negative terminal (refer to *Disconnecting the battery* in the Reference Chapter).

42 Disconnect the sensor wiring plug.

43 Pull the sensor from the housing in the air inlet trunking.

Refitting

44 Refitting is a reversal of removal, but ensure that the sensor is pushed in to the stop in the air inlet trunking.

Coolant temperature sensor

45 Proceed as described in Section 12 for models with single-point fuel injection, but note that the sensor is located in the left-hand end of the cylinder head, below the DIS module **(see illustration)**.

Exhaust gas oxygen sensor

46 Proceed as described in Section 12 for models with single-point fuel injection.

Vehicle speed sensor

47 Proceed as described in Section 12 for models with single-point fuel injection.

Electronic control unit

48 Proceed as described in Section 12 for models with single-point fuel injection.

Emission control system components

49 Details are given in Chapter 4C. Removal and refitting details for the oxygen sensor are given earlier in this Section.

14 Multi-point fuel injection system components (DOHC engines) – removal and refitting

Throttle body

Removal

1 Remove the upper section of the inlet manifold, as described in Section 15.

2 Unbolt the earth cable and the wiring trough from the throttle body.

3 Disconnect the throttle cable at the throttle body with reference to Section 4.

4 Detach the air intake hose.

5 Undo the four throttle body retaining bolts from the mounting flange.

6 Disconnect the wiring plugs at the idle speed control motor and throttle position sensor.

7 Identify the two coolant hoses at the throttle body as an aid to refitting then disconnect them. Be prepared for coolant spillage. Clamp or plug the open ends of the hoses after disconnection.

8 Lift the throttle body from the engine compartment.

Refitting

9 Refitting is a reversal of removal, bearing in mind the following points:
a) *Thoroughly clean the mating faces and use a new throttle body gasket.*
b) *Refit the upper section of the inlet manifold as described in Section 15.*
c) *On completion, check and if necessary adjust the throttle cable free play as described in Section 4. Check and if necessary top-up the coolant level as described in 'Weekly checks'.*

Fuel injectors

Note: *Refer to the precautions given in Section 1 before proceeding. The seals at both ends of the fuel injectors must be renewed on refitting.*

Removal

10 Depressurise the fuel system as described in Section 6.

11 Remove the upper section of the inlet manifold as described in Section 15.

12 Unclip the camshaft position sensor wiring connector from its bracket and separate the two halves of the wiring connector.

13 Remove the two fuel rail securing bolts, then lift the fuel rail complete with the injectors sufficiently to enable the injectors to be removed **(see illustrations)**. Take care not to strain the fuel hoses and the wiring.

14 To remove an injector from the fuel rail,

14.13a Unscrew the fuel rail securing bolts . . .

14.13b . . . then lift the fuel rail from the inlet manifold

14.14a Disconnect the wiring plug . . .

14.14b . . . then remove the securing clip . . .

14.14c . . . and withdraw the injector

first disconnect the wiring plug. Prise out the metal securing clip using a screwdriver or a pair of pliers, and pull the injector from the fuel rail **(see illustrations)**.

15 Overhaul of the fuel injectors is not possible, as no spares are available. If faulty, an injector must be renewed.

16 The fuel rail assembly can be removed from the vehicle after disconnecting the two fuel lines, which are connected to the pipe on the fuel rail, and to the pressure regulator. Mark the hoses for position before disconnecting them, to ensure correct refitting. Similarly, disconnect all wiring, noting its routing and the position of the clips.

Refitting

17 Commence refitting by fitting new seals to both ends of the fuel injectors. Coat the seals with a thin layer of petroleum jelly before fitting.

18 Refitting is a reversal of removal, bearing in mind the following points:

a) *When refitting the injectors to the fuel rail, note that the metal tabs on the fuel rail must engage with the corresponding cut-outs in the fuel injectors (see illustration) – the injectors can only be fitted in one position.*

b) *Ensure that all wiring connectors are securely reconnected, and that the wiring is secured in the relevant brackets as noted before removal.*

c) *Refit the upper section of the inlet manifold, as described in Section 15.*

Fuel pressure regulator

Note: *Refer to the precautions given in Section 1 before proceeding. A new sealing ring must be used on refitting.*

Removal

19 Depressurise the fuel system as described in Section 6.

20 Disconnect the battery negative terminal if not already done (refer to *Disconnecting the battery* in the Reference Chapter).

21 Disconnect the vacuum hose from the fuel pressure regulator.

22 Unscrew the union nut, and disconnect the fuel return line from the fuel pressure regulator, Be prepared for fuel spillage, and take adequate fire precautions. Plug the open end of the fuel line, to prevent dirt ingress and further fuel spillage.

23 Separate the two halves of the connector located above the pressure regulator **(see illustration)**, then unclip the wiring connector from its bracket.

24 Unscrew the pressure regulator securing bolt **(see illustration)**, and withdraw the regulator from the fuel rail, complete with the wiring connector bracket. Recover the sealing ring.

Refitting

25 Refitting is a reversal of removal, but use a new seal when refitting the pressure regulator to the fuel rail, and coat the seal with a thin layer of petroleum jelly before fitting.

Idle speed control motor

Note: *Refer to the precautions given in Section 1 before proceeding. A new O-ring seal must be used when refitting the motor. Suitable thread-locking compound will be required to coat the threads of the motor securing bolts on refitting.*

Removal

26 The idle speed control motor is located on the throttle body, under the inlet manifold at the rear of the engine.

27 Depressurise the fuel system as described in Section 6.

28 Disconnect the battery negative terminal if not already done (refer to *Disconnecting the battery* in the Reference Chapter).

29 Partially drain the cooling system as described in Chapter 1 (drain sufficient coolant to empty the coolant expansion tank).

14.18 The metal tabs must engage with the cut-outs in the injectors (arrowed)

14.23 Separate the two halves of the wiring connector

14.24 Fuel pressure regulator securing bolt (arrowed)

14.32 Disconnecting the wiring plug from the idle speed control motor

14.33 Idle speed control motor securing bolts (arrowed) – viewed with throttle body removed for clarity

14.34 The distance between the end of the motor piston and the end face of the motor body flange should be a maximum of 33.0 mm

30 Disconnect the hoses from the coolant expansion tank, then unscrew the securing nuts, and withdraw the expansion tank.

31 Unscrew the union nut, and disconnect the fuel return line from the fuel pressure regulator. Be prepared for fuel spillage, and take adequate fire precautions. Plug the open end of the fuel line, to prevent dirt ingress and further fuel spillage. Move the fuel line to one side, clear of the working area.

32 Disconnect the wiring plug from the idle speed control motor (see illustration).

33 Remove the two securing bolts, and withdraw the motor from the throttle body (see illustration). Recover the O-ring seal.

Refitting

34 Refitting is a reversal of removal, bearing in mind the following points:

a) *To avoid damaging the housing or the motor during refitting, the distance between the end of the motor piston and the end face of the motor body flange should not be greater than 33.0 mm. Measure the distance shown, and if greater than specified, carefully push the piston into the motor body as far as its stop (see illustration).*

b) *Refit the motor, using a new O-ring seal.*

c) *Coat the threads of the motor securing bolts with a suitable thread-locking compound before fitting.*

d) *On completion, top-up and bleed the cooling system as described in 'Weekly checks' and Chapter 1.*

Throttle position sensor

Note: *Suitable thread-locking compound will be required to coat the threads of the sensor securing screws on refitting.*

Removal

35 Remove the throttle body as described earlier in this Section.

36 Remove the two securing screws, and withdraw the sensor from the throttle body (see illustration).

Refitting

37 Refit the sensor to the throttle body, ensuring that the sensor wiper engages correctly with the throttle valve shaft, and ensuring that the sensor is correctly seated in its location in the throttle body. Coat the threads of the securing screws with suitable thread-locking compound before refitting.

38 Refit the throttle body as earlier in this Section.

Manifold absolute pressure (MAP) sensor

39 Proceed as described in Section 12 for models with single-point fuel injection.

Intake air temperature sensor

40 Proceed as described in Section 13 for SOHC engines.

Crankshaft speed/position sensor

41 Proceed as described in Section 12 for models with single-point fuel injection.

Camshaft position sensor

Removal

42 Disconnect the battery negative terminal (refer to *Disconnecting the battery* in the Reference Chapter).

43 Unclip the sensor wiring connector from its bracket on the fuel rail (at the timing belt end of the engine), and separate the two halves of the wiring connector.

44 Remove the upper outer timing belt cover, with reference to Chapter 2C.

45 Unscrew the two securing bolts, and withdraw the sensor from the rear timing belt cover (see illustration).

Refitting

46 Refitting is a reversal of removal.

Coolant temperature sensor

47 Proceed as described in Section 12 for models with single-point fuel injection, but note that the sensor is located in the thermostat housing (see illustration).

Exhaust gas oxygen sensor

48 Proceed as described in Section 12 for models with single-point fuel injection, but note that the exhaust heat shield must be unbolted from the exhaust manifold for access to the sensor.

Vehicle speed sensor

49 Proceed as described in Section 12 for models with single-point fuel injection.

14.36 Throttle position sensor securing screws (arrowed)

14.45 Removing the camshaft position sensor

14.47 Disconnecting the wiring plug from the coolant temperature sensor

Knock sensor

50 The sensor is part of the knock control system, details of which are given in Chapter 5B.

Electronic control unit

51 Proceed as described in Section 12 for models with single-point fuel injection.

Emission control system components

52 Details are given in Chapter 4C. Removal and refitting details for the oxygen sensor are given earlier in this Section.

15 Inlet manifold – removal and refitting

Models with single-point fuel injection

Note: *A new manifold gasket must be used on refitting.*

Removal

1 Proceed as described for removal of the fuel injection unit in Section 12, paragraphs 6 to 14.

2 For improved access, remove the air cleaner assembly, as described in Section 3.

3 Remove the auxiliary drivebelt as described in Chapter 1.

4 On models with a V-belt alternator drive, unscrew the bolt securing the top of the alternator to the adjuster strut, and recover any washers and insulating bushes, noting their locations. Note the earth strap attached to the bolt. Pivot the alternator downwards, clear of the inlet manifold.

5 On models with a ribbed belt alternator drive, remove the two upper alternator securing bolts **(see illustration)**.

6 Disconnect the throttle cable end from the throttle linkage, then slide the cable grommet from the bracket on the inlet manifold, and move the throttle cable to one side out of the way (refer to Section 4 if necessary).

7 Unscrew the union nut, and disconnect the brake servo vacuum hose from the inlet manifold **(see illustration)**.

8 Disconnect the wiring plug from the exhaust gas recirculation valve.

9 Disconnect the wiring plug from the temperature gauge sender **(see illustration)**.

10 Where applicable, disconnect the wiring from the coolant temperature sensor, located at the right-hand rear of the inlet manifold.

11 Where applicable, separate the two halves of the wiring connector located in the bracket attached to the left-hand end of the inlet manifold **(see illustration)**. Unclip the connector from the bracket.

12 Partially drain the cooling system as described in Chapter 1, then disconnect the coolant hose from the rear of the inlet manifold. Be prepared for coolant spillage,

15.5 Remove the two upper alternator securing bolts (arrowed)

and clamp or plug the open end of the hose, to reduce coolant loss.

13 Make a final check to ensure that all relevant hoses, pipes and wires have been disconnected.

14 Unscrew the securing nuts, and withdraw the manifold from the cylinder head. Note the locations of any brackets secured by the nuts. Recover the gasket.

15 It is possible that some of the manifold studs may be unscrewed from the cylinder head when the manifold securing nuts are unscrewed. In this event, the studs should be screwed back into the cylinder head once the manifold has been removed, using two manifold nuts locked together on the stud.

16 If desired, the fuel injection unit and manifold-mounted ancillary components can be removed from the manifold, with reference to the relevant Sections of this Chapter.

Refitting

17 Refitting is a reversal of removal, bearing in mind the following points:

a) *Clean the gasket faces of the manifold and cylinder head.*

b) *Where applicable, refit any ancillary components to the manifold, with reference to the relevant Sections of this Chapter.*

c) *If the alternator mounting bracket has been unbolted from the manifold, refit it before refitting the manifold, as access is limited once the manifold is in place.*

d) *Refit the manifold using a new gasket.*

e) *Ensure that all relevant hoses, pipes and*

15.7 Brake servo vacuum hose connection (arrowed) at inlet manifold

wires are correctly reconnected and routed.

f) *Refit and tension the auxiliary drivebelt with reference to Chapter 1.*

g) *On completion, top-up and bleed the cooling system as described in 'Weekly checks' and Chapter 1.*

h) *Check and if necessary adjust the throttle cable free play, as described in Section 4.*

SOHC models with multi-point fuel injection

Note: *On models where the inlet manifold is secured by studs (screwed into the cylinder head) and nuts, the studs and nuts should be replaced with bolts on refitting. A new manifold gasket must be used on refitting.*

Removal

18 Depressurise the fuel system as described in Section 6.

19 Disconnect the battery negative terminal if not already done (refer to *Disconnecting the battery* in the Reference Chapter).

20 Remove the auxiliary drivebelt as described in Chapter 1.

21 On models with a V-belt alternator drive, unscrew the bolt securing the top of the alternator to the adjuster strut, and recover any washers and insulating bushes, noting their locations. Note the earth strap attached to the bolt. Pivot the alternator downwards, clear of the inlet manifold.

22 On models with a ribbed belt alternator drive, remove the two upper alternator securing bolts.

15.9 Coolant temperature gauge sender location (arrowed) in inlet manifold

15.11 Separate the two halves of the wiring connector (arrowed) located on the inlet manifold

15.29 Earth lead securing bolts (arrowed) at right-hand end of cylinder head

15.35 Fuel hose bracket securing bolt (arrowed) on underside of inlet manifold

15.37 Inlet manifold securing stud/bolt locations (arrowed) – SOHC engines with multi-point fuel injection

23 Release the securing clip, then disconnect the throttle cable end balljoint from the throttle linkage. Slide the throttle cable grommet from the bracket on the inlet manifold, and move the throttle cable to one side out of the way.

24 Unscrew the union nut, and disconnect the brake servo vacuum hose from the inlet manifold.

25 Disconnect the camshaft cover breather hoses from the throttle body.

26 Disconnect the vacuum hoses from the throttle body, noting their locations to aid refitting.

27 Disconnect the coolant hoses from the throttle body (two hoses) and the inlet manifold (one hose), noting their locations to aid refitting. Be prepared for coolant spillage, and clamp or plug the open ends of the hoses, to prevent further coolant loss. Unclip the coolant hose from the rear of the manifold.

28 Disconnect the wiring plugs from the throttle position sensor, and from the idle speed control motor on the throttle body.

29 Unscrew the two securing bolts, and disconnect the earth leads from the right-hand end of the cylinder head **(see illustration)**.

30 Disconnect the earth lead from the engine lifting eye bolt at the left-hand end of the inlet manifold.

31 Disconnect the wiring from the coolant temperature gauge sender in the inlet manifold.

32 Disconnect the wiring plugs from the fuel injectors.

33 Where applicable, separate the two halves of the wiring connector located in the bracket attached to the upper left-hand inlet manifold stud (or bolt, as applicable).

34 Place a wad of rag beneath the fuel line unions on the fuel pressure regulator and the fuel rail, then slowly loosen the unions. Be prepared for fuel spillage, and take adequate fire precautions. Clamp or plug the open ends of the hoses, to prevent fuel spillage and dirt ingress.

35 Unscrew the bolt securing the fuel hose bracket to the underside of the inlet manifold **(see illustration)**.

36 Make a final check to ensure that all relevant hoses, pipes and wires have been disconnected.

37 On models where the manifold is secured by studs (screwed into the cylinder head) and nuts, the studs must be unscrewed from the cylinder head before the manifold can be removed **(see illustration)**. The studs can be removed using two of the manifold nuts locked together on the studs. Note the location of any brackets secured by the nuts and studs.

38 On models where the manifold is secured by bolts, unscrew the bolts, noting the location of any brackets secured by the bolts.

39 With the securing studs and nuts, or bolts (as applicable) removed, lift the manifold from the cylinder head. Recover the gasket.

40 If desired, the throttle body and manifold-mounted ancillary components can be removed from the manifold, with reference to the relevant Sections of this Chapter.

Refitting

41 Refitting is a reversal of removal, bearing in mind the following points:

a) Clean the gasket faces of the manifold and cylinder head.

b) Where applicable, refit any ancillary components to the manifold, with reference to the relevant Sections of this Chapter.

c) If the alternator mounting bracket has been unbolted from the manifold, refit it before refitting the manifold, as access is limited once the manifold is in place.

d) Refit the manifold using a new gasket.

e) If studs and nuts were originally used to secure the manifold, discard the studs and nuts, and use suitable bolts on refitting.

f) Ensure that all relevant hoses, pipes and wires are correctly reconnected and routed.

g) Refit and tension the auxiliary drivebelt with reference to Chapter 1.

h) On completion, top-up and bleed the cooling system as described in 'Weekly checks' and Chapter 1.

i) Check and if necessary adjust the throttle cable free play, as described in Section 4.

DOHC models – upper section of inlet manifold

Note: A new manifold gasket must be used on refitting.

Removal

42 Disconnect the battery negative terminal (refer to Disconnecting the battery in the Reference Chapter).

43 Partially drain the cooling system as described in Chapter 1 (drain sufficient coolant to empty the coolant expansion tank).

44 Disconnect the hoses from the coolant expansion tank, then unscrew the securing nuts, and withdraw the expansion tank. Note that the lower hose is more easily disconnected once the tank has been removed **(see illustrations)**.

45 Remove the oil filler cap, then remove the two securing screws, and lift off the plastic

15.44a Removing an expansion tank securing nut

15.44b Access to the lower hose is easier once the tank has been removed

15.46a Disconnect the breather hose from the camshaft cover . . .

15.46b . . . and the brake servo vacuum hose from the upper section of the inlet manifold

15.49 Move the fuel tank vent valve to one side

shield which fits over the top of the camshaft cover.

46 Disconnect the breather hose from the camshaft cover, and the brake servo vacuum hose from the upper section of the inlet manifold (see illustrations).

47 Disconnect the manifold vacuum hoses from the fuel pressure regulator and the evaporative emission control solenoid valve, located at the flywheel end of the upper section of the inlet manifold. Alternatively, disconnect these hoses from the manifold itself.

48 Disconnect the breather hose (which runs across the top of the fuel tank vent valve) from the camshaft cover.

49 Release the fuel tank vent valve retaining clip, where fitted (using a screwdriver or similar tool), and withdraw the valve upwards from its mounting bracket. Leave the remaining hose(s) connected, and place the valve to one side, clear of the working area (see illustration).

50 Loosen the clamp screw, and disconnect the air trunking from the lower end of the throttle body.

51 Unscrew the securing bolts, and withdraw the upper section of the inlet manifold (see illustrations).

Refitting

52 Commence refitting by checking the condition of the rubber gasket which fits between the upper and lower sections of the inlet manifold. Renew the gasket if necessary.

53 Refit the upper section of the inlet manifold, ensuring that the gasket between the upper and lower manifold sections locates correctly.

54 Reconnect the air trunking to the lower end of the throttle body, and tighten the securing clamp.

55 Refit the fuel tank vent valve to its bracket, and reconnect the vacuum hose.

56 Reconnect the breather hose to the camshaft cover.

57 Reconnect the fuel pressure regulator vacuum hose.

58 Reconnect the breather hose and the brake servo vacuum hose to the upper section of the inlet manifold.

59 Refit the plastic shield which fits over the top of the camshaft cover, and refit the oil filler cap.

60 Reconnect the hoses to the coolant expansion tank, then refit the expansion tank.

61 Reconnect the battery negative terminal.

62 Top-up and bleed the cooling system as described in Weekly checks and Chapter 1.

DOHC models – lower section of inlet manifold

Removal

63 Depressurise the fuel system as described in Section 6.

64 Remove the upper section of the inlet manifold as described previously in this Section. It should be noted however, that the cooling system should be drained completely.

65 Place a wad of rag beneath the fuel line unions on the fuel pressure regulator and the fuel rail, then slowly loosen the unions. Be prepared for fuel spillage, and take adequate fire precautions. Clamp or plug the open ends of the hoses, to prevent fuel spillage and dirt ingress.

66 Unclip the fuel injector wiring harness, crankshaft speed/position sensor and camshaft position sensor wiring connectors from their brackets, and separate the two halves of the respective connectors.

67 Disconnect the fuel pressure regulator vacuum hose.

68 Disconnect the wiring plug, undo the nut and release the plug bracket from the alternator shackle.

69 Remove the fuel injectors and fuel rail as described in Section 14.

70 Disconnect the throttle cable at the throttle body with reference to Section 4.

71 Unbolt the air intake pipe from the wiring trough bracket. Detach the hose clamp and move the air intake pipe downward away from the throttle body.

72 Undo the four throttle body retaining bolts from the mounting flange.

73 Unbolt the throttle body bracket from the inlet manifold lower section.

74 Remove the wiring trough from the wiring trough bracket and unclip the harness wiring plug. Undo the bolts securing the wiring trough bracket to the inlet manifold lower section and remove the bracket.

75 Disconnect the wiring plug from the exhaust gas recirculation valve.

76 Unscrew the two securing bolts, and

15.51a Remove the securing bolts . . .

15.51b . . . and withdraw the upper section of the inlet manifold

15.51c Recover the gasket

16.3a Exhaust manifold hot-air shroud upper . . .

16.3b . . . and lower securing bolts (arrowed)

16.7 Exhaust manifold securing nuts (arrowed) – DOHC engine, viewed with engine removed for clarity

withdraw the valve from the inlet manifold. Recover the gasket.

77 Remove the intake air temperature sensor from the air intake pipe and remove the pipe towards the left-hand side.

78 Unscrew the nuts securing the lower section of the inlet manifold to the cylinder head. Detach the coolant hose then lift the lower section of the manifold from the engine compartment.

Refitting

79 Refitting is a reversal of removal, bearing in mind the following points:
a) Clean the gasket faces of the exhaust gas recirculation valve, the lower section of the inlet manifold and the cylinder head.
b) Renew all disturbed gaskets..
c) Refit the fuel injectors and fuel rail as described in Section 14.
d) Ensure that all wiring and hoses are correctly reconnected and routed.
e) Refit the upper section of the inlet manifold as described previously in this Section.

16 Exhaust manifold – removal and refitting

Removal

Note: A new gasket must be used on refitting.
1 Disconnect the battery negative terminal (refer to Disconnecting the battery in the Reference Chapter).
2 Unclip the oxygen sensor wiring plug from its bracket on the gearbox/transmission, then separate the two halves of the connector.
3 Where applicable, disconnect the hot-air hose from the hot-air shroud on the exhaust manifold. Remove the securing bolts, and remove the hot-air shroud from the manifold (see illustrations).
4 On DOHC engines with air conditioning, remove the cooling fan and shroud assembly from the radiator as described in Chapter 3.
5 On all DOHC engines, remove the secondary air pipe and combination valve as described in Chapter 4C.
6 Disconnect the exhaust front section from

the manifold, with reference to Section 17.
7 Unscrew the securing nuts, and lift the manifold from the cylinder head (see illustration). Where applicable, note the location of the engine lifting bracket secured by one of the manifold studs. Recover the gasket.

Refitting

8 Refitting is a reversal of removal, bearing in mind the following points:
a) Clean the gasket faces of the manifold and the cylinder head.
b) Refit the manifold using a new gasket.
c) On DOHC engines, refit the secondary air pipe and combination valve as described in Chapter 4C.
d) Reconnect the front section of the exhaust system to the manifold with reference to Section 17.
e) On DOHC engines with air conditioning, refit the cooling fan and shroud to the radiator, with reference to Chapter 3.

17 Exhaust system – general information and component renewal

General information

1 Periodically, the exhaust system should be checked for signs of leaks or damage. Also inspect the system rubber mountings, and renew if necessary.
2 Small holes or cracks can be repaired using proprietary exhaust repair products.

3 On SOHC engine models, the original factory-fitted exhaust system is a one-piece unit, with the exception of the rear silencer. On DOHC engine models, a separate exhaust front section is fitted.
4 Before renewing an individual section of the exhaust system, it is wise to inspect the remaining sections. If corrosion or damage is evident on more than one section of the system, it may prove more economical to renew the entire system.

Component renewal

Note: All relevant gaskets and/or sealing rings should be renewed on refitting.
5 With the exception of the rear silencer box (SOHC engine models), or the rear silencer box and the exhaust front section (DOHC engine models), the exhaust system originally fitted to the vehicle at the factory is a single-section welded unit, which includes the integral catalytic converter (see illustrations).
6 With the exception of the rear silencer box, and the front section (DOHC engines), individual sections of the system can only be removed by cutting the system, and using suitable clamps and sleeves to join the new section to the remainder of the system. Individual sections of the exhaust system are available from Vauxhall/Opel dealers.
7 If any part of the system is to be renewed, it is important to ensure that the correct replacement components are obtained for the particular model concerned.
8 If it proves necessary to cut the system in order to renew a particular components, it is strongly recommended that any such work is

17.5a Typical exhaust system layout – SOHC engine

17.5b Typical exhaust system layout – DOHC engine

entrusted to a Vauxhall/Opel dealer, or exhaust specialist.

9 If work is to be carried out on the exhaust system, first jack up the vehicle and support securely on axle stands (see *Jacking and vehicle support*).

10 The exhaust front section can be disconnected from the manifold after removing the securing bolts. Recover the springs (where applicable) and the gasket. Renew the gasket on refitting. Similarly, on DOHC engine models, the exhaust front section can be disconnected from the intermediate section **(see illustrations)**.

11 To remove the entire exhaust system, disconnect the joints, or cut the system as necessary (with regard to the spare sections available), then unhook the rubber mountings, and withdraw the relevant section of the system. Note that it may be necessary to remove the spring clips from the exhaust mountings before the rubber mountings can be unhooked from the body or the exhaust system **(see illustration)**.

17.10a Recover the springs (arrowed) from the exhaust front section-to-intermediate section joint – DOHC engine

17.10b Use a new gasket (arrowed) when reconnecting the exhaust front section to the manifold – DOHC engine

17.11 Exhaust system rubber mounting spring clip (arrowed)

Chapter 4 Part C:
Emissions control systems

Contents

Degrees of difficulty

| **Easy,** suitable for novice with little experience | **Fairly easy,** suitable for beginner with some experience | **Fairly difficult,** suitable for competent DIY mechanic | **Difficult,** suitable for experienced DIY mechanic | **Very difficult,** suitable for expert DIY or professional |

Specifications

Torque wrench settings	Nm	lbf ft
EGR valve-to-inlet manifold bolts:		
All except 1.0 and 1.2 litre DOHC engines	20	15
EGR valve housing-to-cylinder head bolts:		
1.0 and 1.2 litre DOHC engines	8	6
EGR pipe to EGR valve housing:		
1.2 litre DOHC engine	8	6
Carbon canister strap to bracket	4	3
Carbon canister to wheelarch	4	3
Heat shield to exhaust manifold	8	6
Secondary air combination valve to air pipe	6	4
Secondary air pipe support bracket	8	6
Secondary air pipe to exhaust manifold:		
M6 bolts	8	6
M8 bolts	20	15
Secondary air pump to bracket	20	15
Secondary air switchover valve	5	4

1 General information and precautions

All engines covered by this manual use unleaded petrol and also have various other features built into the fuel/exhaust system to help minimise harmful emissions. The systems are described in more detail in the following paragraphs.

Crankcase emissions control system

A crankcase ventilation system is fitted to all models, but the systems differ in detail according to model.

Oil fumes and blow-by gases (combustion gases which have passed by the piston rings) are drawn from the crankcase into the area of the cylinder head above the camshaft(s) via a hose. From here, the gases are drawn into the inlet manifold/throttle body (as applicable) and/or the airbox on the throttle body, where they are mixed with fresh air/fuel mixture and burnt, reducing harmful exhaust emissions.

Certain models may have a mesh filter inside the camshaft cover, which should be cleaned in paraffin if clogging is evident.

Exhaust emissions control system

To minimise the level of exhaust gas pollutants released into the atmosphere, all models are fitted with a catalytic converter, located in the exhaust system. A 'closed-loop' system is used; an exhaust gas oxygen sensor, mounted in the exhaust manifold, provides a signal to the engine management electronic control unit, to enable it adjust the air/fuel mixture ratio within very fine limits. This enables the catalytic converter to operate at optimum efficiency at all times.

The oxygen sensor senses the level of oxygen in the exhaust gas, which is proportional to the air/fuel mixture ratio. A rich mixture produces exhaust gases with a low oxygen content, the oxygen content rising as the mixture weakens. The catalyst operates at maximum efficiency when the air/fuel mixture ratio is at the chemically-correct ratio for the complete combustion of petrol (14.7 parts of air to 1 part of fuel). The output voltage produced by the oxygen sensor alters sharply when this ratio is achieved. The electronic control unit uses this information to maintain the air/fuel ratio very close to the optimum value under all engine operating conditions, by varying the amount of fuel injected.

Fuel evaporation control system

To minimise the escape into the atmosphere of unburnt hydrocarbons, a fuel evaporation control system is fitted to all models. The fuel tank filler cap is sealed, to prevent the release of fuel vapour into the atmosphere, and a charcoal canister is mounted under the front right-hand wheelarch, to collect the fuel vapours which would otherwise be released from the tank when the vehicle is parked. The vapours are stored in the canister until a vent valve is operated by manifold vacuum, or by the fuel system electronic control unit (depending on engine type). The vent valve releases the vapours into the engine inlet tract, where they are burnt during the normal combustion process.

Exhaust gas recirculation system

The exhaust gas recirculation system, fitted to all engines except the 1.4 litre SOHC engine with multi-point fuel injection (C 14 SE), is designed to recirculate small quantities of exhaust gas into the inlet tract, and therefore into the combustion process. This process reduces the level of oxides of nitrogen present in the final exhaust gas which is released into the atmosphere. The volume of exhaust gas recirculated is controlled by the engine management electronic control unit, via a valve mounted on the inlet manifold.

A tract in the cylinder head allows exhaust gas to pass from the exhaust side of the cylinder head to the exhaust gas recirculation valve in the inlet manifold.

Secondary air injection system

A secondary air injection system is fitted to the 1.4 and 1.6 litre DOHC Ecotec engines (X 14 XE and X 16 XE). It is also known as the Air Injection Reactor (AIR). An electric pump, mounted on the inner wheelarch, forces air into the exhaust manifold, during cold start and run conditions. This quickly increases the exhaust temperature, which enables the catalytic converter to rapidly reach its most effective operating temperature.

2 Crankcase emissions control system – testing and renewal

Testing

1 If the system is thought to be faulty, first check that the hoses are unobstructed. High-mileage vehicles, particularly those regularly used for short journeys, are likely to develop a jelly-like deposit inside the crankcase emissions control system hoses. If excessive deposits are present, the relevant hose(s) should be removed and cleaned.
2 Periodically inspect the system hoses for security and damage, and renew them as necessary. Note that damaged or loose hoses can cause various engine running problems (erratic idle speed, stalling, etc) which can be difficult to trace.

Component renewal

3 The crankcase breather tube can be unbolted from the cylinder block (remove the starter motor for access) after disconnecting the hose. Use a new gasket when refitting.
4 Certain models have a mesh filter inside the camshaft cover, which should be cleaned in paraffin if clogging is evident. For access to the filter, remove the camshaft cover as described in the relevant Part of Chapter 2. The filter can be removed from the camshaft cover for cleaning after unscrewing the securing screws.

3 Exhaust emissions control system – testing and renewal

Testing

1 The system can only be tested accurately using specialist Vauxhall/Opel diagnostic equipment. Any suspected faults should be referred to a Vauxhall/Opel dealer.

Catalytic converter renewal

2 The catalytic converter is located in the exhaust system, and is an integral part of either the exhaust front section or the exhaust intermediate section.
3 Removal and refitting details for the exhaust system components are given in Chapters 4A and 4B.

Oxygen sensor renewal

4 Renewal of the oxygen sensor is described in the relevant fuel system Section of Chapters 4A and 4B.

4 Fuel evaporation control system – testing and renewal

Testing

1 If the system is thought to be faulty, disconnect the hoses from the charcoal canister and vent valve, and check that the hoses are clear by blowing through them. If necessary, clean or renew the hoses (see illustration).
2 If the vent valve or the charcoal canister itself are thought to be faulty, the only course of action available is renewal.

4.1 Disconnecting the fuel vapour vent hose from the fuel injection unit – X 12 SZ engine

4.6 Charcoal canister bracket securing nut (1) and clamp bolt (2)

4.8 Note the locations of the charcoal canister hoses

4.11 Fuel tank vent valve (arrowed) – X 10 XE and X 12 XE engines

Charcoal canister renewal

3 The charcoal canister is located under the front right-hand wheelarch.

4 Apply the handbrake, then jack up the front of the vehicle and support securely on axle stands (see *Jacking and vehicle support*). Remove the front right-hand roadwheel.

5 Remove the wheelarch liner (see Chapter 11) to expose the charcoal canister.

6 Remove the nut securing the canister bracket to the bracket on the body **(see illustration)**.

7 Unscrew the canister clamp bolt, and withdraw the canister from the clamp bracket.

8 Loosen the hose clamps, and disconnect the hoses from the top of the canister, noting their locations to ensure correct refitting **(see illustration)**.

9 Withdraw the canister from under the wheelarch.

10 Fit the new canister using a reversal of the removal procedure. Make sure that the hoses are correctly reconnected, as noted before removal. Ensure that the upper end of the canister clamp bracket locates in the cut-out in the body panel.

Fuel tank vent valve renewal

1.0 and 1.2 litre DOHC engines

11 The valve is located at the left-hand end of the inlet manifold **(see illustration)**.

12 Disconnect the battery negative terminal (refer to *Disconnecting the battery* in the Reference Chapter).

13 Disconnect the upper and lower vent hoses, and the valve wiring plug.

14 Detach the valve from the inlet manifold and remove it from the engine.

15 Refitting is a reversal of removal, ensuring that the hoses are reconnected securely.

1.2 and 1.4 litre SOHC engines

16 The valve is located at the timing belt end of the camshaft housing, at the rear.

17 Disconnect the battery negative terminal (refer to *Disconnecting the battery* in the Reference Chapter).

18 For improved access, remove the breather hose connecting the airbox to the camshaft cover **(see illustration)**.

19 Release the wiring harness from the brackets on the camshaft cover, and lift the harness clear of the fuel tank vent valve **(see illustration)**.

20 Depress the retaining lugs, and slide the

valve rearwards from its mounting bracket **(see illustration)**.

21 Disconnect the valve wiring plug, and the two hoses, noting their locations to ensure correct refitting **(see illustration)**.

22 Withdraw the valve.

23 Refitting is a reversal of removal, ensuring that the hoses are reconnected correctly, as noted before removal.

1.4 and 1.6 litre DOHC engines

24 The valve is located on a bracket attached to the upper section of the inlet manifold.

25 Remove the oil filler cap and the plastic cover from the top of the camshaft cover. The plastic cover is secured by two screws.

26 Disconnect the battery negative terminal (refer to *Disconnecting the battery* in the Reference Chapter), then disconnect the wiring plug from the valve **(see illustration)**.

4.18 Remove the breather hose . . .

4.19 . . . and lift the wiring harness clear for access to the fuel tank vent valve (arrowed) – X 12 SZ and X 14 SZ engines

4.20 Slide the valve from its mounting bracket . . .

4.21 . . . and disconnect the wiring and hoses – X 12 SZ and X 14 SZ engines

4.26 Disconnecting the wiring plug . . .

4.27 . . . and the hoses from the fuel tank vent valve – X 14 XE and X 16 XE engines

27 Disconnect the hoses from the valve, noting their locations to ensure correct refitting **(see illustration)**.
28 Withdraw the valve upwards from its bracket.
29 Refitting is a reversal of removal, ensuring that the hoses are reconnected securely.

5 Exhaust gas recirculation system – testing and renewal

Testing

1 The system can only be tested accurately using specialist Vauxhall/Opel diagnostic equipment. The wiring to the solenoid valve on the inlet manifold can be checked for condition and security, but any further testing should be referred to a Vauxhall/Opel dealer.

Exhaust gas recirculation valve renewal

1.0 and 1.2 litre DOHC engines

Note: *A new EGR housing gasket and EGR pipe gasket must be used on refitting.*
2 The valve is located at the left-hand end of the cylinder head.
3 Disconnect the battery negative terminal (refer to *Disconnecting the battery* in the Reference Chapter).
4 Partially drain the cooling system as described in Chapter 1, then disconnect the coolant hose from the rear of the EGR valve housing **(see illustration)**.
5 Disconnect the wiring plug from the top of the EGR valve and the wiring connector from the adjacent temperature gauge sender.
6 Move the wiring harness to one side for access to the EGR valve housing mounting bolts.
7 On 1.2 litre engines, undo the two bolts securing the EGR pipe to the side of the EGR valve housing **(see illustration)**.
8 Undo the four bolts securing the EGR valve housing to the cylinder head and withdraw the housing assembly **(see illustration)**. Recover the housing gasket and, where applicable, the EGR pipe-to-housing gasket.
9 Refitting is a reversal of removal.

Thoroughly clean the mating faces of the valve, cylinder head and EGR pipe flange, then refit the valve and pipe using new gaskets.
10 On completion, top-up the cooling system as described in *Weekly checks*.

1.2 and 1.4 litre SOHC engines

Note: *A new gasket must be used on refitting.*
11 The valve is located on top of the inlet manifold.
12 Remove the airbox from the top of the fuel injection unit, as described in Chapter 4B.
13 Disconnect the battery negative terminal (refer to *Disconnecting the battery* in the Reference Chapter), then disconnect the wiring plug from the valve **(see illustration)**.
14 Unscrew the two securing bolts, and withdraw the valve from the inlet manifold **(see illustration)**. Recover the gasket.
15 Check the valve vent holes for contamination, and clean if necessary **(see illustration)**.
16 Refitting is a reversal of removal. Thoroughly clean the mating faces of the valve and manifold, then refit the valve using a new gasket.

1.4 and 1.6 litre DOHC engines

17 Depressurise the fuel system as described in Chapter 4B.
18 Disconnect the battery negative terminal if not already done (refer to *Disconnecting the battery* in the Reference Chapter).

5.4 EGR valve coolant hose (1), wiring plug (2) and coolant temperature sensor wiring connector (3) – X 10 XE and X 12 XE engines

5.7 EGR pipe-to-EGR valve housing securing bolts (arrowed) – X 10 XE and X 12 XE engines

5.8 EGR valve housing securing bolts (arrowed) – X 10 XE and X 12 XE engines

5.13 Disconnecting the exhaust gas recirculation valve wiring plug – X 12 SZ and X 14 SZ engines

5.14 Exhaust gas recirculation valve securing bolts (arrowed) – X 12 SZ and X 14 SZ engines

5.15 Check the exhaust gas recirculation valve vent holes (arrowed) for contamination – X 12 SZ and X 14 SZ engines

5.27 Disconnecting the exhaust gas recirculation control module wiring plug – X 12 SZ engines

6.2 Loosen the clamp (arrowed) and remove the air duct hose from the secondary air injection pump – X 14 XE and X 16 XE engines

6.5 Secondary air injection pump mounting bracket nuts – X 14 XE and X 16 XE engines

19 Partially drain the cooling system as described in Chapter 1, then disconnect the coolant hoses and remove the cooling system expansion tank.
20 Unscrew the union nuts and disconnect the fuel feed line from the fuel rail, and the return line from the fuel pressure regulator.
21 Undo the bolts securing the wiring trough and air inlet pipe from the inlet manifold lower section. Detach the air inlet hoses at the inlet pipe and push the pipe downwards slightly for access to the EGR valve.
22 Disconnect the wiring plug from the valve.
23 Unscrew the two securing bolts, and withdraw the valve from the inlet manifold. Recover the gasket.
24 Check the valve vent holes for contamination, and clean if necessary.
25 Refitting is a reversal of removal. Thoroughly clean the mating faces of the valve and manifold, then refit the valve using a new gasket. Top-up the cooling system as described in *Weekly checks* on completion.

Exhaust gas recirculation control module renewal

1.2 litre SOHC engine

26 The module is located on a bracket mounted on the front left-hand wing panel.
27 Disconnect the battery negative terminal (refer to *Disconnecting the battery* in

the Reference Chapter), then disconnect the wiring plug from the module **(see illustration)**.
28 Remove the two securing bolts, and withdraw the module from its mounting bracket.
29 Refitting is a reversal of removal.

6 Secondary air injection pump assembly (1.4 and 1.6 litre DOHC engines) – renewal

1 Disconnect the battery negative terminal (refer to *Disconnecting the battery* in the Reference Chapter).
2 Loosen the hose clamp and remove the air duct hose from the pump, and unclip it from the support bracket **(see illustration)**.
3 Disconnect the air pump wiring plug.
4 Detach the coolant hose from the air pump bracket and move the hose aside.
5 Undo the securing nuts and remove the pump and mounting bracket assembly from its location **(see illustration)**.
6 Detach the air hose then undo the nuts and remove the air pump air cleaner from the pump bracket.
7 Check the pump air cleaner for damage.
8 Refitting is a reversal of removal. Ensure correct alignment of the components.

7 Secondary air switchover valve (1.4 and 1.6 litre DOHC engines) – renewal

1 The switchover valve is mounted on a bracket attached to the suspension strut tower on the left-hand side of the engine compartment **(see illustration)**.
2 Disconnect the battery negative terminal (refer to *Disconnecting the battery* in the Reference Chapter).
3 Disconnect wiring plug from the valve.
4 Mark the location of the vacuum hoses before removing them from the valve.
5 After disconnecting the hoses undo the two bolts, and remove the valve from its bracket.
6 Refitting is a reversal of removal. Ensure hoses are fitted correctly.

8 Secondary air pipe and combination valve (1.4 and 1.6 litre DOHC engines) – renewal

Note: *The gasket should be renewed when refitting the valve.*

1 Release the retaining clip and disconnect the combination valve air duct and the vacuum hose **(see illustration)**.
2 Unbolt the support bracket from the secondary air pipe and exhaust manifold.
3 Mark the location of the valve before removal.
4 Remove the valve from the secondary air pipe.
5 Remove the pipe support bracket by releasing its bolts.
6 Remove the heat shield that is secured by two bolts.
7 The air pipe can now be removed by releasing the two securing bolts.
8 Secure the pipe in the exhaust manifold, coating the bolts with Assembly Paste (Vauxhall P/N 90513210).
9 Using a new gasket, refitting is a reversal of removal, tightening all bolts to the specified torque.

7.1 Secondary air injection switchover valve (arrowed) – X 14 XE and X 16 XE engines

8.1 Disconnect the air duct and vacuum hose from the secondary air combination valve – X 14 XE and X 16 XE engines

9 Catalytic converter – general information and precautions

The catalytic converter is a reliable and simple device which needs no maintenance in itself, but there are some facts of which an owner should be aware if the converter is to function properly for its full service life.

a) DO NOT use leaded petrol in a car equipped with a catalytic converter – the lead will coat the precious metals, reducing their converting efficiency and will eventually destroy the converter.

b) Always keep the ignition and fuel systems well-maintained in accordance with the manufacturer's schedule.

c) If the engine develops a misfire, do not drive the car at all (or at least as little as possible) until the fault is cured.

d) DO NOT push- or tow-start the car – this will soak the catalytic converter in unburned fuel, causing it to overheat when the engine does start.

e) DO NOT switch off the ignition at high engine speeds.

f) DO NOT use fuel or engine oil additives – these may contain substances harmful to the catalytic converter.

g) DO NOT continue to use the car if the engine burns oil to the extent of leaving a visible trail of blue smoke.

h) Remember that the catalytic converter operates at very high temperatures. DO NOT, therefore, park the car in dry undergrowth, over long grass or piles of dead leaves after a long run.

i) Remember that the catalytic converter is FRAGILE – do not strike it with tools during servicing work.

j) In some cases a sulphurous smell (like that of rotten eggs) may be noticed from the exhaust. This is common to many catalytic converter-equipped cars and once the car has covered a few thousand miles the problem should disappear.

k) The catalytic converter, used on a well-maintained and well-driven car, should last for between 50 000 and 100 000 miles – if the converter is no longer effective it must be renewed.

Chapter 5 Part A:
Starting and charging systems

Contents

Degrees of difficulty

| **Easy,** suitable for novice with little experience | | **Fairly easy,** suitable for beginner with some experience | | **Fairly difficult,** suitable for competent DIY mechanic | | **Difficult,** suitable for experienced DIY mechanic | | **Very difficult,** suitable for expert DIY or professional | |

Specifications

General

Electrical system type . . . . 12 volt negative earth

Battery

Type . . . . Lead-acid, 'maintenance-free' (sealed for life)
Battery capacity . . . . 36, 44, 55 or 60 Ah (depending on model)

Alternator

Type . . . . Bosch or Delco-Remy
Maximum output:
  Bosch . . . . 55 or 70 amps (depending on model)
  Delco-Remy . . . . 67 or 100 amps (depending on model)
Regulated voltage . . . . 13.7 to 14.7 volts (approximately)
Brush minimum length:
  Bosch . . . . 5.0 mm
  Delco-Remy:
    67 amp . . . . 12.0 mm
    100 amp . . . . 20.0 mm

Starter motor

Type . . . . Pre-engaged, Delco-Remy or Valeo
Brush minimum length:
  Delco-Remy:
    Except code number 09 000 756 . . . . 4.0 mm
    Code number 09 000 756 . . . . 8.5 mm
  Valeo . . . . 13.0 mm

Torque wrench settings

	Nm	lbf ft
Alternator adjuster strut-to-inlet manifold bolts:		
Models with V-belt	20	15
Alternator (auxiliary) drivebelt tensioner lower mounting bolt:		
Models with ribbed belt	20	15
Alternator (auxiliary) drivebelt tensioner roller-to-engine bolt:		
Models with ribbed belt	20	15
Alternator mounting bracket-to-engine bolts (M10)	40	30
Alternator-to-adjuster strut bolts:		
Models with V-belt	20	15
Alternator-to-mounting bracket bolts:		
M8	30	22
M10	40	30
Alternator upper support bracket to alternator:		
Models with V-belt	20	15
Alternator upper support bracket to inlet manifold:		
Models with V-belt	20	15
Inlet manifold support bracket to cylinder block	20	13
Inlet manifold support bracket to inlet manifold:		
1.0 litre DOHC engines	10	7
1.2 litre DOHC engines	6	4
Starter motor bolts	25	18

1 General information and precautions

General information

The engine electrical system consists mainly of the charging and starting systems (covered in this Part of Chapter 5) and the ignition system (covered in Part B of this Chapter). Because of their engine-related functions, these components are covered separately from the body electrical devices such as the lights, instruments, etc (which are covered in Chapter 12).

The electrical system is of the 12 volt negative earth type.

The battery is of the 'maintenance-free' (sealed for life) type, and is charged by the alternator, which is belt-driven from a crankshaft-mounted pulley.

The starter motor is of the pre-engaged type, incorporating an integral solenoid. On starting, the solenoid moves the drive pinion into engagement with the flywheel ring gear before the starter motor is energised. Once the engine has started, a one-way clutch prevents the motor armature being driven by the engine while the pinion disengages from the flywheel.

Further details of the various systems are given in the relevant Sections of this Chapter. While some repair procedures are given, the usual course of action is to renew the component concerned. The owner whose interest extends beyond mere component renewal should obtain a copy of the *Automobile Electrical & Electronic Systems Manual*, available from the publishers of this manual.

Precautions

It is necessary to take extra care when working on the electrical system, to avoid damage to semi-conductor devices (diodes and transistors), and to avoid the risk of personal injury. In addition to the precautions given in *Safety first!* at the beginning of this manual, observe the following when working on the system:

Always remove rings, watches, etc, before working on the electrical system. Even with the battery disconnected, capacitive discharge could occur if a component's live terminal is earthed through a metal object. This could cause a shock or nasty burn.

Do not reverse the battery connections. Components such as the alternator, ignition system components, or any other components having semi-conductor circuitry, could be irreparably damaged.

If the engine is being started using jump leads and a slave battery, connect the batteries as shown in the preliminary section of this manual (see 'Jump starting'). This also applies when connecting a battery charger.

Never disconnect the battery terminals, the alternator, any electrical wiring, or any test instruments, when the engine is running.

Do not allow the engine to turn the alternator when the alternator is not connected.

Never 'test' for alternator output by 'flashing' the output lead to earth.

Never use an ohmmeter of the type incorporating a hand-cranked generator for circuit or continuity testing.

Always ensure that the battery negative lead is disconnected when working on the electrical system.

Before using electric-arc welding equipment on the car, disconnect the battery, alternator and components such as the engine management and the ABS electronic control units to protect them from the risk of damage.

Several systems fitted to the vehicle require battery power to be available at all times, either to ensure their continued operation (such as the clock) or to maintain control unit memories or security codes which would be wiped if the battery were to be disconnected. To ensure that there are no unforeseen consequences of this action, Refer to 'Disconnecting the battery' in the Reference Chapter for further information.

2 Electrical fault finding – general information

Refer to Chapter 12.

3 Battery – testing and charging

Note: *The following information refers only to the maintenance-free type battery fitted as original equipment.*

1 Topping-up and testing of the electrolyte in each battery cell is not possible. The condition of the battery can therefore only be tested by observing the battery condition indicator.

2 The battery condition indicator is located in the top of the battery casing, and indicates the condition of the battery by its colour **(see illustration)**. If the indicator shows green, then the battery is in a good state of charge. If the indicator turns darker, eventually to black, then the battery requires charging, as described later in this Section. If the indicator shows clear/yellow, then the electrolyte level in the battery is too low to allow further use, and the battery should be renewed. **Do not** attempt to charge, load or jump start a battery when the indicator shows clear/yellow.

3 If the battery is to be charged, remove it from the vehicle, as described in Section 4, and charge it as follows.

4 The maintenance-free type battery takes considerably longer to fully recharge than the standard type, the time taken being dependent on the extent of discharge.

5 A constant-voltage type charger is required; connect it up and set it to 13.9 to 14.9 volts, with a charge current below 25 amps.

6 If the battery is to be charged from a fully-discharged state (less than 12.2 volts output), have it recharged by a Vauxhall/Opel dealer or a competent automotive electrician, as the charge rate is high, and constant supervision during charging is necessary.

4 Battery – removal and refitting

Note: *Refer to 'Disconnecting the battery' in the Reference Section of this manual before proceeding.*

Removal

1 On right-hand drive models, the battery is located on the left-hand side of the engine compartment, towards the rear. On left-hand drive models the battery is located under the windscreen cowl panel on the right-hand side. To remove the cowl panel, undo the five screws, lift the panel up in the centre and remove the right-hand half forwards from the plenum chamber.

2 Disconnect the lead(s) at the negative (earth) terminal by unscrewing the retaining nut and removing the terminal clamp.

3 Disconnect the positive terminal lead(s) in the same way.

4 Unscrew the clamp bolt sufficiently to enable the battery to be lifted from its location **(see illustration)**. Keep the battery upright.

5 If necessary the battery tray can be removed after undoing the four retaining bolts. Release any wiring or hose clips from the tray and lift the tray from the engine compartment.

Refitting

6 Refitting is a reversal of removal, but smear petroleum jelly on the terminals when reconnecting the leads, and always reconnect the positive lead first, and the negative lead last.

5 Charging system – testing

Note: *Refer to the precautions given in 'Safety first!' and in Section 1 of this Chapter before starting work.*

1 If the ignition/no-charge warning light fails to illuminate when the ignition is switched on, first check the alternator wiring connections for security. If satisfactory, check that the warning light bulb has not blown, and that the bulbholder is secure in its location in the instrument panel. If the light still fails to illuminate, check the continuity of the warning light feed wire from the alternator to the bulbholder. If all is satisfactory, the alternator is at fault, and should be renewed, or taken to an auto-electrician for testing and repair.

2 If the ignition warning light illuminates when the engine is running, stop the engine and check that the drivebelt is correctly tensioned (see Chapter 1) and that the alternator connections are secure. If all is so far satisfactory, check the alternator brushes and slip rings (see Section 7). If the fault persists, the alternator should be renewed, or taken to an auto-electrician for testing and repair.

3 If the alternator output is suspect even though the warning light functions correctly, the regulated voltage may be checked as follows.

4 Connect a voltmeter across the battery terminals, and start the engine.

5 Increase the engine speed until the voltmeter reading remains steady; the reading should be approximately 12 to 13 volts, and no more than 14 volts.

6 Switch on as many electrical accessories (eg, the headlights, heated rear window and heater blower) as possible, and check that the alternator maintains the regulated voltage at around 13.5 to 14.5 volts.

7 If the regulated voltage is not as stated, the fault may be due to worn brushes, weak brush springs, a faulty voltage regulator, a faulty diode, a severed phase winding, or worn or damaged slip rings. The brushes and slip rings may be checked (see Section 7), but if the fault persists, the alternator should be renewed, or taken to an auto-electrician for testing and repair.

6 Alternator – removal and refitting

SOHC engines with V-belt
Removal

1 Disconnect the battery negative terminal (refer to *Disconnecting the battery* in the Reference Chapter).

2 Remove the auxiliary drivebelt as described in Chapter 1.

3 Disconnect the wires from their terminals on the rear of the alternator, noting their locations, or disconnect the wiring plug, as applicable. Note that on certain models, access to the alternator wiring may be easier from underneath the vehicle.

4 On models with multi-point fuel injection, remove the throttle body as described in Chapter 4B, Section 13.

5 Unscrew the bolt securing the top of the alternator to the adjuster strut, and recover any washers and insulating bushes, noting their locations. Note the earth strap attached to the bolt.

6 Loosen the bolt securing the adjuster strut to the inlet manifold, and pivot the strut upwards to leave sufficient space to remove the alternator.

7 Undo the bolts securing the alternator upper support bracket to the alternator and inlet manifold and remove the bracket.

8 Support the alternator, then remove the nut and through-bolt securing the alternator to the engine bracket. Again, recover any washers and insulating bushes, noting their locations.

9 Withdraw the alternator from the engine.

Refitting

10 Refitting is a reversal of removal, bearing in mind the following points:
  a) *Ensure that all washers and insulating bushes are refitted in their correct locations, as noted before removal.*
  b) *Ensure that the earth lead is refitted to the top alternator securing bolt.*
  c) *Where applicable, refit the throttle body as described in Chapter 4B.*
  d) *Refit and tension the auxiliary drivebelt as described in Chapter 1.*

3.2 Battery condition indicator (arrowed)

4.4 Unscrewing the battery clamp bolt

6.13 Unbolt the two upper alternator mounting brackets (arrowed) – SOHC engines with ribbed belt alternator drive

SOHC engines with ribbed belt

Removal

11 Proceed as described in paragraphs 1 to 3 inclusive, but note that it is only necessary to release the auxiliary drivebelt from the alternator pulley, it does not have to be removed completely.

12 Remove the nut and through-bolt securing the alternator to the lower bracket. Recover any washers and insulating bushes, noting their locations.

13 Support the alternator, then unbolt the two upper mounting brackets from the alternator, cylinder head and inlet manifold, and withdraw the brackets **(see illustration)**. Again, recover any washers and insulating bushes, noting their locations. Note the earth strap attached to the front mounting bracket bolts.

14 Withdraw the alternator from the engine.

Refitting

15 Refitting is a reversal of removal, bearing in mind the following points:
a) *Ensure that any washers and insulating bushes are refitted in their correct locations, as noted before removal.*
b) *Ensure that the earth lead is refitted to the front mounting bracket.*

6.18 Auxiliary drivebelt automatic tensioner lower mounting bolt (arrowed) – 1.0 and 1.2 litre DOHC engines

c) *Do not fully tighten any of the mounting bolts until the alternator and all mounting brackets are in position.*
d) *Refit the auxiliary drivebelt as described in Chapter 1.*

1.0 and 1.2 litre DOHC engines

16 Proceed as described in paragraphs 1 and 2, but note that it is only necessary to release the auxiliary drivebelt from the alternator pulley, it does not have to be removed completely.

17 If not already done, apply the handbrake, then jack up the front of the vehicle and support securely on axle stands (see *Jacking and vehicle support*).

18 Undo the auxiliary drivebelt automatic tensioner lower mounting bolt, and swing the tensioner upwards to provide access to the lower alternator mounting bolt **(see illustration)**.

19 Disconnect the wires from their terminals on the rear of the alternator, noting their locations.

20 Remove the nut and through-bolt securing the alternator to the lower mounting bracket. Recover any washers and insulating bushes, noting their locations **(see illustration)**.

21 Support the alternator, then remove the nut and through-bolt securing the alternator to the upper mounting bracket. Again, recover

6.20 Alternator upper and lower mounting through-bolt nuts – 1.0 and 1.2 litre DOHC engines

any washers and insulating bushes, noting their locations.

22 Slide the alternator off the mounting brackets and remove it from under the car.

Refitting

23 Refitting is a reversal of removal, bearing in mind the following points:
a) *Ensure that any washers and insulating bushes are refitted in their correct locations, as noted during removal.*
b) *Refit the auxiliary drivebelt as described in Chapter 1.*

1.4 and 1.6 litre DOHC engines

Removal

24 Disconnect the battery negative terminal (refer to *Disconnecting the battery* in the Reference Chapter).

25 Remove the auxiliary drivebelt as described in Chapter 1.

26 Apply the handbrake, then jack up the front of the vehicle and support securely on axle stands (see *Jacking and vehicle support*). Remove the right-hand front roadwheel.

27 Unbolt the crankshaft speed/position sensor bracket from the oil pump, and move the bracket/sensor assembly to one side (take care not to damage the sensor or the wiring) **(see illustration)**.

28 Disconnect the wiring from the oil pressure switch, located in the end of the oil pump.

29 Disconnect the wires from their terminals on the rear of the alternator, noting their locations, or disconnect the wiring plug, as applicable **(see illustration)**.

30 Disconnect the outer end of the driveshaft from the front swivel hub assembly, as described in Chapter 8. There is no need to withdraw the driveshaft from the transmission. Support the end of the driveshaft using wire or string – do not allow the driveshaft to hang down under its own weight, or the joint may be damaged.

31 Unscrew the three securing bolts and remove the upper alternator mounting bracket

6.27 Unbolt the crankshaft speed/position sensor bracket from the oil pump. Securing bolt arrowed – 1.4 and 1.6 litre DOHC engines

6.29 Alternator wiring securing nuts (arrowed) – 1.4 and 1.6 litre DOHC engines (viewed from underneath vehicle)

6.31 Remove the upper alternator mounting bracket (1) – 1.4 and 1.6 litre DOHC engines

34 Manipulate the driveshaft as necessary to allow sufficient clearance for the alternator to pass out through the wheelarch, then withdraw the alternator.

Refitting

35 Refitting is a reversal of removal, bearing in mind the following points:

a) *Refit the nut and through-bolt securing the alternator to the lower mounting bracket before bolting the mounting bracket to the cylinder block. Ensure that any washers and insulating bushes are positioned as noted before removal.*

b) *Ensure that the earth strap is in position when refitting the upper alternator mounting bracket.*

c) *Reconnect the driveshaft to the front swivel hub assembly as described in Chapter 8.*

d) *Refit the auxiliary drivebelt as described in Chapter 1.*

7 Alternator brushes and regulator – inspection and renewal

Standard Bosch alternator

1 The brush holder and voltage regulator are combined in a single assembly, which is bolted to the rear of the alternator **(see**

(see illustration). Note the location of the earth strap secured by the mounting bracket bolts.

32 Remove the nut and through-bolt securing the alternator to the lower mounting bracket. Recover any washers and insulating

bushes, noting their locations.

33 Support the alternator, and unbolt the lower mounting bracket from the cylinder block **(see illustration)**. Withdraw the lower mounting bracket to allow sufficient clearance to remove the alternator.

6.33 Unbolt the alternator lower mounting bracket from the cylinder block – 1.4 and 1.6 litre DOHC engines

A Models without power steering or air conditioning   *B Models with power steering and/or air conditioning*

1 Alternator lower mounting bracket

7.1 Exploded view of the standard Bosch alternator

1 Pulley nut
2 Pulley
3 Fan
4 Drive end housing
5 Bearing
6 Bearing retainer
7 Through-bolts
8 Brush holder/voltage regulator assembly
9 Slip ring end housing
10 Stator endplate
11 Stator
12 Bearing
13 Rotor

illustration). If the voltage regulator is faulty, the complete assembly must be renewed.

2 Disconnect the battery negative terminal (refer to *Disconnecting the battery* in the Reference Chapter).

3 If desired, to improve access further, the alternator can be removed, as described in Section 6.

4 Remove the two securing screws, and withdraw the brush holder/voltage regulator assembly **(see illustrations)**.

5 Check that the brushes move freely in their guides, and that the brush lengths are within the limits given in the Specifications **(see illustration)**. If any doubt exists regarding the condition of the brushes, the best policy is to renew them as follows.

6 Hold the brush wire with a suitable pair of pliers, and unsolder it from the brush holder. Lift away the brush. Repeat for the remaining brush.

7 Note that whenever new brushes are fitted, new brush springs should also be fitted.

8 With the new springs fitted to the brush holder, insert the new brushes, and check that they move freely in their guides. If they bind, polish them lightly with a very fine file or glass paper.

9 Solder the brush wire ends to the brush holder, taking care not to allow solder to pass to the stranded wire.

10 Check the condition of the slip rings, and if necessary clean them with a rag or very fine glass paper **(see illustration)**.

11 Refit the brush holder/voltage regulator assembly, and tighten the securing screws.

12 If the alternator was removed, refit it as described in Section 6.

13 Reconnect the battery negative lead.

7.4a Remove the securing screws ...

7.4b ... and withdraw the brush holder/ voltage regulator – standard Bosch alternator

7.5 Measuring the length of an alternator brush – standard Bosch alternator

7.10 Alternator slip rings (arrowed) – standard Bosch alternator

1 Pulley nut
2 Washer
3 Pulley
4 Bolt
5 Spacer
6 Drive end housing
7 Bearing
8 Bearing cover
9 Rotor
10 Bearing
11 Dust cover
12 Through-bolt
13 Plastic cover
14 Bolt
15 Voltage
   regulator/brush holder
16 Bolt
17 Nut
18 Through-bolt
19 Rectifier
20 Slip ring end housing
21 Bush
22 Stator

H.28/52

7.14 Exploded view of the compact Bosch alternator

Compact Bosch alternator

14 The brush holder and voltage regulator are combined as a single assembly **(see illustration)**. With the alternator removed as described in Section 6, proceed as follows.

15 Remove the three securing nuts, and withdraw the plastic cover from the rear of the alternator **(see illustrations)**. Note that it is possible that the studs may be withdrawn as the nuts are unscrewed – in this case, the studs can be refitted using two nuts locked together on the studs.

16 Remove the two securing screws, and withdraw the brush holder/voltage regulator assembly from the rear of the alternator **(see illustrations)**.

17 Check that the brushes move freely in their guides, and that the brush lengths are within the limits given in the Specifications. If any doubt exists regarding the condition of the brushes, the complete brush holder/voltage regulator assembly must be renewed.

18 Refitting is a reversal of removal.

19 Refit the alternator as described in Section 6.

Standard Delco-Remy alternator

Note: *No spare parts are available for Delco-Remy alternators marked 'Made in Korea'.*

20 The brush holder and voltage regulator

7.15a Unscrew the securing nuts . . .

7.15b . . . and withdraw the plastic cover –
compact Bosch alternator

7.16a Remove the securing screws . . .

7.16b . . . and withdraw the brush holder/
voltage regulator – compact Bosch alternator

7.20 Exploded view of the standard Delco-Remy alternator

1 Pulley nut (not fitted to all models)
2 Pulley
3 Fan
4 Drive end housing
5 Bearing
6 Bearing retainer
7 Rotor
8 Through-bolt
9 Slip ring end housing
10 Brush holder/voltage regulator assembly
11 Diode assembly
12 Stator

are combined in a single assembly **(see illustration)**. For access to the assembly, the alternator must be partially dismantled as follows. If the voltage regulator is faulty, the complete assembly must be renewed.

21 Remove the alternator as described in Section 6.

22 Scribe a line across the drive end housing and the slip ring end housing, to ensure correct alignment when reassembling.

23 Unscrew the three through-bolts, and prise the drive end housing and rotor away from the slip ring end housing and stator **(see illustration)**.

24 Check the condition of the slip rings, and if necessary clean them with a rag or very fine glass paper **(see illustration)**.

25 Remove the three nuts and washers securing the stator leads to the rectifier, and lift away the stator assembly **(see illustration)**.

26 Remove the terminal screw, and lift out the diode assembly.

27 Extract the two screws securing the brush holder and voltage regulator to the slip ring end housing, and remove the brush holder assembly. Note the insulation washers under the screw heads.

28 Check that the brushes move freely in their guides, and that the brush lengths are within the limits given in the Specifications. If any doubt exists regarding the condition of the brushes, the best policy is to renew them.

29 To fit new brushes, unsolder the old brush leads from the brush holder, and solder on the new leads in exactly the same place.

30 Check that the new brushes move freely in the guides.

31 Before refitting the brush holder assembly, retain the brushes in the retracted position using a stiff piece of wire or a twist drill.

32 Refit the brush holder assembly so that the wire or drill protrudes through the slot in the slip ring end housing, and tighten the securing screws.

33 Refit the diode assembly and the stator assembly to the housing, ensuring that the stator leads are in their correct positions, and refit the terminal screw and nuts.

34 Assemble the drive end housing and rotor to the slip ring end housing, ensuring that the previously-made marks are still aligned. Insert and tighten the three through-bolts.

7.23 Separating the drive end housing from the slip ring end housing – standard Delco-Remy alternator

7.24 Alternator slip rings (arrowed) – standard Delco-Remy alternator

7.25 Stator lead securing nuts (A) and brush holder/voltage regulator securing screws (B) – standard Delco-Remy alternator

7.35 Removing the drill bit used to hold brushes in retracted position – standard Delco-Remy alternator

35 Pull the wire or drill (as applicable) from the slot in the slip ring end housing, so that the brushes rest on the rotor slip rings **(see illustration)**.

36 Refit the alternator as described in Section 6.

Compact Delco-Remy alternator

37 With the alternator removed as described in Section 6, proceed as follows **(see illustration)**.

38 Unscrew the securing nuts, and remove the plastic cover from the rear of the alternator.

39 Unscrew the two brush holder securing screws, noting their different lengths. Note that one of the screws also secures the suppressor **(see illustration)**.

40 Unscrew the remaining suppressor securing nut, and lift the suppressor from the rear of the alternator.

41 Using a small screwdriver, or a similar tool, prise up the securing tag at the side of the brush holder, then lift the assembly from the rear of the alternator **(see illustration)**.

42 Check that the brushes move freely in their guides, and that the brush lengths are within the limits given in the Specifications. If any doubt exists regarding the condition of the brushes, the best policy is to renew them. If the brushes are renewed, it is wise to renew the brush springs at the same time.

7.37 Sectional view of the compact Delco-Remy alternator

1 *Drive end housing*	3 *Rotor*	5 *Fan*
2 *Stator*	4 *Slip rings*	6 *Rectifier*

43 To fit new brushes, unsolder the old brush leads from the brush holder, and solder on the new leads in exactly the same place.

44 Check that the new brushes move freely in the guides.

45 Refitting is a reversal of removal.

46 Refit the alternator as described in Section 6.

---

8 Starting system – testing

Note: *Refer to the precautions given in 'Safety first!' and in Section 1 of this Chapter before starting work.*

1 If the starter motor fails to operate when the ignition key is turned to the appropriate position, the possible causes are as follows:

a) *The battery is faulty.*

b) *The electrical connections between the switch, solenoid, battery and starter motor are somewhere failing to pass the necessary current from the battery through the starter to earth.*

c) *The solenoid is faulty.*

d) *The starter motor is mechanically or electrically defective.*

2 To check the battery, switch on the headlights. If they dim after a few seconds, this indicates that the battery is discharged – recharge (see Section 3) or renew the battery. If the headlights glow brightly, operate the starter switch while

7.39 Brush holder securing screws (1) and suppressor (2) – compact Delco-Remy alternator

7.41 Withdraw the brush holder (1) by after releasing the securing tag (2) – compact Delco-Remy alternator

9.3 Starter motor wiring securing nut (arrowed) – viewed from underneath vehicle

watching the headlights. If they dim, then this indicates that current is reaching the starter motor, therefore the fault must lie in the starter motor. If the lights continue to glow brightly (and no clicking sound can be heard from the starter motor solenoid), this indicates that there is a fault in the circuit or solenoid – see the following paragraphs. If the starter motor turns slowly when operated, but the battery is in good condition, then this indicates either that the starter motor is faulty, or there is considerable resistance somewhere in the circuit.

3 If a fault in the circuit is suspected, disconnect the battery leads (including the earth connection to the body), the starter/solenoid wiring and the engine/transmission earth strap. Thoroughly clean the connections, and reconnect the leads and wiring. Use a voltmeter or test light to check that full battery voltage is available at the battery positive lead connection to the solenoid. Smear petroleum jelly around the battery terminals to prevent corrosion – corroded connections are among the most frequent causes of electrical system faults.

4 If the battery and all connections are in good condition, check the circuit by disconnecting the switched feed wire from the solenoid (the thinner wire). Connect a voltmeter or test light between the wire end and a good earth (such as the battery negative terminal), and check that the wire is live when the ignition switch is turned to the 'start' position. If it is, then the circuit is sound – if not, there is a fault in the ignition/starter switch or wiring.

5 The solenoid contacts can be checked by connecting a voltmeter or test light between the battery positive feed connection on the starter side of the solenoid, and earth. When the ignition switch is turned to the 'start' position, there should be a reading or lighted bulb, as applicable. If there is no reading or lighted bulb, the solenoid is faulty and should be renewed.

6 If the circuit and solenoid are proved sound, the fault must lie in the starter motor. Begin checking the starter motor by removing it (see Section 9), and checking the brushes (see Section 10). If the fault does not lie in the brushes, the motor windings must be faulty. In this event, the starter motor must be renewed, unless an auto-electrical specialist can be found who will overhaul the unit at a cost significantly less than that of a new or exchange starter motor.

9 Starter motor – removal and refitting

Removal

1 Disconnect the battery negative terminal (refer to *Disconnecting the battery* in the Reference Chapter).

2 Apply the handbrake, then jack up the front of the vehicle, and support securely on axle stands (see *Jacking and vehicle support*).

3 Note the wiring connections on the solenoid, then unscrew the securing nuts (where applicable) and disconnect them **(see illustration)**.

4 Where applicable, unscrew nut securing the earth cable to the upper starter motor mounting stud. Recover the washer, and disconnect the cable from the stud.

5 On 1.0 and 1.2 litre DOHC engines unbolt the inlet manifold support bracket from the manifold and cylinder block.

6 Unscrew the starter motor mounting stud and bolt, or the two bolts, as applicable, and withdraw the motor from under the vehicle.

Refitting

7 Refitting is a reversal of removal, but where applicable, ensure that the earth cable is reconnected to the stud.

10 Starter motor – brush renewal

Delco-Remy starter motor

1 With the starter motor removed from the vehicle as described in Section 9 and cleaned, grip the unit in a vice fitted with soft jaw protectors **(see illustration)**.

2 Make alignment marks between the main motor casing and the commutator end housing.

3 Unscrew and remove the two through-bolts

1 Solenoid yolk
2 Solenoid return spring
3 Solenoid armature
4 Actuating arm
5 Pivot pin clip
6 Drive end housing
7 Actuating arm pivot pin
8 Shim
9 C-clip
10 Thrust collar
11 Drive pinion and clutch assembly
12 Armature
13 Main motor casing
14 Through-bolt
15 Commutator end housing
16 Brush plate
17 Field coils
18 Permanent magnet

10.1 Exploded view of the Delco-Remy starter motor

10.3 Unscrew the through-bolts . . .

10.4 . . . and extract the two small screws – Delco-Remy starter motor

10.5 Lift the brush plate from the commutator – Delco-Remy starter motor

which hold the components of the starter motor assembly together **(see illustration)**.

4 Extract the two small screws which secure the commutator end housing to the brush plate, then lift off the commutator end housing **(see illustration)**.

5 Lift the brush retaining springs to remove the field brushes from the brush holders, then lift the brush plate from the commutator **(see illustration)**.

6 Remove the remaining springs and brushes from the brush holder.

7 If the brushes have worn to less than the specified minimum length, renew them as a set. To renew the brushes, the leads must be unsoldered from their terminals, and the new brushes must be soldered in place.

8 Clean the brush holder assembly, and wipe the commutator with a petrol-moistened cloth. If the commutator is dirty, it may be

cleaned with fine glass paper, then wiped with the cloth.

9 Check that the brush retaining springs provide adequate pressure on the brushes to maintain good contact with the commutator. Renew any worn springs.

10 Refit the brushes to the brush holder, and refit the retaining springs. To aid refitting of the brush holder assembly, the brushes can be retained in position using a socket or suitable tube of approximately 38.0 mm diameter.

11 Slide the brush holder over the commutator and, where applicable, withdraw the socket or tube.

12 Fit the commutator end housing, ensuring that the marks made on the end housing and the main motor casing are aligned.

13 Fit the two screws securing the end housing to the brush plate.

14 Refit and tighten the two through-bolts.

15 Refit the starter motor as described in Section 9.

Valeo starter motor

16 With the starter motor removed from the vehicle as described in Section 9 and cleaned, proceed as follows.

17 Unscrew the two securing nuts, and withdraw the rear cover from the starter motor **(see illustration)**.

18 Using a suitable screwdriver, lever the brush spring from the brush plate. Recover the insulator plates from under the ends of the spring **(see illustrations)**.

19 Lift the negative brush wiring terminal from the stud on the brush plate, and lift the positive brush terminal from the insulator in the motor body **(see illustrations)**.

20 Lift the brushes from the brush plate. Note the locations of the brushes to ensure correct reassembly **(see illustration)**.

10.17 Removing the rear cover – Valeo starter motor

10.18a Lever the brush spring from the brush plate . . .

10.18b . . . and recover the insulator plates – Valeo starter motor

10.19a Lift the negative brush terminal from the stud . . .

10.19b . . . and the positive brush terminal (arrowed) from the insulator – Valeo starter motor

10.20 Lifting a brush from the brush plate – Valeo starter motor

10.23 Remove the brush plate to enable cleaning of the commutator (arrowed) – Valeo starter motor

10.27 Refitting the brush spring – Valeo starter motor

21 If the brushes have worn to less than the minimum specified length, they must be renewed.

22 If the positive brush is to be renewed, it must be unsoldered from the terminal on the solenoid wiring.

23 If desired, the brush plate can be lifted from the motor to enable the commutator to be cleaned **(see illustration)**. Clean the brush plate assembly, and wipe the commutator with a petrol-moistened cloth. If the commutator is very dirty, it may be cleaned with fine glass paper, then wiped with the cloth.

24 Check that the brush retaining spring provides adequate pressure on the brushes to maintain good contact with the commutator. Renew the spring if it is worn.

25 Commence refitting by refitting the brush plate (where applicable), and placing the brushes in position in the brush plate.

26 Locate the negative brush wiring terminal over the stud on the brush plate, and locate the positive brush terminal in the insulator in the motor body.

27 Fit the insulator plates to the ends of the brushes, then fit the brush spring **(see illustration)**.

28 Ensure that the insulator is in place in the wiring grommet cut-out in the motor rear cover, then refit the cover to the motor.

29 Refit the rear cover securing nuts.

30 Refit the starter motor as described in Section 9.

11 Ignition switch – removal and refitting

The switch is integral with the steering column lock, and removal and refitting is described in Chapter 10.

12 Oil pressure warning light switch – removal and refitting

Removal

1 On SOHC engines, and 1.4 and 1.6 litre DOHC engines, the switch is screwed into the end of the oil pump, on the inlet manifold side of the engine **(see illustration)**. Access is most easily obtained from underneath the vehicle. On 1.0 and 1.2 litre DOHC engines, the switch is screwed into the front right-hand side of the cylinder head **(see illustration)**.

2 Disconnect the battery negative terminal (refer to *Disconnecting the battery* in the Reference Chapter).

3 Disconnect the wiring from the switch.

4 Place a suitable container under the switch, to catch the oil which will be released as the switch is removed.

5 Using a suitable spanner, unscrew the switch. Be prepared for oil spillage, and plug the hole in the oil pump immediately, to minimise oil loss and prevent dirt ingress.

Refitting

6 Refitting is a reversal of removal. On completion, check and if necessary top-up the engine oil level as described in *Weekly checks*.

12.1a Oil pressure warning light switch location (arrowed) – SOHC engines, and 1.4 and 1.6 litre DOHC engines

12.1b Oil pressure warning light switch location (arrowed) – 1.0 and 1.2 litre DOHC engines

Chapter 5 Part B:
Ignition system

Contents

Degrees of difficulty

Easy, suitable for novice with little experience		**Fairly easy,** suitable for beginner with some experience		**Fairly difficult,** suitable for competent DIY mechanic		**Difficult,** suitable for experienced DIY mechanic		**Very difficult,** suitable for expert DIY or professional	

Specifications

General

System type	Distributorless ignition system (DIS)
System application:	
SOHC engines	GM Multec
DOHC engines:	
1.0 and 1.2 litre engines	Bosch Motronic M 1.5.5
1.4 and 1.6 litre engines	GM Multec
Location of No 1 cylinder	Timing belt or timing chain end of engine
Firing order:	
All except 1.0 litre engines	1-3-4-2
1.0 litre engines	1-2-3

Torque wrench settings	Nm	lbf ft
DIS module-to-mounting plate bolts	8	6
DIS module mounting plate-to-camshaft housing bolts	12	9
Knock sensor body to cylinder block	13	10
Knock sensor retaining bolt	20	15
Spark plugs	25	18

1 General information and precautions

Ignition system function

The ignition system is responsible for igniting the air/fuel mixture in each cylinder at the correct moment, in relation to engine speed and load.

The ignition system is based on feeding low-tension voltage from the battery to the coil, where it is converted into high-tension voltage. The high-tension voltage is powerful enough to jump the spark plug gap in the cylinders many times a second under high compression pressures, providing that the system is in good condition.

The low-tension (or primary) circuit consists of the following:

a) The battery.
b) The lead to the ignition switch.
c) The leads from the ignition switch to the DIS module, to the electronic control unit, and to the low-tension coil windings (integral with the DIS module).

The high-tension (or secondary) circuit consists of the following:

a) The high-tension (HT) coil windings (integral with the DIS module).
b) The HT leads (or module connectors) from the DIS module to the spark plugs.
c) The spark plugs.

The system functions in the following manner. Current flowing through the low-tension coil windings produces a magnetic field around the high-tension windings. The electronic control unit produces a signal used to switch off the low-tension circuit.

The subsequent collapse of the magnetic field over the high-tension windings produces a high-tension voltage, which is then fed directly from the coil to the relevant spark plug(s). The low-tension circuit is automatically switched on again by the electronic control unit, to allow the magnetic field to build up again before the firing of the next spark plug(s). The ignition is advanced and retarded automatically, to ensure that the spark occurs at the correct instant in relation to the engine speed and load.

Multec DIS (Distributorless Ignition System)

This system is fitted to models with 1.2 SOHC, 1.4 and 1.6 litre engines.

The system is under the overall control of the Multec electronic control unit, which controls both the ignition and fuel injection systems. The system comprises various sensors (whose inputs also provide data to control the fuel injection system), and the Multec electronic control unit, in addition to the DIS module and spark plugs. Details of the system sensors and the electronic control unit are given in Chapter 4B.

The DIS module is attached to the camshaft housing in the position normally occupied by the distributor, and consists of two ignition coils and an electronic control module, housed in a common casing. Each ignition coil supplies two spark plugs with HT voltage – thus, one spark is provided in a cylinder with its piston on the compression stroke, and one in a cylinder with its piston on the exhaust stroke. This results in a 'wasted spark' being supplied to one cylinder during each ignition cycle, but this has no detrimental effect. This system has the advantage that there are no moving parts – therefore there is no wear, and the system is largely maintenance-free.

Information on crankshaft position, and engine speed and load is supplied to the Multec electronic control unit via inputs from the various system sensors (see Chapter 4B).

The electronic control unit selects the optimum ignition advance setting based on the information received from the various sensors. The degree of advance can thus be constantly varied to suit the prevailing engine operating conditions.

Motronic M 1.5.5 DIS (Distributorless Ignition System)

This system is fitted to models with 1.0 and 1.2 litre DOHC engines (see *Vehicle identification* for details of engine code locations).

The system is under the overall control of the Motronic electronic control unit, which controls both the ignition and fuel injection systems. The system comprises various sensors (whose inputs also provide data to

control the fuel injection system), and the Motronic electronic control unit, in addition to the DIS module and spark plugs. Details of the system sensors and the electronic control unit are given in Chapter 4A.

The DIS module is located centrally on the camshaft cover directly over the spark plugs. The module contains a separate ignition coil for each cylinder which is integral with the spark plug cap, and connected directly to the relevant spark plug. This removes the need for any HT leads connecting the coils to the plugs.

Information on crankshaft position, cylinder identification, and engine speed and load is supplied to the Motronic electronic control unit via inputs from the various system sensors (see Chapter 4A).

The electronic control unit selects the optimum ignition advance setting based on the information received from the various sensors, and fires the relevant ignition coil accordingly. The degree of advance can thus be constantly varied to suit the prevailing engine operating conditions.

2 Ignition system – testing

Warning: The HT voltage generated by an electronic ignition system is extremely high and, in certain circumstances, could prove fatal. Take care to avoid receiving electric shocks from the HT side of the ignition system. Do not handle HT leads, or touch the DIS module, when the engine is running. If tracing faults in the HT circuit, use well-insulated tools to manipulate live leads. Persons with surgically-implanted cardiac pacemaker devices should keep well clear of the ignition circuits, components and test equipment.

General

1 The components of the DIS system are normally very reliable; most faults are far more likely to be due to loose or dirty connections, or to 'tracking' of HT voltage due to dirt, dampness or damaged insulation, than to the failure of any of the system components. **Always** check all wiring thoroughly before condemning an electrical component, and work methodically to eliminate all other possibilities before deciding that a particular component is faulty.

2 The practice of checking for a spark by holding the live end of an HT lead a short distance away from the engine is **not** recommended – not only is there a high risk of a powerful electric shock, but the DIS module or electronic control unit may be damaged.

3 Extreme care should be taken if attempts are to be made to test the system, as the electronic control unit is very sensitive and, if damaged, may prove very costly to renew.

4 Unless the correct special test equipment is available, entrust testing and fault diagnosis to a Vauxhall/Opel dealer. It is far better to pay the labour charges involved in having the vehicle checked by someone suitably qualified, than to risk damage to the system or yourself. The engine management system has a self-diagnostic function, and any problems with the system are stored as fault codes, which can be read using suitable specialist diagnostic equipment. Brief details are given in Chapters 4A and 4B.

Engine fails to start

5 If the engine either will not turn over at all, or only turns over very slowly, check the battery and starter motor. Connect a voltmeter across the battery terminals (meter positive probe to battery positive terminal). Disconnect the wiring plug from the DIS module, then note the voltage reading obtained while turning over the engine on the starter for a few seconds. If the reading obtained is less than approximately 8 volts, check the battery, starter motor and charging system (see Chapter 5A).

6 Testing of the ignition LT and HT circuits can only be carried out safely and effectively using special test equipment, and should be entrusted to a Vauxhall/Opel dealer.

Engine misfires

7 Misfires are usually the result of partial or temporary failures in the system components, and the possible causes are too numerous to be eliminated without the use of special test equipment. The ignition system wiring and the spark plugs can be checked for signs of obvious faults as described in the following paragraphs, but if these checks do not reveal the source of the problem, take the vehicle to a Vauxhall/Opel dealer, who will be able to test the full engine management system using the appropriate equipment.

8 An irregular misfire suggests a loose or dirty connection. With the ignition switched off, check the security and condition of the DIS module wiring, and the HT leads (where applicable).

9 Regular misfiring is most likely to be due to a fault in the HT leads (where applicable) or spark plugs. Check that the HT leads are clean and dry. Check the leads themselves and the spark plugs (by substitution if necessary). Renew the spark plugs as a matter of course if there is any doubt about their condition (refer to Chapter 1 for details of checking spark plugs).

3 DIS module – testing, removal and refitting

Testing

1 Testing of the DIS module can only be carried out safely, and without the risk of

3.4 Disconnecting the DIS module wiring plug – SOHC engine

3.5 HT lead cylinder number identification marks (1) and DIS module securing screws (2) – SOHC engine

3.9 Release the DIS module cover and remove it toward the transmission end of the engine – 1.2 litre DOHC engine

damage to the module, using the appropriate special test equipment. Testing should therefore be entrusted to a Vauxhall/Opel dealer.

Removal

1.2 SOHC, 1.4 and 1.6 litre engines

2 The DIS module is mounted on the left-hand end of the camshaft housing. For improved access on DOHC engines, remove the secondary air injection pump assembly as described in Chapter 4C.
3 Disconnect the battery negative terminal (refer to *Disconnecting the battery* in the Reference Chapter).
4 Disconnect the module wiring plug **(see illustration)**.
5 Disconnect the HT leads from the module, noting their locations to ensure correct refitting. The HT lead cylinder numbers are stamped into the module casing **(see illustration)**.
6 Unscrew the three Torx-type securing screws, and remove the module from its mounting plate.

1.0 and 1.2 litre DOHC engines

7 The DIS module is mounted in the centre of the camshaft cover, directly above the spark plugs.
8 Disconnect the battery negative terminal (refer to *Disconnecting the battery* in the Reference Chapter).
9 Release the DIS module cover and remove

it toward the transmission end of the engine **(see illustration)**.
10 Disconnect the module wiring plug **(see illustration)**.
11 Undo the two module retaining screws, then lift the DIS module upwards and off the spark plugs **(see illustration)**. If necessary, the module may be very carefully eased upwards using a screwdriver. Take care to keep the module level as it is released from the spark plugs to avoid damage to the module connectors and the upper ceramic part of the spark plugs.

Refitting

12 Refitting is a reversal of removal.

4 Knock control system – general information

Note: *For details of engine code locations, refer to 'Vehicle identification'.*

The knock control system forms part of the ignition system, and allows the ignition timing to be advanced to the point at which 'knocking' or 'pre-ignition' is about to occur. This contributes to improved engine efficiency and reduced exhaust emission levels, as it allows the engine to run as close as possible to the 'knock limit' (the point at which 'pre-ignition' or 'pinking' occurs) without the risk of engine damage. The ignition timing is set to a

pre-determined value (stored in the memory of the engine management electronic control unit), which is very close to the knock limit for the engine. Due to slight changes in the combustion process during varying engine operating conditions, and possible slight fuel irregularities, engine knock may occur, and this is detected and controlled by the knock control system.

The system comprises a knock sensor, a separate knock module (X 12 SZ and X 14 SZ engines only), and the Multec or Motronic engine management electronic control unit (see Chapter 4A or 4B). On all engines except X 12 SZ and X 14 SZ the knock module is an integral part of the engine management electronic control unit (ECU).

The knock sensor is located on the cylinder block, and contains a piezo-electric crystal, which has a resonance frequency which corresponds to the engine knock frequency. Mechanical vibrations in the cylinder block are converted by the sensor into an electrical signal. The output signal provided by the sensor increases with an increase in the vibrations in the cylinder block. If the signal increases beyond a preset limit, the sensor indicates the onset of 'knock' to the knock module.

The knock module acts as a signal processor, and modifies the signal produced by the sensor before providing an output to the ECU.

The ECU processes the signals received from the knock module, and retards the ignition timing to prevent knock. From the signals provided by other engine management sensors (see Chapter 4A or 4B), the ECU can determine the cylinder which fired most recently before the knocking occurred, and hence can trace the knocking to that particular cylinder. The ignition timing for the particular cylinder concerned is thus retarded ('selective knock control'), giving independent ignition timing control over all cylinders. Once knocking has been detected and prevented, the ignition timing is progressively advanced to the pre-determined value, or until knocking recurs. The system processes signals many times per second, and is able to react to changes sufficiently quickly to prevent engine

3.10 DIS module wiring plug – 1.2 litre DOHC engine

3.11 Undo the two retaining screws, then lift the DIS module upwards and off the spark plugs – 1.2 litre DOHC engine

damage, with no perceptible effect on engine performance.

If the system develops a fault, the ignition timing is automatically retarded by a pre-determined amount as a safety precaution, and this may be detected as a slight reduction in engine performance.

5 Knock control system components – removal and refitting

Knock sensor

Note: *When refitting the sensor, to ensure correct operation, it is essential to tighten the sensor to the specified torque. On engines where the sensor body is screwed into the cylinder block (rather than being secured by a retaining bolt) Vauxhall/Opel specify the use of tool KM-728 to achieve this. If this tool is not available, it will be necessary to obtain or improvise a suitable alternative.*

Removal

1 The sensor is located centrally at the rear of the cylinder block, below the inlet manifold **(see illustration)**.
2 Disconnect the battery negative terminal

5.5b Knock sensor wiring connector location – SOHC engine

5.1 Knock sensor location (arrowed) – viewed from underneath vehicle – SOHC engine

(refer to *Disconnecting the battery* in the Reference Chapter).
3 Access is most easily obtained from underneath the vehicle. Apply the handbrake, then jack up the front of the vehicle and support securely on axle stands (see *Jacking and vehicle support*).
4 On 1.0 and 1.2 litre DOHC engines, unbolt the inlet manifold support bracket from the manifold and cylinder block.
5 On 1.2 SOHC, 1.4 and 1.6 litre engines, separate the two halves of the sensor wiring connector, which is located on a bracket

5.11 Disconnecting the wiring plug from the knock control system module – 1.2 litre SOHC engine

5.5a Separating the two halves of the knock sensor wiring connector – SOHC engine

either next to the left-hand engine lifting bracket, or behind the inlet manifold **(see illustrations)**.
6 On 1.0 and 1.2 litre DOHC engines, disconnect the wiring connector from the knock sensor body.
7 Undo the sensor retaining bolt, or unscrew the sensor itself and remove it from the cylinder block.

Refitting

8 Refitting is a reversal of removal, but ensure that the sensor body itself, or its retaining bolt is tightened to the specified torque, bearing in mind the note at the beginning of this Section.

Knock control system module
Removal

9 The module is located on a bracket attached to the left-hand side of the engine compartment, in front of the suspension strut turret.
10 Disconnect the battery negative terminal (refer to *Disconnecting the battery* in the Reference Chapter).
11 Disconnect the module wiring plug **(see illustration)**.
12 Remove the two securing screws, and withdraw the module from its bracket.
Refitting
13 Refitting is a reversal of removal.

Chapter 6
Clutch

Contents

Degrees of difficulty

| **Easy,** suitable for novice with little experience | | **Fairly easy,** suitable for beginner with some experience | | **Fairly difficult,** suitable for competent DIY mechanic | | **Difficult,** suitable for experienced DIY mechanic | | **Very difficult,** suitable for expert DIY or professional | |

Specifications

General
Type . . . .   Single dry plate, cable-operated

Clutch disc
Diameter:
    1.4 and 1.6 litre DOHC engines . . . .   200.0 mm
     All other engines . . . .   190.0 mm
Lining thickness (new – all models) . . . .   3.5 mm

Torque wrench settings	Nm	lbf ft
Clutch bellhousing cover plate bolts	7	5
Clutch cover-to-flywheel bolts	15	11
Clutch release fork-to-pivot shaft bolt	35	26

2.2a Measuring the length of threaded rod protruding through the plastic block at the end of the clutch cable . . .

2.2b . . . or protruding through the end of the damper block (arrowed) on certain later models

2.3 Remove the clip (1) from the threaded rod, slide the threaded rod (2) from the release arm, and pull the assembly from the lug (3)

1 General information

All manual gearbox models are fitted with a single dry plate clutch, which consists of five main components; friction disc, pressure plate, diaphragm spring, cover and release bearing.

The friction disc is free to slide along the splines of the gearbox input shaft, and is held in position between the flywheel and the pressure plate by the pressure exerted on the pressure plate by the diaphragm spring. Friction lining material is riveted to both sides of the friction disc, and spring cushioning between the friction linings and the hub absorbs transmission shocks, and helps to ensure a smooth take-up of power as the clutch is engaged.

The diaphragm spring is mounted on pins, and is held in place in the cover by annular fulcrum rings.

The release bearing is located on a guide sleeve at the front of the gearbox. The bearing is free to slide on the sleeve, under the action of the release arm, which pivots inside the clutch bellhousing.

The release arm is operated by the clutch pedal, via a cable. As wear takes place on the friction disc over a period of time, the clutch pedal will rise progressively, relative to its original position. Cable adjustment should be periodically checked as described in Chapter 1.

When the clutch pedal is depressed, the release arm is actuated by means of the cable. The release arm pushes the release bearing to bear against the centre of the diaphragm spring, thus pushing the centre of the diaphragm spring inwards. The diaphragm spring acts against the fulcrum rings in the cover. As the centre of the spring is pushed in, the outside of the spring is pushed out, so allowing the pressure plate to move backwards away from the friction disc.

When the clutch pedal is released, the diaphragm spring forces the pressure plate into contact with the friction linings on the friction disc, and simultaneously pushes the friction disc forwards on its splines, forcing it against the flywheel. The friction disc is now firmly sandwiched between the pressure plate and the flywheel, and drive is taken up.

2 Clutch cable – removal and refitting

Removal

1 Depending on model, to improve access to the clutch cable at the gearbox end, it may be beneficial to release the power steering fluid reservoir from its clamp and move it to one side, or remove the secondary air injection components as described in Chapter 4C.

2 Working in the engine compartment, measure the length of the threaded rod protruding through the plastic block at the release arm end of the cable (see illustration). This will enable approximate pre-setting of the cable when refitting. On certain later models a damper block is fitted to the end of the cable (see illustration). On these models, measure the length of threaded rod protruding through the end of the damper block.

3 Remove the clip from the threaded rod at the release arm, then slide the rod from the release arm (see illustration). Push the release arm towards the engine; if necessary, slacken the cable adjuster to aid removal.

4 Pull the cable assembly from the lug on the clutch bellhousing.

5 From inside the car, disconnect the cable end from the plastic segment at the top of the pedal. Access is limited, and it may prove easier to remove the clutch pedal, as described in Section 3, before disconnecting the cable.

6 The cable assembly can now be withdrawn into the engine compartment, by pulling it through the bulkhead. Take care not to damage the bulkhead grommet as the cable is withdrawn. Unclip the cable from any support brackets, and take note of the cable routing to aid refitting.

Refitting

7 Refitting is a reversal of removal, bearing in mind the following points:
  a) Ensure that the cable is routed as noted before removal.
  b) Position the threaded rod so that the length of thread protruding through the plastic block, or damper block is as noted before removal, then adjust the cable as described in Chapter 1.
  c) Ensure that the bulkhead grommet is correctly seated.
  d) Refit any components removed for access.

3 Clutch pedal – removal and refitting

Removal

1 Proceed as described in paragraphs 1 to 4 in the previous Section. Then, working in the driver's footwell, remove the locking clip from the right-hand end of the clutch pedal pivot shaft, then unscrew the pedal retaining nut and recover the washer(s).

2 Push the pivot shaft out of the pedal bracket (to the left), then lower the pedal and return spring. Note the position of any washers and/or spacers on the pivot shaft, so that they can be refitted in their original positions.

3 Disconnect the cable end from the pedal, and withdraw the pedal and return spring from the vehicle (see illustration).

3.3 Clutch pedal pivot components

Refitting

4 Refitting is a reversal of removal, but before inserting the pedal pivot shaft, smear the surface with a little molybdenum disulphide grease.

5 On completion, adjust the clutch cable if necessary, as described in Chapter 1.

---

4 Clutch assembly – removal, inspection and refitting

4.3 Stamped mark on flywheel (arrowed) aligned with notch in clutch cover

4.4 With all the bolts removed, lift off the clutch assembly

> ⚠ **Warning: Dust created by clutch wear (which gets deposited on the clutch components) may contain asbestos, which is a health hazard. DO NOT blow it out with compressed air, or inhale any of it. DO NOT use petrol (or petroleum-based solvents) to clean off the dust. Brake system cleaner or methylated spirit should be used to flush the dust into a suitable receptacle. After the clutch components are wiped clean with rags, dispose of the contaminated rags and cleaner in a sealed, marked container.**

Removal

1 Access to the clutch can be obtained by removing the gearbox (Chapter 7A) or the complete engine/gearbox assembly, and then separating the gearbox from the engine after removal (Chapter 2D or 2E).

2 With the gearbox detached from the engine, proceed as follows.

3 Where applicable (and if the original clutch is to be refitted), note the position of the mark on the flywheel which aligns with the notch in the rim of the clutch cover, then progressively unscrew the six bolts and spring washers which secure the clutch cover to the flywheel **(see illustration)**.

4 With all the bolts removed, lift off the clutch assembly **(see illustration)**. Be prepared to catch the friction disc as the cover assembly is lifted from the flywheel, and note which way round the friction disc is fitted. The greater-projecting side of the hub should face away from the flywheel.

Inspection

5 With the clutch assembly removed, clean off all traces of dust using a dry cloth. Although most friction discs now have asbestos-free linings, some do not, and it is wise to take suitable precautions; *asbestos dust is harmful, and must not be inhaled.*

6 Examine the linings of the clutch disc for wear and loose rivets, and the disc for distortion, cracks, broken torsion springs and worn splines. The surface of the friction linings may be highly glazed, but, as long as the friction material pattern can be clearly seen, this is satisfactory. If there is any sign of oil contamination, indicated by a continuous, or patchy, shiny black discolouration, the disc must be renewed. The source of the

contamination must be traced and rectified before fitting new clutch components; typically, a leaking crankshaft oil seal or gearbox input shaft oil seal – or both – will be to blame (renewal procedures are given in Chapters 2A, 2B or 2C, and 7A respectively). The disc must also be renewed if the lining thickness has worn down to, or just above, the level of the rivet heads.

7 Check the machined faces of the flywheel and pressure plate. If either is grooved, or heavily scored, renewal is necessary. The pressure plate must also be renewed if any cracks are apparent, if the diaphragm spring is damaged, or its pressure suspect.

8 With the clutch removed, it is advisable to check the condition of the release bearing, as described in Section 5.

Refitting

9 It is important to ensure that no oil or grease gets onto the friction disc linings, or the pressure plate and flywheel faces. It is advisable to refit the clutch assembly with clean hands, and to wipe down the pressure plate and flywheel faces with a clean rag before assembly begins.

10 Apply a smear of molybdenum disulphide grease to the splines of the friction disc hub, then offer the disc to the flywheel, with the greater-projecting side of the hub facing away from the flywheel **(see illustration)**. Hold the friction disc against the flywheel while the cover/pressure plate assembly is offered into position.

11 Fit the clutch cover assembly, where

applicable aligning the mark on the flywheel with the notch in the rim of the clutch cover. Insert the six bolts and spring washers, and tighten them finger-tight, so that the friction disc is gripped, but can still be moved.

12 The friction disc must now be centralised, so that when the engine and gearbox are mated, the gearbox input shaft splines will pass through the splines in the friction disc hub.

13 Centralisation can be carried out by inserting a round bar or a long screwdriver through the hole in the centre of the friction disc, so that the end of the bar rests in the spigot in the centre of the crankshaft **(see illustration)**. Where possible, use a blunt instrument – if a screwdriver or similar is used, wrap tape around the blade to prevent damage to the bearing surface. Moving the bar/screwdriver sideways or up-and-down as necessary, move the friction disc as necessary to achieve centralisation. With the bar removed, view the friction disc hub in relation to the hole in the centre of the crankshaft and the circle created by the ends of the diaphragm spring fingers. When the hub appears exactly in the centre, all is correct. Alternatively, if a suitable clutch alignment tool can be obtained, this will eliminate all the guesswork, and obviate the need for visual alignment. Note, however, that on some engines, the diameter of the crankshaft spigot is larger than the diameter of the friction disc hub, and not all commercially available clutch alignment tools will be suitable.

4.10 Place the friction disc on the flywheel, with the greater-projecting side of the hub facing away from the flywheel

4.13 Centralising the clutch friction disc using a screwdriver

14 Tighten the cover retaining bolts gradually in a diagonal sequence to the specified torque. Remove the alignment tool (if used).

15 Refit the engine or the gearbox, as described in the relevant Chapter.

16 On completion, check the clutch cable adjustment, as described in Chapter 1.

5 Clutch release bearing – removal, inspection and refitting

Note: *Refer to the note and warning at the beginning of Section 4 before proceeding.*

Removal

1 The gearbox must be removed for access to the release bearing. Unless the complete engine/gearbox assembly is to be removed from the vehicle and separated for major overhaul (see Chapter 2D or 2E), access to the clutch is most easily obtained by removing the gearbox, as described in Chapter 7A.

2 Unscrew the clamp bolt securing the release fork to the release arm pivot shaft.

3 Pull the release arm pivot shaft up and out of the bellhousing, then withdraw the release fork and the bearing. Where necessary, slide the bearing from the release fork, and where applicable, pull the bearing from the plastic collar.

4 If desired, the gearbox input shaft oil seal can be renewed after removing the release bearing guide sleeve, as described in Chapter 7A.

Inspection

5 Spin the release bearing, and check it for excessive roughness. Hold the outer race, and attempt to move it laterally against the inner race. If any excessive movement or roughness is evident, renew the bearing. If a new clutch has been fitted, it is wise to renew the release bearing as a matter of course.

6 The nylon bushes supporting the release arm pivot shaft can be renewed if necessary, by tapping them from their lugs in the bellhousing using a suitable drift. Drive the new bushes into position, ensuring that their locating tabs engage with the slots in the bellhousing lugs.

Refitting

7 Refitting of the release bearing and arm is a reversal of the removal procedure, bearing in mind the following points:

a) *Lightly smear the inner surfaces of the release arm pivot bushes, and the outer surfaces of the release bearing guide sleeve, with molybdenum disulphide grease.*

b) *Where applicable, fit the release bearing to the plastic collar, then fit the release bearing and fork together, and tighten the release fork clamp bolt to the specified torque.*

c) *Refit the gearbox as described in Chapter 7A, or the engine/gearbox assembly as described in Chapter 2D or 2E, as applicable.*

d) *On completion, check the clutch cable adjustment as described in Chapter 1.*

Chapter 7 Part A:
Manual gearbox

Contents

Degrees of difficulty

Easy, suitable for novice with little experience	**Fairly easy,** suitable for beginner with some experience	**Fairly difficult,** suitable for competent DIY mechanic	**Difficult,** suitable for experienced DIY mechanic	**Very difficult,** suitable for expert DIY or professional

Specifications

General

Type	Five forward speeds and one reverse, synchromesh on all forward gears. Integral differential

Manufacturer's designation:
1.0 and 1.2 litre DOHC engine	F 13/5 CR
1.2 litre SOHC	F 13/5 CR or F 13/5 WR
1.4 litre SOHC multi-point fuel injection engine	F 13/5 CR or F 15/5 CR
1.4 litre SOHC single-point fuel injection engine	F 13/5 WR
1.4 litre DOHC engine	F 13/5 CR, F 15/5 CR or F 17/5 CR
1.6 litre DOHC engine	F 15/5 CR or F 17/5 CR

Gear ratios

F 13/5 WR gearbox:
1st	3.73:1
2nd	1.96:1
3rd	1.31:1
4th	0.95:1
5th	0.76:1
Reverse	3.31:1

F 13/5 CR, F 15/5 CR and F 17/5 CR gearbox:
1st	3.73:1
2nd	2.14:1
3rd	1.41:1
4th	1.12:1
5th	0.89:1
Reverse	3.31:1

Final drive ratios (typical)

F 13/5 WR gearbox	3.94:1 or 4.18:1
F 13/5 CR and F 15/5 CR gearboxes	3.74:1 or 3.94:1
F 17/5 CR gearbox	3.74:1

Torque wrench settings

	Nm	lbf ft
Clutch bellhousing cover plate bolts	7	5
Clutch release bearing guide sleeve bolts	5	4
Differential housing cover plate bolts:		
Steel plate	30	22
Alloy plate	18	13
Engine/gearbox mountings:		
Left-hand:		
Gearbox bracket-to-gearbox bolts	60	44
Gearbox bracket-to-mounting block bolts	60	44
Mounting block-to-body bolts*	65	48
Rear:		
Gearbox bracket-to-gearbox bolts	70	52
Gearbox bracket-to-mounting block bolts	65	48
Mounting block-to-body bolts	65	48
Engine-to-gearbox bolts	60	44
Gearchange lever housing-to-floorpan bolts	6	4
Speedometer drivegear retaining plate bolt	4	3
Reversing light switch	20	15

Use thread-locking compound.

1 General information

One of three different CR (close ratio) or WR (wide ratio) manual gearboxes may be fitted, depending on model and engine fitted (see Specifications); there are only minor internal differences between the gearbox types.

Drive from the clutch is transmitted to the input shaft, which runs in parallel with the mainshaft. The input shaft and mainshaft gears are in constant mesh, and selection of gears is by sliding synchromesh hubs, which lock the appropriate mainshaft gear to the mainshaft.

The 5th speed gear components are located in an extension housing at the end of the gearbox.

Reverse gear is obtained by sliding an idler gear into mesh with two straight-cut gears on the input shaft and mainshaft.

The differential is mounted in the main gearbox casing, and drive is transmitted to the differential by a pinion gear on the end of the mainshaft. The inboard ends of the driveshafts locate directly into the differential. The gearbox and differential unit share the same lubricating oil.

Gear selection is by a floor-mounted gearchange lever, via a remote control linkage.

2 Gearbox oil – draining and refilling

Draining

1 Place a suitable container under the differential cover plate. Unscrew the securing bolts and withdraw the cover plate, allowing the gearbox oil to drain into the container (see illustration).

2 Refit the differential cover plate, and tighten the securing bolts when the oil has drained.

Refilling

3 Proceed as described for the gearbox oil level check in Chapter 1.

3 Gearchange linkage/mechanism – adjustment

Note: *According to gearbox type (see text), a new plug should be fitted to the gear linkage adjuster hole in the gear selector housing on completion of adjustment.*

1 On models equipped with secondary air injection, remove the necessary air injection components as described in Chapter 4C, for access to the top of the gearbox.

2 Observe the gear selector housing on the top of the gearbox, adjacent to the clutch cable. On the front or rear of the housing there should be a spring-loaded adjustment plunger (usually coloured orange) protruding from the edge of the housing (see illustration). If an adjustment plunger is not present, observe the rear of the housing where there will be a plastic plug. Extract this plug, if present, from the adjuster hole (see illustration). If necessary, for improved access to the gear selector housing, remove the battery with reference to Chapter 5A.

2.1 Differential cover plate securing bolts (arrowed)

3.2a Spring-loaded type gearchange linkage adjustment plunger (arrowed)

3.2b Extract the plastic plug (where fitted) from the adjuster hole

3.4 Gear selector rod-to-clamp sleeve clamp nut (arrowed)

3.5 Insert a twist drill to engage with the selector lever – viewed with gearbox removed for clarity

3.7 Using a pin punch to lock the gearchange lever in position

3 Jack up the front of the vehicle and support securely on axle stands (see *Jacking and vehicle support*).

4 Working underneath the vehicle, loosen the clamp nut and bolt securing the gear selector rod to the clamp sleeve **(see illustration)**.

5 Looking towards the engine compartment bulkhead, with the selector rod in the neutral plane, grip the gear selector rod, and twist it clockwise. If the housing has an adjustment plunger, move the selector rod back-and-forth slightly until the plunger can be pushed fully into the housing to engage with a corresponding hole in the selector rod. Release the selector rod and the plunger should remain in engagement. Alternatively, insert a 4.5 mm diameter twist drill through the adjuster hole at the rear of the gear selector housing, to engage with the hole in the selector lever **(see illustration)**.

6 Working inside the vehicle, pull back on the front edge of the gearchange lever gaiter, and free its lower end from the centre console, to allow access to the base of the gearchange lever.

7 Move the gearchange lever to the neutral position in the 1st/2nd gear plane. Adjust the position of the lever until a suitable tool can be inserted through the holes in the base of the lever assembly and the lever housing to lock the lever in position **(see illustration)**.

8 Without moving the gearchange lever, tighten the clamp bolt and nut securing the gear selector rod to the clamp sleeve in the engine compartment.

9 Pull out the adjustment plunger, or remove the twist drill from the adjuster hole in the gear selector housing. Seal the hole with a new plug.

10 Refit the gearchange lever gaiter to the centre console.

11 Where applicable, refit the secondary air injection components as described in Chapter 4C.

12 Refit the battery (if removed), and reconnect the battery leads.

13 Finally check that all gears can be engaged easily, first with the engine off, then with the engine running.

4 Gearchange linkage/mechanism – removal, overhaul and refitting

Gearchange lever

Removal

1 Ensure that the lever is in neutral.

2 Pull back on the front edge of the gearchange lever gaiter, and free its lower end from the centre console to allow access to the base of the lever.

3 Release the clip from the base of the lever shaft, then withdraw the pivot pin, and lift out the lever **(see illustrations)**.

Overhaul

4 To renew the gearchange lever gaiter and/or the knob, proceed as follows. **Note:**

There is a strong possibility that the knob will be destroyed during the removal process.

5 On models with a plastic lever knob, immerse the knob in hot water (approximately 80°C) for a few minutes, then twist the knob and tap it from the lever. On models with a leather-covered lever knob, clamp the lever in a vice fitted with soft jaw protectors, and place an open-ended spanner under the metal insert at the bottom of the knob; tap the knob from the lever, using the spanner as an insulator to protect the knob.

6 If renewing the gaiter, slide the old gaiter from the lever, and fit the new one. Use a little liquid detergent (eg, washing-up liquid) to aid fitting if necessary.

7 Refit the knob (or fit the new knob, as applicable). When fitting a plastic knob, preheat it in hot water, as during removal. When fitting a leather-covered knob, preheat the metal insert at the base of the knob using a hair drier or hot-air gun. Ensure that the knob is fitted the correct way round.

Refitting

8 Refitting the lever is a reversal of removal.

Gearchange lever housing assembly

Removal

9 Working in the engine compartment, loosen the clamp bolt securing the gear selector rod to the clamp sleeve.

10 Remove the gearchange lever, as described previously in this Section.

4.3a Release the gearchange lever securing clip (arrowed) . . .

4.3b . . . then withdraw the pivot pin . . .

4.3c . . . and lift out the lever (viewed with centre console removed)

4.12 Two of the gearchange lever housing securing bolts (arrowed)

11 Remove the centre console, as described in Chapter 11.
12 Unscrew the four bolts securing the gearchange lever housing to the floorpan **(see illustration)**.
13 The housing and clamp sleeve can now be withdrawn. Pull the assembly towards the rear of the vehicle, to feed the clamp sleeve through the bulkhead. As the clamp sleeve is fed through the bulkhead, have an assistant remove the clamp from the end of the clamp sleeve in the engine compartment, to avoid damage to the rubber boot on the bulkhead.

Overhaul

14 If desired, the rubber boot can be renewed by pulling the old boot from the bulkhead, and pushing the new boot into position, ensuring that it is correctly seated.

5.1 Disconnecting the speedometer cable from the gearbox

4.18 Gear linkage universal joint pin retaining lug (1)

15 The clamp sleeve bush in the gearchange lever housing can be renewed after sliding the clamp sleeve from the housing. Prise the bush insert from the front of the housing, then prise the bush from the insert. Fit the new bush using a reversal of the removal procedure, but lubricate the inside of the bush with a little silicone grease.

Refitting

16 Refitting of the assembly is a reversal of removal, but before tightening the clamp bolt, adjust the gear selector linkage as described in Section 3.

Gear selector linkage

Removal

17 Ensure that the gearchange lever is in neutral.
18 Remove the securing pin (squeeze the two retaining lugs to release the pin), and separate the two sections of the linkage universal joint **(see illustration)**.
19 Loosen the clamp bolt securing the clamp sleeve to the linkage, and pull the clamp sleeve from the selector rod.
20 Release the spring clip, then pull the bellcrank pivot pin from the bracket on the rear engine/gearbox mounting.
21 Withdraw the linkage from the vehicle.

Overhaul

22 Check the linkage components for wear, and renew as necessary. The pivot bushes can be renewed by prising out the old bushes and pressing in the new, and the link can be renewed by pulling it from the balljoints. Further dismantling is not recommended.

Refitting

23 Refitting is a reversal of removal, but lubricate all moving components with a little grease and, before tightening the clamp bolt, adjust the gear selector linkage as described in Section 3.

5 Speedometer drive – removal and refitting

Removal

Note: *On later models the speedometer drive is replaced by an electronic vehicle speed sensor. The removal and refitting procedures are basically the same except that there is no speedometer cable or speedometer driven gear on the vehicle speed sensor.*

1 Unscrew the securing sleeve, and disconnect the speedometer cable from the top of the gearbox **(see illustration)**. If a vehicle speed sensor is fitted, disconnect the wiring connector from the sensor.
2 Unbolt the retaining plate, and withdraw the speedometer drive/vehicle speed sensor assembly **(see illustrations)**.
3 Where applicable, the speedometer driven gear can be withdrawn from its sleeve, in which case note the thrustwasher under the gear **(see illustration)**.

Refitting

4 If the driven gear has been removed from the sleeve, lubricate the gear shaft with a little silicone grease, then slide the gear into the sleeve, ensuring that the thrustwasher is in place on the gear shaft.
5 Inspect the O-ring seal on the sleeve, and renew if worn or damaged.
6 Further refitting is a reversal of removal.

5.2a Unbolt the retaining plate . . .

5.2b . . . and withdraw the speedometer drive assembly

5.3 Withdrawing the speedometer driven gear from its sleeve. Note thrustwasher (arrowed)

6.3 Prising out a differential side oil seal

6.4 Driving a new differential side oil seal into position

6.8a Withdraw the clutch release bearing guide sleeve . . .

6 Oil seals – renewal

Differential side (driveshaft) oil seals

1 Apply the handbrake, then jack up the front of the vehicle and support securely on axle stands (see *Jacking and vehicle support*). Remove the relevant front roadwheel.
2 Disconnect the inner end of the relevant driveshaft from the differential as described in Chapter 8. There is no need to disconnect the driveshaft from the swivel hub. Support the driveshaft by suspending it with wire or string – do not allow the driveshaft to hang down under its own weight, or the joints may be damaged.
3 Prise the now-exposed oil seal from the differential housing, using a screwdriver or similar instrument **(see illustration)**.
4 Smear the sealing lip of the new oil seal with a little gearbox oil, then using a metal tube or socket of suitable diameter, drive the new seal into the differential casing until the outer surface of the seal is flush with the outer surface of the differential casing **(see illustration)**.
5 Reconnect the driveshaft to the differential as described in Chapter 8.
6 Refit the roadwheel, then lower the vehicle to the ground.

Input shaft (clutch) oil seal

7 Remove the gearbox as described in Section 8.
8 Unscrew the securing bolts, and withdraw the clutch release bearing guide sleeve from the bellhousing. Recover the O-ring which fits between the guide sleeve and the bellhousing **(see illustrations)**.
9 Drive the old seal from the guide sleeve **(see illustration)**, and fit a new seal using a suitable tube or socket. Press the new seal into position – do not drive it in, as the seal is easily damaged.
10 Fill the space between the lips of the new seal with lithium-based grease, then refit the guide sleeve using a new O-ring. The O-ring should be fitted dry.
11 Refit the guide sleeve to the bellhousing, and tighten the securing bolts.
12 Refit the gearbox as described in Section 8.

7 Reversing light switch – testing, removal and refitting

Testing

1 The reversing light circuit is operated by a plunger-type switch, mounted in the front of the gearbox casing.
2 To test the switch, disconnect the wiring, and use a suitable meter or a battery-and-bulb test circuit to check for continuity between the switch terminals. Continuity should only exist when reverse gear is selected. If this is not the case, and there are no obvious breaks or other damage to the wires, the switch is faulty and must be renewed.

Removal

3 The reversing light switch is located in the front of the gearbox casing, and is accessible from the engine compartment.
4 Disconnect the battery negative terminal (refer to *Disconnecting the battery* in the Reference Chapter).
5 Disconnect the wiring from the switch, then unscrew the switch from the gearbox **(see illustration)**.

Refitting

6 Refitting is a reversal of removal.

8 Manual gearbox – removal and refitting

Note: *This is an involved procedure, and it may prove easier in many cases (particularly with DOHC engine models) to remove the gearbox complete with the engine as an assembly, as described in Chapter 2D or 2E. If removing the gearbox on its own, it is*

6.8b . . . and recover the O-ring

6.9 Driving the oil seal from the clutch release bearing guide sleeve

7.5 Disconnect the wiring from the reversing light switch (arrowed)

8.3a Slide the clutch cable from the release lever . . .

8.3b . . . and pull the cable support (1) from the bracket (2) on the gearbox casing

8.5 Speedometer cable connector (arrowed) – viewed with engine removed

suggested that this Section is read through thoroughly before commencing work. Suitable equipment will be required to support the engine and gearbox, and the help of an assistant will be required.

Removal

1 Disconnect the battery negative terminal (refer to *Disconnecting the battery* in the Reference Chapter).

2 On models equipped with secondary air injection, remove the necessary air injection components as described in Chapter 4C, for access to the top of the gearbox.

3 Remove the retaining clip (where applicable), then slide the clutch cable from the release lever, pushing the release lever back towards the bulkhead, if necessary, to allow the cable to be disconnected. Pull the cable support from the bracket on the

8.7a It may be necessary to move the coolant gallery (arrowed) . . .

gearbox casing, then move the cable to one side out of the way, taking note of its routing **(see illustrations)**.

4 Disconnect the wiring from the reversing light switch, located at the front of the gearbox, above the mounting bracket (see Section 7).

5 Disconnect the wiring from the vehicle speed sensor or, alternatively, unscrew the securing sleeve, and disconnect the speedometer cable from the top of the gearbox. Note that on certain models, the cable is in two sections, joined by a connector near the engine compartment bulkhead – in this case, it may be easier to separate the two cable sections at the connector, rather than to disconnect the cable from the gearbox **(see illustration)**.

6 On 1.4 and 1.6 litre DOHC engine models, to gain better access to the upper engine-to-gearbox bolts, proceed as follows:

a) Drain the cooling system as described in Chapter 1, then disconnect the coolant hoses from the side of the expansion tank. Remove the expansion tank securing nuts, then move the tank to allow the lower coolant hose to be disconnected. Withdraw the tank.

b) Remove the two securing screws, and withdraw the plastic shield from the camshaft cover.

c) Disconnect the HT leads from the spark plugs, using the tool provided (attached to one of the leads).

d) Disconnect the breather hose which runs across the HT leads at the left-hand end

of the cylinder head, to allow the HT leads to be moved clear of the engine.

e) Disconnect the wiring plug from the DIS ignition module, located at the left-hand end of the cylinder head. Unscrew the three securing bolts and remove the module, complete with the HT leads.

7 Unscrew and remove the three upper engine-to-gearbox bolts, noting the locations of any brackets secured by the bolts. On certain models (1.4 and 1.6 litre DOHC engine models in particular), the plastic coolant gallery may prevent access to the centre upper bolt **(see illustrations)** in which case, proceed as follows:

a) Drain the cooling system as described in Chapter 1 (if not already done), then disconnect the radiator hose from the front of the coolant gallery.

b) Remove the rear upper engine-to-gearbox bolt, which also secures the coolant gallery and a clutch cable bracket. Note that on DOHC engine models, access to this bolt is most easily obtained by reaching down through the hole in the battery tray.

c) Move the coolant gallery as necessary to enable access to the centre upper engine-to-gearbox bolt.

8 Apply the handbrake, then jack up the front of the vehicle, and support securely on axle stands (see *Jacking and vehicle support*). Note that the vehicle must be raised sufficiently high to enable the gearbox be withdrawn from under the front of the vehicle. Remove the roadwheels.

8.7b . . . to allow access to one of the engine-to-gearbox bolts

8.7c Oxygen sensor bracket . . .

8.7d . . . and coolant gallery and clutch cable brackets located on upper engine-to-gearbox bolts

8.9 Vauxhall/Opel tool No KM-263-B used to support engine

8.12 Removing the engine-to-gearbox blanking plate

8.13 Pull the selector tube (1) from the gear linkage (2)

9 The engine must now be supported. Ideally, the engine should be supported using chains suspended from a strong wooden or metal beam resting on blocks positioned securely in the channels at the sides of the engine compartment. A Vauxhall/Opel special tool is available for this purpose (see illustration). Alternatively, the engine can be supported using a suitable hoist and lifting tackle, but the hoist must be capable of supporting the engine with the front of the vehicle raised off the ground, leaving sufficient clearance to withdraw the gearbox from under the front of the vehicle (see previous paragraph). As a further alternative, the engine can be supported using a jack and interposed block of wood under the sump, but great care must be taken when removing the gearbox, not to move the engine off the jack – it is strongly recommended that the engine is additionally supported using a hoist or bar as described previously, to avoid any possibility of injury. Note that if a hoist is used to support the engine, a further hoist will be required to carry out removal of the gearbox safely. (The alternative to all this is to remove the engine and gearbox as an assembly, as described in Chapter 2D or 2E.)

10 With the engine supported, proceed as follows.

11 Where applicable, unbolt the earth strap from the end of the gearbox.

12 On engines with a steel sump, unscrew the securing bolts, and remove the engine-to-gearbox blanking plate from the bellhousing (see illustration).

13 Loosen the clamp nut and bolt securing the gear selector rod to the linkage, then pull the selector tube towards the engine compartment bulkhead to separate it from the linkage (see illustration).

14 On SOHC engine models, and 1.0 and 1.2 litre DOHC engine models, disconnect the exhaust front section from the manifold as described in Chapter 4A or 4B, and release the system from the forward rubber mountings – this will allow the engine to be lowered later in the procedure.

15 On 1.4 and 1.6 litre DOHC engine models, remove the exhaust front section as described in Chapter 4B.

16 Place a suitable container under the differential cover plate, then remove the securing bolts, and withdraw the cover plate to drain the gearbox oil. Refit the differential cover plate on completion of draining.

17 Remove the front anti-roll bar as described in Chapter 10.

18 Remove the left-hand front suspension lower arm and tie-bar as described in Chapter 10.

19 Disconnect the inner ends of the driveshafts from the gearbox as described in Chapter 8. There is no need to disconnect the driveshafts from the swivel hubs. Be prepared for oil spillage, and plug the openings in the gearbox, to prevent dirt ingress and further oil loss. Do not allow the driveshafts to hang down under their own weight, or the joints may be damaged – support the driveshafts with wire or string.

20 Support the gearbox with a trolley jack, with an interposed block of wood to spread the load. Ensure that the engine is adequately supported as described in paragraph 9.

21 Additionally, the gearbox should be supported from above, using a hoist. Fit a suitable strap around the gearbox casing, passing it through the hole in the battery tray (remove the battery as described in Chapter 5A, if not already done), and suspend the strap from the hoist (see illustration). This will enable the gearbox to be lowered safely during removal.

22 Remove the left-hand engine/gearbox mounting bracket completely, by unscrewing the two bolts securing the bracket to the rubber mounting, and the three bolts securing the mounting bracket to the gearbox (see illustration).

23 Remove the nut and through-bolt securing the rear engine/gearbox mounting bracket to the mounting on the body (see illustration).

24 Release the spring clip, then pull the gear linkage pivot pin from the bracket on the rear engine/gearbox mounting.

25 Remove the two bolts securing the rear engine/gearbox mounting bracket to the gearbox, and withdraw the mounting bracket.

26 Make a final check to ensure that all relevant wiring, hoses, etc, have been disconnected to facilitate gearbox removal. Note that on certain models, the wiring for the oxygen sensor may be secured to the lug on the gearbox with a cable-tie.

27 Using the lifting tackle, and the jack(s), lower the engine and gearbox slightly.

8.21 Strap passed through battery tray and around gearbox casing to support gearbox

8.22 Removing the left-hand engine/gearbox mounting bracket

8.23 Remove the nut and through-bolt securing the rear engine/gearbox mounting

8.28 Removing one of the lower engine-to-gearbox bolts

28 Unscrew and remove the remaining engine-to-gearbox bolts **(see illustration)**, noting the locations of any brackets secured by the bolts.

29 With the aid of an assistant, carefully separate the gearbox from the engine (use the hoist to take the weight of the gearbox). It may be necessary to rock the gearbox a little to release it from the engine. Take care not to allow the weight of the gearbox to hang on the input shaft as the gearbox is separated from the engine.

30 Lower the gearbox from the engine compartment, taking care not to damage surrounding components.

Refitting

31 Before refitting, check that the left-hand engine/gearbox mounting-to-body bolts rotate freely in their threaded holes in the body. If necessary, re-cut the threaded holes in the body using a suitable tap.

32 Commence refitting by positioning the gearbox under the front of the vehicle, supporting with the hoist and strap, and the trolley jack and interposed block of wood, as during removal.

33 Raise the gearbox sufficiently to enable the engine and gearbox to be mated together. Ensure that the gearbox input shaft engages correctly with the clutch friction disc as the gearbox is joined to the engine.

34 Refit the lower engine-to-gearbox bolts, but do not fully tighten them at this stage. Ensure that any brackets or clips noted during removal are in place on the bolts.

35 Coat the threads of the left-hand engine/gearbox mounting-to-body bolts with thread-locking compound, then raise the engine and gearbox sufficiently to enable the mounting bracket to be refitted.

36 Refit the left-hand engine/gearbox mounting, and tighten the mounting bolts to the specified torque.

37 Refit the rear engine/gearbox mounting bracket to the gearbox, and tighten the bolts to the specified torque.

38 Refit the through-bolt and nut securing the rear engine/gearbox mounting to the mounting on the body.

39 Refit the gear linkage to the bracket on the rear engine/gearbox mounting, and secure with the pivot pin.

40 The hoist and jack used to support the gearbox can now be withdrawn.

41 Tighten the lower engine-to-gearbox bolts to the specified torque.

42 Refit the left-hand front suspension lower arm and tie-bar as described in Chapter 10.

43 Refit the front anti-roll bar as described in Chapter 10.

44 Reconnect the inner ends of the driveshafts to the gearbox as described in Chapter 8.

45 Refit or reconnect the exhaust front section as described in Chapter 4A or 4B.

46 Reconnect the gear selector rod to the gear linkage, and adjust the linkage as described in Section 3.

47 On engines with a steel sump, refit the engine-to-gearbox blanking plate to the bellhousing.

48 Where applicable, reconnect the earth strap to the end of the gearbox.

49 Remove or disconnect the equipment used to support the engine, and lower the vehicle to the ground.

50 Refit and tighten the three upper engine-to-gearbox bolts (where necessary, gaining access as described during removal); ensure that the coolant gallery (where applicable) and any brackets noted during removal are in place on the bolts. Where applicable, reconnect the radiator hose to the coolant gallery.

51 On 1.4 and 1.6 litre DOHC engine models,

H23097

9.2a Exploded view of F 13/5 CR gearbox

refit the DIS module and HT leads, and the expansion tank, using a reversal of the removal procedure.

52 Where fitted, reconnect the speedometer cable to the gearbox, or reconnect the two sections of the cable, as applicable, with reference to Chapter 12. Alternatively, reconnect the wiring to the vehicle speed sensor.

53 Reconnect the reversing light switch wiring.

54 Reconnect the clutch cable to the release lever, and check the clutch cable adjustment as described in Chapter 1. Ensure that the cable is routed as noted during removal.

55 Where applicable, refit the secondary air injection components as described in Chapter 4C.

56 Where applicable, refill the cooling system as described in Chapter 1.

57 Refill the gearbox with oil as described in Section 2.

58 Refit the battery (if removed), then reconnect the battery terminals.

9 Manual gearbox overhaul – general information

1 The complete overhaul of a manual gearbox is a complicated task, requiring a number of special tools, and previous experience is a great help. It is therefore recommended that owners remove the gearbox themselves, if wished, but then either fit a new or reconditioned unit, or have the existing unit overhauled by a Vauxhall/Opel dealer or gearbox specialist.

2 The dismantling of the gearbox into its major assemblies is a reasonably straightforward operation, and can be carried out to enable an assessment of wear or damage to be made (suitable exploded views of the gearboxes are provided to assist owners who wish to do this) **(see illustrations)**. From this assessment, a decision can be taken on whether or not to proceed with a full overhaul. Note, however, that any overhaul work will require the dismantling and reassembly of many small and intricate assemblies, as well as taking several precise measurements to assess wear. This will require a number of special tools, and previous experience will prove invaluable. As a minimum, the following tools will be required:

a) *Internal and external circlip pliers.*
b) *A selection of pin punches.*
c) *A selection of Torx and splined bits.*
d) *A bearing puller.*
e) *A hydraulic press.*
f) *A slide hammer.*
g) *A selection of heat-sensitive marker pencils.*

3 While the *Fault finding* Section at the end of this manual should help to isolate most gearbox faults to enable a decision to be taken on what course of action to follow, remember that economic considerations may rule out an apparently-simple repair. For example, a common reason for gearbox dismantling is to renew the synchromesh units, wear or faults in these assemblies being indicated by noise when changing gear. Jumping out of gear or similar gear selection faults may be due to worn selector forks, or synchro-sleeves. General noise during operation may be due to worn bearings, shafts or gears. The cumulative cost of renewing all worn components may make it more economical to renew the gearbox complete.

4 To establish whether gearbox overhaul is economically viable, first establish the cost of a complete replacement gearbox, comparing the cost of a new unit with that of an exchange reconditioned unit (if available), or even a good secondhand unit (with a guarantee) from a vehicle breaker. Compare these costs with the likely cost of the replacement parts which will be required if the existing gearbox is overhauled; do not forget to include all items which must be renewed when they are disturbed, such as oil seals, O-rings, roll pins, circlips, snaprings, etc.

9.2b Exploded view of F 15/5 CR gearbox

Notes

Chapter 7 Part B:
Automatic transmission

Contents

Degrees of difficulty

| Easy, suitable for novice with little experience | Fairly easy, suitable for beginner with some experience | Fairly difficult, suitable for competent DIY mechanic | Difficult, suitable for experienced DIY mechanic | Very difficult, suitable for expert DIY or professional |

Specifications

General

Type .... Hydrodynamic torque converter with electronically-controlled mechanical lock-up system, two epicyclic gearsets giving four forward speeds and reverse, integral final drive. Gearchanging under full electronic control, with three 'driving' modes selectable

Manufacturer's designation .... AF 13

Gear ratios
1st	2.81:1
2nd	1.48:1
3rd	1.00:1
4th	0.74:1
Reverse	2.77:1
Final drive	4.12:1

Torque wrench settings

	Nm	lbf ft
Engine/transmission mountings:		
Left-hand:		
Mounting block-to-body bolts**	65	48
Transmission bracket-to-mounting block bolts	60	44
Transmission bracket-to-transmission bolts	60	44
Rear:		
Mounting block-to-body bolts	65	48
Transmission bracket-to-mounting block bolts	65	48
Transmission bracket-to-transmission bolts	70	52
Fluid cooler pipe union bolts	25	18
Selector lever housing nuts	8	6
Selector lever position switch actuating lever to selector lever shaft	8	6
Selector lever position switch to transmission	25	18
Torque converter-to-driveplate bolts*	50	37
Transmission bellhousing cover plate bolts	7	5
Transmission-to-engine bolts	60	44

*Use new bolts
**Use thread-locking compound

1.1 Cutaway view of the AF 13 automatic transmission

1 Gear assembly
2 Multi-disc brake
3 Multi-plate clutch
4 Multi-plate clutch
5 Multi-plate clutch
6 Freewheel assembly
7 Freewheel assembly
8 Multi-plate clutch
9 Differential
10 Brake band
11 Fluid pump
12 Torque converter

1.4 Automatic transmission electronic control system

1 Diagnostic plug
2 Brake light switch
3 Kickdown switch
4 Transmission input speed sensor
5 Speedometer cable or vehicle speed sensor connection
6 Economy/Sport mode switch
7 Winter mode switch
8 Automatic transmission electronic control unit
9 Engine management electronic control unit
10 Throttle position sensor
11 DIS ignition module
12 Selector lever position switch
13 Solenoid valve connection
14 Transmission output speed sensor

1 General information

1 A 4-speed fully-automatic transmission is available as an option on certain Corsa models. The transmission consists of a torque converter, an epicyclic geartrain and hydraulically-operated clutches and brakes. The differential is integral with the transmission, and is similar to that used in manual gearbox models **(see illustration)**.

2 The torque converter provides a fluid coupling between the engine and transmission which acts as an automatic 'clutch', and also provides a degree of torque multiplication when accelerating.

3 The epicyclic geartrain provides either one of the four forward gear ratios, or reverse gear, according to which of its component parts are held stationary or allowed to turn. The components of the geartrain are held or released by brakes and clutches, which are activated by a hydraulic control unit. A fluid pump within the transmission provides the necessary hydraulic pressure to operate the brakes and clutches.

4 The transmission is electronically-controlled, and three driving modes – 'Economy', 'Sport' and 'Winter' – are provided. The transmission electronic control unit (ECU) operates in conjunction with the engine management ECU to control the gearchanges. The transmission ECU receives information on transmission fluid temperature, throttle position, engine coolant temperature, and input-versus-output speed. The ECU controls the hydraulically-operated clutches and brakes via four solenoids. The control system can also retard the engine ignition timing, via the engine management ECU, to permit smoother gearchanges **(see illustration)**.

5 Due to the complexity of the automatic transmission, any repair or overhaul work must be entrusted to a Vauxhall/Opel dealer, who will have the necessary specialist equipment and knowledge for fault diagnosis and repair. Refer to the *Fault finding* section at the end of this manual for further information.

2 Selector cable – removal and refitting

Removal

1 Apply the handbrake, and ensure that the transmission selector lever is in position N.

2 Disconnect the battery negative terminal (refer to *Disconnecting the battery* in the Reference Chapter).

3 On models equipped with secondary air injection, remove the necessary air injection components as described in Chapter 4C, for access to the top of the transmission.

2.9 Release the selector cable end fitting (arrowed) from the selector lever ball stud, then depress the locking tags (1) and release the cable trunion from the housing

4 On right-hand drive models, remove the battery as described in Chapter 5A.

5 Carefully prise the selector cable end fitting from the ball stud on the selector lever position switch actuating lever.

6 Using a screwdriver, extract the retaining clip securing the selector cable trunion to the bracket on the transmission. Depress the two locking tags on the side of the trunion and release the cable from the bracket.

7 Remove the selector lever cover from the centre console, and disconnect the transmission Winter mode switch wiring connector.

8 Remove the centre console, as described in Chapter 11.

9 Using a screwdriver, release the selector cable end fitting from the ball stud on the selector lever (see illustration).

10 Depress the two locking tags on the side of the outer cable trunion and release the cable from the selector lever housing. Withdraw the cable from the housing.

Refitting

11 Refitting Is a reversal of the removal procedure.

3 Selector lever housing – removal and refitting

Removal

1 Apply the handbrake, and ensure that the transmission selector lever is in position N.

2 Disconnect the battery negative terminal (refer to *Disconnecting the battery* in the Reference Chapter).

3 Release the two catches on the side of the selector lever cover, lift the cover from the centre console, and disconnect the transmission Winter mode switch wiring connector.

4 Remove the centre console as described in Chapter 11.

5 Using a screwdriver, release the selector cable end fitting from the ball stud on the selector lever.

6 Depress the two locking tags on the side of

the outer cable trunion and release the cable from the selector lever housing. Withdraw the cable from the housing.

7 Disconnect the selector lever housing wiring plug.

8 Undo the four retaining nuts and withdraw the housing from the car.

Refitting

9 Refitting is a reversal of removal.

4 Selector lever lock components – removal and refitting

General

1 The transmission selector lever assembly incorporates an electrically-operated selector lever lock mechanism that prevents the lever being moved out of the P position unless the ignition is switched on and the brake pedal is depressed. The components associated with the system are as follows:

a) Selector lever lock contact switch.
b) Selector lever lock solenoid switch.
c) Ignition key contact switch.
d) Brake stop-light switch.

2 Apart from the brake stop-light switch, all the components are located on the selector lever housing, and removal and refitting is described in the following sub-Sections. Stop-light switch removal and refitting procedures are given in Chapter 9.

3 If the selector lever is in the P position and there is an interruption of the power supply to the ignition switch (ie, if the battery is disconnected, or if the battery is flat) it will not be possible to move the selector lever out of position P by the normal means. To overcome this problem, it is possible, in an emergency,

to manually release the selector lever lock solenoid switch as described in *Selector lever lock manual override* later in this Section.

4 If the battery is to be disconnected, or if the vehicle is to be left unused for some time, always ensure that the selector lever is moved to the neutral N position.

Selector lever lock contact switch

Removal

Note: *New contact switch retaining clip washers will be required for refitting.*

5 Remove the selector lever housing as described in Section 3.

6 Disconnect the earth lead from the earth terminal on the base of the selector lever housing (see illustration).

7 Disconnect the wiring connector from the side of the housing.

8 Release the two securing clip washers and press the selector lever contact switch out of the housing. Note that new clip washers will be required for refitting.

Refitting

9 Locate the switch on the housing ensuring that it is positioned correctly and secure with two new clip washers.

10 Reconnect the wiring connector and the earth lead.

11 Refit the selector lever housing as described in Section 3.

Selector lever lock solenoid switch

Removal

12 Remove the selector lever housing as described in Section 3.

13 Disconnect the wiring connector from the side of the housing.

4.6 Selector lever lock contact switch details

1 Selector lever lock contact switch
2 Securing clip washers
3 Wiring connector
Arrow indicates earth lead connection

4.30 To release the selector lever lock, depress the plunger (inset) on the selector lever lock solenoid switch

14 Undo the two bolts and withdraw the solenoid switch from the housing.
15 Release the solenoid switch wiring contact pin from the wiring connector (pin 8 in the connector). Vauxhall/Opel special tool MKM-923-22 is available for releasing the contact pin, but it should be possible to carefully release the pin using conventional tools.
16 Withdraw the contact pin and wiring lead from the wiring connector and remove the solenoid switch from the lever housing.

Refitting

17 Push the wiring contact pin into the appropriate location in the wiring plug ensuring that it locks into place.
18 Refit the solenoid switch to the housing and secure with the two bolts.
19 Reconnect the wiring connector, then refit the selector lever housing as described in Section 3.

Ignition key contact switch

Removal

20 Remove the selector lever housing as described in Section 3.
21 Disconnect the wiring connector from the side of the housing.
22 Undo the two bolts and withdraw the contact switch from the housing.
23 Release the switch wiring contact pin from the wiring connector (pin 1 in the connector). Vauxhall/Opel special tool MKM-923-22 is available for releasing the contact pin, but it should be possible to carefully release the pin using conventional tools.
24 Withdraw the contact pin and wiring lead from the wiring connector and remove the contact switch from the lever housing.

Refitting

25 Push the wiring contact pin into the appropriate location in the wiring plug ensuring that it locks into place.
26 Refit the contact switch to the housing and secure with the two bolts.

27 Reconnect the wiring connector, then refit the selector lever housing as described in Section 3.

Selector lever lock manual override

28 If it is not possible to move the selector lever out of the P position due to a disconnected or flat battery, proceed as follows.
29 Release the two catches on the side of the selector lever cover, and lift the cover from the centre console. Turn the cover through 90° taking care not to strain the Winter mode switch wiring connector.
30 Insert a small screwdriver down the side of the selector lever housing and depress the plunger on the selector lever lock solenoid switch (see illustration). With the plunger depressed, move the selector lever into the N position in the normal way.
31 Refit the selector lever cover to the centre console. Do not move the selector lever back into the P position until battery power is restored.

5 Speedometer drive – removal and refitting

The procedure is as described for manual gearbox models in Chapter 7A.

6 Differential side (driveshaft) oil seals – renewal

1 The procedure is as described for manual gearbox models in Chapter 7A, bearing in mind the following points:
a) *Drain the transmission fluid into a suitable container by removing the drain plug located at the lower right-hand side of the transmission housing (see illustration).*
b) *Smear the sealing ring of the new oil seal with transmission fluid.*
c) *On completion, refill the transmission through the dipstick tube with the correct quantity and type of fluid, and check the level as described in Chapter 1.*

6.1 Automatic transmission fluid drain plug (1)

7 Fluid cooler – general information

The transmission fluid cooler is an integral part of the radiator assembly; radiator removal and refitting is described in Chapter 3.
The hoses running from the transmission to the cooler should be checked at regular intervals, and renewed if there is any doubt about their condition.
Always take note of the pipe and hose connections before disturbing them, and take note of the hose routing.
To minimise the loss of fluid, and to prevent the entry of dirt into the system, clamp the hoses before disconnecting them, and plug the unions once the hoses have been disconnected.
When reconnecting the hoses, ensure that they are connected to their original locations, and route them so that they are not kinked or twisted. Also allow for the movement of the engine on its mountings, ensuring that the hoses will not be stretched or fouled by surrounding components.
Always renew the sealing washers if the banjo union bolts (where fitted) are disturbed, and tighten the bolts to their specified torque wrench setting. Be particularly careful when tightening the cooler unions.

8 Kickdown switch – removal and refitting

The kickdown switch is integral with the throttle cable. Refer to Chapter 4A or 4B for throttle cable removal, refitting and adjustment procedures.

9 Selector lever position switch – adjustment, removal and refitting

Adjustment

1 Adjustment of the switch entails the use of Vauxhall/Opel special tool KM-962, which is then connected to the selector lever position switch wiring connector on the transmission. The tool contains a series of LEDs (light emitting diodes), that illuminate in sequence, with the ignition switched on, as each selector position is engaged. If the LEDs do not illuminate correctly in each selector lever position, the position switch securing screws must be slackened and the switch repositioned accordingly. As accurate adjustment of the position switch can only be carried out using this tool, the work should be entrusted to a Vauxhall/Opel dealer.

Removal

Note: *It will be necessary to have the adjustment of the switch carried out by a Vauxhall/Opel dealer on completion (see adjustment above). Bearing this in mind, it may be beneficial to have the complete operation (removal, refitting and adjustment) carried out by the dealer at the same time.*

2 Apply the handbrake, and select position N with the gear selector lever.

3 Disconnect the battery negative terminal (refer to *Disconnecting the battery* in the Reference Chapter).

4 On models equipped with secondary air injection, remove the necessary air injection components as described in Chapter 4C, for access to the top of the transmission.

5 On right-hand drive models, remove the battery as described in Chapter 5A.

6 Carefully prise the selector cable end fitting from the ball stud on the selector lever position switch actuating lever.

7 Using a screwdriver, extract the retaining clip securing the selector cable trunion to the bracket on the transmission. Depress the two locking tags on the side of the trunion and release the cable from the bracket.

8 Disconnect the selector lever position switch wiring connector.

9 Using pliers to counterhold the shaft, unscrew the nut securing the actuating lever to the selector lever shaft and remove the lever.

10 Mark the position of the selector lever position switch in relation to the transmission housing, then undo the two bolts and remove the switch from the transmission.

Refitting

11 Ensure that the selector lever shaft is in position N (the third detent from the front). Lower the switch onto the shaft, and rotate it until the shaft's flattened surface is aligned with the groove in the switch housing.

12 Refit the nut securing the actuating lever to the selector lever shaft. Use pliers to counterhold the shaft as the nut is tightened, as during removal.

13 Align the switch body with the marks made during removal, then refit and tighten the two switch mounting bolts. If a new switch is being fitted, obtain an approximate position from the marks made on the old switch.

14 Reconnect the switch wiring connector, then refit the selector cable to the transmission bracket and switch actuating lever. Secure the cable trunion with the retaining clip.

15 On models equipped with secondary air injection, refit the air injection components as described in Chapter 4C.

16 On right-hand drive models, refit the battery with reference to Chapter 5A.

17 Take the vehicle to a Vauxhall/Opel dealer for accurate adjustment of the switch.

10 Transmission 'mode' switches – removal and refitting

Economy/Sport mode switch

1 Removal of the Economy/Sport mode switch entails complete dismantling of the selector lever housing so that the switch can be pushed out of the selector lever using a length of welding rod, or similar. The switch wires must then be unsoldered from the switch. It is recommended that this operation is entrusted to a Vauxhall/Opel dealer.

Winter mode switch

Removal

2 Disconnect the battery negative terminal (refer to *Disconnecting the battery* in the Reference Chapter).

3 Remove the selector lever cover from the centre console, and disconnect the Winter mode switch wiring connector.

4 Carefully push the switch from the selector lever cover.

Refitting

5 Refitting is a reversal of removal.

11 Electronic control unit – removal and refitting

Removal

1 The electronic control unit is located on the right-hand side of the heater air distribution housing.

2 Disconnect the battery negative terminal (refer to *Disconnecting the battery* in the Reference Chapter).

3 Open the right-hand front door and, where applicable, remove the storage tray from under the facia.

4 Remove the screw securing the front of the sill trim panel and lift up the front edge of the panel.

5 Remove the screw and plastic clip securing the footwell trim panel. Carefully pull back the weatherstrip from the front edge of the door aperture to expose the edge of the footwell trim panel, then withdraw the trim panel from the footwell.

6 Undo the two screws and remove the air distribution housing right-hand side cover panel.
Remove the two retaining buttons and remove the carpet from the right-hand side footwell.

7 Unclip the electronic control unit from the mounting bracket on the air distribution housing.

8 Disconnect the wiring connector and remove the control unit from the car.

Refitting

9 Refitting is a reversal of removal.

12 Automatic transmission – removal and refitting

Removal

Note: *This is an involved procedure, and it may prove easier in many cases to remove the transmission complete with the engine as an assembly, as described in Chapter 2D or 2E. If removing the transmission on its own, it is suggested that this Section is read through thoroughly before commencing work. Suitable equipment will be required to support the engine and transmission, and the help of an assistant will be required. New torque converter-to-driveplate bolts must be used on refitting, and if the original torque converter is being used, an M10 x 1.25 mm tap will be required.*

1 Disconnect the battery negative terminal (refer to *Disconnecting the battery* in the Reference Chapter).

2 On models equipped with secondary air injection, remove the necessary air injection components as described in Chapter 4C, for access to the top of the transmission.

3 On right-hand drive models, remove the battery as described in Chapter 5A.

4 Carefully prise the selector cable end fitting from the ball stud on the selector lever position switch actuating lever.

5 Using a screwdriver, extract the retaining clip securing the selector cable trunion to the bracket on the transmission. Depress the two locking tags on the side of the trunion and release the cable from the bracket.

6 Disconnect the vent hose from the front of the transmission **(see illustration)**.

7 Disconnect the transmission wiring harness plugs, and unbolt the wiring harness brackets from the transmission.

8 Unclip the oxygen sensor wiring connector from the bracket on the transmission, and separate the two halves of the connector.

9 Unscrew and remove the three upper engine-to-transmission bolts, noting the locations of any brackets or clips attached to the bolts. Note that on certain models, one of the bolts secures the dipstick tube. On certain models, the plastic coolant gallery may prevent access to the centre upper bolt, in which case, proceed as follows:

12.6 Transmission vent hose (arrowed)

12.19 Transmission bellhousing cover plate securing bolts (arrowed)

12.21 Torque converter-to-driveplate bolt (arrowed)

a) *Drain the cooling system as described in Chapter 1 (if not already done), then disconnect the radiator hose from the front of the coolant gallery.*

b) *Remove the rear upper engine-to-transmission bolt, which also secures the coolant gallery and a clutch cable bracket.*

c) *Move the coolant gallery as necessary to enable access to the centre upper engine-to-transmission bolt.*

10 Remove the dipstick and its tube from the transmission casing. Recover the O-ring.

11 Apply the handbrake, then jack up the front of the vehicle, and support securely on axle stands (see *Jacking and vehicle support*). Note that the vehicle must be raised sufficiently high to enable the transmission to be withdrawn from under the front of the vehicle. Remove the roadwheels.

12 The engine must now be supported. Ideally, the engine should be supported using chains suspended from a strong wooden or metal beam resting on blocks positioned securely in the channels at the sides of the engine compartment. A Vauxhall/Opel special tool is available for this purpose. Alternatively, the engine can be supported using a suitable hoist and lifting tackle, but the hoist must be capable of supporting the engine with the front of the vehicle raised off the ground, leaving sufficient clearance to withdraw the transmission from under the front of the vehicle (see previous paragraph). A further alternative is to support the engine using a jack and interposed block of wood under the sump, but great care must be taken when removing the transmission not to move the engine off the jack – it is strongly recommended that the engine is additionally supported using a hoist or bar as described previously, to avoid any possibility of injury. Note that if a hoist is used to support the engine, a further hoist will be required to carry out removal of the transmission safely. (The alternative to all this is to remove the engine and transmission as an assembly, as described in Chapter 2D or 2E.)

13 Where applicable, disconnect the speedometer cable from the top of the transmission, with reference to Chapter 12. Note that on certain models, the cable is in two sections, joined by a connector near the engine compartment bulkhead – in this case, it may be easier to separate the two cable sections at the connector, rather than to disconnect the cable from the transmission. On later models, disconnect the vehicle speed sensor wiring connector from the sensor.

14 Disconnect the exhaust front section from the manifold as described in Chapter 4A or 4B, and release the system from the forward rubber mountings – this will allow the engine to be lowered later in the procedure.

15 Remove the front anti-roll bar as described in Chapter 10.

16 Remove the left-hand front suspension lower arm and tie-bar as described in Chapter 10.

17 Disconnect the inner ends of the driveshafts from the transmission as described in Chapter 8. There is no need to disconnect the driveshafts from the swivel hubs. Be prepared for transmission fluid spillage, and plug the openings in the transmission, to prevent dirt ingress and further fluid loss. Do not allow the driveshafts to hang down under their own weight, or the joints may be damaged – support the driveshafts with wire or string.

18 Place a suitable container beneath the transmission fluid cooler hose connections at the transmission. Clamp the transmission fluid cooler hoses, then disconnect them from the transmission, noting their locations. Be prepared for fluid spillage, and plug the open ends of the hoses and transmission, to minimise fluid loss and prevent dirt ingress.

19 Where a metal sump is fitted, unscrew the securing bolts, and remove the transmission bellhousing cover plate **(see illustration)**. Where an aluminium sump is fitted, pull out the rubber access plug.

20 If the original torque converter and

driveplate are to be refitted, make alignment marks between the torque converter and the driveplate, to ensure that the components are reassembled in their original positions.

21 Working through the bottom of the bellhousing, unscrew the three torque converter-to-driveplate bolts. It will be necessary to turn the engine, using a suitable spanner or socket on the crankshaft pulley or sprocket bolt (as applicable), to gain access to each bolt in turn through the aperture **(see illustration)**. Turning the engine will be much easier if the spark plugs are removed first (see Chapter 1). Use a screwdriver or a similar tool to jam the driveplate ring gear, preventing the driveplate from rotating as the bolts are loosened. Discard the bolts.

22 Support the transmission with a trolley jack, with an interposed block of wood to spread the load. Ensure that the engine is adequately supported as described in paragraph 12.

23 Additionally, the transmission should be supported from above, using a hoist. Fit a suitable strap around the transmission casing, passing it through the hole in the battery tray (remove the battery as described in Chapter 5A, if not already done), and suspend the strap from the hoist. This will enable the transmission to be lowered safely during removal.

24 Remove the left-hand engine/transmission mounting bracket completely, by unscrewing the two bolts securing the bracket to the rubber mounting, and the three bolts securing the mounting bracket to the transmission.

25 Remove the nut and through-bolt securing the rear engine/transmission mounting bracket to the mounting on the body.

26 Remove the two bolts securing the rear engine/transmission mounting bracket to the transmission, and withdraw the mounting bracket.

27 Make a final check to ensure that all

relevant wiring, hoses, etc, have been disconnected to facilitate transmission removal. Note that on certain models, the wiring for the oxygen sensor may be secured to the lug on the transmission with a cable-tie.

28 Using the lifting tackle and the jack(s), lower the engine and transmission slightly.

29 Ensure that the transmission is adequately supported, then unscrew and remove the three lower engine-to-transmission bolts (note the location of any brackets secured by the bolts). Ensure that the torque converter is held firmly in place in the transmission casing as the engine and transmission are separated, otherwise it could fall out, resulting in fluid spillage and possible damage. Retain the torque converter while the transmission is removed by bolting a strip of metal across the transmission bellhousing end face.

30 The transmission can now be lowered and withdrawn from under the front of the vehicle. The help of an assistant will greatly ease this operation.

Refitting

31 Before refitting, check that the left-hand engine/transmission mounting-to-body bolts rotate freely in their threaded holes in the body. If necessary, re-cut the threaded holes in the body using a suitable tap.

32 If the original torque converter is being refitted, commence refitting by recutting the torque converter-to-driveplate bolt threads in the torque converter using an M10 x 1.25 mm tap **(see illustration)**.

33 If a new transmission is being fitted, the manufacturers recommend that the radiator's fluid cooler passages are flushed clean before the new transmission is installed. Ideally, compressed air should be used (in which case, ensure that adequate safety precautions are taken; in particular, eye protection should be worn). Alternatively, the cooler can be flushed with clean automatic transmission

12.32 Torque converter-to-driveplate bolt threads (arrowed) must be recut on refitting

fluid until all the old fluid has been expelled, and fresh fluid runs clear from the cooler outlet.

34 Commence refitting by positioning the transmission under the front of the vehicle, and support with a trolley jack and interposed block of wood, as during removal.

35 Where applicable, remove the strip of metal retaining the torque converter in the transmission, and hold the torque converter in position as the transmission is mated to the engine.

36 On models where the dipstick tube is secured by one of the engine-to-transmission bolts, fit the dipstick tube to the transmission, using a new O-ring.

37 Raise the engine and transmission sufficiently to enable the lower engine-to-transmission bolts to be fitted, but do not tighten them fully at this stage. Ensure that any brackets or clips (as applicable) noted during removal are in place on the bolts.

38 Coat the threads of the left-hand engine/transmission mounting-to-body bolts with suitable thread-locking compound, then raise the engine and transmission sufficiently to enable the mounting bracket to be refitted.

39 Refit the left-hand engine/transmission mounting, and tighten the bolts to the specified torque.

40 Refit the rear engine/transmission mounting bracket to the transmission, and tighten the bolts to the specified torque.

41 Refit the nut and through-bolt securing the rear engine/transmission mounting to the mounting on the body.

42 Tighten the previously-fitted engine-to-transmission bolts to the specified torque, then withdraw the trolley jack and the hoist used to support the transmission.

43 If the original torque converter and driveplate have been refitted, carefully turn the engine to align the marks made before removal, before fitting the torque converter-to-driveplate bolts.

44 Fit **new** torque converter-to-driveplate bolts, and tighten them to the specified torque. Turn the engine for access to each bolt in turn, and prevent the driveplate from turning as during removal.

45 Refit the transmission bellhousing cover plate or the access plug.

46 Reconnect the fluid cooler hoses to the transmission. Ensure that the hoses are reconnected to their correct locations, as noted before removal.

47 Refit the suspension lower arm and tie-bar as described in Chapter 10.

48 Refit the front anti-roll bar as described in Chapter 10.

49 Reconnect the inner end of the driveshafts to the transmission as described in Chapter 8.

50 Reconnect the front section of the

exhaust system to the manifold as described in Chapter 4A or 4B, and reconnect the system to the forward rubber mountings.

51 Where fitted, reconnect the speedometer cable to the top of the transmission, or reconnect the two halves of the cable at the connector, as applicable. On later models, reconnect the vehicle speed sensor wiring connector.

52 Refit the roadwheels, then lower the vehicle to the ground.

53 Remove or disconnect the equipment used to support the engine, if not already done.

54 Refit and tighten the three upper engine-to-transmission bolts (where necessary gaining access as described during removal), ensuring that the coolant gallery, dipstick tube, and any brackets (as applicable) noted during removal are in place on the bolts. Where applicable, reconnect the radiator hose to the coolant gallery.

55 Reconnect the oxygen sensor wiring connector, and refit it to its bracket.

56 Reconnect the transmission wiring harness plugs, and secure the wiring harness brackets to the transmission.

57 Reconnect the transmission vent hose.

58 If not already done, refit the dipstick tube, using a new O-ring.

59 Refit the selector cable trunion and refit the retaining clip securing the trunion to the bracket on the transmission. Refit the selector cable end fitting to the ball stud on the selector lever position switch actuating lever

60 On models equipped with secondary air injection, refit the disturbed air injection components as described in Chapter 4C.

61 Where applicable, refill the cooling system as described in Chapter 1.

62 Refit the battery, where applicable, then reconnect the battery negative terminal.

63 Check the automatic transmission fluid level, and top-up if necessary as described in Chapter 1.

13 Automatic transmission overhaul – general information

In the event of a fault occurring on the transmission, it is first necessary to determine whether it is of an electrical, mechanical or hydraulic nature, and to achieve this, special test equipment is required. It is therefore essential to have the work carried out by a Vauxhall/Opel dealer if a transmission fault is suspected.

Do not remove the transmission from the car for possible repair before professional fault diagnosis has been carried out, since most tests require the transmission to be in the vehicle.

Notes

Chapter 8
Driveshafts

Contents

Degrees of difficulty

Easy, suitable for novice with little experience	Fairly easy, suitable for beginner with some experience	Fairly difficult, suitable for competent DIY mechanic	Difficult, suitable for experienced DIY mechanic	Very difficult, suitable for expert DIY or professional

Specifications

Type
All except 1.0 litre models . . . . Unequal length shafts with ball-and-cage type constant velocity joint at each end

1.0 litre models . . . . Unequal length shafts with ball-and-cage type outer, and tripod type inner, constant velocity joints

Lubrication (overhaul only – see text)
Lubricant type/specification . . . . Use only special grease supplied in sachets with gaiter kits – joints are otherwise pre-packed with grease and sealed

Torque wrench settings

	Nm	lbf ft
Driveshaft retaining nut:*		
Stage 1	130	96
Stage 2	Slacken the nut completely	
Stage 3	20	15
Stage 4	Angle-tighten through a further 90°	
Lower arm balljoint clamp bolt nut*	30	22
Roadwheel bolts	110	81

*Use new nuts/bolts.

1 General information

Drive is transmitted from the differential to the front wheels by means of two solid steel driveshafts of unequal length. The right-hand driveshaft is longer than the left-hand one, due to the position of the transmission unit.

Both driveshafts are splined at their outer ends to accept the wheel hubs, and are threaded so that each hub can be fastened by a large nut. The inner end of each driveshaft is splined to accept the differential sun gear.

Constant velocity (CV) joints are fitted to each end of the driveshafts, to ensure the smooth and efficient transmission of drive at all the angles possible as the roadwheels move up-and-down with the suspension, and as they turn from side-to-side under steering. Both inner and outer constant velocity joints are of the ball-and-cage type on all except 1.0 litre models; on these vehicles, the inner constant velocity joints are of the tripod type.

2 Driveshafts – removal and refitting

Note: *A new driveshaft retaining nut and balljoint clamp bolt nut will be needed on refitting.*

Removal

HAYNES HiNT *If work is being carried out without the aid of an assistant, remove the wheel trim/hub cap (as applicable) then withdraw the split pin and slacken the driveshaft retaining nut with the vehicle resting on its wheels.*

1 Firmly apply the handbrake, then jack up the front of the car and support it securely on axle stands (see *Jacking and vehicle support*). Remove the relevant front roadwheel.
2 Extract the split pin from the driveshaft

2.2 Extract the split pin from the driveshaft retaining nut

retaining nut and discard it; a new one must be used on refitting **(see illustration)**.
3 Refit at least two roadwheel bolts to the front hub, and tighten them securely. Have an assistant firmly depress the brake pedal to prevent the front hub from rotating, then using a socket and extension bar, slacken and remove the driveshaft retaining nut. Alternatively, a tool can be fabricated from two lengths of steel strip (one long, one short) and a nut an bolt; the nut and bolt forming the pivot of a forked tool. Bolt the tool to the hub using two wheel bolts, and hold the tool to prevent the hub from rotating as the driveshaft retaining nut is undone **(see illustration)**.
4 Unscrew the driveshaft retaining nut, and remove the washer. Discard the nut; a new one must be used on refitting.
5 Slacken and remove the lower arm balljoint clamp nut and bolt, and free the lower arm from the swivel hub **(see illustration)**. Discard the clamp bolt nut; a new one must be used on refitting.
6 Carefully pull the swivel hub assembly outwards, and withdraw the driveshaft outer constant velocity joint from the hub assembly. If necessary, the shaft can be tapped out of the hub using a soft-faced mallet. Support the driveshaft by suspending it with wire or string; do not allow it to hang under its own weight, or the joints may be damaged.
7 A suitable tool will now be required to release the inner end of the driveshaft from the differential. To release the right-hand driveshaft, a flat steel bar with a good chamfer

2.3 Using a fabricated tool to hold the front hub stationary whilst the driveshaft retaining nut is slackened

H30004

on one end can be used. The left-hand driveshaft may prove more difficult to release, and a suitable square- or rectangular-section bar may be required.
8 Lever between the driveshaft and the differential housing to release the driveshaft circlip from the differential. Carefully withdraw the driveshaft from the transmission unit, taking great care not to damage the driveshaft oil seal, and remove the driveshaft from underneath the vehicle **(see illustrations)**.
9 Plug the opening in the differential, to prevent further oil loss and dirt ingress.
10 **Do not** *allow the vehicle to rest on its wheels with one or both driveshaft(s) removed, as damage to the wheel bearing(s) may result.* If moving the vehicle is unavoidable, temporarily insert the outer end of the driveshaft(s) in the hub(s), and tighten the hub nut(s): in this case, the inner end(s) of the driveshaft(s) must be supported, for example by suspending with string from the vehicle underbody. **Do not** *allow the driveshaft to hang down under its own weight, or the joints may be damaged.*

Refitting

11 Before installing the driveshaft, examine the driveshaft oil seal in the transmission for signs of damage or deterioration. Renew if necessary, referring to the relevant part of Chapter 7 for further information.
12 Check the circlip fitted to the inner constant velocity joint splines for signs of damage, and renew if necessary. Ensure that

2.5 Withdraw the clamp bolt, and free the lower arm balljoint from the swivel hub

2.8a Lever the driveshaft CV joint out from the transmission to release its circlip from the differential . . .

2.8b . . . then withdraw the shaft, taking great care not to damage the oil seal in the transmission

2.12 Prior to refitting, ensure that the circlip (arrowed) is correctly located in the inner CV joint groove

2.15 Using a screwdriver on the CV joint weld bead to drive the joint into the differential until the snap-ring engages positively

2.18a Working in the stages given in the Specifications, tighten the driveshaft retaining nut to the specified torque setting . . .

the circlip is correctly seated in its groove **(see illustration)**.

13 Thoroughly clean the driveshaft splines, and the apertures in the transmission unit and hub assembly. Apply a thin film of grease to the oil seal lips, and to the driveshaft splines and shoulders. Check that all gaiter clips are securely fastened.

14 Remove the plug from the transmission (see paragraph 9) and offer up the driveshaft. Locate the joint splines with those of the differential sun gear, taking great care not to damage the oil seal.

15 Place a screwdriver or similar tool on the weld bead of the inner driveshaft joint, not the metal cover, and drive the shaft into the differential until the retaining snap-ring engages positively **(see illustration)**. Pull on the joint, not the shaft, to make sure that the joint is securely retained by the circlip.

16 Locate the outer constant velocity joint splines with those of the swivel hub, and slide the joint back into position in the hub. Fit the washer and new driveshaft retaining nut, tightening it by hand only at this stage.

17 Locate the lower arm balljoint in the swivel hub, and insert the clamp bolt from the rear of the swivel hub, so that its threads are facing forwards. Fit a new nut to the clamp bolt, and tighten it to the specified torque setting.

18 Using the method employed on removal to prevent rotation, tighten the driveshaft retaining nut through the stages given in the Specifications at the start of this Chapter **(see illustrations)**.

19 With the nut correctly tightened, secure it in position with a new split pin **(see illustrations)**. If the holes in the driveshaft are not aligned with any of the slots in the nut, loosen **(do not tighten)** the nut by the *smallest possible amount* until the split pin can be inserted.

20 Refit the roadwheel, then lower the vehicle to the ground and tighten the roadwheel bolts to the specified torque.

21 Top-up the transmission with the specified type of oil/fluid using the information given in Chapter 1.

3 Driveshaft rubber gaiters – renewal

All except 1.0 litre models

Note: *If both driveshaft gaiters are to renewed at the same time, it is only necessary to remove one of the constant velocity joints. The second gaiter can then be slid along and removed from the exposed end of the driveshaft. The inner and outer CV joints are identical and the following procedure can be used for either joint.*

1 Remove the driveshaft from the car as described in Section 2.

2 Secure the driveshaft in a vice equipped with soft jaws, and release the two retaining clips on the gaiter which is to be renewed. If

2.18b . . . and then through the specified angle (note the use of an angle gauge)

necessary, the retaining clips can be cut to release them.

3 Slide the rubber gaiter down the shaft to expose the constant velocity joint. Scoop out any excess grease.

4 Using circlip pliers, expand the circlip which secures the joint to the driveshaft **(see illustration)**.

5 Using a soft-faced mallet, tap the joint off the end of the driveshaft.

6 Slide the rubber gaiter off the driveshaft, and discard it.

7 If both gaiters are to be renewed, release the retaining clips, then slide the second gaiter along the driveshaft and remove it. If the driveshaft is fitted with a vibration damper, mark the damper fitted position, then unbolt and remove it from the driveshaft.

8 Thoroughly clean the constant velocity

2.19a Insert a new split pin . . .

2.19b . . . and secure in position by bending over the split pin ends

3.4 Expand the CV joint circlip, and tap the joint off the end of the driveshaft

3.9 Examine the constant velocity joint balls and cage for signs of wear or damage

3.11 Components required for driveshaft gaiter renewal

3.14 Slide the gaiter onto the end of the driveshaft

joint(s) using paraffin, or a suitable solvent, and dry thoroughly. Carry out a visual inspection as follows.

9 Move the inner splined driving member from side-to-side, to expose each ball in turn at the top of its track. Examine the balls for cracks, flat spots, or signs of surface pitting (see illustration).

10 Inspect the ball tracks on the inner and outer members. If the tracks have widened, the balls will no longer be a tight fit. At the same time, check the ball cage windows for wear or cracking between the windows.

11 If on inspection any of the constant velocity joint components are found to be worn or damaged, it will be necessary to renew the complete joint assembly (refer to the Note at the end of Section 4). If the joint is in satisfactory condition, obtain a repair kit

consisting of a new gaiter and retaining clips, a constant velocity joint circlip, and the correct type and quantity of grease (see illustration).

12 Wind tape around the splines on the end of the driveshaft, to protect the gaiter as it is slid into place.

13 Where both gaiters have been removed, slide on the first gaiter and proceed as described in paragraphs 15 to 18.

14 Slide the (second) gaiter onto the end of the driveshaft (see illustration), then remove the tape from the driveshaft splines.

15 Fit a new circlip to the constant velocity joint, then tap the joint onto the driveshaft until the circlip engages in its groove (see illustrations). Make sure that the joint is securely retained by the circlip, by pulling on the joint, not the shaft.

16 Pack the joint with the specified type of grease (see illustration). Work the grease well into the bearing tracks whilst twisting the joint, and fill the rubber gaiter with any excess.

17 Ease the gaiter over the joint, and ensure that the gaiter lips are correctly located in the grooves on both the driveshaft and constant velocity joint. Lift the outer sealing lip of the gaiter, to equalise air pressure within the gaiter.

18 Fit the large metal retaining clip to the gaiter. Pull the clip as tight as possible, and locate the hooks on the clip in their slots. Remove any slack in the gaiter retaining clip by carefully compressing the raised section of the clip. In the absence of the special tool, a pair of side cutters may be used. Secure the small retaining clip using the same procedure (see illustrations).

3.15a Fit a new circlip . . .

3.15b . . . ensuring it is correctly located in the joint inner member

3.15c Slide the joint onto the driveshaft until the circlip is correctly located in the driveshaft groove

3.16 Pack the CV joint and gaiter with the grease supplied

3.18a Hook the large outer retaining clip ends together . . .

3.18b . . . then secure the clip in position by compressing the raised section of the clip

3.18c Small inner retaining clip is secured in position in the same way

3.24a Make alignment marks between the tripod joint and the driveshaft . . .

3.24b . . . then prise the circlip from the end of the driveshaft

19 Check that both constant velocity joints move freely in all directions then, where applicable, refit the vibration damper its original position on the driveshaft. On completion, refit the driveshaft to the car as described in Section 2.

1.0 litre models

20 Remove the driveshaft from the car as described in Section 2.

21 The outer CV joint on 1.0 litre models is of the same ball-and-cage type as used on all other models. Both rubber gaiters can therefore be renewed after removing the outer CV joint as described previously in paragraphs 1 to 19.

22 If the inner rubber gaiter is being renewed, and an initial inspection indicates possible wear in the inner joint, remove the joint for a detailed inspection as follows.

23 With the rubber gaiter released from the joint, mark the joint outer member in relation to the driveshaft, to ensure correct refitting. Withdraw the joint outer member from the tripod and driveshaft. As the outer member is withdrawn, take precautions to prevent the bearing rollers falling off the tripod. Wipe away all excess grease and, if necessary, wrap tape around the tripod joint to secure the rollers in position.

24 Using a punch, paint or a suitable marker pen, make alignment marks between the tripod joint and driveshaft, and also identify which way round the tripod is fitted. Prise the circlip from the end of the driveshaft, then remove the tripod joint assembly **(see illustrations)**. If the joint is a tight fit, it maybe necessary to use a puller to draw it off the shaft – if a puller is used, take great care not to damage the rollers.

25 Slide the gaiter off the end of the driveshaft.

26 Where applicable, remove the tape from the joint, and thoroughly clean the constant velocity joint components using paraffin, or a suitable solvent, and dry the components thoroughly.

27 Check the spider, rollers and outer member for signs of wear, pitting or scuffing on their bearing surfaces. Also check that the spider rollers rotate smoothly and easily, with no traces of roughness.

28 If any of the constant velocity joint components are found to be worn or damaged, it will be necessary to renew the complete joint assembly. If the joint is in satisfactory condition, obtain a repair kit consisting of a new gaiter and retaining clips, circlips, and the correct type and quantity of grease.

29 Clean the driveshaft, and tape over the splines on its inner end to protect the new gaiter as it is fitted.

30 Slide the new gaiter onto the driveshaft then remove the tape from the driveshaft end.

31 If necessary, again wind tape around the tripod to retain the rollers then, with the previously-made marks on the tripod and driveshaft aligned, push the tripod onto the driveshaft splines. If necessary use a soft-faced mallet to drive the tripod fully onto the splines. Secure the tripod in position using the new circlip, making sure that the circlip locates correctly in the driveshaft groove.

32 Where applicable, remove the tape from around the tripod, then work the grease supplied with the repair kit fully into the roller bearings. Fill the joint outer member with any excess grease.

33 Locate the outer member over the tripod, making sure that the previously-made marks are aligned.

34 Slide the gaiter along the driveshaft, and locate it in the recesses on the driveshaft and joint outer member.

35 Ensure that the gaiter is not twisted or distorted, then carefully lift the lip of the gaiter at the outer member end to equalise air pressure in the gaiter.

36 Fit the large metal retaining clip to the gaiter. Remove any slack in the gaiter retaining clip by carefully compressing the raised section of the clip. In the absence of the special tool, a pair of side cutters may be used. Secure the small retaining clip using the same procedure.

37 The driveshaft can now be refitted to the car as described in Section 2.

4 Driveshaft overhaul – general information

1 If any of the checks described in Chapter 1 reveal wear in a driveshaft joint, first remove the roadwheel trim or centre cap (as appropriate).

2 If the split pin is in position, the driveshaft nut should be correctly tightened. If in doubt, the only alternative is to obtain a new nut and split pin, then fit and tighten the nut using the procedures described in Section 2. Once tightened, secure the nut in position with the new split pin, and refit the centre cap or trim. Repeat this check on the other driveshaft nut.

3 Road test the vehicle, and listen for a metallic clicking from the front as the vehicle, is driven slowly in a circle on full-lock. If a clicking noise is heard, this indicates wear in the outer constant velocity joint. This means that the joint must be renewed; as reconditioning is not possible.

4 If vibration, consistent with road speed, is felt through the car when accelerating, there is a possibility of wear in the inner constant velocity joints.

5 To check the joints for wear, remove the driveshafts, then dismantle them as described in Section 3; if any wear or free play is found, the affected joint must be renewed. **Note:** *If driveshaft joint wear is apparent on a vehicle which has covered in excess of 50 000 miles (80 000 km), the manufacturer recommends that the complete driveshaft is renewed.*

Chapter 9
Braking system

Contents

Degrees of difficulty

Easy, suitable for novice with little experience	**Fairly easy,** suitable for beginner with some experience	**Fairly difficult,** suitable for competent DIY mechanic	**Difficult,** suitable for experienced DIY mechanic	**Very difficult,** suitable for expert DIY or professional

Specifications

Front brakes

Type	Disc, with single-piston sliding caliper
Disc diameter:	
1.0, 1.2 and 1.4 litre models	236 mm
1.6 litre models	256 mm
Disc thickness:	
New:	
Solid disc	12.7 mm
Ventilated disc	20.0 mm
Minimum thickness:	
Solid disc	9.7 mm
Ventilated disc	17.0 mm
Maximum disc run-out	0.1 mm
Brake pad minimum thickness (including backing plate)	7.0 mm

Rear brakes

Type	Single leading shoe drum
Drum diameter:	
New:	
Corsa and Corsavan models	200 mm
Combo Van models	230 mm
Maximum diameter:	
Corsa and Corsavan models	201 mm
Combo Van models	231 mm
Maximum drum out-of-round	0.1 mm
Minimum friction material thickness	2.5 mm
Minimum friction material-to-rivet depth	0.5 mm

Torque wrench settings

	Nm	lbf ft
ABS components:		
ECU-to-modulator retaining screws*	3	2
Front wheel sensor bolt	8	6
Modulator block retaining nuts	8	6
Rear wheel sensor screw	4	3
Brake hose union bolt	40	30
Brake pedal pivot shaft nut	18	13
Brake pipe union nut	16	12
Front brake caliper:		
Guide bolts	30	22
Mounting bracket-to-swivel hub bolts*	95	70
Front brake disc screw	7	5
Master cylinder mounting nuts*	22	16
Master cylinder reservoir support bracket:		
Bracket-to-bulkhead nut*	20	15
Bracket-to-reservoir bolt	12	9
Pressure-regulating valve:*		
Mounting bolts	20	15
Spring bolt (Corsa and Corsavan)	20	15
Spring clamp nuts (Combo Van)	20	15
Rear hub nut (pre-load)	25	18
Rear wheel cylinder bolts	9	7
Roadwheel bolts	110	81
Servo unit mounting nuts	22	16

*Use new nuts/bolts

1 General information

The braking system is of the servo-assisted, dual-circuit hydraulic type. The arrangement of the hydraulic system is such that each circuit operates one front and one rear brake from a tandem master cylinder. Under normal circumstances, both circuits operate in unison. However, in the event of hydraulic failure in one circuit, full braking force will still be available at two wheels.

All models have front disc brakes and rear drum brakes. An Anti-lock Braking System (ABS) is fitted as standard or optional equipment, according to model (refer to Section 19 for further information on ABS operation).

The front disc brakes are actuated by single-piston sliding type calipers, which ensure that equal pressure is applied to each disc pad.

The rear drum brakes incorporate leading and trailing shoes, which are actuated by twin-piston wheel cylinders. A self-adjust mechanism is incorporated to automatically compensate for brake shoe wear. As the brake shoe linings wear, the footbrake operation automatically operates the adjuster mechanism, which effectively lengthens the shoe strut, and repositions the brake shoes to maintain the lining-to-drum clearance.

Pressure-regulating valves are situated in the hydraulic lines to control the pressure applied to the rear brakes. The regulating valves help to prevent rear wheel lock-up during emergency braking. On 1.0 and 1.2 litre models, the valves are of the pressure-dependent type; on all other models, they are of the load-dependent type, which actually alter the pressure to suit the load being carried by the vehicle.

The cable-operated handbrake provides an independent mechanical means of rear brake application.

Note: *When servicing any part of the system, work carefully and methodically; also observe scrupulous cleanliness when overhauling any part of the hydraulic system. Always renew components (in axle sets, where applicable) if in doubt about their condition, and use only genuine Vauxhall/Opel replacement parts, or at least those of known good quality. Note the warnings given in 'Safety first!' and at relevant points in this Chapter concerning the dangers of asbestos dust and hydraulic fluid.*

2 Hydraulic system – bleeding

Note: *Hydraulic fluid is poisonous; wash off immediately and thoroughly in the case of skin contact, and seek immediate medical advice if any fluid is swallowed or gets into the eyes. Certain types of hydraulic fluid are inflammable, and may ignite when allowed into contact with hot components. When servicing any hydraulic system, it is safest to assume that the fluid IS inflammable, and to take precautions against the risk of fire as though it is petrol that is being handled. Finally, it is hygroscopic (it absorbs moisture from the air) – old fluid may be contaminated, and unfit for further use. When topping-up or renewing the fluid, always use the recommended type, and ensure that it comes from a freshly-opened sealed container.*

HAYNES HiNT *Hydraulic fluid is also an effective paint stripper, and will attack plastics; if any is spilt, it should be washed off immediately using copious quantities of water.*

General

1 Any hydraulic system will only function correctly once all the air has been removed from the components and circuit; this is achieved by bleeding the system.

2 During the bleeding procedure, add only clean, fresh hydraulic fluid of the recommended type; never use old fluid, nor re-use any which has already been bled from the system. Ensure that sufficient fresh fluid is available before starting work.

3 If there is any possibility of the wrong fluid being in the system, the brake components and circuit must be flushed completely with uncontaminated, correct fluid, and new seals should be fitted to the various components.

4 If hydraulic fluid has been lost from the system (or if air has entered) because of a leak, ensure that the fault is cured before proceeding further.

5 Park the vehicle on level ground, switch off the engine and select first or reverse gear, then chock the wheels and release the handbrake.

6 Check that all pipes and hoses are secure, that the pipe unions are tight, and that the bleed screws are closed. Clean any dirt from around the bleed screws.

7 Unscrew the master cylinder reservoir cap, and top the master cylinder reservoir up to the MAX level line; refit the cap loosely, and remember to maintain the fluid level at least above the MIN level line throughout the procedure, to avoid the risk of further air entering the system.

8 There are a number of one-man, do-it-yourself brake bleeding kits currently available from motor accessory shops. It is recommended that one of these kits is used whenever possible, as they greatly simplify the bleeding operation, and also reduce the risk of expelled air and fluid being drawn back into the system. If such a kit is not available, the basic (two-man) method must be used, which is described in detail below.

Caution: Vauxhall/Opel recommend using a pressure bleeding kit for this operation (see paragraphs 24 to 27).

9 If a kit is to be used, prepare the vehicle as described previously, and follow the kit manufacturer's instructions, as the procedures may vary slightly according to the type being used; generally, they will be as outlined below in the relevant sub-section.

10 Whichever method is used, the same sequence must be followed (paragraphs 11 and 12) to ensure the removal of all air from the system.

Bleeding sequence

11 If the system has been only partially disconnected, and suitable precautions were taken to minimise fluid loss, it should only be necessary to bleed that part of the system (ie, the primary or secondary circuit).

12 If the complete system is to be bled, then it should be done working in the following sequence:

a) Right-hand rear brake.
b) Left-hand rear brake.
c) Right-hand front brake.
d) Left-hand front brake.

Bleeding – basic (two-man) method

13 Collect a clean glass jar, a suitable length of plastic or rubber tubing which is a tight fit over the bleed screw, and a ring spanner to fit the bleed screw. The help of an assistant will also be required.

14 Remove the dust cap from the first screw in the sequence. Fit the spanner and tube to the screw, place the other end of the tube in the jar, and pour in sufficient fluid to cover the end of the tube.

15 Ensure that the master cylinder reservoir fluid level is maintained at least above the MIN level line throughout the procedure.

16 Have the assistant fully depress the brake pedal several times to build up pressure, then maintain it on the final stroke.

17 While pedal pressure is maintained, unscrew the bleed screw (approximately one turn) and allow the compressed fluid and air to flow into the jar. The assistant should maintain pedal pressure, following it down to the floor if necessary, and should not release it until instructed to do so. When the flow stops, tighten the bleed screw again; the pedal should then be released slowly, and the reservoir fluid level checked and topped-up.

18 Repeat the steps given in paragraphs 16 and 17 until the fluid emerging from the bleed screw is free from air bubbles. If the master cylinder has been drained and refilled, and air is being bled from the first screw in the sequence, allow approximately five seconds between cycles for the master cylinder passages to refill.

19 When no more air bubbles appear, tighten the bleed screw securely, remove the tube and spanner, and refit the dust cap. Do not overtighten the bleed screw.

20 Repeat the procedure on the remaining screws in the sequence, until all air is removed from the system and the brake pedal feels firm again.

Bleeding – using a one-way valve kit

21 As their name implies, these kits consist of a length of tubing with a one-way valve fitted, to prevent expelled air and fluid being drawn back into the system; some kits include a translucent container, which can be positioned so that the air bubbles can be more easily seen flowing from the end of the tube.

22 The kit is connected to the bleed screw, which is then opened **(see illustration)**. The user returns to the driver's seat, depresses the brake pedal with a smooth, steady stroke, then slowly releases it; this is repeated until the expelled fluid is clear of air bubbles.

23 These kits simplify work so much that it is easy to forget the master cylinder reservoir fluid level; ensure that this is maintained at least above the MIN level line at all times, or air will be drawn into the system.

Bleeding – using a pressure bleeding kit

24 These kits are usually operated by the

2.22 Using a one-way valve kit to bleed the rear brake

reservoir of pressurised air contained in the spare tyre, noting that it will probably be necessary to reduce the pressure to less than normal; refer to the instructions supplied with the kit.

25 By connecting a pressurised, fluid-filled container to the master cylinder reservoir, bleeding can be carried out simply by opening each screw in turn (in the specified sequence) and allowing the fluid to flow out until no more air bubbles can be seen in the expelled fluid.

26 This method has the advantage that the large reservoir of fluid provides an additional safeguard against air being drawn into the system during bleeding.

27 Pressure bleeding is particularly effective when bleeding 'difficult' systems, or when bleeding the complete system at the time of routine fluid renewal.

All methods

28 When bleeding is complete and firm pedal feel is restored, wash off any spilt fluid, tighten the bleed screws securely, and refit their dust caps.

29 Check the hydraulic fluid level, and top-up if necessary (see *Weekly checks*).

30 Discard any hydraulic fluid that has been bled from the system; it will not be fit for re-use. Bear in mind that this fluid may be inflammable.

31 Check the feel of the brake pedal. If it feels at all spongy, air must still be present in the system, and further bleeding is required. Failure to bleed satisfactorily after a reasonable repetition of the bleeding procedure may be due to worn master cylinder seals.

3 Hydraulic pipes and hoses – renewal

Note: *Before starting work, refer to the note at the beginning of Section 2 concerning the dangers of hydraulic fluid.*

1 If any pipe or hose is to be renewed, minimise fluid loss by first removing the master cylinder reservoir cap and screwing it down onto a piece of polythene. Alternatively, flexible hoses can be sealed, if required, using a proprietary brake hose clamp. Metal brake pipe unions can be plugged (if care is taken not to allow dirt into the system) or capped immediately they are disconnected. Place a wad of rag under any union that is to be disconnected, to catch any spilt fluid.

2 If a flexible hose is to be disconnected, unscrew the brake pipe union nut before removing the spring clip which secures the hose to its mounting bracket.

3 To unscrew the union nuts, it is preferable to obtain a brake pipe spanner of the correct size; these are available from most large motor accessory shops. Failing this, a close-fitting open-ended spanner will be required, though if the nuts are tight or corroded, their

4.2 Using a screwdriver, carefully prise out the pad retaining spring from the caliper

4.3 Remove the guide bolt dust caps . . .

4.4a . . . then unscrew the guide bolts . . .

flats may be rounded-off if the spanner slips. In such a case, a self-locking wrench is often the only way to unscrew a stubborn union, but it follows that the pipe and the damaged nuts must be renewed on reassembly. Always clean a union and surrounding area before disconnecting it. If disconnecting a component with more than one union, make a careful note of the connections before disturbing any of them.

4 If a brake pipe is to be renewed it can be obtained, cut to length and with the union nuts and end flares in place, from Vauxhall/Opel dealers. All that is then necessary is to bend it to shape, following the line of the original, before fitting it to the car. Alternatively, most motor accessory shops can make up brake pipes from kits, but this requires very careful measurement of the original to ensure that the replacement is of the correct length. The safest answer is usually to take the original to the shop as a pattern.

5 On refitting, do not overtighten the union nuts. It is not necessary to exercise brute force to obtain a sound joint.

6 Ensure that the pipes and hoses are correctly routed, with no kinks, and that they are secured in the clips or brackets provided. After fitting, remove the polythene from the reservoir, and bleed the hydraulic system as described in Section 2. Wash off any spilt fluid, and check carefully for fluid leaks.

4 Front brake pads – renewal

⚠️ *Warning: Renew BOTH sets of front brake pads at the same time – NEVER renew the pads on only one wheel, as uneven braking may result. Note that the dust created by wear of the pads may contain asbestos, which is a health hazard. Never blow it out with compressed air, and don't inhale any of it. An approved filtering mask should be worn when working on the brakes. DO NOT use petroleum-based solvents to clean brake parts – use brake cleaner or methylated spirit only.*

1 Firmly apply the handbrake, then jack up the front of the car and support it securely on axle stands (see *Jacking and vehicle support*). Remove the front roadwheels.

2 Using a screwdriver, prise the pad retaining spring from the outer edge of the caliper, noting its correct fitted position **(see illustration)**.

3 Prise out the two guide bolt dust caps from the inner edge of the caliper **(see illustration)**.

4 Unscrew the guide bolts from the caliper, and lift the caliper and inner pad away from the mounting bracket. Tie the caliper to the suspension strut using a suitable piece of wire **(see illustrations)**. Do not allow the

caliper to hang unsupported on the flexible brake hose.

5 Remove the inner pad from the caliper piston, noting that it is retained by a clip attached to the pad backing plate, and recover the outer pad from the mounting bracket.

6 Brush the dirt and dust from the caliper mounting bracket, but take care not to inhale it. Carefully remove any rust from the edge of the brake disc.

7 First measure the thickness of each brake pad (friction material and backing plate) **(see illustration)**. If either pad is worn at any point to the specified minimum thickness or less, all four pads must be renewed. The pads should also be renewed if any are fouled with oil or grease; there is no satisfactory way of degreasing friction material, once contaminated. If any of the brake pads are worn unevenly, or fouled with oil or grease, trace and rectify the cause before reassembly. The pad retaining spring should also be renewed if new pads are to be fitted. New brake pads and retaining springs are available from Vauxhall/Opel dealers.

8 If the brake pads are still serviceable, carefully clean them using a clean, fine wire brush or similar, paying particular attention to the sides and back of the metal backing. Clean out the grooves in the friction material, and pick out any large embedded particles of dirt or debris. Carefully clean the pad

4.4b . . . and slide off the caliper and inner pad assembly

4.4c Tie the caliper to the suspension strut, to avoid placing any strain on the hydraulic brake hose

4.7 Measuring brake pad thickness

4.11 Clip the inner pad securely into the caliper piston . . .

4.12 . . . and fit the outer pad to the caliper mounting bracket

4.14 Slide the caliper into position and install the guide bolts, tightening them to the specified torque setting

locations in the caliper body/mounting bracket.

9 Prior to fitting the pads, check that the guide bolts are a snug fit in the caliper bushes. Brush the dust and dirt from the caliper and piston, but do not inhale it, as it is injurious to health. Inspect the dust seal around the piston for damage, and the piston for evidence of fluid leaks, corrosion or damage. If attention to any of these components is necessary, refer to Section 8.

10 If new brake pads are to be fitted, the caliper piston must be pushed back into the cylinder to make room for them. *It is imperative that the caliper piston is pushed back as slowly as possible, using minimal force.* Either use a G-clamp or similar tool, or use suitable pieces of wood as levers. Provided that the master cylinder reservoir has not been overfilled with hydraulic fluid, there should be no spillage, but keep a careful watch on the fluid level while retracting the piston. If the fluid level rises above the MAX level line at any time, the surplus should be syphoned off or ejected via a plastic tube connected to the bleed screw (see Section 2). **Note:** *Do not syphon the fluid by mouth, as it is poisonous; use a syringe or an old poultry baster.*

11 Fit the inner pad to the caliper, ensuring that its clip is correctly located in the caliper piston **(see illustration)**.

12 Fit the outer pad to the caliper mounting bracket, ensuring that its friction material is facing the brake disc **(see illustration)**.

13 Slide the caliper and inner pad into position over the outer pad, and locate it in the mounting bracket.

14 Install the caliper guide bolts, and tighten them to the specified torque setting **(see illustration)**.

15 Refit the guide bolt dust caps to the caliper.

16 Refit the pad retaining spring to the caliper, ensuring that its ends are correctly located in the caliper holes **(see illustration)**.

17 Depress the brake pedal repeatedly, until normal (non-assisted) pedal pressure is restored, and the pads are pressed into firm contact with the brake disc.

18 Repeat the above procedure on the remaining front brake caliper.

19 Refit the roadwheels, aligning the marks made on removal, then lower the vehicle to the ground and tighten the roadwheel bolts to the specified torque setting.

20 Check the hydraulic fluid level as described in *Weekly checks*.

---

5 Rear brake shoes – renewal

> ⚠️ **Warning: Brake shoes must be renewed on BOTH rear wheels at the same time – NEVER renew the shoes on only one**

wheel, as uneven braking may result. The dust created as the shoes wear may contain asbestos, which is a health hazard. Never blow it out with compressed air, and don't inhale any of it. An approved filtering mask should be worn when working on the brakes. DO NOT use petroleum-based solvents to clean brake parts – use brake cleaner or methylated spirit only.

1 Remove the brake drum as described in Section 7.

2 Working carefully and taking the necessary precautions, remove all traces of brake dust from the brake drum, backplate and shoes.

3 Measure the thickness of the friction material of each brake shoe, at several points. If the friction material thickness or the depth from the friction material surface to any of the of rivet heads is equal to or less than the specified minimum, all four shoes must be renewed as a set **(see illustrations)**. Also, the shoes should be renewed if any are fouled with oil or grease; there is no satisfactory way of degreasing friction material, once contaminated.

4 If any of the brake shoes are worn unevenly, or fouled with oil or grease, trace and rectify the cause before reassembly. If the shoes are to be renewed proceed as described below. If all is well refit the drums as described in Section 7.

5 Note the location and orientation of all

4.16 When refitting, ensure that the pad retaining spring ends are correctly located in the caliper holes (arrowed)

5.3a Brake shoe wear can be assessed by measuring the thickness of the friction material . . .

5.3b . . . or by measuring the depth from the friction material surface to the rivet heads (a tyre tread depth indicator may be used)

5.5 Prior to disturbing the shoes, note the correct fitted locations of all components, paying particular attention to the adjuster strut components

5.6 Unhook the upper return spring, and remove it from the brake shoes

5.7 Remove the retaining spring, followed by the lever and return spring (arrowed)

components before dismantling, as an aid to reassembly **(see illustration)**.

6 Using a pair of pliers, carefully unhook the upper shoe return spring, and remove it from the brake shoes **(see illustration)**.

7 Prise the adjusting lever retaining spring out of the front shoe, and remove the retaining spring, lever and return spring from the brake shoe, noting each component's correct fitted position **(see illustration)**.

8 Prise the upper ends of the brake shoes apart, and withdraw the adjuster strut from between the shoes.

9 Using a pair of pliers, remove the front shoe retainer spring cup by depressing and turning it through 90º. With the cup removed, lift off

the spring and withdraw the retainer pin **(see illustrations)**.

10 Detach the front shoe from the lower return spring, and remove both the shoe and return spring.

11 Remove the rear shoe retainer spring cup, spring and retainer pin as described in paragraph 9, then remove the shoe, detaching it from the handbrake cable.

12 Do not depress the brake pedal until the brakes are reassembled. As a precaution, wrap a strong elastic band around the wheel cylinder pistons to retain them.

13 Although linings are available separately (without shoes), renewal of the shoes complete with linings is to be preferred, unless the necessary skills and equipment are available to fit new linings to the old shoes.

14 If both brake assemblies are dismantled at the same time, take care not to mix up the components. Note that the left-hand and right-hand adjuster components are marked as such; the threaded rod is marked L or R, and the other 'handed' components are colour-coded black for the left-hand side, and silver for the right-hand side **(see illustration)**.

15 Dismantle and clean the adjuster strut. Apply a smear of silicone-based grease to the adjuster threads **(see illustration)**.

16 Examine the return springs. If they are distorted, or if they have seen extensive service, renewal is advisable. Weak springs may cause the brakes to bind.

17 If a new handbrake operating lever was not supplied with the new shoes (where applicable), transfer the lever from the old shoes. The lever may be secured with a pin and circlip, or by a rivet, which will have to be drilled out. It may also be necessary to transfer the adjusting lever pivot pin and clip from the original front shoe to the new shoe **(see illustration)**.

18 Peel back the rubber protective caps, and check the wheel cylinder for fluid leaks or other damage. Ensure that both cylinder pistons are free to move easily. Refer to Section 9, if necessary, for information on wheel cylinder overhaul.

19 Prior to installation, clean the backplate thoroughly. Apply a thin smear of high-temperature copper-based brake grease or anti-seize compound to all those surfaces of

5.9a Using pliers, remove the spring cup . . .

5.9b . . . then lift off the spring and retainer pin

5.14 Left-hand adjuster strut assembly is marked L (arrowed)

5.15 Dismantling the adjuster strut for cleaning

5.17 It may be necessary to transfer the adjusting lever pivot pin and clip (arrowed) from the original shoes to the new ones

5.19 Apply a smear of anti-seize compound to the contact surfaces of the backplate (arrowed). Note the elastic band wrapped around the wheel cylinder

5.20 Engage the rear brake shoe with the handbrake cable, and locate the shoe on the backplate

5.22a Install the front shoe and lower return spring . . .

the backplate which bear on the shoes, particularly the wheel cylinder pistons and lower pivot point **(see illustration)**. Do not allow the lubricant to foul the friction material.
20 Ensure that the handbrake cable is correctly retained by the clip on the lower brake shoe pivot point, then engage the rear shoe with the cable. Locate the shoe on the backplate **(see illustration)**.
21 Install the rear shoe retainer pin and spring, and secure it in position with the spring cup.
22 Hook the lower return spring onto the rear shoe, then engage the front shoe with the return spring. Locate the front shoe on the backplate, and secure it in position with its

5.22b . . . and secure it in position with the retainer pin, spring and spring cup

retainer pin, spring and spring cup **(see illustrations)**.
23 Screw the adjuster strut wheel fully onto the forked end of the adjuster, so that the adjuster strut is set to its shortest possible length. Back the wheel off a half a turn, and check that it is free to rotate easily.
24 Manoeuvre the adjuster strut assembly into position between the brake shoes. Make sure that both ends of the strut are correctly engaged with the shoes, noting that the forked end of the strut must be positioned so that its longer, straight fork is to the back of the shoe **(see illustration)**.
25 Engage the adjusting lever return spring with the front shoe and adjusting lever, and locate the lever on its pivot pin **(see illustration)**. Check that the lever and spring are correctly located, and secure the lever in position with the retaining spring, making sure the spring ends are securely located in the retaining pin and shoe **(see illustration 5.5)**.
26 Remove the rubber band from the wheel cylinder. Make sure that both shoes are correctly positioned on the wheel cylinder pistons, then fit the upper return spring **(see illustration)**.
27 Ensure that the handbrake operating lever stop peg is correctly positioned against the edge of the shoe web, then refit the brake drum as described in Section 7.
28 Repeat the operation on the remaining brake.

29 Once both sets of rear shoes have been renewed, with the handbrake fully released, adjust the lining-to-drum clearance by repeatedly depressing the brake pedal 20 to 25 times. Whilst depressing the pedal, have an assistant listen to the rear drums, to check that the adjuster strut is functioning correctly; if so, a clicking sound will be emitted by the strut as the pedal is depressed.
30 Check and, if necessary, adjust the handbrake as described in Section 14.
31 On completion, check the hydraulic fluid level as described in *Weekly checks*.

6 Front brake disc – inspection, removal and refitting

Note: *Before starting work, refer to the note at the beginning of Section 4 concerning the dangers of asbestos dust.*

Inspection

Note: *If either disc requires renewal, BOTH should be renewed at the same time, to ensure even and consistent braking.*
1 Chock the rear wheels, firmly apply the handbrake, then jack up the front of the car and support it on axle stands. Remove the appropriate front roadwheel.
2 Slowly rotate the brake disc so that the full area of both sides can be checked; remove

5.24 Refit the adjuster strut, noting that the longer, straight part of the fork (arrowed) must be behind the shoe

5.25 Refit the adjusting lever and spring, making sure that the spring is correctly engaged in the front brake shoe hole (arrowed)

5.26 Make sure that both shoes are correctly aligned with the wheel cylinder, then install the upper return spring

6.6a Slacken and remove the two bolts (arrowed) securing the brake caliper mounting bracket to the hub . . .

6.6b . . . then slide the caliper assembly off the brake disc

6.7a Undo the retaining screw . . .

the brake pads if better access is required to the inner surface. Light scoring is normal in the area swept by the brake pads, but if heavy scoring is found, the disc must be renewed.

3 It is normal to find a lip of rust and brake dust around the disc's perimeter; this can be scraped off if required. If, however, a lip has formed due to excessive wear of the brake pad swept area, then the disc's thickness must be measured using a micrometer. Take measurements at several places around the disc, at the inside and outside of the pad swept area; if the disc has worn at any point to the specified minimum thickness or less, the disc must be renewed.

4 If the disc is thought to be warped, it can be checked for run-out either using a dial gauge mounted on any convenient fixed point, while the disc is slowly rotated, or by using feeler gauges to measure (at several points all around the disc) the clearance between the disc and a fixed point such as the caliper mounting bracket. To ensure that the disc is squarely seated on the hub, fit two wheel bolts, complete with spacers approximately 10 mm thick, and tighten them securely. If the measurements obtained are at the specified maximum or beyond, the disc is excessively warped and must be renewed; however, it is worth checking first that the hub bearing is in good condition (Chapters 1 and/or 10).

5 Check the disc for cracks, especially around the wheel bolt holes, and for any other wear or damage, and renew if necessary.

Removal

Note: *New brake caliper mounting bracket-to-swivel hub bolts will be required when refitting.*

6 Unscrew the two bolts securing the brake caliper assembly to the swivel hub, and slide the caliper assembly off the disc **(see illustrations)**. Using a piece of wire or string, tie the caliper to the front suspension coil spring, to avoid placing any strain on the hydraulic brake hose. Discard the caliper mounting bolts; they must be renewed whenever they are disturbed.

7 Remove the screw securing the brake disc to the hub, and remove the disc. If it is tight, lightly tap its rear face with a hide or plastic mallet **(see illustrations)**.

Refitting

8 Refitting is the reverse of the removal procedure, noting the following points:
a) Ensure that the mating surfaces of the disc and hub are clean and flat.
b) Tighten the disc retaining screw to the specified torque setting.
c) If a new disc has been fitted, use a suitable solvent to wipe any preservative coating from the disc before refitting the caliper.
d) Remove all traces of old thread-locking compound from the brake caliper holes in the swivel hub, ideally by running a tap of

the correct size and pitch through them. If the threads of the new caliper mounting bracket bolts are not already pre-coated with compound, apply a suitable thread-locking compound to them. Slide the caliper assembly into position over the disc, then fit the mounting bolts and tighten them to the specified torque setting **(see illustrations)**.
e) Refit the roadwheel, aligning the marks made on removal, then lower the vehicle to the ground and tighten the roadwheel bolts to the specified torque. On completion, repeatedly depress the brake pedal until normal (non-assisted) pedal pressure returns.

7 Rear brake drum – removal, inspection and refitting

Note: *Before starting work, refer to the note at the beginning of Section 5 concerning the dangers of asbestos dust.*

Removal

1 Chock the front wheels, then jack up the rear of the vehicle and support it on axle stands. Remove the appropriate rear wheel and release the handbrake. Proceed as described under the relevant sub-heading.

6.7b . . . and remove the brake disc from the hub

6.8a Apply thread-locking compound to the threads of the brake caliper mounting bracket bolts . . .

6.8b . . . and tighten them to the specified torque setting

7.2 Remove the cap from the centre of the drum to gain access to the hub nut

7.4a Slacken and remove the hub nut and washer . . .

7.4b . . . followed by the outer bearing

Corsa and Corsavan

2 Prise out the cap from the centre of the drum (see illustration).

3 Extract the split pin from the hub nut and discard it; a new one must be used on refitting.

4 Slacken and remove the rear hub nut, then slide off the toothed washer and remove the outer bearing from the centre of the drum (see illustrations).

5 It should now be possible to withdraw the brake drum assembly from the stub axle by hand. It may be difficult to remove the drum, due to the brake shoes binding on the inner circumference of the drum. If the brake shoes are binding, first check that the handbrake is fully released, then proceed as follows.

6 Referring to Section 14 for further information, fully slacken the handbrake cable adjuster nut to obtain maximum free play in the cable.

7 Remove the plug from the inspection hole in the brake backplate, and push the handbrake operating lever outwards away from the brake shoe. This will release the handbrake lever stop-peg from the edge of the brake shoe, and further collapse the shoes (see illustrations). The brake drum can then be withdrawn from the stub axle.

Combo Van

8 Slacken and remove the drum retaining

screw, and remove the drum from the vehicle. It may be difficult to remove the drum due to the brake shoes binding on the inner circumference of the drum. If the brake shoes are binding, first check that the handbrake is fully released, then proceed as described above in paragraphs 6 and 7.

Inspection

Note: *If either drum requires renewal, BOTH should be renewed at the same time, to ensure even and consistent braking.*

9 Working carefully, remove all traces of brake dust from the drum, but *avoid inhaling the dust, as it is a health-hazard.*

10 Scrub clean the outside of the drum, and check it for obvious signs of wear or damage (such as cracks around the roadwheel bolt holes); renew the drum if necessary.

11 Examine the inside of the drum carefully. Light scoring of the friction surface is normal, but if heavy scoring is found, the drum must be renewed. It is usual to find a lip on the drum's inboard edge which consists of a mixture of rust and brake dust; this should be scraped away, to leave a smooth surface which can be polished with fine (120- to 150-grade) emery paper. If, however, the lip is due to the friction surface being recessed by excessive wear, then the drum must be renewed.

12 If the drum is thought to be excessively

worn, or oval, its internal diameter must be measured at several points using an internal micrometer. Take measurements in pairs, the second at right-angles to the first, and compare the two to check for signs of ovality. Provided that it does not enlarge the drum to beyond the specified maximum diameter, it may be possible to have the drum refinished by skimming or grinding; if this is not possible, the drums on both sides must be renewed. Note that if the drum is to be skimmed, both drums must be refinished, to maintain a consistent internal diameter on both sides.

Refitting

13 If a new brake drum is to be installed, use a suitable solvent to remove any preservative coating that may have been applied to its interior. Note that it may also be necessary to shorten the adjuster strut length by rotating the strut wheel, to allow the new drum to pass over the brake shoes.

Corsa and Corsavan

14 Ensure that the handbrake lever stop-peg is correctly repositioned against the edge of the brake shoe web (see illustration), and apply a smear of grease to the drum oil seal.

15 Slide the drum into position, then refit the outer bearing and toothed thrustwasher,

7.7a If necessary, release the handbrake lever stop-peg by inserting a screwdriver in through the hole in the rear of the backplate . . .

7.7b . . . and use screwdriver (A) to push handbrake lever away from the brake shoe in the direction of arrow (B) – shown with drum removed

7.14 Prior to refitting the drum, check that the handbrake lever is correctly positioned on the shoe

7.15 Fit the toothed washer, making sure its tooth is correctly engaged with the stub axle slot

7.16a Tighten the hub nut to the specified torque setting while rotating the drum

7.16b Gradually slacken the hub nut until the position is found where it is just possible to move the toothed washer

ensuring that its tooth is correctly engaged in the axle slot **(see illustration)**.

16 Refit the hub nut, and tighten it to the specified pre-load torque setting, while rotating the brake drum to settle the hub bearings in position. Gradually slacken the hub nut until the position is found where it is just possible to move the toothed washer from side-to-side using a screwdriver **(see illustrations)**. **Note:** *Only a small amount of force should be needed to move the washer; do not use the screwdriver as a lever to move the washer.* When the hub nut is correctly positioned, secure it in position with a new split pin.

17 If the stub axle holes are not aligned with any of the slots in the hub nut, tighten the nut by the *smallest amount possible* until the split pin can be inserted. With the nut in this position, check that it is still possible to move the toothed washer. If it is, insert the split pin and secure it in position. If it is not possible to move the washer, slacken the nut slightly until the next hub nut slot/axle hole aligns. Check that it is possible to move the toothed washer, then secure the hub nut in position with the new split pin **(see illustration)**.

18 Fit the cap to the centre of the brake drum.

19 With the handbrake fully released, adjust the lining-to-drum clearance by repeatedly depressing the brake pedal 20 to 25 times. Whilst depressing the pedal, have an assistant listen to the rear drums, to check

that the adjuster strut is functioning correctly; if so, a clicking sound will be emitted by the strut as the pedal is depressed.

20 With the lining-to-drum clearance set, check and, if necessary, adjust the handbrake as described in Section 14.

21 Refit the roadwheel, aligning the marks made on removal, then lower the vehicle to the ground and tighten the roadwheel bolts to the specified torque setting.

Combo Van

22 Ensure that the drum and hub flange mating surfaces are clean and dry, and remove all traces of corrosion.

23 Ensure that the handbrake lever stop-peg is correctly repositioned against the edge of the brake shoe web, and locate the drum on the hub. Refit the drum retaining screw, and tighten it securely.

24 Carry out the operations described in paragraphs 19 to 21.

---

8 Front brake caliper –
removal, overhaul and refitting

Note: *New brake hose sealing washers will be required when refitting. Before starting work, refer to the note at the beginning of Section 2 concerning the dangers of hydraulic fluid, and to the warning at the beginning of Section 4 concerning the dangers of asbestos dust.*

Removal

1 Chock the rear wheels, apply the handbrake, then jack up the front of the vehicle and support it on axle stands. Remove the appropriate roadwheel.

2 Minimise fluid loss by first removing the master cylinder reservoir cap, then tightening it down onto a piece of polythene to obtain an airtight seal. Alternatively, use a brake hose clamp, a G-clamp or a similar tool to clamp the flexible hose.

3 Clean the area around the caliper brake hose union. Slacken and remove the union bolt, and recover the sealing washer from either side of the hose union. Discard the washers; new ones must be used on refitting. Plug the hose end and caliper hole, to minimise fluid loss and prevent the ingress of dirt into the hydraulic system.

4 Remove the brake pads as described in paragraphs 2 to 5 of Section 4, and remove the caliper from the vehicle.

Overhaul

5 With the caliper on the bench, wipe away all traces of dust and dirt, but *avoid inhaling the dust, as it is a health hazard.*

6 Withdraw the partially-ejected piston from the caliper body, and remove the dust seal. The piston can be withdrawn by hand, or if necessary pushed out by applying compressed air to the brake hose union hole. Only low pressure should be required, such as is generated by a foot pump.

7 Using a small screwdriver, carefully remove the piston seal from the caliper, taking great care not mark the bore **(see illustration)**.

8 Carefully press the guide bushes out of the caliper body.

9 Thoroughly clean all components, using only methylated spirit, isopropyl alcohol or clean hydraulic fluid as a cleaning medium. Never use mineral-based solvents such as petrol or paraffin, which will attack the hydraulic system's rubber components. Dry the components immediately, using compressed air or a clean, lint-free cloth. Use compressed air to blow clear the fluid passages, if available (wear eye protection).

10 Check all components, and renew any

7.17 When the hub bearing is correctly adjusted, secure the nut in position with a new split pin

8.7 Removing the piston seal from the caliper body

9.4 Rear wheel cylinder retaining bolt (A) and brake pipe union nut (B)

that are worn or damaged. Check particularly the cylinder bore and piston; these should be renewed (note that this means the renewal of the complete body assembly) if they are scratched, worn or corroded in any way. Similarly check the condition of the guide bushes and bolts; both bushes and bolts should be undamaged and (when cleaned) a reasonably tight sliding fit in each other. If there is any doubt about the condition of any component, renew it.

11 If the assembly is fit for further use, obtain the necessary components from your Vauxhall/Opel dealer. Renew the caliper seals as a matter of course; these should never be re-used.

12 On reassembly, ensure that all components are absolutely clean and dry.

13 Soak the piston and the new piston (fluid) seal in clean hydraulic fluid. Smear clean fluid on the cylinder bore surface.

14 Fit the new piston (fluid) seal, using only the fingers to manipulate it into the cylinder bore groove.

15 Fit the new dust seal to the piston, refit it to the cylinder bore using a twisting motion, and ensure that the piston enters squarely into the bore. Press the dust seal fully into the caliper body, and push the piston fully into the caliper bore.

16 Ease the guide bushes into position in the caliper body.

Refitting

17 Refit the caliper and brake pads as described in paragraphs 11 to 16 of Section 4.

18 Position a new sealing washer on each side of the hose union, and connect the brake hose to the caliper. Ensure that the hose is correctly positioned against the caliper body lug, then install the union bolt and tighten it to the specified torque setting.

19 Remove the brake hose clamp or the polythene, where fitted, and bleed the hydraulic system as described in Section 2. Note that, providing the precautions described were taken to minimise brake fluid loss, it should only be necessary to bleed the relevant front brake.

20 Refit the roadwheel, aligning the marks made on removal, then lower the vehicle to the ground and tighten the roadwheel bolts to the specified torque.

H.28158

9.6 Exploded view of a rear brake wheel cylinder

9 Rear wheel cylinder – removal, overhaul and refitting

Note: *Before starting work, refer to the note at the beginning of Section 2 concerning the dangers of hydraulic fluid, and to the warning at the beginning of Section 5 concerning the dangers of asbestos dust.*

Removal

1 Remove the brake drum as described in Section 7.

2 Using pliers, carefully unhook the upper brake shoe return spring, and remove it from both brake shoes. Pull the upper ends of the shoes away from the wheel cylinder to disengage them from the pistons.

3 Minimise fluid loss by first removing the master cylinder reservoir cap, then tightening it down onto a piece of polythene to obtain an airtight seal. Alternatively, use a brake hose clamp, a G-clamp or a similar tool to clamp the flexible hose at the nearest convenient point to the wheel cylinder.

4 Wipe away all traces of dirt around the brake pipe union at the rear of the wheel cylinder, and unscrew the union nut. Carefully ease the pipe out of the wheel cylinder, and plug or tape over its end to prevent dirt entry. Wipe off any spilt fluid immediately **(see illustration)**.

5 Unscrew the two wheel cylinder retaining bolts from the rear of the backplate, and remove the cylinder, taking great care not to allow surplus hydraulic fluid to contaminate the brake shoe linings.

Overhaul

6 Brush the dirt and dust from the wheel cylinder, but take care not to inhale it **(see illustration)**.

7 Pull the rubber dust seals from the ends of the cylinder body.

8 The pistons will normally be ejected by the pressure of the coil spring, but if they are not,

tap the end of the cylinder body on a piece of wood, or apply low air pressure (eg, from a foot pump) to the hydraulic fluid union hole to eject the pistons from their bores.

9 Inspect the surfaces of the pistons and their bores in the cylinder body for scoring, or evidence of metal-to-metal contact. If evident, renew the complete wheel cylinder assembly.

10 If the pistons and bores are in good condition, discard the seals and obtain a repair kit, which will contain all the necessary renewable items.

11 Lubricate the piston seals with clean brake fluid, and insert them into the cylinder bores, with the spring between them, using finger pressure only.

12 Dip the pistons in clean brake fluid, and insert them into the cylinder bores.

13 Fit the dust seals, and check that the pistons can move freely in their bores.

Refitting

14 Ensure that the backplate and wheel cylinder mating surfaces are clean, then spread the brake shoes and manoeuvre the wheel cylinder into position.

15 Engage the brake pipe, and screw in the union nut two or three turns to ensure that the thread has started.

16 Insert the two wheel cylinder retaining bolts, and tighten them to the specified torque setting. Now tighten the brake pipe union nut to the specified torque.

17 Remove the clamp from the flexible brake hose, or the polythene from the master cylinder reservoir (as applicable).

18 Ensure that the brake shoes are correctly located in the cylinder pistons, then carefully refit the brake shoe upper return spring, using a screwdriver to stretch the spring into position.

19 Refit the brake drum as described in Section 7.

20 Bleed the brake hydraulic system as described in Section 2. Providing suitable precautions were taken to minimise loss of fluid, it should only be necessary to bleed the relevant rear brake.

10.2 Disconnecting the master cylinder brake fluid level sender wiring connector

10.12a On right-hand drive models, unscrew the retaining bolt and nut . . .

10.12b . . . and remove the support bracket from the master cylinder

10 Master cylinder – removal, overhaul and refitting

Note: *New master cylinder retaining nuts will be required when refitting. Before starting work, refer to the warning at the beginning of Section 2 concerning the dangers of hydraulic fluid.*

Removal

1 Remove the master cylinder reservoir cap, and syphon the hydraulic fluid from the reservoir. **Note:** *Do not syphon the fluid by mouth, as it is poisonous; use a syringe or an old poultry baster.* Alternatively, open any convenient bleed screw in the system, and gently pump the brake pedal to expel the fluid through a plastic tube connected to the screw (see Section 2).

10.13a Undo the two retaining nuts (arrowed) . . .

2 Disconnect the battery negative terminal (refer to *Disconnecting the battery* in the Reference Chapter), and the wiring connector from the brake fluid level sender unit **(see illustration)**. Proceed as described under the relevant sub-heading.

Left-hand drive models

3 Wipe clean the area around the brake pipe unions on the side of the master cylinder, and place absorbent rags beneath the pipe unions to catch any surplus fluid. Make a note of the correct fitted positions of the unions, then unscrew the union nuts and carefully withdraw the pipes. Plug or tape over the pipe ends and master cylinder orifices, to minimise the loss of brake fluid and to prevent the entry of dirt into the system. Wash off any spilt fluid immediately with cold water.

4 Slacken and remove the two nuts securing the master cylinder to the vacuum servo unit and discard them; new ones must be used on refitting. Withdraw the master cylinder assembly from the engine compartment, noting that on models with ABS it will be necessary to undo the two retaining nuts securing the fluid reservoir to the engine compartment bulkhead.

5 Recover the seal which is fitted between the master cylinder and servo. If the servo unit pushrod has come away with the master cylinder, remove it and refit it to the centre of the servo.

Right-hand drive models

6 Remove both windscreen wiper arms as described in Chapter 12.

7 Carefully prise out the wiper spindle sealing grommets from the windscreen cowl panel.

8 Undo the retaining screws, and remove both halves of the windscreen cowl panel from the vehicle.

9 Peel the bonnet seal off the engine compartment bulkhead, and remove it from the vehicle.

10 Unscrew the large plastic nut from each wiper spindle.

11 Prise out the two retaining clips from the centre of the water deflector shield, then release the shield from the engine compartment bulkhead and wiper spindles, and remove it from the vehicle.

12 Unscrew the nut and bolt, and remove the support bracket from the top of the master cylinder fluid reservoir **(see illustrations)**.

13 Remove the master cylinder as described above in paragraphs 3 to 5, ignoring the note concerning models fitted with ABS **(see illustrations)**.

Overhaul

Models with ABS

14 Master cylinder overhaul on models with ABS is not possible, as no spares are available. If the cylinder is thought to be faulty, it must be renewed.

15 The only parts available individually are the fluid reservoir and its mounting seals. These can be renewed as described below for the non-ABS models.

Models without ABS

16 Unhook the clip (where necessary), and

10.13b . . . and remove the master cylinder from the servo unit

10.13c Where necessary, recover the pushrod . . .

10.13d . . . and rubber seal from the servo unit

1 Cap
2 Reservoir
3 Seals
4 Master cylinder body
5 Primary piston and springs
6 Secondary piston
7 Circlip
8 Seal

H.28161

10.16 Exploded view of the master cylinder – models without ABS

remove the fluid reservoir and reservoir seals from the master cylinder body **(see illustration)**.

17 Carefully prise the seal out of the end of the master cylinder.

18 Using a wooden dowel, press the piston assembly into the master cylinder body, then extract the circlip from the end of the master cylinder bore.

19 Noting the order of removal and the direction of fitting of each component, withdraw the piston assemblies, complete with springs and seals. Tap the body on to a clean wooden surface to dislodge them. If necessary, clamp the master cylinder body in a vice (fitted with soft jaw covers) and use compressed air (applied through the one of the fluid ports) to assist the removal of the piston assemblies. Wear eye protection if compressed air is used.

20 Thoroughly clean all components, using only methylated spirit, isopropyl alcohol or clean hydraulic fluid as a cleaning medium. Never use mineral-based solvents such as petrol or paraffin, which will attack the hydraulic system's rubber components. Dry the components immediately, using compressed air (wear eye protection) or a clean, lint-free cloth.

21 Check all components, and renew any that are worn or damaged. Check particularly

the cylinder bores and pistons; the complete assembly should be renewed if these are scratched, worn or corroded. If there is any doubt about the condition of the assembly or of any of its components, renew it. Check that the body's fluid passages are clear.

22 If the assembly is fit for further use, obtain a repair kit from your Vauxhall/Opel dealer. The kit consists of both piston assemblies and springs, as well as a new circlip. Renew all seals disturbed on dismantling, and the piston circlip, as a matter of course; these should never be re-used.

23 On reassembly, soak the piston assemblies in clean hydraulic fluid. Smear clean fluid into the cylinder bore.

24 Insert the pistons into the bore, using a twisting motion to avoid trapping the seal lips. Ensure that all components are refitted in the correct order and the right way round.

25 Press the piston assemblies fully into the bore using a clean wooden dowel, and secure them in position with the new circlip. Ensure that the circlip is correctly located in the groove in the cylinder bore.

26 Fit the new seal to the end of the master cylinder bore.

27 Fit the new mounting seals to the master cylinder body, then refit the reservoir, ensuring it's clipped securely in position.

Refitting

Left-hand drive models

28 Remove all traces of dirt from the master cylinder and servo unit mating surfaces, and check that the pushrod is in position in the servo unit. Inspect the master cylinder seal for signs of wear or damage, and renew if necessary.

29 Fit the seal to the servo and refit the master cylinder, ensuring that the pushrod enters the master cylinder bore centrally. Fit the new master cylinder mounting nuts, and tighten them to the specified torque. On models with ABS, securely tighten the fluid reservoir retaining nuts.

30 Wipe clean the brake pipe unions, refit them to the master cylinder ports, and tighten them to the specified torque.

31 Refill the master cylinder reservoir with new fluid, and bleed the complete hydraulic system as described in Section 2.

Right-hand drive models

32 Refit the master cylinder as described in paragraphs 28 to 30, ignoring the note concerning models with ABS.

33 Refit the fluid reservoir support bracket, tightening its retaining nut and bolt to the specified torque setting.

34 Install the components removed for access by reversing the removal procedure.

11 Brake pedal – removal and refitting

Removal

Left-hand drive models

1 Unhook the return spring from the brake pedal.

2 Slide off the spring clip, and withdraw the clevis pin securing the pedal to the servo unit pushrod **(see illustration)**.

3 Remove the locking clip from the brake pedal pivot shaft, then slacken and remove

11.2 Slide off the spring clip, and withdraw the clevis pin (arrowed) securing the servo pushrod to the pedal

11.3a Withdraw the locking clip . . .

11.3b . . . then slacken and remove the pivot shaft nut and washer

11.4a Withdraw the pivot shaft . . .

11.4b . . . and remove the pedal and return spring from the mounting bracket

11.7 On right-hand drive models, it will be necessary to first remove the clutch pedal bracket in order to remove the brake pedal

11.10 Tighten the pivot shaft nut to the specified torque setting, and secure it in position with the locking clip

11.11 Ensure that the servo pushrod clevis pin is securely retained by its spring clip

the nut and washer from the shaft (see illustrations).

4 Slide the pivot shaft to the left, and remove the brake pedal and return spring from underneath the facia (see illustrations).

5 Inspect the pedal pivot bush and shaft for signs of wear, and renew if necessary.

Right-hand drive models

6 On models with manual transmission, detach the clutch cable from the pedal as described in Chapter 6, and unhook the return spring from the pedal.

7 Working in the engine compartment, unscrew the clutch pedal mounting bracket retaining nuts and washers. From inside the vehicle, undo the bracket retaining bolt(s) and remove the bracket assembly from the vehicle (see illustration). Note: This bracket is fitted

on models with automatic transmission, even though the clutch pedal is not present.

8 Remove the brake pedal as described above in paragraphs 1 to 5.

Refitting

Left-hand drive models

9 Apply a smear of multi-purpose grease to the pedal pivot bush, and fit the return spring to the pedal.

10 Manoeuvre the pedal and spring into position, ensuring it is correctly engaged with the servo pushrod, and insert the pivot shaft bolt from the left-hand side. Fit the washer and nut. Tighten the pivot shaft nut to the specified torque setting, and secure it in position with the locking clip (see illustration).

11 Align the pedal hole with the pushrod end, and insert the clevis pin. Secure the pin in position with the spring clip (see illustration).

12 Hook the return spring over the pedal, and check the operation of the brake pedal.

Right-hand drive models

13 Refit the brake pedal as described above in paragraphs 9 to 12.

14 Refit the clutch pedal mounting bracket, tightening its retaining nuts and bolts securely.

15 Where necessary, connect the clutch cable to the clutch pedal, and hook the return spring back into position on the pedal. Adjust the clutch cable as described in Chapter 1.

12 Vacuum servo unit – testing, removal and refitting

Testing

1 To test the operation of the servo unit, with the engine off, depress the footbrake several times to exhaust the vacuum. Now start the engine, keeping the pedal firmly depressed. As the engine starts, there should be a noticeable 'give' in the brake pedal as the vacuum builds up. Allow the engine to run for at least two minutes, then switch it off. The brake pedal should now feel normal, but further applications should result in the pedal feeling firmer, the pedal stroke decreasing with each application.

2 If the servo does not operate as described, first inspect the servo unit check valve as described in Section 13.

3 If the servo unit still fails to operate satisfactorily, the fault lies within the unit itself. Repairs to the unit are not possible; if faulty, the servo unit must be renewed.

Removal

Left-hand drive models

4 On models with ABS, remove the master cylinder as described in Section 10.

5 On models without ABS, undo the two master cylinder retaining nuts, and disengage the unit from the front of the vacuum servo unit. Release the brake pipes from their

12.16 Servo unit retaining nuts (arrowed, one hidden) – right-hand drive models

12.19 Prior to refitting the servo unit, ensure that the pushrod length (1) is correctly set – see text

retaining clips on the bulkhead and body, and position the master cylinder clear of the servo unit, ensuring that no excess strain is placed on the brake pipes. Keep the master cylinder upright, to prevent fluid loss. Discard the retaining nuts; new ones must be used on refitting.

6 Carefully ease the vacuum hose out of the servo unit, taking care not to displace the sealing grommet.

7 Release the cooling system expansion tank from the bulkhead, and position it clear of the servo.

8 Release the clutch cable from its retainer, and remove the retainer. Also remove the frame.

9 Working from inside the vehicle, slide off the spring clip and withdraw the clevis pin securing the brake pedal to the servo unit pushrod.

10 Slacken and remove the nuts securing the servo unit to the brake pedal mounting bracket, then return to the engine compartment and manoeuvre the servo unit out of position. Recover the gasket from the rear of the servo unit. Discard the gasket and retaining nuts; new ones should be used on refitting.

Right-hand drive models

11 Remove the windscreen wiper motor assembly as described in Chapter 12.

12 Remove the master cylinder as described in Section 10. On some models, it may prove sufficient to unbolt the master cylinder and position it clear of the servo, taking great care not to strain the brake pipes. This removes the need to disconnect the brake pipes and open the hydraulic system.

13 On models with manual transmission, detach the clutch cable from the pedal as described in Chapter 6, and unhook the return spring from the pedal.

14 Working in the engine compartment, unscrew the clutch pedal mounting bracket retaining nuts and washers. From inside the vehicle, undo the bracket retaining bolt(s) and remove the bracket from the vehicle. **Note:** *This bracket is fitted on models with automatic transmission, even though the clutch pedal is not present.*

15 Unhook the return spring from the brake pedal, then slide off the spring clip and withdraw the clevis pin securing the pedal to the servo unit pushrod.

16 Slacken and remove the nuts securing the servo unit to the pedal mounting bracket, and remove the bracket **(see illustration)**.

17 Return to the engine compartment, and lift the servo unit out of position. Recover the gasket from the rear of the servo unit. Discard the gasket and retaining nuts; new ones should be used on refitting.

Refitting

18 Before refitting the servo, check that the pushrod fork dimension is correct, as follows.

19 Measure the distance from the end face of the servo casing to the centre of the clevis pin hole in the pushrod fork **(see illustration)**. This distance should be 141.5 mm on left-hand drive models and 133.0 mm on right-hand drive models. To make accurate measurement easier, insert a bolt or bar of suitable diameter through the pivot pin hole, and measure to the centre of the bolt or bar.

20 If adjustment is necessary, slacken the locknut, and turn the fork to give the specified dimension. Hold the fork and securely tighten the locknut.

21 Inspect the servo unit check valve sealing grommet for signs of damage or deterioration, and renew if necessary. Proceed as described under the relevant sub-heading.

Left-hand drive models

22 Ensure that the servo and bulkhead mating surfaces are clean and dry.

23 Fit a new gasket to the rear of the servo, and reposition the unit in the engine compartment.

24 From inside the vehicle, ensure that the servo unit pushrod is correctly engaged with the brake pedal, then offer up the pedal mounting bracket and fit the new servo unit mounting nuts. Tighten the nuts to the specified torque setting.

25 Refit the servo unit pushrod-to-brake pedal clevis pin, and secure it in position with the spring clip.

26 Install the frame and clutch cable retainer. Clip the clutch cable back into position.

27 Refit the expansion tank in its original position.

28 Ease the vacuum hose end piece into place in the servo unit, taking great care not to displace or damage the grommet.

29 On models without ABS, refit the master cylinder to the front of the servo unit, ensuring that the servo pushrod enters the master cylinder squarely. Fit the new master cylinder mounting nuts, and tighten them to the specified torque setting. Ensure that the brake pipes are correctly clipped back into position in all the relevant retaining clips.

30 On models with ABS, refit the master cylinder as described in Section 10.

31 On completion, start the engine and check for air leaks at the vacuum hose-to-servo unit connection. Check the operation of the braking system.

Right-hand drive models

32 Install the servo unit as described above in paragraphs 22 to 24.

33 Refit the clutch pedal mounting bracket, tightening its retaining nuts and bolts securely.

34 Where necessary, reconnect the clutch cable to the pedal, and hook the return spring back over the pedal (see Chapter 6). Adjust the clutch cable as described in Chapter 1.

35 Refit the master cylinder as described in Section 10.

36 Refit the windscreen wiper motor as described in Chapter 12.

37 On completion, start the engine and check for air leaks at the vacuum hose-to-servo unit connection. Check the operation of the braking system.

13 Vacuum servo unit check valve – removal, testing and refitting

1 The check valve is located in the vacuum hose running from the inlet manifold to the brake servo. Although the valve is available separately from the hoses, in order to remove the valve, the hoses must be cut, and therefore renewed on reassembly. If the valve is to be renewed, it is therefore easier to remove the complete hose/valve assembly, and renew it complete **(see illustration)**.

13.1 Vacuum servo unit check valve is integral with the hose, and cannot be renewed separately

13.2 Ease the vacuum hose out from the servo unit, taking care not to displace the grommet (arrowed)

Removal

2 Carefully ease the vacuum hose out of the servo unit, taking care not to displace the grommet **(see illustration)**.

3 Note the correct routing of the hose, then undo the union nut securing the hose to the inlet manifold and remove the hose assembly from the vehicle.

Testing

4 Examine the check valve and vacuum hose for signs of damage, and renew if necessary.

5 The valve may be tested by blowing through it in both directions. Air should flow through the valve in one direction only: when blown through from the servo unit end of the valve. Renew the valve if this is not the case.

6 Examine the servo unit rubber sealing grommet for signs of damage or deterioration, and renew as necessary.

Refitting

7 Ensure that the sealing grommet is correctly fitted to the servo unit.

8 Ease the hose union into position in the servo, taking great care not to displace or damage the grommet.

9 Ensure that the hose is correctly routed, and connect it to the inlet manifold, tightening its union nut securely.

10 On completion, start the engine and check for air leaks at the check valve-to-servo unit connection.

14.4 Adjusting the handbrake cable – Corsa and Corsavan models

14 Handbrake – adjustment

1 To check the handbrake adjustment, fully release the handbrake lever, and apply the footbrake firmly several times. This will establish correct shoe-to-drum clearance, and ensure that the self-adjust mechanism is fully adjusted. Applying normal, moderate pressure, pull the handbrake lever to the fully-applied position, counting the number of clicks emitted from the handbrake ratchet mechanism. If adjustment is correct, there should be 8 clicks before the handbrake is fully applied; if this is not the case, adjust as follows.

2 Chock the front wheels, then jack up the rear of the vehicle, and support securely on axle stands.

3 On Corsa and Corsavan models, the handbrake cable adjuster nut is situated above the rear axle crossmember. On Combo Van models, the handbrake cable adjuster nut is situated directly underneath the handbrake lever; if necessary, unscrew the retaining nuts and remove the exhaust heat shield to improve access to the nut.

4 With the handbrake set on the fourth notch of the ratchet mechanism, rotate the adjusting nut until a reasonable amount of force is required to turn each wheel/hub **(see illustration)**. **Note:** *The force required should be equal for each wheel.* Once this is so, fully

release the handbrake lever and check that the wheels/hubs rotate freely. Check the adjustment by applying the handbrake fully whilst counting the clicks emitted from the handbrake ratchet and, if necessary, re-adjust.

5 On completion of adjustment, check the handbrake cables for free movement, and apply a little grease to the adjuster threads and exposed cable ends to prevent corrosion.

6 Refit the exhaust heat shield and/or roadwheels (as applicable) and lower the vehicle to the ground. If the roadwheels have been removed, tighten the roadwheel bolts to the specified torque setting.

15 Handbrake lever – removal, overhaul and refitting

Removal

1 Chock the front wheels, then jack up the rear of the vehicle, and support securely on axle stands.

2 Undo the retaining nuts, and remove the exhaust heat shield from underneath the vehicle to gain access to the underside of the handbrake lever.

3 On Corsa and Corsavan models, fully slacken the handbrake cable adjuster nut. Remove the grommet from the connecting link joining the front end of the cable to the handbrake lever, and detach the cable **(see illustration)**. Detach the connecting joint from the handbrake lever rod, and remove it from underneath the vehicle.

4 On Combo Van models, slacken and remove the handbrake cable adjuster nut, and detach the cable equaliser plate from the handbrake rod.

5 Remove the left-hand front seat as described in Chapter 11.

6 Peel back the carpet situated at the base of the handbrake lever, to gain access to the handbrake lever mounting bolts via the holes in the vehicle body. If necessary, cut flaps in the carpet using a sharp knife **(see illustration)**.

7 Unscrew the handbrake lever mounting bolts and withdraw the lever, disconnecting the wiring connector from the handbrake warning light switch as it becomes accessible **(see illustrations)**.

15.3 On Corsa and Corsavan models, remove the grommet and free the cable and connecting link from the handbrake lever

15.6 Note that it will probably be necessary to cut holes in the carpet to gain access to the handbrake lever retaining bolts

15.7a Unscrew the two retaining bolts . . .

15.7b . . . and remove them through the access holes . . .

15.7c . . . then lift the handbrake lever out of position

Overhaul

8 A worn ratchet segment can be renewed by driving the securing sleeve from the handbrake lever, using a metal rod or a bolt of suitable diameter.

9 Drive the new sleeve supplied with the new segment into the lever, to permit a little play between the segment and lever.

10 If desired, a new pawl can be fitted after drilling out the original pivot rivet.

11 Rivet the new pawl so that it is still free to move.

12 The handbrake warning light switch can be removed from the lever assembly after unscrewing its retaining bolt.

Refitting

13 Refitting is a reversal of the removal procedure, adjusting the cable as described in Section 14.

16 Handbrake cables – removal and refitting

Corsa and Corsavan

1 The handbrake cable consists of two sections, a long cable (complete with equaliser plate) linking the handbrake lever to the left-hand drum brake, and a short cable linking the right-hand drum brake to the equaliser plate. The equaliser plate links both cables together, and is situated above the rear axle crossmember. Each cable can be renewed individually as follows.

Long cable

2 Undo the retaining nuts, and remove the exhaust heat shield from underneath the vehicle to gain access to the underside of the handbrake lever.

3 Unscrew the handbrake cable adjuster nut, and detach the short cable from the equaliser plate.

4 Remove the left-hand rear brake drum as described in Section 7.

5 Referring to Section 5, remove the upper and lower return springs, then remove the spring cup, spring and retainer pin, and remove the rear brake shoe. Note that the

front shoe and adjuster strut mechanism can be left in position on the backplate.

6 Free the handbrake cable from the retaining clip on the shoe lower pivot, then remove the retaining clip and withdraw the cable from the rear of the backplate **(see illustration)**.

7 Work back along the cable, releasing it from any relevant retaining clips and ties, whilst noting its correct routing **(see illustration)**.

8 Remove the grommet from the connecting link, and detach the front end of the cable from the connecting joint. Remove the cable from underneath the vehicle. Free the connecting link from the handbrake lever rod, and store it with the cable for safe-keeping.

9 On refitting, attach the connecting link to the handbrake lever, then hook the cable into the connecting link. Secure the cables in position with the grommet

10 Work back along the cable, securing it in position with all the relevant clips and ties, and routing it as noted on removal.

11 Insert the cable through the backplate, and secure it in position with the clip. Insert the short cable in the equaliser plate, and screw the adjuster nut onto the cable threads.

12 Ensure that the cable is securely retained by the clip on the shoe lower pivot point, and refit the rear brake shoe as described in Section 5.

13 Ensure that the brake shoes and adjuster strut components are correctly fitted, then refit the brake drum as described in Section 7.

14 Adjust the handbrake cable as described in Section 14.

16.6 Each handbrake cable is secured to the backplate by a retaining clip

Short cable

15 Remove the cable as described above in paragraphs 3 to 7, removing the right-hand brake drum instead of the left-hand drum.

16 Refit the cable as described in paragraphs 10 to 14.

Combo Van

17 The handbrake cable consists of two sections of equal length, which run from each rear brake to the equaliser plate. The equaliser plate is secured to the handbrake lever rod by the adjuster nut. The cables cannot be separated from the equaliser plate, and therefore the cable arrangement can only be removed and refitted as an assembly.

Removal

18 Undo the retaining nuts, and remove the exhaust heat shield from underneath the vehicle to gain access to the underside of the handbrake lever.

19 Unscrew the handbrake cable adjuster nut, and detach the equaliser plate from the handbrake lever.

20 Remove the left-hand rear brake drum as described in Section 7.

21 Referring to Section 5, remove the upper and lower return springs, then remove the spring cup, spring and retainer pin, and remove the rear brake shoe. Note that the front shoe and adjuster strut mechanism can be left in position on the backplate.

22 Free the handbrake cable from the retaining clip on the shoe lower pivot, then remove the retaining clip and withdraw the cable from the rear of the backplate.

23 Repeat the operations in paragraphs 20 to 22 on the right-hand rear brake.

24 Work back along both cables, releasing them from any relevant retaining clips and ties, whilst noting the correct routing. Remove the cable/equaliser plate assembly from underneath the vehicle.

Refitting

25 Connect the equaliser plate to the handbrake lever, and screw on the adjuster nut.

26 Work back along both cables, securing them in position with all the relevant clips and ties, and routing them as noted on removal.

27 Insert the cable through the left-hand

16.7 Free the cable from any relevant clips or brackets securing it to the vehicle underbody

17.1 Rear brake pressure-regulating valves (arrowed) – 1.0 and 1.2 litre models

17.8 Rear brake pressure-regulating valve assembly – 1.4 and 1.6 litre Corsa and Corsavan models

17.18 On Corsa and Corsavan models, slacken the pivot bolt . . .

backplate, and secure it in position with the clip.

28 Ensure that the cable is securely retained by the clip on the shoe lower pivot point, and refit the rear brake shoe as described in Section 5.

29 Ensure that the brake shoes and adjuster strut components are correctly fitted, then refit the left-hand brake drum as described in Section 7. **Note:** *Do not apply the brake pedal until the right-hand drum has also been installed.*

30 Repeat the operations in paragraphs 27 to 29 on the right-hand brake.

31 Once both drums are in position, with the handbrake fully released, adjust the lining-to-drum clearance by repeatedly depressing the brake pedal 20 to 25 times. Whilst depressing the pedal, have an assistant listen to the rear drums, to check that the adjuster strut is functioning correctly; if so, a clicking sound will be emitted by the strut as the pedal is depressed

32 Adjust the handbrake cable as described in Section 14.

17 Rear brake pressure-regulating valve(s) – removal and refitting

Note: *Before starting work, refer to the warning at the beginning of Section 2 concerning the dangers of hydraulic fluid.*

Removal

1.0 and 1.2 litre models

1 The rear brake pressure-regulating valves are of the pressure-dependent type, and are located underneath the vehicle, directly above the rear axle on the left-hand side of the vehicle **(see illustration)**. There are two valves, one for each rear brake. The purpose of the valves is to prevent the rear wheels locking up under heavy braking.

2 Chock the front wheels, then jack up the rear of the vehicle and support it on axle stands.

3 Minimise fluid loss by first removing the master cylinder reservoir cap and screwing it down onto a piece of polythene.

4 Wipe clean the area around the brake pipe unions on the relevant valve, and place absorbent rags beneath the pipe unions to catch any surplus fluid.

5 Retain the relevant pressure-regulating valve with a suitable open-ended spanner, slacken the union nuts and disconnect both brake pipes, and remove the valve from underneath the vehicle. Plug or tape over the pipe ends and valve orifices, to minimise the loss of brake fluid and to prevent the entry of dirt into the system. Wash off any spilt fluid immediately with cold water.

6 Where necessary, remove the other valve in the same way.

7 If renewal is necessary, both valves should be renewed as a matched pair. The lead and switching pressures are stamped on the body of each valve (lead pressure in front of the slash, and switching pressure after the dash). Ensure that both valves are stamped with exactly the same pressures.

1.4 and 1.6 litre models

8 The pressure-regulating valve is of the load-dependent type, and is mounted underneath the rear of the vehicle. The valve is mounted onto the vehicle underbody, and is connected to the rear axle (Corsa Corsavan) or leaf spring (Combo Van) by a spring **(see illustration)**. As the load being carried by the vehicle is altered, the suspension moves in relation to the vehicle body, altering the tension in the spring. The spring then adjusts the pressure-regulating valve lever so that the correct pressure is applied to the rear brakes to suit the load being carried. The purpose of the valve is to prevent the rear wheels locking up under heavy braking.

9 Minimise fluid loss by first removing the master cylinder reservoir cap and screwing it down onto a piece of polythene.

10 Using pliers, carefully unhook the spring and detach it from the valve.

11 Wipe clean the area around the brake pipe unions on the valve, and place absorbent rags beneath the pipe unions to catch any surplus fluid. Make identification marks on the brake pipes; these marks can then be used on

refitting to ensure that each pipe is correctly reconnected.

12 Slacken the union nuts, and disconnect the brake pipes from the valve. Plug or tape over the pipe ends and valve orifices, to minimise the loss of brake fluid and to prevent the entry of dirt into the system. Wash off any spilt fluid immediately with cold water.

13 Undo the two bolts, and remove the pressure-regulating valve from underneath the vehicle.

Refitting

1.0 and 1.2 litre models

14 Refitting is the reverse of the removal procedure, tightening the pipe union nuts to the specified torque setting. On completion, bleed the complete hydraulic system as described in Section 2.

1.4 and 1.6 litre models

15 Refitting is the reverse of the removal procedure, noting the following points:

a) *Tighten the valve mounting bolts to the specified torque.*

b) *Ensure that the brake pipes are correctly connected to the valve, and tighten the union nuts to the specified torque settings.*

c) *Coat the ends of the spring with grease prior to installation.*

d) *Bleed the complete hydraulic system as described in Section 2.*

16 On completion, adjust the valve as follows.

17 With the vehicle completely unladen, position the car over an inspection pit, or drive it onto ramps so that it is resting on all four wheels.

18 On Corsa and Corsavan models, slacken the front pivot bolt, which secures the valve spring to the axle **(see illustration)**. On Combo Van models, slacken the nuts securing the spring clamp to the right-hand leaf spring.

19 Remove all tension from the spring, then push the pressure-regulating valve lever towards the pivot bolt/clamp (as applicable) until the lever reaches its stop. Hold it there, then position the pivot bolt/clamp so that all clearance between the spring and valve is

17.19a . . . and adjust the valve as described in the text

17.19b On Combo van models, adjust the valve as described in the text by repositioning the clamp (arrowed) on the leaf spring

removed, without tensioning the spring **(see illustrations)**.

20 On Corsa and Corsavan models, hold the bolt in this position and tighten it to the specified torque setting. On Combo Van models, tighten the spring clamp nuts to the specified torque setting.

18 Stop-light switch – removal, refitting and adjustment

Removal

1 The stop-light switch is located on the pedal bracket behind the facia. To remove the switch, first disconnect the battery negative terminal (refer to *Disconnecting the battery* in the Reference Chapter).

2 Disconnect the wiring plug from the stop-light switch, then unscrew the switch from its mounting bracket **(see illustrations)**.

Refitting and adjustment

3 Refitting is a reversal of removal, adjusting the switch as follows.

4 The switch should be positioned so that the stop-lights are illuminated after the brake pedal has travelled approximately 20 mm. Adjust the position of the switch as required until the stop-lights are functioning correctly.

19 Anti-lock braking system (ABS) – description and system operation

General description

1 The anti-lock braking system fitted to Corsa models covered by this manual is the Bosch 5.3 type, comprising a hydraulic modulator assembly, electronic control unit and four wheel speed sensors, in addition to the normal braking system components.

2 The purpose of the system is to apply the vehicle brakes at maximum efficiency without wheel lock or loss of directional stability. Inductive type wheel speed sensors monitor the speed of the roadwheels by generating an electrical signal as the wheel is rotated. This information is passed to the ABS electronic control unit (ECU) which compares the signals received from each wheel and uses the speed of the fastest wheel as a reference value. The ECU continually monitors the speed of each wheel and if the onset of lock at any wheel is detected (a received speed signal being less than the reference value) a signal is sent to the hydraulic modulator which regulates the brake pressure for the relevant wheel(s).

Electronic control unit

3 The ECU continually monitors wheel speed from the signals provided by the wheel speed sensors, and brake application from the brake light switch signal. If the ECU detects the incidence of wheel lock on one or more wheels, a signal is sent to the hydraulic modulator to regulate the hydraulic pressure to the brake of the locking wheel(s). The ECU contains two microprocessors and uses digital technology to complete this function and other functions such as, fault code memory and power modules for valve and relay activity.

4 To reduce external electrical connections to a minimum and improve reliability, the ECU is integral with the hydraulic modulator **(see illustration)**.

5 The ECU is equipped with a self-test capability that initially examines the ABS system when the ignition is switched on, and then examines the wheel speed sensor signals after a wheel speed of approximately 4 mph is reached from all wheels. The ABS self-test program continues to examine the signals from the various components as long as the ignition is switched on. If self-test determines that faults are not present, the ABS is ready for operation once a specified vehicle speed has been achieved.

18.2a Disconnect the wiring connector from the stop-light switch . . .

18.2b . . . and unscrew the switch from the pedal bracket

Eq44093

19.4 ABS ECU (1) and integral hydraulic modulator (2)

19.8 ABS hydraulic circuit schematic

1 Pump motor 2 Inlet and outlet solenoid valves 3 Pulsation damper

19.11 Sectional view of a wheel speed sensor

1 Mounting bolt location   5 Coil
2 Permanent magnet   6 Sensor tip
3 Wiring harness   7 Toothed sensor ring
4 O-ring

6 If the ECU detects that a fault is present, all ABS functions are switched off and the warning lamp is turned on. The conventional braking system continues to operate as normal without ABS assistance.

7 If the ECU detects a fault during the self-test routine, an internal fault code is stored in the ECU memory. Stored fault codes can be retrieved from the vehicle diagnostic connector with the aid of a suitable fault code reader. If the fault clears, the code will remain stored until cleared with the fault code reader.

Hydraulic modulator

8 Bosch 5.3 is a four-channel system with a separate hydraulic circuit for each brake. The hydraulic modulator consists of an electric motor and radial piston return pump, inlet and outlet solenoid valves, pressure accumulators and pulsation dampers **(see illustration)**. The unit controls the hydraulic pressure applied to the brake for each individual front wheel and each individual rear wheel. The return pump is switched on when the ABS is activated and returns hydraulic fluid, drained off during the pressure reduction phase, back into the brake circuit.

9 The 'select-low' principle is employed for control of the rear brakes during ABS operation. With the 'select-low' principle, the wheel with the lowest adhesion determines the amount of hydraulic pressure to be supplied to both rear brakes during a controlled ABS cycle.

Wheel speed sensors

10 The rotational speed of the roadwheels and any changes in the rotational speed are recorded by inductive wheel speed sensors, one located at each roadwheel.

11 Each wheel speed sensor assembly comprises a toothed sensor ring which rotates at roadwheel speed, and an adjacent sensor mounted a set distance from the sensor ring **(see illustration)**.

12 The sensors are permanent magnet pulse generator types producing an AC voltage sine wave as the sensor ring teeth pass through the magnetic field of the sensor.

13 The frequency of the waveform produced by the wheel speed sensor is proportional to the road speed. This AC voltage signal is continually being delivered to the ECU for processing.

14 The peak-to-peak voltage of the speed signal can vary considerably according to wheel speed and an analogue-to-digital converter in the ECU transforms the AC pulse into a digital signal.

Wiring, switches and warning lamps

15 An integrated main wiring harness is used for ECU power supply and earth connections, and enables sensor signals to reach the ECU and the ECU, in turn, to send output signals to the ABS warning lamp and diagnostic connector. The main relay and return pump relay are an integral part of the ECU and cannot be separately removed. Internal connections between the ECU and hydraulic modulator are used to activate the return pump motor.

16 The stop-light switch comprises a switch body and contact pin and is located above the brake pedal. When the brake pedal is depressed, closing the stop light switch, a signal is sent to the ECU indicating that the brakes are being applied. Once this signal is received, the ECU will begin monitoring the wheel speed via the wheel speed sensors and activate the ABS if necessary.

17 After the ignition is switched on, the ABS warning lamp on the instrument panel is illuminated for approximately 2 to 4 seconds during the system initial self-test cycle, then extinguished. During vehicle operation above a pre-determined wheel speed, the ECU continues the self-test cycle whereby the system status is continually monitored. If a fault is detected, the ECU illuminates the warning lamp on the instrument panel. The ECU switches off the ABS, however the conventional braking system continues to operate as normal. The warning lamp will remain illuminated until the fault is no longer present.

18 When the ECU detects a fault, the fault code is stored and the ABS warning lamp activated. If the fault no longer exists after the next system start (ignition on/off) the ABS warning lamp is extinguished after the self-test cycle, however the fault code remains stored in the ECU memory.

System operation

19 The ECU continually monitors wheel speed from the signals provided by the wheel speed sensors. If the ECU detects the incidence of wheel lock on one or more wheels, ABS is automatically initiated in three phases. As the system operates individually on each wheel, all or any of the wheels could be in any one of the following phases at any particular moment.

First ABS phase, pressure holding

20 To prevent any further build-up of hydraulic pressure in the circuit being controlled, the ECU closes the inlet solenoid valve and allows the outlet solenoid valve to remain closed. The hydraulic fluid line from the master cylinder to the brake caliper or

19.20 ABS operation – first phase, pressure holding

1 Inlet solenoid valve   *2 Outlet solenoid valve*   *3 Wheel speed sensor*

wheel cylinder is closed, and the hydraulic fluid in the controlled circuit is maintained at a constant pressure. This effectively removes the braking force from the controlled circuit. The pressure cannot now be increased in that circuit by any further application of the brake pedal **(see illustration)**.

21 If the wheel speed sensor signals indicate that wheel rotation has now stabilised, the ECU will instigate the pressure build-up phase, allowing braking to continue. If wheel lock is still detected after the pressure holding phase, the ECU instigates the pressure reduction phase.

Second ABS phase, pressure reduction

22 If the ECU detects wheel instability, a pressure reduction phase is initiated. The inlet solenoid valve remains closed and the outlet solenoid valve is opened by means of a series of short activation pulses. The pressure in the controlled circuit decreases rapidly as the fluid flows from the brake caliper or wheel cylinder into the pressure accumulator. At the same

time, the ECU actuates the electric motor to operate the return pump. The hydraulic fluid is then pumped back into the pressure side of the master cylinder. This process creates a pulsation which can be felt in the brake pedal action, but which is softened by the pulsation damper **(see illustration)**.

Third ABS phase, pressure build-up

23 The pressure build-up phase is instigated after the wheel rotation has stabilised. The inlet and outlet solenoid valves are returned to the at rest position (inlet solenoid valve open and outlet solenoid valve closed) which re-opens the hydraulic fluid line from the master cylinder to the brake caliper or wheel cylinder. Hydraulic pressure is reinstated, thus re-introducing operation of the brake. After a brief period, a short pressure holding phase is re-introduced and the ECU continually shifts between pressure build-up and pressure holding until the wheel has decelerated to a sufficient degree where pressure reduction is once more required **(see illustration)**.

24 The whole ABS control cycle takes place 4 to 10 times per second for each affected wheel and this ensures maximum braking effect and control during ABS operation.

20 Anti-lock Braking system (ABS) components – removal and refitting

Modulator assembly

Note: *Before starting work, refer to the note at the beginning of Section 2 concerning the dangers of hydraulic fluid.*

19.22 ABS operation – second phase, pressure reduction

1 Inlet solenoid valve	*4 Pump motor*
2 Outlet solenoid valve	*5 Return pump*
3 Pressure accumulator	*6 Pulsation damper*

19.23 ABS operation – third phase, pressure build-up

1 Inlet solenoid valve   *2 Outlet solenoid valve*

Removal

1 Disconnect the battery negative terminal (refer to *Disconnecting the battery* in the Reference Chapter).

2 Pull out the locking bar and disconnect the wiring harness multi-plug connector from the electronic control unit located on the hydraulic modulator.

3 Unscrew the master cylinder reservoir filler cap, and top-up the reservoir to the MAX mark (see *Weekly checks*). Place a piece of polythene over the filler neck, and secure the polythene with the filler cap. This will minimise brake fluid loss during subsequent operations. As a precaution, place absorbent rags beneath the modulator brake pipe unions when unscrewing them.

4 Wipe clean the area around the modulator brake pipe unions, then make a note of how the pipes are arranged, to use as a reference on refitting. Unscrew the union nuts, and carefully withdraw the pipes.

5 Plug or tape over the pipe ends and modulator orifices, to minimise the loss of brake fluid and to prevent the entry of dirt into the system. Wash off any spilt fluid immediately with cold water.

6 Slacken and remove the mounting nuts, and release the modulator assembly from its mounting bracket. Remove the assembly from the engine compartment.

Refitting

7 Refitting is the reverse of the removal procedure, noting the following points:

  a) *Tighten the modulator block mounting nuts to the specified torque setting.*

  b) *Refit the brake pipes to their respective unions, and tighten the union nuts to the specified torque.*

  c) *Ensure that the wiring is correctly routed, and that the multi-plug connector is firmly pressed into position and secured with the locking bar.*

  d) *On completion, and prior to refitting the battery, bleed the complete hydraulic system as described in Section 2. Ensure that the system is bled in the correct order, to prevent air entering the modulator return pump.*

Electronic control unit (ECU)

Removal

Caution: Separation of the ECU from the hydraulic modulator is not recommended by the manufacturers of the ABS system (Bosch). Information on this operation is, however, given by Vauxhall/Opel. If difficulties are experienced when refitting the ECU to the modulator, it may be necessary to renew the complete assembly.

Note: *New ECU retaining screws and a new gasket will be required for refitting.*

8 Remove the hydraulic modulator from the car as described previously in this Section.

9 Disconnect the return pump motor wiring plug from the ECU.

10 Undo the six retaining screws and carefully withdraw the ECU upwards and off the hydraulic modulator. Recover the gasket.

Refitting

11 Prior to refitting, clean and then carefully inspect, the condition of the gasket sealing surfaces on the ECU and hydraulic modulator. If the surfaces are in any way deformed, damaged, or rough to the extent that a perfect gasket seal cannot be maintained, the complete modulator and ECU assembly must be renewed.

12 Check to see if there is a spring plate located over the solenoid valves on the hydraulic modulator. If a spring plate is present, it should be removed and discarded.

13 With a new gasket in position, and holding the ECU centrally, carefully lower it over the solenoid valves on the modulator, keeping it square and level.

14 Fit the six new retaining screws, and tighten the four screws around the solenoid area of the modulator, evenly and progressively until they all just make contact with the ECU body. Continue tightening these four screws alternately and progressively until the ECU body just makes contact with the hydraulic modulator. Now tighten the remaining two screws until they also just make contact with the ECU body.

15 Progressively, and working in a diagonal sequence, tighten the four screws in the vicinity of the solenoid area to the specified torque. Now tighten the remaining two screws to the specified torque. The ECU must make complete contact with the hydraulic modulator, with no visible gap around any of the sealing area. If this cannot be achieved, release all the screws and tighten them progressively again. If it is still not possible to obtain correct seating of the unit, the complete assembly must be renewed.

16 Reconnect the return pump motor wiring plug, then refit the hydraulic modulator as described previously in this Section.

Front wheel speed sensor

Removal

17 Disconnect the battery negative terminal (refer to *Disconnecting the battery* in the Reference Chapter).

18 Firmly apply the handbrake, then jack up the front of the car and support it securely on axle stands (see *Jacking and vehicle support*). Remove the appropriate front roadwheel.

19 Trace the wheel speed sensor wiring back to its wiring connector, and release it from its retaining clip. Disconnect the connector **(see illustration)**, and work back along the sensor wiring, freeing it from all the relevant retaining clips and ties.

20 Slacken and remove the bolt securing the sensor to the mounting bracket, and remove the sensor and lead assembly from the vehicle **(see illustrations)**.

Refitting

21 Prior to refitting, apply a thin coat of multi-purpose grease to the sensor mounting bracket.

22 Ensure that the sensor and mounting bracket sealing faces are clean, then fit the sensor to the hub. Refit the retaining bolt, and tighten it to the specified torque.

23 Ensure that the sensor wiring is correctly routed, and retained by all the necessary clips. Reconnect it to its wiring connector, and fit the connector into the retaining clip.

24 Refit the roadwheel, aligning the marks made on removal, then lower the vehicle to the ground and tighten the roadwheel bolts to the specified torque.

20.19 Disconnect the wiring connector . . .

20.20a . . . then undo the retaining bolt (arrowed) . . .

20.20b . . . and remove the front wheel speed sensor from the vehicle

20.26 Disconnecting a rear wheel speed sensor wiring connector

20.28 Removing the sensor from the rear of the backplate

20.30 Turn the sensor in the direction of the arrow, so that the retaining clip (A) is freed from the mounting bracket

Rear wheel speed sensor

Removal

25 Chock the front wheels then jack up the rear of the car and support it on axle stands (see *Jacking and vehicle support*).

26 Trace the wiring back from the sensor to its wiring connector, which is situated just near the spare wheel well. Free the connector from its retaining clip, and disconnect the wiring from the main wiring loom **(see illustration)**.

27 Work back along the sensor wiring, and free it from any relevant retaining clips.

28 Slacken and remove the screw securing the sensor unit to the backplate, and withdraw the sensor from the backplate. Remove the sensor and lead assembly from the vehicle **(see illustration)**.

Refitting

29 Prior to refitting, apply a thin coat of multi-purpose grease to the sensor tip. Ensure that the sensor and backplate mating faces are clean.

30 Turn the sensor anti-clockwise to release it from the retaining clip on the mounting bracket. This is vital to ensure that the sensor is correctly positioned on refitting **(see illustration)**.

31 Push the sensor in lightly until it seats, then refit its retaining screw and tighten it to the specified torque setting. With the screw tightened, rotate the sensor clockwise until it engages with the retaining clip **(see illustration)**. As the sensor engages with the clip, it will move out slightly, to leave the correct air gap between the sensor tip and toothed ring on the drum.

32 Ensure that the sensor wiring is correctly routed and retained by all the necessary retaining clips. Reconnect the wiring connector, and fit it back into the retaining clip.

33 Lower the vehicle to the ground.

Front wheel speed sensor toothed rings

34 The front toothed rings are an integral part of the driveshaft outer constant velocity (CV) joints, and cannot be renewed separately. Examine the rings for such damage as chipped or missing teeth. If renewal is necessary, the complete outer constant velocity joint must be renewed, as described in Chapter 8.

Rear wheel speed sensor toothed rings

35 The rear toothed rings are an integral part of the rear brake drum, and cannot be renewed separately **(see illustration)**. Examine the rings for signs of damage such as chipped or missing teeth. If renewal is necessary, the rear brake drum must be renewed as described in Section 7.

20.31 With the sensor in position and the screw tightened, turn the sensor in the direction of the arrow so that the clip (A) engages with the mounting bracket and the correct air gap is set

20.35 Rear wheel speed sensor toothed ring is an integral part of the brake drum

Notes

Chapter 10
Suspension and steering

Contents

Degrees of difficulty

Easy, suitable for novice with little experience	**Fairly easy,** suitable for beginner with some experience	**Fairly difficult,** suitable for competent DIY mechanic	**Difficult,** suitable for experienced DIY mechanic	**Very difficult,** suitable for expert DIY or professional

Specifications

Front suspension

Type .... Independent, with MacPherson struts and forward-facing tie-bars. Anti-roll bar fitted to most models

Rear suspension

Type:
  Corsa and Corsavan .... Semi-independent torsion beam, with trailing arms, coil springs and telescopic shock absorbers. Anti-roll bar on some models
  Combo Van models .... Tubular axle and leaf springs with telescopic shock absorbers

Steering

Type .... Rack-and-pinion. Power assistance standard on certain models, optional on others

Roadwheels

Type .... Pressed-steel or aluminium alloy (depending on model)
Size .... 5J x 13, 5.5J x 13 and 5.5J x 14

Front wheel alignment and steering angles

Camber angle:
  All models except Sport:
    Corsa and Corsavan .... -25' ± 45'
    Combo Van .... -40' ± 45'
  Sport models .... -35' ± 45'
  Maximum difference between sides .... 1°
Castor angle:
  All models except Sport:
    Corsa and Corsavan .... 1°50' ± 1°
    Combo Van .... 10' ± 10'
  Sport models .... 1°55' ± 1°
  Maximum difference between sides .... 1°
Toe setting .... -10' ± 10' (1.0 mm toe-out ± 1.0 mm)

Rear wheel alignment

Camber angle:
  Corsa and Corsavan .... -1°30' ± 30'
  Combo Van .... -25' ± 25'
Maximum difference between sides .... 30'
Toe setting:
  Corsa and Corsavan .... 10' +30' -15' (1.0 mm toe-in +3 mm -1.5 mm)
  Combo Van .... 15' ± 10' (1.5 mm toe-in ± 1.0 mm)

Tyres

Pressures .... See end of *Weekly Checks*
Corsa and Corsavan:
  1.0 litre models .... 145/80 R 13-75 T
                                               165/70 R 13-79 T
                                               165/65 R 14-78 T
  1.2 litre SOHC models .... 145/80 R 13-75 T
                                               165/70 R 13-79 T
                                               165/65 R 14-78 T
  1.2 litre DOHC models .... 165/70 R 13-79 T
                                               165/65 R 14-78 T
  1.4 litre SOHC models with single-point fuel injection (X 14 SZ) .... 145/80 R 13-75 T
                                               165/70 R 13-79 T
                                               165/65 R 14-78 T
  1.4 litre SOHC models with multi-point fuel injection (C 14 SE) ..... 145/80 R 13-75 T
                                               165/70 R 13-79 T
  1.4 litre DOHC models .... 165/70 R 13-79 T
                                               165/65 R 14-78 T
                                               185/60 R 14-82 H
  1.6 litre models .... 165/65 R 14-78 Q
                                               175/65 R 14-78 Q
                                               185/60 R 14-82 H
Combo Van .... 165 R 13-86 R

Torque wrench settings

	Nm	lbf ft
Front suspension		
Anti-roll bar clamp nuts*	20	15
Lower arm balljoint clamp bolt nut*	30	22
Lower arm pivot bolt nut:*		
Stage 1	45	33
Stage 2	Angle-tighten a further 45°	
Stage 3	Angle-tighten a further 15°	
Lower arm-to-balljoint/tie-bar bolts:*		
Stage 1	90	66
Stage 2	Angle-tighten a further 30°	
Stage 3	Angle-tighten a further 15°	
Suspension strut-to-swivel hub bolts:*		
Stage 1	50	37
Stage 2	90	66
Stage 3	Angle-tighten a further 45°	
Stage 4	Angle-tighten a further 15°	
Suspension strut upper mounting nuts*	30	22
Tie-bar front nut*	90	66
Tie-bar mounting bush bracket bolts:*		
Stage 1	50	37
Stage 2	Angle-tighten a further 90°	
Stage 3	Angle-tighten a further 15°	
Rear suspension – Corsa and Corsavan models		
Anti-roll bar bolts:*		
Stage 1	60	44
Stage 2	Angle-tighten a further 60°	
Stage 3	Angle-tighten a further 15°	
Hub nut (pre-load)	25	18
Shock absorber:		
Lower bolt	65	48
Upper nut	20	15
Stub axle bolts:*		
Stage 1	50	37
Stage 2	Angle-tighten a further 30°	
Stage 3	Angle-tighten a further 15°	
Trailing arm pivot bolts:*		
Stage 1	50	37
Stage 2	Angle-tighten a further 45°	
Stage 3	Angle-tighten a further 15°	
Rear suspension – Combo Van models		
Bump stop bolt	50	37
Bump stop seat nut	20	15
Hub nut (pre-load)	25	18
Leaf spring pivot bolts	65	48
Shackle nut	35	26
Shock absorber:		
Lower bolt	65	48
Upper bolt	70	52
U-bolt nuts	45	33
Steering		
Intermediate shaft clamp bolt	22	16
Power steering pipe union nuts	28	21
Power steering pump bolts	20	15
Steering column and column clamp bolts	22	16
Steering gear mountings	22	16
Steering wheel nut	20	15
Track rod balljoint locknut	50	37
Track rod balljoint-to-swivel hub nut*	35	26
Roadwheels		
Roadwheel bolts	110	81

Use new nuts/bolts.

1 General information

1 The independent front suspension is of the MacPherson strut type, incorporating coil springs and integral telescopic shock absorbers **(see illustration)**. The MacPherson struts are located by transverse lower suspension arms, which utilise rubber inner mounting bushes, and incorporate a balljoint at the outer ends. The front swivel hubs, which carry the wheel bearings, brake calipers and the hub/disc assemblies, are bolted to the MacPherson struts, and connected to the lower arms via the balljoints. A forward-facing tie-bar connects each lower suspension arm to the vehicle body. On most models, a front anti-roll bar is fitted. The anti-roll bar is rubber-mounted onto the tie-bars by mounting clamps.

2 On Corsa and Corsavan models, the rear suspension is of semi-independent type, consisting of a torsion beam axle and trailing arms, with double-conical coil springs and telescopic shock absorbers **(see illustration)**. The front ends of the trailing arms are attached to the vehicle underbody by horizontal bushes; the rear ends are located by the shock absorbers, which are bolted to the underbody at their upper ends. The coil springs are mounted independently of the shock absorbers, and act directly between the trailing arms and the underbody. Certain models are fitted with an anti-roll bar, which is bolted onto the underside of each trailing arm.

3 On Combo Van models, the rear

1 MacPherson strut
2 Lower arm
3 Tie-bar
4 Anti-roll bar

1.1 Front suspension components

suspension consists of a tubular axle and leaf spring arrangement, with telescopic shock absorbers **(see illustration opposite)**. The front end of each leaf spring is bolted directly to the vehicle underbody, and the rear end is attached by a shackle arrangement to allow movement of the spring. The axle is secured to each leaf spring by two U-bolts. The shock absorber upper ends are bolted to the vehicle underbody; the lower ends are bolted to the axle.

4 The steering column is linked to the steering gear by an intermediate shaft. The intermediate shaft has a universal joint fitted to its upper end, and is secured to the column by a clamp bolt. The lower end of the intermediate shaft is attached to the steering gear pinion by means of a clamp bolt.

5 The rack-and-pinion type steering gear is rubber-mounted onto the engine compartment bulkhead, and is connected by two track rods, with balljoints at their outer ends, to the steering arms projecting rearwards from the swivel hubs. The track rod ends are threaded, to facilitate adjustment.

6 Power-assisted steering is fitted as standard or optional equipment, according to model. On all except 1.0 litre models, the power steering is of the conventional hydraulic type, powered by a belt-driven pump, which is driven off the crankshaft pulley. On 1.0 litre models, electronic power steering is fitted whereby an electric motor, drive gear assembly and torque sensor, incorporated in the upper steering column, provide a variable degree of power assistance according to road speed. The system is controlled by an electronic control unit with self-diagnostic capability, located behind the footwell trim on the driver's side.

1 Shock absorber
2 Coil spring
3 Torsion beam axle
4 Anti-roll bar (where fitted)
5 Trailing arm

1.2 Rear suspension components – Corsa and Corsavan models

1 *Leaf spring front pivot and bush*
2 *Leaf spring*
3 *Bump stop*
4 *Shackle*
5 *Rear hub assembly*
6 *Shock absorber*
7 *Bump stop seat*
8 *Retaining plate*
9 *U-bolts*

H.28162

1.3 Rear suspension components – Combo Van models

2 Front swivel hub assembly – removal and refitting

Note: *New retaining nuts and/or bolts will be required for most attachments when refitting (see text).*

Removal

> **HAYNES HINT**
> *If work is being carried out without the aid of an assistant, remove the wheel trim/hub cap (as applicable), then withdraw the split pin and slacken the driveshaft retaining nut prior to jacking up the vehicle.*

1 Firmly apply the handbrake, then jack up the front of the car and support it securely on axle stands (see *Jacking and vehicle support*). Remove the appropriate front roadwheel.
2 Extract the split pin from the driveshaft retaining nut and discard it; a new one must be used on refitting.
3 Refit at least two roadwheel bolts to the front hub, and tighten them securely. Have an assistant firmly depress the brake pedal to prevent the front hub from rotating, then using a socket and extension bar, slacken and remove the driveshaft retaining nut. Alternatively, a tool can be fabricated from two lengths of steel strip (one long, one short) and a nut and bolt; the nut and bolt forming the pivot of a forked tool. Bolt the tool to the hub using two wheel bolts, and hold the tool to prevent the hub from rotating as the driveshaft retaining nut is undone **(see illustration 2.3 in Chapter 8)**.
4 Unscrew the two bolts securing the brake caliper mounting bracket to the swivel hub, and slide the caliper assembly off the disc. Using a piece of wire or string, tie the caliper to the front suspension coil spring to avoid placing any strain on the hydraulic brake hose **(see illustrations)**. Discard the caliper mounting bracket bolts – they must be renewed whenever they are disturbed. If the

2.4a Undo the bolts (arrowed) securing the caliper bracket to the swivel hub . . .

2.4b . . . then slide the caliper off the disc, and hook it onto the strut spring using a piece of wire

2.6 Withdraw the clamp bolt, and free the lower arm balljoint from the swivel hub

2.7a On models with ABS, slacken and remove the retaining bolt . . .

2.7b . . . and release the wheel speed sensor mounting bracket from the swivel hub

2.9 Unscrew the nuts and withdraw the bolts securing the suspension strut to the swivel hub

2.10 Free the swivel hub from the end of the driveshaft, and withdraw it from the vehicle

hub bearings are to be disturbed, remove the brake disc as described in Chapter 9.

5 Unscrew the driveshaft retaining nut, and remove the washer. Discard the nut; a new one must be used on refitting.

6 Slacken and remove the lower arm balljoint clamp nut and bolt, and free the lower arm from the swivel hub **(see illustration)**. Discard the clamp bolt nut; a new one must be used on refitting.

7 On models with ABS, undo the bolt securing the wheel speed sensor mounting bracket to the swivel hub, and position the sensor assembly clear of the hub **(see illustrations)**.

8 On all models, slacken and remove the nut securing the steering gear track rod balljoint to the swivel hub, and release the balljoint tapered shank using a universal balljoint separator. Discard the nut; it should be renewed whenever it is disturbed.

9 Slacken and remove the two nuts and bolts securing the suspension strut to the swivel hub, noting which way around the bolts are inserted **(see illustration)**. Discard the nuts and bolts; they should be renewed whenever they are disturbed.

10 Carefully pull the swivel hub assembly outwards, and withdraw the driveshaft outer constant velocity joint from the hub assembly. If necessary, the shaft can be tapped out of the hub using a soft-faced mallet. Support the driveshaft by suspending it with wire or string, and do not allow it to hang under its own weight. Remove the hub assembly from the vehicle **(see illustration)**.

Refitting

11 Ensure that the driveshaft outer constant velocity joint and hub splines are clean, then slide the hub onto the driveshaft splines. Fit the washer and new driveshaft retaining nut, tightening it by hand only at this stage **(see illustration)**.

12 Engage the swivel hub with the suspension strut, and insert the new bolts from the rear of the strut so that their threads are facing forwards. Fit the new nuts, tightening them by hand only at this stage.

13 Locate the lower arm balljoint in the swivel hub. Insert the clamp bolt from the rear of the swivel hub, so that its threads are facing forwards. Fit the new nut to the clamp bolt, and tighten it to the specified torque setting **(see illustration)**.

14 With the hub correctly located, tighten the strut-to-swivel hub bolts through the various stages given in the Specifications at the start of this Chapter.

15 Engage the track rod balljoint in the swivel hub, then fit the new retaining nut and tighten it to the specified torque setting.

2.11 Engage the swivel hub with the driveshaft constant velocity joint, and fit the washer and new retaining nut

2.13 Fit a new nut to the lower arm balljoint clamp bolt, and tighten it to the specified torque setting

If a suitable tap is not available, cut two slots into the threads of one of the original mounting bolts, and use the bolt to remove the locking compound from the threads.

16 Refit the brake disc (where removed) to the hub, referring to Chapter 9 for further information.

17 Remove all traces of old thread-locking compound from the brake caliper mounting bracket holes in the swivel hub, ideally by running a tap of the correct size and pitch through them (see Haynes Hint).

18 If the threads of the new caliper mounting bracket bolts are not already pre-coated with thread-locking compound, apply a suitable locking compound to them. Slide the caliper assembly into position over the disc, then fit the mounting bolts and tighten them to the specified torque setting (Chapter 9 Specifications).

19 Where necessary, refit the ABS wheel speed sensor bracket to the hub, making sure its locating peg is correctly engaged (see illustration), and tighten the mounting bracket retaining bolt to the specified torque (Chapter 9 Specifications).

20 Using the method employed on removal to prevent rotation, tighten the driveshaft retaining nut through the stages given in the Specifications shown in Chapter 8.

21 With the nut correctly tightened, secure it in position with a new split pin. If the holes in the driveshaft are not aligned with any of the slots in the nut, loosen (do not tighten) the nut by the *smallest possible amount* until the split pin can be inserted.

22 Refit the roadwheel, then lower the vehicle to the ground and tighten the roadwheel bolts to the specified torque. Refit the wheel trim/hub cap, where applicable.

3 Front hub bearings – renewal

Note: *The bearing is sealed, pre-adjusted and pre-lubricated. Never overtighten the driveshaft nut beyond the specified torque wrench setting in an attempt to 'adjust' the bearing.*

Note: *A press will be required to dismantle and rebuild the assembly; if such a tool is not available, a large bench vice and spacers (such as large sockets) will serve as an adequate substitute. The bearing's inner races are an interference fit on the hub; if the inner race remains on the hub when it is pressed out of the hub carrier, a knife-edged bearing puller will be required to remove it.*

1 Remove the swivel hub assembly as described in Section 2.

2 Undo the screws and remove the brake disc shield from the hub (see illustration). Discard the screws; new ones should be used on refitting.

3 Support the swivel hub securely on blocks or in a vice. Using a tubular spacer which bears only on the inner end of the hub flange, press the hub flange out of the bearing. If the bearing's outboard inner race remains on the hub, remove it using a bearing puller (see note above).

4 Extract the bearing retaining circlips from the swivel hub assembly (see illustration).

5 Where necessary, refit the inner race back in position over the ball cage, and securely support the inner face of the swivel hub. Using a tubular spacer which bears only on the inner race, press the complete bearing assembly out of the swivel hub.

6 Thoroughly clean the hub and swivel hub, removing all traces of dirt and grease. Polish away any burrs or raised edges which might hinder reassembly. Check both assemblies for cracks or any other signs of wear or damage,

and renew as necessary. Renew the circlips regardless of their apparent condition.

7 On reassembly, apply a light film of oil to the bearing outer race and hub flange shaft, to aid installation of the bearing. Remove all traces of old thread-locking compound from the disc shield retaining screw holes, ideally by running a tap of the correct size and pitch through them.

8 Install the new outer circlip in the swivel hub. Make sure that the circlip is correctly located in its groove, with its holes situated at the bottom of the hub.

9 Securely support the swivel hub, and locate the bearing in the hub. Press the bearing fully into position, ensuring that it enters the hub squarely, using a tubular spacer which bears only on the bearing outer race.

10 Once the bearing is correctly seated against the outer circlip, secure the bearing in position with the new inner circlip. Make sure that the circlip is correctly located in its groove, with its holes situated at the bottom of the hub.

11 Securely support the outer face of the hub flange, and locate the swivel hub bearing inner race over the end of the hub flange. Press the bearing onto the hub, using a tubular spacer which bears only on the inner race of the hub bearing, until it seats against the hub shoulder. Check that the hub flange rotates freely, and wipe off any excess oil or grease.

12 Fit the disc shield to the hub assembly, and apply a few drops of thread-locking compound to the new screws. Fit the screws, and tighten them securely.

13 Refit the swivel hub assembly as described in Section 2.

4 Front strut – removal, overhaul and refitting

Note: *When refitting, new strut-to-swivel hub bolts and nuts, and strut upper mounting nuts, will be required.*

Removal

1 Firmly apply the handbrake, then jack up the front of the car and support it securely on

2.19 On models with ABS, ensure that the sensor bracket pin (arrowed) is correctly located in the hub hole when refitting the bracket to the swivel hub

3.2 Disc shield retaining screws are accessed through holes in the hub flange

3.4 Hub bearing is retained by a circlip (arrowed)

4.2 On models with ABS, free the sensor wiring from its clip on the base of the strut

4.4a On some models, it may be necessary to undo the nuts (arrowed) . . .

4.4b . . . and reposition the wiring loom tray to gain access to the strut upper mounting nuts (arrowed)

axle stands (see *Jacking and vehicle support*). Remove the appropriate roadwheel.

2 On models with ABS, release the front wheel speed sensor wiring from its clip on the suspension strut **(see illustration)**.

3 Slacken and remove the two nuts and bolts securing the suspension strut to the swivel hub. Discard both nuts and bolts; these must be renewed whenever they are disturbed.

4 From within the engine compartment, unscrew the two suspension strut upper mounting nuts and discard them; new ones should be used on refitting. On some models, it may be necessary to reposition the wiring loom tray to improve access to the strut upper mounting; the tray is retained by plastic nuts **(see illustrations)**.

5 Release the strut from the swivel hub, and withdraw it from under the wheelarch **(see illustrations)**.

Overhaul

6 Overhaul of the strut should be entrusted to a Vauxhall/Opel dealer or suitably-equipped garage. A spring compressor and numerous other special tools are necessary to ensure correct fitting and torque setting of the upper spring seat and strut piston retaining nut. Any attempt to dismantle the strut without such tools is likely to result in damage or personal injury.

Refitting

7 Manoeuvre the strut assembly into position, ensuring that the top mounting plate is

correctly located. Fit the washers and new strut upper mounting nuts, and tighten them to the specified torque setting **(see illustration)**. Refit the wiring loom tray to its original location, where applicable.

8 Engage the lower end of the strut with the swivel hub. Insert the new bolts from the rear of the strut so that their threads are facing forwards. Fit the new nuts to the bolts, and tighten them through the various stages given in the Specifications at the start of this Chapter **(see illustrations)**.

9 On models with ABS, clip the sensor wiring back into its retaining clip.

10 Refit the roadwheel, then lower the vehicle to the ground and tighten the roadwheel bolts to the specified torque.

4.5a Release the lower end of the strut from the swivel hub . . .

4.5b . . . and manoeuvre the strut out from underneath the wheelarch

4.7 Tighten the strut upper mounting nuts to the specified torque setting

4.8a Insert the new bolts from the rear of the strut, so their threads are facing forwards

4.8b Tighten the bolts first to the specified torque settings . . .

4.8c . . . and then through the specified angles

5.4 Examine the lower arm pivot bush for signs of damage or deterioration, and if necessary renew

5.6 Engage the outer end of the lower arm with the balljoint and tie-bar, and insert the new bolts . . .

5.7 . . . then align the inner end of the arm, and insert the pivot bolt so its threads are facing towards the rear of the vehicle

5 Front lower arm – removal, overhaul and refitting

Note: *When refitting, a new pivot bolt nut, and new lower arm-to-balljoint/tie-bar nuts and bolts, will be required.*

Removal

1 Firmly apply the handbrake, then jack up the front of the car and support it securely on axle stands (see *Jacking and vehicle support*). Remove the appropriate front roadwheel.
2 Unscrew the nut and withdraw the pivot bolt securing the lower arm to the vehicle body. Discard the nut; a new one should be used on refitting.
3 Slacken and remove the two nuts and bolts securing the balljoint and tie-bar to the lower arm, and remove the lower arm from the vehicle. Discard the nuts and bolts; new ones should be used on refitting.

Overhaul

4 Thoroughly clean the lower arm and the area around the arm mountings, removing all traces of dirt and underseal if necessary. Check carefully for cracks, distortion, or any other signs of wear or damage, paying particular attention to the pivot bush **(see illustration)**. If bush renewal is necessary, the lower arm should be taken to a Vauxhall/Opel dealer or suitably-equipped garage. A hydraulic press and spacers are required to

5.9a Position a jack beneath the lower arm, and raise it until the angle at the arm is at approximately 80° to the vertical . . .

press the bush out of the arm, and to install the new one.
5 Examine the shank of the pivot bolt for signs of wear or scoring, and renew if necessary.

Refitting

6 Offer up the lower arm, aligning it with the tie-bar and balljoint, and install the new bolts and nuts **(see illustration)**.
7 Align the inner end of the arm with its mounting, and insert the pivot bolt from the front of the vehicle, so that its threads are facing towards the rear of the vehicle **(see illustration)**.
8 Tighten the balljoint/tie-bar-to-lower arm bolt nuts through the various stages given in the Specifications at the start of this Chapter
9 Position a jack underneath the outer end of the lower arm. Raise the jack so that the lower

5.9b . . . then fit a new nut to the pivot bolt, and tighten it through the various stages given in the Specifications

arm is positioned as shown in illustration 5.9a. With the arm correctly positioned, fit the new nut to the pivot bolt, and tighten it through the various stages given in the Specifications at the start of this Chapter **(see illustrations)**.
10 Remove the jack from underneath the arm, then refit the roadwheel, aligning the marks made on removal.
11 Lower the vehicle to the ground, and tighten the roadwheel bolts to the specified torque setting.

6 Front lower arm balljoint – removal and refitting

Note: *When refitting, a new clamp bolt nut and new balljoint/tie-bar to lower arm nuts and bolts will be required.*

Removal

1 Firmly apply the handbrake, then jack up the front of the car and support it securely on axle stands (see *Jacking and vehicle support*). Remove the appropriate front roadwheel.
2 Slacken and remove the lower arm balljoint clamp nut and bolt, and free the balljoint from the swivel hub **(see illustration)**. Discard the clamp bolt nut; a new one must be used on refitting.
3 Slacken and remove the two nuts and bolts securing the balljoint and tie-bar to the lower arm **(see illustration)**. Discard the nuts and

6.2 Slacken and remove the nut and clamp bolt . . .

6.3 . . . then remove the balljoint-to-lower arm/tie-bar bolts (arrowed) . . .

6.4 . . . and withdraw the balljoint from the end of the lower arm

6.5 Insert the balljoint into the end of the lower arm, and fit the new retaining bolts

6.7 Fit a new nut to the balljoint clamp bolt, and tighten it to the specified torque setting

bolts; these should be renewed whenever they are disturbed.

4 Withdraw the balljoint from the lower arm, and remove it from the vehicle (see illustration).

Refitting

5 Align the balljoint with the lower arm and tie-bar, then insert the new bolts (see illustration). Fit the new nuts to the bolts, tightening them by hand only at this stage.

6 Locate the balljoint shank in the swivel hub, and insert the clamp bolt from the rear of the swivel hub, so that its threads are facing forwards.

7 Fit the new nut to the balljoint clamp bolt, and tighten it to the specified torque setting (see illustration). Tighten the balljoint-to-lower arm/tie-bar bolt nuts through the

7.4 Unscrew the retaining nut from the front end of the tie-bar

various stages given in the Specifications at the start of this Chapter.

8 Refit the roadwheel, then lower the vehicle to the ground and tighten the roadwheel bolts to the specified torque setting.

9 Check the front wheel alignment and steering angles as described in Section 27.

---

7 Front tie-bar – removal, overhaul and refitting

Note: *When refitting, a new tie-bar front mounting nut and anti-roll bar mounting clamp nuts will be required. The balljoint/tie-bar-to-lower arm nuts and bolts must also be renewed, as must the front mounting bracket bolts.*

Removal

1 Firmly apply the handbrake, then jack up the front of the car and support it securely on axle stands (see *Jacking and vehicle support*).

2 Prior to removal, mark the position of the anti-roll bar mounting clamp rubbers on the tie-bar.

3 Unscrew the two nuts from each anti-roll bar clamp, and remove both halves of the clamp. Discard the nuts; new ones must be used on refitting.

4 Slacken the nut securing the front of the tie-bar to its mounting bracket, and remove the nut (see illustration). Discard the nut; a new one should be used on refitting.

5 Slacken and remove the two nuts and bolts securing the tie-bar and balljoint to the lower arm (see illustration). Discard the nuts and bolts; these should be renewed whenever they are disturbed. **Note:** *On some models, it may be necessary to disconnect the lower arm balljoint from the swivel hub to enable the bolts to be withdrawn (see Section 6).*

6 Free the front end of the tie-bar from its mounting bush, and remove it from the vehicle (see illustration). Slide the washer off the end of the tie-bar.

Overhaul

7 Inspect the tie-bar for signs of damage, paying particular attention to the threads, and renew if necessary. If the anti-roll bar clamp rubbers show any signs of damage or deterioration, they must also be renewed.

8 Examine the front mounting bush and bracket for signs of wear and damage. The bush cannot be renewed separately, and if wear or damage is evident, obtain a new bracket and bush as an assembly. To renew the bracket, undo the three bolts and withdraw the bracket from the crossmember (see illustration). Discard the bracket retaining bolts; they must be renewed whenever they are disturbed. On refitting, remove all traces of old thread-locking compound from the retaining bolt holes in the crossmember, ideally by running a tap of the correct size and pitch through them. Locate the bracket in position and fit the new retaining bolts. Tighten the bolts hand tight only at this stage.

7.5 Slacken and remove the two bolts (arrowed) securing the tie-bar and balljoint to the lower arm . . .

7.6 . . . then free the front end of the bar from its mounting bush, and recover the washer (arrowed)

7.8 Tie-bar front mounting bush bracket is retained by three bolts (arrowed)

8.3a Unscrew the anti-roll bar clamp retaining nuts . . .

8.3b . . . and free the bar and lower clamp halves from the tie-bar

8.3c Recover the upper half of each clamp . . .

HAYNES HINT

If a suitable tap is not available, cut two slots into the threads of one of the original mounting bolts, and use the bolt to remove the locking compound from the threads.

Refitting

9 Fit the washer to the threaded end of the tie-bar, and insert the tie-bar into its mounting bush.

10 Align the tie-bar with the lower arm and balljoint, and insert the new retaining bolts. Fit new nuts to the bolts, and tighten the nuts through the various stages given in the Specifications at the start of this Chapter.

11 Fit the new nut to the front of the tie-bar, and tighten it hand tight only at this stage.

12 Install and tighten the anti-roll bar mounting clamps using the information given in Section 8.

13 If not previously done, unscrew the three bolts securing the tie-bar mounting bush bracket to the crossmember. Remove all traces of old thread-locking compound from the retaining bolt holes in the crossmember, ideally by running a tap of the correct size and pitch through them. Fit the new retaining bolts and tighten them hand tight only at this stage.

14 Lower the car to the ground and tighten the three tie-bar mounting bush bracket bolts through the various stages given

in the Specifications at the start of this Chapter.

15 Finally, tighten the tie-bar front mounting nut to the specified torque.

8 Front anti-roll bar – removal and refitting

Note: *When refitting, new anti-roll bar mounting clamp nuts will be required.*

Removal

1 Firmly apply the handbrake, then jack up the front of the car and support it securely on axle stands (see *Jacking and vehicle support*).

2 Prior to removal, mark the position of each anti-roll bar mounting clamp rubber on the tie-bars.

3 Unscrew the two nuts from each mounting clamp, and remove both halves of the clamp. As the last clamp is removed, support the anti-roll bar and remove it from underneath the vehicle **(see illustrations)**. Discard all clamp nuts; new ones must be used on refitting.

4 Inspect the mounting clamp rubbers for signs of damage and deterioration, and renew if necessary **(see illustration)**.

Refitting

5 Align all the mounting rubbers with the marks made on the tie-bars prior to removal.

Ensure that the flat edge of each rubber is facing downwards.

6 Fit the upper half of each mounting clamp to its relevant rubber.

7 On 1.0 and 1.2 litre DOHC engine models, position the anti-roll bar so that, when fitted, the end having the curved section will be on the right-hand side of the car, with the curved end facing down.

8 Offer up the anti-roll bar, and fit the lower half of the mounting clamp. Ensure that the clamp half is correctly engaged with the anti-roll bar flats, then couple both halves of each clamp together **(see illustration)**. Fit the new clamp nuts, tightening them by hand only at this stage.

9 With all the clamps loosely installed, check that the distance between the right-and left-hand rear clamps and the tie-bar inner bolt is as follows **(see illustration)**:

1.0 and 1.2 litre DOHC models: 110 mm
All other models: 121 mm

Reposition the anti-roll bar as required until both the right- and left-hand clamps are correctly positioned, then go around and tighten all the clamp nuts to the specified torque setting.

10 Lower the vehicle to the ground.

8.4 . . . and remove the mounting rubber from the tie-bar

8.8 When refitting, ensure that each lower clamp is correctly engaged with the anti-roll bar flats

8.9 Position the anti-roll bar so that the distance between the left- and right-hand rear clamp and each tie-bar inner bolt (A) is as given in the text. Inset (B) shows cross-sectional view of anti-roll bar and tie-bar

9 Rear hub assembly – removal and refitting

Removal

Corsa and Corsavan models

1 On these models, the rear hub is an integral part of the brake drum. Refer to Chapter 9 for drum removal and refitting details.
2 Check the hub bearing for signs of roughness or damage, and renew if necessary as described in Section 10.
3 With the hub removed, examine the stub axle shaft for signs of wear or damage and, if necessary, renew it as described in Section 11.

Combo Van models

4 Remove the rear brake drum as described in Chapter 9.
5 Prise out the cap from the centre of the hub.
6 Extract the split pin from the hub nut, then slacken and remove the nut.
7 Slide the hub assembly, complete with the toothed washer and outer bearing, off the stub axle.
8 Check the hub bearing for signs of roughness or damage, and renew if necessary as described in Section 10.
9 With the hub removed, examine the stub axle shaft for signs of wear or damage. If renewal is necessary, the complete rear axle must be renewed; it is not possible to separate the stub axles from the axle.

Refitting

Corsa and Corsavan models

10 Refit the brake drum as described in Chapter 9.

Combo Van models

11 Ensure that the stub axle is clean, and apply a smear of grease to the lip of the hub oil seal.
12 Slide the hub, outer bearing and toothed washer onto the stub axle, ensuring that the toothed washer is correctly engaged with the stub axle slot.
13 Refit the hub nut, tightening it to the specified pre-load torque setting whilst rotating the hub to settle the bearings in position. Gradually slacken the hub nut until the position is found where it is just possible to move the toothed washer from side-to-side using a screwdriver. **Note:** *Only a small amount of force should be needed to move the washer; do not use the screwdriver as a lever to move the washer.* When the hub nut is correctly positioned, secure it in position with a new split pin.
14 If the stub axle holes are not aligned with any of the slots in the hub nut, tighten the nut by the *smallest possible amount* until the split

10.3 Lever the oil seal out from the hub with a flat-bladed screwdriver

pin can be inserted. With the nut in this position, check that it is still possible to move the toothed washer. If it is, insert the split pin and secure it in position. If it is not possible to move the washer, slacken the nut slightly until the next hub nut slot/axle hole aligns. Check that it is possible to move the toothed washer, then secure the hub nut in position with the new split pin.
15 Fit the cap to the centre of the hub.
16 Install the brake drum as described in Chapter 9.

10 Rear hub bearings – renewal

1 On Corsa and Corsavan models, remove the rear brake drum as described in Chapter 9. On Combo Van models, remove the hub as described in Section 9.
2 If not already done, remove the toothed washer from the drum/hub, and lift out the outer taper roller bearing.
3 Using a suitable flat-bladed screwdriver, lever the oil seal out of the rear of the drum/hub, noting which way around it is fitted **(see illustration)**.
4 Remove the inner taper roller bearing from the inside of the drum/hub.
5 Support the drum/hub, and tap the outer bearing outer race out of position, using a hammer and metal drift which just passes

10.9a Insert the outer race into the hub . . .

10.5 Support the hub on blocks of wood, and drift out the outer races using a hammer and punch

through the centre of the inner bearing outer race **(see illustration)**.
6 Turn the drum/hub over, and tap the inner bearing outer race out of position.
7 Thoroughly clean the hub, removing all traces of dirt and grease. Polish away any burrs or raised edges which might hinder reassembly. Check the drum/hub surface for cracks or any other signs of wear or damage, and renew it if necessary. The bearings and oil seal must be renewed whenever they are disturbed, as removal will almost certainly damage the outer races. Obtain new bearings, an oil seal, and a small quantity of the special bearing grease (90 510 336) from your Vauxhall/Opel dealer. In the absence of the special grease, a good-quality lithium-based grease may be used instead.
8 On reassembly, apply a light film of clean engine oil to each bearing outer race, to aid installation.
9 Securely support the drum/hub, and locate the outer bearing outer race in the hub. Tap the outer race fully into position, using a tubular spacer which bears only on the outer edge of the race, and ensuring that it enters the hub squarely **(see illustrations)**.
10 Turn the drum/hub over, and install the inner bearing outer race in the same way.
11 Ensure that both outer races are correctly seated in the hub, and wipe them clean.
12 Work the grease well into both the taper

10.9b . . . and drift it into position using a hammer and tubular drift

10.12a Work the grease well into the roller bearings . . .

10.12b . . . and smear the outer race surfaces

10.13 Fit the taper roller bearing to the innermost outer race . . .

10.14 . . . then press the oil seal into position

roller bearings, and apply a smear of grease to the outer races **(see illustrations)**.

13 Fit the taper roller bearing to the innermost outer race **(see illustration)**.

14 Press the oil seal into the rear of the drum/hub, ensuring that its sealing lip is facing inwards **(see illustration)**. Position the seal so that it is flush with the hub face, or until its lip abuts the rear of the drum/hub. If necessary, the seal can be tapped into position using a suitable tubular drift which bears only on the hard outer edge of the seal.

15 Turn the drum/hub over, fit the taper roller bearing to the outer race, and install the toothed washer.

16 Pack the hub bearings with a suitable grease.

17 On Corsa and Corsavan models, install the brake drum as described in Chapter 9.

18 On Combo Van models, refit the hub assembly as described in Section 9.

11 Rear stub axle – removal and refitting

Corsa and Corsavan models

Note: *When refitting, new stub axle retaining bolts must be used.*

Removal

1 Remove the brake drum as described in Chapter 9.

2 Position a jack underneath the relevant trailing arm, and raise the jack until it is just supporting the weight of the arm.

3 Undo the lower shock absorber mounting bolt, and swing the shock absorber away from the trailing arm to gain access to the stub axle retaining bolts.

4 Slacken and remove the retaining bolts, and remove the stub axle from the trailing arm **(see illustrations)**. Discard the retaining bolts; new ones must be used on refitting.

5 Inspect the stub axle surface for signs of damage such as scoring, and renew if necessary.

Refitting

6 Ensure that the mating surfaces of the stub axle and backplate are clean and dry. Check the backplate for signs of damage, and remove any burrs with a fine file or emery cloth.

7 Offer up the stub axle, and fit the new retaining bolts. Tighten the retaining bolts through the various stages given in the Specifications at the start of this Chapter.

8 Align the shock absorber with the trailing arm, then fit its lower mounting bolt, tightening it to the specified torque.

9 Remove the jack from underneath the trailing arm, and refit the brake drum as described in Chapter 9.

Combo Van models

10 On Combo Van models, the stub axles are an integral part of the rear axle, and cannot be removed separately. If a stub axle is damaged, the complete axle assembly must be renewed. Refer to Section 15 for axle removal and refitting details.

11.4a On Corsa and Corsavan models, undo the four retaining bolts (arrowed) . . .

11.4b . . . and remove the stub axle (shown with brake shoes removed)

12.3a On Corsa models, unclip the trim cover . . .

12.3b . . . and remove the cap to gain access to the shock absorber upper mounting nut

12 Rear shock absorber – removal, testing and refitting

Removal

Corsa and Corsavan models

1 Chock the front wheels then jack up the rear of the car and support it on axle stands (see *Jacking and vehicle support*).

2 Position a jack underneath the relevant trailing arm, and raise the jack until it is just supporting the weight of the arm.

3 Working in the luggage compartment, prise out the trim cover and/or remove the trim cap (as applicable) to gain access to the shock absorber upper mounting nut **(see illustrations)**.

4 Slacken and remove the nut, and lift off the plate and rubber mounting damper. If necessary, to prevent the shock absorber piston rotating as the nut is slackened, retain it using an open-ended spanner on the flats on the upper end of the piston **(see illustration)**.

5 Slacken and remove the lower shock absorber mounting bolt, then lower the shock absorber out of position and remove it from underneath the vehicle **(see illustrations)**.

6 Remove the rubber damper, spacer and dust cover from the shock absorber piston.

Combo Van

7 Chock the front wheels then jack up the rear of the car and support it on axle stands (see *Jacking and vehicle support*).

8 Position a jack underneath the axle, and raise the jack until it is just supporting the weight of the axle.

9 Note the orientation of the shock absorber, then slacken and remove the upper and lower shock absorber mounting bolts, and remove the shock absorber from underneath the vehicle **(see illustrations)**.

12.4 Slacken the mounting nut whilst retaining the piston with an open-ended spanner

12.5a Remove the lower mounting bolt . . .

12.5b . . . then free the shock absorber from the trailing arm, and manoeuvre it out from underneath the vehicle

12.9a On Combo Van models, slacken and remove the upper (arrowed) . . .

12.9b . . . and lower mounting bolts . . .

12.9c . . . and remove the shock absorber from underneath the vehicle

12.15 Tightening the shock absorber lower mounting bolt – Corsa models

12.21 Tightening the shock absorber lower mounting bolt – Combo Van models

Testing

10 Examine the shock absorber for signs of fluid leakage or damage. Test the operation of the strut, while holding it in an upright position, by moving the piston through a full stroke, and then through short strokes of 50 to 100 mm. In both cases, the resistance felt should be smooth and continuous. If the resistance is jerky, or uneven, or if there is any visible sign of wear or damage to the strut, renewal is necessary. Also check the rubber mounting bush(es) for damage and deterioration. If the bushes are damaged or worn, the complete shock absorber will have to be renewed, as the mounting bushes are not available separately. Inspect the shanks of the mounting bolts for signs of wear or damage, and renew as necessary.

11 On Corsa and Corsavan models, examine the upper mounting rubber dampers for signs of damage or deterioration, and renew if necessary.

Refitting

Corsa and Corsavan

12 Ensure that the rubber bump stops are in position on the piston, then operate the piston fully through several strokes to prime it.

13 Fully extend the piston, then slide the dust cover, spacer and rubber damper onto the piston.

14 Manoeuvre the shock absorber into position, ensuring that the piston is correctly located in the hole in the vehicle body.

15 Insert the shock absorber lower mounting bolt, and tighten it to the specified torque setting **(see illustration)**.

16 From inside the luggage compartment, refit the rubber mounting damper and plate to the piston.

17 Fit the upper mounting nut, and tighten it to the specified torque setting. If necessary, prevent the piston rotating as described in paragraph 4.

18 Refit the trim cap/cover (as applicable).

19 Remove the jack from underneath the trailing arm, and lower the vehicle to the ground.

Combo Van

20 Operate the shock absorber fully through several strokes to prime it, then manoeuvre it into position underneath the vehicle.

21 Ensure that the shock absorber is positioned the correct way up, and insert both the upper and lower mounting bolts. Tighten both mounting bolts to their specified torque settings **(see illustration)**.

22 Remove the jack from underneath the axle, and lower the vehicle to the ground.

13 Rear coil spring (Corsa and Corsavan) – removal and refitting

Note: *Both coil springs are removed at the same time.*

Removal

1 Chock the front wheels then jack up the rear of the car and support it on axle stands (see *Jacking and vehicle support*). Remove both rear roadwheels.

2 Position a jack underneath the right-hand trailing arm, and raise the jack until it is just supporting the weight of the arm.

3 Undo the shock absorber lower mounting bolt, and disengage the right-hand shock absorber from the trailing arm.

4 On 1.4 and 1.6 litre models, remove the spring connecting the rear brake pressure-regulating valve to the axle (Chapter 9) **(see illustration)**.

5 Detach the rear brake pipes from their clips on the vehicle underbody and axle **(see illustrations)**, then slowly lower the jack until it is no longer supporting the trailing arm. With the trailing arm unsupported, check that no excess strain is being placed on the brake pipes.

13.4 On 1.4 and 1.6 litre models, unhook the spring from the rear brake pressure-regulating valve

13.5a Slide out the retaining clips . . .

13.5b . . . and free the rear brake pipes from the vehicle underbody brackets

13.9a Lower the rear axle, then remove the coil springs . . .

13.9b . . . and recover the upper . . .

13.9c . . . and lower spring seats

6 Position the jack underneath the left-hand trailing arm, and raise the jack until it is supporting the weight of the arm.

7 Undo the lower shock absorber mounting bolt, and disengage the left-hand shock absorber from the trailing arm.

8 Slowly lower the jack, keeping watch on the brake pipes to ensure no excess strain is placed on them, until it is possible to withdraw the right-hand coil spring. Note which way around the spring is installed, and recover the upper and lower spring seats.

9 Remove the left-hand spring, noting which way around it is installed, and recover both the upper and lower spring seats **(see illustrations)**.

10 If the vehicle is to be left for some time with the springs removed, lift up the trailing

14.2a Undo the two retaining nuts (arrowed) . . .

arms and refit the shock absorber lower mounting bolts. **Note:** *Do not allow the rear axle assembly to hang unsupported.*

11 Inspect the springs closely for signs of damage, such as cracking, and check the spring seats for signs of wear or damage. Renew worn components as necessary.

Refitting

12 If the shock absorber lower bolts were refitted in paragraph 10, remove them now, and lower the trailing arms.

13 Install the upper and lower spring seats in position on the underbody and trailing arms.

14 Manoeuvre the left-hand coil spring into position, noting that the smaller-diameter end of the spring must be uppermost (towards the vehicle body). Ensure that the spring is correctly located in both the upper and lower seats.

15 Fit the right-hand spring in the same way.

16 With both springs correctly seated, lift the left-hand trailing arm up on the jack, and align the shock absorber with its mounting bracket. Refit the shock absorber lower mounting bolt, and tighten it to the specified torque setting.

17 Repeat the operation on the right-hand side, and remove the jack.

18 Locate the rear brake pipes back in position, and secure them with the retaining clips.

19 On 1.4 and 1.6 litre models, refit the brake pressure-regulating valve spring, and adjust the valve as described in Chapter 9.

20 Refit the roadwheels, then lower the vehicle to the ground, and tighten the roadwheel bolts to the specified torque.

14 Rear leaf spring and bump stop (Combo Van) – removal, inspection and refitting

Removal

1 Chock the front wheels then jack up the rear of the car and support it on axle stands (see *Jacking and vehicle support*). Remove the relevant rear roadwheel, then proceed as described under the relevant sub-heading.

Leaf spring

2 Unscrew the two retaining nuts, and release the handbrake cable bracket from the spring **(see illustrations)**.

3 If the right-hand leaf spring is being removed, unscrew the two retaining nuts, and detach the rear brake pressure-regulating valve spring clamp from the leaf spring **(see illustration)**.

4 Place a jack underneath the rear axle, and raise the jack so that it is supporting the weight of the axle.

5 Slacken and remove the front pivot bolt securing the leaf spring to the vehicle body, and the rear pivot bolt securing the spring to the shackle **(see illustrations)**.

6 Lower the axle slightly, then unscrew the

14.2b . . . and detach the handbrake cable bracket from the leaf spring

14.3 If the right-hand spring is being removed, also remove the brake pressure-regulating valve spring clamp

14.5a Slacken and remove the front pivot bolt . . .

nut and remove the bump stop seat from the top of the leaf spring **(see illustration)**.

7 Unscrew the four U-bolt retaining nuts, then remove both U-bolts and the retaining plate **(see illustrations)**.

8 Remove the leaf spring from underneath the vehicle.

9 Undo the shackle nut, and remove both halves of the shackle from underneath the vehicle **(see illustration)**.

Bump stop

10 Unscrew the bump stop retaining bolt, and remove the stop from the vehicle **(see illustration)**. Withdraw the bolt, and recover the spacer and washer.

Inspection

11 Closely inspect the leaf spring and shackle for signs of damage, such as cracking, especially around the pivot points. Renew components as necessary.

12 Inspect the spring and shackle pivot bushes for signs of wear, and renew if necessary. A hydraulic press and spacers will be required to renew the leaf spring bushes, but the shackle-to-body bush halves can be easily levered out of position and the new ones installed **(see illustration)**.

13 Examine the pivot bolts and shackle stud for signs of scoring, and renew worn components as necessary.

14 Check the rubber bump stop, and renew it if the rubber shows signs of damage or deterioration.

Refitting

Leaf spring

15 Insert the shackle plate with the stud through from the inboard side of the bracket, and fit the plain plate on the outside. Fit the nut, tightening it by hand only at this stage **(see illustrations)**.

16 Engage the leaf spring with the shackle and front mounting bracket. Note that the locating pin on the base of the spring is offset. Make sure that the spring is fitted with the shorter distance between the spring pivot bush and locating pin facing towards the front of the vehicle.

17 Insert the front and rear spring pivot bolts, and tighten the pivot bolts and shackle nut to the specified torque setting **(see illustrations)**.

14.5b . . . and the rear bolt securing the spring to the shackle

14.6 Undo the nut (arrowed) and remove the bump stop seat from the spring

14.7a Undo the retaining nuts, then withdraw both U-bolts . . .

14.7b . . . and remove the retaining plate

14.9 Undo the nut (arrowed) and remove the shackle

14.10 Unscrew the retaining bolt from the centre of the bump stop, and remove the stop from the vehicle

14.12 Remove the shackle bushes from the vehicle, and inspect them for wear

14.15a Insert the shackle plate from the inboard side . . .

14.15b . . . and fit the plain plate on the outside

14.17a Tighten the rear pivot bolt . . .

14.17b . . . and the front pivot bolt to the specified torque

14.18 Lift the axle into position, making sure that the spring locating pin is correctly located in the axle hole (arrowed) – shown with spring removed

18 Lift the axle into position, ensuring its hole is correctly engaged with the locating pin on the base of the leaf spring **(see illustration)**.

19 Refit the retaining plate to the top of the spring, and install both the U-bolts and retaining nuts. Tighten the retaining nuts evenly and progressively to the specified torque **(see illustration)**, ensuring that an equal length of thread is visible above each nut. If there is a difference of more than 3 mm between any two, slacken the retaining nuts and repeat the tightening sequence.

20 Fit the bump stop seat to the retaining plate, aligning its locating peg with innermost retaining plate hole, and tighten its retaining nut to the specified torque **(see illustration)**.

21 Refit the handbrake cable clamp to the

leaf spring, and securely tighten its retaining nuts.

22 On the right-hand spring, refit the brake pressure-regulating valve clamp to the spring, and adjust the valve as described in Chapter 9.

23 Refit the roadwheel, then lower the vehicle to the ground, and tighten the roadwheel bolts to the specified torque.

Bump stop

24 Insert the washer into the bump stop, and fit the spacer and retaining bolt **(see illustrations)**.

25 Fit the bump stop to the vehicle, and tighten the retaining bolt to the specified torque.

26 Refit the roadwheel, then lower the vehicle to the ground, and tighten the roadwheel bolts to the specified torque.

15 Rear axle – removal and refitting

Removal

1 Chock the front wheels then jack up the rear of the car and support it on axle stands (see *Jacking and vehicle support*). Remove both rear roadwheels.

2 Unscrew the brake master cylinder fluid reservoir cap and screw it down onto a piece of polythene to minimise fluid loss during the following procedure. Proceed as described under the relevant sub-heading.

Corsa and Corsavan models

Note: *New trailing arm pivot bolts and nuts will be required when refitting.*

3 Undo the retaining nuts, and remove the exhaust heat shield from underneath the vehicle to gain access to the underside of the handbrake lever.

4 Referring to Chapter 9, unscrew the handbrake cable adjuster nut, then remove the grommet from the connecting link, and detach the front end of the cable from the connecting joint. Work back along the cable, releasing it from any relevant retaining clips and ties, so that the cable is free to be removed with the axle.

5 On models with ABS, disconnect the rear wheel speed sensors at the wiring connectors. Free the sensor wiring from all its retaining clips, so that it is free to be removed with the axle.

6 Trace the brake pipes back from the backplates to their unions situated directly above the axle. Slacken the union nuts, and disconnect the pipes. Plug the pipe ends, to minimise fluid loss and prevent the entry of dirt into the hydraulic system. Remove the retaining clips, and release the pipes from the axle/vehicle body.

7 Remove the left- and right-hand coil springs as described in Section 13, then place the jack underneath the centre of the axle.

8 Slacken and remove the nut and pivot bolt securing each trailing arm to the vehicle

14.19 Tighten the U-bolt retaining nuts to the specified torque as described in text

14.20 Fit the bump stop seat, making sure its locating peg is engaged with the inner retaining plate hole (arrowed)

14.24a When refitting the bump stop, do not omit the washer from inside the stop . . .

14.24b . . . or the spacer from the top of the bump stop

underbody **(see illustration)**. Discard the nuts and bolts; new ones should be used on refitting.

9 Make a final check that all necessary components have been disconnected and positioned so that they will not hinder the removal procedure. Carefully lower the axle assembly out of position, and remove it from underneath the vehicle.

10 Inspect the trailing arm bushes for signs of damage or deterioration, and renew if necessary. Bush renewal should be entrusted to a Vauxhall/Opel dealer, or to a suitably-equipped garage with access to a hydraulic press and spacers.

Combo Van

11 Undo the retaining nuts, and remove the exhaust heat shield from underneath the vehicle to gain access to the underside of the handbrake lever and cable.

12 Referring to Chapter 9, unscrew the handbrake cable adjuster nut, then remove the equaliser plate from the handbrake lever. Work back along each cable, releasing it from any relevant retaining clips and ties, so that the cable assembly is free to be removed with the axle.

13 Trace the brake pipes back from the backplates to their unions on the top of the axle. Slacken the union nuts, and disconnect the pipes. Plug the pipe ends, to minimise fluid loss and prevent the entry of dirt into the hydraulic system. Remove the retaining clips, and release the pipes from the axle **(see illustration)**.

14 Unscrew both the left- and right-hand shock absorber lower mounting bolts, and free both shock absorbers from the axle.

15 Position a jack beneath the centre of the axle, and raise the jack until it is supporting the weight of the axle.

16 Unscrew the nut, and remove the bump stop seat from the top of the both the left- and right-hand leaf springs.

17 Unscrew the four U-bolt retaining nuts, then remove both U-bolts and the retaining plate from the left-hand leaf spring. Remove the U-bolts and retaining plate from the right-hand leaf spring in the same way.

18 Make a final check that all necessary components have been disconnected and positioned so that they will not hinder the removal procedure. Carefully lower the axle assembly out of position, and remove it from underneath the vehicle.

Refitting

Corsa and Corsavan models

19 Refitting is a reverse of the removal procedure, bearing in mind the following points:
a) Ensure that the trailing arm and mounting bracket surfaces are clean and dry. Raise the axle assembly into position, and insert the new trailing arm pivot bolts, tightening them by hand only at this stage.

15.8 Trailing arm pivot bolt (arrowed) – Corsa and Corsavan models

b) Ensure that the brake pipes, handbrake cables and wiring (as applicable) are correctly routed, and retained by all the necessary retaining clips.
c) Tighten all the brake pipe union nuts to the specified torque, and bleed the braking system, with reference to Chapter 9.
d) Adjust the handbrake cable as described in Chapter 9. On 1.4 and 1.6 litre models, also adjust the rear brake pressure-regulating valve once the vehicle is on the ground.
e) On completion, lower the vehicle to the ground, and tighten the roadwheel bolts to the specified torque.
f) With the vehicle resting on its wheels and two assistants seated in the front seats, tighten the trailing arm pivot bolts through the various stages given in the Specifications at the start of this Chapter.

Combo Van models

20 Refitting is a reverse of the removal procedure, bearing in mind the following points:
a) Ensure that the holes in the axle are correctly aligned with the locating pegs on the leaf springs when raising the axle into position.
b) Install the U-bolts, retaining plates and bump stop seats as described in Section 14.
c) Ensure that the brake pipes, handbrake cables and wiring (as applicable) are

16.2 Prior to removal, mark the positions (arrowed) of the rubber dampers on the axle crossmember

15.13 Remove the retaining clips (arrowed), and release the brake pipes from the top of the axle

correctly routed and retained by all the necessary retaining clips.
d) Tighten all the brake pipe union nuts to the specified torque, and bleed the braking system, with reference to Chapter 9.
e) Adjust the handbrake cable and rear brake pressure-regulating valve as described in Chapter 9.
f) On completion, lower the vehicle to the ground, and tighten the roadwheel bolts to the specified torque.

16 Rear anti-roll bar (Corsa and Corsavan) – removal and refitting

Note: New retaining bolts will be required on refitting.

Removal

1 Chock the front wheels then jack up the rear of the car and support it on axle stands (see Jacking and vehicle support). Remove one of the rear roadwheels.

2 Prior to removal, mark the position of the rubber dampers on the axle crossmember **(see illustration)**.

3 Slacken and remove the bolts securing the anti-roll bar to the trailing arms **(see illustration)**. Discard the bolts; new ones must be used on refitting.

4 Withdraw the bar from the side on which the roadwheel has been removed. If the bar is

16.3 Slacken and remove the nut and bolt securing the anti-roll bar to each trailing arm . . .

16.4a . . . then withdraw the anti-roll bar . . .

16.4b . . . and recover the rubber dampers

16.9a Insert the new anti-roll bar retaining bolts . . .

tight, remove the opposite roadwheel, and drift the bar out using a hammer and soft metal drift. Recover the dampers from the bar as they are released **(see illustrations)**.

5 Inspect the rubber dampers for signs of damage or deterioration, and renew as necessary.

Refitting

6 To ease installation, coat the anti-roll bar with soapy water.

7 Insert the anti-roll bar in through the trailing arm, and locate the rubber dampers on the bar. Align the rubber dampers with the marks made prior to removal, and seat them in the axle crossmember.

8 Slide the anti-roll bar fully into position, so that it is correctly engaged in the opposite trailing arm.

9 Install the new retaining bolts, then refit the washers and nuts. Tighten both bolts first to the specified torque, and then through the specified angles given in the Specifications at the start of this Chapter **(see illustrations)**.

10 Refit the roadwheel(s), aligning the marks made on removal. Lower the vehicle to the ground, and tighten the roadwheel bolts to the specified torque.

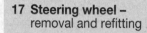

17 Steering wheel – removal and refitting

Note: *A puller will be required to draw the steering wheel off the column splines. A new retaining nut lockwasher will be required when refitting.*

Models without an air bag
Removal

1 Disconnect the battery negative terminal (refer to *Disconnecting the battery* in the Reference Chapter).

2 Set the front wheels in the straight-ahead position, and release the steering lock by inserting the ignition key.

3 Carefully ease the horn button out from the steering wheel, and disconnect its wiring **(see illustration)**.

4 Using a screwdriver, prise back the tabs on the retaining nut lockwasher **(see illustration)**.

5 Unscrew the retaining nut, and lift off the lockwasher. Discard the lockwasher; a new one should be used on refitting.

6 Make alignment marks between the steering wheel and steering column shaft.

7 A 2-legged puller will now be required to free the steering wheel from its splines. Locate the legs of the puller in the holes in the centre of the wheel, and draw the steering wheel off the column splines. Lift off the steering wheel, and remove the spring from the column shaft **(see illustration)**.

Refitting

8 Check that the indicator cancelling lug/horn button contact pad fitted to the rear of steering wheel is in good condition, and if necessary renew it. To release the pad, depress the two clips located inside the steering wheel **(see illustration)**.

9 Ensure that the indicator switch stalk is in

16.9b . . . and tighten them to the specified torque, and then through the specified angles

17.3 Ease the horn button out from the steering wheel, and disconnect its wiring

17.4 Using a screwdriver, bend down the tabs of the lockwasher from the steering wheel nut

17.7 With the steering wheel removed, lift the spring from the column

17.8 Removing the indicator cancelling lug/horn button contact pad from the steering wheel

17.11 Fit the new lockwasher, engaging its tabs with the wheel cut-outs (arrowed)

its central (OFF) position. Failure to do this could lead to the steering wheel lug breaking the switch tab as the steering wheel is refitted.
10 Fit the spring to the column, then locate the wheel on the column splines, aligning the marks made on removal.
11 Fit the new lockwasher, and screw on the retaining nut **(see illustration)**. Tighten the retaining nut to the specified torque, and secure it in position with the lockwasher tabs.
12 Reconnect the wiring connectors to the horn button, and refit the button in the centre of the steering wheel.
13 Reconnect the battery, and check the operation of the horn.

Models with an air bag

⚠ **Warning: Make sure that the safety recommendations given in Chapter 12 are followed, to prevent personal injury.**

Removal

14 Remove the air bag as described in Chapter 12.
15 Set the front wheels in the straight-ahead position, then lock the column in position after removing the ignition key.
16 Slacken and remove the two screws securing the wiring contact unit to the steering wheel.
17 Release the horn wiring connector from the steering wheel, and disconnect it.
18 Remove the steering wheel as described above in paragraphs 4 to 7, taking great care not to damage the wiring contact unit.
19 Disconnect the contact unit wiring

18.4a Insert the rod (arrowed) into the lock housing hole, then with the ignition key correctly positioned (see text) . . .

17.20 Air bag wiring contact unit. Centralise the unit as described in text before fitting it to the steering wheel

1 Arrow markings *3 Centre*
2 Contact unit

connectors, and slide the contact unit off the steering column, noting its correct fitted position.

Refitting

20 Prior to installation, it is necessary to set the contact unit to its centre position. To do this, hold the outside of the unit, and rotate the centre of the contact unit anti-clockwise until sharp resistance is felt. From this point, turn the centre back through two-and-a-half turns in a clockwise direction, and align the arrow markings on the centre and outer parts of the contact unit **(see illustration)**.
21 With the contact unit correctly centralised, install the unit in the rear of the steering wheel, routing the wiring connectors through the relevant wheel aperture, and secure it in position with the retaining screws. Reconnect the horn wiring connector and clip it into the steering wheel recess.
22 Ensure that the indicator switch stalk is in its central (OFF) position, then refit the steering wheel to the column, aligning the marks made prior to removal. When locating the steering wheel on the splines, make sure that the contact unit is correctly engaged with both the steering column and indicator switch.
23 Fit the new lockwasher, and screw on the retaining nut. Tighten the retaining nut to the specified torque, and secure it in position with the lockwasher tabs.
24 Reconnect the contact unit wiring

18.4b . . . withdraw the lock cylinder

18.2 Removing an upper steering column shroud retaining screw

connectors, and clip them into position on the steering column.
25 Release the steering lock, and refit the air bag as described in Chapter 12.

18 Ignition switch/steering column lock – removal and refitting

Removal

1 Disconnect the battery negative terminal (refer to *Disconnecting the battery* in the Reference Chapter).
2 With the steering wheel in the straight-ahead position, turn the wheel 90° to the left, then prise off the trim cap and remove the left upper shroud screw **(see illustration)**. Turn the wheel 180° to the right and remove the right upper screw. Remove the rubber seal from the ignition switch/lock, then undo the lower retaining screws and remove the lower steering column shroud. Proceed as described under the relevant sub-heading.

Lock cylinder

3 Insert the ignition key into the ignition switch/lock, and turn it to position I.
4 Insert a thin rod into the hole in the lock housing, press the rod to release the detent spring, and pull out the lock cylinder using the key **(see illustrations)**. If the lock cylinder will not come out easily, turn the key to position II and try and withdraw it.

Ignition switch wiring block

5 Disconnect the wiring connector from the ignition switch wiring block **(see illustration)**.

18.5 Disconnect the wiring connector . . .

18.6a ... then undo the grub screws ...

18.6b ... and remove the ignition switch wiring block

18.7 Later type of lock cylinder. Early types have a hook cast onto the end of the lock cylinder in the position indicated by the arrow

6 Slacken the two grub screws (one at the front and one at the rear), and withdraw the wiring block from the end of the switch housing **(see illustrations)**.

Refitting

Lock cylinder

7 Insert the ignition key into the lock cylinder. There are two different types of lock cylinder; early types have a hook on the inner end of the lock cylinder housing, and later types do not **(see illustration)**. The early-type cylinder must be installed with the key in position II, while the later type is installed with the key in position I.
8 Ensure that the centre of the ignition switch wiring block is correctly aligned with the lock cylinder rod flats. If necessary, rotate the switch centre using a suitable screwdriver. If the steering column lock has been actuated,

18.8 Prior to installing the lock cylinder, depress the steering lock mechanism block with a screwdriver

release the lock by depressing the locking mechanism block in the column housing **(see illustration)**.
9 Insert the cylinder into the housing until the detent spring clicks into position, then check the operation of the lock cylinder and steering lock.
10 Refit the steering column shroud, tightening its retaining screws securely, and fit the rubber to the switch/lock. Reconnect the battery.

Ignition switch wiring block

11 Refit the ignition switch to the housing, ensuring that the switch centre is correctly engaged with lock cylinder rod flats.
12 Insert both grub screws, and tighten them securely.
13 Reconnect the wiring connector to ignition switch.
14 Refit the steering column shroud, tightening its retaining screws securely. Refit the rubber to the switch/lock, and the trim caps to the upper screws.
15 Reconnect the battery negative terminal, and check the operation of the switch.

---

19 Steering column – removal, inspection and refitting

Note: *The following procedures are applicable to models with manual steering, or conventional hydraulic power steering only. On models with electronic power steering (1.0 litre*

models), steering column removal and refitting should be entrusted to a Vauxhall/Opel dealer. The procedure is complex and numerous special tools are essential, which makes the operation beyond the scope of this manual.

Removal

1 Disconnect the battery negative terminal (refer to *Disconnecting the battery* in the Reference Chapter).
2 Remove the steering wheel as described in Section 17. On models with an air bag, also remove the contact unit from the steering column.
3 On models without an air bag, remove the rubber seal from the ignition switch/lock, then undo the retaining screws and remove the upper and lower steering column shrouds.
4 Where necessary, undo the nut and release the support bar from the column.
5 Depress the retaining clips, and release the left- and right-hand combination switches from the column. Disconnect the wiring connectors, and remove the switches from the vehicle **(see illustration)**.
6 Disconnect the wiring connectors from the ignition switch wiring block and the horn contact, then release the wiring from the steering column **(see illustration)**.
7 Using paint or similar, make alignment marks between the steering column and intermediate shaft, then slacken and remove the clamp bolt securing the intermediate shaft to the steering column **(see illustration)**.

19.5 Depress the retaining clips, and slide the combination switches out from the column ...

19.6 ... and disconnect the wiring connector from the horn contact pin (arrowed)

19.7 Steering column-to-intermediate shaft clamp bolt (arrowed)

19.8 Steering column lower mounting bolt

19.9 Steering column upper mounting nut (A) and shear-head bolt (B)

19.11 Removing the steering column

8 Unscrew the lower mounting bolt securing the steering column to the bulkhead **(see illustration)**.

9 Two fasteners must now be extracted from the column upper mounting bracket. A conventional nut is used on one side of the column, and a shear-head type bolt is used on the other side **(see illustration)**.

10 The shear-head bolt must be removed by drilling down the centre of the bolt, and then using a suitable bolt/stud extractor (sometimes called 'easy-outs'). When drilling the bolt, take care not to damage the facia panel or steering column. A new shear-head bolt will obviously be required for refitting.

11 Release the column assembly from its mountings, then detach it from the intermediate shaft and remove it from the vehicle **(see illustration)**. Handle the column carefully, avoiding knocks or impact of any kind, which may damage the collapsible section of the column housing.

Inspection

12 The steering column incorporates a telescopic safety section. In the event of a front-end crash, the shaft housing collapses, and prevents the steering wheel injuring the driver. Before refitting the steering column,

examine the column and mountings for signs of damage and deformation, and check the steering shaft for signs of free play in the column bushes **(see illustration)**. If there are signs of damage or play, the column must be renewed. On models not fitted with an air bag, overhaul of the column is possible, but this is a difficult task which should really be entrusted to a Vauxhall/Opel dealer. Consult your dealer for further information.

Refitting

13 Manoeuvre the steering column into position, and engage it with the intermediate shaft universal joint, aligning the marks made on removal.

14 Refit the column upper and lower mounting nut/bolts, and the new shear-head bolt. Tighten all bolts by hand only at this stage **(see illustration)**.

15 Align the intermediate shaft bolt hole with the steering column shaft cut-out so that the clamp bolt can be slid into position. Tighten the bolt by hand only.

16 Tighten the column mounting bolts to the specified torque setting. Tighten the shear-head bolt until its head breaks off.

17 Tighten the clamp bolt to the specified torque setting.

18 Ensure that the wiring is correctly routed, and reconnect it to the ignition switch wiring block and horn contact.

19 Clip the left-and right-hand switches back into position, and reconnect their wiring connectors.

20 Where necessary, refit the support strut to the column, and securely tighten its retaining nut.

21 On models without an air bag, clip the steering column shrouds into position, and securely tighten the retaining screws. Refit the rubber seal to the ignition switch/lock, then refit the steering wheel as described in Section 17.

22 On models with an air bag, refit the contact unit and steering wheel as described in Section 17.

20 Steering column intermediate shaft – removal, inspection and refitting

Removal

1 Set the front wheels in the straight-ahead position.

2 Using paint or a suitable marker pen, make

19.12 Inspect the collapsible section of the column for signs of damage, and renew the column assembly if necessary

19.14 Use a new shear-head bolt when refitting the column

20.3a Slacken and remove the steering column-to-intermediate shaft clamp bolt . . .

20.3b . . . and the intermediate shaft-to-steering gear clamp bolt and nut (arrowed)

20.4 Free the intermediate shaft from the column and steering gear, and remove it from under the facia

alignment marks between the intermediate shaft joints and the steering column and steering gear shafts.

3 Slacken and remove the upper clamp bolt and the lower clamp bolt and nut (see illustrations).

4 Disengage the shaft universal joint from the steering column, then slide the shaft from the steering gear pinion and remove it from the vehicle (see illustration).

Inspection

5 Inspect the intermediate shaft universal joint for signs of roughness in its bearings and ease of movement. If either joint is damaged in any way, the complete shaft assembly must be renewed.

Refitting

6 Check that the front wheels are still in the straight-ahead position, and that the steering wheel is correctly positioned.

7 Aligning the marks made on removal, engage the shaft with the steering gear pinion, then locate the universal joint on the steering column end. Install both clamp bolts, tightening them to the specified torque setting.

21 Steering gear assembly – removal, overhaul and refitting

Note: New track rod balljoint-to-swivel hub nuts will be required when refitting.

Removal

1 Firmly apply the handbrake, then jack up the front of the car and support it securely on axle stands (see Jacking and vehicle support). Remove both front roadwheels.

Manual steering gear

2 Referring to Chapter 2A, 2B or 2C, as applicable, support the weight of the engine/transmission unit, and remove the rear engine/transmission mounting rubber and bracket from the vehicle.

3 On models with manual transmission, disconnect the gearchange linkage from the transmission as described in Chapter 7A.

4 Slacken and remove the nuts securing the steering gear track rod balljoints to the swivel hubs (see illustration), and release the balljoint tapered shanks using a universal balljoint separator. Discard the nuts; they should be renewed whenever they are disturbed.

5 Remove the intermediate shaft as described in Section 20.

6 Prior to removal, mark the position of the mounting rubbers on the steering gear housing. These marks can then be used on refitting to ensure that the steering gear is correctly positioned in the clamps.

7 Slacken and remove the four nuts and washers securing the steering gear to the bulkhead. Note the correct fitted locations of any relevant brackets retained by the nuts, then remove the steering gear mounting clamp(s) (see illustration).

8 Detach the rubber gaiter from the bulkhead, and free the steering gear pinion from the intermediate shaft.

9 Move the steering gear towards the right-hand side of the engine compartment, then lower the left-hand end of the assembly, and manoeuvre the assembly out from underneath the vehicle. Note that it may be necessary to lower the engine slightly to gain the necessary clearance for removal.

Power-assisted steering gear

10 Remove the air cleaner assembly as described in Chapter 4A or 4B.

11 On left-hand drive models, to improve access to the steering gear, remove the

21.4 Unscrew the retaining nuts securing each track rod balljoint to the swivel hubs

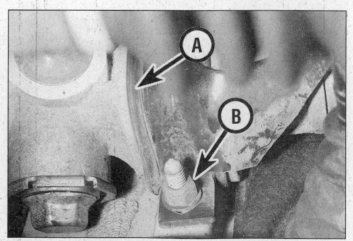

21.7 Steering gear mounting rubber (A) and mounting clamp and nut (B) – viewed from underneath

braking system vacuum servo unit as described in Chapter 9.

12 Remove the intermediate shaft as described in Section 20.

13 On models with manual transmission, disconnect the gearchange linkage from the transmission as described in Chapter 7A, and unbolt the clutch cable bracket from the bulkhead. Additionally, on models with electronic power steering, disconnect the end of the clutch cable from the gearbox as described in Chapter 6.

14 Slacken and remove the nuts securing the steering gear track rod balljoints to the swivel hubs, and release the balljoint tapered shanks using a universal balljoint separator. Discard the nuts; they should be renewed whenever they are disturbed.

15 On models with hydraulic power steering, using brake hose clamps, clamp both the supply and return hoses near the power steering fluid reservoir. Mark the unions to ensure that they are correctly positioned on reassembly, then unscrew the feed and return pipe union nuts from the steering gear assembly; be prepared for fluid spillage, and position a suitable container beneath the pipes whilst unscrewing the union nuts **(see illustration)**. Disconnect both pipes, and plug the pipe ends and steering gear orifices, to prevent excessive fluid leakage and the entry of dirt into the hydraulic system.

16 Free the power steering pipes from any relevant retaining clips, and position them clear of the steering gear so that they will not hinder the removal procedure.

17 Referring to Chapter 2A, 2B or 2C, as applicable, support the weight of the engine/transmission unit, and remove the rear engine/transmission mounting rubber and bracket from the vehicle.

18 Prior to removal, mark the position of the mounting rubbers on the steering gear housing. These marks can then be used on refitting to ensure that the steering gear is correctly positioned in the clamps.

19 Slacken and remove the four nuts and washers securing the steering gear to the

21.15 Hydraulic power-assisted steering gear fluid feed and return pipe unions (arrowed) – shown with engine removed for clarity

bulkhead. Note the correct fitted locations of any relevant brackets retained by the nuts, then remove the steering gear mounting clamp(s).

20 On models with air conditioning, release the refrigerant pipes from their retaining clips on the bulkhead. **Note:** *Refer to the warning notes in Chapter 3 – do not attempt to disconnect any of the pipes.*

21 Release the rubber gaiter from the bulkhead, then move the steering gear fully towards the right on right-hand drive models, or the left on left-hand drive models. Lower the opposite end of the steering gear, and manoeuvre the assembly out from underneath the vehicle. Note that on 1.6 litre DOHC engine models, it may be necessary to unbolt the remaining engine/transmission mountings and lower the engine slightly to gain the necessary clearance for removal (see Chapter 2C).

Overhaul

22 Examine the steering gear assembly for signs of wear or damage, and check that the rack moves freely throughout the full length of its travel, with no signs of roughness or excessive free play between the steering gear pinion and rack. It is possible to overhaul the steering gear assembly housing components, but this task should be entrusted to a Vauxhall/Opel dealer. The only components which can be renewed easily by the home mechanic are the steering gear gaiters, the track rod balljoints and the track rods (manual steering gear only). Steering gear gaiter, track rod balljoint and track rod renewal procedures are covered in Sections 24, 25 and 26 respectively.

23 On models with hydraulic power-assisted steering, inspect all the steering gear fluid unions for signs of leakage, and check that all union nuts are securely tightened.

24 Inspect the rubber mountings and pinion gear rubber gaiter, and renew them if they show signs of wear or deterioration.

Refitting

Manual steering gear

25 Fit the mounting rubbers to the steering gear, and align them with the marks made prior to removal. If a new steering gear assembly is being installed, transfer the marks from the original onto the new assembly.

26 Manoeuvre the steering gear assembly back into position on the bulkhead. With the pinion correctly located in the bulkhead aperture, refit the mounting clamps and retaining nuts, not forgetting to fit the necessary brackets to steering gear mounting studs.

27 Ensure that the rubbers are correctly aligned with the marks made on removal, and tighten the mounting clamp nuts to the specified torque setting.

28 The remainder of refitting is reverse of the removal procedure, noting the following points:

a) *Refit the intermediate shaft as described in Section 20.*

b) *Locate the track rod balljoints in position, fit the new nuts and tighten them to the specified torque.*

c) *Connect the gearchange linkage as described in Chapter 7A.*

d) *Refit the engine/transmission mounting as described in Chapter 2A, 2B or 2C.*

e) *Refit the air cleaner assembly as described in Chapter 4A or 4B.*

f) *On completion, check and, if necessary, adjust the front wheel alignment as described in Section 27.*

Power-assisted steering gear

29 Install the steering gear as described above in paragraphs 25 to 27.

30 Wipe clean the feed and return pipe unions, and refit them to their respective unions on the steering gear. Tighten the union nuts to the specified torque setting, and ensure that the pipes are securely retained by all the necessary retaining clips.

31 The remainder of the refitting procedure is a direct reversal of the removal sequence, noting the following points:

a) *Refit the intermediate shaft as described in Section 20, and ensure that the rubber gaiter is correctly seated in the bulkhead.*

b) *On models with air conditioning, ensure that the refrigerant pipes are securely retained by all the necessary clips.*

c) *Locate the track rod balljoints in position, fit the new nuts and tighten them to the specified torque.*

d) *Connect the gearchange linkage as described in Chapter 7A.*

e) *Refit the engine/transmission mounting(s) as described in Chapter 2A, 2B or 2C.*

f) *On completion, remove the clamps from the hoses, and bleed the hydraulic system as described in Section 23.*

g) *Check and, if necessary, adjust the front wheel alignment as described in Section 27.*

22 Power steering pump – removal and refitting

Removal

1 Remove the auxiliary drivebelt as described in Chapter 1.

2 Using brake hose clamps, clamp both the supply and return hoses near the power steering fluid reservoir. This will minimise fluid loss during subsequent operations.

3 Slacken the retaining clip, and disconnect the fluid supply hose from the rear of the pump. Slacken the union nut, and disconnect the feed pipe from the pump, along with its O-

22.3 Power steering pump fluid supply hose retaining clip (A) and feed pipe union nut (B)

22.4 Typical power steering pump rear mounting bolts (arrowed) – shown with coolant hose removed

25.4 Release the track rod balljoint from the swivel hub using a universal balljoint separator

ring (see illustration). Be prepared for some fluid spillage as the pipe and hose are disconnected, and plug the hose/pipe end and pump unions, to minimise fluid loss and prevent the entry of dirt into the system.

4 Slacken and remove the front and rear retaining bolts securing the power steering pump to its mounting bracket (see illustration), and remove the pump from the engine compartment.

Refitting

5 Manoeuvre the pump into position and refit its mounting bolts, tightening them to the specified torque setting.

6 Fit a new O-ring to the feed pipe union, then reconnect the pipe to the pump, and tighten the union nut to the specified torque setting. Refit the supply hose to the pump, and securely tighten its retaining clip. Remove the brake hose clamps used to minimise fluid loss.

7 Refit the auxiliary drivebelt as described in Chapter 1.

8 On completion, bleed the hydraulic system as described in Section 23.

23 Power steering system – bleeding

1 With the engine stopped, fill the fluid reservoir right up to the brim with the specified type of fluid. This is more important if fluid has been lost after work has been carried out, or if the system has been leaking. Otherwise, top the level up to the relevant mark (see paragraph 5).

2 Have an assistant start the engine, while you keep watch on the fluid level. Be prepared to add more fluid as the engine starts, as the fluid level may drop quickly. The fluid level must be kept above the MIN mark at all times, or air will be drawn into the system.

3 With the engine running at idle speed, turn the steering wheel slowly two or three times approximately 45° to the left and right of the

centre, then turn the wheel twice from lock-to-lock. Do not hold the wheel on either lock, as this places strain on the hydraulic system. Repeat this procedure until bubbles cease to appear in fluid reservoir, topping-up as necessary.

4 If, when turning the steering, an abnormal noise is heard from the fluid lines, it indicates that there is still air in the system. Check this by turning the wheels to the straight-ahead position and switching off the engine. If the fluid level in the reservoir rises, then air is present in the system, and further bleeding is necessary.

5 Once all air is removed from the system, stop the engine and check the fluid level. With the fluid at operating temperature (80°C), the level should be on the MAX mark; with the fluid cold (20°C), the level should be on the MIN mark. Correct the level by topping-up, or by removing fluid using a syringe or similar, as necessary.

24 Steering gear rubber gaiters – renewal

1 Remove the track rod balljoint as described in Section 25.

2 Mark the correct fitted position of the gaiter on the track rod, then release the retaining clips, and slide the gaiter off the steering gear housing and track rod end.

3 Thoroughly clean the track rod and the steering gear housing, using fine abrasive paper to polish off any corrosion, burrs or sharp edges which might damage the new gaiter's sealing lips on installation. Scrape off all grease from the old gaiter, and apply to the track rod inner balljoint.

4 Carefully slide the new gaiter onto the track rod end, and locate it on the steering gear housing. Align the outer edge of the gaiter with the mark made on the track rod prior to removal, then secure it in position with new retaining clips.

5 Refit the track rod balljoint as described in Section 25.

25 Track rod balljoint – removal and refitting

Note: A new track rod balljoint-to-swivel hub nut will be required when refitting.

Removal

1 Firmly apply the handbrake, then jack up the front of the car and support it securely on axle stands (see Jacking and vehicle support). Remove the appropriate front roadwheel.

2 If the balljoint is to be re-used, use a straight-edge and a scriber, or similar, to mark its relationship to the track rod.

3 Hold the track rod, and unscrew the balljoint locknut by a quarter of a turn.

4 Slacken and remove the nut securing the track rod balljoint to the swivel hub, and release the balljoint tapered shank using a universal balljoint separator (see illustration). Discard the nut; a new one must be used of refitting.

5 Counting the exact number of turns necessary to do so, unscrew the balljoint from the track rod end.

6 Count the number of exposed threads between the end of the track rod and the locknut, and record this figure. If a new gaiter is to be fitted, unscrew the locknut from the track rod.

7 Carefully clean the balljoint and the track rod threads. Renew the balljoint if there is excessive free play of the balljoint shank, or if the shank is excessively stiff. If the balljoint gaiter is damaged, the complete balljoint assembly must be renewed; it is not possible to obtain the gaiter separately.

Refitting

8 If it was removed, screw the locknut onto the track rod threads, and position it so that the same number of exposed threads are visible as was noted prior to removal.

9 Screw the balljoint into the track rod by the number of turns noted on removal. This should bring the balljoint locknut to within a quarter of a turn from the locknut, with the alignment marks that were made (if applicable) on removal lined up.

10 Refit the balljoint shank to the swivel hub, then fit a new retaining nut and tighten it to the specified torque setting.

11 Refit the roadwheel, then lower the vehicle to the ground and tighten the roadwheel bolts to the specified torque setting.

12 Check and, if necessary, adjust the front wheel toe setting as described in Section 27. Tighten the balljoint locknut to the specified torque setting on completion.

26 Track rod – renewal

Manual steering gear

Note: *When refitting, a new track rod balljoint-to-swivel hub nut, and new gaiter retaining clips, will be required.*

1 Remove the track rod balljoint as described in Section 25.

2 Release the retaining clips, and slide the steering gear gaiter off the end of the track rod as described in Section 24.

3 Extend the steering rack from the housing. Prevent the rack from rotating using an open-ended spanner located on the rack flats, and slacken the track rod inner balljoint from the rack end.

4 Unscrew the track rod assembly, and remove it along with its spacer.

5 Remove the track rod assembly, and examine the track rod inner balljoint for signs of slackness or tight spots. Check that the track rod itself is straight and free from damage. If necessary, renew the track rod; it is also recommended that the steering gear gaiter/dust cover is renewed.

6 Locate the spacer on the end of the steering rack, and screw the balljoint into the steering rack. Tighten the track rod balljoint to the specified torque, whilst retaining the steering rack with an open-ended spanner.

7 Install the steering gaiter and track rod balljoint as described in Sections 24 and 25.

Power-assisted steering gear

8 On models with either hydraulic, or electronic power-assisted steering, the track rods are not available separately. If a track rod is damaged in any way, the complete steering gear assembly must be renewed. Refer to your Vauxhall/Opel dealer for further information on parts availability.

27 Wheel alignment and steering angles – general information

1 Accurate front wheel alignment is essential for precise steering and handling, and for even tyre wear. Before carrying out any checking or adjusting operations, make sure that the tyres are correctly inflated, that all steering and suspension joints and linkages are in sound condition, and that the wheels are not buckled or distorted, particularly around the rims. It will also be necessary to have the vehicle positioned on flat, level ground, with enough space to push the car backwards and forwards through about half its length.

2 Front wheel alignment consists of four factors **(see illustration)**:

Camber is the angle at which the roadwheels are set from the vertical, when viewed from the front or rear of the vehicle. Positive camber is the angle (in degrees) that the wheels are tilted outwards at the top from the vertical.

27.2 Wheel alignment and steering angles

Castor is the angle between the steering axis and a vertical line when viewed from each side of the vehicle. Positive castor is indicated when the steering axis is inclined towards the rear of the vehicle at its upper end.

Steering axis inclination is the angle, when viewed from the front or rear of the vehicle, between the vertical and an imaginary line drawn between the upper and lower front suspension strut mountings.

Toe setting is the amount by which the distance between the front inside edges of the roadwheels differs from that between the rear inside edges, when measured at hub height. If the distance between the front edges is less than at the rear, the wheels are said to 'toe-in'. If it is greater than at the rear, the wheels are said to 'toe-out'.

3 Camber, castor and steering axis inclination are set during manufacture, and are not adjustable. Unless the vehicle has suffered accident damage, or there is gross wear in the suspension mountings or joints, it can be assumed that these settings are correct. If for any reason it is believed that they are not correct, the task of checking them should be left to a Vauxhall/Opel dealer, who will have the necessary special equipment needed to measure the small angles involved.

4 It is, however, within the scope of the home mechanic to check and adjust the front wheel toe setting. To do this, a tracking gauge must first be obtained. Two types of gauge are available, and can be obtained from motor accessory shops. The first type measures the distance between the front and rear inside edges of the roadwheels, as previously described, with the vehicle stationary. The second type, known as a 'scuff plate', measures the actual position of the contact surface of the tyre, in relation to the road surface, with the vehicle in motion. This is achieved by pushing or driving the front tyre over a plate, which then moves slightly according to the scuff of the tyre, and shows this movement on a scale. Both types have their advantages and disadvantages, but either can give satisfactory results if used correctly and carefully.

5 Many tyre specialists will also check toe settings free, or for a nominal charge. Considering the initial cost of obtaining a tracking gauge, and then becoming experienced with its use, it may actually be beneficial to have the whole job done by a tyre specialist or similar company. The actual procedure for using a tracking gauge is, however, outlined in the following paragraphs to show the work involved.

6 Make sure that the steering is in the straight-ahead position when making measurements.

7 If adjustment is necessary, chock the rear wheels, apply the handbrake, then jack up the front of the vehicle and support it securely on axle stands. Turn the steering wheel onto full-left lock, and record the number of exposed threads on the right-hand track rod end. Now turn the steering onto full-right lock, and record the number of threads on the left-hand side. If there are the same number of threads visible on both sides, then subsequent adjustment should be made equally on both sides. If there are more threads visible on one side than the other, it will be necessary to compensate for this during adjustment. It is most important that, after adjustment, the same number of threads are visible on each track rod end.

8 First clean the track rod threads; if they are corroded, apply penetrating fluid before starting adjustment. Release the rubber gaiter outer clips, then peel back the gaiters and apply a smear of grease, so that the gaiters will not be twisted or strained as their respective track rods are rotated.

9 Use a straight-edge and a scriber, or similar, to mark the relationship of each track rod to its balljoint then, holding each track rod in turn, unscrew its locknut fully.

10 Alter the length of the track rods, bearing in mind the note made in paragraph 7, screwing them into or out of the balljoints by rotating the track rod using an open-ended spanner fitted to the track rod flats provided. Shortening the track rods (screwing them into their balljoints) will reduce toe-in/increase toe-out.

11 When the setting is correct, hold the track rods and securely tighten the balljoint locknuts. Check that the balljoints are seated correctly in their sockets, and count the exposed threads to check the length of both track rods. If they are not the same, then the adjustment has not been made equally, and problems will be encountered with tyre scrubbing in turns; also, the steering wheel spokes will no longer be horizontal when the wheels are in the straight-ahead position.

12 If the track rod lengths are the same, check that the toe setting has been correctly adjusted by lowering the vehicle to the ground and re-checking the toe setting; re-adjust if necessary. If the setting is correct, tighten the track rod balljoint locknuts to the specified torque setting. Ensure that the rubber gaiters are seated correctly and are not twisted or strained, and secure them in position with the retaining clips.

Chapter 11
Bodywork and fittings

Contents

Degrees of difficulty

Easy, suitable for novice with little experience	**Fairly easy,** suitable for beginner with some experience	**Fairly difficult,** suitable for competent DIY mechanic	**Difficult,** suitable for experienced DIY mechanic	**Very difficult,** suitable for expert DIY or professional

Specifications

Torque wrench settings	Nm	lbf ft
Facia fasteners:		
Facia end screws	6	4
Facia-to-bulkhead nuts	22	16
Support bracket screws	6	4
Front seat bolts	20	15
Rear seat:		
Corsa and Corsavan (split rear seat):		
Seat back-to-bracket bolts	30	22
Seat back-to-hinge bolts	20	15
Combo Van:		
Seat back bolts	20	15
Tailgate lock cylinder/handle nuts	4	3
Seat belt anchorage bolts	35	26
Seat belt height adjuster ratchet bolts	20	15
Seat belt inertia reel bolt	35	26

1 General information

The bodyshell is made of pressed-steel sections, and is available in three- and five-door Hatchback versions, as well as two different forms of Van. Most components are welded together, but some use is made of structural adhesives; the front wings are bolted on.

The bonnet, doors, and some other vulnerable panels, are made of zinc-coated metal, and are further protected by being coated with an anti-chip primer, prior to being sprayed.

Extensive use is made of plastic materials, mainly on the interior, but also in exterior components. The front and rear bumpers are injection-moulded from a synthetic material which is very strong and yet light. Plastic components such as wheelarch liners are fitted to the underside of the vehicle, to improve the body's resistance to corrosion.

2 Maintenance – bodywork and underframe

The general condition of a vehicle's bodywork is the one thing that significantly affects its value. Maintenance is easy, but needs to be regular. Neglect, particularly after minor damage, can lead quickly to further deterioration and costly repair bills. It is important also to keep watch on those parts of the vehicle not immediately visible, for instance the underside, inside all the wheelarches, and the lower part of the engine compartment.

The basic maintenance routine for the bodywork is washing – preferably with a lot of water, from a hose. This will remove all the loose solids which may have stuck to the vehicle. It is important to flush these off in such a way as to prevent grit from scratching the finish. The wheelarches and underframe need washing in the same way, to remove any accumulated mud, which will retain moisture and tend to encourage rust. Paradoxically enough, the best time to clean the underframe and wheelarches is in wet weather, when the mud is thoroughly wet and soft. In very wet weather, the underframe is usually cleaned of large accumulations automatically, and this is a good time for inspection.

Periodically, except on vehicles with a wax-based underbody protective coating, it is a good idea to have the whole of the underframe of the vehicle steam-cleaned, engine compartment included, so that a thorough inspection can be carried out to see what minor repairs and renovations are necessary. Steam-cleaning is available at many garages, and is necessary for the removal of the accumulation of oily grime, which sometimes is allowed to become thick in certain areas. If steam-cleaning facilities are not available, there are some excellent grease solvents available

which can be brush-applied; the dirt can then be simply hosed off. Note that these methods should not be used on vehicles with wax-based underbody protective coating, or the coating will be removed. Such vehicles should be inspected annually, preferably just prior to Winter, when the underbody should be washed down, and any damage to the wax coating repaired. Ideally, a completely fresh coat should be applied. It would also be worth considering the use of such wax-based protection for injection into door panels, sills, box sections, etc, as an additional safeguard against rust damage, where such protection is not provided by the vehicle manufacturer.

After washing paintwork, wipe off with a chamois leather to give an unspotted clear finish. A coat of clear protective wax polish will give added protection against chemical pollutants in the air. If the paintwork sheen has dulled or oxidised, use a cleaner/polisher combination to restore the brilliance of the shine. This requires a little effort, but such dulling is usually caused because regular washing has been neglected. Care needs to be taken with metallic paintwork, as special non-abrasive cleaner/polisher is required to avoid damage to the finish. Always check that the door and ventilator opening drain holes and pipes are completely clear, so that water can be drained out. Brightwork should be treated in the same way as paintwork. Windscreens and windows can be kept clear of the smeary film which often appears, by the use of proprietary glass cleaner. Never use any form of wax or other body or chromium polish on glass.

3 Maintenance – upholstery and carpets

Mats and carpets should be brushed or vacuum-cleaned regularly, to keep them free of grit. If they are badly stained, remove them from the vehicle for scrubbing or sponging, and make quite sure they are dry before refitting. Seats and interior trim panels can be kept clean by wiping with a damp cloth. If they do become stained (which can be more apparent on light-coloured upholstery), use a little liquid detergent and a soft nail brush to scour the grime out of the grain of the material. Do not forget to keep the headlining clean in the same way as the upholstery. When using liquid cleaners inside the vehicle, do not over-wet the surfaces being cleaned. Excessive damp could get into the seams and padded interior, causing stains, offensive odours or even rot.

> **HAYNES HINT** *If the inside of the vehicle gets wet accidentally, it is worthwhile taking some trouble to dry it out properly, particularly where carpets are involved. Do not leave oil or electric heaters inside the vehicle for this purpose.*

4 Minor body damage – repair

Repairs of minor scratches in bodywork

If the scratch is very superficial, and does not penetrate to the metal of the bodywork, repair is very simple. Lightly rub the area of the scratch with a paintwork renovator, or a very fine cutting paste, to remove loose paint from the scratch, and to clear the surrounding bodywork of wax polish. Rinse the area with clean water.

Apply touch-up paint to the scratch using a fine paint brush; continue to apply fine layers of paint until the surface of the paint in the scratch is level with the surrounding paintwork. Allow the new paint at least two weeks to harden, then blend it into the surrounding paintwork by rubbing the scratch area with a paintwork renovator or a very fine cutting paste. Finally, apply wax polish.

Where the scratch has penetrated right through to the metal of the bodywork, causing the metal to rust, a different repair technique is required. Remove any loose rust from the bottom of the scratch with a penknife, then apply rust-inhibiting paint to prevent the formation of rust in the future. Using a rubber or nylon applicator, fill the scratch with bodystopper paste. If required, this paste can be mixed with cellulose thinners to provide a very thin paste which is ideal for filling narrow scratches. Before the stopper-paste in the scratch hardens, wrap a piece of smooth cotton rag around the top of a finger. Dip the finger in cellulose thinners, and quickly sweep it across the surface of the stopper-paste in the scratch; this will ensure that the surface of the stopper-paste is slightly hollowed. The scratch can now be painted over as described earlier in this Section.

Repairs of dents in bodywork

When deep denting of the vehicle's bodywork has taken place, the first task is to pull the dent out, until the affected bodywork almost attains its original shape. There is little point in trying to restore the original shape completely, as the metal in the damaged area will have stretched on impact, and cannot be reshaped fully to its original contour. It is better to bring the level of the dent up to a point which is about 3 mm below the level of the surrounding bodywork. In cases where the dent is very shallow anyway, it is not worth trying to pull it out at all. If the underside of the dent is accessible, it can be hammered out gently from behind, using a mallet with a wooden or plastic head. Whilst doing this, hold a suitable block of wood firmly against the outside of the panel, to absorb the impact from the hammer blows and thus prevent a large area of the bodywork from being 'belled-out'.

Should the dent be in a section of the bodywork which has a double skin, or some other factor making it inaccessible from behind, a different technique is called for. Drill several small holes through the metal inside the area – particularly in the deeper section. Then screw long self-tapping screws into the holes, just sufficiently for them to gain a good purchase in the metal. Now the dent can be pulled out by pulling on the protruding heads of the screws with a pair of pliers.

The next stage of the repair is the removal of the paint from the damaged area, and from an inch or so of the surrounding 'sound' bodywork. This is accomplished most easily by using a wire brush or abrasive pad on a power drill, although it can be done just as effectively by hand, using sheets of abrasive paper. To complete the preparation for filling, score the surface of the bare metal with a screwdriver or the tang of a file, or alternatively, drill small holes in the affected area. This will provide a really good 'key' for the filler paste.

To complete the repair, see the Section on filling and respraying.

Repairs of rust holes or gashes in bodywork

Remove all paint from the affected area, and from an inch or so of the surrounding 'sound' bodywork, using an abrasive pad or a wire brush on a power drill. If these are not available, a few sheets of abrasive paper will do the job most effectively. With the paint removed, you will be able to judge the severity of the corrosion, and therefore decide whether to renew the whole panel (if this is possible) or to repair the affected area. New body panels are not as expensive as most people think, and it is often quicker and more satisfactory to fit a new panel than to attempt to repair large areas of corrosion.

Remove all fittings from the affected area, except those which will act as a guide to the original shape of the damaged bodywork (eg headlight shells etc). Then, using tin snips or a hacksaw blade, remove all loose metal and any other metal badly affected by corrosion. Hammer the edges of the hole inwards, in order to create a slight depression for the filler paste.

Wire-brush the affected area to remove the powdery rust from the surface of the remaining metal. Paint the affected area with rust-inhibiting paint, if the back of the rusted area is accessible, treat this also.

Before filling can take place, it will be necessary to block the hole in some way. This can be achieved by the use of aluminium or plastic mesh, or aluminium tape.

Aluminium or plastic mesh, or glass-fibre matting, is probably the best material to use for a large hole. Cut a piece to the approximate size and shape of the hole to be filled, then position it in the hole so that its edges are below the level of the surrounding

bodywork. It can be retained in position by several blobs of filler paste around its periphery.

Aluminium tape should be used for small or very narrow holes. Pull a piece off the roll, trim it to the approximate size and shape required, then pull off the backing paper (if used) and stick the tape over the hole; it can be overlapped if the thickness of one piece is insufficient. Burnish down the edges of the tape with the handle of a screwdriver or similar, to ensure that the tape is securely attached to the metal underneath.

Bodywork repairs – filling and respraying

Before using this Section, see the Sections on dent, deep scratch, rust holes and gash repairs.

Many types of bodyfiller are available, but generally speaking, those proprietary kits which contain a tin of filler paste and a tube of resin hardener are best for this type of repair. A wide, flexible plastic or nylon applicator will be found invaluable for imparting a smooth and well-contoured finish to the surface of the filler.

Mix up a little filler on a clean piece of card or board – measure the hardener carefully (follow the maker's instructions on the pack), otherwise the filler will set too rapidly or too slowly. Using the applicator, apply the filler paste to the prepared area; draw the applicator across the surface of the filler to achieve the correct contour and to level the surface. As soon as a contour that approximates to the correct one is achieved, stop working the paste – if you carry on too long, the paste will become sticky and begin to 'pick-up' on the applicator. Continue to add thin layers of filler paste at 20-minute intervals, until the level of the filler is just proud of the surrounding bodywork.

Once the filler has hardened, the excess can be removed using a metal plane or file. From then on, progressively-finer grades of abrasive paper should be used, starting with a 40-grade production paper, and finishing with a 400-grade wet-and-dry paper. Always wrap the abrasive paper around a flat rubber, cork, or wooden block – otherwise the surface of the filler will not be completely flat. During the smoothing of the filler surface, the wet-and-dry paper should be periodically rinsed in water. This will ensure that a very smooth finish is imparted to the filler at the final stage.

At this stage, the 'dent' should be surrounded by a ring of bare metal, which in turn should be encircled by the finely 'feathered' edge of the good paintwork. Rinse the repair area with clean water, until all of the dust produced by the rubbing-down operation has gone.

Spray the whole area with a light coat of primer – this will show up any imperfections in the surface of the filler. Repair these imperfections with fresh filler paste or

bodystopper, and once more smooth the surface with abrasive paper. Repeat this spray-and-repair procedure until you are satisfied that the surface of the filler, and the feathered edge of the paintwork, are perfect. Clean the repair area with clean water, and allow to dry fully.

 HAYNES HiNT *If bodystopper is used, it can be mixed with cellulose thinners to form a really thin paste which is ideal for filling small holes.*

The repair area is now ready for final spraying. Paint spraying must be carried out in a warm, dry, windless and dust-free atmosphere. This condition can be created artificially if you have access to a large indoor working area, but if you are forced to work in the open, you will have to pick your day very carefully. If you are working indoors, dousing the floor in the work area with water will help to settle the dust which would otherwise be in the atmosphere. If the repair area is confined to one body panel, mask off the surrounding panels; this will help to minimise the effects of a slight mis-match in paint colours. Bodywork fittings (eg chrome strips, door handles etc) will also need to be masked off. Use genuine masking tape, and several thicknesses of newspaper, for the masking operations.

Before commencing to spray, agitate the aerosol can thoroughly, then spray a test area (an old tin, or similar) until the technique is mastered. Cover the repair area with a thick coat of primer; the thickness should be built up using several thin layers of paint, rather than one thick one. Using 400-grade wet-and-dry paper, rub down the surface of the primer until it is really smooth. While doing this, the work area should be thoroughly doused with water, and the wet-and-dry paper periodically rinsed in water. Allow to dry before spraying on more paint.

Spray on the top coat, again building up the thickness by using several thin layers of paint. Start spraying at one edge of the repair area, and then, using a side-to-side motion, work until the whole repair area and about 2 inches of the surrounding original paintwork is covered. Remove all masking material 10 to 15 minutes after spraying on the final coat of paint.

Allow the new paint at least two weeks to harden, then, using a paintwork renovator, or a very fine cutting paste, blend the edges of the paint into the existing paintwork. Finally, apply wax polish.

Plastic components

With the use of more and more plastic body components by the vehicle manufacturers (eg bumpers, spoilers, and in some cases major body panels), rectification of more serious damage to such items has become a matter of either entrusting repair work to a specialist in this field, or renewing complete

6.2a Unclip the access cover in the wheelarch liner . . .

6.2b . . . to gain access to the bumper retaining nut (viewed from underneath the wheelarch liner)

6.3 Unscrew the bolts securing the bumper mounting brackets to the crossmember, one on each side of the radiator grille aperture

components. Repair of such damage by the DIY owner is not really feasible, owing to the cost of the equipment and materials required for effecting such repairs. The basic technique involves making a groove along the line of the crack in the plastic, using a rotary burr in a power drill. The damaged part is then welded back together, using a hot-air gun to heat up and fuse a plastic filler rod into the groove. Any excess plastic is then removed, and the area rubbed down to a smooth finish. It is important that a filler rod of the correct plastic is used, as body components can be made of a variety of different types (eg polycarbonate, ABS, polypropylene).

Damage of a less serious nature (abrasions, minor cracks etc) can be repaired by the DIY owner using a two-part epoxy filler repair material. Once mixed in equal proportions, this is used in similar fashion to the bodywork filler used on metal panels. The filler is usually cured in twenty to thirty minutes, ready for sanding and painting.

If the owner is renewing a complete component himself, or if he has repaired it with epoxy filler, he will be left with the problem of finding a suitable paint for finishing which is compatible with the type of plastic used. At one time, the use of a universal paint was not possible, owing to the complex range of plastics encountered in body component applications. Standard paints, generally speaking, will not bond to plastic or rubber satisfactorily. However, it is now possible to obtain a plastic body parts finishing kit which

consists of a pre-primer treatment, a primer and coloured top coat. Full instructions are normally supplied with a kit, but basically, the method of use is to first apply the pre-primer to the component concerned, and allow it to dry for up to 30 minutes. Then the primer is applied, and left to dry for about an hour before finally applying the special-coloured top coat. The result is a correctly-coloured component, where the paint will flex with the plastic or rubber, a property that standard paint does not normally possess.

5 Major body damage – repair

Where serious damage has occurred, or large areas need renewal due to neglect, it means that complete new panels will need welding-in, and this is best left to professionals. If the damage is due to impact, it will also be necessary to check completely the alignment of the bodyshell, and this can only be carried out accurately by a Vauxhall/Opel dealer, using special jigs. If the body is left misaligned, it is primarily dangerous as the car will not handle properly, and secondly, uneven stresses will be imposed on the steering, suspension and possibly transmission, causing abnormal wear, or complete failure, particularly to such items as the tyres.

6 Front bumper – removal and refitting

Removal

1 Firmly apply the handbrake, then jack up the front of the car and support it securely on axle stands (see *Jacking and vehicle support*).
2 Unclip the access covers, situated at the top of each wheelarch liner, and unscrew the two plastic nuts (one on each side) securing either end of the bumper to the vehicle **(see illustrations)**. Note that the plastic retaining nuts should be discarded, and new ones used on refitting.
3 Remove the radiator grille as described in Section 22, then unscrew the two bolts securing the bumper mounting brackets to the crossmember, one located on each side of the radiator grille aperture **(see illustration)**.
4 Slacken and remove the three bolts securing the bottom of the bumper to the vehicle body **(see illustration)**.
5 On models with front foglights, disconnect the wiring connector from each light unit.
6 Undo the four screws (two on either side) securing the ends of the bumper to the wheelarch liner **(see illustration)**.
7 With the aid of an assistant, release the bumper ends from the wheelarch outer trim covers, and remove the bumper from the front of the vehicle **(see illustration)**. On models

6.4 Front bumper-to-body bolts (arrowed)

6.6 Unscrewing a bumper-to-wheelarch liner lower screw

6.7 Carefully ease the wheelarch outer trim covers away from the vehicle, then release the bumper ends and remove the bumper from the vehicle

7.2 Rear bumper upper retaining screws (arrowed)

7.3 Unscrew the four screws securing the bottom of the bumper to the vehicle . . .

7.4 . . . and the plastic nut securing each end of the bumper to the wheelarch

with headlight washers, note that it will be necessary to disconnect the supply hose from the T-piece as it becomes accessible.

Refitting

8 Refitting is a reversal of the removal procedure, using new plastic nuts, and ensuring that all bumper fasteners are securely tightened.

7 Rear bumper – removal and refitting

Removal

Corsa and Corsavan

1 Remove the number plate light unit as described in Chapter 12.

2 Open the tailgate, and undo the three screws securing the top of the bumper to the vehicle **(see illustration)**.

3 Slacken and remove the four screws securing the bottom of the bumper to the vehicle body **(see illustration)**.

4 Unscrew the two plastic nuts (one on either side) securing the ends of the bumper to the inside of the wheelarch **(see illustration)**. Note that the plastic nuts should be discarded, and new ones used on refitting.

5 With the aid of an assistant, unclip the bumper ends from the wheelarch outer trim

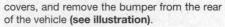

7.5 Release the bumper ends from the wheelarch outer trim covers, and remove the rear bumper

covers, and remove the bumper from the rear of the vehicle **(see illustration)**.

Combo Van

6 Remove both rear number plate light units as described in Chapter 12.

7 Prise out the trim plug from either end of the bumper to gain access to the bumper retaining bolts, then slacken and remove the two mounting bolts (one on either end) **(see illustrations)**.

8 Undo the three screws securing the bottom of the bumper to the vehicle, and the four screws securing the top of the bumper to the vehicle **(see illustration)**.

9 Lift the bumper away from the rear of the vehicle **(see illustration)**.

7.7a On Combo Van models, prise out the trim plug from either end of the bumper . . .

7.7b . . . then slacken and remove the bumper end bolts

7.8 Unscrew the four upper screws (arrowed) and the lower screws . . .

7.9 . . . and remove the bumper

7.10a Remove the foam wedges . . .

7.10b . . . then undo the two retaining bolts (arrowed) . . .

7.10c . . . and unhook the bumper mounting from the vehicle

10 If necessary, slide the foam wedges out from between the bumper mountings, and unbolt the mountings from the vehicle body. Each mounting is retained by two bolts **(see illustrations)**.

Refitting

11 Refitting is a reverse of the relevant removal procedure, ensuring that all disturbed fasteners are securely tightened. Before bolting the bumper in position, ensure that the number plate light wiring is fed through the bumper aperture(s).

8 Bonnet – removal, refitting and adjustment

Removal

1 Open the bonnet, and have an assistant support it. Using a pencil or felt-tip pen, mark the outline position of each bonnet hinge relative to the bonnet, to use as a guide on refitting.
2 Undo the retaining screws, and lift the left-hand windscreen cowl panel to improve access to the washer reservoir. Undo the reservoir retaining nut, then disconnect the windscreen washer supply pipe from the reservoir pump, and release it from the bonnet hinge **(see illustration)**.
3 Undo the bonnet retaining bolts and, with the help of an assistant, carefully lift the bonnet clear **(see illustrations)**. Store the bonnet out of the way, in a safe place. Inspect the hinge for signs of wear or damage. If hinge renewal is necessary, the vehicle must be taken to a Vauxhall/Opel dealer, as renewal requires the windscreen to be removed (see Section 20).

Refitting and adjustment

4 With the aid of an assistant, offer up the bonnet, and loosely fit the retaining bolts. Align the hinges with the marks made on removal, then tighten the retaining bolts securely. Reconnect the windscreen washer supply pipe.
5 Close the bonnet, and check for alignment with the adjacent panels. If necessary,

slacken the bonnet support bolts, and realign the bonnet to suit. Once the bonnet is correctly aligned, securely tighten the bolts.
6 Once the bonnet is correctly aligned, check that the bonnet fastens and releases in a satisfactory manner, and if necessary adjust the lock striker as described in Section 10.

9 Bonnet release cable – removal and refitting

Removal

1 Open the bonnet, and unscrew the release cable retaining clamp screw from the body crossmember **(see illustration)**.
2 Release the outer cable from the clamp, then detach the inner cable from the lock spring.

8.2 Disconnect the washer hose from the reservoir pump . . .

8.3b . . . and lift the bonnet away from the vehicle with the aid of an assistant

3 Work back along the cable, releasing it from all the relevant retaining clips and ties, whilst noting its correct routing. Release the rubber sealing grommet from the engine compartment bulkhead, and tie a piece of string to the cable end, this can then be used to draw the cable back into position.
4 From inside the vehicle, unclip the bonnet release lever from the side of the driver's footwell.
5 Withdraw the lever and cable assembly from inside the vehicle. Once the cable end appears, untie the string and leave it in position in the vehicle; the string can then be used to draw the new cable back into position.

Refitting

6 Tie the string to the end of the cable, and use the string to draw the bonnet release cable through from inside the vehicle into the

8.3a . . . then undo the bonnet retaining bolts . . .

9.1 Slackening the bonnet release cable clamp screw

engine compartment. Once the cable is through, untie the string.

7 Ensure that the cable is correctly routed and retained by all the relevant clips and ties, then seat the outer cable grommet in the engine compartment bulkhead.

8 Connect the inner cable to the lock spring, and seat the outer cable in its retaining clamp. Position the outer cable so that all free play is removed from the inner cable, then securely tighten its clamp screw.

9 Check the operation of the bonnet release lever before shutting the bonnet.

10 Bonnet lock components – removal and refitting

Bonnet lock hook

1 Drill out the pivot pin, and remove the lock hook and return spring from the bonnet (see illustration).

2 On refitting, locate the hook and spring in the bonnet bracket, and insert a new pivot pin. Secure the pin in position by flattening its end with a suitable pair of pliers.

Lock striker

3 Slacken the striker locknut, then unscrew the striker from the bonnet and recover the washer. If necessary, unscrew the locknut from the end of the striker, and remove the spring and spring seats.

4 Where necessary, fit the spring and spring seats to the striker, and screw on the locknut. Fit the washer to the striker, and screw the striker into position in the bonnet, tightening it only lightly at this stage.

5 Hold the locknut, and adjust the position of the striker so that the distance from the lower spring seat to the inside of the bonnet is 40 to 45 mm (see illustration).

6 When the striker is correctly positioned, securely tighten the locknut.

Lock spring

7 Unhook the spring from the body crossmember, then free it from the release cable and remove it from the vehicle.

10.1 Bonnet lock hook is removed by drilling out its pivot pin (arrowed)

8 On refitting, ensure that the spring is correctly engaged with the cable and crossmember. Check the operation of the bonnet release lever before shutting the bonnet.

11 Door – removal, refitting and adjustment

Removal

All front and Corsa rear doors

1 Open the door to gain access to the wiring connector which is fitted to the front edge of the door.

2 Disconnect the wiring connector from the

11.2 Release the locking ring, and disconnect the wiring connector from the door

10.5 When refitting, adjust the position of the bonnet lock striker as described in text

front edge of the door. To do this, unscrew the connector locking ring, then pull the connector away from the door (see illustration).

3 Using a suitable hammer and punch, tap out the roll pin securing the door check link to the vehicle body (see illustration).

4 Remove the plastic covers (where fitted) from the door hinge pins. Have an assistant support the door, then drive both hinge pins out of position using a hammer and suitable punch (see illustrations). Remove the door from the vehicle.

5 Inspect the hinge pins for signs of wear or damage, and renew if necessary. The check link roll pin should be renewed as a matter of course.

Combo Van rear door

6 Open the rear door, and release the

11.3 Tap out the check link roll pin using a suitable hammer and punch

11.4a Remove the upper plastic cover . . .

11.4b . . . and lower plastic cover . . .

11.4c . . . then tap out the hinge pins whilst an assistant supports the weight of the door

11.6 On the Combo Van rear door, release the check link spring from the door pin

11.7a Unclip the wiring from the vehicle body . . .

11.7b . . . then release the grommet . . .

11.7c . . . and disconnect the relevant rear door wiring

11.8 Unscrew the hinge retaining bolts and remove the door

check link spring from the door pin **(see illustration)**.

7 Where necessary, trace the wiring back from the door to its wiring connectors in the main vehicle body. Disconnect the wiring connectors, then free the grommet from the vehicle body, and withdraw the wiring loom so that it is free to be removed with the door **(see illustrations)**.

8 Have an assistant support the door, then slacken and remove the four hinge retaining bolts and remove the door from the vehicle **(see illustration)**.

9 If necessary, the hinge(s) can then be unbolted and removed.

Refitting

All front and Corsa rear doors

10 Refitting is the reversal of removal, using a new check link roll pin.

Combo Van rear door

11 Refitting is a reversal of the removal procedure, tightening the hinge bolts securely, and ensuring that the wiring is securely reconnected.

Adjustment

All front and Corsa rear doors

12 Adjustment of the door position is not possible; the hinges are welded to the vehicle

body and door, and cannot be repositioned. Misalignment of the door can only be caused by accident damage or wear of the hinge pins.

13 Door closure may be adjusted by altering the position of the door lock striker on the body. Slacken the striker retaining bolts, reposition the striker as required, then securely retighten the bolts.

Combo Van rear door

14 Slight adjustment of the doors can be achieved by slackening the hinge retaining bolts and repositioning the hinge/door.

15 Door closure may be adjusted by altering the position of the door lock striker on the door/body (as applicable). Slacken the striker retaining bolts, reposition the striker as required, then securely retighten the bolts **(see illustrations)**.

12 Door inner trim panel – removal and refitting

Removal

Front door

1 Unscrew the door pocket retaining screws, and pull the pocket downwards and away from the door to release its retaining clips. On models with electric windows, disconnect the

11.15a Rear door lock striker – Combo Van

11.15b Rear door latch striker – Combo Van

12.1a Undo the retaining screws (arrowed) and remove the door pocket

12.1b Where necessary, disconnect the electric window switch wiring connectors as the pocket is removed

window switch wiring connectors as the pocket is removed **(see illustrations)**.

2 Lift the inner door lock handle, and carefully prise the handle trim cover out from the door trim panel **(see illustration)**.

3 Where necessary, remove the loudspeaker from the armrest handle as described in Chapter 12, and free the electric exterior mirror or passenger side window switch (as applicable) from the armrest **(see illustration)**.

4 Undo the three retaining screws, and remove the armrest handle from the door **(see illustration)**.

5 Undo the retaining screw (where fitted) and unclip the exterior mirror inner trim panel from the door. On models with manually-operated mirrors, it will be necessary to pull the knob off the adjusting lever in order to remove the panel **(see illustrations)**.

6 On models with manual windows, release the retaining clip and remove the window regulator handle. To release the clip, fabricate a hook from a piece of welding rod, and use the rod to hook the clip out from between the handle and bezel **(see illustration)**. Slide the handle off the regulator, and remove the handle bezel.

7 Carefully prise the window inner sealing strip from the top edge of the door trim panel **(see illustration)**.

8 Slacken and remove the retaining screws

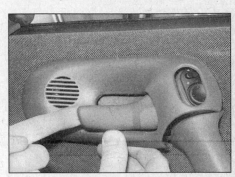

12.2 Lift the handle, and unclip the handle trim cover from the door panel

12.3 Where necessary, carefully prise the exterior mirror switch out of the armrest

12.4 Undo the retaining screws (arrowed) and remove the armrest – three-door model shown

12.5a On models with manually-operated exterior mirrors, it will be necessary to remove the knob from the adjusting lever . . .

12.5b . . . in order to remove the inner trim panel

12.6 On models with manual windows, unhook the regulator handle retaining clip using a piece of welding rod

12.7 Carefully prise out the window sealing strip from the top of the inner trim panel

12.8a Undo the front . . .

12.8b . . . and rear retaining screws from the trim panel . . .

12.8c . . . and remove the trim panel from the door – three-door model shown

12.9 Undo the two screws, and remove the handle from the rear door

12.10 Unclip the trim cover from the door inner handle

12.12 Unclip the inner trim panel from the rear door . . .

12.13 . . . then prise out the window sealing strip from the top of the door

on the rear edge of the panel, and at the front of the panel, directly below the exterior mirror, and remove the trim panel from the door (see illustrations).

Rear door

9 Undo the retaining screws, and remove the handle from the rear door (see illustration).
10 Lift the inner door lock handle, and carefully prise the handle trim cover out from the door trim panel (see illustration).
11 Remove the window regulator handle as described in paragraph 6.
12 Carefully prise the inner trim panel away from the rear of the door (see illustration).

13 Carefully prise the window inner sealing strip from the top edge of the door trim panel (see illustration). The strip retaining clips should stay in position on the door; if they are loose, remove then and store with the sealing strip.
14 Unscrew the retaining screws from the edge of the door trim panel, and remove the panel from the door (see illustration).

Refitting

15 Refitting is the reverse of the relevant removal procedure. On models with manual windows, fit the retaining clip to the regulator handle before fitting the handle onto the regulator (see illustration).

12.14 Undo the retaining screws (arrowed) and remove the inner trim panel from the rear door

12.15 When refitting, fit the clip (arrowed) to the regulator handle before fitting the handle to the door

13.2 Carefully peel the weathershield away from the door to gain access to the lock components

13.4 The interior handle simply unclips from the door

13.8a Undo the two nuts . . .

13 Door handle and lock components – removal and refitting

Removal

Interior handle

1 Remove the door inner trim panel as described in Section 12.

2 Peel the polythene weathershield away from the door to gain access to the door lock components **(see illustration)**. Where necessary, cut around the trim panel screw brackets, using a sharp knife, to release the weathershield.

3 Release the retaining clip by pivoting it away from the link rod, and detach the rod from the lock assembly.

4 Unclip the interior handle from the door, and remove it complete with the rod **(see illustration)**.

Front exterior handle

5 Remove the door inner trim panel as described in Section 12, and peel back the weathershield (see paragraph 2).

6 With the window fully raised, undo the retaining bolt(s) from the base of the window guide, and manoeuvre the guide out from the door.

7 Release the retaining clips by pivoting them away from the link rods, and free the link rods from the lock assembly.

13.8b . . . then free the lock cylinder mounting plate from the rear of the exterior door handle

8 Unscrew the two handle retaining nuts, and detach the lock cylinder mounting plate from the rear of the handle **(see illustrations)**.

9 Lift the retaining clips on the base of the handle, and remove the handle from the outside of the door.

Front lock cylinder

10 Remove the exterior door handle as described above, then manoeuvre the lock cylinder mounting plate out of the door. Where necessary, trace the wiring back from the central locking/alarm microswitch, and disconnect it at the wiring connector to enable the plate to be removed.

11 With the mounting plate removed, insert the key into the lock cylinder, then prise off the C-clip from rear of the mounting plate. Lift

13.11a Remove the C-clip . . .

off the link rod bracket and spring, noting their correct fitted locations, and withdraw the lock cylinder **(see illustrations)**.

Front lock

12 Remove the door inner trim panel as described in Section 12, and peel back the weathershield (see paragraph 2).

13 Remove the window guide as described in paragraph 6.

14 Undo the three retaining screws, and manoeuvre the lock assembly out of the door. On models with central locking, disconnect the wiring connector from the servo unit as it becomes accessible **(see illustrations)**.

Rear exterior handle (Corsa)

15 Remove the door inner trim panel as

13.11b . . . then lift off the link rod bracket and spring, noting its correct fitted position . . .

13.11c . . . and withdraw the lock cylinder

13.14a Undo the three retaining screws . . .

13.14b . . . then remove the lock assembly from the door

13.14c On models with central locking, disconnect the wiring connector from the servo unit before removing the lock

13.16 Free the sealing strip from the rear of the door to gain access to the guide upper retaining bolt

13.17a Slacken and remove the upper window guide retaining bolt . . .

13.17b . . . and lower retaining bolt . . .

described in Section 12, and peel back the weathershield (see paragraph 2). Carefully prise the outer trim panel away from the door.

16 Wind the window fully down, and release the window sealing strip from the rear of the door and guide, to gain access to the retaining bolt **(see illustration)**.

17 Undo the two guide retaining bolts, and manoeuvre the guide upwards and out from the door **(see illustrations)**.

18 Release the retaining clips by pivoting them away from the link rods, and free the link rods from the lock assembly **(see illustration)**.

19 Undo the two nuts, and free the mounting plate assembly from the rear of the handle **(see illustration)**.

20 Lift the retaining clips on the base of the handle, then remove the handle from the outside of the door, freeing its link rod from the lock **(see illustration)**.

Rear lock (Corsa)

21 Remove the exterior handle as described above, and manoeuvre out the mounting plate assembly **(see illustration)**.

22 Undo the three retaining screws, and remove the lock assembly **(see illustrations)**. On models with central locking, disconnect the wiring connector from the servo unit as it becomes accessible.

13.17c . . . and manoeuvre the guide upwards and out of the rear door

13.18 Pivot the retaining clip (arrowed) away from each link rod, and disconnect the rods from the lock

13.19 Undo the two nuts, and free the mounting plate from the rear of the exterior handle

13.20 Remove the exterior handle from the door, freeing its link rod from the lock

13.21 Remove the lock cylinder mounting plate from the door to improve access to the rear door lock

13.22a Undo the three retaining screws ...

13.22b ... and remove the lock assembly from the rear door

13.23a On Combo Van models, prise out the access cover ...

Rear lock and lock cylinder (Combo Van)

23 Carefully prise the access cover out from the rear door. To further improve access, prise out the retaining clips and remove the trim panel from the centre of the door (see illustrations).

24 Release the retaining clips by pivoting them away from the link rods, and free the link rods from the lock assembly (see illustration).

25 Undo the two retaining nuts, then free the lock cylinder mounting plate from the rear of the handle. Undo the three lock assembly retaining screws, and manoeuvre the lock and cylinder mounting plate assembly out of the door (see illustrations).

26 Release the retaining clip, and separate the lock and mounting plate (see illustration).

27 If necessary, to remove the lock cylinder, insert the key into the lock cylinder, then prise off the C-clip from rear of the mounting plate. Lift off the link rod bracket and spring, noting their correct fitted locations, and withdraw the lock cylinder (see illustration).

Rear handle (Combo Van)

28 Remove the lock and lock cylinder mounting plate as described above.

29 Lift the retaining clips on the base of the

13.23b ... and remove the trim panel to gain access to the lock

13.24 Link rod pivot clips (arrowed) are released by pivoting them away from the rod

13.25a Free the lock cylinder mounting plate from the handle ...

13.25b ... then undo the three lock retaining screws ...

13.25c ... and manoeuvre the lock and cylinder mounting plate assembly out of the door

13.26 Release the retaining clip (arrowed), and separate the lock from the lock cylinder mounting plate

13.27 Lock cylinder and associated components are retained by a C-clip

13.29 Door handle is retained by two clips (locations arrowed)

13.30 Remove the access cover to reveal the latch lock

13.31 Release the retaining clip, and slide the knob off the latch lock handle

handle, and remove the handle from the outside of the door **(see illustration)**.

Rear latch lock (Combo Van)

30 Carefully prise the access cover from the rear door **(see illustration)**. To further improve access, prise out the retaining clips and remove the trim panel from the centre of the door.

31 Release the retaining clip, and pull the knob off the latch handle **(see illustration)**.

32 Release the retaining clips by pivoting them away from the link rods, and free both link rods from the lock **(see illustration)**.

33 Undo the three retaining screws, and manoeuvre the latch lock out from the door **(see illustration)**.

Rear latches (Combo Van)

34 Remove the access cover and trim panel as described in paragraph 30.

13.32 Detach both link rods (arrowed) from the lock . . .

13.33 . . . and manoeuvre the lock out from the door

35 Release the relevant retaining clip by pivoting it away from the link rod, and free the link rod from the lock.

36 Undo the screws securing the latch to the door, and guide the latch and link rod out of position **(see illustrations)**.

37 If necessary, remove the second latch in the same way.

Refitting

38 Refitting is the reverse of the removal sequence, noting the following points:

a) *If a lock cylinder has been removed, on refitting ensure that the spring and link rod bracket are correctly positioned and are securely held by the C-clip. Check the operation of the lock cylinder, making sure that the spring returns the cylinder to its central position, before refitting the plate to the door.*

b) *Ensure that all link rods are securely held in position by their retaining clips.*

c) *Apply grease to all lock and link rod pivot points.*

d) *Before installing the relevant trim panel, thoroughly check the operation of all the door lock handles and, where necessary, the central locking system, and ensure that the weathershield is correctly positioned.*

e) *On models with side air bags incorporated in the front seats, it is vitally important that the polythene weathershield fitted behind the trim panel is undamaged and perfectly sealed to the door around its complete contact area. If this is not the case the side air bag impact*

13.36a Undo the two bolts . . .

sensor may not function correctly. If the weathershield was damaged in any way during removal, or if a perfect seal cannot be made, renew the weathershield.

14 Door window glass and regulator – removal and refitting

Removal

1 Remove the door inner trim panel as described in Section 12.

2 Peel the polythene weathershield away from the door to gain access to the door lock components. Where necessary, cut around the trim panel screw brackets, using a sharp knife, to release the weathershield. Proceed as described under the relevant sub-heading.

Front manual window

3 With the window fully raised, undo the retaining bolt(s) from the base of the window rear guide, and manoeuvre the guide out from the door.

4 Wind the window down, and position it so its guide is in the centre of the door aperture.

5 Mark the position of the regulator guide retaining bolts on the door, then undo the two bolts and release the regulator bracket from the door. The marks can then be used on refitting to make sure the bracket is correctly positioned.

6 Release the regulator rollers from the ends of the window glass guide rail, then lift the glass and manoeuvre it out from the door.

13.36b . . . and slide the latch and link rod out from the door

14.7 Removing the front door window glass

14.12a Undo the two retaining bolts (arrowed) . . .

14.12b . . . then manoeuvre the window guide out from the door

14.14a Mark the position of the regulator guide bolts on the door, then undo the bolts . . .

14.14b . . . and remove the guide

Front electric window

7 Remove the regulator assembly as described below. The glass can then be lifted out from the door (**see illustration**).

Rear

8 Carefully prise the outer trim panel away from the door.
9 Wind the window fully down, then release

the window sealing strip from the rear of the door and guide, to gain access to the guide retaining bolt.
10 Undo the two bolts, and remove the window guide from the door (**see illustrations 13.17a, 13.17b and 13.17c**).
11 Tilt the window glass forwards, and free the window guide from the regulator mechanism. The glass can then be manoeuvred out from the door.

Front regulator

Note: A pop-rivet gun and suitable rivets will be required when refitting. The rivet heads should be approximately 4.8 mm in diameter and 11 mm in length.
12 With the window fully raised, undo the retaining bolt(s) from the base of the window guide, and manoeuvre the guide out from the door (**see illustrations**).
13 Position the window so that its guide rail is in the centre of the door aperture, and wedge it in position with a suitable wooden or rubber wedge.
14 Mark the position of the regulator guide retaining bolts on the door, then undo the two bolts and remove the guide (**see illustrations**).
15 Using an 8.5 mm drill bit, drill out the rivets securing the regulator assembly to the door, taking great care not to damage the door panel. With all the rivets removed, free the regulator rollers from the ends of the window glass guide rail, and manoeuvre the regulator assembly out through the door aperture. On models with electric windows, disconnect the wiring connector from the regulator as it becomes accessible (**see illustrations**).

14.15a Front door window regulator retaining rivets (arrowed) – manual window

14.15b Carefully drill out the rivets with a suitable drill . . .

14.15c . . . then free the regulator rollers from the window glass . . .

14.15d . . . and remove the regulator assembly from the door

14.15e On models with electric windows, disconnect the wiring connector from the regulator as it is removed

Rear regulator

Note: *A pop-rivet gun and suitable rivets will be required when refitting. The rivet heads should be approximately 4.8 mm in diameter and 11 mm in length.*

16 Position the window so that its guide rail is in the centre of the lower door aperture, and wedge it in position with a suitable wooden or rubber wedge.

17 Using an 8.5 mm drill bit, drill out the rivets securing the regulator assembly to the door, taking great care not to damage the door panel **(see illustration)**.

18 With all the rivets removed, free the regulator from the glass guide rail, and manoeuvre it out through the door aperture.

Refitting

19 Refitting is the reverse of the removal procedure, noting the following points:

a) *Where the regulator has been removed, remove the remains of the old rivets before fitting the regulator to the door. Engage the regulator with the window glass, and secure it in position with new pop-rivets.*

b) *On the front window, align the regulator guide bolts with the marks made on removal, then tighten them securely.*

c) *Check the window moves smoothly and easily up and down, without any sign of tight spots. If the window movement is stiff, trace and rectify the cause. On the front window, movement is adjustable by slackening the regulator guide bolts and*

14.17 Rear door window regulator retaining rivets (arrowed) – five-door models

moving the bolts up and down the slotted holes. Find the position where the window movement is the easiest, then securely tighten the bolts.

d) *Refit the weathershield, making sure it is securely stuck to the door, then install the trim panel as described in Section 12.*

15 Tailgate and support struts – removal and refitting

Removal

Tailgate

1 Disconnect the battery negative terminal

(refer to *Disconnecting the battery* in the Reference Chapter).

2 Open the tailgate, and detach the parcel shelf cords. Undo the retaining screws, and remove the lifter hooks from the tailgate **(see illustration)**.

3 Carefully prise out the retaining clips, and remove the inner trim panel from the tailgate **(see illustration)**.

4 Disconnect the wiring connectors from the tailgate wiper motor, central locking components and/or courtesy light switch (as applicable). Undo the relevant tailgate wiper motor bolt, and free the earth lead. Also disconnect the wiring connector from the heated rear window element. Tie a suitable length of string to the end of the wiring loom, then free the grommet from the top of the tailgate and withdraw the wiring loom **(see illustrations)**. When the end of the loom appears, untie the string and leave it in position in the tailgate; it can then be used to draw the wiring back into position when refitting.

5 Where necessary, prise out the washer jet from the tailgate/spoiler (as applicable), and disconnect it from the washer hose **(see illustrations)**. Tie a suitable length of string to the hose end, then withdraw the hose, leaving the string in position in the same way as for the wiring.

6 Have an assistant support the tailgate, then raise the spring clips and pull the support struts off their balljoint mountings on the tailgate. Prise out the hinge pin retaining clips,

15.2 Undo the retaining screws, and remove the parcel shelf lifter hooks from the tailgate . . .

15.3 . . . then prise out the retaining clips and remove the inner trim panel

15.4a Disconnect the various wiring connectors situated behind the trim panel . . .

15.4b . . . and the heated rear window wiring connector . . .

15.4c . . . then remove the grommet and withdraw the wiring from the tailgate

15.5a Prise the washer jet out from the tailgate . . .

15.5b . . . and disconnect it from the hose (1.6 litre DOHC model – jet mounted in spoiler)

15.6a Remove the retaining clips . . .

15.6b . . . then withdraw the hinge pin and lift off the tailgate

then tap both hinge pins out of position and remove the tailgate from the vehicle (see illustrations).

7 Examine the hinge pins for signs of wear or damage, and renew if necessary.

Support struts

8 Support the tailgate in the open position using a stout piece of wood, or with the help of an assistant.

9 Raise the spring clips, and pull the support strut off its balljoint mountings on the tailgate and vehicle body (see illustration).

Refitting

Tailgate

10 Refitting is a reversal of the removal procedure, noting the following points:

a) Prior to refitting, apply a smear of multi-purpose grease to the hinge pins.

b) Ensure that the hinge pins are securely retained by their clips, and that the support struts are securely held in position by their spring clips.

c) Use the string to draw the wiring loom and washer hose through into position, and ensure that all wiring connectors are correctly reconnected.

Support struts

11 Refitting is a reverse of the removal procedure, ensuring that the strut is securely retained by its spring clips.

15.9 Lift the retaining clip, and free the support strut from its balljoints

16 Tailgate lock components – removal and refitting

Removal

1 Release the rear parcel shelf lifting cords from the tailgate, then unclip the shelf and remove it from the vehicle.

2 Undo the retaining screws, and remove the parcel shelf lifting cord hooks from the tailgate trim panel.

3 Carefully prise out the retaining clips, and remove the trim panel from the tailgate. Proceed as described under the relevant sub-heading.

16.5 Tailgate lock is retained by three screws (arrowed)

Lock

4 From inside the tailgate, release the retaining clip by pivoting it away from the link rod, and detach the rod from the lock assembly.

5 Slacken and remove the three screws, and remove the lock from the tailgate (see illustration).

Lock cylinder

6 From inside the tailgate, release the retaining clip by pivoting it away from the link rod, and detach the rod from the lock cylinder (see illustration).

7 Where necessary, release the retaining clip and detach the central locking/alarm microswitch from the top of the lock cylinder (see illustration).

16.6 Release the retaining clip (arrowed) and detach the link rod from the tailgate lock cylinder casting

16.7 Where necessary, release the microswitch from the top of the casting

16.8a Undo the three nuts (arrowed), then remove the lock cylinder casting from inside the tailgate . . .

16.8b . . . and the exterior handle from the outside

16.9 Lock cylinder roll pin can be tapped out with a suitable punch

8 Undo the three nuts and remove the exterior handle; the lock cylinder casting can then be manoeuvred out of the tailgate (see illustrations).

9 To dismantle the assembly, insert the key into the lock cylinder, then tap out the roll pin from the rear of the cylinder housing using a suitable pin punch, and remove the link rod bracket from the rear of the cylinder (see illustration). Note which way around the bracket is fitted. Discard the roll pin; a new one should be used on refitting.

10 Release the retaining catches, remove the trim cover, and free the lock cylinder housing from the casting. The lock cylinder can then be withdrawn from its housing.

Refitting

Lock

11 Refitting is a reverse of the removal procedure.

Lock cylinder

12 Insert the lock cylinder into its housing, and insert the housing and spring into the main casting. Refit the link rod bracket, making sure it is fitted the correct way around, and secure it in position with a new roll pin. Check the operation of the lock, then refit the trim cover.

13 Refit the lock cylinder casting and exterior handle to the tailgate, then fit the retaining nuts and tighten them to the specified torque.

On models with central locking, make sure that the casting is correctly engaged with the servo unit rod before tightening the retaining nuts.

14 Connect the link rod, and secure it in position with the clip.

15 Where necessary, clip the alarm/central locking switch back onto the lock assembly.

16 Refit the trim panel and parcel shelf.

17 Central locking components – removal and refitting

Electronic control unit

1 Ensure that the ignition is switched off. Remove the fuel injection ECU as described in Chapter 4A or 4B.

2 Release the retaining clip, then remove the ECU mounting bracket from the side of the footwell and withdraw the insulation panel (see illustrations).

3 Undo the two bolts and remove the central locking ECU from the vehicle, disconnecting the wiring connector as it becomes accessible (see illustration).

4 Refitting is the reverse of removal.

Front door servo

5 Remove the relevant lock assembly as described in Section 13.

6 Undo the two retaining screws, and detach the servo unit from the lock (see illustration).

7 Refitting is the reverse of removal.

Rear door servo

Corsa

8 Remove the relevant lock assembly as described in Section 13.

9 Undo the two retaining screws, and detach the servo unit from the lock.

10 Refitting is the reverse of removal.

Combo Van

11 Carefully prise the access cover out from the rear door. To further improve access, prise out the retaining clips and remove the trim

17.2a Unclip the ECU mounting bracket . . .

17.2b . . . and remove the insulation panel . . .

17.3 . . . to gain access to the central locking control unit (retaining bolts arrowed)

17.6 Front door lock servo unit is retained by two screws (arrowed)

17.11a On Combo Van rear door, unclip the access cover . . .

17.11b . . . and remove the trim panel to improve access to the servo unit

17.13a Detach the link rod (A) and undo the retaining screws (B) . . .

panel from the centre of the door (see illustrations).

12 Release the retaining clip by pivoting it away from the link rod, and free the servo unit link rod from the lock assembly.

13 Undo the two retaining screws and remove the servo unit from the door, disconnecting its wiring connector as it becomes accessible (see illustrations).

14 Refitting is the reverse of removal. Prior to installing the trim panel, check the operation of the servo unit.

Tailgate servo

15 Remove the tailgate inner trim panel as described in paragraphs 1 to 3 of Section 16.

16 Undo the two bolts and manoeuvre the servo unit out of position, disconnecting the wiring connector as it becomes accessible (see illustrations).

17 Refitting is the reverse of removal, ensuring that the servo rod is correctly engaged with the lock casting (see illustration). Prior to installing the trim panel, check the operation of the servo unit.

Fuel filler cap servo

18 Remove the right-hand rear light unit as described in Chapter 12.

19 Disconnect the servo unit wiring connector, then undo the retaining screws and manoeuvre the servo out through the rear light aperture (see illustrations).

17.13b . . . then remove the servo unit and disconnect its wiring connector

17.16b . . . and remove the servo unit from the tailgate

17.16a Disconnect the wiring connector, then undo the retaining bolts (arrowed) . . .

17.17 When refitting, ensure that the servo unit rod (arrowed) is correctly engaged with the lock

17.19a Disconnect the wiring connector . . .

17.19b . . . then undo the two retaining screws (arrowed) . . .

17.19c . . . and remove the fuel filler cap servo unit

17.24a When refitting, ensure that the microswitch is correctly located on the pins . . .

17.24b . . . and secure it in position with the retaining clip

17.24c Make sure that the switch wiring is correctly routed, and reconnect the wiring connector

20 Refitting is the reverse of removal, ensuring that the servo unit rod is correctly engaged with the filler cap hole. Check the operation of the servo unit before refitting the light unit.

Door microswitch

21 Remove the door inner trim panel as described in Section 12.
22 Peel the polythene weathershield away from the door to gain access to the door lock. Where necessary, cut around the trim panel screw brackets, using a sharp knife, to release the weathershield.
23 Using a suitable screwdriver, prise off the switch retaining clip, and disengage the switch from the lock cylinder mounting plate. Trace the wiring back to its connector, then disconnect it and remove the switch from the door.
24 Refitting is the reverse of the removal, making sure that the switch is correctly located on the mounting plate pins. Also ensure that the wiring is routed around the back of the window guide so that it doesn't foul the window movement **(see illustrations)**.

Tailgate lock microswitch

25 Remove the tailgate trim panel as described in paragraphs 1 to 3 of Section 16.
26 Using a suitable screwdriver, prise off the switch retaining clip, and disengage the

switch from the lock cylinder mounting plate **(see illustration)**. Trace the wiring back to its connector, then disconnect it and remove the switch from the tailgate.
27 Refitting is the reverse of the removal, making sure that the switch is correctly located and securely retained by its clip.

18 Electric window components – removal and refitting

Note: *Every time the battery is disconnected, or the electric window motors are disconnected, it will be necessary when reconnecting to reprogramme the motors, to restore the one-touch function of the buttons. To do this, fully close both front windows. With the windows closed, depress the up button of the driver's side window for approximately 5 seconds, then release it and depress the passenger side window up button for approximately 5 seconds.*

Window switches

1 Refer to Chapter 12.

Window winder motors

2 Remove the regulator mechanism as described in Section 14.
3 Prior to removing the motor, it is necessary to secure the regulator arm to the mounting

bracket, to prevent it moving as the motor is removed. The arm is spring-loaded, and if it is not secured in position, it will be forcibly twisted as the motor is removed, and could severely damage your hands.
4 With the regulator arm secured, slacken and remove the three retaining screws, and separate the motor and regulator **(see illustration)**. Do not attempt to dismantle the motor assembly, as it is a sealed unit.
5 Fit the motor assembly to the regulator, and securely tighten its retaining screws.
6 Release the regulator arm, and install the regulator mechanism as described in Section 14.

19 Exterior mirror and associated components – removal and refitting

Note: *There are two different manufacturers of the exterior mirrors fitted to Corsa models, and the individual mirror components are not interchangeable between the two types. This mirror type is indicated by a symbol on the rubber seal located on the inside of the mirror (the mirror must be removed to see this) (see illustration). Identify the mirror type before ordering mirror spares.*

17.26 Release the retaining clip and remove the microswitch from the tailgate lock

18.4 Electric window motor retaining screws (arrowed)

19.0 Exterior mirror manufacturer's identification markings

1 Engelmann   2 Fico

19.3 Exterior mirror retaining bolts (arrowed) – manually-operated mirror

19.5 Disconnect the wiring connector, then undo the three retaining bolts (arrowed) . . .

19.6 . . . and remove the mirror from the door

Manually-operated mirror

1 Pull off the knob from the mirror adjusting lever.
2 Undo the screw (where fitted), and unclip the inner trim panel from the door.
3 Undo the retaining bolts, and remove the mirror assembly from the outside of the door (see illustration).
4 Refitting is the reverse of removal.

Electrically-operated mirror

5 Undo the retaining screw (where fitted), and unclip the exterior mirror inner trim panel from the door. Disconnect the wiring connector from the mirror (see illustration).
6 Undo the three retaining bolts, and remove the mirror assembly from the outside of the door (see illustration).

19.8 Using a wooden wedge to prise the window glass out of position. Inset shows heating element wiring connections on electrically-operated mirror

19.10 Align the balljoints and sockets (arrowed) when refitting the mirror glass

7 Refitting is a reverse of the removal procedure.

Mirror glass

8 Insert a wide plastic or wooden wedge between the mirror glass and mirror housing, and carefully prise the glass from its balljoints (see illustration). Take great care when removing the glass; do not use excessive force, as the glass is easily broken (wear thick gloves, particularly if removing an already-broken mirror glass).
9 Remove the glass from the mirror. On models with electric mirrors, disconnect the wiring connectors from the mirror heating element as they become accessible (see illustration).
10 When refitting, carefully clip the glass

19.9 Disconnecting the heating element wiring connections – electrically-operated mirrors

19.12 Motor retaining screws (arrowed) – electrically-operated mirror

back into position, ensuring that it is correctly located on each of its balljoints (see illustration).

Mirror motor

11 Remove the mirror glass as described above.
12 Undo the three screws and remove the motor assembly, disconnecting its wiring connectors as they become accessible (see illustration).
13 Refitting is the reverse of removal.

Mirror switch

14 Refer to Chapter 12.

20 Windscreen, tailgate and fixed window glass – general information

1 These areas of glass are secured by the tight fit of the weatherstrip in the body aperture, and are bonded in position with a special adhesive. The removal and refitting of these areas of fixed glass is a difficult, messy and time-consuming task, which is considered beyond the scope of the home mechanic. It is difficult, unless one has plenty of practice, to obtain a secure, waterproof fit. Furthermore, the task carries a high risk of breakage; this applies especially to the laminated glass windscreen. In view of this, owners are strongly advised to have this sort of work carried out by one of the many specialist windscreen fitters, or a Vauxhall/Opel dealer.

21 Sunroof – general information

1 A manual or electric sunroof was offered as an optional extra on most models, and is fitted as standard equipment on some models.
2 Due to the complexity of the sunroof mechanism, considerable expertise is needed to repair, replace or adjust the sunroof components successfully. Removal of the roof first requires the headlining to be removed,

which is a complex and tedious operation in itself, and not a task to be undertaken lightly (See Section 26). Therefore, any problems with the sunroof should be referred to a Vauxhall/Opel dealer.

3 On models with an electric sunroof, if the sunroof motor fails to operate, first check the relevant fuse. If the fault cannot be traced and rectified, the sunroof can be opened and closed manually using a suitable Allen wrench to turn the motor spindle. To gain access to the motor spindle, carefully prise out the trim cover situated at the rear of the sunroof. Insert the Allen key in the motor spindle, and turn to move the sunroof to the required position. A suitable Allen key is supplied with the vehicle, and should be found in the glovebox.

22 Body exterior fittings – removal and refitting

Radiator grille

1 Open the bonnet and unscrew the two bolts securing the radiator grille to the engine compartment front crossmember.
2 Similarly unscrew the two bolts securing the bumper mounting brackets to the crossmember, one located on each side of the radiator grille.
3 Ease the bumper mounting brackets forward slightly and release the radiator grille lower retaining clip strip.
4 Lift the radiator grille upwards from its location.
5 Refitting is a reversal of removal.

Wheelarch liners and body under-panels

6 The various plastic covers fitted to the underside of the vehicle are secured in position by a mixture of screws, nuts and retaining clips, and removal will be fairly obvious on inspection. Work methodically around the liner/panel, removing its retaining screws and releasing its retaining clips until it is free to be removed from the underside of the vehicle. Most clips used on the vehicle, with the exception of the fasteners which are used to secure the wheelarch liners, are simply prised out of position. The wheelarch liner clips are released by tapping their centre pins through the clip, and then removing the outer section of the clip; new clips will be required on refitting if the centre pins are not recovered.
7 When refitting, renew any retaining clips that may have been broken on removal, and ensure that the panel is securely retained by all the relevant clips, nuts and screws. Vauxhall/Opel also recommend that plastic nuts (where used) are renewed, regardless of their apparent condition, whenever they are disturbed.

Body trim strips and badges

8 The various body trim strips and badges are held in position with a special adhesive tape. Removal requires the trim/badge to be heated, to soften the adhesive, and then cut away from the surface. Due to the high risk of damage to the vehicle's paintwork during this operation, it is recommended that this task should be entrusted to a Vauxhall/Opel dealer.

23 Seats – removal and refitting

⚠ **Warning: Depending on model, the front seats may be equipped with mechanical or pyrotechnic seat belt tensioners, and side air bags may be built into the outer sides of the seats. The seat belt tensioners and side air bags may cause injury if triggered accidentally. Before carrying out any work on the front seats, always ensure that the safety fork is inserted in the seat belt tensioner cylinder, to prevent the possibility of the tensioner being accidentally triggered (see paragraphs 2 and 3 below). Seats should always be transported and installed with the safety fork in place. If the tensioner has been triggered due to a sudden impact or accident, the unit must be renewed, as it cannot be reset. A triggered tensioner mechanism can be identified by the yellow tongue which will be visible on the seat belt stalk buckle. If a seat is to be disposed of, the tensioner must be triggered before the seat is removed from the vehicle. Due to safety considerations, tensioner renewal or seat disposal must be entrusted to a Vauxhall/Opel dealer. Where side air bags are fitted, refer to Chapter 12 for the precautions which should be observed when dealing with an air bag system.**

Removal

Front seat

1 On models with side air bags or pyrotechnic seat belt tensioners, observe the following precautions before attempting to remove the seat:
a) Remove the ignition key.
b) Disconnect the battery negative terminal (refer to 'Disconnecting the battery' in the Reference Section of this manual), and wait for two minutes before carrying out any further work.
2 Undo the retaining screws, and remove the trim panel from the outside of the seat to gain access to the outer seat guide rail bolt. Locate the plastic safety fork, which is clipped onto the rear of the tensioner. Insert the safety fork into the slot provided in the tensioner cylinder, ensuring that the fork engages securely **(see illustrations)**.
3 On models with side air bags, pyrotechnic seat belt tensioners or heated seats, disconnect the wiring connector which is situated underneath the seat.
4 Slide the seat fully forwards, then slacken and remove the seat rear retaining bolts.
5 Move the seat forwards to disengage the seat guide rails from the floor brackets, and lift the seat out of the vehicle.

Rear seat cushion – Corsa and Corsavan

6 Prise off the trim covers from the rear seat cushion hinges.
7 Slacken and remove the two retaining bolts, then release the seat cushion clips and remove the cushion from the vehicle.

One-piece rear seat backrest – Corsa and Corsavan

8 Open up the tailgate, and remove the rear parcel shelf.
9 Fold the rear seat backrest forwards, and remove the spring clip from the left- and right-hand seat backrest pivot pins.
10 Using a small flat-bladed screwdriver, release the retaining clips, and remove the left- and right-hand pivot pin guides from the vehicle. The seat backrest can then be manoeuvred out of the vehicle.

Two-piece (split folding) rear seat backrest – Corsa and Corsavan

11 Open up the tailgate, and remove the rear parcel shelf.
12 Unclip the trim covers from the left- and right-hand seat backrest hinges.

23.2a Unclip the safety fork from the rear of the seat belt tensioner . . .

23.2b . . . and insert it into the slot, making sure that it is correctly engaged with the tensioner pin (arrowed)

13 Prise out the retaining clips, and peel back the carpet from the rear of the seats to gain access to the centre pivot of the seat. Undo the four retaining screws, and remove the hinge.

14 Undo the left- and right-hand seat backrest retaining bolts, and remove the seat assembly.

Rear seat cushion – Combo Van

15 Fold back the carpet from front of the seat to gain access to the seat pivot pins.

16 Prise off the C-clip from each pin, then withdraw both pins and remove the seat cushion from the vehicle.

Rear seat backrest – Combo Van

17 Where necessary, undo the retaining bolts and remove the luggage compartment grille from the vehicle.

18 Fold the seat backrest forwards, then undo the retaining bolts from the left- and right-hand seat hinges and remove the backrest from the vehicle.

Refitting

Front seats

19 Refitting is a reverse of the removal procedure, noting the following points:

a) *Remove all traces of old thread-locking compound from the threads of the seat retaining bolts, and clean the threaded holes in the vehicle floor, ideally by running a tap of the correct size and pitch down them.*

b) *Apply a suitable thread-locking compound to the threads of the seat bolts. Refit the bolts, and tighten them to the specified torque setting.*

c) *Prior to refitting the trim panel, remove the safety fork from the seat belt tensioner, and clip it back into position on the outside of the tensioner.*

d) *Reconnect the battery negative terminal.*

Rear seats – all models

21 Refitting is a reverse of the removal procedure, tightening the seat mounting bolts to the specified torque (where applicable).

24.1 Seat belt tensioner mechanism components

1 *Tensioner unit, containing*   2 *Cable*
  pre-tensioned spring   3 *Pivot*

24 Front seat belt tensioning mechanism – general information

All models covered in this manual are fitted with a front seat belt tensioner system. On pre-1999 models a mechanical system is used and on 1999 models onward, pyrotechnic tensioners are fitted. Both systems are designed to instantaneously take up any slack in the seat belt in the case of a sudden frontal impact, therefore reducing the possibility of injury to the front seat occupants. Each front seat is fitted with its own system, the components of which are mounted in the seat frame **(see illustration)**.

The seat belt tensioner is triggered by a frontal impact causing a deceleration of six times the force of gravity or greater. Lesser impacts, including impacts from behind, will not trigger the system.

On the mechanical type tensioners, when the system is triggered, a pre-tensioned spring draws back the seat belt via a cable

25.1 On three-door models, unscrew the front seat belt upper mounting bolt, and recover the spacer and washer from behind the belt anchorage

which acts on the seat belt stalk. The cable can move by up to 80,0 mm, which therefore reduces the slack in the seat belt around the shoulders and waist of the occupant by a similar amount.

On the pyrotechnic type seat belt tensioner, the tensioner is actuated by a gas generator cartridge connected to the seat belt stalk.

There is a risk of injury if the system is triggered inadvertently when working on the vehicle, and it is therefore strongly recommended that any work involving the seat belt tensioner system is entrusted to a Vauxhall/Opel dealer. Refer to the warning given at the beginning of Section 23 before contemplating any work on the front seats.

25 Seat belt components – removal and refitting

Removal

Front seat belt – three-door models

1 Prise off the trim cover from the upper seat belt mounting. Unscrew the mounting bolt, and recover the washer and spacer from behind the belt anchorage **(see illustration)**.

2 Remove the trim cap, then slacken and remove bolt and washer securing the seat belt mounting rail to the floor. Disengage the rail from the floor and the seat belt, and remove it **(see illustrations)**.

25.2a Remove the trim cap . . .

25.2b . . . then unscrew the retaining bolt and washer . . .

25.2c . . . and disengage the seat belt mounting rail from the floor and seat belt, and remove it from the vehicle

25.5a Unscrew the retaining nut and washer . . .

25.5b . . . and remove the seat pin and washer (where fitted)

25.6a Prise out the circular plug (where fitted) from the front of the luggage compartment side trim panel

25.6b Prise out the three retaining clips (arrowed) from the rear of the panel . . .

25.6c . . . then undo the retaining screws (arrowed) and remove the panel

from the relevant luggage compartment side trim panel. Where necessary, undo the retaining nut and washer, and remove the seat pin and washer from the vehicle **(see illustrations)**.

6 Prise out the retaining clips from the rear of the panel, and the circular plug/seat stop buffer (as applicable) from the front of the panel. Slacken and remove all the panel retaining screws, then release the panel from the vehicle body and disconnect the speaker wiring connector (where fitted) **(see illustrations)**.

7 Position the luggage compartment panel clear of the rear seat side trim panel. There is no need to undo the rear seat belt anchorages.

8 Undo the two screws, and release the sill trim panel from the front edge of the rear seat side trim panel **(see illustration)**.

9 Slacken and remove the rear retaining screw from the base of the panel **(see illustration)**.

10 Peel the door sealing strip away from the front edge of the rear seat side panel, then unclip the top of the panel and remove it from the vehicle **(see illustrations)**.

11 Undo the inertia reel retaining bolt, and remove the seat belt assembly from the vehicle. If necessary, the seat belt height adjuster ratchet can be removed as follows.

12 Prise out the hook from the top of the door pillar panel. Undo the upper and lower retaining screws, and remove the trim panel to gain access to the seat belt height adjuster ratchet. Undo the two bolts and remove the ratchet **(see illustrations)**.

25.8 Undo the two screws, and release the sill trim panel from the rear seat side trim panel

25.9 Undo the rear retaining screw . . .

3 Remove the rear seat backrest as described in Section 23.

4 If the left-hand seat belt is to be removed,

remove the interior light unit from the luggage compartment trim panel as described in Chapter 12.

5 Remove the rear shock absorber access panel

25.10a . . . then peel the door sealing strip away from the front of the panel . . .

25.10b . . . and unclip the panel from the vehicle

25.12a Remove the hook from the door pillar panel, and unscrew the upper retaining screw . . .

25.12b . . . then undo the lower retaining screw . . .

25.12c . . . and remove the door pillar trim panel

25.12d Seat belt height adjuster ratchet is retained by two bolts (arrowed)

Front seat belt – five-door and Combo Van models

13 Prise off the trim cap from the seat belt upper mounting. Unscrew the mounting bolt, and recover the washer and spacer from behind the belt anchorage (**see illustrations**).

14 Remove the trim caps from the door pillar trim panel to reveal the retaining screws, then undo both screws and free the panels. Unclip the two panel sections, and remove them from the vehicle (**see illustration**).

15 Prise off the trim cap from the lower seat belt mounting. Unscrew the mounting bolt, and recover the washer, spacer and trim cover from behind the belt anchorage.

16 Undo the inertia reel retaining bolt, and remove the seat belt assembly from the vehicle (**see illustration**). If necessary, undo the retaining bolts and remove the seat belt ratchet mechanism from the door pillar.

Rear seat side belt – three-door and five-door models

17 Carry out the operations described above in paragraphs 3 to 6.

18 Prise off the trim cover from the upper seat belt mounting. Unscrew the mounting bolt, and recover the washer and spacer from behind the belt anchorage (**see illustration**).

19 Unscrew the lower seat belt mounting bolt and washer, then undo the inertia reel retaining bolt. Remove the guide from the luggage compartment trim panel, then free the belt and remove it from the vehicle (**see illustrations**). If necessary, the seat belt

25.13a Unclip the trim cap . . .

25.13b . . . then unscrew the mounting bolt, and recover the washer and spacer from behind the belt anchorage

25.14 Unclip the two halves of the door pillar trim panel, and remove them

25.16 Undo the inertia reel retaining bolt (arrowed) and remove the seat belt assembly

25.18 Unscrew the rear seat belt upper mounting bolt, noting the correct fitted position of the washer and spacer

25.19a Unscrew the lower mounting bolt . . .

25.19b . . . and the inertia reel retaining bolt . . .

25.19c . . . then remove the guide, and feed the belt through the luggage compartment trim panel

25.20a On three-door models, prise out the trim cap . . .

25.20b . . . then undo the upper retaining screw . . .

25.20c . . . and the lower retaining screw . . .

25.20d . . . and unclip the trim panel from the vehicle

25.21 Rear seat belt height adjuster mechanism is retained by two bolts (arrowed)

height adjuster ratchet can be removed as follows.

20 On three-door models, prise out the trim cap from the top of the rear window trim panel, then undo both the upper and lower panel retaining screws. Unclip the retaining clips, situated along the top edge of the panel, and free it from the door pillar trim panel (see illustrations). Note: *It may be necessary to remove the hook and undo the door pillar panel upper screw first (see paragraph 12).* Undo the two retaining bolts and remove the ratchet.

21 On five-door models, prise out the trim caps, then undo the retaining screws and remove the rear quarter window trim panel. Undo the two retaining bolts, and remove the ratchet (see illustration).

Rear seat side belt – Combo Van models

22 Where necessary, undo the retaining bolts and remove the luggage compartment grille from the vehicle.

23 Fold the rear seat cushion forwards, then prise out the retaining clips and remove the trim panel from either side of the seat belt inertia reel.

24 Undo the retaining screws, and remove the cover from the inertia reel.

25 Unclip the trim cover from the upper belt mounting. Undo the bolt, and recover the washer and spacer from behind the belt anchorage.

26 Undo the lower seat belt and inertia reel retaining bolts, and remove the seat belt from the vehicle.

Rear seat centre belt and buckles – all models

27 Fold the rear seat cushion forwards, and unscrew the relevant bolt securing the belt or buckle to the floor (see illustration).

Refitting

28 Refitting is a reversal of the removal procedure, ensuring that all the mounting bolts are tightened to the specified torque, where applicable (see illustration). Make sure that any trim panels disturbed during removal are securely retained by all the relevant retaining clips.

26 Interior trim – removal and refitting

Interior trim panels

1 The interior trim panels are secured using either screws or various types of trim fasteners, usually studs or clips.

2 Check that there are no other panels overlapping the one to be removed; usually there is a sequence that has to be followed that will become obvious on close inspection.

3 Remove all obvious fasteners, such as screws. If the panel will not come free, it is held by hidden clips or fasteners. These are usually situated around the edge of the panel, and can be prised up to release them; note,

25.27 Rear seat belt buckle retaining bolt

25.28 When refitting, tighten the seat belt mounting bolts to their specified torque settings

26.6 Unscrew the glovebox lower retaining screws (arrowed) . . .

26.7a . . . then undo the three upper retaining screws (arrowed) . . .

26.7b . . . and withdraw the glovebox, disconnecting the wiring connector from the illumination light as it becomes accessible

however, that they can break quite easily, so replacements should be available. The best way of releasing such clips (in the absence of the correct type of tool) is to use a large flat-bladed screwdriver. Note in many cases that the adjacent sealing strip must be prised back to release a panel.

4 When removing a panel, **never** use excessive force, or the panel may be damaged; always check carefully that all fasteners have been removed or released before attempting to withdraw a panel.

5 Refitting is the reverse of the removal procedure; secure the fasteners by pressing them firmly into place, and ensure that all disturbed components are secured correctly, to prevent rattles.

Glovebox

6 Slacken and remove the two glovebox lower retaining screws (**see illustration**).

7 Open up the glovebox lid, and undo the three upper retaining screws situated inside the glovebox (on models with a passenger's air bag, the centre screw is not fitted). Slide the glovebox out of position, disconnecting the wiring connectors from the glovebox illumination light and anti-theft warning system control unit (where fitted) as they becomes accessible (**see illustrations**).

8 Refitting is the reverse of removal.

Carpets

9 The passenger compartment floor carpet is

in one piece, and is secured at its edges by screws or clips, usually the same fasteners used to secure the various adjoining trim panels.

10 Carpet removal and refitting is reasonably straightforward, but very time-consuming. All adjoining trim panels must be removed first, as must components such as the seats, the centre console and seat belt lower anchorages.

Headlining

11 The headlining is clipped to the roof, and can only be withdrawn once all fittings such as the grab handles, sunvisors, sunroof (if fitted), windscreen and rear quarterwindows and related trim panels have been removed, and the door, tailgate and sunroof aperture sealing strips have been prised clear.

12 Note that headlining removal requires considerable skill and experience if it is to be carried out without damage, and is therefore best entrusted to an expert.

27 Centre console – removal and refitting

Removal

1 Firmly apply the handbrake, and slide both front seats fully rearwards.

2 Prise out the trim cap from the front of the centre console storage compartment, and unscrew the retaining screw (**see illustrations**).

3 On models with manual transmission, unclip the gear lever gaiter from the centre console, and fold it back over the gear lever (**see illustration**).

4 On all models, slide the console to the rear to disengage it from its retaining clip, and lift it upwards and over the gear/selector lever (**see illustration**).

Refitting

5 Refitting is the reverse of removal.

27.2a Prise out the trim cap from the centre console storage compartment . . .

27.2b . . . to gain access to the retaining screw

27.3 On models with manual transmission, unclip the gaiter and fold it back over the gear lever

27.4 Move the centre console to the rear to free it from its retaining clips, and lift it over the gear lever

28.6a Undo the two lower retaining screws . . .

28.6b . . . then open up the ashtray, and undo the two upper retaining screws

28.6c Withdraw the ashtray from the facia, and disconnect its wiring connectors

28 Facia panel assembly – removal and refitting

 Label each wiring connector as it is disconnected from its relevant component. The labels will prove useful when refitting, as a guide to routing the wiring and feeding it through the facia apertures.

28.10a Prise out the two retaining clips . . .

28.10b . . . then turn the combination switch mounting bracket anti-clockwise, and slide it off the steering column

Removal

1 Disconnect the battery negative terminal (refer to *Disconnecting the battery* in the Reference Chapter).
2 Remove the following components as described in Chapter 12:
 a) *Instrument panel.*
 b) *Windscreen wiper motor.*
 c) *Radio/cassette player.*
 d) *Clock/multi/function unit display.*
 e) *Steering column combination switches.*
3 Remove the following components as described in Chapter 3:
 a) *Heater/ventilation control unit.*
 b) *Driver's side vent housing.*
 c) *Passenger side heater duct.*
4 Remove the glovebox as described in Section 26.
5 Remove the storage compartment (where fitted) from underneath the passenger side of

the facia. The compartment is secured in position by a retaining screw and clip.
6 Undo the two lower ashtray retaining screws, then open up the ashtray and remove the two upper retaining screws. Withdraw the ashtray from the centre of the facia, disconnecting the wiring connectors from the rear of the unit as they become accessible **(see illustrations)**.
7 Remove the centre console as described in Section 27.
8 Undo the retaining screws, and release the fusebox from the driver's side of the facia, and the relay carrier from the top of the glovebox aperture. See Section 3 of Chapter 12 for further information. There is no need to disconnect any of the above components – they can be left in position
9 Remove the steering wheel as described in Chapter 10.

10 Prise out the two retaining clips from the combination switch mounting bracket, then twist the bracket anti-clockwise and slide it off the top of the steering column **(see illustrations)**.
11 Disconnect the wiring connector from the stop-light switch. On models with an air bag, disconnect the control unit wiring connector, then undo the retaining screws and remove the control unit from the vehicle.
12 Undo the retaining screws, and remove the support bracket from the base of the centre of the facia **(see illustration)**.
13 Where necessary, undo the screw securing the radio/cassette mounting bracket in position, then slide out the bracket, freeing it from the aerial lead and wiring connector **(see illustrations)**.
14 Release the retaining clips and, noting its

28.12 Removing the support bracket from the centre of the facia

28.13a Undo the retaining screw (arrowed), then slide out the radio/cassette bracket, freeing the wiring connector . . .

28.13b . . . and aerial lead from the rear of the bracket

correct routing, free the wiring loom from the metal frame of the facia panel. Also slide the instrument panel wiring connector out from its clip on the facia **(see illustrations)**.

15 Undo the two retaining screws from the left-hand end of the facia panel, and the two screws from the facia right-hand end **(see illustration)**.

16 Return to the engine compartment, and undo the three retaining nuts securing the facia to the bulkhead **(see illustration)**.

17 The facia panel is now free to be removed. Pull the panel away from the bulkhead, then remove the facia assembly, noting the correct routing of the wiring harnesses, and feeding the wiring back through the facia apertures.

Refitting

18 Refitting is a reversal of the removal procedure, noting the following points:

a) *Manoeuvre the facia into position and, using the labels stuck on during removal, ensure that the wiring is correctly routed and fed through the relevant facia apertures.*

b) *Clip the facia back into position, then refit all the facia fasteners and tighten them to their specified torque settings.*

c) *On completion, reconnect the battery and check that all the electrical components and switches function correctly.*

28.14a Release the retaining clips and ties, and free the wiring from the facia metal frame . . .

28.14b . . . and the instrument panel wiring connector from the facia

28.15 Undo the facia side retaining screws . . .

28.16 . . . then undo the nuts securing the facia assembly to the engine compartment bulkhead

Chapter 12
Body electrical systems

Contents

Degrees of difficulty

Easy, suitable for novice with little experience	**Fairly easy,** suitable for beginner with some experience	**Fairly difficult,** suitable for competent DIY mechanic	**Difficult,** suitable for experienced DIY mechanic	**Very difficult,** suitable for expert DIY or professional

Specifications

System type	12 volt negative earth

Bulbs	**Wattage**
Headlight	60/55
Front foglight	55
Front sidelight	5
Direction indicator	21
Direction indicator side repeater	5
Stop/tail light	21/5
Reversing light	21
Rear foglight	21
Number plate light	10
Interior lights	10
Instrument panel illumination lights	2
Instrument panel warning lights	1.2

Torque wrench settings	**Nm**	**lbf ft**
Air bag unit retaining screws	10	7
Windscreen wiper motor	25	18

1 General information and precautions

Warning: Before carrying out any work on the electrical system, read through the precautions given in 'Safety first!' at the beginning of this manual, and in Chapter 5A.

1 The electrical system is of the 12 volt negative earth type. Power for the lights and all electrical accessories is supplied by a lead-acid type battery, which is charged by the engine-driven alternator.

2 This Chapter covers repair and service procedures for the various electrical components not associated with the engine. Information on the battery, alternator and starter motor can be found in Chapter 5A.

3 It should be noted that, prior to working on any component in the electrical system, the battery negative terminal should first be disconnected, to prevent the possibility of electrical short-circuits and/or fires.

Caution: Before proceeding, refer to 'Disconnecting the battery' in the Reference Chapter for further information.

2 Electrical fault finding – general information

Note: *Refer to the precautions given in 'Safety first!' and in Section 1 before starting work. The following tests relate to testing of the main electrical circuits, and should not be used to test delicate electronic circuits (such as the anti-lock braking system or fuel injection system), particularly where an electronic control module is used.*

General

1 A typical electrical circuit consists of an electrical component, any switches, relays, motors, fuses, fusible links or circuit breakers related to that component, and the wiring and connectors which link the component to both the battery and the vehicle body. To help to pinpoint a problem in an electrical circuit, wiring diagrams are included at the end of this Chapter.

2 Before attempting to diagnose an electrical fault, first study the appropriate wiring diagram to obtain a complete understanding of the components included in the particular circuit concerned. The possible sources of a fault can be narrowed down by noting if other components related to the circuit are operating properly. If several components or circuits fail at one time, the problem is likely to be related to a shared fuse or earth connection.

3 Electrical problems usually stem from simple causes, such as loose or corroded connections, a faulty earth connection, a blown fuse, a melted fusible link, or a faulty relay (refer to Section 3 for details of testing relays). Inspect the condition of all fuses, wires and connections in a problem circuit before testing the components. Use the wiring diagrams to determine which terminal connections will need to be checked in order to pinpoint the trouble-spot.

4 The basic tools required for electrical fault-finding include a circuit tester or voltmeter (a 12 volt bulb with a set of test leads can also be used for certain tests); a self-powered test light (sometimes known as a continuity tester); an ohmmeter (to measure resistance); a battery and set of test leads; and a jumper wire, preferably with a circuit breaker or fuse incorporated, which can be used to bypass suspect wires or electrical components. Before attempting to locate a problem with test instruments, use the wiring diagram to determine where to make the connections.

5 To find the source of an intermittent wiring fault (usually due to a poor or dirty connection, or damaged wiring insulation), a 'wiggle' test can be performed on the wiring. This involves wiggling the wiring by hand to see if the fault occurs as the wiring is moved. It should be possible to narrow down the source of the fault to a particular section of wiring. This method of testing can be used in conjunction with any of the tests described in the following sub-Sections.

6 Apart from problems due to poor connections, two basic types of fault can occur in an electrical circuit – open-circuit, or short-circuit.

7 Open-circuit faults are caused by a break somewhere in the circuit, which prevents current from flowing. An open-circuit fault will prevent a component from working, but will not cause the relevant circuit fuse to blow.

8 Short-circuit faults are caused by a 'short' somewhere in the circuit, which allows the current flowing in the circuit to 'escape' along an alternative route, usually to earth. Short-circuit faults are normally caused by a breakdown in wiring insulation, which allows a feed wire to touch either another wire, or an earthed component such as the bodyshell. A short-circuit fault will normally cause the relevant circuit fuse to blow.

Finding an open-circuit

9 To check for an open-circuit, connect one lead of a circuit tester or voltmeter to either the negative battery terminal or a known good earth.

10 Connect the other lead to a connector in the circuit being tested, preferably nearest to the battery or fuse.

11 Switch on the circuit, bearing in mind that some circuits are live only when the ignition switch is turned to a particular position.

12 If voltage is present (indicated either by the tester bulb lighting or a voltmeter reading, as applicable), this means that the section of the circuit between the relevant connector and the battery is problem-free.

13 Continue to check the remainder of the circuit in the same fashion.

14 When a point is reached at which no voltage is present, the problem must lie between that point and the previous test point with voltage. Most problems can be traced to a broken, corroded or loose connection.

Finding a short-circuit

15 To check for a short-circuit, first disconnect the load(s) from the circuit (loads are the components which draw current from a circuit, such as bulbs, motors, heating elements, etc).

16 Remove the relevant fuse from the circuit, and connect a circuit tester or voltmeter to the fuse connections.

17 Switch on the circuit, bearing in mind that some circuits are live only when the ignition switch is turned to a particular position.

18 If voltage is present (indicated either by the tester bulb lighting or a voltmeter reading, as applicable), this means that there is a short-circuit.

19 If no voltage is present, but the fuse still blows with the load(s) connected, this indicates an internal fault in the load(s).

Finding an earth fault

20 The battery negative terminal is connected to 'earth' – the metal of the engine/transmission unit and the car body – and most systems are wired so that they only receive a positive feed, the current returning via the metal of the car body. This means that the component mounting and the body form part of that circuit. Loose or corroded mountings can therefore cause a range of electrical faults, ranging from total failure of a circuit, to a puzzling partial fault. In particular, lights may shine dimly (especially when another circuit sharing the same earth point is in operation), motors (eg, wiper motors or the radiator cooling fan motor) may run slowly, and the operation of one circuit may have an apparently-unrelated effect on another. Note that on many vehicles, earth straps are used between certain components, such as the engine/transmission and the body, usually where there is no metal-to-metal contact between components, due to flexible rubber mountings, etc.

21 To check whether a component is properly earthed, disconnect the battery, and connect one lead of an ohmmeter to a known good earth point. Connect the other lead to the wire or earth connection being tested. The resistance reading should be zero; if not, check the connection as follows.

22 If an earth connection is thought to be faulty, dismantle the connection, and clean back to bare metal both the bodyshell and the wire terminal or the component earth connection mating surface. Be careful to remove all traces of dirt and corrosion, then use a knife to trim away any paint, so that a clean metal-to-metal joint is made. On reassembly, tighten the joint fasteners securely; if a wire terminal is being refitted, use serrated washers between the terminal

Body electrical systems 12•3

o the retaining bolt, and remove
brake warning light switch from
the lever

4.25 Withdraw the courtesy light switch
from the door pillar, and disconnect its
wiring connector

4.28 Removing the luggage compartment
light switch – Combo Van models

ake warning light switch

ve the handbrake lever as described
9.

the bolt, and remove the switch
ever **(see illustration)**.

the new switch, securely tightening
g bolt, and refit the handbrake lever
ed in Chapter 9.

ght switch

to Chapter 9.

sy light switch

the door, then undo the switch
screw. Withdraw the switch from the
connecting its wiring connector as it
accessible **(see illustration)**. Tie a
string to the wiring, to prevent it
ack into the door pillar.
ting is a reverse of the removal
re.

ge compartment light

Corsa and Corsavan models, the
s fitted to the bottom of the tailgate.
bo Van models, the switch is fitted to
-hand side of the vehicle body, on the
edge of the rear door.
o the retaining screw, then withdraw
ch and disconnect it from its wiring
tor **(see illustration)**. Tie a piece of

string to the wiring, to prevent it falling back
into the tailgate/vehicle body (as applicable).
29 Refitting is a reverse of the removal
procedure.

Driver's door electric window switch

30 Unscrew the door pocket retaining
screws, and pull the pocket downwards and
away from the door to release its retaining
clips **(see illustration)**. Disconnect the switch
wiring connectors.
31 Release the retaining clips, and remove
the relevant switch from the panel **(see
illustration)**.
32 Refitting is the reverse of removal,
ensuring that the wiring is correctly routed
inside the door pocket.

Passenger door electric window switch

33 Remove the door inner trim panel as
described in Chapter 11.
34 Disconnect the switch wiring connector,
and remove the switch from the vehicle.
35 Refitting is the reverse of removal.

Electric mirror switch

36 Remove the door inner trim panel as
described in Chapter 11.
37 Disconnect the switch wiring connector,
and remove the switch from the vehicle **(see
illustration)**.
38 Refitting is the reverse of removal.

Electric sunroof switch

39 Carefully prise the sunroof switch out of
position, and disconnect it from its wiring
connector.
40 When refitting, connect the wiring connector,
and clip the switch back into position.

Air conditioning system switch

41 The air conditioning system control switch is
an integral part of the heating/ventilation control
unit, and cannot be removed. Should the switch
become faulty, the complete control unit
assembly must be renewed (see Chapter 3),

Horn switch

Models without driver's air bag

42 Carefully ease the horn button out from
the steering wheel, and disconnect its wiring
connector.
43 Reconnect the wiring connector and push
the button back into position.

Models with driver's air bag

44 Remove the driver's air bag as described
in Section 27.
45 Using a small screwdriver, carefully
release the relevant switch from the switch
holder in the steering wheel.
46 Disconnect the wiring connector and
remove the switch.
47 Refit the wiring connector and switch,
then refit the air bag as described in Section 27.

To remove the driver's door electric
window switches, remove the
door pocket . . .

4.31 . . . then release the retaining clips,
and slide the relevant switch out of
the pocket

4.37 Disconnect the wiring connector, and
remove the electric mirror switch from
the door

---

and the bodyshell, to ensure a clean and
secure connection. When the connection is
remade, prevent the onset of corrosion in the
future by applying a coat of petroleum jelly or
silicone-based grease. Alternatively, at regular
intervals, spray on a proprietary ignition sealer
or a water-dispersant lubricant.

3 Fuses and relays – general information

Fuses

1 Most of the fuses are located behind the
driver's side lower facia panel, with additional
fuses on some models being located in the
junction box in the engine compartment **(see
illustrations)**. The junction box is located next
to the master cylinder brake fluid reservoir.
2 To gain access to fusebox, unclip the
access panel from the driver's side of the
facia. To gain access to those in the junction
box, unclip the junction box lid.

3.7a Fusebox relay locations and
identification numbers

1 Exterior mirror heating timer relay (K35)
2 Turn signal relay (K10)
3 Tailgate wiper relay (K30)
4 Not used
5 Front foglight relay (K5)
6 Rear foglight relay (K89)
7 Windscreen wiper relay (K8)
8 Heated rear window relay (K1)
9 'Lights-on' warning buzzer (H19)
10 Anti-theft alarm horn relay (K63)
11 Headlight washer system relay (K97)
12 Anti-theft alarm immobiliser relay (K3)
13 Daytime driving light relay (K59)
14 Diagnostic plug (for use by Vauxhall/Opel dealer)

3.1a Unclip the cover from the driver's
side of the facia to gain access to most of
the fuses

3 The fuse number is marked on the fusebox
next to each fuse. A list of the circuits each
fuse protects is given in the Specifications at
the start of this Chapter.
4 To remove a fuse, first switch off the circuit
concerned (or the ignition), then pull the fuse
out of its terminals. The wire within the fuse is
clearly visible; if the fuse is blown, it will be
broken or melted.
5 Always renew a fuse with one of an
identical rating; never use a fuse with a
different rating from the original, nor
substitute anything else. Never renew a fuse
more than once without tracing the source of

3.7b Relay carrier relay locations and
identification numbers

1 Cooling fan relay (K51)
2 Cooling fan relay (K52)
3 Cooling fan relay (K26)
4 Anti-theft alarm control unit
5 Air conditioning relay (K6)
6 Air conditioning cooling fan relay (K7)
7 Cooling fan relay (high-speed) (K67)

3.1b Additional fuses and relays are
located in the junction box in the engine
compartment (right-hand drive model)

the trouble. The fuse rating is stamped on top
of the fuse; note that the fuses are also
colour-coded for easy recognition.
6 If a new fuse blows immediately, find the
cause before renewing it again; a short to
earth as a result of faulty insulation is most
likely. Where a fuse protects more than one
circuit, try to isolate the defect by switching
on each circuit in turn (if possible) until the
fuse blows again. Always carry a supply of
spare fuses of each relevant rating on the
vehicle, a spare of each rating should be
clipped into the base of the fusebox.

Relays

7 The majority of relays are located in the top
of the fusebox behind the driver's side lower
facia panel. Additional relays may be located
on the relay carriers which are situated behind
the facia above the glovebox, behind the
right-hand footwell trim panel, or in the engine
compartment junction box. Full details of relay
locations are given in the Specifications at the
start of this Chapter, and in the accompanying
illustrations **(see illustrations)**.
8 To gain access to the fusebox relays, unclip
the fusebox access panel from the facia,
then undo the two retaining screws and lower
the fusebox out from the facia **(see
illustrations)**.
9 To gain access to the facia relay carrier,
remove the glovebox as described in Chapter 11, Section 26. Undo the two retaining
screws, and lower the anti-theft alarm control
unit (where fitted) out from the top of the
glovebox aperture. Undo the two screws, and

3.8a Undo the two retaining screws
(arrowed) . . .

3.8b . . . and lower the fusebox out of position to gain access to the relays

3.9a Undo the two retaining screws (arrowed) . . .

3.9b . . . and lower the anti-theft alarm control unit out of position to gain access to the relay carrier

lower the relay carrier plate out from the top of the glovebox aperture **(see illustrations)**.

10 To gain access to the relay carrier behind the right-hand footwell trim panel, open the front door and where applicable, remove the storage tray from under the facia. Remove the screw securing the front of the sill trim panel and lift up the front edge of the panel. Remove the screw and plastic clip securing the footwell trim panel. Carefully pull back the weatherstrip from the front edge of the door aperture to expose the edge of the footwell trim panel, then withdraw the trim panel from the footwell.

11 If a circuit or system controlled by a relay

develops a fault and the relay is suspect, operate the system; if the relay is functioning, it should be possible to hear it click as it is energised. If this is the case, the fault lies with the components or wiring of the system. If the relay is not being energised, then either the relay is not receiving a main supply or a switching voltage, or the relay itself is faulty. Testing is by the substitution of a known good unit, but be careful; while some relays are identical in appearance and in operation, others look similar but perform different functions.

12 To renew a relay, first ensure that the ignition switch is off. The relay can then

simply be pulled out from the socket and the new relay pressed in.

---

4 Switches –
removal and refitting

Note: *Disconnect the battery negative terminal (refer to 'Disconnecting the battery' in the Reference Chapter) before removing any switch, and reconnect the terminal after refitting.*

Ignition switch/steering column lock

1 Refer to Chapter 10.

Steering column switch

2 With the steering wheel in the straight-ahead position, turn the wheel 90° to the left, then prise off the trim cap and remove the left upper shroud screw. Turn the wheel 180° to the right, and remove the right upper screw. Remove the rubber seal from the ignition switch/lock, then undo the lower retaining screws and remove the steering column shrouds **(see illustrations)**.

3 Depress the retaining clips, and release the relevant switch assembly from the column bracket. Disconnect the wiring connector, and

4.2a Prise out the trim plugs from the top of the steering column shrouds . . .

4.2b . . . and unscrew the upper shroud screws

4.2c Unscrew the three lower shroud retaining screws (arrowed) . . .

4.2d . . . then remove the rubber seal from the ignition switch/lock . . .

4.2e . . . and remove both shrouds from the column

4.3a Depress the retaining clips, then slide out the switch (shown with steering wheel removed for clarity) . . .

4.3b . . . and disconnect its wiring connector

4.7 Release the re bladed screwdr lighting

4.22 Un the han

remove the switch assembly from the vehicle **(see illustrations)**.

4 If necessary, remove the opposite switch assembly in the same way.

5 Refitting is a reversal of the removal procedure.

Lighting switch (incorporating instruments dimmer and interior lights)

6 Turn the knob to the headlight 'on' position, and pull the knob out.

7 Insert a small screwdriver or suitable rod through the hole in the bottom of the knob, then depress the switch knob retaining clip and remove the knob **(see illustration)**.

8 Depress the switch retaining clips, pull the

switch out from the facia, and disconnect the wiring connector **(see illustration)**.

9 Note that the switch assembly cannot be dismantled; if any of its functions are faulty, the complete assembly must be renewed.

10 Refitting is a reversal of the removal procedure.

Foglight, heated seat and headlight beam adjuster switches

11 To remove the facia pushbutton switches, a suitable hooked tool is needed. A suitable tool can be fabricated from a strip of 2 mm steel which is approximately 5 mm in width (a small hacksaw blade works well). Bend the end of the strip through 90° so that there is a

hook approximately angle to the strip.

21 Rem in Chapte
22 Undo from the
23 Insta its retain as desc

Stop-l

24 Refe

Court

25 Ope retaining pillar, d become piece fa falling b
26 Ref proced

Lugg swit

27 On switch On Co the rig outside
28 U the sw conne

hook approximately 4 angle to the strip.
12 Manoeuvre the s great care not to dam panel. Locate the hoo use it to pull the swit **illustration)**.
13 On refitting, push until it clicks into posit

Hazard warning

14 Depress the switc 'on' position.
15 Using a small flat carefully lever the sw taking great care not t vent panel **(see illustrat**
16 On refitting, push clicks into position.

Heated rear wind motor switch

17 Pull the switch out 'on' position.
18 Insert a small screw through the hole in the then depress the switch and remove the knob **(see**
19 Depress the switch pull the switch out fro **illustration)**.
20 Refitting is the reverse

4.8 Depress the retaining clips, and withdraw the lighting switch from the facia

4.12 Using the hooked tool to withdraw the front foglight switch

4.15 Removing the hazard warning light switch. Note the use of a piece of card to avoid marking the switch surround

4.18 Release the retaining clip with a suitable screwdriver, and pull off the knob

4.19 Depress the retainin withdraw the heated rear w motor switch from th

4.30

5.2a To improve access to the right-hand headlight unit, release the fastener . . .

5.2b . . . and remove the intake duct from the air cleaner housing

5.2c Disconnect the wiring connector . . .

5 Bulbs (exterior lights) – renewal

General

1 Whenever a bulb is renewed, note the following points:

a) *Disconnect the battery negative terminal (refer to 'Disconnecting the battery' in the Reference Chapter).*

b) *Remember that if the light has just been in use, the bulb may be extremely hot.*

c) *Always check the bulb contacts and holder, ensuring that there is clean metal-to-metal contact between the bulb and its live(s) and earth. Clean off any corrosion or dirt before fitting a new bulb.*

5.2d . . . and remove the rubber cover from the rear of the headlight

d) *Wherever bayonet-type bulbs are fitted, ensure that the live contact(s) bear firmly against the bulb contact.*

e) *Always ensure that the new bulb is of the correct rating, and that it is completely clean before fitting it; this applies particularly to headlight/foglight bulbs (see below).*

Headlight

2 Working in the engine compartment, disconnect the wiring connector from the rear of the headlight, then remove the rubber dust cover. Note that if the right-hand bulb is being renewed, it will be necessary to unclip the intake duct from the air cleaner housing to improve access **(see illustrations)**.

3 Unhook and release the ends of the bulb retaining clip, and release it from the rear of the light unit.

4 Withdraw the bulb **(see illustration)**.

5 When handling the new bulb, use a tissue or clean cloth to avoid touching the glass with the fingers; moisture and grease from the skin can cause blackening and rapid failure of this type of bulb. If the glass is accidentally touched, wipe it clean using methylated spirit.

6 Install the new bulb, ensuring that its locating tabs are correctly located in the light cut-outs.

7 Refit the dust cover to the rear of the light unit, and reconnect the wiring connector.

Front sidelight

8 Working in the engine compartment, push

the bulbholder inwards, then twist it anti-clockwise to release it from the rear of the headlight unit **(see illustration)**. Note that if the right-hand bulb is being renewed, it will be necessary to unclip the intake duct from the air cleaner housing to improve access.

9 The bulb is of the capless (push-fit) type, and can be removed by simply pulling it out of the bulbholder.

10 Refitting is the reverse of the removal procedure, ensuring that the bulbholder is securely clipped into position.

Front direction indicator

11 Working in the engine compartment, twist the bulbholder anti-clockwise, and remove it from the rear of the headlight unit. Note that if the right-hand bulb is being renewed, it will be necessary to unclip the intake duct from the air cleaner housing to improve access.

12 The bulb is a bayonet fit in the holder, and can be removed by pressing it and twisting in an anti-clockwise direction **(see illustration)**.

13 Refitting is a reverse of the removal procedure.

Front direction indicator side repeater

14 Carefully prise the rear edge of the indicator side repeater light out from the wing, if necessary using a suitable plastic wedge,

5.4 Release the retaining clip (arrowed) and withdraw the headlight bulb

5.8 Removing the sidelight bulbholder from the headlight unit

5.12 Front direction turn signal bulb is a bayonet fit in its holder

5.14 Lift the rear of the indicator side repeater light to release it from the wing

5.15a Release the bulbholder from the rear of the light unit . . .

5.15b . . . then pull the bulb out of the holder

taking great care not damage the painted finish of the wing **(see illustration)**.

15 Withdraw the light unit from the wing, and pull the bulbholder out of the light unit. The bulb is of the capless (push-fit) type, and can be removed by simply pulling it out of the bulbholder **(see illustrations)**.

16 Refitting is a reverse of the removal procedure.

Front foglight

17 If necessary, to improve access to the rear of the foglight, firmly apply the handbrake, then jack up the front of the car and support it securely on axle stands (see *Jacking and vehicle support*).

18 Disconnect the wiring connector from the rear of the foglight unit. Twist the cover anti-

clockwise, and free it from the rear of the foglight **(see illustration)**.

19 Disconnect the bulb wire from the cover terminal, then release the spring clip and withdraw the foglight bulb from the rear of the light unit **(see illustrations)**.

20 When handling the new bulb, use a tissue or clean cloth to avoid touching the glass with the fingers; moisture and grease from the skin can cause blackening and rapid failure of this type of bulb. If the glass is accidentally touched, wipe it clean using methylated spirit.

21 Insert the new bulb, making sure it is correctly located, and secure it in position with the spring clip.

22 Connect the bulb wire to the cover terminal, then refit the cover to the rear of the

unit. Connect the wiring connector to the cover, and lower the vehicle to the ground (where applicable).

Rear light cluster

23 From inside the vehicle luggage compartment, depress the retaining catches, and open the trim panel flap to gain access to the rear of the light unit **(see illustration)**.

24 Release the rear light cluster retaining catch(es), and free the bulbholder assembly from the rear of the light unit **(see illustration)**.

25 The relevant bulb can then be renewed; all bulbs have a bayonet fitting **(see illustration)**. Note that the stop/tail light bulb has offset locating pins, to prevent it being installed incorrectly.

5.18 Twist the cover anti-clockwise to release it from the rear of the foglight

5.19a Disconnect the bulb from the cover . . .

5.19b . . . then release the retaining clip . . .

5.19c . . . and withdraw the foglight bulb from the rear of the unit

5.23 Release the retaining clips, and remove the trim cover to gain access to the rear of the rear light cluster – Combo Van models

5.24 Depress the retaining catches (arrowed) . . .

5.25 . . . then withdraw the bulbholder and remove the relevant bulb

5.27 On Corsa and Corsavan models, carefully prise the rear number plate light out from the bumper . . .

5.28a . . . then unclip the lens . . .

5.28b . . . and remove the bulb, which is a bayonet fit in the light unit

5.30 On Combo Van models, release the relevant number plate light from the bumper as described in the text . . .

5.31a . . . then unclip the cover . . .

26 Refitting is the reverse of the removal sequence, ensuring that the bulbholder is securely clipped into position.

Number plate light

Corsa and Corsavan models

27 Using a small flat-bladed screwdriver, carefully prise the light out from the rear bumper **(see illustration)**.

28 Unclip the lens from the light unit, and remove the bulb. The bulb is a bayonet fit in the holder, and can be removed by pressing it and twisting anti-clockwise **(see illustrations)**.

29 Refitting is a reverse of the removal procedure.

Combo Van models

30 On the left-hand side, lift up the light unit, and prise out the base of the unit from the bumper. On the right-hand side, push down on the light unit, and prise out the top of the unit from the bumper **(see illustration)**.

31 Withdraw the light unit, then release the retaining clips and open it up. The bulb is a bayonet fit in the holder, and can be removed by pressing it and twisting anti-clockwise **(see illustrations)**.

32 Refitting is a reverse of the removal procedure.

High-level stop-light

33 The high-level stop-light bulbs are of the LED (light emitting diode) type and cannot be individually renewed.

6 Bulbs (interior lights) – renewal

General

1 Refer to Section 5, paragraph 1.

Front courtesy light

2 Using a suitable screwdriver, carefully prise the light unit out of position, and release the bulb from the light unit contacts **(see illustrations)**.

3 Install the new bulb, ensuring that it is securely held in position by the contacts, and clip the light unit back into position.

5.31b . . . and remove the bulb

6.2a Carefully prise the courtesy light unit out of position using a small screwdriver . . .

6.2b . . . and release the bulb from its wiring contacts

6.10 Removing an instrument panel illumination/warning light bulb

6.14 Removing the clock/multi-function display illumination bulb

6.17 Withdraw the ashtray unit from the facia . . .

Rear courtesy light

4 Using a small flat-bladed screwdriver, carefully prise the light unit out from its surround. Disconnect the wiring connector, and remove the light.
5 Unclip the heat shield from the light unit, and release the bulb from its contacts.
6 Install the new bulb, ensuring that it is securely held in position by the contacts, and clip the heat shield back into position.
7 Connect the wiring connector, and clip the light back into position in the surround.

Luggage compartment light

8 Refer to the information given above in paragraphs 2 and 3.

Instrument panel illumination/warning lights

9 Remove the instrument panel as described in Section 9.
10 Twist the relevant bulbholder anti-clockwise, and withdraw it from the rear of the panel **(see illustration)**.
11 All bulbs are integral with their holders. Be very careful to ensure that the new bulbs are of the correct rating, the same as those removed; this is especially important in the case of the ignition/no-charge warning light.
12 Refit the bulbholder to the rear of the instrument panel, then refit the instrument panel as described in Section 9.

Clock/multi-function display illumination

13 Remove the clock/multi-function display unit as described in Section 11.
14 Twist the bulbholder anti-clockwise, and withdraw it from the rear of the clock **(see illustration)**. The bulb is integral with its holder.
15 Refit the bulbholder to the rear of the unit, then refit the unit as described in Section 11.

Cigarette light/ashtray illumination

16 Open the ashtray, and remove the cigarette lighter insert.
17 Undo the retaining screws, and withdraw the ashtray from the centre of the facia, disconnecting the wiring connectors from the rear of the unit as they become accessible **(see illustration)**.

18 Slide the illumination bulbholder out of the panel, and renew the bulb **(see illustration)**. The bulbs is of the capless (push-fit) type; pull the old bulb out of the holder, and press the new one into position.
19 Slide the illumination bulbholder back into position, and refit the ashtray by reversing the removal procedure.

Heater control panel illumination

20 Withdraw the heater control panel as described in Chapter 3, so that access to the rear of the panel can be gained. Note there is no need to remove the panel completely; the control cables can be left attached.
21 Unclip the bulbholder from the rear of the control unit **(see illustration)**. The bulbs are of the capless (push-fit) type; pull the relevant bulb out of the holder, and press the new one into position.
22 Refit the bulbholder, and install the control panel as described in Chapter 3.

Glovebox illumination light

23 Open the glovebox. Using a small flat-bladed screwdriver, carefully prise the light unit out of position, then release the bulb from its contacts.
24 Install the new bulb, ensuring it is securely held in position by the contacts, and clip the light unit back into position.

Switch illumination

25 All the switches are fitted with illumination bulbs; some are also fitted with a bulb to

6.18 . . . then disconnect the wiring connectors and remove the illumination bulb from the rear of the unit

show when the circuit concerned is operating. These bulbs are an integral part of the switch assembly, and cannot be obtained separately. Bulb replacement will therefore require the renewal of the complete switch assembly.

Automatic transmission selector housing illumination

26 Remove the centre console as described in Chapter 11.
27 Unclip the selector lever cover from the selector housing and lift it upwards.
28 Withdraw the relevant bulbholder from the underside of the selector lever cover and release the bulb from the bulbholder.
29 Install the new bulb, refit the bulbholder and clip the selector lever cover back into position.
30 Refit the centre console as described in Chapter 11.

---

7 Exterior light units – removal and refitting

Note: *Disconnect the battery negative terminal (refer to 'Disconnecting the battery' in the Reference Chapter) before removing any light unit, and reconnect the terminal after refitting.*

Headlight

1 Unscrew the two screws securing the relevant end of the front bumper to the wheelarch liner. Unclip the access cover from

6.21 Release the retaining clips (arrowed), and withdraw the bulbholder from the rear of the heater control panel

7.2a Undo the bolts securing the radiator grille section of the front bumper to the crossmember . . .

7.2b . . . then undo the two headlight unit retaining bolts (arrowed)

7.3a Release the end of the bumper from the wheelarch outer trim cover . . .

7.3b . . . then push the bumper down and withdraw the headlight unit . . .

7.3c . . . disconnecting the wiring connectors as they become accessible

7.4 Where fitted, remove the headlight beam adjustment motor as described in text

the top of the liner, and unscrew the plastic nut securing the bumper to the vehicle. Discard the nut; a new one should be used on refitting.
2 Open the bonnet, then slacken and remove the bolts securing the radiator grille section of the bumper to the crossmember, and the two bolts securing the headlight to the crossmember **(see illustrations)**.
3 Release the bumper end from the wheelarch outer trim cover, then hold and push down on the bumper end, and manoeuvre the headlight out of position. Disconnect the wiring connectors from rear of the unit as they become accessible, and remove the headlight unit from the vehicle **(see illustrations)**.
4 On models with a headlight beam adjustment system, if necessary, rotate the adjustment motor clockwise to free the motor from the rear of the headlight unit, and pull the motor squarely away to disconnect its

balljoint **(see illustration)**. On refitting, align the motor balljoint with the light unit socket, and clip it into position. Engage the motor assembly with the light, and twist it anti-clockwise to secure it in position.
5 Refitting is a direct reversal of the removal procedure. On completion, check the headlight beam alignment using the information given in Section 8.

Front direction indicator light

6 The front direction indicator lights are integral with the headlight units. Removal and refitting is as described above.

Front direction side repeater light

7 Carefully prise the rear edge of the indicator side repeater light out from the wing, if necessary using a suitable plastic wedge,

taking great care not damage the painted finish of the wing.
8 Withdraw the light unit from the wing, and disconnect its wiring connector. Tie a piece of string to the wiring, to prevent it falling back into the wing.
9 On refitting, connect the wiring connector, and clip the light unit back into position.

Front foglight

10 Release the relevant end of the front bumper from the vehicle, as described above in paragraphs 1 to 3, ignoring the references to the headlight. If necessary, jack up the front of the vehicle and support it on axle stands to improve access to the foglight.
11 Disconnect the wiring connector, then undo the three foglight retaining screws and remove the light unit from the bumper **(see illustrations)**.

7.11a Disconnect the foglight wiring connector . . .

7.11b . . . then undo the three retaining screws (arrowed) . . .

7.11c . . . and remove the light unit from the rear of the bumper

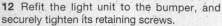

7.13 Foglight aim is adjusted using the adjuster on the rear of the unit

7.16 Rear light unit wiring connector (A) and retaining bolts (B) – Combo Van models

7.18 Removing the rear number plate light unit – Corsa and Corsavan models

12 Refit the light unit to the bumper, and securely tighten its retaining screws.
13 Secure the front bumper in position, and adjust the foglight aim using the adjuster on the rear of the light unit **(see illustration)**.

Rear light cluster

14 From inside the luggage compartment, depress the retaining catches and open up the trim panel flap to gain access to the rear of the light unit.
15 Disconnect the wiring connector from the rear of the bulbholder.
16 Slacken and remove the rear light unit retaining bolts, and withdraw the light unit from the rear of the vehicle **(see illustration)**.
17 Refitting is a reverse of the removal procedure, tightening the retaining bolts securely.

Number plate light

Corsa and Corsavan models

18 Using a small flat-bladed screwdriver, carefully prise the light out from the rear bumper, and disconnect it from the wiring connectors **(see illustration)**.
19 When refitting, connect the wiring connector, and clip the light back into the bumper.

Combo Van models

20 On the left-hand side, lift up the light unit, and prise out the base of the unit from the bumper. On the right-hand side, push the light

unit down, and prise out the top of the unit from the bumper.
21 Withdraw the light unit, and disconnect the wiring connectors **(see illustration)**.
22 When refitting, connect the wiring connectors, and clip the light back into the bumper.

High-level stop-light

23 Open the tailgate or rear doors as applicable.
24 Undo the screw at each end securing the light body to the mounting brackets and withdraw the light unit from its location.
25 Release the wiring harness, disconnect the wiring connector and remove the light unit.
26 Refitting is a reversal of removal.

---

8 Headlight beam alignment –
general information

1 Accurate adjustment of the headlight beam is only possible using optical beam-setting equipment, and this work should therefore be carried out by a Vauxhall/Opel dealer or suitably-equipped workshop.
2 For reference, the headlights can be adjusted using the adjuster assemblies fitted to the top and bottom of each light unit. The top adjuster, accessed through a hole in

the crossmember, alters the horizontal position of the beam. The bottom adjuster alters the vertical aim of the beam **(see illustration)**.
3 Some models have an electrically-operated headlight beam adjustment system, controlled via a switch in the facia. The recommended settings are as follows.

Corsa and Corsavan with rear seats

0 Front seat(s) occupied
1 All seats occupied
2 All seats occupied, and load in luggage compartment
3 Driver's seat occupied and load in the luggage compartment

Combo Van and Corsavan without rear seats

0 Seat(s) occupied
1 Seats occupied and load compartment approximately half-loaded
2 Seats occupied and luggage compartment fully loaded
3 Driver's seat only occupied and luggage compartment fully loaded

Note: *When adjusting the headlight aim, ensure that the switch is set to position 0.*

---

9 Instrument panel –
removal and refitting

Removal

1 Disconnect the battery negative terminal (refer to *Disconnecting the battery* in the Reference Chapter).
2 With the steering wheel in the straight-ahead position, turn the wheel 90° to the left, then prise off the trim cap and remove the left upper shroud screw. Turn the wheel 180° to the right, and remove the right upper screw. Remove the rubber seal from the ignition switch/lock, then undo the lower retaining screws and remove the steering column shrouds.
3 Undo the three retaining screws, and remove the instrument panel shroud from the

7.21 Removing a rear number plate light unit – Combo Van models

8.2 Adjusting the headlight horizontal beam using a suitable screwdriver (vertical beam adjuster arrowed)

9.3a Undo the three instrument panel shroud retaining screws (shown with steering wheel removed for clarity) . . .

9.3b . . . and manoeuvre the shroud out of position

9.5 Undo the panel retaining screws (A), then release the clip (B) . . .

facia **(see illustrations)**. Recover the two shroud retaining clips.

4 On early models with a cable-driven mechanical speedometer, unscrew the speedometer cable lower end from the transmission unit. If necessary, remove the battery, then jack up the front of the vehicle and support it on axle stands to improve access to the cable.

5 Unscrew the two retaining screws from the base of the instrument panel **(see illustration)**.

6 Using a small flat-bladed screwdriver, depress the panel upper retaining clip, and withdraw the panel from the facia. The wiring connector disconnects automatically as the panel is removed **(see illustration)**.

7 Depress the retaining clip, disconnect the

speedometer cable (where applicable), and remove the instrument panel from the vehicle.

Refitting

8 Where applicable, connect the speedometer cable to the rear of the panel, making sure it is securely retained by the clip, and connect the panel wiring connectors.

9 Clip the panel back into position, aligning it with its wiring connector, and secure it in position with the two retaining screws.

10 Refit the instrument panel shroud, and securely tighten its retaining screws.

11 Install the upper and lower steering column shrouds, and securely tighten all the retaining screws. Fit the rubber seal to the ignition switch/lock and the trim caps to the upper screws.

12 Connect the lower end of the speedometer cable to the transmission, and tighten it securely.

13 Reconnect the battery, and check the operation of the panel warning lights to ensure that they are functioning correctly.

10 Instrument panel components – removal and refitting

General

1 Remove the instrument panel as described in Section 9, then proceed as described under the relevant sub-heading.

Speedometer

2 Remove the reset pin for the trip odometer, then carefully release the retaining clips and remove the lens from the front of the instrument panel **(see illustrations)**.

3 Carefully detach the printed circuit from the speedometer housing **(see illustration)**.

4 Undo the retaining screws, and remove the speedometer from the rear of the instrument panel **(see illustration)**.

5 Refitting is a reverse of the removal procedure. Do not overtighten the instrument panel fasteners, as the plastic is easily cracked.

9.6 . . . and withdraw the instrument panel from the facia

10.2a Pull out the trip odometer reset pin . . .

10.4 Instrument panel components (high-specification panel with tachometer)

A Speedometer retaining screws
B Temperature gauge nuts
C Fuel gauge nuts
D Voltage stabiliser

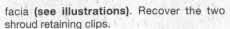

10.2b . . . then release the retaining clips and remove the lens from the front of the instrument panel

10.3 Carefully detach the printed circuit from the top of the speedometer housing

10.15 Undo the retaining screw (arrowed) and disconnect the voltage stabiliser from the rear of the instrument panel

Tachometer

6 Remove the lens from the panel as described in paragraph 2.

7 Undo the retaining screws, and lift the tachometer out from the panel assembly.

8 When refitting, ensure that the tachometer pins are correctly aligned with the panel housing, then refit the retaining screws. Do not overtighten the screws, as the plastic is easily cracked. Clip the lens back onto the panel, and refit the trip odometer reset pin.

Temperature gauge

9 Remove the lens from the panel as described in paragraph 2.

10 Undo the retaining nuts securing the wiring to the temperature gauge terminals, and lift the gauge out from the panel (see illustration 10.4).

11 Refitting is the reverse of removal. Do not overtighten the retaining nuts, as the plastic is easily cracked.

Fuel gauge

12 Remove the lens from the panel as described in paragraph 2.

13 Undo the retaining nuts securing the wiring to the fuel gauge terminals, and lift the gauge out from the panel (see illustration 10.4).

14 Refitting is the reverse of removal. Do not overtighten the retaining nuts, as the plastic is easily cracked.

Voltage stabiliser

15 Undo the retaining screw, then carefully pull the stabiliser from the instrument panel wiring pins (see illustration).

16 When refitting, ease the stabiliser onto the pins, and secure it in position with the retaining screw.

Printed circuit

17 Remove all the instruments and the voltage stabiliser as described above.

18 Remove all the bulbholders from the rear of the case by twisting them in an anti-clockwise direction. Release the printed circuit from its retaining pins, and remove it from the rear of the case.

19 Refitting is a reversal of the removal procedure, ensuring that the printed circuit is correctly located on all the necessary retaining pins.

11 Clock/multi-function display components – removal and refitting

1 The clock/multi-function display unit is fitted to the centre of the facia. The display panel shows the time; on higher-specification models, it also shows the outside air temperature and/or the radio station.

Clock/multi-function display unit

Removal

2 Disconnect the battery negative terminal (refer to *Disconnecting the battery* in the Reference Chapter).

3 Remove both the centre heater/ventilation vents from the facia, as described in Chapter 3.

4 Undo the two retaining screws located in the vent apertures, then withdraw the clock/multi-function display from the facia (see illustrations).

5 Disconnect the wiring connector, and remove the unit from the vehicle (see illustration).

Refitting

6 Reconnect the wiring connector, then manoeuvre the unit back into position.

7 Securely tighten the screws, and install the vents as described in Chapter 3.

8 Reconnect the battery negative terminal, then reset the clock and enter the radio security code.

Air temperature sensor

Removal

9 The multi-function unit air temperature sensor is mounted in the front of the vehicle, directly behind the centre of the bumper. The sensor is accessible through the bumper grille.

10 Depress the retaining clips, then free the sensor from the rear of its bracket. Disconnect the sensor from its wiring connector, and remove it from the vehicle.

Refitting

11 Connect the sensor to the wiring connector, and clip it back into position in the bumper.

12 'Lights-on' warning system – general information

1 Most vehicles covered in this manual are equipped with a 'lights-on' warning system. The purpose of the system is to warn the driver that the lights have been left on. Once the ignition switch has been turned off; the buzzer will sound when a door is opened. The system consists of a buzzer unit which is linked to the driver's door courtesy light switch.

2 To gain access to the buzzer unit, unclip the fusebox access panel from the facia, then undo the two retaining screws and lower the fusebox out from the facia. The buzzer is the third unit from the left in the lower row of relays. The unit is a push-fit in the fusebox.

3 Refer to Section 4 for information on courtesy light switch removal.

13 Cigarette lighter – removal and refitting

Removal

1 Open the ashtray, and remove the cigarette lighter insert.

2 Undo the retaining screws, and withdraw the ashtray from the centre of the facia.

11.4a Undo the two retaining screws (arrowed) . . .

11.4b . . . then lift the multi-function display away from the facia . . .

11.5 . . . and disconnect its wiring connector

14.2 Horn unit is retained by a single bolt (arrowed)

Disconnect the wiring connectors from the rear of the unit as they become accessible.
3 Release the retaining tangs and push out the metal insert, then remove the plastic outer section of the lighter.

Refitting

4 Refitting is a reversal of the removal procedure.

14 Horn – removal and refitting

Removal

1 Remove the front bumper as described in Chapter 11.
2 Undo the retaining bolt and remove the horn, disconnecting its wiring connectors as they become accessible (**see illustration**).

Refitting

3 Refitting is the reverse of removal.

15 Speedometer drive cable – removal and refitting

Removal

Note: *The following procedure is only applicable to early models with a mechanical speedometer. An electric speedometer is fitted to later models and is operated by the vehicle speed sensor on the gearbox/transmission.*

16.3 Lift the nut cover, then undo the retaining nut and lift off the wiper arm

1 Remove the instrument panel as described in Section 9. Tie a piece string to the upper end of the cable; this can then be used to draw the cable back into position.
2 Free the speedometer cable from any relevant retaining clips and ties, noting its correct routing.
3 Release the cable grommet from the engine compartment bulkhead, and withdraw the cable forwards and out through the bulkhead. Once the cable is free, untie the string and leave it in position in the vehicle; the string can then be used to draw the new cable back into position.

Refitting

4 Tie the string to the end of the cable, then use the string to draw the speedometer cable through from the engine compartment and into position. Once the cable is through, untie the string.
5 Ensure that the cable is correctly routed, and retained by all the relevant clips and ties, then seat the outer cable grommet in the engine compartment bulkhead.
6 Refit the instrument panel as described in Section 9.

16 Wiper arm – removal and refitting

Removal

1 Operate the wiper motor, then switch it off so that the wiper arm returns to the at-rest (parked) position.

 HAYNES HiNT *Stick a piece of masking tape along the edge of the wiper blade, to use as an alignment aid on refitting.*

2 Lift up the wiper arm spindle nut cover, then slacken and remove the spindle nut.
3 Lift the blade off the glass, and pull the wiper arm off its spindle (**see illustration**). If necessary, the arm can be levered off the spindle using a suitable flat-bladed screwdriver.
Note: *If both windscreen wiper arms are to be removed at the same time, mark them for identification. The arms are not interchangeable; the passenger-side wiper arm is longer than the driver's-side arm, and its shaft is also cranked slightly.*

Refitting

4 Ensure that the wiper arm and spindle splines are clean and dry, then refit the arm to the spindle, aligning the wiper blade with the tape fitted on removal. Refit the spindle nut, tightening it securely, and clip the nut cover back in position.

17 Windscreen wiper motor and linkage – removal and refitting

Removal

1 Disconnect the battery negative terminal (refer to *Disconnecting the battery* in the Reference Chapter).
2 Remove the wiper arms as described in the previous Section.
3 Undo the retaining screws, and remove both halves of the windscreen cowl panel from the vehicle (**see illustration**).
4 Peel the bonnet seal off the engine compartment bulkhead, and remove it from the vehicle.
5 Unscrew the large plastic nut from each wiper spindle (**see illustration**).
6 Prise out the two clips from the centre of the water deflector shield. Release the shield from the engine compartment bulkhead and wiper spindles, and remove it from the vehicle (**see illustrations**).

17.3 Removing the right-hand windscreen cowl panel

17.5 Unscrew the large plastic nut from each wiper spindle . . .

17.6a . . . then prise out the two clips . . .

17.6b . . . and remove the water deflector shield from the vehicle

17.7a Disconnect the wiring connector . . .

17.7b . . . then undo the three retaining bolts (arrowed) . . .

7 Disconnect the wiring connector from the wiper motor. Undo the three retaining bolts, and remove the wiper motor and linkage assembly out from the vehicle (see illustrations).

8 If necessary, mark the relative positions of the motor shaft and linkage arm, then unscrew the retaining nut from the motor spindle. Free the wiper linkage from the spindle, then remove the three motor retaining bolts, and separate the motor and linkage (see illustration). Note: *It is not necessary to remove the linkage assembly from the vehicle to remove the motor.*

Refitting

9 Where necessary, assemble the motor and linkage, and securely tighten the motor retaining bolts. Locate the linkage arm on the

motor spindle, aligning the marks made prior to removal, and securely tighten its retaining nut.

10 Manoeuvre the motor assembly back into position in the vehicle. Refit the three retaining bolts, and tighten them to the specified torque setting.

11 Reconnect the wiper motor wiring connector.

12 Refit the water deflector, making sure it is correctly located on the bulkhead and wiper spindles, and secure it in position with the two clips and wiper spindle nuts.

13 Install both halves of the windscreen cowl, and securely tighten the retaining screws.

14 Refit the bonnet seal to the engine compartment bulkhead.

15 Install both the wiper arms as described in Section 16, and reconnect the battery negative terminal.

18 Tailgate wiper motor – removal and refitting

Removal

1 Remove the wiper arm as described in Section 16.

2 Remove the plastic cover from the wiper spindle, then unscrew the retaining nut, and lift the washer and outer mounting rubber off the spindle (see illustrations).

3 Open the tailgate, and detach the parcel shelf cords. Undo the retaining screws, and remove the lifter hooks from the tailgate (see illustration).

4 Carefully prise out the retaining clips, and remove the inner trim panel from the tailgate.

17.7c . . . and remove the wiper motor and linkage assembly from the vehicle (right-hand drive model)

17.8 Windscreen wiper motor spindle nut (A) and retaining bolts (B)

18.2a Remove the plastic cover from the tailgate wiper motor spindle . . .

18.2b . . . then undo the retaining nut . . .

18.2c . . . and lift off the washer and outer mounting rubber (arrowed)

18.3 Undo the retaining screws, and remove the parcel shelf lifter cords from the tailgate

18.6a Undo the wiper motor mounting bolts, noting the correct fitted positions of the earth leads (arrowed)

18.6b Remove the wiper motor from the tailgate, and slide off the inner mounting rubber

19.2 Undo the retaining nut (arrowed) . . .

5 Disconnect the wiper motor wiring connector, and release the wiring from any relevant retaining clips.

6 Slacken and remove the wiper motor mounting bolts, noting the correct fitted location of the earth leads, and remove the wiper motor. Recover the collars from either side of each motor mounting rubber, and slide the inner mounting rubber off the motor spindle **(see illustrations)**.

7 Examine the motor mounting rubbers for signs of damage or deterioration, and renew as necessary.

Refitting

8 Slide the inner mounting rubber onto the motor spindle, and ensure that the rubbers are correctly fitted to the motor mountings.

9 Position a collar on each side of the motor mounting rubbers, and refit the motor to the tailgate. Fit the mounting bolts, not forgetting to fit the earth leads to the bolts, and tighten them securely.

10 Reconnect the wiper motor wiring connector.

11 Refit the trim panel to the tailgate, ensuring that it is securely retained by all of its clips. Install the lifter cords.

12 Slide the outer mounting rubber and washer onto the wiper spindle, then fit the retaining nut. Securely tighten the retaining nut, and refit the plastic cover.

13 Refit the wiper arm as described in Section 16.

19 Windscreen/tailgate washer system components – removal and refitting

Washer system reservoir

1 Remove the windscreen cowl panels as described in paragraphs 1 to 4 of Section 17.

2 Unscrew the fluid reservoir retaining nut **(see illustration)**, then release the reservoir from its retaining bracket.

3 Disconnect the wiring connector from the washer pump, then disconnect the hose(s) from the base of the pump and remove the reservoir from the vehicle **(see illustrations)**. Wash off any spilt fluid with cold water.

4 Refitting is the reverse of removal, ensuring that the washer hose(s) are securely connected.

Washer pump

5 Remove the washer reservoir as described above.

6 Tip out the contents of the reservoir, then carefully ease the pump out from the reservoir and recover its sealing grommet **(see illustration)**.

7 Refitting is the reverse of removal, using a new sealing grommet if the original one shows signs of damage or deterioration.

Windscreen washer jets

8 Carefully prise the nozzle from the bonnet,

taking great care not to damage the paintwork.

9 Disconnect the nozzle from its fluid hose, and remove it from the vehicle. Tie a piece of string to the hose, to prevent it falling back into the bonnet.

10 On refitting, securely connect the nozzle to the hose, and clip it into position in the bonnet. Check the operation of the jet. If necessary, adjust the nozzle using a pin, aiming the spray to a point slightly above the centre of the swept area.

Tailgate washer jet

11 Carefully prise the washer jet out of the top of the tailgate/spoiler (as applicable), and disconnect it from its supply pipe. Whilst the jet is removed, tie a piece of string to the supply pipe, to ensure that it does not fall back into the tailgate.

12 When refitting, ensure that the jet is clipped securely in position. Check the operation of the jet. If necessary, adjust the nozzle using a pin, aiming the spray to a point slightly above the centre of the swept area.

20 Headlight washer system components – removal and refitting

Washer system reservoir

1 Firmly apply the handbrake, then jack up

19.3a . . . disconnect the washer pump wiring connector . . .

19.3b . . . then lift out the washer reservoir, and disconnect hoses from the pump

19.6 Ease the pump out of the reservoir, and recover the sealing grommet (arrowed)

21.4 Removing the radio/cassette player using the special DIN tools

22.2a Unclip the small (treble) loudspeaker from the door panel . . .

22.2b . . . and disconnect its wiring connector

the front of the car and support it securely on axle stands (see *Jacking and vehicle support*). Remove the left-hand front roadwheel, making alignment marks between the wheel and hub.

2 Undo the retaining nuts and screws, then release the retaining fasteners and remove the left-hand wheelarch liner (see Chapter 11, Section 22). Discard the nuts and fasteners; new ones should be used on refitting.

3 Remove the front bumper as described in Chapter 11.

4 Slacken and remove the retaining bolts, then lower the reservoir out from underneath the wing to gain access to the washer pump.

5 Slacken the retaining clip, and disconnect the hose from the washer pump. Disconnect the pump wiring connector, and remove the reservoir from the vehicle.

6 Refitting is the reverse of removal.

Washer pump

7 Remove the washer reservoir as described above.

8 Tip out the contents of the reservoir, then carefully ease the pump out from the reservoir and recover its sealing grommet.

9 Refitting is the reverse of removal. Use a new sealing grommet if the original one shows signs of damage or deterioration.

Washer nozzles

10 Remove the front bumper as described in Chapter 11.

11 Undo the two retaining bolts, and remove the nozzle from the bumper.

12 On refitting, securely tighten the retaining bolts and refit the bumper as described in Chapter 11.

21 Radio/cassette player – removal and refitting

Note: *The following removal and refitting procedure is for the range of radio/cassette units which Vauxhall/Opel fit as standard equipment. Removal and refitting procedures of non-standard units may differ slightly.*

Removal

1 All the radio/cassette players fitted by Vauxhall/Opel have DIN standard fixings. Two special tools, obtainable from most car accessory shops, are required for removal. Alternatively, suitable tools can be fabricated from 3 mm diameter wire, such as welding rod.

2 Disconnect the battery negative terminal (refer to *Disconnecting the battery* in the Reference Chapter).

3 Unscrew the four grub screws from the corners of the radio/cassette player, using a suitable Allen key.

4 Insert the tools into the holes exposed by removal of the grub screws, and push them until they snap into place. The radio/cassette

player can then be slid out of the facia **(see illustration)**.

Refitting

5 To refit the radio/cassette player, simply push the unit into the facia until the retaining lugs snap into place, then refit the grub screws. On completion, reconnect the battery and enter the radio security code, where applicable.

22 Speakers – removal and refitting

Front small (treble) speaker

1 Lift the front door inner handle, and carefully prise the handle trim cover out from the door trim panel.

2 Unclip the speaker from the handle, disconnecting its wiring connectors as they become accessible **(see illustrations)**.

3 Refitting is the reverse of removal.

Front large (bass) speaker

4 Undo the retaining screws, and free the door pocket from the inner trim panel, disconnecting the window switch wiring connector(s) (where applicable) as they become accessible.

5 Undo the retaining screws, then free the speaker from the door. Disconnect the wiring connectors and remove the speaker **(see illustrations)**.

6 Refitting is the reverse of removal.

Rear speaker

7 Remove the rear parcel shelf. If the left speaker is to be removed, remove the interior light unit from the trim panel as described in Section 6.

8 Remove the rear shock absorber access panel from the trim panel.

9 Prise out the retaining clips from the rear of the panel, and the circular plug/seat stop buffer (as applicable) from the front of the panel. Slacken and remove all the panel retaining screws, and release the panel from the vehicle body. Disconnect the

22.5a Undo the three retaining screws (arrowed) . . .

22.5b . . . then withdraw the large (bass) loudspeaker from the door, and disconnect its wiring connector

22.9a Release the luggage compartment trim panel from the vehicle . . .

22.9b . . . then turn it around and disconnect the wiring connector from the rear loudspeaker

22.10 Undo the three retaining screws, and remove the speaker from the trim panel

speaker wiring connector, and turn the panel around to gain access to the speaker (**see illustrations**). Note that it is not necessary to detach the seat belt unless the trim panel is to be removed.

10 Undo the three retaining screws, and remove the speaker from the trim panel (**see illustration**).

11 Refitting is a reverse of the removal procedure. Make sure that the trim panel is securely retained by all the relevant clips and screws. If the left trim panel is being installed, do not forget to feed the interior light wiring through the trim panel aperture before fastening the panel in position.

23 Radio aerial – removal and refitting

Corsa and Corsavan

Removal

1 Open the tailgate, then prise out the trim clips and release the rear of the headlining from the roof. Carefully peel the headlining back until access is gained to the aerial retaining nut and wiring connectors.

2 Disconnect both wiring connectors, then undo the retaining nut and remove the aerial from the roof.

Refitting

3 Locate the aerial in roof hole and refit its retaining nut, tightening it securely. Reconnect the wiring connectors, then clip the headlining back into position

Combo Van

Removal

4 Firmly apply the handbrake, then jack up the front of the car and support it securely on axle stands (see *Jacking and vehicle support*). Remove the left-hand front roadwheel.

5 Undo the retaining nuts and screws, then release the retaining fasteners and remove the left-hand wheelarch liner (refer to Chapter 11, Section 22). Discard the nuts and fasteners; new ones should be used when refitting.

6 From inside the vehicle, release the retaining clips and remove the trim panel from the left-hand front footwell.

7 Reach up behind the facia, and disconnect the aerial lead from the rear of the radio/cassette player. Work back along the aerial lead, releasing it from the all the relevant retaining clips and ties, noting how the lead is routed. If necessary, to improve access, remove the storage compartment from underneath the facia; the compartment is retained by a single screw and retaining clip.

8 From underneath the wing, release the grommet and withdraw the aerial lead. Unscrew the aerial nut, remove the washer and rubber, then release the aerial from its lower retaining clip. Remove the aerial and lead from underneath the wing.

Refitting

9 Insert the aerial from underneath the wing, and clip it into position. Fit the rubber and washer onto the aerial, and securely tighten the retaining nut.

10 Pass the aerial lead through into the vehicle, and seat the rubber grommet in the vehicle body.

11 From inside the vehicle, ensure that the lead is correctly routed, and secure it in position with all the necessary clips and ties. Reconnect the lead to the rear of the radio/cassette player. Where necessary, refit the storage compartment.

12 Refit the footwell trim panel, making sure that it is securely retained by its clips.

13 Install the wheelarch liner, securing it in position with new nuts and clips.

14 Refit the roadwheel, then lower the vehicle to the ground and tighten the roadwheel bolts to the specified torque.

24 Anti-theft alarm system – general information

Note: *This information is applicable only to the anti-theft alarm system fitted by Vauxhall/Opel as standard equipment.*

1 Some models in the range are fitted with an anti-theft alarm system as standard equipment. The alarm is automatically armed and disarmed when the deadlocks are locked and unlocked using the driver's door lock. The alarm has switches on all the doors (including the tailgate), the bonnet, the radio/cassette player and the ignition and starter circuits. If the tailgate, bonnet or any of the doors are opened whilst the alarm is set, the alarm horn will sound and the hazard warning lights will flash. The alarm also has an immobiliser function which makes the ignition and starter circuits inoperable whilst the alarm is triggered.

2 The alarm system performs a self-test every time it is switched on; this test takes approximately 10 seconds. During the self-test, the LED (light emitting diode) in the hazard warning light switch will come on. If the LED flashes, then either the tailgate, bonnet or one of the doors is open, or there is a fault in the circuit. After the initial 10-second period, the LED will flash to indicate that the alarm is switched on. On unlocking the driver's door lock, the LED will illuminate for approximately 1 second, then go out, indicating that the alarm has been switched off.

3 With the alarm set, if the tailgate is unlocked, the tailgate switch sensing will automatically be switched off, but the door and bonnet switches will still be active. Once the tailgate is shut and locked again, the tailgate switch sensing will be switched back on after approximately 10 seconds.

4 Should the alarm system develop a fault, the vehicle should be taken to a Vauxhall/Opel dealer for examination.

25 Heated front seat components – removal and refitting

Heater mats

1 On models with heated front seats, a heater mat is fitted to the both the seat back and seat cushion. Renewal of either heater mat involves peeling back the upholstery, removing the old mat, sticking the new mat in position and then refitting the upholstery.

Note that upholstery removal and refitting requires considerable skill and experience if it is to be carried out successfully, and is therefore best entrusted to your Vauxhall/Opel dealer. In practice, it will be very difficult for the home mechanic to carry out the job without ruining the upholstery.

Heated seat switches

2 Refer to Section 4.

26 Air bag system – general information and precautions

General information

A driver's air bag is fitted as standard equipment on certain models, and is an option on all other models. The air bag is fitted in the steering wheel centre pad. Additionally, a passenger's air bag located in the facia, and side air bags located in the front seats are also optionally available.

The system is armed only when the ignition is switched on, however, a reserve power source maintains a power supply to the system in the event of a break in the main electrical supply. The steering wheel and facia air bags are activated by a 'g' sensor (deceleration sensor), and controlled by an electronic control unit located under the centre console. The side air bags are activated by severe side impact and operate independently of the main system and of each other. A separate electrical supply, control unit and sensor is provided for each side air bag.

The air bags are inflated by a gas generator, which forces the bag out from its location in the steering wheel, facia or seat back frame.

Precautions

Warning: The following precautions must be observed when working on vehicles equipped with an air bag system, to prevent the possibility of personal injury.

General precautions

The following precautions **must** be observed when carrying out work on a vehicle equipped with an air bag:

a) *Do not disconnect the battery with the engine running.*
b) *Before carrying out any work in the vicinity of the air bag, removal of any of the air bag components, or any welding work on the vehicle, de-activate the system as described in the following sub-Section.*
c) *Do not attempt to test any of the air bag system circuits using test meters or any other test equipment.*
d) *If the air bag warning light comes on, or any fault in the system is suspected,*

consult a Vauxhall/Opel dealer without delay. **Do not** attempt to carry out fault diagnosis, or any dismantling of the components.

Precautions to be taken when handling an air bag

a) *Transport the air bag by itself, bag upward.*
b) *Do not put your arms around the air bag.*
c) *Carry the air bag close to the body, bag outward.*
d) *Do not drop the air bag or expose it to impacts.*
e) *Do not attempt to dismantle the air bag unit.*
f) *Do not connect any form of electrical equipment to any part of the air bag circuit.*

Precautions to be taken when storing an air bag unit

a) *Store the unit in a cupboard with the air bag upward.*
b) *Do not expose the air bag to temperatures above 80°C.*
c) *Do not expose the air bag to flames.*
d) *Do not attempt to dispose of the air bag – consult a Vauxhall/Opel dealer.*
e) *Never refit an air bag which is known to be faulty or damaged.*

De-activation of air bag system

The system must be de-activated before carrying out any work on the air bag components or surrounding area:

a) *Switch on the ignition and check the operation of the air bag warning light on the instrument panel. The light should illuminate when the ignition is switched on, then extinguish.*
b) *Switch off the ignition.*
c) *Remove the ignition key.*
d) *Switch off all electrical equipment.*
e) *Disconnect the battery negative terminal (refer to 'Disconnecting the battery' in the Reference Section of this manual).*
f) *Insulate the battery negative terminal and the end of the battery negative lead to prevent any possibility of contact.*
g) *Wait for at least two minutes before carrying out any further work. Wait at least ten minutes if the air bag warning light did not operate correctly.*

Activation of air bag system

To activate the system on completion of any work, proceed as follows:

a) *Ensure that there are no occupants in the vehicle, and that there are no loose objects around the vicinity of the steering wheel. Close the vehicle doors and windows.*
b) *Ensure that the ignition is switched off then reconnect the battery negative terminal.*
c) *Open the driver's door and switch on the ignition, without reaching in front of the steering wheel. Check that the air bag*

warning light illuminates briefly then extinguishes.
d) *Switch off the ignition.*
e) *If the air bag warning light does not operate as described in paragraph c), consult a Vauxhall/Opel dealer before driving the vehicle.*

27 Air bag system components – removal and refitting

Warning: Refer to the precautions given in Section 26 before attempting to carry out work on any of the air bag components.

1 De-activate the air bag system as described in the previous Section, then proceed as described under the relevant heading.

Driver's air bag

2 With the steering wheel in the straight-ahead position, turn the wheel 90° to the left, then prise off the trim cap and remove the left upper shroud screw. Turn the wheel 180° to the right, and remove the right upper screw. Remove the rubber seal from the ignition switch/lock, then undo the lower retaining screws and remove the steering column shrouds.

3 With the steering wheel positioned in the straight-ahead position, turn the wheel 90° to the right to gain access to the left-hand air bag retaining bolt. Unscrew the bolt from the rear of the steering wheel, then turn the wheel 180° to the left to gain access to the right-hand air bag retaining bolt. Unscrew the right-hand retaining bolt, then return the steering wheel to the straight-ahead position.

4 Carefully lift the air bag assembly away from the steering wheel, and disconnect the wiring connector from the rear of the unit. Note that the air bag must not be knocked or dropped, and should be stored the correct way up, with its padded surface uppermost.

5 Refitting is a reversal of the removal procedure. Tighten the air bag retaining screws to the specified torque setting.

Passenger's air bag

6 Remove the battery as described in Chapter 5A.

7 Remove the glovebox as described in Chapter 11, Section 26.

8 Remove the heater/ventilation vent and duct on the passenger's side as described in Chapter 3.

9 Remove the windscreen cowl panel and the water deflector shield as described in Section 17 of this Chapter.

10 From the engine compartment side, undo the nuts securing the air bag mounting brackets, and facia panel fastening to the bulkhead.

11 Unscrew the facia panel attachments on the passenger's side.

12 Disconnect the air bag wiring plug from the side of the unit.

13 Undo the nuts securing the air bag to the mounting brackets, Ease the facia away from the bulkhead as necessary and remove the air bag from the mounting brackets. Note that the air bag must not be knocked or dropped, and should be stored the correct way up (as mounted in the vehicle).

14 Refitting is a reversal of the removal procedure. Tighten the air bag retaining nuts to the specified torque setting.

Side air bags

15 The side air bags are located internally within the front seat back and no attempt should be made to remove them. Any suspected problems with the side air bag system should be referred to a Vauxhall/Opel dealer.

Air bag control unit

16 Remove the centre console as described in Chapter 11.

17 Disconnect the control unit wiring connector, then undo the retaining screws and remove the control unit from the vehicle.

18 Refitting is the reverse of removal. If a new control unit is being installed, the vehicle must be taken to a Vauxhall/Opel dealer for the control unit to be reprogrammed at the earliest possible opportunity. **Note:** *The air bag system will not be operational until the new control unit is reprogrammed; this will be indicated by the warning light in the instrument panel being illuminated.*

Air bag wiring contact unit

19 The wiring contact unit is fitted to the underside of the steering wheel, and provides the electrical supply to both the air bag and horn buttons. The unit is removed and refitted with the steering wheel (see Chapter 10).

Vauxhall Corsa 1997 to 2000 wiring diagrams

Diagram 1

Key to symbols

Bulb	⊗
Switch	
Multiple contact switch (ganged)	
Fuse/fusible link and current rating	F5 30A
Resistor	
Variable resistor	
Connecting wires	
Plug and socket contact	
Item no.	2
Pump/motor	M
Earth point and location	E22
Gauge/meter	
Diode	
Wire splice or soldered joint	
Solenoid actuator	
Light emitting diode (LED)	
Wire colour (brown with black tracer)	Br/Sw
Screened cable	

Dashed outline denotes part of a larger item, containing in this case an electronic or solid state device.
6 - unspecified connector pin 6.
T14/9 - 14 pin connector, pin 9.

Earth locations

E1	Right bulkhead
E2	Left bulkhead
E3	Tunnel
E4	Left engine earth
E5	Right engine earth
E6	Body rear
E7	Steering column

Relays

Relay	Location
Air conditioning	Behind right-hand footwell trim panel
Air conditioning cooling fan	Behind right-hand footwell trim panel
Air conditioning compressor relay	Engine compartment junction box
Anti-theft alarm horn	Fusebox
Anti-theft alarm immobiliser	Fusebox
Cooling fan	Behind right-hand footwell trim panel
Cooling fan	Relay carrier above glovebox
Cooling fan	Relay carrier above glovebox
Cooling fan high speed	Relay carrier above glovebox
Daytime driving light	Behind fusebox
Exterior mirror heating	Fusebox
Front foglight	Fusebox
Fuel pump	Behind right-hand footwell trim panel
Headlight washer pump	Fusebox
Heated rear screen	Fusebox
'Lights-on' buzzer	Fusebox
Rear foglight	Fusebox
Tailgate wiper	Fusebox
Turn signal	Fusebox
Windscreen wiper	Fusebox

Fuses

Fuse	Rating	Circuit protected
F1	20A	Direction indicators, diagnostic connector, interior lights, horn, triple info display and radio
F2	10A	Automatic transmission
F3	30A	Trunk lamp, heated rear window
F5	10A	Automatic transmission
F6	10A	Rear fog lights
F7	30A	Engine cooling
F8	10A	LH parking/tail light
F9	20A	Front fog lights
F10	10A	LH high beam headlight
F11	30A	Headlight washer
F12	10A	LH low beam headlight
F13	20A	Central locking
F14	50A	Power steering
F15	30A	Air conditioning, heating
F16	30A	Wash/wipe
F17	10A	Electric mirrors, interior lights, electric windows, triple info display, air conditioning, engine cooling, power steering, instrument cluster
F18	20A	Central locking, reversing lights, heated rear window, air conditioning, cigarette lighter, speed sensor, automatic transmission, seat heating
F20	30A	Engine cooling, air conditioning
F21	15A	Stop lights, hazard warning lights, instrument cluster
F22	10A	ABS
F23	10A	RH parking/tail light
F24	15A	Air conditioning
F25	10A	RH high beam headlight
F26	20A	Fuel pump
F27	10A	RH low beam headlight
F28	30A	Electric windows
F49	50A	Secondary air injection

H32293

Wire colours

Bl	Blue	Pu	Purple
Br	Brown	Ro	Red
Ge	Yellow	Sw	Black
Gr	Grey	Vi	Violet
Gn	Green	Ws	White
Or	Orange		

Key to items

1. Battery
2. Ignition switch
3. Main fuse box
4. Alternator
5. Starter motor
6. Aerial amplifier
7. Radio
8. Diagnostic connector
9. Telephone connection
10. LH rear speaker
11. RH rear speaker
12. LH front speaker
13. LH front tweeter
14. RH front tweeter
15. RH front speaker
16. Passenger's airbag
17. Passenger's side airbag
18. Driver's side airbag
19. Passenger's side airbag sensor
20. Airbag module
21. LH seatbelt pretensioner
22. RH seatbelt pretensioner
23. Driver's airbag
24. Airbag contact unit
25. Driver's side airbag sensor

Diagram 2

* Manual only
** Auto only

MTS
H32294

Starting and charging

Typical radio

See diagram 8
Triple info display

See diagram 14
Instrument cluster

See diagram 11
F19

See diagram 15
Automatic transmission

See diagram 8
Triple info display

See diagram 14
Instrument cluster

Airbag system

See diagram 14
Instrument cluster

Wire colours

Bl	Blue	**Pu**	Purple
Br	Brown	**Ro**	Red
Ge	Yellow	**Sw**	Black
Gr	Grey	**Vi**	Violet
Gn	Green	**Ws**	White
Or	Orange		

Key to items

1 Battery
2 Ignition switch
3 Main fuse box
8 Diagnostic connector
26 Motronic control module
27 Ignition coil
28 Spark plugs

29 Fuel injector relay
30 Fuel pump relay
31 Fuel pump
32 Camshaft position sensor
33 Tank vent valve
34 Fuel injector cylinder 1

35 Fuel injector cylinder 2
36 Fuel injector cylinder 3
37 Oxygen sensor
38 EGR solenoid valve
39 Throttle position sensor
40 Coolant temperature sensor
41 Knock sensor

42 Idle speed stepper motor
43 Air mass meter
44 Crankshaft sensor

* Manual only
** Auto only

MTS
H32295

Diagram 3

Engine management system Motronic X10XE engines

Wire colours

Bl Blue
Br Brown
Ge Yellow
Gr Grey
Gn Green
Or Orange
Pu Purple
Ro Red
Sw Black
Vi Violet
Ws White

Key to items

1 Battery
2 Ignition switch
3 Main fuse box
8 Diagnostic connector
26 Motronic control module
27 Ignition coil
28 Spark plugs
29 Fuel injector relay
30 Fuel pump relay
31 Fuel pump
32 Camshaft position sensor
33 Tank vent valve
34 Fuel injector cylinder 1
35 Fuel injector cylinder 2
36 Fuel injector cylinder 3
37 Oxygen sensor
38 EGR solenoid valve
39 Throttle position sensor
40 Coolant temperature sensor
41 Knock sensor
42 Idle speed stepper motor
43 Air mass meter
44 Crankshaft sensor
45 Fuel injector cylinder 4

* Manual only
** Auto only

Diagram 4

MTS
H32296

Engine management system Motronic X12XE engines

Wire colours

Bl Blue   **Pu** Purple
Br Brown   **Ro** Red
Ge Yellow   **Sw** Black
Gr Grey   **Vi** Violet
Gn Green   **Ws** White
Or Orange

Key to items

1 Battery
2 Ignition switch
3 Main fuse box
8 Diagnostic connector
27 Ignition coil
28 Spark plugs

30 Fuel pump relay
31 Fuel pump
33 Tank vent valve
37 Oxygen sensor
38 EGR solenoid valve
39 Throttle position sensor

40 Coolant temperature sensor
41 Knock sensor
44 Crankshaft sensor
46 Multec control module
47 Single point fuel injector
48 Knock signal filter

49 EGR amplifier
50 MAP sensor
51 Idle speed actuator

Diagram 5

MTS
H32297

Engine management system Multec X12SZ engines

Wire colours

Bl	Blue	Pu	Purple
Br	Brown	Ro	Red
Ge	Yellow	Sw	Black
Gr	Grey	Vi	Violet
Gn	Green	Ws	White
Or	Orange		

Key to items

1 Battery
2 Ignition switch
3 Main fuse box
8 Diagnostic connector
27 Ignition coil
28 Spark plugs

30 Fuel pump relay
31 Fuel pump
33 Tank vent valve
37 Oxygen sensor
38 EGR solenoid valve
39 Throttle position sensor

40 Coolant temperature sensor
41 Knock sensor
44 Crankshaft sensor
46 Multec control module
47 Single point fuel injector
50 MAP sensor

51 Idle speed actuator

Diagram 6

MTS
H32298

Engine management system Multec X14SZ engines

Wire colours

Bl	Blue	**Pu**	Purple
Br	Brown	**Ro**	Red
Ge	Yellow	**Sw**	Black
Gr	Grey	**Vi**	Violet
Gn	Green	**Ws**	White
Or	Orange		

Key to items

1 Battery
2 Ignition switch
3 Main fuse box
8 Diagnostic connector
27 Ignition coil
28 Spark plugs
30 Fuel pump relay

31 Fuel pump
32 Camshaft position sensor
33 Tank vent valve
34 Fuel injector cylinder 1
35 Fuel injector cylinder 2
36 Fuel injector cylinder 3
37 Oxygen sensor

38 EGR solenoid valve
39 Throttle position sensor
40 Coolant temperature sensor
41 Knock sensor
44 Crankshaft sensor
45 Fuel injector cylinder 4
46 Multec control module

50 MAP sensor
51 Idle speed actuator
52 Engine fuse box
53 Secondary air injection relay
54 Secondary air injection pump

Diagram 7

MTS
H32299

Engine management system Multec X14XE & X16XE engines

Wire colours

Bl	Blue
Br	Brown
Ge	Yellow
Gr	Grey
Gn	Green
Or	Orange

Pu	Purple
Ro	Red
Sw	Black
Vi	Violet
Ws	White

Key to items

1 Battery
2 Ignition switch
3 Main fuse box
8 Diagnostic connector
55 Driver's window switch
56 Passenger's window switch
57 Drivers window motor

58 Passenger window motor
59 ABS control module
60 Front left wheel sensor
61 Front right wheel sensor
62 Rear left wheel sensor
63 Rear right wheel sensor
64 Speed sensor

65 Fuel solenoid valve
66 Triple info display
67 Outside temperature sensor

Diagram 8

MTS
H32300

Electric windows

ABS

See diagram 14
Instrument cluster

See diagram 12
Stop lights

Vehicle speed sensor

Triple info display

See diagram 14
Instrument cluster

See diagram 2
Radio

See diagram 11
Light switch

See diagram 14
Instrument cluster

Wire colours

Bl	Blue	**Pu**	Purple
Br	Brown	**Ro**	Red
Ge	Yellow	**Sw**	Black
Gr	Grey	**Vi**	Violet
Gn	Green	**Ws**	White
Or	Orange		

Key to items

1 Battery
2 Ignition switch
3 Main fuse box
68 Blower switch
69 Blower motor
70 Air conditioning switch, & temp. lever switch
71 Air conditioning relay
72 Pressure switches
73 Coolant solenoid valve
74 Coolant temp. switch
75 Compressor clutch diode
76 Compressor clutch
77 Air con. compressor relay
78 Power steering pressure switch
79 Revolution acceleration pressure switch
80 Radiator fan test connector
81 Radiator fan
82 Radiator fan relay 1
83 Radiator fan relay 2
84 Radiator fan relay 3
85 Radiator fan relay 4

* X14NZ & X14SZ only

Diagram 9

MTS
H32301

Air conditioning

Engine cooling (air con. only)

Wire colours

Bl	Blue	**Pu**	Purple
Br	Brown	**Ro**	Red
Ge	Yellow	**Sw**	Black
Gr	Grey	**Vi**	Violet
Gn	Green	**Ws**	White
Or	Orange		

Key to items

1 Battery
2 Ignition switch
3 Main fuse box
24 Airbag contact unit
74 Coolant temp. switch
80 Radiator fan test connector
81 Radiator fan
86 Headlight washer relay
87 Headlight washer pump
88 Washer pump
89 Wash/wipe switch
90 Rear window wiper
91 Rear window wiper relay
92 Windscreen wiper
93 Windscreen wiper relay
94 Bridging connector
95 Cigarette lighter
96 Horn
97 Horn relay
98 Horn switch

Diagram 10

* 1999 on only
** Without item 93
***Airbag only

H32302

Wire colours

Bl	Blue	**Pu**	Purple
Br	Brown	**Ro**	Red
Ge	Yellow	**Sw**	Black
Gr	Grey	**Vi**	Violet
Gn	Green	**Ws**	White
Or	Orange		

Key to items

1 Battery
2 Ignition switch
3 Main fuse box
99 Light switch
100 Signal switch
101 Headlight levelling switch
102 LH headlight levelling motor
103 RH headlight levelling motor
104 LH front light cluster
  a) low beam
  b) high beam
  c) parking light
105 RH front light cluster
  as 104
106 LH rear light cluster
  a) tail light
  c) reversing light
  e) fog light
107 RH rear light cluster
  as 106
108 Licence plate light
109 Front fog light switch
110 Front fog light relay
111 Front fog light
112 Rear fog light switch
113 Rear fog light relay
114 Reverse light switch

Diagram 11

MTS
H32503

Exterior lights

Fog lights

Reversing lights

Wire colours

Bl	Blue	Pu	Purple
Br	Brown	Ro	Red
Ge	Yellow	Sw	Black
Gr	Grey	Vi	Violet
Gn	Green	Ws	White
Or	Orange		

Key to items

1 Battery
2 Ignition switch
3 Main fuse box
68 Heated rear window switch
99 Light switch
100 Signal switch
104 LH front light cluster
  d) direction indicator
105 RH front light cluster (as 104)
106 LH rear light cluster
  b) stop light
  d) direction indicator
107 RH rear light cluster (as 106)
115 LH side direction indicator
116 RH side direction indicator
117 Hazard warning switch
118 Direction indicator unit
119 Stop light switch
120 Centre stop light
121 Passenger light
122 Rear reading lights
123 Boot light
124 Boot light switch
125 Warning buzzer
126 LH rear door switch
127 LH front door switch
128 RH rear door switch
129 Drivers door switch
130 Heated rear window relay
131 Heated rear window

Diagram 12

★ Auto only

MTS H32304

Direction indicators

Stop lights

See diagram 14 Instrument cluster

See diagram 8, 15 ABS, Automatic transmission

Interior lights

See diagram 11 Fuse 19

Heated rear window

Wire colours

Bl	Blue	**Pu**	Purple
Br	Brown	**Ro**	Red
Ge	Yellow	**Sw**	Black
Gr	Grey	**Vi**	Violet
Gn	Green	**Ws**	White
Or	Orange		

Key to items

1 Battery
2 Ignition switch
3 Main fuse box
8 Diagnostic connector
132 Heated power mirror relay
133 Heated power mirror switch
134 Drivers power mirror
135 Passenger power mirror
136 Torque sensor
137 Power steering control unit
138 Power steering motor
139 Central locking control unit
140 Front passenger switch
141 Drivers switch
142 Drivers door lock motor
143 Passenger door lock motor
144 RH rear door lock motor
145 LH rear door lock motor
146 Trunk lid lock motor
147 Fuel flap lock motor
148 LH front seat heating switch
149 LH front seat heater
150 RH front seat heating switch
151 RH front seat heater

Diagram 13

MTS
H32305

Wire colours

Bl	Blue	Pu	Purple
Br	Brown	Ro	Red
Ge	Yellow	Sw	Black
Gr	Grey	Vi	Violet
Gn	Green	Ws	White
Or	Orange		

Key to items

1 Battery
2 Ignition switch
3 Main fuse box
152 Instrument cluster
  a) turn signal light
  b) charge warning light
  c) brake warning light
  d) ABS warning light
  e) oil pressure warning light
  f) auto transmission
    power program

152 Instrument cluster cont.
  g) power steering warning light
  h) airbag warning light
  i) engine warning light
  j) low fuel warning light
  k) fuel gauge
  l) coolant temp gauge
  m) speedometer
  n) tachometer
  o) instrument illumination
  p) high beam warning light

152 Instrument cluster cont.
  q) fog light warning light
153 Brake fluid switch
154 Handbrake switch
155 Oil pressure switch
156 Fuel level sensor
157 Coolant temp sensor

★ Airbag only
★★ Without airbag

Diagram 14

MTS
H32306

Wire colours

Bl	Blue	**Pu**	Purple
Br	Brown	**Ro**	Red
Ge	Yellow	**Sw**	Black
Gr	Grey	**Vi**	Violet
Gn	Green	**Ws**	White
Or	Orange		

Key to items

1 Battery
2 Ignition switch
3 Main fuse box
8 Diagnostic connector
158 Automatic transmission control unit
159 Selector lever
160 Ignition key locking magnet

161 Ignition key locking magnet switch
162 Selector lever magnet
163 Selector lever magnet switch
164 Selector lever light
165 Start assistance switch
166 Program switch
167 Kick down switch

168 Valve body assembly
169 Transmission output sensor
170 Transmission input sensor

Diagram 15

* Motronic only
** Multec only
*** X12XE only

MTS
H32307

Automatic transmission

Dimensions and Weights

Note: *All figures are approximate and may vary according to model. Refer to manufacturer's data for exact figures.*

Dimensions

Overall length:
All models except Combo Van	3741 mm
Combo Van models	4231 mm

Overall width:

All models except Combo Van:
Excluding door mirrors	1608 mm
Including door mirrors	1768 mm

Combo Van models:
Excluding door mirrors	1688 mm
Including door mirrors	2060 mm

Dimensions (continued)

Overall height (unladen):

    All models except Combo Van .... 1420 mm

    Combo Van models .... 1840 mm

Wheelbase:

    All models except Combo Van .... 2443 mm

    Combo Van models .... 2480 mm

Front track:

    All models .... 1387 mm

Rear track:

    All except Combo Van models .... 1388 mm

    Combo Van models .... 1427 mm

Weights

Kerb weight:*

    3-door Hatchback:

        1.0 litre models .... 857 to 906 kg

        1.2 litre manual gearbox models .... 835 to 916 kg

        1.2 litre automatic transmission models .... 896 to 995 kg

        1.4 litre manual gearbox models .... 840 to 1057 kg

        1.4 litre automatic transmission models .... 875 to 1048 kg

        1.6 litre models .... 945 to 1021 kg

    5-door Hatchback:

        1.0 litre models .... 887 to 936 kg

        1.2 litre manual gearbox models .... 860 to 946 kg

        1.2 litre automatic transmission models .... 981 to 1025 kg

        1.4 litre manual gearbox models .... 865 to 1043 kg

        1.4 litre automatic transmission models .... 900 to 1078 kg

    Corsavan models .... 940 to 950 kg

    Combo Van models .... 1030 to 1075 kg

Maximum gross vehicle weight:*

    3-door Hatchback:

        1.0 litre models .... 1360 kg

        1.2 litre manual gearbox models .... 1370 kg

        1.2 litre automatic transmission models .... 1405 kg

        1.4 litre manual gearbox models .... 1455 kg

        1.4 litre automatic transmission models .... 1490 kg

        1.6 litre models .... 1465 kg

    5-door Hatchback:

        1.0 litre models .... 1390 kg

        1.2 litre manual gearbox models .... 1340 kg

        1.2 litre automatic transmission models .... 1430 kg

        1.4 litre manual gearbox models .... 1485 kg

        1.4 litre automatic transmission models .... 1520 kg

    Corsavan models:

        1.2 litre models .... 1330 kg

        1.4 litre models .... 1375 kg

    Combo Van models .... 1620 kg

Maximum roof rack load:

    All models .... 100 kg

Maximum towing weights:*

    Braked trailer:

        1.0 and 1.2 litre models .... 500 to 650 kg

        1.4 litre models .... 900 kg

        1.6 litre models .... 1000 kg

    Unbraked trailer:

        1.0 and 1.2 litre models .... 400 kg

        1.4 and 1.6 litre models .... 450 kg

Maximum towing hitch downward load (nose weight):

    All models .... 50 kg

*Depending on model and specification. Refer to the VIN plate or a Vauxhall/Opel dealer for exact recommendations.

Length (distance)

Inches (in)	x 25.4	=	Millimetres (mm)	x 0.0394	= Inches (in)
Feet (ft)	x 0.305	=	Metres (m)	x 3.281	= Feet (ft)
Miles	x 1.609	=	Kilometres (km)	x 0.621	= Miles

Volume (capacity)

Cubic inches (cu in; in³)	x 16.387	=	Cubic centimetres (cc; cm³)	x 0.061	= Cubic inches (cu in; in³)
Imperial pints (Imp pt)	x 0.568	=	Litres (l)	x 1.76	= Imperial pints (Imp pt)
Imperial quarts (Imp qt)	x 1.137	=	Litres (l)	x 0.88	= Imperial quarts (Imp qt)
Imperial quarts (Imp qt)	x 1.201	=	US quarts (US qt)	x 0.833	= Imperial quarts (Imp qt)
US quarts (US qt)	x 0.946	=	Litres (l)	x 1.057	= US quarts (US qt)
Imperial gallons (Imp gal)	x 4.546	=	Litres (l)	x 0.22	= Imperial gallons (Imp gal)
Imperial gallons (Imp gal)	x 1.201	=	US gallons (US gal)	x 0.833	= Imperial gallons (Imp gal)
US gallons (US gal)	x 3.785	=	Litres (l)	x 0.264	= US gallons (US gal)

Mass (weight)

Ounces (oz)	x 28.35	=	Grams (g)	x 0.035	= Ounces (oz)
Pounds (lb)	x 0.454	=	Kilograms (kg)	x 2.205	= Pounds (lb)

Force

Ounces-force (ozf; oz)	x 0.278	=	Newtons (N)	x 3.6	= Ounces-force (ozf; oz)
Pounds-force (lbf; lb)	x 4.448	=	Newtons (N)	x 0.225	= Pounds-force (lbf; lb)
Newtons (N)	x 0.1	=	Kilograms-force (kgf; kg)	x 9.81	= Newtons (N)

Pressure

Pounds-force per square inch (psi; lbf/in²; lb/in²)	x 0.070	=	Kilograms-force per square centimetre (kgf/cm²; kg/cm²)	x 14.223	= Pounds-force per square inch (psi; lbf/in²; lb/in²)
Pounds-force per square inch (psi; lbf/in²; lb/in²)	x 0.068	=	Atmospheres (atm)	x 14.696	= Pounds-force per square inch (psi; lbf/in²; lb/in²)
Pounds-force per square inch (psi; lbf/in²; lb/in²)	x 0.069	=	Bars	x 14.5	= Pounds-force per square inch (psi; lbf/in²; lb/in²)
Pounds-force per square inch (psi; lbf/in²; lb/in²)	x 6.895	=	Kilopascals (kPa)	x 0.145	= Pounds-force per square inch (psi; lbf/in²; lb/in²)
Kilopascals (kPa)	x 0.01	=	Kilograms-force per square centimetre (kgf/cm²; kg/cm²)	x 98.1	= Kilopascals (kPa)
Millibar (mbar)	x 100	=	Pascals (Pa)	x 0.01	= Millibar (mbar)
Millibar (mbar)	x 0.0145	=	Pounds-force per square inch (psi; lbf/in²; lb/in²)	x 68.947	= Millibar (mbar)
Millibar (mbar)	x 0.75	=	Millimetres of mercury (mmHg)	x 1.333	= Millibar (mbar)
Millibar (mbar)	x 0.401	=	Inches of water (inH₂O)	x 2.491	= Millibar (mbar)
Millimetres of mercury (mmHg)	x 0.535	=	Inches of water (inH₂O)	x 1.868	= Millimetres of mercury (mmHg)
Inches of water (inH₂O)	x 0.036	=	Pounds-force per square inch (psi; lbf/in²; lb/in²)	x 27.68	= Inches of water (inH₂O)

Torque (moment of force)

Pounds-force inches (lbf in; lb in)	x 1.152	=	Kilograms-force centimetre (kgf cm; kg cm)	x 0.868	= Pounds-force inches (lbf in; lb in)
Pounds-force inches (lbf in; lb in)	x 0.113	=	Newton metres (Nm)	x 8.85	= Pounds-force inches (lbf in; lb in)
Pounds-force inches (lbf in; lb in)	x 0.083	=	Pounds-force feet (lbf ft; lb ft)	x 12	= Pounds-force inches (lbf in; lb in)
Pounds-force feet (lbf ft; lb ft)	x 0.138	=	Kilograms-force metres (kgf m; kg m)	x 7.233	= Pounds-force feet (lbf ft; lb ft)
Pounds-force feet (lbf ft; lb ft)	x 1.356	=	Newton metres (Nm)	x 0.738	= Pounds-force feet (lbf ft; lb ft)
Newton metres (Nm)	x 0.102	=	Kilograms-force metres (kgf m; kg m)	x 9.804	= Newton metres (Nm)

Power

Horsepower (hp)	x 745.7	=	Watts (W)	x 0.0013	= Horsepower (hp)

Velocity (speed)

Miles per hour (miles/hr; mph)	x 1.609	=	Kilometres per hour (km/hr; kph)	x 0.621	= Miles per hour (miles/hr; mph)

Fuel consumption*

Miles per gallon, Imperial (mpg)	x 0.354	=	Kilometres per litre (km/l)	x 2.825	= Miles per gallon, Imperial (mpg)
Miles per gallon, US (mpg)	x 0.425	=	Kilometres per litre (km/l)	x 2.352	= Miles per gallon, US (mpg)

Temperature

Degrees Fahrenheit = (°C x 1.8) + 32   Degrees Celsius (Degrees Centigrade; °C) = (°F - 32) x 0.56

It is common practice to convert from miles per gallon (mpg) to litres/100 kilometres (l/100km), where mpg x l/100 km = 282

Spare parts are available from many sources, including maker's appointed garages, accessory shops, and motor factors. To be sure of obtaining the correct parts, it will sometimes be necessary to quote the vehicle identification number. If possible, it can also be useful to take the old parts along for positive identification. Items such as starter motors and alternators may be available under a service exchange scheme - any parts returned should be clean.

Our advice regarding spare parts is as follows.

Officially appointed garages

This is the best source of parts which are peculiar to your car, and which are not otherwise generally available (eg, badges, interior trim, certain body panels, etc). It is also the only place at which you should buy parts if the vehicle is still under warranty.

Accessory shops

These are very good places to buy materials and components needed for the maintenance of your car (oil, air and fuel filters, light bulbs, drivebelts, greases, brake pads, touch-up paint, etc). Components of this nature sold by a reputable shop are usually of the same standard as those used by the car manufacturer.

Besides components, these shops also sell tools and general accessories, usually have convenient opening hours, charge lower prices, and can often be found close to home. Some accessory shops have parts counters where components needed for almost any repair job can be purchased or ordered.

Motor factors

Good factors will stock all the more important components which wear out comparatively quickly, and can sometimes supply individual components needed for the overhaul of a larger assembly (eg, brake seals and hydraulic parts, bearing shells, pistons, valves). They may also handle work such as cylinder block reboring, crankshaft regrinding, etc.

Tyre and exhaust specialists

These outlets may be independent, or members of a local or national chain. They frequently offer competitive prices when compared with a main dealer or local garage, but it will pay to obtain several quotes before making a decision. When researching prices, also ask what "extras" may be added - for instance fitting a new valve and balancing the wheel are both commonly charged on top of the price of a new tyre.

Other sources

Beware of parts or materials obtained from market stalls, car boot sales or similar outlets. Such items are not invariably sub-standard, but there is little chance of compensation if they do prove unsatisfactory. in the case of safety-critical components such as brake pads, there is the risk not only of financial loss, but also of an accident causing injury or death.

Second-hand components or assemblies obtained from a car breaker can be a good buy in some circumstances, but this sort of purchase is best made by the experienced DIY mechanic.

Vehicle Identification

Modifications are a continuing and unpublished process in vehicle manufacture, quite apart from major model changes. Spare parts manuals and lists are compiled upon a numerical basis, the individual vehicle numbers being essential to correct identification of the component required.

When ordering spare parts, always give as much information as possible. Quote the car model, year of manufacture and vehicle identification and/or engine numbers as appropriate.

The *vehicle identification plate* is riveted on top of the front body panel and includes the Vehicle Identification Number (VIN), vehicle weight information and paint and trim colour codes.

The *Vehicle Identification Number (VIN)* is given on the vehicle identification plate and is also stamped into the body floor panel between the right-hand front seat and the door sill panel; lift the flap in the carpet to see it.

The engine number is stamped on a horizontal flat located on the exhaust manifold side of the cylinder block, at the distributor end. The first part of the engine number gives the engine code – eg X 12 XE **(see illustration)**. Engine codes are as follows:

1.0 litre DOHC engine	X 10 XE
1.2 litre SOHC engine	X 12 SZ
1.2 litre DOHC engine	X 12 XE
1.4 litre SOHC engine	
multi-point fuel injection	C 14 SE
single-point fuel injection	X 14 SZ
1.4 litre DOHC engine	X 14 XE
1.6 litre DOHC engine	X 16 XE

Vauxhall/Opel use a 'Car pass' scheme for vehicle identification. This is a card which is issued to the customer when the car is first purchased. It contains important information, eg, VIN number, key number and radio code. It also includes a special code for diagnostic equipment, therefore it must be kept in a secure place and not in the vehicle.

Vehicle Identification Number (VIN) plate (1) and engine number (2) locations

Whenever servicing, repair or overhaul work is carried out on the car or its components, observe the following procedures and instructions. This will assist in carrying out the operation efficiently and to a professional standard of workmanship.

Joint mating faces and gaskets

When separating components at their mating faces, never insert screwdrivers or similar implements into the joint between the faces in order to prise them apart. This can cause severe damage which results in oil leaks, coolant leaks, etc upon reassembly. Separation is usually achieved by tapping along the joint with a soft-faced hammer in order to break the seal. However, note that this method may not be suitable where dowels are used for component location.

Where a gasket is used between the mating faces of two components, a new one must be fitted on reassembly; fit it dry unless otherwise stated in the repair procedure. Make sure that the mating faces are clean and dry, with all traces of old gasket removed. When cleaning a joint face, use a tool which is unlikely to score or damage the face, and remove any burrs or nicks with an oilstone or fine file.

Make sure that tapped holes are cleaned with a pipe cleaner, and keep them free of jointing compound, if this is being used, unless specifically instructed otherwise.

Ensure that all orifices, channels or pipes are clear, and blow through them, preferably using compressed air.

Oil seals

Oil seals can be removed by levering them out with a wide flat-bladed screwdriver or similar implement. Alternatively, a number of self-tapping screws may be screwed into the seal, and these used as a purchase for pliers or some similar device in order to pull the seal free.

Whenever an oil seal is removed from its working location, either individually or as part of an assembly, it should be renewed.

The very fine sealing lip of the seal is easily damaged, and will not seal if the surface it contacts is not completely clean and free from scratches, nicks or grooves. If the original sealing surface of the component cannot be restored, and the manufacturer has not made provision for slight relocation of the seal relative to the sealing surface, the component should be renewed.

Protect the lips of the seal from any surface which may damage them in the course of fitting. Use tape or a conical sleeve where possible. Lubricate the seal lips with oil before fitting and, on dual-lipped seals, fill the space between the lips with grease.

Unless otherwise stated, oil seals must be fitted with their sealing lips toward the lubricant to be sealed.

Use a tubular drift or block of wood of the appropriate size to install the seal and, if the seal housing is shouldered, drive the seal down to the shoulder. If the seal housing is unshouldered, the seal should be fitted with its face flush with the housing top face (unless otherwise instructed).

Screw threads and fastenings

Seized nuts, bolts and screws are quite a common occurrence where corrosion has set in, and the use of penetrating oil or releasing fluid will often overcome this problem if the offending item is soaked for a while before attempting to release it. The use of an impact driver may also provide a means of releasing such stubborn fastening devices, when used in conjunction with the appropriate screwdriver bit or socket. If none of these methods works, it may be necessary to resort to the careful application of heat, or the use of a hacksaw or nut splitter device.

Studs are usually removed by locking two nuts together on the threaded part, and then using a spanner on the lower nut to unscrew the stud. Studs or bolts which have broken off below the surface of the component in which they are mounted can sometimes be removed using a stud extractor. Always ensure that a blind tapped hole is completely free from oil, grease, water or other fluid before installing the bolt or stud. Failure to do this could cause the housing to crack due to the hydraulic action of the bolt or stud as it is screwed in.

When tightening a castellated nut to accept a split pin, tighten the nut to the specified torque, where applicable, and then tighten further to the next split pin hole. Never slacken the nut to align the split pin hole, unless stated in the repair procedure.

When checking or retightening a nut or bolt to a specified torque setting, slacken the nut or bolt by a quarter of a turn, and then retighten to the specified setting. However, this should not be attempted where angular tightening has been used.

For some screw fastenings, notably cylinder head bolts or nuts, torque wrench settings are no longer specified for the latter stages of tightening, "angle-tightening" being called up instead. Typically, a fairly low torque wrench setting will be applied to the bolts/nuts in the correct sequence, followed by one or more stages of tightening through specified angles.

Locknuts, locktabs and washers

Any fastening which will rotate against a component or housing during tightening should always have a washer between it and the relevant component or housing.

Spring or split washers should always be renewed when they are used to lock a critical component such as a big-end bearing retaining bolt or nut. Locktabs which are folded over to retain a nut or bolt should always be renewed.

Self-locking nuts can be re-used in non-critical areas, providing resistance can be felt when the locking portion passes over the bolt or stud thread. However, it should be noted that self-locking stiffnuts tend to lose their effectiveness after long periods of use, and should then be renewed as a matter of course.

Split pins must always be replaced with new ones of the correct size for the hole.

When thread-locking compound is found on the threads of a fastener which is to be re-used, it should be cleaned off with a wire brush and solvent, and fresh compound applied on reassembly.

Special tools

Some repair procedures in this manual entail the use of special tools such as a press, two or three-legged pullers, spring compressors, etc. Wherever possible, suitable readily-available alternatives to the manufacturer's special tools are described, and are shown in use. In some instances, where no alternative is possible, it has been necessary to resort to the use of a manufacturer's tool, and this has been done for reasons of safety as well as the efficient completion of the repair operation. Unless you are highly-skilled and have a thorough understanding of the procedures described, never attempt to bypass the use of any special tool when the procedure described specifies its use. Not only is there a very great risk of personal injury, but expensive damage could be caused to the components involved.

Environmental considerations

When disposing of used engine oil, brake fluid, antifreeze, etc, give due consideration to any detrimental environmental effects. Do not, for instance, pour any of the above liquids down drains into the general sewage system, or onto the ground to soak away. Many local council refuse tips provide a facility for waste oil disposal, as do some garages. If none of these facilities are available, consult your local Environmental Health Department, or the National Rivers Authority, for further advice.

With the universal tightening-up of legislation regarding the emission of environmentally-harmful substances from motor vehicles, most vehicles have tamperproof devices fitted to the main adjustment points of the fuel system. These devices are primarily designed to prevent unqualified persons from adjusting the fuel/air mixture, with the chance of a consequent increase in toxic emissions. If such devices are found during servicing or overhaul, they should, wherever possible, be renewed or refitted in accordance with the manufacturer's requirements or current legislation.

OIL CARE

FOLLOW THE CODE

OIL BANK LINE
0800 66 33 66
www.oilbankline.org.uk

Note: It is antisocial and illegal to dump oil down the drain. To find the location of your local oil recycling bank, call this number free.

The jack supplied with the vehicle tool kit should only be used for changing roadwheels – see *Wheel changing* at the front of this manual. When carrying out any other kind of work, raise the vehicle using a hydraulic jack, and always supplement the jack with axle stands positioned under the vehicle jacking points.

When jacking up the vehicle with a trolley jack, position the jack head under one of the relevant jacking points (note that the jacking points for use with a hydraulic jack are different to those for use with the vehicle jack). **Do not** jack the vehicle under the sump or any of the steering or suspension components. Supplement the jack using axle stands (**see illustrations**).

 Warning: Never work under, around, or near a raised vehicle, unless it is adequately supported in at least two places.

Rear jacking point for hydraulic jack or axle stands

Front jacking point for hydraulic jack or axle stands

Axle stands should be placed under, or adjacent to the jacking point (arrowed)

Disconnecting the battery

Numerous systems fitted to the vehicle require battery power to be available at all times, either to ensure their continued operation (such as the clock) or to maintain control unit memories which would be erased if the battery were to be disconnected. Whenever the battery is to be disconnected therefore, first note the following, to ensure that there are no unforeseen consequences of this action:

a) *First, on any vehicle with central locking, it is a wise precaution to remove the key from the ignition, and to keep it with you, so that it does not get locked in, if the central locking should engage accidentally when the battery is reconnected.*

b) *Depending on model and specification, the Vauxhall anti-theft alarm system may be of the type which is automatically activated when the vehicle battery is disconnected and/or reconnected. To prevent the alarm sounding on models so equipped, switch the ignition on, then off, and disconnect the battery within 15 seconds. If the alarm is activated when the battery is reconnected, switch the ignition on then off to deactivate the alarm.*

c) *If a security-coded audio unit is fitted, and the unit and/or the battery is disconnected, the unit will not function again on reconnection until the correct security code is entered. Details of this procedure, which varies according to the*

unit fitted, are given in the vehicle audio system operating instructions. Ensure you have the correct code before you disconnect the battery. If you do not have the code or details of the correct procedure, but can supply proof of ownership and a legitimate reason for wanting this information, a Vauxhall dealer may be able to help.

d) *The engine management electronic control unit is of the 'self-learning' type, meaning that as it operates, it also monitors and stores the settings which give optimum engine performance under all operating conditions. When the battery is disconnected, these settings are lost and the ECU reverts to the base settings programmed into its memory at the factory. On restarting, this may lead to the engine running/idling roughly for a short while, until the ECU has re-learned the optimum settings. This process is best accomplished by taking the vehicle on a road test (for approximately 15 minutes), covering all engine speeds and loads, concentrating mainly in the 2500 to 3500 rpm region.*

e) *On models equipped with automatic transmission, the transmission selector lever assembly incorporates an electrically-operated selector lever lock mechanism that prevents the lever being moved out of the P position unless the ignition is switched on and the brake pedal is depressed. If the selector lever is*

in the P position and the battery is disconnected, it will not be possible to move the selector lever out of position P by the normal means. Although it is possible to manually override the system (see Chapter 7B), it is sensible to move the selector lever to the N position before disconnecting the battery.

f) *On all models, when reconnecting the battery after disconnection, switch on the ignition and wait 10 seconds to allow the electronic vehicle systems to stabilise and re-initialise.*

Devices known as 'memory-savers' (or 'code-savers') can be used to avoid some of the above problems. Precise details vary according to the device used. Typically, it is plugged into the cigarette lighter, and is connected by its own wires to a spare battery; the vehicle's own battery is then disconnected from the electrical system, leaving the 'memory-saver' to pass sufficient current to maintain audio unit security codes and any other memory values, and also to run permanently-live circuits such as the clock.

⚠ **Warning: Some of these devices allow a considerable amount of current to pass, which can mean that many of the vehicle's systems are still operational when the main battery is disconnected. If a 'memory saver' is used, ensure that the circuit concerned is actually 'dead' before carrying out any work on it!**

Introduction

A selection of good tools is a fundamental requirement for anyone contemplating the maintenance and repair of a motor vehicle. For the owner who does not possess any, their purchase will prove a considerable expense, offsetting some of the savings made by doing-it-yourself. However, provided that the tools purchased meet the relevant national safety standards and are of good quality, they will last for many years and prove an extremely worthwhile investment.

To help the average owner to decide which tools are needed to carry out the various tasks detailed in this manual, we have compiled three lists of tools under the following headings: *Maintenance and minor repair, Repair and overhaul*, and *Special*. Newcomers to practical mechanics should start off with the *Maintenance and minor repair* tool kit, and confine themselves to the simpler jobs around the vehicle. Then, as confidence and experience grow, more difficult tasks can be undertaken, with extra tools being purchased as, and when, they are needed. In this way, a *Maintenance and minor repair* tool kit can be built up into a *Repair and overhaul* tool kit over a considerable period of time, without any major cash outlays. The experienced do-it-yourselfer will have a tool kit good enough for most repair and overhaul procedures, and will add tools from the *Special* category when it is felt that the expense is justified by the amount of use to which these tools will be put.

Maintenance and minor repair tool kit

The tools given in this list should be considered as a minimum requirement if routine maintenance, servicing and minor repair operations are to be undertaken. We recommend the purchase of combination spanners (ring one end, open-ended the other); although more expensive than open-ended ones, they do give the advantages of both types of spanner.

- [ ] *Combination spanners:*
  Metric - 8 to 19 mm inclusive
- [ ] *Adjustable spanner - 35 mm jaw (approx.)*
- [ ] *Spark plug spanner (with rubber insert) - petrol models*
- [ ] *Spark plug gap adjustment tool - petrol models*
- [ ] *Set of feeler gauges*
- [ ] *Brake bleed nipple spanner*
- [ ] *Screwdrivers:*
  Flat blade - 100 mm long x 6 mm dia
  Cross blade - 100 mm long x 6 mm dia
  Torx - various sizes (not all vehicles)
- [ ] *Combination pliers*
- [ ] *Hacksaw (junior)*
- [ ] *Tyre pump*
- [ ] *Tyre pressure gauge*
- [ ] *Oil can*
- [ ] *Oil filter removal tool*
- [ ] *Fine emery cloth*
- [ ] *Wire brush (small)*
- [ ] *Funnel (medium size)*
- [ ] *Sump drain plug key (not all vehicles)*

Repair and overhaul tool kit

These tools are virtually essential for anyone undertaking any major repairs to a motor vehicle, and are additional to those given in the *Maintenance and minor repair* list. Included in this list is a comprehensive set of sockets. Although these are expensive, they will be found invaluable as they are so versatile - particularly if various drives are included in the set. We recommend the half-inch square-drive type, as this can be used with most proprietary torque wrenches.

The tools in this list will sometimes need to be supplemented by tools from the *Special* list:

- [ ] *Sockets (or box spanners) to cover range in previous list (including Torx sockets)*
- [ ] *Reversible ratchet drive (for use with sockets)*
- [ ] *Extension piece, 250 mm (for use with sockets)*
- [ ] *Universal joint (for use with sockets)*
- [ ] *Flexible handle or sliding T "breaker bar" (for use with sockets)*
- [ ] *Torque wrench (for use with sockets)*
- [ ] *Self-locking grips*
- [ ] *Ball pein hammer*
- [ ] *Soft-faced mallet (plastic or rubber)*
- [ ] *Screwdrivers:*
  Flat blade - long & sturdy, short (chubby), and narrow (electrician's) types
  Cross blade – long & sturdy, and short (chubby) types
- [ ] *Pliers:*
  Long-nosed
  Side cutters (electrician's)
  Circlip (internal and external)
- [ ] *Cold chisel - 25 mm*
- [ ] *Scriber*
- [ ] *Scraper*
- [ ] *Centre-punch*
- [ ] *Pin punch*
- [ ] *Hacksaw*
- [ ] *Brake hose clamp*
- [ ] *Brake/clutch bleeding kit*
- [ ] *Selection of twist drills*
- [ ] *Steel rule/straight-edge*
- [ ] *Allen keys (inc. splined/Torx type)*
- [ ] *Selection of files*
- [ ] *Wire brush*
- [ ] *Axle stands*
- [ ] *Jack (strong trolley or hydraulic type)*
- [ ] *Light with extension lead*
- [ ] *Universal electrical multi-meter*

Sockets and reversible ratchet drive

Brake bleeding kit

Torx key, socket and bit

Hose clamp

Angular-tightening gauge

Special tools

The tools in this list are those which are not used regularly, are expensive to buy, or which need to be used in accordance with their manufacturers' instructions. Unless relatively difficult mechanical jobs are undertaken frequently, it will not be economic to buy many of these tools. Where this is the case, you could consider clubbing together with friends (or joining a motorists' club) to make a joint purchase, or borrowing the tools against a deposit from a local garage or tool hire specialist. It is worth noting that many of the larger DIY superstores now carry a large range of special tools for hire at modest rates.

The following list contains only those tools and instruments freely available to the public, and not those special tools produced by the vehicle manufacturer specifically for its dealer network. You will find occasional references to these manufacturers' special tools in the text of this manual. Generally, an alternative method of doing the job without the vehicle manufacturers' special tool is given. However, sometimes there is no alternative to using them. Where this is the case and the relevant tool cannot be bought or borrowed, you will have to entrust the work to a dealer.

- ☐ Angular-tightening gauge
- ☐ Valve spring compressor
- ☐ Valve grinding tool
- ☐ Piston ring compressor
- ☐ Piston ring removal/installation tool
- ☐ Cylinder bore hone
- ☐ Balljoint separator
- ☐ Coil spring compressors (where applicable)
- ☐ Two/three-legged hub and bearing puller
- ☐ Impact screwdriver
- ☐ Micrometer and/or vernier calipers
- ☐ Dial gauge
- ☐ Stroboscopic timing light
- ☐ Dwell angle meter/tachometer
- ☐ Fault code reader
- ☐ Cylinder compression gauge
- ☐ Hand-operated vacuum pump and gauge
- ☐ Clutch plate alignment set
- ☐ Brake shoe steady spring cup removal tool
- ☐ Bush and bearing removal/installation set
- ☐ Stud extractors
- ☐ Tap and die set
- ☐ Lifting tackle
- ☐ Trolley jack

Buying tools

Reputable motor accessory shops and superstores often offer excellent quality tools at discount prices, so it pays to shop around.

Remember, you don't have to buy the most expensive items on the shelf, but it is always advisable to steer clear of the very cheap tools. Beware of 'bargains' offered on market stalls or at car boot sales. There are plenty of good tools around at reasonable prices, but always aim to purchase items which meet the relevant national safety standards. If in doubt, ask the proprietor or manager of the shop for advice before making a purchase.

Care and maintenance of tools

Having purchased a reasonable tool kit, it is necessary to keep the tools in a clean and serviceable condition. After use, always wipe off any dirt, grease and metal particles using a clean, dry cloth, before putting the tools away. Never leave them lying around after they have been used. A simple tool rack on the garage or workshop wall for items such as screwdrivers and pliers is a good idea. Store all normal spanners and sockets in a metal box. Any measuring instruments, gauges, meters, etc, must be carefully stored where they cannot be damaged or become rusty.

Take a little care when tools are used. Hammer heads inevitably become marked, and screwdrivers lose the keen edge on their blades from time to time. A little timely attention with emery cloth or a file will soon restore items like this to a good finish.

Working facilities

Not to be forgotten when discussing tools is the workshop itself. If anything more than routine maintenance is to be carried out, a suitable working area becomes essential.

It is appreciated that many an owner-mechanic is forced by circumstances to remove an engine or similar item without the benefit of a garage or workshop. Having done this, any repairs should always be done under the cover of a roof.

Wherever possible, any dismantling should be done on a clean, flat workbench or table at a suitable working height.

Any workbench needs a vice; one with a jaw opening of 100 mm is suitable for most jobs. As mentioned previously, some clean dry storage space is also required for tools, as well as for any lubricants, cleaning fluids, touch-up paints etc, which become necessary.

Another item which may be required, and which has a much more general usage, is an electric drill with a chuck capacity of at least 8 mm. This, together with a good range of twist drills, is virtually essential for fitting accessories.

Last, but not least, always keep a supply of old newspapers and clean, lint-free rags available, and try to keep any working area as clean as possible.

Micrometers

Dial test indicator ("dial gauge")

Strap wrench

Compression tester

Fault code reader

This is a guide to getting your vehicle through the MOT test. Obviously it will not be possible to examine the vehicle to the same standard as the professional MOT tester. However, working through the following checks will enable you to identify any problem areas before submitting the vehicle for the test.

Where a testable component is in borderline condition, the tester has discretion in deciding whether to pass or fail it. The basis of such discretion is whether the tester would be happy for a close relative or friend to use the vehicle with the component in that condition. If the vehicle presented is clean and evidently well cared for, the tester may be more inclined to pass a borderline component than if the vehicle is scruffy and apparently neglected.

It has only been possible to summarise the test requirements here, based on the regulations in force at the time of printing. Test standards are becoming increasingly stringent, although there are some exemptions for older vehicles.

An assistant will be needed to help carry out some of these checks.

The checks have been sub-divided into four categories, as follows:

1 Checks carried out **FROM THE DRIVER'S SEAT**

2 Checks carried out **WITH THE VEHICLE ON THE GROUND**

3 Checks carried out **WITH THE VEHICLE RAISED AND THE WHEELS FREE TO TURN**

4 Checks carried out on **YOUR VEHICLE'S EXHAUST EMISSION SYSTEM**

1 Checks carried out **FROM THE DRIVER'S SEAT**

Handbrake

☐ Test the operation of the handbrake. Excessive travel (too many clicks) indicates incorrect brake or cable adjustment.
☐ Check that the handbrake cannot be released by tapping the lever sideways. Check the security of the lever mountings.

Footbrake

☐ Depress the brake pedal and check that it does not creep down to the floor, indicating a master cylinder fault. Release the pedal, wait a few seconds, then depress it again. If the pedal travels nearly to the floor before firm resistance is felt, brake adjustment or repair is necessary. If the pedal feels spongy, there is air in the hydraulic system which must be removed by bleeding.

☐ Check that the brake pedal is secure and in good condition. Check also for signs of fluid leaks on the pedal, floor or carpets, which would indicate failed seals in the brake master cylinder.
☐ Check the servo unit (when applicable) by operating the brake pedal several times, then keeping the pedal depressed and starting the engine. As the engine starts, the pedal will move down slightly. If not, the vacuum hose or the servo itself may be faulty.

Steering wheel and column

☐ Examine the steering wheel for fractures or looseness of the hub, spokes or rim.
☐ Move the steering wheel from side to side and then up and down. Check that the steering wheel is not loose on the column, indicating wear or a loose retaining nut. Continue moving the steering wheel as before, but also turn it slightly from left to right.
☐ Check that the steering wheel is not loose on the column, and that there is no abnormal

movement of the steering wheel, indicating wear in the column support bearings or couplings.

Windscreen, mirrors and sunvisor

☐ The windscreen must be free of cracks or other significant damage within the driver's field of view. (Small stone chips are acceptable.) Rear view mirrors must be secure, intact, and capable of being adjusted.

☐ The driver's sunvisor must be capable of being stored in the "up" position.

Seat belts and seats

Note: *The following checks are applicable to all seat belts, front and rear.*

☐ Examine the webbing of all the belts (including rear belts if fitted) for cuts, serious fraying or deterioration. Fasten and unfasten each belt to check the buckles. If applicable, check the retracting mechanism. Check the security of all seat belt mountings accessible from inside the vehicle.
☐ Seat belts with pre-tensioners, once activated, have a "flag" or similar showing on the seat belt stalk. This, in itself, is not a reason for test failure.
☐ The front seats themselves must be securely attached and the backrests must lock in the upright position.

Doors

☐ Both front doors must be able to be opened and closed from outside and inside, and must latch securely when closed.

2 Checks carried out WITH THE VEHICLE ON THE GROUND

Vehicle identification

☐ Number plates must be in good condition, secure and legible, with letters and numbers correctly spaced – spacing at (A) should be at least twice that at (B).

☐ The VIN plate and/or homologation plate must be legible.

Electrical equipment

☐ Switch on the ignition and check the operation of the horn.
☐ Check the windscreen washers and wipers, examining the wiper blades; renew damaged or perished blades. Also check the operation of the stop-lights.

☐ Check the operation of the sidelights and number plate lights. The lenses and reflectors must be secure, clean and undamaged.
☐ Check the operation and alignment of the headlights. The headlight reflectors must not be tarnished and the lenses must be undamaged.
☐ Switch on the ignition and check the operation of the direction indicators (including the instrument panel tell-tale) and the hazard warning lights. Operation of the sidelights and stop-lights must not affect the indicators - if it does, the cause is usually a bad earth at the rear light cluster.
☐ Check the operation of the rear foglight(s), including the warning light on the instrument panel or in the switch.
☐ The ABS warning light must illuminate in accordance with the manufacturers' design. For most vehicles, the ABS warning light should illuminate when the ignition is switched on, and (if the system is operating properly) extinguish after a few seconds. Refer to the owner's handbook.

Footbrake

☐ Examine the master cylinder, brake pipes and servo unit for leaks, loose mountings, corrosion or other damage.

☐ The fluid reservoir must be secure and the fluid level must be between the upper (A) and lower (B) markings.

☐ Inspect both front brake flexible hoses for cracks or deterioration of the rubber. Turn the steering from lock to lock, and ensure that the hoses do not contact the wheel, tyre, or any part of the steering or suspension mechanism. With the brake pedal firmly depressed, check the hoses for bulges or leaks under pressure.

Steering and suspension

☐ Have your assistant turn the steering wheel from side to side slightly, up to the point where the steering gear just begins to transmit this movement to the roadwheels. Check for excessive free play between the steering wheel and the steering gear, indicating wear or insecurity of the steering column joints, the column-to-steering gear coupling, or the steering gear itself.
☐ Have your assistant turn the steering wheel more vigorously in each direction, so that the roadwheels just begin to turn. As this is done, examine all the steering joints, linkages, fittings and attachments. Renew any component that shows signs of wear or damage. On vehicles with power steering, check the security and condition of the steering pump, drivebelt and hoses.
☐ Check that the vehicle is standing level, and at approximately the correct ride height.

Shock absorbers

☐ Depress each corner of the vehicle in turn, then release it. The vehicle should rise and then settle in its normal position. If the vehicle continues to rise and fall, the shock absorber is defective. A shock absorber which has seized will also cause the vehicle to fail.

Exhaust system

☐ Start the engine. With your assistant holding a rag over the tailpipe, check the entire system for leaks. Repair or renew leaking sections.

3 Checks carried out
WITH THE VEHICLE RAISED AND THE WHEELS FREE TO TURN

Jack up the front and rear of the vehicle, and securely support it on axle stands. Position the stands clear of the suspension assemblies. Ensure that the wheels are clear of the ground and that the steering can be turned from lock to lock.

Steering mechanism

☐ Have your assistant turn the steering from lock to lock. Check that the steering turns smoothly, and that no part of the steering mechanism, including a wheel or tyre, fouls any brake hose or pipe or any part of the body structure.

☐ Examine the steering rack rubber gaiters for damage or insecurity of the retaining clips. If power steering is fitted, check for signs of damage or leakage of the fluid hoses, pipes or connections. Also check for excessive stiffness or binding of the steering, a missing split pin or locking device, or severe corrosion of the body structure within 30 cm of any steering component attachment point.

Front and rear suspension and wheel bearings

☐ Starting at the front right-hand side, grasp the roadwheel at the 3 o'clock and 9 o'clock positions and rock gently but firmly. Check for free play or insecurity at the wheel bearings, suspension balljoints, or suspension mountings, pivots and attachments.

☐ Now grasp the wheel at the 12 o'clock and 6 o'clock positions and repeat the previous inspection. Spin the wheel, and check for roughness or tightness of the front wheel bearing.

☐ If excess free play is suspected at a component pivot point, this can be confirmed by using a large screwdriver or similar tool and levering between the mounting and the component attachment. This will confirm whether the wear is in the pivot bush, its retaining bolt, or in the mounting itself (the bolt holes can often become elongated).

☐ Carry out all the above checks at the other front wheel, and then at both rear wheels.

Springs and shock absorbers

☐ Examine the suspension struts (when applicable) for serious fluid leakage, corrosion, or damage to the casing. Also check the security of the mounting points.

☐ If coil springs are fitted, check that the spring ends locate in their seats, and that the spring is not corroded, cracked or broken.

☐ If leaf springs are fitted, check that all leaves are intact, that the axle is securely attached to each spring, and that there is no deterioration of the spring eye mountings, bushes, and shackles.

☐ The same general checks apply to vehicles fitted with other suspension types, such as torsion bars, hydraulic displacer units, etc. Ensure that all mountings and attachments are secure, that there are no signs of excessive wear, corrosion or damage, and (on hydraulic types) that there are no fluid leaks or damaged pipes.

☐ Inspect the shock absorbers for signs of serious fluid leakage. Check for wear of the mounting bushes or attachments, or damage to the body of the unit.

Driveshafts (fwd vehicles only)

☐ Rotate each front wheel in turn and inspect the constant velocity joint gaiters for splits or damage. Also check that each driveshaft is straight and undamaged.

Braking system

☐ If possible without dismantling, check brake pad wear and disc condition. Ensure that the friction lining material has not worn excessively, (A) and that the discs are not fractured, pitted, scored or badly worn (B).

☐ Examine all the rigid brake pipes underneath the vehicle, and the flexible hose(s) at the rear. Look for corrosion, chafing or insecurity of the pipes, and for signs of bulging under pressure, chafing, splits or deterioration of the flexible hoses.

☐ Look for signs of fluid leaks at the brake calipers or on the brake backplates. Repair or renew leaking components.

☐ Slowly spin each wheel, while your assistant depresses and releases the footbrake. Ensure that each brake is operating and does not bind when the pedal is released.

☐ Examine the handbrake mechanism, checking for frayed or broken cables, excessive corrosion, or wear or insecurity of the linkage. Check that the mechanism works on each relevant wheel, and releases fully, without binding.

☐ It is not possible to test brake efficiency without special equipment, but a road test can be carried out later to check that the vehicle pulls up in a straight line.

Fuel and exhaust systems

☐ Inspect the fuel tank (including the filler cap), fuel pipes, hoses and unions. All components must be secure and free from leaks.

☐ Examine the exhaust system over its entire length, checking for any damaged, broken or missing mountings, security of the retaining clamps and rust or corrosion.

Wheels and tyres

☐ Examine the sidewalls and tread area of each tyre in turn. Check for cuts, tears, lumps, bulges, separation of the tread, and exposure of the ply or cord due to wear or damage. Check that the tyre bead is correctly seated on the wheel rim, that the valve is sound and properly seated, and that the wheel is not distorted or damaged.

☐ Check that the tyres are of the correct size for the vehicle, that they are of the same size and type on each axle, and that the pressures are correct.

☐ Check the tyre tread depth. The legal minimum at the time of writing is 1.6 mm over at least three-quarters of the tread width. Abnormal tread wear may indicate incorrect front wheel alignment.

Body corrosion

☐ Check the condition of the entire vehicle structure for signs of corrosion in load-bearing areas. (These include chassis box sections, side sills, cross-members, pillars, and all suspension, steering, braking system and seat belt mountings and anchorages.) Any corrosion which has seriously reduced the thickness of a load-bearing area is likely to cause the vehicle to fail. In this case professional repairs are likely to be needed.

☐ Damage or corrosion which causes sharp or otherwise dangerous edges to be exposed will also cause the vehicle to fail.

4 Checks carried out on YOUR VEHICLE'S EXHAUST EMISSION SYSTEM

Petrol models

☐ Have the engine at normal operating temperature, and make sure that it is in good tune (ignition system in good order, air filter element clean, etc).

☐ Before any measurements are carried out, raise the engine speed to around 2500 rpm, and hold it at this speed for 20 seconds. Allow the engine speed to return to idle, and watch for smoke emissions from the exhaust tailpipe. If the idle speed is obviously much too high, or if dense blue or clearly-visible black smoke comes from the tailpipe for more than 5 seconds, the vehicle will fail. As a rule of thumb, blue smoke signifies oil being burnt (engine wear) while black smoke signifies unburnt fuel (dirty air cleaner element, or other carburettor or fuel system fault).

☐ An exhaust gas analyser capable of measuring carbon monoxide (CO) and hydrocarbons (HC) is now needed. If such an instrument cannot be hired or borrowed, a local garage may agree to perform the check for a small fee.

CO emissions (mixture)

☐ At the time of writing, for vehicles first used between 1st August 1975 and 31st July 1986 (P to C registration), the CO level must not exceed 4.5% by volume. For vehicles first used between 1st August 1986 and 31st July 1992 (D to J registration), the CO level must not exceed 3.5% by volume. Vehicles first

used after 1st August 1992 (K registration) must conform to the manufacturer's specification. The MOT tester has access to a DOT database or emissions handbook, which lists the CO and HC limits for each make and model of vehicle. The CO level is measured with the engine at idle speed, and at "fast idle". The following limits are given as a general guide:

At idle speed -
CO level no more than 0.5%
At "fast idle" (2500 to 3000 rpm) -
CO level no more than 0.3%
(Minimum oil temperature 60ºC)

☐ If the CO level cannot be reduced far enough to pass the test (and the fuel and ignition systems are otherwise in good condition) then the carburettor is badly worn, or there is some problem in the fuel injection system or catalytic converter (as applicable).

HC emissions

☐ With the CO within limits, HC emissions for vehicles first used between 1st August 1975 and 31st July 1992 (P to J registration) must not exceed 1200 ppm. Vehicles first used after 1st August 1992 (K registration) must conform to the manufacturer's specification. The MOT tester has access to a DOT database or emissions handbook, which lists the CO and HC limits for each make and model of vehicle. The HC level is measured with the engine at "fast idle". The following is given as a general guide:

At "fast idle" (2500 to 3000 rpm) -
HC level no more than 200 ppm
(Minimum oil temperature 60ºC)

☐ Excessive HC emissions are caused by incomplete combustion, the causes of which can include oil being burnt, mechanical wear and ignition/fuel system malfunction.

Diesel models

☐ The only emission test applicable to Diesel engines is the measuring of exhaust smoke density. The test involves accelerating the engine several times to its maximum unloaded speed.

Note: *It is of the utmost importance that the engine timing belt is in good condition before the test is carried out.*

☐ The limits for Diesel engine exhaust smoke, introduced in September 1995 are:
Vehicles first used before 1st August 1979:
Exempt from metered smoke testing, but must not emit "dense blue or clearly visible black smoke for a period of more than 5 seconds at idle" or "dense blue or clearly visible black smoke during acceleration which would obscure the view of other road users".
Non-turbocharged vehicles first used after 1st August 1979: 2.5m-1
Turbocharged vehicles first used after 1st August 1979: 3.0m-1

☐ Excessive smoke can be caused by a dirty air cleaner element. Otherwise, professional advice may be needed to find the cause.

Engine

- [ ] Engine fails to rotate when attempting to start
- [ ] Engine rotates, but will not start
- [ ] Engine difficult to start when cold
- [ ] Engine difficult to start when hot
- [ ] Starter motor noisy or excessively-rough in engagement
- [ ] Engine starts, but stops immediately
- [ ] Engine idles erratically
- [ ] Engine misfires at idle speed
- [ ] Engine misfires throughout the driving speed range
- [ ] Engine hesitates on acceleration
- [ ] Engine stalls
- [ ] Engine lacks power
- [ ] Engine backfires
- [ ] Oil pressure warning light illuminated with engine running
- [ ] Engine runs-on after switching off
- [ ] Engine noises

Cooling system

- [ ] Overheating
- [ ] Overcooling
- [ ] External coolant leakage
- [ ] Internal coolant leakage
- [ ] Corrosion

Fuel and exhaust systems

- [ ] Excessive fuel consumption
- [ ] Fuel leakage and/or fuel odour
- [ ] Excessive noise or fumes from exhaust system

Clutch

- [ ] Pedal travels to floor – no pressure or very little resistance
- [ ] Clutch fails to disengage (unable to select gears)
- [ ] Clutch slips (engine speed increases, with no increase in vehicle speed)
- [ ] Judder as clutch is engaged
- [ ] Noise when depressing or releasing clutch pedal

Manual gearbox

- [ ] Noisy in neutral with engine running
- [ ] Noisy in one particular gear
- [ ] Difficulty engaging gears
- [ ] Jumps out of gear
- [ ] Vibration
- [ ] Lubricant leaks

Automatic transmission

- [ ] Fluid leakage
- [ ] Transmission fluid brown, or has burned smell
- [ ] General gear selection problems
- [ ] Transmission will not downshift (kickdown) with accelerator pedal fully depressed
- [ ] Engine will not start in any gear, or starts in gears other than Park or Neutral
- [ ] Transmission slips, shifts roughly, is noisy, or has no drive in forward or reverse gears

Driveshafts

- [ ] Clicking or knocking noise on turns (at slow speed on full-lock)
- [ ] Vibration when accelerating or decelerating

Braking system

- [ ] Vehicle pulls to one side under braking
- [ ] Noise (grinding or high-pitched squeal) when brakes applied
- [ ] Excessive brake pedal travel
- [ ] Brake pedal feels spongy when depressed
- [ ] Excessive brake pedal effort required to stop vehicle
- [ ] Judder felt through brake pedal or steering wheel when braking
- [ ] Brakes binding
- [ ] Rear wheels locking under normal braking

Suspension and steering systems

- [ ] Vehicle pulls to one side
- [ ] Wheel wobble and vibration
- [ ] Excessive pitching and/or rolling around corners, or during braking
- [ ] Wandering or general instability
- [ ] Excessively-stiff steering
- [ ] Excessive play in steering
- [ ] Lack of power assistance
- [ ] Tyre wear excessive

Electrical system

- [ ] Battery will not hold a charge for more than a few days
- [ ] Ignition/no-charge warning light remains illuminated with engine running
- [ ] Ignition/no-charge warning light fails to come on
- [ ] Lights inoperative
- [ ] Instrument readings inaccurate or erratic
- [ ] Horn inoperative, or unsatisfactory in operation
- [ ] Windscreen/tailgate wipers inoperative, or unsatisfactory in operation
- [ ] Windscreen/tailgate washers inoperative, or unsatisfactory in operation
- [ ] Electric windows inoperative, or unsatisfactory in operation
- [ ] Central locking system inoperative, or unsatisfactory in operation

Introduction

The vehicle owner who does his or her own maintenance according to the recommended service schedules should not have to use this section of the manual very often. Modern component reliability is such that, provided those items subject to wear or deterioration are inspected or renewed at the specified intervals, sudden failure is comparatively rare. Faults do not usually just happen as a result of sudden failure, but develop over a period of time. Major mechanical failures in particular are usually preceded by characteristic symptoms over hundreds or even thousands of miles. Those components which do occasionally fail without warning are often small and easily carried in the vehicle.

With any fault-finding, the first step is to decide where to begin investigations. This may be obvious, but some detective work may be necessary. The owner who makes half a dozen haphazard adjustments or replacements may be successful in curing a fault (or its symptoms), but will be none the wiser if the fault recurs, and ultimately may have spent more time and money than was necessary. A calm and logical approach will be found to be more satisfactory in the long run. Always take into account any warning signs that may have been noticed in the period preceding the fault – power loss, high or low gauge readings, unusual smells, etc – and remember – failure of components such as fuses or spark plugs may only be pointers to some underlying fault.

The pages which follow provide an easy-reference guide to the more common problems which may occur during the operation of the vehicle. These problems and their possible causes are grouped under headings denoting various components or systems, such as Engine, Cooling system, etc. The Chapter which deals with the problem is shown in brackets, but in some instances it will be necessary to refer to the specific Chapter Part, depending on model or system, as applicable. Some problems may be more obvious, such as loose or disconnected wiring, and in these instances a Chapter reference may not be given as the problem can be simply overcome by dealing with the fault as it stands. Whatever the problem, certain basic principles apply. These are as follows:

Verify the fault. This is simply a matter of being sure that you know what the symptoms are before starting work. This is particularly important if you are investigating a fault for someone else, who may not have described it very accurately.

Don't overlook the obvious. For example, if the vehicle won't start, is there fuel in the tank? (Don't take anyone else's word on this particular point, and don't trust the fuel gauge either!) If an electrical fault is indicated, look for loose or broken wires before digging out the test gear.

Cure the disease, not the symptom. Substituting a flat battery with a fully-charged one will get you off the hard shoulder, but if the underlying cause is not attended to, the new battery will go the same way. Similarly, changing oil-fouled spark plugs for a new set will get you moving again, but remember that the reason for the fouling (if it wasn't simply an incorrect grade of plug) will have to be established and corrected.

Don't take anything for granted. Particularly, don't forget that a 'new' component may itself be defective (especially if it's been rattling around in the boot for months), and don't leave components out of a fault diagnosis sequence just because they are new or recently-fitted. When you do finally diagnose a difficult fault, you'll probably realise that all the evidence was there from the start.

Engine

Engine fails to rotate when attempting to start

- [ ] Battery terminal connections loose or corroded (Weekly checks).
- [ ] Battery discharged or faulty (Chapter 5).
- [ ] Broken, loose or disconnected wiring in the starting circuit (Chapter 5).
- [ ] Defective starter solenoid or switch (Chapter 5).
- [ ] Defective starter motor (Chapter 5).
- [ ] Starter pinion or flywheel ring gear teeth loose or broken (Chapters 2 and 5).
- [ ] Engine earth strap broken or disconnected (Chapter 5).
- [ ] Automatic transmission not in Park/Neutral position or starter inhibitor switch faulty (Chapter 7).

Engine rotates, but will not start

- [ ] Fuel tank empty.
- [ ] Battery discharged (engine rotates slowly) (Chapter 5).
- [ ] Battery terminal connections loose or corroded (*Weekly checks*).
- [ ] Ignition components damp or damaged (Chapters 1 and 5).
- [ ] Broken, loose or disconnected wiring in the ignition circuit (Chapters 1 and 5).
- [ ] Worn, faulty or incorrectly-gapped spark plugs (Chapter 1).
- [ ] Fuel injection system fault (Chapter 4).
- [ ] Major mechanical failure (eg camshaft drive) (Chapter 2).

Engine difficult to start when cold

- [ ] Battery discharged (Chapter 5).
- [ ] Battery terminal connections loose or corroded (*Weekly checks*).
- [ ] Worn, faulty or incorrectly-gapped spark plugs (Chapter 1).
- [ ] Fuel injection system fault (Chapter 4).
- [ ] Other ignition system fault (Chapters 1 and 5).
- [ ] Low cylinder compressions (Chapter 2).

Engine difficult to start when hot

- [ ] Air filter element dirty or clogged (Chapter 1).
- [ ] Fuel injection system fault (Chapter 4).
- [ ] Low cylinder compressions (Chapter 2).

Starter motor noisy or excessively-rough in engagement

- [ ] Starter pinion or flywheel ring gear teeth loose or broken (Chapters 2 and 5).
- [ ] Starter motor mounting bolts loose or missing (Chapter 5).
- [ ] Starter motor internal components worn or damaged (Chapter 5).

Engine starts, but stops immediately

- [ ] Loose or faulty electrical connections in the ignition circuit (Chapters 1 and 5).
- [ ] Vacuum leak at the fuel injection unit/throttle body or inlet manifold (Chapter 4).
- [ ] Fuel injection system fault (Chapter 4).

Engine idles erratically

- [ ] Air filter element clogged (Chapter 1).
- [ ] Vacuum leak at the fuel injection unit/throttle body, inlet manifold or associated hoses (Chapter 4).
- [ ] Worn, faulty or incorrectly-gapped spark plugs (Chapter 1).
- [ ] Uneven or low cylinder compressions (Chapter 2).
- [ ] Camshaft lobes worn (Chapter 2).
- [ ] Timing belt/chain incorrectly tensioned (Chapter 2).
- [ ] Fuel injection system fault (Chapter 4).

Engine misfires at idle speed

- [ ] Worn, faulty or incorrectly-gapped spark plugs (Chapter 1).
- [ ] Faulty spark plug HT leads – where applicable (Chapter 1).
- [ ] Engine management system fault (Chapters 1 and 5)
- [ ] Vacuum leak at the fuel injection unit/throttle body, inlet manifold or associated hoses (Chapter 4).
- [ ] Distributor cap cracked or tracking internally – where applicable (Chapter 1).
- [ ] Uneven or low cylinder compressions (Chapter 2).
- [ ] Disconnected, leaking, or perished crankcase ventilation hoses (Chapter 4).
- [ ] Fuel injection system fault (Chapter 4).

Engine misfires throughout the driving speed range

- [ ] Fuel filter choked (Chapter 1).
- [ ] Fuel pump faulty, or delivery pressure low (Chapter 4).
- [ ] Fuel tank vent blocked, or fuel pipes restricted (Chapter 4).
- [ ] Vacuum leak at the fuel injection unit/throttle body, inlet manifold or associated hoses (Chapter 4).
- [ ] Worn, faulty or incorrectly-gapped spark plugs (Chapter 1).
- [ ] Faulty spark plug HT leads – where applicable (Chapter 1).
- [ ] Distributor cap cracked or tracking internally – where applicable (Chapter 1).
- [ ] Faulty ignition coil or DIS module (Chapter 5).
- [ ] Uneven or low cylinder compressions (Chapter 2).
- [ ] Fuel injection system fault (Chapter 4).

Engine (continued)

Engine hesitates on acceleration

☐ Worn, faulty or incorrectly-gapped spark plugs (Chapter 1).
☐ Vacuum leak at the fuel injection unit/throttle body, inlet manifold or associated hoses (Chapter 4).
☐ Fuel injection system fault (Chapter 4).

Engine stalls

☐ Vacuum leak at the fuel injection unit/throttle body, inlet manifold or associated hoses (Chapter 4).
☐ Fuel filter choked (Chapter 1).
☐ Fuel pump faulty, or delivery pressure low (Chapter 4).
☐ Fuel tank vent blocked, or fuel pipes restricted (Chapter 4).
☐ Fuel injection system fault (Chapter 4).

Engine lacks power

☐ Engine management system fault (Chapters 1 and 5).
☐ Timing belt/chain incorrectly fitted or tensioned (Chapter 2).
☐ Fuel filter choked (Chapter 1).
☐ Fuel pump faulty, or delivery pressure low (Chapter 4).
☐ Uneven or low cylinder compressions (Chapter 2).
☐ Worn, faulty or incorrectly-gapped spark plugs (Chapter 1).
☐ Vacuum leak at the fuel injection unit/throttle body, inlet manifold or associated hoses (Chapter 4).
☐ Brakes binding (Chapters 1 and 9).
☐ Clutch slipping (Chapter 6).
☐ Automatic transmission fluid level incorrect (Chapter 1).
☐ Fuel injection system fault (Chapter 4).

Engine backfires

☐ Engine management system fault (Chapters 1 and 5).
☐ Timing belt/chain incorrectly fitted or tensioned (Chapter 2).
☐ Vacuum leak at the fuel injection unit/throttle body, inlet manifold or associated hoses (Chapter 4).
☐ Fuel injection system fault (Chapter 4).

Oil pressure warning light illuminated with engine running

☐ Low oil level, or incorrect oil grade (*Weekly checks*).
☐ Faulty oil pressure warning light switch (Chapter 5).
☐ Worn engine bearings and/or oil pump (Chapter 2).
☐ High engine operating temperature (Chapter 3).

☐ Oil pressure relief valve defective (Chapter 2).
☐ Oil pick-up strainer clogged (Chapter 2).

Engine runs-on after switching off

☐ Excessive carbon build-up in engine (Chapter 2).
☐ High engine operating temperature (Chapter 3).
☐ Fuel injection system fault (Chapter 4).

Engine noises

Pre-ignition (pinking) or knocking during acceleration or under load

☐ Engine management system fault (Chapters 1, 4 and 5)
☐ Incorrect grade of fuel (Chapter 1).
☐ Vacuum leak at the fuel injection unit/throttle body, inlet manifold or associated hoses (Chapter 4).
☐ Excessive carbon build-up in engine (Chapter 2).
☐ Worn or damaged distributor (where applicable) or other ignition system component (Chapter 5).
☐ Fuel injection system fault (Chapter 4).

Whistling or wheezing noises

☐ Leaking inlet manifold or fuel injection unit/throttle body gasket (Chapter 4).
☐ Leaking exhaust manifold gasket or pipe-to-manifold joint (Chapter 4).
☐ Leaking vacuum hose (Chapters 4, 5 and 9).
☐ Blowing cylinder head gasket (Chapter 2).

Tapping or rattling noises

☐ Worn valve gear or camshaft (Chapter 2).
☐ Ancillary component fault (coolant pump, alternator, etc) (Chapters 3, 5, etc).

Knocking or thumping noises

☐ Worn big-end bearings (regular heavy knocking, perhaps less under load) (Chapter 2).
☐ Worn main bearings (rumbling and knocking, perhaps worsening under load) (Chapter 2).
☐ Piston slap (most noticeable when cold) (Chapter 2).
☐ Ancillary component fault (coolant pump, alternator, etc) (Chapters 3, 5, etc).

Cooling system

Overheating

☐ Insufficient coolant in system (*Weekly checks*).
☐ Thermostat faulty (Chapter 3).
☐ Radiator core blocked, or grille restricted (Chapter 3).
☐ Electric cooling fan or thermoswitch faulty (Chapter 3).
☐ Pressure cap faulty (Chapter 3).
☐ Ignition timing incorrect (engine management system fault) (Chapters 1 and 5).
☐ Inaccurate temperature gauge sender unit (Chapter 3).
☐ Airlock in cooling system (Chapter 1).

Overcooling

☐ Thermostat faulty (Chapter 3).
☐ Inaccurate temperature gauge sender unit (Chapter 3).

External coolant leakage

☐ Deteriorated or damaged hoses or hose clips (Chapter 1).
☐ Radiator core or heater matrix leaking (Chapter 3).
☐ Pressure cap faulty (Chapter 3).
☐ Coolant pump seal leaking (Chapter 3).
☐ Boiling due to overheating (Chapter 3).
☐ Core plug leaking (Chapter 2).

Internal coolant leakage

☐ Leaking cylinder head gasket (Chapter 2).
☐ Cracked cylinder head or cylinder bore (Chapter 2).

Corrosion

☐ Infrequent draining and flushing (Chapter 1).
☐ Incorrect coolant mixture or inappropriate coolant type (*Weekly checks*).

Fuel and exhaust systems

Excessive fuel consumption

- [ ] Air filter element dirty or clogged (Chapter 1).
- [ ] Fuel injection system fault (Chapter 4).
- [ ] Ignition timing incorrect (engine management system fault) (Chapters 1 and 5).
- [ ] Tyres under-inflated (*Weekly checks*).

Fuel leakage and/or fuel odour

- [ ] Damaged or corroded fuel tank, pipes or connections (Chapter 4).
- [ ] Fuel injection system fault (Chapter 4).

Excessive noise or fumes from exhaust system

- [ ] Leaking exhaust system or manifold joints (Chapters 1 and 4).
- [ ] Leaking, corroded or damaged silencers or pipe (Chapters 1 and 4).
- [ ] Broken mountings causing body or suspension contact (Chapter 1).

Clutch

Pedal travels to floor – no pressure or very little resistance

- [ ] Broken clutch cable (Chapter 6).
- [ ] Incorrect clutch cable adjustment (Chapter 1).
- [ ] Broken clutch release bearing or fork (Chapter 6).
- [ ] Broken diaphragm spring in clutch pressure plate (Chapter 6).

Clutch fails to disengage (unable to select gears)

- [ ] Incorrect clutch cable adjustment (Chapter 1).
- [ ] Clutch disc sticking on gearbox input shaft splines (Chapter 6).
- [ ] Clutch disc sticking to flywheel or pressure plate (Chapter 6).
- [ ] Faulty pressure plate assembly (Chapter 6).
- [ ] Clutch release mechanism worn or incorrectly assembled (Chapter 6).

Clutch slips (engine speed increases, with no increase in vehicle speed)

- [ ] Incorrect clutch cable adjustment (Chapter 1).

- [ ] Clutch disc linings excessively worn (Chapter 6).
- [ ] Clutch disc linings contaminated with oil or grease (Chapter 6).
- [ ] Faulty pressure plate or weak diaphragm spring (Chapter 6).

Judder as clutch is engaged

- [ ] Clutch disc linings contaminated with oil or grease (Chapter 6).
- [ ] Clutch disc linings excessively worn (Chapter 6).
- [ ] Clutch cable sticking or frayed (Chapter 6).
- [ ] Faulty or distorted pressure plate or diaphragm spring (Chapter 6).
- [ ] Worn or loose engine or gearbox mountings (Chapter 2).
- [ ] Clutch disc hub or gearbox input shaft splines worn (Chapter 6).

Noise when depressing or releasing clutch pedal

- [ ] Worn clutch release bearing (Chapter 6).
- [ ] Worn or dry clutch pedal bushes (Chapter 6).
- [ ] Faulty pressure plate assembly (Chapter 6).
- [ ] Pressure plate diaphragm spring broken (Chapter 6).
- [ ] Broken clutch disc cushioning springs (Chapter 6).

Manual gearbox

Noisy in neutral with engine running

- [ ] Input shaft bearings worn (noise apparent with clutch pedal released, but not when depressed) (Chapter 7).*
- [ ] Clutch release bearing worn (noise apparent with clutch pedal depressed, possibly less when released) (Chapter 6).

Noisy in one particular gear

- [ ] Worn, damaged or chipped gear teeth (Chapter 7).*

Difficulty engaging gears

- [ ] Clutch fault (Chapter 6).
- [ ] Worn or damaged gear linkage (Chapter 7).
- [ ] Incorrectly-adjusted gear linkage (Chapter 7).
- [ ] Worn synchroniser units (Chapter 7).*

Vibration

- [ ] Lack of oil (Chapter 1).
- [ ] Worn bearings (Chapter 7).*

Jumps out of gear

- [ ] Worn or damaged gear linkage (Chapter 7).
- [ ] Incorrectly-adjusted gear linkage (Chapter 7).
- [ ] Worn synchroniser units (Chapter 7).*
- [ ] Worn selector forks (Chapter 7).*

Lubricant leaks

- [ ] Leaking differential output oil seal (Chapter 7).
- [ ] Leaking housing joint (Chapter 7).*
- [ ] Leaking input shaft oil seal (Chapter 7).*

Although the corrective action necessary to remedy the symptoms described is beyond the scope of the home mechanic, the above information should be helpful in isolating the cause of the condition, so that the owner can communicate clearly with a professional mechanic.

Automatic transmission

Note: *Due to the complexity of the automatic transmission, it is difficult for the home mechanic to properly diagnose and service this unit. For problems other than the following, the vehicle should be taken to a dealer service department or automatic transmission specialist.*

Fluid leakage

☐ Automatic transmission fluid is usually dark in colour. Fluid leaks should not be confused with engine oil, which can easily be blown onto the transmission by air flow.

☐ To determine the source of a leak, first remove all built-up dirt and grime from the transmission housing and surrounding areas, using a degreasing agent, or by steam-cleaning. Drive the vehicle at low speed, so air flow will not blow the leak far from its source. Raise and support the vehicle, and determine where the leak is coming from. The following are common areas of leakage.

   a) *Oil pan.*
   b) *Dipstick tube (Chapter 1).*
   c) *Transmission-to-oil cooler fluid pipes/unions (Chapter 7).*

Transmission fluid brown, or has burned smell

☐ Transmission fluid level low, or fluid in need of renewal (Chapter 1).

General gear selection problems

☐ Chapter 7 deals with checking and adjusting the selector cable on automatic transmissions. The following are common problems which may be caused by a poorly-adjusted cable.

   a) *Engine starting in gears other than Park or Neutral.*
   b) *Indicator on gear selector lever pointing to a gear other than the one actually being used.*
   c) *Vehicle moves when in Park or Neutral.*
   d) *Poor gearshift quality or erratic gearchanges.*

Refer to Chapter 7 for the selector cable adjustment procedure.

Transmission will not downshift (kickdown) with accelerator pedal fully depressed

☐ Low transmission fluid level (Chapter 1).
☐ Incorrect selector cable adjustment (Chapter 7).

Engine will not start in any gear, or starts in gears other than Park or Neutral

☐ Incorrect starter inhibitor switch adjustment (Chapter 7).
☐ Incorrect selector cable adjustment (Chapter 7).

Transmission slips, shifts roughly, is noisy, or has no drive in forward or reverse gears

☐ There are many probable causes for the above problems, but the home mechanic should be concerned with only one possibility – fluid level. Before taking the vehicle to a dealer or transmission specialist, check the fluid level and condition of the fluid as described in Chapter 1. Correct the fluid level as necessary, or change the fluid and filter if needed. If the problem persists, professional help will be necessary.

Driveshafts

Clicking or knocking noise on turns (at slow speed on full-lock)

☐ Lack of constant velocity joint lubricant, possibly due to damaged gaiter (Chapter 8).
☐ Worn outer constant velocity joint (Chapter 8).

Vibration when accelerating or decelerating

☐ Worn inner constant velocity joint (Chapter 8).
☐ Bent or distorted driveshaft (Chapter 8).

Braking system

Note: *Before assuming that a brake problem exists, make sure that the tyres are in good condition and correctly inflated, that the front wheel alignment is correct, and that the vehicle is not loaded with weight in an unequal manner. Apart from checking the condition of all pipe and hose connections, any faults occurring on the anti-lock braking system should be referred to a Vauxhall/Opel dealer for diagnosis.*

Vehicle pulls to one side under braking

☐ Worn, defective, damaged or contaminated front brake pads or rear brake shoes on one side (Chapters 1 and 9).
☐ Seized or partially-seized front brake caliper or rear wheel cylinder piston (Chapters 1 and 9).
☐ A mixture of brake pad/shoe lining materials fitted between sides (Chapters 1 and 9).
☐ Front brake caliper mounting bolts loose (Chapter 9).
☐ Rear brake backplate mounting bolts loose (Chapter 9).
☐ Worn or damaged steering or suspension components (Chapters 1 and 10).

Noise (grinding or high-pitched squeal) when brakes applied

☐ Brake pad or shoe friction lining material worn down to metal backing (Chapters 1 and 9).
☐ Excessive corrosion of brake disc or drum. (May be apparent after the vehicle has been standing for some time (Chapters 1 and 9).
☐ Foreign object (stone chipping, etc) trapped between brake disc and shield (Chapters 1 and 9).

Excessive brake pedal travel

☐ Inoperative rear brake self-adjust mechanism (Chapters 1 and 9).
☐ Faulty master cylinder (Chapter 9).
☐ Air in hydraulic system (Chapters 1 and 9).
☐ Faulty vacuum servo unit (Chapter 9).

Brake pedal feels spongy when depressed

☐ Air in hydraulic system (Chapters 1 and 9).
☐ Deteriorated flexible rubber brake hoses (Chapters 1 and 9).
☐ Master cylinder mounting nuts loose (Chapter 9).
☐ Faulty master cylinder (Chapter 9).

Excessive brake pedal effort required to stop vehicle

☐ Faulty vacuum servo unit (Chapter 9).
☐ Disconnected, damaged or insecure brake servo vacuum hose (Chapter 9).
☐ Primary or secondary hydraulic circuit failure (Chapter 9).
☐ Seized brake caliper or wheel cylinder piston(s) (Chapter 9).
☐ Brake pads or brake shoes incorrectly fitted (Chapters 1 and 9).
☐ Incorrect grade of brake pads or brake shoes fitted (Chapters 1 and 9).
☐ Brake pads or brake shoe linings contaminated (Chapters 1 and 9).

Braking system (continued)

Rear wheels locking under normal braking

☐ Rear brake shoe linings contaminated (Chapters 1 and 9).
☐ Faulty rear brake pressure-regulating valve(s) (Chapter 9).

Judder felt through brake pedal or steering wheel when braking

☐ Excessive run-out or distortion of front discs or rear drums (Chapters 1 and 9).
☐ Brake pad or brake shoe linings worn (Chapters 1 and 9).

☐ Brake caliper or rear brake backplate mounting bolts loose (Chapter 9).
☐ Wear in suspension or steering components or mountings (Chapters 1 and 10).

Brakes binding

☐ Seized brake caliper or wheel cylinder piston(s) (Chapter 9).
☐ Incorrectly-adjusted handbrake mechanism (Chapter 9).
☐ Faulty master cylinder (Chapter 9).

Suspension and steering systems

Note: *Before diagnosing suspension or steering faults, be sure that the trouble is not due to incorrect tyre pressures, mixtures of tyre types, or binding brakes.*

Vehicle pulls to one side

☐ Defective tyre (*Weekly checks*).
☐ Excessive wear in suspension or steering components (Chapters 1 and 10).
☐ Incorrect front wheel alignment (Chapter 10).
☐ Accident damage to steering or suspension components (Chapter 1).

Wheel wobble and vibration

☐ Front roadwheels out of balance (vibration felt mainly through the steering wheel) (*Weekly checks*, Chapters 1 and 10).
☐ Rear roadwheels out of balance (vibration felt throughout the vehicle) (*Weekly checks*, Chapters 1 and 10).
☐ Roadwheels damaged or distorted (*Weekly checks*, Chapters 1 and 10).
☐ Faulty or damaged tyre (*Weekly checks*).
☐ Worn steering or suspension joints, bushes or components (Chapters 1 and 10).
☐ Wheel bolts loose (Chapters 1 and 10).

Excessive pitching and/or rolling around corners, or during braking

☐ Defective shock absorbers (Chapters 1 and 10).
☐ Broken or weak spring and/or suspension component (Chapters 1 and 10).
☐ Worn or damaged anti-roll bar or mountings (Chapter 10).

Wandering or general instability

☐ Incorrect front wheel alignment (Chapter 10).
☐ Worn steering or suspension joints, bushes or components (Chapters 1 and 10).
☐ Roadwheels out of balance (*Weekly checks*, Chapters 1 and 10).
☐ Faulty or damaged tyre (*Weekly checks*).
☐ Wheel bolts loose (Chapters 1 and 10).
☐ Defective shock absorbers (Chapters 1 and 10).

Excessively-stiff steering

☐ Lack of steering gear lubricant (Chapter 10).
☐ Seized track rod end balljoint or suspension balljoint (Chapters 1 and 10).

☐ Broken or incorrectly-adjusted auxiliary drivebelt (Chapter 1).
☐ Incorrect front wheel alignment (Chapter 10).
☐ Steering rack or column bent or damaged (Chapter 10).
☐ Faulty power steering pump (Chapter 10).

Excessive play in steering

☐ Worn steering column intermediate shaft universal joint (Chapter 10).
☐ Worn steering track rod end balljoints (Chapters 1 and 10).
☐ Worn rack-and-pinion steering gear (Chapter 10).
☐ Worn steering or suspension joints, bushes or components (Chapters 1 and 10).

Lack of power assistance

☐ Broken or incorrectly-adjusted auxiliary drivebelt (Chapter 1).
☐ Incorrect power steering fluid level (*Weekly checks*).
☐ Restriction in power steering fluid hoses (Chapter 1).
☐ Faulty power steering pump (Chapter 10).
☐ Faulty rack-and-pinion steering gear (Chapter 10).

Tyre wear excessive

Tyres worn on inside or outside edges

☐ Tyres under-inflated (wear on both edges) (*Weekly checks*).
☐ Incorrect camber or castor angles (wear on one edge only) (Chapter 10).
☐ Worn steering or suspension joints, bushes or components (Chapters 1 and 10).
☐ Excessively-hard cornering.
☐ Accident damage.

Tyre treads exhibit feathered edges

☐ Incorrect toe setting (Chapter 10).

Tyres worn in centre of tread

☐ Tyres over-inflated (*Weekly checks*).

Tyres worn on inside and outside edges

☐ Tyres under-inflated (*Weekly checks*).

Tyres worn unevenly

☐ Tyres/wheels out of balance (*Weekly checks*).
☐ Excessive wheel or tyre run-out (*Weekly checks*).
☐ Worn shock absorbers (Chapters 1 and 10).
☐ Faulty tyre (*Weekly checks*).

Electrical system

Note: *For problems associated with the starting system, refer to the faults listed under 'Engine' earlier in this Section.*

Battery will not hold a charge for more than a few days

- ☐ Battery defective internally (Chapter 5).
- ☐ Battery terminal connections loose or corroded (*Weekly checks*).
- ☐ Auxiliary drivebelt worn or incorrectly adjusted (Chapter 1).
- ☐ Alternator not charging at correct output (Chapter 5).
- ☐ Alternator or voltage regulator faulty (Chapter 5).
- ☐ Short-circuit causing continual battery drain (Chapters 5 and 12).

Ignition/no-charge warning light remains illuminated with engine running

- ☐ Auxiliary drivebelt broken, worn, or incorrectly adjusted (Chapter 1).
- ☐ Alternator brushes worn, sticking, or dirty (Chapter 5).
- ☐ Alternator brush springs weak or broken (Chapter 5).
- ☐ Internal fault in alternator or voltage regulator (Chapter 5).
- ☐ Broken, disconnected, or loose wiring in charging circuit (Chapter 5).

Ignition/no-charge warning light fails to come on

- ☐ Warning light bulb blown (Chapter 12).
- ☐ Broken, disconnected, or loose wiring in warning light circuit (Chapter 12).
- ☐ Alternator faulty (Chapter 5).

Lights inoperative

- ☐ Bulb blown (Chapter 12).
- ☐ Corrosion of bulb or bulbholder contacts (Chapter 12).
- ☐ Blown fuse (Chapter 12).
- ☐ Faulty relay (Chapter 12).
- ☐ Broken, loose, or disconnected wiring (Chapter 12).
- ☐ Faulty switch (Chapter 12).

Instrument readings inaccurate or erratic

Instrument readings increase with engine speed

- ☐ Faulty voltage regulator (Chapter 12).

Fuel or temperature gauges give no reading

- ☐ Faulty gauge sender unit (Chapters 3 or 4).
- ☐ Wiring open-circuit (Chapter 12).
- ☐ Faulty gauge (Chapter 12).

Fuel or temperature gauges give continuous maximum reading

- ☐ Faulty gauge sender unit (Chapters 3 or 4).
- ☐ Wiring short-circuit (Chapter 12).
- ☐ Faulty gauge (Chapter 12).

Horn inoperative, or unsatisfactory in operation

Horn operates all the time

- ☐ Horn push either earthed or stuck down (Chapter 12).
- ☐ Horn cable-to-horn push earthed (Chapter 12).

Horn fails to operate

- ☐ Blown fuse (Chapter 12).
- ☐ Cable or cable connections loose, broken or disconnected (Chapter 12).
- ☐ Faulty horn (Chapter 12).

Horn emits intermittent or unsatisfactory sound

- ☐ Cable connections loose (Chapter 12).
- ☐ Horn mountings loose (Chapter 12).
- ☐ Faulty horn (Chapter 12).

Windscreen/tailgate wipers inoperative, or unsatisfactory in operation

Wipers fail to operate, or operate very slowly

- ☐ Wiper blades stuck to screen, or linkage seized or binding.
- ☐ Blown fuse (Chapter 12).
- ☐ Cable or cable connections loose, broken or disconnected (Chapter 12).
- ☐ Faulty relay (Chapter 12).
- ☐ Faulty wiper motor (Chapter 12).

Wiper blades sweep over too large or too small an area of the glass

- ☐ Wiper arms incorrectly positioned on spindles.
- ☐ Excessive wear of wiper linkage (Chapter 12).
- ☐ Wiper motor or linkage mountings loose or insecure (Chapter 12).

Wiper blades fail to clean the glass effectively

- ☐ Wiper blade rubbers worn or perished (*Weekly checks*).
- ☐ Wiper arm tension springs broken, or arm pivots seized (Chapter 12).
- ☐ Insufficient windscreen washer additive to adequately remove road film (*Weekly checks*).

Windscreen/tailgate washers inoperative, or unsatisfactory in operation

One or more washer jets inoperative

- ☐ Blocked washer jet (Chapter 12).
- ☐ Disconnected, kinked or restricted fluid hose (Chapter 12).
- ☐ Insufficient fluid in washer reservoir (*Weekly checks*).

Washer pump fails to operate

- ☐ Broken or disconnected wiring or connections (Chapter 12).
- ☐ Blown fuse (Chapter 12).
- ☐ Faulty washer switch (Chapter 12).
- ☐ Faulty washer pump (Chapter 12).

Washer pump runs for some time before fluid is emitted from jets

- ☐ Faulty one-way valve in fluid supply hose (Chapter 12).

Electric windows inoperative, or unsatisfactory in operation

Window glass will only move in one direction

- ☐ Faulty switch (Chapter 12).

Window glass slow to move

- ☐ Incorrectly-adjusted door glass guide channels (Chapter 11).
- ☐ Regulator seized or damaged, or in need of lubrication (Chapter 11).
- ☐ Door internal components or trim fouling regulator (Chapter 11).
- ☐ Faulty motor (Chapter 11).

Window glass fails to move

- ☐ Incorrectly-adjusted door glass guide channels (Chapter 11).
- ☐ Blown fuse (Chapter 12).
- ☐ Faulty relay (Chapter 12).
- ☐ Broken or disconnected wiring or connections (Chapter 12).
- ☐ Faulty motor (Chapter 11).

Electrical system (continued)

Central locking system inoperative, or unsatisfactory in operation

Complete system failure

- [ ] Blown fuse (Chapter 12).
- [ ] Faulty relay (Chapter 12).
- [ ] Broken or disconnected wiring or connections (Chapter 12).
- [ ] Faulty control unit (Chapter 11).

Latch locks but will not unlock, or unlocks but will not lock

- [ ] Faulty master switch (Chapter 12).

- [ ] Broken or disconnected latch operating rods or levers (Chapter 11).
- [ ] Faulty relay (Chapter 12).
- [ ] Faulty control unit (Chapter 11).

One solenoid/motor fails to operate

- [ ] Broken or disconnected wiring or connections (Chapter 12).
- [ ] Faulty solenoid/motor (Chapter 11).
- [ ] Broken, binding or disconnected latch operating rods or levers (Chapter 11).
- [ ] Fault in door latch (Chapter 11).

A

ABS (Anti-lock brake system) A system, usually electronically controlled, that senses incipient wheel lockup during braking and relieves hydraulic pressure at wheels that are about to skid.

Air bag An inflatable bag hidden in the steering wheel (driver's side) or the dash or glovebox (passenger side). In a head-on collision, the bags inflate, preventing the driver and front passenger from being thrown forward into the steering wheel or windscreen.

Air cleaner A metal or plastic housing, containing a filter element, which removes dust and dirt from the air being drawn into the engine.

Air filter element The actual filter in an air cleaner system, usually manufactured from pleated paper and requiring renewal at regular intervals.

Air filter

Allen key A hexagonal wrench which fits into a recessed hexagonal hole.

Alligator clip A long-nosed spring-loaded metal clip with meshing teeth. Used to make temporary electrical connections.

Alternator A component in the electrical system which converts mechanical energy from a drivebelt into electrical energy to charge the battery and to operate the starting system, ignition system and electrical accessories.

Ampere (amp) A unit of measurement for the flow of electric current. One amp is the amount of current produced by one volt acting through a resistance of one ohm.

Anaerobic sealer A substance used to prevent bolts and screws from loosening. Anaerobic means that it does not require oxygen for activation. The Loctite brand is widely used.

Antifreeze A substance (usually ethylene glycol) mixed with water, and added to a vehicle's cooling system, to prevent freezing of the coolant in winter. Antifreeze also contains chemicals to inhibit corrosion and the formation of rust and other deposits that would tend to clog the radiator and coolant passages and reduce cooling efficiency.

Anti-seize compound A coating that reduces the risk of seizing on fasteners that are subjected to high temperatures, such as exhaust manifold bolts and nuts.

Asbestos A natural fibrous mineral with great heat resistance, commonly used in the composition of brake friction materials. Asbestos is a health hazard and the dust created by brake systems should never be inhaled or ingested.

Axle A shaft on which a wheel revolves, or which revolves with a wheel. Also, a solid beam that connects the two wheels at one end of the vehicle. An axle which also transmits power to the wheels is known as a live axle.

Axleshaft A single rotating shaft, on either side of the differential, which delivers power from the final drive assembly to the drive wheels. Also called a driveshaft or a halfshaft.

B

Ball bearing An anti-friction bearing consisting of a hardened inner and outer race with hardened steel balls between two races.

Bearing The curved surface on a shaft or in a bore, or the part assembled into either, that permits relative motion between them with minimum wear and friction.

Bearing

Big-end bearing The bearing in the end of the connecting rod that's attached to the crankshaft.

Bleed nipple A valve on a brake wheel cylinder, caliper or other hydraulic component that is opened to purge the hydraulic system of air. Also called a bleed screw.

Brake bleeding Procedure for removing air from lines of a hydraulic brake system.

Brake bleeding

Brake disc The component of a disc brake that rotates with the wheels.

Brake drum The component of a drum brake that rotates with the wheels.

Brake linings The friction material which contacts the brake disc or drum to retard the vehicle's speed. The linings are bonded or riveted to the brake pads or shoes.

Brake pads The replaceable friction pads that pinch the brake disc when the brakes are applied. Brake pads consist of a friction material bonded or riveted to a rigid backing plate.

Brake shoe The crescent-shaped carrier to which the brake linings are mounted and which forces the lining against the rotating drum during braking.

Braking systems For more information on braking systems, consult the *Haynes Automotive Brake Manual*.

Breaker bar A long socket wrench handle providing greater leverage.

Bulkhead The insulated partition between the engine and the passenger compartment.

C

Caliper The non-rotating part of a disc-brake assembly that straddles the disc and carries the brake pads. The caliper also contains the hydraulic components that cause the pads to pinch the disc when the brakes are applied. A caliper is also a measuring tool that can be set to measure inside or outside dimensions of an object.

Camshaft A rotating shaft on which a series of cam lobes operate the valve mechanisms. The camshaft may be driven by gears, by sprockets and chain or by sprockets and a belt.

Canister A container in an evaporative emission control system; contains activated charcoal granules to trap vapours from the fuel system.

Canister

Carburettor A device which mixes fuel with air in the proper proportions to provide a desired power output from a spark ignition internal combustion engine.

Castellated Resembling the parapets along the top of a castle wall. For example, a castellated balljoint stud nut.

Castor In wheel alignment, the backward or forward tilt of the steering axis. Castor is positive when the steering axis is inclined rearward at the top.

Catalytic converter A silencer-like device in the exhaust system which converts certain pollutants in the exhaust gases into less harmful substances.

Catalytic converter

Circlip A ring-shaped clip used to prevent endwise movement of cylindrical parts and shafts. An internal circlip is installed in a groove in a housing; an external circlip fits into a groove on the outside of a cylindrical piece such as a shaft.

Clearance The amount of space between two parts. For example, between a piston and a cylinder, between a bearing and a journal, etc.

Coil spring A spiral of elastic steel found in various sizes throughout a vehicle, for example as a springing medium in the suspension and in the valve train.

Compression Reduction in volume, and increase in pressure and temperature, of a gas, caused by squeezing it into a smaller space.

Compression ratio The relationship between cylinder volume when the piston is at top dead centre and cylinder volume when the piston is at bottom dead centre.

Constant velocity (CV) joint A type of universal joint that cancels out vibrations caused by driving power being transmitted through an angle.

Core plug A disc or cup-shaped metal device inserted in a hole in a casting through which core was removed when the casting was formed. Also known as a freeze plug or expansion plug.

Crankcase The lower part of the engine block in which the crankshaft rotates.

Crankshaft The main rotating member, or shaft, running the length of the crankcase, with offset "throws" to which the connecting rods are attached.

Crankshaft assembly

Crocodile clip See Alligator clip

D

Diagnostic code Code numbers obtained by accessing the diagnostic mode of an engine management computer. This code can be used to determine the area in the system where a malfunction may be located.

Disc brake A brake design incorporating a rotating disc onto which brake pads are squeezed. The resulting friction converts the energy of a moving vehicle into heat.

Double-overhead cam (DOHC) An engine that uses two overhead camshafts, usually one for the intake valves and one for the exhaust valves.

Drivebelt(s) The belt(s) used to drive accessories such as the alternator, water pump, power steering pump, air conditioning compressor, etc. off the crankshaft pulley.

Accessory drivebelts

Driveshaft Any shaft used to transmit motion. Commonly used when referring to the axleshafts on a front wheel drive vehicle.

Drum brake A type of brake using a drum-shaped metal cylinder attached to the inner surface of the wheel. When the brake pedal is pressed, curved brake shoes with friction linings press against the inside of the drum to slow or stop the vehicle.

E

EGR valve A valve used to introduce exhaust gases into the intake air stream.

Electronic control unit (ECU) A computer which controls (for instance) ignition and fuel injection systems, or an anti-lock braking system. For more information refer to the *Haynes Automotive Electrical and Electronic Systems Manual*.

Electronic Fuel Injection (EFI) A computer controlled fuel system that distributes fuel through an injector located in each intake port of the engine.

Emergency brake A braking system, independent of the main hydraulic system, that can be used to slow or stop the vehicle if the primary brakes fail, or to hold the vehicle stationary even though the brake pedal isn't depressed. It usually consists of a hand lever that actuates either front or rear brakes mechanically through a series of cables and linkages. Also known as a handbrake or parking brake.

Endfloat The amount of lengthwise movement between two parts. As applied to a crankshaft, the distance that the crankshaft can move forward and back in the cylinder block.

Engine management system (EMS) A computer controlled system which manages the fuel injection and the ignition systems in an integrated fashion.

Exhaust manifold A part with several passages through which exhaust gases leave the engine combustion chambers and enter the exhaust pipe.

F

Fan clutch A viscous (fluid) drive coupling device which permits variable engine fan speeds in relation to engine speeds.

Feeler blade A thin strip or blade of hardened steel, ground to an exact thickness, used to check or measure clearances between parts.

Feeler blade

Firing order The order in which the engine cylinders fire, or deliver their power strokes, beginning with the number one cylinder.

Flywheel A heavy spinning wheel in which energy is absorbed and stored by means of momentum. On cars, the flywheel is attached to the crankshaft to smooth out firing impulses.

Free play The amount of travel before any action takes place. The "looseness" in a linkage, or an assembly of parts, between the initial application of force and actual movement. For example, the distance the brake pedal moves before the pistons in the master cylinder are actuated.

Fuse An electrical device which protects a circuit against accidental overload. The typical fuse contains a soft piece of metal which is calibrated to melt at a predetermined current flow (expressed as amps) and break the circuit.

Fusible link A circuit protection device consisting of a conductor surrounded by heat-resistant insulation. The conductor is smaller than the wire it protects, so it acts as the weakest link in the circuit. Unlike a blown fuse, a failed fusible link must frequently be cut from the wire for replacement.

G

Gap The distance the spark must travel in jumping from the centre electrode to the side electrode in a spark plug. Also refers to the spacing between the points in a contact breaker assembly in a conventional points-type ignition, or to the distance between the reluctor or rotor and the pickup coil in an electronic ignition.

Adjusting spark plug gap

Gasket Any thin, soft material - usually cork, cardboard, asbestos or soft metal - installed between two metal surfaces to ensure a good seal. For instance, the cylinder head gasket seals the joint between the block and the cylinder head.

Gasket

Gauge An instrument panel display used to monitor engine conditions. A gauge with a movable pointer on a dial or a fixed scale is an analogue gauge. A gauge with a numerical readout is called a digital gauge.

H

Halfshaft A rotating shaft that transmits power from the final drive unit to a drive wheel, usually when referring to a live rear axle.

Harmonic balancer A device designed to reduce torsion or twisting vibration in the crankshaft. May be incorporated in the crankshaft pulley. Also known as a vibration damper.

Hone An abrasive tool for correcting small irregularities or differences in diameter in an engine cylinder, brake cylinder, etc.

Hydraulic tappet A tappet that utilises hydraulic pressure from the engine's lubrication system to maintain zero clearance (constant contact with both camshaft and valve stem). Automatically adjusts to variation in valve stem length. Hydraulic tappets also reduce valve noise.

I

Ignition timing The moment at which the spark plug fires, usually expressed in the number of crankshaft degrees before the piston reaches the top of its stroke.

Inlet manifold A tube or housing with passages through which flows the air-fuel mixture (carburettor vehicles and vehicles with throttle body injection) or air only (port fuel-injected vehicles) to the port openings in the cylinder head.

J

Jump start Starting the engine of a vehicle with a discharged or weak battery by attaching jump leads from the weak battery to a charged or helper battery.

L

Load Sensing Proportioning Valve (LSPV) A brake hydraulic system control valve that works like a proportioning valve, but also takes into consideration the amount of weight carried by the rear axle.

Locknut A nut used to lock an adjustment nut, or other threaded component, in place. For example, a locknut is employed to keep the adjusting nut on the rocker arm in position.

Lockwasher A form of washer designed to prevent an attaching nut from working loose.

M

MacPherson strut A type of front suspension system devised by Earle MacPherson at Ford of England. In its original form, a simple lateral link with the anti-roll bar creates the lower control arm. A long strut - an integral coil spring and shock absorber - is mounted between the body and the steering knuckle. Many modern so-called MacPherson strut systems use a conventional lower A-arm and don't rely on the anti-roll bar for location.

Multimeter An electrical test instrument with the capability to measure voltage, current and resistance.

N

NOx Oxides of Nitrogen. A common toxic pollutant emitted by petrol and diesel engines at higher temperatures.

O

Ohm The unit of electrical resistance. One volt applied to a resistance of one ohm will produce a current of one amp.

Ohmmeter An instrument for measuring electrical resistance.

O-ring A type of sealing ring made of a special rubber-like material; in use, the O-ring is compressed into a groove to provide the sealing action.

Overhead cam (ohc) engine An engine with the camshaft(s) located on top of the cylinder head(s).

Overhead valve (ohv) engine An engine with the valves located in the cylinder head, but with the camshaft located in the engine block.

Oxygen sensor A device installed in the engine exhaust manifold, which senses the oxygen content in the exhaust and converts this information into an electric current. Also called a Lambda sensor.

P

Phillips screw A type of screw head having a cross instead of a slot for a corresponding type of screwdriver.

Plastigage A thin strip of plastic thread, available in different sizes, used for measuring clearances. For example, a strip of Plastigage is laid across a bearing journal. The parts are assembled and dismantled; the width of the crushed strip indicates the clearance between journal and bearing.

Plastigage

Propeller shaft The long hollow tube with universal joints at both ends that carries power from the transmission to the differential on front-engined rear wheel drive vehicles.

Proportioning valve A hydraulic control valve which limits the amount of pressure to the rear brakes during panic stops to prevent wheel lock-up.

R

Rack-and-pinion steering A steering system with a pinion gear on the end of the steering shaft that mates with a rack (think of a geared wheel opened up and laid flat). When the steering wheel is turned, the pinion turns, moving the rack to the left or right. This movement is transmitted through the track rods to the steering arms at the wheels.

Radiator A liquid-to-air heat transfer device designed to reduce the temperature of the coolant in an internal combustion engine cooling system.

Refrigerant Any substance used as a heat transfer agent in an air-conditioning system. R-12 has been the principle refrigerant for many years; recently, however, manufacturers have begun using R-134a, a non-CFC substance that is considered less harmful to the ozone in the upper atmosphere.

Rocker arm A lever arm that rocks on a shaft or pivots on a stud. In an overhead valve engine, the rocker arm converts the upward movement of the pushrod into a downward movement to open a valve.

Rotor In a distributor, the rotating device inside the cap that connects the centre electrode and the outer terminals as it turns, distributing the high voltage from the coil secondary winding to the proper spark plug. Also, that part of an alternator which rotates inside the stator. Also, the rotating assembly of a turbocharger, including the compressor wheel, shaft and turbine wheel.

Runout The amount of wobble (in-and-out movement) of a gear or wheel as it's rotated. The amount a shaft rotates "out-of-true." The out-of-round condition of a rotating part.

S

Sealant A liquid or paste used to prevent leakage at a joint. Sometimes used in conjunction with a gasket.

Sealed beam lamp An older headlight design which integrates the reflector, lens and filaments into a hermetically-sealed one-piece unit. When a filament burns out or the lens cracks, the entire unit is simply replaced.

Serpentine drivebelt A single, long, wide accessory drivebelt that's used on some newer vehicles to drive all the accessories, instead of a series of smaller, shorter belts. Serpentine drivebelts are usually tensioned by an automatic tensioner.

Serpentine drivebelt

Shim Thin spacer, commonly used to adjust the clearance or relative positions between two parts. For example, shims inserted into or under bucket tappets control valve clearances. Clearance is adjusted by changing the thickness of the shim.

Slide hammer A special puller that screws into or hooks onto a component such as a shaft or bearing; a heavy sliding handle on the shaft bottoms against the end of the shaft to knock the component free.

Sprocket A tooth or projection on the periphery of a wheel, shaped to engage with a chain or drivebelt. Commonly used to refer to the sprocket wheel itself.

Starter inhibitor switch On vehicles with an automatic transmission, a switch that prevents starting if the vehicle is not in Neutral or Park.

Strut See MacPherson strut.

T

Tappet A cylindrical component which transmits motion from the cam to the valve stem, either directly or via a pushrod and rocker arm. Also called a cam follower.

Thermostat A heat-controlled valve that regulates the flow of coolant between the cylinder block and the radiator, so maintaining optimum engine operating temperature. A thermostat is also used in some air cleaners in which the temperature is regulated.

Thrust bearing The bearing in the clutch assembly that is moved in to the release levers by clutch pedal action to disengage the clutch. Also referred to as a release bearing.

Timing belt A toothed belt which drives the camshaft. Serious engine damage may result if it breaks in service.

Timing chain A chain which drives the camshaft.

Toe-in The amount the front wheels are closer together at the front than at the rear. On rear wheel drive vehicles, a slight amount of toe-in is usually specified to keep the front wheels running parallel on the road by offsetting other forces that tend to spread the wheels apart.

Toe-out The amount the front wheels are closer together at the rear than at the front. On front wheel drive vehicles, a slight amount of toe-out is usually specified.

Tools For full information on choosing and using tools, refer to the *Haynes Automotive Tools Manual*.

Tracer A stripe of a second colour applied to a wire insulator to distinguish that wire from another one with the same colour insulator.

Tune-up A process of accurate and careful adjustments and parts replacement to obtain the best possible engine performance.

Turbocharger A centrifugal device, driven by exhaust gases, that pressurises the intake air. Normally used to increase the power output from a given engine displacement, but can also be used primarily to reduce exhaust emissions (as on VW's "Umwelt" Diesel engine).

U

Universal joint or U-joint A double-pivoted connection for transmitting power from a driving to a driven shaft through an angle. A U-joint consists of two Y-shaped yokes and a cross-shaped member called the spider.

V

Valve A device through which the flow of liquid, gas, vacuum, or loose material in bulk may be started, stopped, or regulated by a movable part that opens, shuts, or partially obstructs one or more ports or passageways. A valve is also the movable part of such a device.

Valve clearance The clearance between the valve tip (the end of the valve stem) and the rocker arm or tappet. The valve clearance is measured when the valve is closed.

Vernier caliper A precision measuring instrument that measures inside and outside dimensions. Not quite as accurate as a micrometer, but more convenient.

Viscosity The thickness of a liquid or its resistance to flow.

Volt A unit for expressing electrical "pressure" in a circuit. One volt that will produce a current of one ampere through a resistance of one ohm.

W

Welding Various processes used to join metal items by heating the areas to be joined to a molten state and fusing them together. For more information refer to the *Haynes Automotive Welding Manual*.

Wiring diagram A drawing portraying the components and wires in a vehicle's electrical system, using standardised symbols. For more information refer to the *Haynes Automotive Electrical and Electronic Systems Manual*.

Haynes Manuals – The Complete UK Car List

Title	Book No.
ALFA ROMEO Alfasud/Sprint (74 - 88) up to F *	0292
Alfa Romeo Alfetta (73 - 87) up to E *	0531
AUDI 80, 90 & Coupe Petrol (79 - Nov 88) up to F	0605
Audi 80, 90 & Coupe Petrol (Oct 86 - 90) D to H	1491
Audi 100 & 200 Petrol (Oct 82 - 90) up to H	0907
Audi 100 & A6 Petrol & Diesel (May 91 - May 97) H to P	3504
Audi A3 Petrol & Diesel (96 - May 03) P to 03	4253
Audi A4 Petrol & Diesel (95 - Feb 00) M to V	3575
AUSTIN A35 & A40 (56 - 67) up to F *	0118
Austin/MG/Rover Maestro 1.3 & 1.6 Petrol (83 - 95) up to M	0922
Austin/MG Metro (80 - May 90) up to G	0718
Austin/Rover Montego 1.3 & 1.6 Petrol (84 - 94) A to L	1066
Austin/MG/Rover Montego 2.0 Petrol (84 - 95) A to M	1067
Mini (59 - 69) up to H *	0527
Mini (69 - 01) up to X	0646
Austin/Rover 2.0 litre Diesel Engine (86 - 93) C to L	1857
Austin Healey 100/6 & 3000 (56 - 68) up to G *	0049
BEDFORD CF Petrol (69 - 87) up to E	0163
Bedford/Vauxhall Rascal & Suzuki Supercarry (86 - Oct 94) C to M	3015
BMW 316, 320 & 320i (4-cyl) (75 - Feb 83) up to Y *	0276
BMW 320, 320i, 323i & 325i (6-cyl) (Oct 77 - Sept 87) up to E	0815
BMW 3- & 5-Series Petrol (81 - 91) up to J	1948
BMW 3-Series Petrol (Apr 91 - 99) H to V	3210
BMW 3-Series Petrol (Sept 98 - 03) S to 53	4067
BMW 520i & 525e (Oct 81 - June 88) up to E	1560
BMW 525, 528 & 528i (73 - Sept 81) up to X *	0632
BMW 5-Series 6-cyl Petrol (April 96 - Aug 03) N to 03	4151
BMW 1500, 1502, 1600, 1602, 2000 & 2002 (59 - 77) up to S *	0240
CHRYSLER PT Cruiser Petrol (00 - 03) W to 53	4058
CITROËN 2CV, Ami & Dyane (67 - 90) up to H	0196
Citroën AX Petrol & Diesel (87 - 97) D to P	3014
Citroën Berlingo & Peugeot Partner Petrol & Diesel (96 - 05) P to 55	4281
Citroën BX Petrol (83 - 94) A to L	0908
Citroën C15 Van Petrol & Diesel (89 - Oct 98) F to S	3509
Citroën C3 Petrol & Diesel (02 - 05) 51 to 05	4197
Citroën CX Petrol (75 - 88) up to F	0528
Citroën Saxo Petrol & Diesel (96 - 04) N to 54	3506
Citroën Visa Petrol (79 - 88) up to F	0620
Citroën Xantia Petrol & Diesel (93 - 01) K to Y	3082
Citroën XM Petrol & Diesel (89 - 00) G to X	3451
Citroën Xsara Petrol & Diesel (97 - Sept 00) R to W	3751
Citroën Xsara Picasso Petrol & Diesel (00 - 02) W to 52	3944
Citroën ZX Diesel (91 - 98) J to S	1922
Citroën ZX Petrol (91 - 98) H to S	1881
Citroën 1.7 & 1.9 litre Diesel Engine (84 - 96) A to N	1379
FIAT 126 (73 - 87) up to E *	0305
Fiat 500 (57 - 73) up to M *	0090
Fiat Bravo & Brava Petrol (95 - 00) N to W	3572
Fiat Cinquecento (93 - 98) K to R	3501
Fiat Panda (81 - 95) up to M	0793
Fiat Punto Petrol & Diesel (94 - Oct 99) L to V	3251
Fiat Punto Petrol (Oct 99 - July 03) V to 03	4066
Fiat Regata Petrol (84 - 88) A to F	1167
Fiat Tipo Petrol (88 - 91) E to J	1625
Fiat Uno Petrol (83 - 95) up to M	0923

Title	Book No.
Fiat X1/9 (74 - 89) up to G *	0273
FORD Anglia (59 - 68) up to G *	0001
Ford Capri II (& III) 1.6 & 2.0 (74 - 87) up to E *	0283
Ford Capri II (& III) 2.8 & 3.0 V6 (74 - 87) up to E	1309
Ford Cortina Mk III 1300 & 1600 (70 - 76) up to P *	0070
Ford Escort Mk I 1100 & 1300 (68 - 74) up to N *	0171
Ford Escort Mk I Mexico, RS 1600 & RS 2000 (70 - 74) up to N *	0139
Ford Escort Mk II Mexico, RS 1800 & RS 2000 (75 - 80) up to W *	0735
Ford Escort (75 - Aug 80) up to V *	0280
Ford Escort Petrol (Sept 80 - Sept 90) up to H	0686
Ford Escort & Orion Petrol (Sept 90 - 00) H to X	1737
Ford Escort & Orion Diesel (Sept 90 - 00) H to X	4081
Ford Fiesta (76 - Aug 83) up to Y	0334
Ford Fiesta Petrol (Aug 83 - Feb 89) A to F	1030
Ford Fiesta Petrol (Feb 89 - Oct 95) F to N	1595
Ford Fiesta Petrol & Diesel (Oct 95 - Mar 02) N to 02	3397
Ford Fiesta Petrol & Diesel (Apr 02 - 05) 02 to 54	4170
Ford Focus Petrol & Diesel (98 - 01) S to Y	3759
Ford Focus Petrol & Diesel (Oct 01 - 04) 51 to 54	4167
Ford Galaxy Petrol & Diesel (95 - Aug 00) M to W	3984
Ford Granada Petrol (Sept 77 - Feb 85) up to B *	0481
Ford Granada & Scorpio Petrol (Mar 85 - 94) B to M	1245
Ford Ka (96 - 02) P to 52	3570
Ford Mondeo Petrol (93 - Sept 00) K to X	1923
Ford Mondeo Petrol & Diesel (Oct 00 - Jul 03) X to 03	3990
Ford Mondeo Diesel (93 - 96) L to N	3465
Ford Orion Petrol (83 - Sept 90) up to H	1009
Ford Sierra 4-cyl Petrol (82 - 93) up to K	0903
Ford Sierra V6 Petrol (82 - 91) up to J	0904
Ford Transit Petrol (Mk 2) (78 - Jan 86) up to C	0719
Ford Transit Petrol (Mk 3) (Feb 86 - 89) C to G	1468
Ford Transit Diesel (Feb 86 - 99) C to T	3019
Ford 1.6 & 1.8 litre Diesel Engine (84 - 96) A to N	1172
Ford 2.1, 2.3 & 2.5 litre Diesel Engine (77 - 90) up to H	1606
FREIGHT ROVER Sherpa Petrol (74 - 87) up to E	0463
HILLMAN Avenger (70 - 82) up to Y	0037
Hillman Imp (63 - 76) up to R *	0022
HONDA Civic (Feb 84 - Oct 87) A to E	1226
Honda Civic (Nov 91 - 96) J to N	3199
Honda Civic Petrol (Mar 95 - 00) M to X	4050
HYUNDAI Pony (85 - 94) C to M	3398
JAGUAR E Type (61 - 72) up to L *	0140
Jaguar MkI & II, 240 & 340 (55 - 69) up to H *	0098
Jaguar XJ6, XJ & Sovereign; Daimler Sovereign (68 - Oct 86) up to D	0242
Jaguar XJ6 & Sovereign (Oct 86 - Sept 94) D to M	3261
Jaguar XJ12, XJS & Sovereign; Daimler Double Six (72 - 88) up to F	0478
JEEP Cherokee Petrol (93 - 96) K to N	1943
LADA 1200, 1300, 1500 & 1600 (74 - 91) up to J	0413
Lada Samara (87 - 91) D to J	1610
LAND ROVER 90, 110 & Defender Diesel (83 - 95) up to N	3017
Land Rover Discovery Petrol & Diesel (89 - 98) G to S	3016
Land Rover Discovery Diesel (99 - 04) S to 54	4606
Land Rover Freelander Petrol & Diesel (97 - 02) R to 52	3929
Land Rover Series IIA & III Diesel (58 - 85) up to C	0529
Land Rover Series II, IIA & III 4-cyl Petrol (58 - 85) up to C	0314
MAZDA 323 (Mar 81 - Oct 89) up to G	1608
Mazda 323 (Oct 89 - 98) G to R	3455
Mazda 626 (May 83 - Sept 87) up to E	0929

Title	Book No.
Mazda B1600, B1800 & B2000 Pick-up Petrol (72 - 88) up to F	0267
Mazda RX-7 (79 - 85) up to C *	0460
MERCEDES-BENZ 190, 190E & 190D Petrol & Diesel (83 - 93) A to L	3450
Mercedes-Benz 200D, 240D, 240TD, 300D & 300TD 123 Series Diesel (Oct 76 - 85) up to C	1114
Mercedes-Benz 250 & 280 (68 - 72) up to L *	0346
Mercedes-Benz 250 & 280 123 Series Petrol (Oct 76 - 84) up to B *	0677
Mercedes-Benz 124 Series Petrol & Diesel (85 - Aug 93) C to K	3253
Mercedes-Benz C-Class Petrol & Diesel (93 - Aug 00) L to W	3511
MGA (55 - 62) *	0475
MGB (62 - 80) up to W	0111
MG Midget & Austin-Healey Sprite (58 - 80) up to W *	0265
MINI Petrol (July 01 - 05) Y to 05	4273
MITSUBISHI Shogun & L200 Pick-Ups Petrol (83 - 94) up to M	1944
MORRIS Ital 1.3 (80 - 84) up to B	0705
Morris Minor 1000 (56 - 71) up to K	0024
NISSAN Almera Petrol (95 - Feb 00) N to V	4053
Nissan Bluebird (May 84 - Mar 86) A to C	1223
Nissan Bluebird Petrol (Mar 86 - 90) C to H	1473
Nissan Cherry (Sept 82 - 86) up to D	1031
Nissan Micra (83 - Jan 93) up to K	0931
Nissan Micra (93 - 02) K to 52	3254
Nissan Primera Petrol (90 - Aug 99) H to T	1851
Nissan Stanza (82 - 86) up to D	0824
Nissan Sunny Petrol (May 82 - Oct 86) up to D	0895
Nissan Sunny Petrol (Oct 86 - Mar 91) D to H	1378
Nissan Sunny Petrol (Apr 91 - 95) H to N	3219
OPEL Ascona & Manta (B Series) (Sept 75 - 88) up to F *	0316
Opel Ascona Petrol (81 - 88)	3215
Opel Astra Petrol (Oct 91 - Feb 98)	3156
Opel Corsa Petrol (83 - Mar 93)	3160
Opel Corsa Petrol (Mar 93 - 97)	3159
Opel Kadett Petrol (Nov 79 - Oct 84) up to B	0634
Opel Kadett Petrol (Oct 84 - Oct 91)	3196
Opel Omega & Senator Petrol (Nov 86 - 94)	3157
Opel Rekord Petrol (Feb 78 - Oct 86) up to D	0543
Opel Vectra Petrol (Oct 88 - Oct 95)	3158
PEUGEOT 106 Petrol & Diesel (91 - 04) J to 53	1882
Peugeot 205 Petrol (83 - 97) A to P	0932
Peugeot 206 Petrol & Diesel (98 - 01) S to X	3757
Peugeot 206 Petrol & Diesel (01 - 06) Y to 56	4613
Peugeot 306 Petrol & Diesel (93 - 02) K to 02	3073
Peugeot 307 Petrol & Diesel (01 - 04) Y to 54	4147
Peugeot 309 Petrol (86 - 93) C to K	1266
Peugeot 405 Petrol (88 - 97) E to P	1559
Peugeot 405 Diesel (88 - 97) E to P	3198
Peugeot 406 Petrol & Diesel (96 - Mar 99) N to T	3394
Peugeot 406 Petrol & Diesel (Mar 99 - 02) T to 52	3982
Peugeot 505 Petrol (79 - 89) up to G	0762
Peugeot 1.7/1.8 & 1.9 litre Diesel Engine (82 - 96) up to N	0950
Peugeot 2.0, 2.1, 2.3 & 2.5 litre Diesel Engines (74 - 90) up to H	1607
PORSCHE 911 (65 - 85) up to C	0264
Porsche 924 & 924 Turbo (76 - 85) up to C	0397
PROTON (89 - 97) F to P	3255
RANGE ROVER V8 Petrol (70 - Oct 92) up to K	0606

* Classic reprint

Preserving Our Motoring Heritage

< The Model J Duesenberg Derham Tourster. Only eight of these magnificent cars were ever built – this is the only example to be found outside the United States of America

Almost every car you've ever loved, loathed or desired is gathered under one roof at the Haynes Motor Museum. Over 300 immaculately presented cars and motorbikes represent every aspect of our motoring heritage, from elegant reminders of bygone days, such as the superb Model J Duesenberg to curiosities like the bug-eyed BMW Isetta. There are also many old friends and flames. Perhaps you remember the 1959 Ford Popular that you did your courting in? The magnificent 'Red Collection' is a spectacle of classic sports cars including AC, Alfa Romeo, Austin Healey, Ferrari, Lamborghini, Maserati, MG, Riley, Porsche and Triumph.

A Perfect Day Out

Each and every vehicle at the Haynes Motor Museum has played its part in the history and culture of Motoring. Today, they make a wonderful spectacle and a great day out for all the family. Bring the kids, bring Mum and Dad, but above all bring your camera to capture those golden memories for ever. You will also find an impressive array of motoring memorabilia, a comfortable 70 seat video cinema and one of the most extensive transport book shops in Britain. The Pit Stop Cafe serves everything from a cup of tea to wholesome, home-made meals or, if you prefer, you can enjoy the large picnic area nestled in the beautiful rural surroundings of Somerset.

> John Haynes O.B.E., Founder and Chairman of the museum at the wheel of a Haynes Light 12.

< Graham Hill's Lola Cosworth Formula 1 car next to a 1934 Riley Sports.

The Museum is situated on the A359 Yeovil to Frome road at Sparkford, just off the A303 in Somerset. It is about 40 miles south of Bristol, and 25 minutes drive from the M5 intersection at Taunton.
Open 9.30am - 5.30pm (10.00am - 4.00pm Winter) 7 days a week, *except Christmas Day, Boxing Day and New Years Day*
Special rates available for schools, coach parties and outings Charitable Trust No. 292048